Organisation

IM

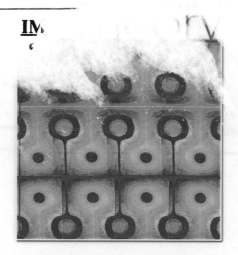

To Olly

Organisation Theory

fourth edition

Concepts and cases

Stephen P. Robbins

Neil Barnwell

Pearson Education Australia
Unit 4, Level 2
14 Aquatic Drive
Frenchs Forest NSW 2086

www.pearsoned.com.au

Senior Acquisitions Editor: Alison Green
Project Editor: Jane Roy
Editorial co-ordinator: Marji Backer
Copy Editor: Kate Ormston-Jeffery
Proofreader: Ron Buck
Cover and Internal Design: Dizign Pty Ltd
Cover painting: *The most beautiful carpet that I have ever seen* by Peter Atkins, courtesy of the artist and Sherman Galleries, Sydney.
Instructional Design: Linda Chaousis
Typeset by Midland Typesetters, Maryborough, Vic.

Printed in China

3 4 5 06 05 04

National Library of Australia
Cataloguing-in-Publication Data

Robbins, Stephen P., 1943– .
    Organisation Theory: concepts and cases.

    4th ed.
    Includes index.
    ISBN 1 74009 545 6.

    1. Organizational behaviour. 2. Organizational change—Australia
    I. Barnwell, Neil. II. Title.

658.00994

An imprint of Pearson Education Australia

Contents

Preface

We are pleased to present the fourth edition of *Organisation Theory: Concepts and Cases* to our Australian and New Zealand readers. This edition follows a similar approach to that used in previous editions. It is intended to mainly be of use to business students and the material has been selected and interpreted to assist them in understanding organisations and their management. It is expected that it will be of most use to undergraduate and early stage post-graduate students.

All texts need a theme and the one we follow in this edition is to select material that will be of practical value to those faced with the task of managing organisations. In the case of organisation theory, this is not as easy as it may appear. Organisation theory is a multidisciplinary study that includes elements of sociology, anthropology, corporate strategy and, in the case of post-modernism, philosophy. This contributes to organisation theory being a contested terrain, where various approaches vie to attract the attention of those concerned with organisations. Inevitably in drawing upon this material, judgements must be made as to what is important and of value to students. In this task we have been guided by the material's practical value.

This does not mean that the text does not have a firm academic base. The material is drawn from studies published in respected academic journals and, in some cases, business publications. Each chapter is extensively referenced and contains a guide to further reading for those interested in broadening their study of the topic.

Although most of those using the text will be undertaking business degrees, the basic principles and theories discussed apply to all organisations. The book is therefore of use to those charged with managing government departments, charities and various non-government organisations.

As with previous editions we open each chapter with an illustrative case study and we conclude with a closing case study which is intended to be discussed in class. Each chapter also contains review questions which test student's knowledge of the material. The book contains many illustrative boxes dispersed throughout the text which show how the material may be applied in current business situations. The book also contains concluding case studies and a useful glossary.

In order to reflect advances in organisation theory, a number of chapters have been amalgamated whilst others have been expanded. All parts of the book have been updated to reflect current thinking, research and practice. Particular attention has been paid to the impact of information technologies on organisations. Major changes have been made to the chapter on organisational culture in order to incorporate advances in this area. And a new chapter has been devoted to explain how changes in environments and technology have led to changes in the way that organisations are structured and managed. But the book still incorporates many of the standard studies and theories upon which organisation theory is based and which still inform much of the teaching in the subject.

We hope that students and instructors find this book both useful and easy to read. And as with all authorship tasks, we extend our thanks to those too many to mention, who have provided support and encouragement throughout its writing and production.

Stephen P. Robbins
Neil Barnwell (neil.barnwell@uts.edu.au)

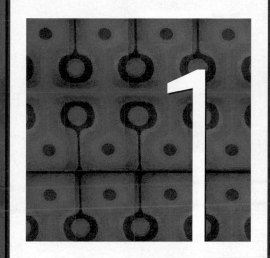

1

Introduction to Organisation Theory

part 1

CHAPTER 1

An overview

After reading this chapter you should be able to:

1 define organisation theory;

2 compare organisation theory and organisational behaviour;

3 explain the value in studying organisation theory;

4 describe the systems perspective;

5 describe the life-cycle perspective;

6 discuss how systems and life cycles are part of the biological metaphor;

7 introduce the concepts of critical theory and postmodernism.

Introduction

Virgin Blue takes to the skies

One of the most prominent businessmen of the past 20 years is Sir Richard Branson, the originator of the widely known Virgin brand. Virgin brand goods and services range from a cola drink to banking and mobile phones.[1] Branson's business approach is to take on dominant players in established industries and carve out a niche for himself. In some cases the name is used as a marketing tool, with services and expertise provided by specialists. But in other cases entirely new organisations are created.

One of Branson's early ventures was into the airline industry, through the establishment of Virgin Atlantic. This pitted him in head-to-head competition against British Airways, a competitive stoush which he immensely enjoyed. He also operates a European airline, Virgin Express, which he uses when travelling around the region. As owner of the airline he often sits and chats with the pilots during the flight. On one such flight in the late 1990s one of the pilots, an Australian, was complaining about the fact that there were only two airlines in Australia and that as a result air travel was expensive. There seemed to be room for at least one more airline offering a cheaper product. Branson's entrepreneurial spirit was aroused, and he determined on the spur of the moment to start a new airline to service the Australian market.

Air transportation is not an industry for the faint-hearted. It is legendary for the enormous amount of capital it consumes, often with little return. It is also difficult to be a small player. Economies favour established airlines with large fleets, extensive networks and frequency of service. Owing to the distance of Australia from the rest of his airline operations, Branson's new airline could not be an extension of one he already owned; he had to start a new organisation from scratch.

His first move was to appoint a chief executive. He chose Brett Godfrey, a 37-year-old finance manager with Virgin Express. Godfrey's task was formidable. He needed to identify essential tasks and refine these into areas of responsibility. Managers were then appointed to be responsible for those areas. They in turn had to build their departments by hiring the appropriate staff, allocating tasks and recommending investment decisions. A decision had to be made on the location of the head office and appropriate accommodation found. Suitable aircraft had to be leased and maintenance facilities established. One of the greatest hurdles for the new company was negotiating with the various government bodies that control aviation. Procedure manuals had to be written and presented to the Civil Aviation and Safety Authority for approval. Test flights were needed to prove the capacity of the airline to perform and to handle emergencies appropriately before an air operator's certificate could be issued. Landing slots had to be negotiated with the various airport authorities, a particular problem in Sydney with its capacity constraints. Suitable terminal access had to arranged—no easy task, given that most airports catered only for the then two dominant carriers, Ansett and Qantas. In addition, IT systems had to be developed and hardware and software purchased and installed. Booking and information systems were put on line. A call centre had to be established, maintenance and supply contracts negotiated and HRM policies written.

The airline even needed a new name. Singapore Airlines owned a 49% share of Virgin Atlantic and the right to the Virgin brand name as it applied to airlines. The

Virgin airline in Australia would be totally financed by Sir Richard Branson himself, with no direct relationship to his other aviation investments. Thus the name Virgin Blue was born.

If Virgin Blue was to be successful, it had to seek points of difference between itself and the other airlines. One of these points was obvious: it was to pitch its price lower than Ansett and Qantas. The other was the feel of the airline: being a new start-up, Virgin Blue could hire those who reflected the image it wanted to create. This was particularly relevant to those who worked at the customer interface. Not surprisingly, Virgin Blue wanted to create a youthful persona, full of smiles and freshness and not too bureaucratic. It was also important that staff possess a can-do approach, that goals be met and, through their efforts, the start-up airline be successful. The feeling that they were part of a historic shift in the airline industry was a major motivator.

Virgin Blue also used its choice of head office location to advantage. Drawn to Brisbane by concessions and grants from the Queensland government, it identified considerable advantages to weaving itself into the fabric of Queensland society. All of its initial routes originated from Brisbane, and it promoted itself heavily in that state as a local airline for local people. The atmosphere of the 'sunshine state' started to permeate its culture.

The sudden collapse of Ansett created new opportunities and challenges for Virgin. It could greatly expand its operations but this required capital, which was in short supply. It needed outside shareholders to provide more money for capital equipment. It also required hiring and training new staff; this was not something which could be achieved overnight. Balancing this unexpected windfall was the downturn in travel following the attacks on the World Trade Center in New York. This stretched almost every airline and put many into bankruptcy. Virgin Blue had to grow up very fast or face extinction.

Brett Godfrey created an organisation. Within 18 months of the idea being formed, the red aircraft of Virgin Blue became a familiar sight in Australian skies. The task was beyond the capacity of any one person. We can see in Virgin Blue's formation all the features of an organisation that we will discuss in this book. Goals had to be set and key areas of responsibility identified. Departments were formed and coordination mechanisms established. The environment put pressure on the organisation which required a response. As well, the culture of the organisation needed to reflect the values and attitudes necessary for the organisation's survival. Although there were many factors responsible for Virgin Blue's successful establishment, the correct organisational structure and design played a prominent part. And although many other factors will determine whether Virgin Blue survives, the discipline of organisation theory, which is the subject of this book, will have a major part to play.

Some basic definitions

The Virgin Blue story illustrates the creation and growth of an organisation. But what precisely do we mean by the term *organisation*? Perhaps not so obviously, Virgin Blue's senior management was also involved with *organisation structure, organisation design* and *organisation theory*. As all four terms are important and are often confused, let's clarify them.

What is an organisation?

organisation a consciously coordinated social entity with a relatively identifiable boundary, that functions on a relatively continuous basis to achieve a common goal or set of goals

An **organisation** is a consciously coordinated social entity, with a relatively identifiable boundary, that functions on a relatively continuous basis to achieve a common goal or set of goals. That's a mouthful of words, so let us break it down into its more relevant parts.

The words *consciously coordinated* imply actions of management. *Social entity* means that the unit is composed of people or groups of people who interact with each other. The interaction patterns that people follow in an organisation do not just emerge—rather, they are deliberately established. Therefore, because organisations are social entities, the interaction patterns of their members must be balanced and harmonised to minimise duplication yet ensure that critical tasks are completed. The result is that our definition assumes explicitly the need for coordinating the interaction patterns of people.

An organisation has a *relatively identifiable boundary*. This boundary can change over time and may not always be perfectly clear, but a definable boundary must exist in order to distinguish members from non-members. Such a boundary tends to be created through explicit or implicit contracts between members and their organisations. In most employment relationships, there is an explicit contract whereby work is exchanged for pay. In social or voluntary organisations, members contribute in return for prestige, social interaction or the satisfaction of helping others. But every organisation has a boundary that differentiates who is and who is not part of that organisation.

People in an organisation have some *continuing bond*. This bond, of course, does not mean lifelong membership. On the contrary, organisations face constant change in their memberships, although while they are members the people in an organisation participate with some degree of regularity. For a clerk in the National Australia Bank, that may require being at work eight hours a day, five days a week. At the other extreme, someone functioning on a relatively continuous basis as a member of the Country Women's Association may attend only a few meetings a year or merely pay the annual dues.

Finally, organisations exist to achieve something. These 'somethings' are *goals*, and they are usually unattainable by individuals working alone or, if attainable individually, are achieved more efficiently through group effort. While it is not necessary for all members to endorse the organisation's goals fully, our definition implies that disagreement with the goals of the organisation would lead to a person terminating their membership.

Notice how all the parts of our definition align with our description of the development of Virgin Blue. The goals of Virgin Blue are to provide cost-effective air travel to the people of Australia, achieve an adequate market share and make an acceptable return on funds employed. Staff were hired and inducted into the Virgin Blue vision and values. In undertaking their tasks they developed a formal set of relationships which were the patterns of interaction of the organisation. These patterns included people undertaking specialised tasks and a hierarchy of workers and managers.

Members of Virgin Blue are identified as employees, owners or board members. In return for their work effort or other contribution they receive pay and other forms of compensation. Finally, the organisation's life exists beyond that of any of its members. Employees may leave, but they can be replaced so that the activities they perform can continue. Even the ownership of Virgin Blue may change, with little effect on its day-to-day operations.

What is organisation structure?

Our definition of *organisation* recognises the need for formally coordinating the interaction patterns of organisation members. **Organisation structure** defines how tasks are to be allocated, areas of responsibility and authority, who reports to whom, and the formal coordinating mechanisms and interaction patterns that will be followed. We define an organisation's structure as having three components: complexity, formalisation, and centralisation. (We review each of these in detail in Chapter 4.)

Complexity considers the extent of differentiation within the organisation. This includes the degree of specialisation or division of labour, the number of levels in the organisation's hierarchy and the extent to which the organisation's units are dispersed geographically. As tasks at Virgin Blue became increasingly specialised and more levels were added to the hierarchy, the organisation became increasingly complex. Complexity, of course, is a relative term. A small business, for instance, has a long way to go to approach the complexity of BHP Billiton or the ANZ Bank, where there are hundreds of occupational specialties, nearly a dozen management levels between production workers and the chief executive officer, and organisational units dispersed in countries throughout the world.

The degree to which an organisation relies on rules and procedures to direct the behaviour of employees is *formalisation*. Some organisations operate with a minimum of such standardised guidelines; others, even those quite small in size, have all kinds of regulations instructing employees as to what they can and cannot do.

Centralisation considers where the responsibility for decision-making authority lies. In some organisations, decision making is highly centralised. Problems flow upwards and the senior executives choose the appropriate action. In other cases, decision making is decentralised. Authority is dispersed downwards in the hierarchy. It is important to recognise that, as with complexity and formalisation, an organisation is not *either* centralised or decentralised. Centralisation and decentralisation represent two extremes on a continuum. Organisations *tend* to be centralised or *tend* to be decentralised. The placement of the organisation on this continuum, however, is one of the major factors in determining what type of structure exists.

What is organisation design?

Our third term, organisation design, emphasises the management side of organisation theory. **Organisation design** is concerned with constructing and changing an organisation's structure to achieve the organisation's goals. Constructing or changing an organisation is not unlike building or remodelling a house: both begin with a goal;

organisation structure the degree of complexity, formalisation and centralisation in an organisation

organisation design the construction and change of an organisation's structure

the designer then creates a means or plan for achieving that goal. In house construction, that plan is a blueprint; in organisation building, the corresponding document is an organisation chart.

As you proceed through this text, you will see a consistent concern with offering prescriptions for how organisations can be *designed* to facilitate the attainment of their goals. The concern should not be surprising, as this book is intended for business students and managers. You are probably more interested in learning how to design organisations than in merely knowing how they function. You have a managerial perspective, consistently looking for the application potential in concepts. When organisation theory is studied from the perspective of the needs of managers and future managers, it is heavily oriented towards organisation design.

What is organisation theory?

organisation theory the discipline that studies the structure and design of organisations

From our previous definitions, it is not too difficult to identify that **organisation theory** is the study of the structure and design of organisations. But organisations have a life which is far more complex than that laid down in the formal organisational design. Organisations develop personalities, which we call culture. Whether or not the culture assists an organisation in attaining its goals is important to managers. And as environments and technologies are never fixed, so organisations must adapt to the changes that affect them. These include changes in societal attitudes and expectations which require organisations to respond to them. Hence areas such as sustainability and gender, which were previously not of any great importance, are attracting greater research interest. So, in addition to structure and design, organisational theory includes the study of these less clearly defined areas and makes suggestions as to how they can contribute to organisational effectiveness.

At the end of this chapter, we introduce a model that identifies explicitly the major subparts that make up this discipline we call organisation theory. Chapter 2 presents a brief overview of the evolution of organisation theory over time.

Contrasting organisation theory and organisational behaviour

As we are clarifying terminology, it might be helpful in this section to differentiate between the subject matter of organisation theory and that of organisational behaviour. Many students of management and organisations will take courses in both areas, and a brief comparison of the two should assist you in understanding their different emphases as well as their areas of overlap.

organisational behaviour a field of study that investigates the impact of individuals and small-group factors on employee performance and attitudes

Organisational behaviour is the study of the way in which individuals and teams behave in the workplace. It focuses on behaviour in organisations and on a narrow set of employee performance and attitude variables—employee productivity, absenteeism, turnover and job satisfaction are those most often looked at. Individual behaviour topics typically studied in organisational behaviour include perception, values, learning, motivation and personal attributes. Group topics include roles, status, leadership, power, communication and conflict.

In contrast, organisation theory takes a macro-perspective. Its unit of analysis is the organisation itself or its primary subunits. Organisation theory focuses on the behaviour of organisations and uses a broader definition of organisational effectiveness. It is concerned not only with employee performance and attitudes but also with the overall organisation's ability to adapt and achieve its goals.

This micro–macro distinction creates some overlap; for instance, structural factors have an impact on employee behaviour. Students of organisational behaviour should therefore consider the structure–behaviour relationship. Similarly, some micro-topics are relevant to the study of organisation theory. However, where micro- and macro-issues overlap, their emphasis is often different: for instance, the topic of culture in organisational behaviour tends to focus on the way that culture influences interpersonal and intragroup relationships. When studied by organisational theorists, on the other hand, the emphasis is on how culture contributes to the organisation's goals and the extent to which it is manageable. While the student of organisational behaviour is likely to see culture as arising from the actions of individuals and being a people issue, the student of organisation theory tends to see the same culture as arising from the way that tasks and departments are structured, the way that the organisation manages rewards, and the patterns of communication and reporting relationships. The issue of course is not that one is right and the other wrong. Rather, organisational behaviour and theory emphasise different levels of organisational analysis.

The biological metaphor

Organisations are intangible: that is, they do not exist as a physical presence but as a set of relationships among people. Given this intangibility, a **metaphor** is a popular device for making comparisons. The use of metaphors can be extremely helpful in explaining or providing insight into the workings of two phenomena, one of which you already understand fairly well. In this section we are going to look at organisations (a phenomenon we will assume you are technically unfamiliar with) as if they were living organisms, like plants, animals or human beings (phenomena we will assume you *are* reasonably familiar with). We call this comparison the biological metaphor.

metaphor is a figure of speech in which a descriptive term is used to refer to another object to which it seems to bear no relationship

A word of warning before we proceed. Some scholars have questioned whether the biological metaphor is appropriate for application to organisations.[2] For example, while few would dispute that organisations are born, grow and require continual nourishment for survival, organisations are not predestined to die, as all living organisms are. Death may be a part of biological life, but it is not inevitable for organisations. Churches for instance seem to have an almost indefinite life, and constant mergers and acquisitions in business make defining organisational death problematic. So while the biological metaphor is not perfect, it has nevertheless become an increasingly popular conceptual framework for understanding organisations. As you will see, just like living organisms, organisations grow, pass through predictable stages of development, undergo a series of predictable transitions and deteriorate if the energy they put out is not replaced by new inputs. Describing organisations as systems and as proceeding through a life cycle should give you new insight into their make-up.

The systems perspective

There is wide agreement among organisational theorists that a systems perspective offers important insight into the workings of an organisation.[3] The following pages introduce the idea of systems, contrast *open* and *closed* systems, and demonstrate how an open-systems approach can help you to conceptualise better just what it is that organisations do.

OT CLOSEUP

Ten different ways of looking at organisations, or what you see is what you get!

Organisations have been conceptualised in numerous ways.[4] The following represent some of the more OFTEN used descriptions:

Rational entities in pursuit of goals. Organisations exist to achieve goals, and the behaviour of organisational members can be explained as the rational pursuit of those goals.

Coalitions of powerful constituencies. Organisations are made up of groups, each of which seeks to satisfy its own self-interest. These groups use their power to influence the distribution of resources within the organisation.

Open systems. Organisations are input-output transformation systems that depend on their environment for survival.

Meaning-producing systems. Organisations are artificially created entities. Their goals and purposes are symbolically created and maintained by management.

Loosely coupled systems. Organisations are made up of relatively independent units that can pursue dissimilar or even conflicting goals.

Political systems. Organisations are composed of internal constituencies that seek control over the decision process in order to enhance their position.

Instruments of domination. Organisations place members in job 'boxes' that constrain what they can do and with whom they can interact. Additionally, they are given a boss who has authority over them.

Information-processing units. Organisations interpret their environment, coordinate activities and facilitate decision making by processing information horizontally and vertically through a structural hierarchy.

Psychic prisons. Organisations constrain members by constructing job descriptions, departments, divisions, and standards of acceptable and unacceptable behaviours. When accepted by members, they become artificial barriers that limit choices.

Social contracts. Organisations are composed of sets of unwritten agreements whereby members perform certain behaviours in return for compensation.

Definition of a system

system a set of interrelated and interdependent parts arranged in a manner that produces a unified whole

A **system** is a set of interrelated and interdependent parts arranged in a manner that produces a unified whole. Societies are systems, and so too are cars, plants and human bodies. They take inputs, transform them and produce an output.

The unique characteristic of the systems viewpoint is the interrelationship of parts within the system. Every system is characterised by two diverse forces: differentiation and integration. A system is differentiated into specialised functions. In the human body, for instance, the lungs, heart and liver are all distinct functions. Similarly, organisations have divisions and departments with each performing specialised activities. At the same time, in order to maintain unity among the differentiated parts and to form a complete whole, every system has a process of integration. In organisations, this integration is typically achieved through coordinating devices such as levels of hierarchy, direct supervision, and rules, procedures and policies. Every system, therefore, requires differentiation to identify its subparts and integration to ensure that the system does not break down into separate elements.

The subsystems of an organisation may in turn be broken down into further subsystems. The Commonwealth Bank, for instance, may be viewed as a system; funds management as a subsystem; and parts of funds management, such as marketing, as yet a further subsystem. This highlights a dilemma for both managers and researchers: what is to be our level of analysis? Through examining the complete system we may be taking too broad a view for effective analysis. But if we concentrate on minor subsystems, we may miss important features of the whole system that impinge on subsystem effectiveness.

Types of systems

Systems are classified typically as either closed or open. Closed-system thinking stems primarily from the physical sciences. It views the system as self-contained. Its dominant characteristic is that it essentially ignores the effect of the environment on the system. A **closed system** would be one that received no energy from an outside source and from which no energy was released into its surroundings. More idealistic than practical, the closed-system perspective has little applicability to the study of organisations.

An **open system** recognises the dynamic interaction of a system with its environment. A simplified graphic representation of the open system appears in Figure 1.1.

closed system a self-contained system that ignores its environment

open system a dynamic system that interacts with and responds to its environment

FIGURE 1.1 Basic open system

No student of organisations could build much of a defence for viewing organisations as closed systems. Even isolated, self-sufficient monasteries rely on the environment for new members as existing ones age and die. Business organisations in contemporary society obtain their raw materials and human resources from the environment. They depend on clients and customers in the environment to absorb their output. Banks take in deposits, convert them into loans and other investments, and use the resulting profits to maintain themselves, to grow and to pay dividends and taxes. The bank system, for example, interacts actively with its environment, which is made up of people with savings to invest, other people in need of loans, potential employees looking for work, the Reserve Bank, and increasingly public attitudes which may be critical of the various banks' attitudes towards customers.

An organisation's environment is far more complex than obtaining raw materials and inputs into the productive process and distributing outputs. Major environmental changes that have occurred in recent years have included deregulation, privatisation of government enterprises and the growth in globalisation. These have generally combined to greatly increase the levels of competition and, hence, environmental interaction. Community expectations are also a significant environmental influence on organisations, with those which can exploit new attitudes and values, such as The Body Shop, generally performing extremely well.

Figure 1.2 provides a more complex picture of an open system as it would apply to an industrial organisation. We see inputs of materials, labour and capital. We see a technological process created for transforming raw materials into finished product. The finished product, in turn, is sold to a customer. Financial institutions, the labour force, suppliers and customers are all part of the environment, as is government.

FIGURE 1.2 An industrial organisation as an open system

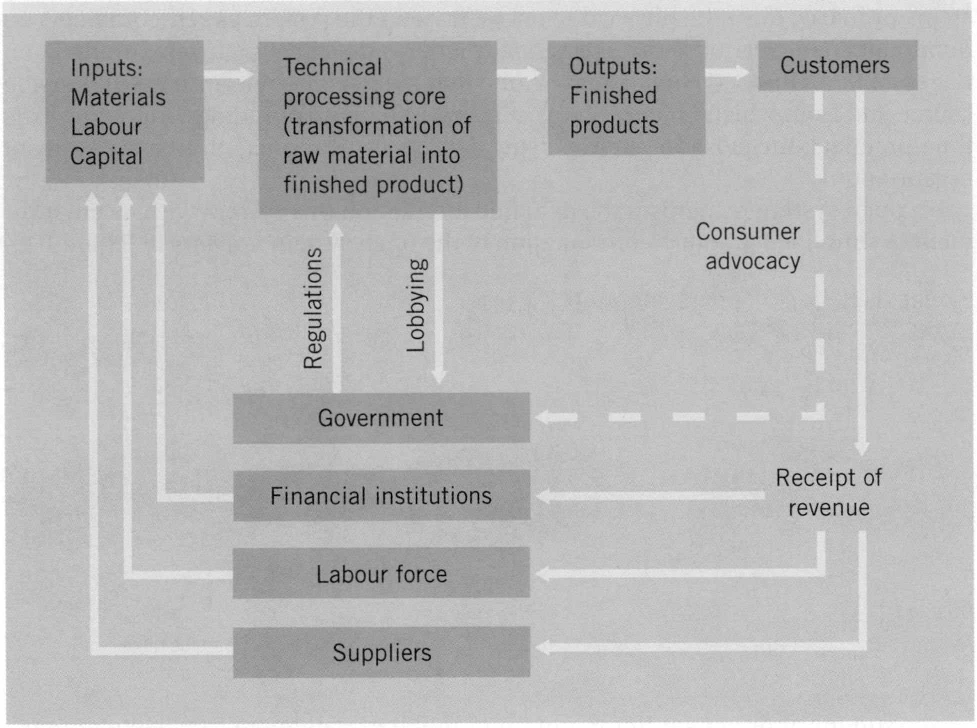

As we have seen, it is difficult to conceive of any system as being fully closed. All systems must have some interaction with their environments if they are to survive. Probably the most relevant way in which to look at the closed–opened dichotomy is to consider it as a range rather than as two clearly separate classifications. In this way, we can explain that the degree to which a system is open or closed varies within systems. An open system, for instance, may become more closed if contact with the environment is reduced over time. The reverse would also be true. The experience of many government instrumentalities, such as electricity-generating authorities, illustrates this point.

In Australia, electricity was initially generated by local councils, but after World War II, the various state governments undertook responsibility for the task. Private generation of electricity for public sale was prohibited. Each state was to be self-sufficient in electricity, and the electricity distribution network was not connected to allow interstate trade. The state electricity-generating boards were set up as statutory authorities. In effect this meant that they were subject to very little oversight by the politicians of the day. While this system allowed the unfettered growth of the electricity-generating industry, by the 1990s it became apparent that some states were capable of generating electricity at lower cost than others. New South Wales, for instance, with its large deposits of cheap thermal coal, generally had a lower cost of electricity than South Australia, which lacked such resources. The price of electricity was also felt to be too high and the various generating boards unresponsive to customer needs.

As a result of both state and federal government initiatives the generators of electricity were either privatised or corporatised, depending on various state political priorities. Interconnections between the states were established to enable interstate trade in electricity. The generators of electricity were then forced to compete for major customers. A hedge market for electricity was generated and various private operators entered the industry. Levels of competition greatly increased, and a number of generators experienced the unpleasant consequences of losing money. Downsizing of workforces was widespread, and high-cost generating plant was closed. Those working in the industry experienced rapid and unanticipated change, which radically altered the nature of the organisations they worked for. They still generated electricity, with much the same plant, but the organisations were radically different places from those of 10 years before. They had seen their environments move to being far more open.

Characteristics of an open system

TABLE 1.1 Characteristics of an open system

Environmental awareness: the organisation consistently interacts with its environment	**Movement towards growth and expansion:** the more sophisticated the system, the more it is likely to grow and expand
Feedback: the system adjusts to information from its environment	**Balance of maintenance and adaptive activities:** to be effective the system must ensure that its subparts are in balance and that it maintains its ability to adapt to the environment
Cyclical character: the system consists of cycles of events	
Tendency towards growth: without active intervention, the system runs down or disintegrates	
Steady state: there is an input or energy to counteract the winding-down properties	**Equifinality:** there are a number of ways to achieve the same objective

Adapted from Daniel Katz and Robert L. Khan, The Social Psychology of Organizations, 2nd Edition, New York, John Wiley, 1978.

All systems have inputs, transformation processes and outputs. They take such things as raw materials, energy, information and human resources and convert them into goods and services, profits, waste materials and the like. Open systems, however, have some additional characteristics of relevance to those of us studying organisations.[5]

- *Environment awareness.* One of the most obvious characteristics of an open system is its recognition of the interdependence between the system and its environment. Changes in the environment affect one or more of the systems or subsystems. Conversely, changes in the system affect its environment. Some companies make major technological innovations, for instance, which affect other organisational environments.

Without a boundary there is no system, and the boundary or boundaries determine where systems and subsystems start and stop. Boundaries can be legal, in that companies are legal entities entitled to employ staff and own assets. Boundaries can also be physical, such as the international boundaries that may form an impediment to trade. They can also be maintained psychologically through symbols, such as titles, uniforms and indoctrination rituals. At this point, it is sufficient to acknowledge that the concept of boundaries is required for an understanding of systems. Somehow we must make a judgement as to what is part of the system and what is not.

- *Feedback.* Open systems continually receive information from their environment. This helps the system to adjust and allows it to take corrective actions to rectify deviations from its prescribed course. We call this receipt of environmental information **feedback**—that is, a process that allows a portion of the output to be returned to the system as input (e.g. information or money) so as to modify succeeding outputs from the system.

- *Cyclical character.* Open systems consist of cycles of events. The system's outputs furnish the means for new inputs that permit the repetition of the cycle. This is demonstrated in Figure 1.2; the revenue received from the customers of the industrial firm must be sufficient to pay creditors and the wages of employees and to repay loans if the cycle is to be perpetuated and the organisation to survive.

- *Tendency towards growth.* A closed system, because it does not import energy or new inputs from its environment, will run down over time as equipment wears out, workforces age and products become dated. In contrast, an open system is able to import energy from its environment. As a consequence it can repair itself, maintain its structure, avoid death and even grow, because it has the ability to import more energy than it puts out. In technical terms, this tendency towards growth is called negative entropy.

- *Steady state.* There is generally a balance between inputs from the environment and those expended to counteract the winding down of the system. This results in a relatively steady state. With the character of the system remaining almost unchanged over long periods of time. Most motor vehicle and oil companies, although involved in major interactions with their environment, maintain their character over long periods of time. Many organisations draw resources from their environment, not with the intention of undergoing radical change but to expand existing operations. Thus, while an open system is active in processing inputs to outputs, the system tends to maintain itself over time.

- *Movement towards growth and expansion.* To ensure their survival, large and complex systems operate in such a way as to acquire some margin of safety beyond the immediate level of existence. The many subsystems within the system—to avoid entropy, or winding down—tend to import more energy from the environment than is required for the system's output. The result is that the steady state is applicable to simple systems but, at more complex levels, becomes one of preserving the character of the system through growth and expansion. We see this in large corporations and government bureaucracies which, not satisfied with the status quo, attempt to increase their chances of survival by actively seeking growth and expansion.

feedback receipt of information pertaining to individual or system effectiveness

A final point on this characteristic needs to be made: the basic system does not change directly as a result of expansion. The most common growth pattern is one in which there is merely a multiplication of the same type of cycles or subsystems. The quantity of the system changes while the quality remains the same. Most colleges and universities, for instance, expand by doing more of the same thing rather than by pursuing new or innovative activities.

- *Balance of maintenance and adaptive activities.* Open systems seek to reconcile two, often conflicting, sets of activities. **Maintenance activities** ensure that the various subsystems are in balance and that the total system conforms to its environment. This, in effect, prevents rapid changes that may unbalance the system. In contrast, **adaptive activities** are necessary so that the system can adjust over time to variations in internal and external demands. Maintenance activities seek stability and preservation of the status quo through the purchase, maintenance and overhaul of machinery, the recruitment and training of employees, and mechanisms such as the provision and enforcement of rules and procedures. Adaptive activities focus on change through planning, market research, recruitment and training, new product development and the like.

  maintenance activities activities that provide stability to a system and preserve the status quo

  adaptive activities change activities that allow the system to adapt over time

  Both maintenance and adaptive activities are required if a system is to survive. Stable and well-maintained organisations that do not adapt as conditions change will not be long-lasting. Similarly, the adaptive but unstable organisation will be inefficient and unlikely to survive for long.

- *Equifinality.* The concept of **equifinality** argues that a system can reach the same final state from differing initial conditions and by a variety of paths. This means that an organisational system can accomplish its objectives with varied inputs and transformation processes. Thus different car companies can use different design and production methods and be organised in different ways but still produce a mass market car. As we discuss the managerial implications of organisation theory, it will be valuable for you to keep the idea of equifinality in mind. It will encourage you to consider a variety of solutions to a given problem rather than to seek some rigid optimal solution.

  equifinality a system can reach the same final state from differing initial conditions and by a variety of paths

Importance of the systems perspective

The systems point of view is a useful framework for students of management trying to conceptualise organisations. For managers and future managers, the systems perspective makes it possible to see the organisation as a whole with interdependent parts—a system composed of subsystems. It prevents, or at least deters, lower-level managers from viewing their jobs as managing static, isolated elements of the organisation. It encourages all managers to identify and understand the environment in which their system operates. It helps them to see the organisation as stable patterns and actions within boundaries and to gain insight into why organisations are resistant to change. Finally, it directs their attention to alternative inputs and processes for reaching their goals.

However, the systems perspective is not the only way in which we can view organisations. One of its greatest limitations is that it is an abstract concept. When viewing an organisation using a systems perspective, an observer sees a complex interaction of systems, subsystems and environments. The tendency is to consider that everything depends on everything else. This makes it difficult to isolate specific problems and to offer to management suggestions as to what precisely will change and to what degree, if a certain action is taken. Its value, therefore, lies more in its conceptual framework than in its direct applicability to solving managers' organisational problems.

The life-cycle perspective

As noted earlier in this chapter, organisations are born, grow and eventually die (though it may take 100 years or more). New organisations are formed daily. At the same time, hundreds of organisations close their doors each day never to open again. We see this birth and death phenomenon especially among small businesses. They pop up and disappear in every community. In this section, we will build on the biological metaphor of organisations proceeding through life-cycle stages. Like human beings, we will argue, all organisations are born, live and die. Like human beings, some develop faster than others and some do a far better job of ageing than others. Also as with human growth and ageing, there are also predictable phases that organisations pass through. As a result, the metaphor of the human life cycle remains an interesting way to conceptualise the life of an organisation.

Definition of a life cycle

organisational life cycle the pattern of predictable change through which the organisation moves from start-up to dissolution

The **organisational life cycle** refers to the pattern of predictable change through which the organisation moves from start-up to dissolution. We propose that organisations evolve through a standardised sequence of transitions as they develop over time. By applying the life-cycle metaphor to organisations, we are saying that there are distinct stages through which organisations proceed, that the stages follow a consistent pattern, and that the transitions from one stage to another are predictable rather than random occurrences.

Life-cycle stages

The life-cycle concept has received a great deal of attention in the strategy and marketing literature. The life cycle is used to show how products move through four stages: birth or formation, growth, maturity, and decline. The implication for management is that the continual introduction of new products is required if the organisation is to survive over the long run.

We could use the same four stages in describing organisations, but organisations are not products, and they have some unique characteristics which require some modifications in our description. Research into the organisation life cycle leads us to a five-stage model:[6]

1 *Entrepreneurial stage.* This stage is synonymous with the formation stage in the product life cycle. The organisation is in its infancy. Goals tend to be fluid or ambiguous. Creativity and managerial input is high. Progress to the next stage demands acquiring and maintaining a steady supply of resources.

2 *Collectivity stage.* This stage continues the innovation of the earlier stage, but now the organisation's mission is clarified. Communication and structure within the organisation remain essentially informal. Members put in long hours and demonstrate high commitment to the organisation. The organisation is generally quite small, with intensive, hands-on management.

3 *Formalisation-and-control stage.* The structure of the organisation stabilises in the third stage. Predictability increases, permitting formal rules and procedures to

be imposed. Innovation is de-emphasised, while efficiency and stability are emphasised. Decision makers are now more entrenched, with those in senior authority positions in the organisation holding power. Decision making also takes on a more conservative posture. At this stage, the organisation exists beyond the presence of any one individual. Roles have been clarified so that changes in organisational membership causes no severe threat to the organisation.

4 *Elaboration-of-structure stage.* In this stage the organisation diversifies its product or service markets. Management searches for new products and growth opportunities. The organisation structure becomes more complex and elaborated. Decision making is decentralised.

5 *Decline stage.* As a result of competition, technological obsolescence or similar forces, the organisation in the decline stage finds the demand for its products or services shrinking. Management searches for ways to hold markets and looks for new opportunities. Employee turnover, especially among those with the most saleable skills, escalates. Conflicts increase within the organisation. New people assume leadership in an attempt to arrest the decline. Decision making is centralised in this new leadership.

Do all organisations proceed through the five stages? Not necessarily! If possible, management would like to avoid having the organisation reach stage 5. However, excluding this stage from our model assumes that organisations follow an unending growth curve or at least remain stable. This obviously is an optimistic assumption. No organisation, or society for that matter, can endure for eternity. But some can last for a very long time and outlive any of their members. The National Australia Bank and Westpac (formerly the Bank of New South Wales) date back to the middle of the 19th century. The Universities of Sydney and Melbourne are well over 100 years old, quite young compared with their European counterparts, such as Oxford and the Sorbonne. Whether these examples are now in the decline stage is questionable, as these organisations are still doing basically the same thing as they did when they started in business. What is apparent is that if basic technologies or competitive conditions change, organisations can face rapid decline and death. Steam locomotive manufacturers entered the 1950s as major industrial enterprises. By the beginning of the 1960s, most had passed from the scene. Within the space of 20 years, companies in the United Kingdom passed from dominating world ship-building to almost ceasing to exist. When the transistor was introduced to commercial production in the late 1950s, it foreshadowed the end of many manufacturers of technologically out-of-date thermionic valves.

Do the life-cycle stages correlate with an organisation's chronological age? Not at all! Observation confirms that some organisations have reached stages 3 and 4 less than five years after being formed, while others are 40 years old and still in their collectivity stage. In fact, some successful organisations seek to stay in the early stages. For example, Country Road, the successful designer, manufacturer and retailer of fashion clothing products, realises that it must retain many of the attributes of a stage 2 company to remain competitive. In considering this issue, it is sometimes not easy to determine the stage a company is in. Is Microsoft still at the growth stage or at the maturity or even decline stage? BP, an oil company with an almost 100-year history, is positioning itself to be a major player in sustainable energy. Where does this place the company in relation to our model? On the other hand, some organisations never die. Police services, for instance, are often subject to various inquiries into corruption, misuse of power, neglect of duty and selective enforcement of justice. Regardless of the criticisms sustained by police forces, the need for their services guarantees their existence.

A final question: can we reconcile our five-stage organisation life-cycle model with the more traditional four-stage model of formation, growth, maturity, and decline? The answer is yes. As shown in Figure 1.3, formation and the entrepreneurial stage are synonymous. Collectivity is essentially comparable with growth. Stages 3 and 4 in our model—formalisation and elaboration—appear to align reasonably well with maturity. Finally, of course, decline, and death, is consistent in both models.

FIGURE 1.3 Organisational life cylce

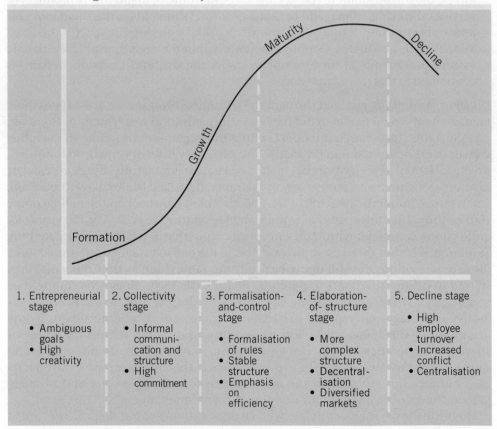

1. Entrepreneurial stage	2. Collectivity stage	3. Formalisation-and-control stage	4. Elaboration-of- structure stage	5. Decline stage
• Ambiguous goals • High creativity	• Informal communi-cation and structure • High commitment	• Formalisation of rules • Stable structure • Emphasis on efficiency	• More complex structure • Decentral-isation • Diversified markets	• High employee turnover • Increased conflict • Centralisation

Importance of the life-cycle perspective

Viewing organisations in a life-cycle perspective offsets the tendency to look at them as static entities. Organisations are not snapshots of images frozen in time; they are motion pictures. They evolve and change. Using the life-cycle perspective makes us aware when we assess or describe an organisation that it hasn't always been the way it is, nor will it always be the same in the future.

Additionally, the life-cycle metaphor is valuable when we consider what management can do to make an organisation more effective. The actions that are appropriate for a given problem when the organisation is growing may be very different if that problem occurs in the decline stage. As a case in point, Chapter 14 will specifically address how managing in a declining organisation makes very different demands on a manager from managing during the growth phase.

Positivism, postmodernism and critical theory

This book presents and discusses, systematically, research undertaken by organisational theory scholars. Most of the research we draw on has been undertaken on profit-seeking business organisations. By definition, this makes them capitalistic in nature. But we also include work undertaken on government organisations and, to a certain extent, charities and other not-for-profit organisations. We have defined organisations as being coordinated entities with identifiable boundaries and a continuing ongoing bond between members. In doing this, we imply an important and central role for management. Indeed, an organisation without management and control is almost a contradiction in terms. Many reading this book will be seeking a career in management or at least a role in the business world. In the general community, business issues and the actions undertaken by managers are widely discussed in the popular press. Many accept this situation as normal; it reflects the world they see around them and is accepted as the conventional way in which industrial societies are structured.

The empirical studies that form the basis of this book share the same methodology: they seek to identify the common features which organisations share and then determine what may give rise to these common features. These techniques are called observational, in that the researcher observes various organisational practices. As a result of this form of inquiry we find that organisations in turbulent and changing environments share certain commonalities, as do those which undertake routine tasks such as mass production manufacturing or the operation of rail systems. The subject of research may be a sample of organisations, parts of organisations or one organisation studied intensively. In many cases, we proceed from a series of propositions or hypotheses which are logical statements of association and which are then tested for their accuracy. In either case, data are gathered and often statistical analysis is conducted with conclusions drawn from the data.

We undertake research of this nature to expand our understanding of what influences organisational structure and practices. In doing this we can develop theories that contribute to the more effective management of organisations. An additional reason for undertaking research of this nature is that it satisfies our curiosity about the world around us.

This approach has certain shortcomings. In many instances, correlations and other statistical tests have identified only weak associations between variables. This does not provide us with a high level of confidence that an unambiguous cause-and-effect relationship exists. It also often occurs that a hypothesis that is strongly supported by theory has received little support when subjected to experimental investigation. Methodological difficulties also create problems. We often have to contend with problems such as how to measure intangibles, like the relationships between people and the structures of organisations. Nevertheless, a number of landmark theories have been developed from this process, which will be discussed in subsequent chapters.

The process we describe has been called a *positivist* approach, which leads to the development of *normative* theories. These words require explanation. Positivist implies that we are attempting to do things which lead to some improvement. In this case we are trying to improve organisational effectiveness. Normative means that we are trying to develop theories which may be applied across a wide range of situations.

There are many organisational theorists, however, who would not agree with our approach. A brief glance through academic journals dealing with matters relating to organisational theory will show that only some studies actually follow the methodology we have described. Some researchers have no doubt been discouraged by the lack of strong associations, and have diverted their attention to other areas of interest and forms of inquiry. Some have moved from analysing populations of organisations to methodologies concentrating on smaller groups or even individuals. But other researchers now promote the position that the future of organisational theory lies not with positivism but with postmodernism and critical theory. These later approaches to organisational theory stand as a counterpoint to that taken by this book. It is therefore worthwhile identifying what these approaches are.

Post means after, so postmodernism is the period after modernism. This leads to the question: what is modernism? The modern world started to emerge in the 18th century, when ideas of individual responsibility and the rights of 'man' (as they were referred to then) were widely debated. The Industrial Revolution was gathering pace at that time and modern capitalism began to emerge. Over the next 200 years or so, significant scientific discoveries were made, and their commercialisation saw the growth of the business corporation with which we are familiar. Accompanying the Industrial Revolution was a great expansion of world trade as companies sought materials and markets for finished products. Modernism is the period associated with this economic expansion. The institutions and organisations that grew to dominance during this period are also called modern. These organisations generally are profit seeking, have private ownership, are actively managed and respond to market forces. Although most people work in small organisations, it is the large organisations that dominate the business landscape and capture most researchers' attentions.

You would probably agree that we live in a world dominated by modernist thought and institutions. But the expansion of capitalism has not been without its critics. These critics—among the more widely known being Marx and Engels—viewed capitalism as a passing phase of economic organisation. They observed that increasingly workers were becoming marginalised and exploited in the interests of capital. The workers, which they called the proletariat, would eventually rise up and overthrow the existing order. Thus capitalism was just one stage in an evolution. Both postmodernism and critical theory in their own way draw on the idea of the evolution of capitalism to another state. Postmodernism promotes a world after modern institutions have been overtaken by events. But we will start our discussion with critical theory, as it is perhaps easiest to place within this evolution.

critical theory an approach to studying organisations which concentrates on their perceived shortcomings and deficiencies

Critical theory

It is obvious from its name that **critical theory** sets out to criticise.[7] So what is it criticising? There is wide discussion about of the benefits and disadvantages of capitalism and the modern and increasingly multinational orientation of business enterprise. It is not the intention of this book to engage in this particular debate. However, critical theory attempts to highlight one particular aspect of capitalism, which is the experience of lower-level workers within organisations.

So here is one of the counterpoints to this book. Assess the material contained in it for a moment from the viewpoint of a worker. To locate this worker's experience, let's say this person is a call centre operator. The worker may be low-paid, subject to constant surveillance and control, and located in an area—as many call centres are—with few other employment opportunities. If we give this person (let's call him Peter) *voice*, that is the opportunity to be heard, he may view the material in this book as irrelevant. He may consider that it acts against his interests by promoting a system that keeps him in tedious work, lacking challenge and choice. Peter may prefer an approach to teaching that promotes greater awareness of organisational control and surveillance and be more sensitive to the social problems arising from low wages and lack of choice. Critical theorists would take the point of view of the worker; what they are criticising is the capitalist system, which they see as exploiting and marginalising (i.e. pushed to the edge of discussion so their opinions are not heard) those hired to work in the lower level of organisations.

Critical theorists, along with postmodernists, would attack positivist methodologies as laying false scientific claims to world knowledge. The idea that we can quantify, categorise and analyse organisations or social systems to any degree of accuracy is considered by them to be misleading. Much exists within organisations that defies easy explanation. Further, much of the research on organisations serves the narrow interests of managers and the owners of capital, rather than the wider interests of the worker. Its methodologies are generally familiar to most researchers but its assumptions of exploitation and marginalisation, although of course true in many instances, have a political commitment when applied to the economic system in its entirety.

Critical theory therefore has a heavy social activist overlay. It considers that work in a capitalist system is inherently dehumanising and oppressing, but most critical theorists do not seek an overthrow of the social system. They seek to create conditions which promote the emancipation of people. This is done by theorising, research and awareness building.

Postmodernism

We often speak of critical theory and **postmodernism** in the same breath, but they have different origins.[8] A group of philosophers, later known as postmodernists, emerged in Europe after World War II ended in 1945. The most widely known and quoted are Wittgenstein, Lyotard, Foucault and Derrida. They came to maturity at a tumultuous time, with the war in Europe having devastated populations and created human suffering on a scale impossible to imagine. The end of the war brought further tensions as Europe became one of the main arenas of conflict between communism and capitalism. The age in which they lived was characterised by abuse of power, so it is not surprising that power became a central focus in their writings.

Their philosophies envisaged a social system which was shorn of much of the prejudice and power relations of the past. We have used the term philosophy in the sense that these were philosophers in the traditional sense of the word, not management researchers seeking better ways to manage. Consequently, postmodernism should be seen as part of a philosophical system with its own

post modernism an approach to studying organisations which emerged from European philosophical origins and which rejects traditional approaches to studying organisations

language, jargon and terminology. The use of postmodernist language enables easy identification of papers written from this perspective.

In reviewing postmodernism, it is helpful to remember that organisational theory is not just a subset of management inquiry. It is a cross-disciplinary study, drawing on sociology, anthropology and social psychology. Each of these disciplines contributes in its own way to knowledge in the area and each, in turn, influences the way that knowledge evolves. As the functioning of organisations is of great importance to management researchers, they in turn have influenced the way that organisational theory has been constructed, researched and interpreted. In some ways it is helpful to view postmodernist approaches as emerging from the non-management disciplines.

Postmodernism is not an easy approach to describe. There are different schools of thought, each with its own interpretation. We will concentrate on describing the four areas of postmodernism relevant to this book. These are how knowledge is generated and defined, the power/knowledge connection, the role of language in researching organisations, and postmodernism's political agenda.

OT CLOSEUP

A postmodernist glossary

Postmodernists have developed their own vocabulary, which is used in their publications. Some of the more commonly used and easy to describe terms are listed below. A number of these terms are not exclusive to postmodernism and have quite wide application, but an understanding of them is necessary to appreciate the meanings behind postmodernist writing. Many postmodernist articles are difficult to interpret, not because the ideas behind them are hard to grasp but because meanings are hidden behind arcane terminology.

Deconstruction. Pulling apart in order to understand. Anything may be deconstructed, including society, but postmodernists generally apply the word to the use of language.

Discourse. Communication through words. The wider meaning is associated with not just sentences but streams of thought.

Domination. One group attempting to rule or govern another.

Elite. Those holding power and influence.

Hegemony. Dominance over a group of people.

Marginalisation. Ignoring the attitudes and experiences of groups or individual.

Metanarratives. A group of narratives or stories which inform the dominant discourse or communication

Other. Those excluded by the dominant group.

Postcolonial analysis. Attitudes and values attributed to the Third (postcolonial) World. Most research is oriented to First World experience.

Privileged position. Those whose opinions, or voice, are heard. Often refers to those whose opinions dominate research.

Reflexivity. Derives from the word 'reflect' and refers to the need for researchers constantly to consider the implications and effectiveness of their research.

Reification. Converting something intangible into concrete form.

Signification. The meaning behind something.

Voice. An opinion or point of view. When a group or person does not have voice, it implies that their opinions or attitudes are not being heard.

The generation of knowledge

Earlier we described the way that most of the knowledge in this text has been generated. Postmodernists would consider that this approach has major flaws. Postmodernists challenge the claim that science is objective and impartial. They claim it falsely promotes the concept that the world is capable of being known and controlled through reason. They propose that positivist approaches structure knowledge in ways that do not represent what is occurring in organisations. This is called *reification*—that is, giving physical attributes to something which does not exist in a tangible form. Through the process of reification we have shaped knowledge into certain forms that suit the researcher's purpose. This has become the way we have learnt to know the world and the way in which reality is represented. This leads to one of the central points of difference between postmodernism and scientific methodology: that is, that postmodernists consider knowledge to be socially constructed. This social construction of knowledge has generated a view of organisations which reflects the interests of management and perpetuates the interests of those who traditionally exercise power in organisations. This group is generally termed the elite.

Postmodernists consider that this process of inquiry has devalued the other—those silent voices which have not participated in our research. Postmodernists would consider that we have created a situation where a managerial elite exerts hegemony and domination over marginalised groups and have ignored the issues of class, gender and ethnicity.

The power/knowledge connection

Power is at the heart of postmodernist concerns. Power is generally seen in a negative light, as a vehicle for exploitation rather than as a means of achieving goals. Power becomes the way in which domination is exercised in organisations. There is a power/knowledge connection. Power emerges from knowledge and knowledge is kept within the empowered group by the control of language.

The role of language

In undertaking empirical research, we use language as representation; it represents certain things we wish to research. Postmodernists, in contrast, claim that language shapes our concept of reality, and that reality is a social construction based on language. Control of language in turn controls the way in which events are interpreted and acted on. By such use of language we have generated an image of organisations that serve the interests of the elite.

Postmodernists regard language not as a passive describer of objects and events but as a changing, living representation of relationships within organisations. Consequently, we should concentrate on language as action. It is primarily through language that knowledge and power is exercised and through minutely analysing language that true knowledge of organisational practices will be revealed. This process is called deconstruction.

The political agenda

We mentioned earlier that the study of organisations is cross-disciplinary. A number of these disciplines generally do not view business activities in a sympathetic light.

Many researchers in these disciplines consider business organisations as inherently discriminatory and management as an exploitative elite seeking to reproduce its own privileges. Given this, it is not surprising that postmodernism has a political edge and has developed as a form of opposition to capitalistic business enterprises. Postmodernists are particularly concerned with the modern organisation as being a form of social control. The strongest evidence in this may be found in the language used by postmodernists. Such terms as elites, marginalisation, power, domination and hegemony reveal a preoccupation with stratified social processes rather than goals, means and ends. Most postmodernists accept that their approach involves the active promotion of a political agenda.

One school of postmodernist thought makes its political agenda explicit: this is critical postmodernism. It combines the political activism of critical theory with postmodernist thought to form a critique of modern business. It actively seeks to promote research and theorising aimed at demonstrating the inherent inequality of business organisations. The aim is not to develop ways of making large organisations less oppressive but to engineer their replacement with smaller, more inclusive units.

Overall, the view of human nature taken by postmodernists is not particularly complimentary. They view the world as being divided between the oppressed and the oppressor, the elite and the marginalised, the powered and the disempowered. The only purposeful activity that is acknowledged by them is the exercise and reinforcement of power by elites for reasons which are never articulated but which may be assumed to be for the purposes of exploitation. The marginalised, downtrodden and victims of the exercise of power are assumed to have neither the power nor the ability to change their situation. As a result, power and control are viewed in a negative light.

Postmodernist research

Postmodernism has found its expression more in theorising than in research output. There are a number of studies, however, which illustrate a postmodernist approach. One study identified that 'just-in-time' inventory management and 'total quality control' are associated with an increase in management control and reduced worker autonomy.[9] But there is very little research that can specifically be identified as postmodern.

Postmodernists reject the positivist approach to research and advocate that researchers concentrate their efforts on micro-texts and individual encounters rather than on researching total organisations. As a result, postmodernist researchers concentrate on analysis of text and vocabulary in order to peel away layers of meanings. One of the reasons for the low volume of postmodernist research may be that many organisational researchers lack skills in language interpretation and text analysis. Another is that the focus of postmodernist inquiry leads to research difficulties. It is tricky, for instance, to measure such phenomena as power, influence and exploitation. Not only are these subjective, but they are constantly shifting within organisations.

Yet another postmodernism

Some researchers apply a different interpretation to the term postmodernism.[10] They regard modernism as the period dominated by large bureaucratic organisations. They see such organisations as being outdated, inefficient and unable to respond to change. They are characterised by high levels of control and provide low levels of autonomy to workers. The current age, which is that after modernism, is characterised by fast-changing technologies and environments and higher levels of competition. Modernist, bureaucratic organisations are seen to be ill-suited to this environment. This has led to the emergence of the postmodernist organisation. These are small, nimble organisations with low levels of hierarchy and control, increased worker autonomy, and fewer rules and regulations.

It can be seen that this interpretation of postmodernism is different from that previously discussed. It approaches business organisations in a conventional manner and proposes that a new organisational form is emerging in response to environmental changes. We will expand on the new organisational forms in later chapters.

Postmodernism and this book

Researchers and theorists study organisations for many different reasons. As forming organisations is a fundamental human activity, it is not surprising that so many different disciplines have an interest in the area. It is also understandable that the study of organisations has been influenced by political considerations.

This book draws on one subset of organisational inquiry. It uses as its subject organisations which operate within a business environment. These are primarily business organisations but may include non-profit organisations such as hospitals, educational institutions and government departments. We consider that the structure and management of these organisations reflect certain patterns and that these patterns are capable of rational inquiry and interpretation. The results of research to determine these patterns form a coherent discipline, which is the subject of this book. Hence we are relying on scientific methodology.

We study organisations from the point of view of their management. We take a sympathetic view of the manager's task, not in the sense that managers deserve sympathy but in the sense that managers in the current environment face a difficult task. Our aim is to assist managers, and those likely to be managers later in their career, in unravelling some of the difficulties associated with the organisational part of their job. Where postmodernist interpretation assists this, and it does in areas such as culture, we will include it in the text. However, remember that this book is about the total organisation and its structure. Much postmodernist theorising has greater relevance to the individual–organisational interface. This area is more the concern of organisational behaviour.

There is much that is not understood about organisations. They are, after all, an abstract construct, a human invention that exists within our imagination; it is this abstract nature that leads to the manipulative and political behaviour characteristic of organisational life. But they do exist to achieve goals. They use technologies that are measurable and observable and have structures that may be traced through areas of responsibilities and reporting relationships. They exist within environments that may be classified and apply strategies that may be categorised. It is at this level of application that this book is aimed.

Coming attractions: the plan of this book

This book is concerned with applying organisation theory to answering the following five questions:

1 How do we know whether an organisation is successful?
2 How can we classify and describe the components of an organisation?

3   What influences the structure an organisation adopts?
4   What options do managers have for designing their organisation, and when should each be used?
5   How do you apply knowledge of organisation theory to help managers to solve current management problems?

The issue of an organisation's success is subsumed under the topic of *organisational effectiveness*. This is *the* dependent variable; it is the primary object of our attention. However, what constitutes organisational effectiveness is itself not easy to determine. In Chapter 3, four approaches to defining and measuring organisational effectiveness are presented. We consider what it is that organisations are trying to do and how various constituencies may define and appraise the same organisation's effectiveness differently. We also provide guidelines to help you evaluate an organisation's effectiveness.

Organisation structure has a definite but complicated meaning. As noted previously, the three primary components or *dimensions of an organisation* are complexity, formalisation and centralisation. They represent the variables that, when combined, create different organisational designs. Chapter 4 takes an in-depth look at each of these dimensions of organisation structure. We also describe the five basic structural forms that an organisation adopts.

The most vocal debate in organisational theory surrounds the question of what determines structure. Attention has focused on five determinants: the organisation's overall *strategy*; *size*, or the number of people employed by the organisation; the degree of routineness in the *technology* used by the organisation to transform its inputs into finished products or services; the degree of uncertainty in the organisation's *environment*; and the self-serving preferences of those individuals or groups who hold *power and control* in the organisation. The first four of these determinants have been labelled 'contingency variables' because their supporters argue that structure will change to reflect changes in them.[11] So, for example, if structure is contingent on size, a change in size will result in a change in the organisation's structure. The power-control perspective, however, is non-contingent. Its supporters propose that, in all instances, an organisation's structure is determined by the interests of those in power and that these individuals will always prefer the structural design that maximises their control. In Chapters 5 to 9, we review the five determinants and assess under what conditions each can become the major cause of an organisation's structure. Chapter 10 integrates the previous chapters by discussing how environmental and technological changes have led to new, emergent forms of organisations.

Certain issues are currently receiving the bulk of attention by organisational theorists as they attempt to offer solutions to organisational problems currently challenging managers. These include *managing the environment, organisational change, organisational culture, evolution*, and *gender in organisations*. Chapters 11 to 15 look at each of these issues and demonstrate how organisational theory concepts can assist in their management. Following Chapter 15 you'll find a set of cases. These provide additional opportunities to apply the concepts introduced in the book to the solution of management problems.

Figure 1.4 summarises the plan of this book and how it has been translated into topics and chapters. Our primary concern is with the impact of various structures

FIGURE 1.4 Framework for analysing organisation theory

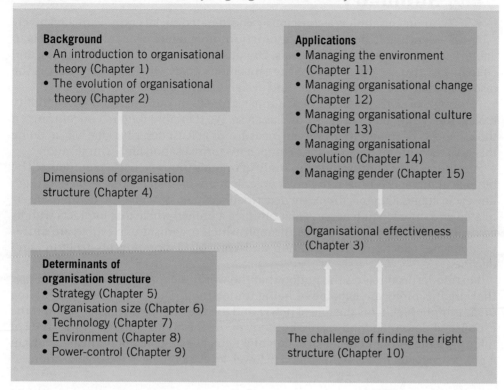

on effectiveness. Therefore, we begin with a discussion of organisational effectiveness. Then we define structural components and the determinants of structure. This is followed by a section on the various design options that can be constructed out of the structural components. Attention is continually focused on linking structural designs with effectiveness; after reviewing the various structural options, you should be able to ascertain under what conditions each is preferable. The section on applications demonstrates how organisation theory concepts relate to five current managerial issues.

A final point needs to be made here: organisational theory concepts apply to subunits of an organisation as well as to the overall organisation. Although we will focus in this book on the structure and design of entire organisations, that is not the only level of analysis to which this book is applicable. The concepts to which you will be introduced in the following chapters are relevant to analysing divisions, departments and similar subunits within organisations as well as to organisations in their entirety. In fact, most large organisations are too diverse and internally heterogeneous to be treated as a singular structural entity. Consequently, when we say that an organisation is structured in a certain singular way, in many cases this is a generalisation. A closer look typically reveals several different structural forms within most organisations, especially the large and complex ones.

Summary

An organisation is a consciously coordinated social entity, with a relatively identifiable boundary, that functions on a relatively continuous basis to achieve a common goal or set of goals. Organisation design is the constructing and changing of structure to achieve the organisation's goals. Organisation theory is the discipline that studies the structure and design of organisations.

Although organisations influence most aspects of our life, their intangibility makes them difficult to describe and analyse. We therefore tend to concentrate on those aspects of organisations we can measure, or at least describe. One way of doing this is to measure an organisation's complexity, formalisation and centralisation.

Another way of approaching the study of organisations is to use metaphors. The biological metaphor is used to depict organisations as systems that evolve through life-cycle stages. Organisations are described as open systems—made up of inter-related and interdependent parts that produce a unified whole that interacts with its environment. The distinct stages through which organisations evolve are entrepreneurial, collectivity, formalisation-and-control, elaboration-of-structure, and decline.

Postmodernism rejects the notion that the world is capable of being known and that organisations are capable of being understood. Their approach to studying organisations highlights the role of power and the way that language perpetuates the exercise of power. They advocate the study of organisations through the analysis of micro-interactions and deconstruction of language. Most postmodernists maintain a political agenda that is sympathetic to lower-level members of the organisation.

For review and discussion

1 Are all groups organisations? Discuss.
2 Is a small business, with only two or three employees, an organisation? Discuss.
3 What research methodologies are generally used to study organisation theory?
4 How can the systems perspective help you better understand organisations?
5 Compare *open* and *closed* systems.
6 What are the characteristics of an open system?
7 Why do organisations tend towards growth?
8 Give an example of how the environment affects an organisation you are familiar with.
9 At what stage of their life cycle are the following organisations?
   • Qantas
   • the educational institution you are studying at
   • Shell
   • the Department of Foreign Affairs and Trade
   • the ABC.
10 Is organisational decline inevitable? Defend your position.
11 Contrast organisation structure and design.
12 Contrast organisational behaviour and organisation theory.

13 Describe the approach of critical theory. Does it complement organisation theory or does it replace it?

14 Identify the way that postmodernists approach organisation theory. In what way may postmodernist theories be of use to managers?

15 For each of the following organisations, identify their inputs, transformation processes, outputs, relevant subsystems and environment. Be as specific as possible.
   • the Smith Family
   • the Greek Orthodox Church
   • the Carlton Football Club
   • the Royal Australian Navy
   • St Vincent's Hospital
   • a local pharmacist.

 CASE FOR CLASS DISCUSSION
'Tell your friends about One-Tel'

You may remember One-Tel, a telecommunications company started by Jodee Rich and Brad Keeling. It was founded in 1995 and aimed to take advantage of the deregulation of the telecommunications industry that had occurred in the early 1990s. It attracted the backing of the Murdoch and Packer families, which subscribed more than $600 million dollars in capital to help the company get established.

The deregulation of the telecommunications market seemed to offer unlimited opportunity. Telstra was felt to be a bureaucratic dinosaur, slow to adapt to the pressure of competition. One-Tel's business plan aimed to take advantage of this. As it did not have its own network, it would buy capacity from Telstra and then resell it to retail customers. It aimed primarily at the youth market, and its 'dude', the bearded, beret-wearing young man, became a well-known advertising icon, along with the jingle 'Tell your friends about One-Tel'. The advertising did not come cheap however, with over $40 million being spent annually on promoting the company.

Like a lot of companies at the time, One-Tel was basically established as a 'flip' company: that is, once it had proved it was viable and was starting to generate cash, the founders would sell their shares at a handy markup, possibly to Telstra or Optus or some other interested party. It was never a technology-based company; the founders and most of the employees viewed their main challenges as being marketing and not technical in nature. Most of the 1700 employees worked in call centres, with the technology being provided by suppliers.

From 1996, One-Tel's ambitions started to expand at an alarming rate. It replicated its Australian operations in Britain and France, building a good-sized retail presence. It also decided to build its own Australian telecommunications network, costing almost $1 billion. Finding this amount of money was easy: Lucent, the supplier of the equipment, provided vendor finance and did not expect payment until the system was up and running and generating revenue. One-Tel also spent up big on 3G licences, which enabled large amounts of data to be transmitted to a mobile phone. But it also needed large amounts of capital to develop the infrastructure before it could be used.

While it would be wrong to say that One-Tel was a market darling, most felt that it had a good chance of surviving. Even allowing for the irrational exuberance of the time, it was considered that the founders had a sound business model. But all was not well with the One-Tel dude. It had a high level of cash burn, a finance term describing the rate at which more cash is being spent than earned. It was purchasing capacity from Telstra at 18.5 cents per call but charging its customers 17c per call—that is, if the customer actually received the bill. One-Tel's billing system hardly worked, and invoices were generally late and incorrect. And even when they were delivered, there was a high level of bad debts among its youth-oriented customers. One-Tel never managed to focus its energies on its revenue problem.

Indeed, one of the criticisms of the company was that Rich and Keeling never listened to anyone. Neither had much in the way of experience in running a large corporation. They seemed to rely on faith and time rather than management skills to solve the company's problems. They continually produced unrealistic, almost misleading, financial forecasts and never brought skilled management to bear on the fundamentally important issues facing the company. While large amounts were being spent on expanding capacity, there was underinvestment in the core business, including billing and customer service. As a result, systems were never put in place to manage what turned out to be uncontrolled growth. These shortcomings were made worse by Jodee Rich's refusal to listen to advice.

Despite frantic attempts to raise extra capital, an insolvent One-Tel finally called in administrators, who subsequently liquidated the company in June 2001. Most of its assets were sold by auction in an attempt to repay its $633 million in debt. In addition to the mundane office equipment, purchasers bought a life-sized model of the dude, a vintage motor cycle and 21 feng shui dragons.

Adapted from: John Durie, 'One-Tel a Lesson for Media Heirs', *The Australian Financial Review*, 31 May 2001, p. 64.

QUESTIONS

1 Looking back on One-Tel's experience, what contributions could have been made to keeping the company solvent using techniques drawn from organisation theory, organisational behaviour and other disciplines?

2 Show how the characteristics of open-systems theory could be applied in this case.

3 Show how this case illustrates the life-cycle perspective of organisations.

FURTHER READING

Robert Chia, 'From Modern to Post Modern Organizational Analysis', *Organization Studies*, 16(4), 1995, pp. 580–604.

Robert Gephart, 'Critical Management Studies', *Academy of Management Review*, 18(4), 1993, pp. 798–803.

Daniel Katz & R.L. Khan, *The Social Psychology of Organizations*, 2nd edn, New York: Wiley, 1978.

John Kimberley & R.H. Miles, eds, *The Organizational Life Cycle*, San Francisco: Jossey-Bass, 1980.

Gareth Morgan, *Images of Organizations*, Beverly Hills, CA: Sage, 1986.

NOTES

1 The material for this case study has been drawn from Ben Sandilands. 'Virgin Fills Airline Brand Vacuum', *The Australian Financial Review*, 13 September 2000; Sharon McDonald-Leigh, 'My Job', *The Sydney Morning Herald*, 23 September 2000; Lachlan Colquhoun, 'Newcomers Score in Dogfights: Early Rounds', *Business Review Weekly*, 13 October 2000.

2 John R. Kimberly, 'The Life Cycle Analogy and the Study of Organizations: Introduction', in J.R. Kimberly & R.H. Miles, eds, *The Organizational Life Cycle*, San Francisco: Jossey-Bass, 1980, pp. 6–9.

3 See Donde P. Ashmos & George P. Huber, 'The Systems Paradigm in Organization Theory: Correcting the Record and Suggesting the Future', *Academy of Management Review*, October 1987, pp. 607–21.

4 See, for example, Gareth Morgan, *Images of Organizations*, Beverly Hills, CA.: Sage, 1986.

5 This section is adapted from Daniel Katz & Robert L. Kahn, *The Social Psychology of Organizations*, 2nd edn, New York: John Wiley, 1978, pp. 22–30.

6 Adapted from Kim S. Cameron & David A. Whetten, 'Models of the Organization Life Cycle: Applications to Higher Education', *Research in Higher Education*, June 1983, pp. 211–24.

7 Robert Gephart, 'Critical Management Studies', *Academy of Management Review*, 18(4), 1993, pp. 798–803.

8 The following are a selection of articles relevant to the postmodernist approach to organisation theory: John Hassard, 'Post Modern Organizational Analysis: Towards a Conceptual Framework', *Journal of Management Studies*, 31(3), 1994, pp. 303–24; Robert Chia, 'From Modern to Postmodern Organizational Analysis', *Organization Studies*, 16(4), 1995, pp. 580–604; Howard Schwartz, 'The Postmodern Organization: Mastering the Art of Irreversible Change; Managing in the Postmodern World: America's Revolution Against Exploitation', *Academy of Management Review*, 20(1), 1995, pp. 215–21; Kenneth Gergen & Tojo Thatchenkery, 'Organization, Science as Social Construction: Postmodern Potentials', *Journal of Applied Behavioural Science*, 32(4), 1996, pp. 356–77; Marta Calas & Linda Smircich, 'Past Postmodernism? Reflections and Tentative Directions', *Academy of Management Review*, 24(4), 1999, pp. 649–71; Mats Alvesson & Stanley Deetz, 'Critical Theory and Postmodernism: Approaches to Organizational Studies' in Stewart Clegg, Cynthia Hardy & Walter Nord, eds, *Handbook of Organizational Studies*, London: Sage 1996; and Steven Feldman, 'The Levelling of Organization Culture: Egalitarianism in Critical Postmodern Organization Theory', *Journal of Applied Behavioural Sciences*, 35(2), 1999, pp. 228–44.

9 Thomas Lawrence & Nelson Phillips, 'Commentary: Separating Play and Critique: Postmodern and Critical Perspectives on TQM/BPR', *Journal of Management Inquiry*, 7(2), 1998, pp. 154–60.

10 Richard Daft & Arie Lewin, 'Where are the Theories for the "New" Organizational Forms: An Editorial Essay', *Organizational Science*, 4(4), 1993, i–iv.

11 See, for instance, George Schreyogg, 'Contingency and Choice in Organization Theory', *Organization Studies*, No. 3, 1980, pp. 305–26; and Henry L. Tosi, Jr & John W. Slocum, Jr, 'Contingency Theory: Some Suggested Directions', *Journal of Management*, Spring 1984, pp. 9–26.

CHAPTER 2

The evolution of organisation theory

After reading this chapter you should be able to:

1 describe the evolution of the different approaches to organisation theory;

2 identify Adam Smith's contribution to organisation theory;

3 explain how the Industrial Revolution changed organisations;

4 define the four principles of scientific management;

5 describe Henri Fayol's contribution to organisation theory;

6 define Max Weber's bureaucracy;

7 describe the Hawthorne studies;

8 contrast Theory X and Theory Y;

9 identify the major contributors to the contingency approach;

10 contrast the rational and political perspectives of organisations;

11 look at some contemporary organisational approaches.

Introduction

Telstra and organisation theory

Telstra is one of Australia's largest companies, with a dominant position in the telecommunications industry. Looking at the way in which Telstra manages its operations we can identify most of the streams of management thought that emerged during the 20th century. Few of Telstra's lower ranking employees are unaffected by the need for efficiency. Ways of undertaking tasks are carefully researched and laid down. Technical standards demand that all staff be adequately trained for their job and fully supported with the appropriate tools and equipment. Call centres are monitored to ensure that customer service is being maintained, with careful attention being paid to work stations and ergonomics. Staff are selected on the basis of skill sets most appropriate to the job.

But Telstra also has other management tasks to undertake. Staff are not automatons; the needs of people need to be taken into account. Telstra must constantly balance the needs of its employees with its requirement to constantly improve productivity and lower costs. The basic choices it makes in this area have far-reaching effects on issues such as industrial relations and staff motivation and commitment. An examination of the structure of Telstra would reveal that it was not a random agglomeration of departments and relationships between people. We could, with sufficient research, identify the influence of Telstra's technology, its environment, its strategy and also that of its enormous size. Telstra has over 40 000 employees.

As with all organisations, decision making in Telstra can be highly political. There would be few major decisions, such as those concerned with strategy or the direction and nature of major investments, in which there were not different attitudes and opinions. These must be worked through the political process to arrive at a course of action. And the size of Telstra, its complexity and technological sophistication mean that it is impossible for one person, or even a group of people, to fully grasp what is happening within the organisation. This is a further impetus to political action.

Our observation of Telstra has highlighted the mainstreams of organisational inquiry over the past 100 years. The earliest of these was the quest for efficiency, as proposed by Frederick Taylor and the scientific management school. The second, starting in the 1930s, introduced the human needs of employees as a concern for management. The third was the influence of contingency factors such as technology and environment on structure. And the fourth was the way in which power and politics shaped decision making. Although these approaches came in waves, and may be identified with a particular time frame, they did not replace or supplant the previous approaches. Each provided new insight, and, as we shall see, in their own way influence organisations even now.

The study of organisational theory has undergone an evolutionary process. The current state of inquiry is a result of different perspectives that have emerged in response to technological, environmental and social changes. The attention given to analysing organisations by both academics and practitioners has gathered pace over the past century. Not surprisingly, as those who comment and theorise on organisations come from a wide variety of backgrounds, there are often divergent views as to how best to study organisations and for whose purpose they should be analysed. The purpose of this chapter is to provide a brief overview of the main contributions and demonstrate how we got to where we are today. In doing this we will show how technological and environmental changes have influenced the study of organisations. One of the themes of this chapter will be that current organisation theories reflect a cumulative developmental pattern. Theories have been introduced, evaluated and refined over time, with new insight reflecting areas that earlier theories overlooked. Although organisational theory is subject to fashions and fads in thinking and research, few approaches are entirely discredited; generally the more innovative and useful parts of each theory find a continuing place in management thought. So if you want to understand what is happening today in organisation theory, you need to look back along the path from which it has come.

Developing a framework

Most systematic study of organisation theory has taken place since about 1900. This is not surprising, as by this time the industrialised world started to take the form with which we are familiar. Most inventions that were to shape the 20th century had been devised and it was left to subsequent efforts to commercialise them. There were a few major pre-20th-century milestones, and we will discuss them in the next section. However, for us the real problem lies in developing a framework that can adequately demonstrate the evolutionary nature of contemporary organisation theory. That is, how do you *organise* organisation theory?

It has been suggested that there are two underlying dimensions in the evolution of organisation theory and that each dimension, in turn, has opposing perspectives.[1] The first dimension reflects the fact that organisations are *systems*. We described the systems perspective in Chapter 1. We saw that organisations can be viewed as open systems, which interact with their environment. Or they may be viewed as closed systems, which are almost self-sufficient entities. Before about 1960, organisation theory tended to be dominated by a closed-system perspective. Organisations were seen as essentially autonomous and sealed off from their environment, or at least that was what management attempted to achieve. In about 1960, however, organisation theory began to take on a distinctly open-systems perspective. Analyses that had previously placed the primary focus on the internal characteristics of organisation gave way to approaches that emphasised the importance for the organisation of events and processes external to it.

The second dimension deals with the *ends* of organisation structure. Here again are two opposed positions. The rational or strategic perspective argues that the structure of an organisation is conceived as a vehicle for effectively achieving specified objectives and that this perspective is the main influence on organisational design. In contrast, the social perspective emphasises that structure is primarily the result of conflicting forces of the organisation's constituents, who seek power and control.

In addition to viewing the evolution of organisation theory along these two dimensions, we shall identify the main environmental, technological and political forces that have influenced ways of thinking in relation to organisations. By doing this we are developing tools of analysis that enable us to understand the current state of research and practice.

Early contributions

The concept of a person whose main task was to 'manage' is of quite recent origin. It evolved with the growth of the modern industrial undertaking, whose complex operations required large numbers of administrators. Prior to this, managerial tasks were undertaken as a byproduct of the position a person held. If people were civil engineers, they oversaw the work of those constructing their projects. If people were naval architects, they superintended the construction of ships.

There is no shortage of examples of organisational structures in classical times. Both the words 'administrator' and 'superintendent' have Latin origins. The structure of organisations was even referred to in the bible, where Moses' father-in-law refers to leaders of tens, fifties, hundreds and thousands. The Roman army had a similar structure, with the centurion being the leader of the 'hundreds'. Until the growth of the modern corporation, the largest organisations were associated with the church and the army (and sometimes navy). The structures and practices of these organisations provided the template for most organisations that followed. They inducted members and socialised them into their ways. Membership implied disciplined conformance. There was a ranking of administrators and managers according to levels of responsibility, with each level of management having its badges of rank and symbols of office. This led to pyramid-shaped organisations. Loyalty and predictable performance was an outcome of the culture of the organisation, enabling management to take place over a wide geographic spread. Armies also developed the concept of line and staff, with the 'line' being those engaged in actual warfare and 'staff' describing those who provided the services supporting them, such as planning, victualling and transport.

The experience of preindustrial organisations foreshadowed many of the problems faced by modern managers.[2] The English East India Company, for instance, incorporated in the 1600s, was faced with the problem of profitably exploiting trade with the Far East, the region stretching from India to China. Its greatest problems were those of maintaining discipline among its workforce, determining where it was making and losing money, and managing significant cultural diversity. It never surmounted the first problem: distances were too great, and a sense of entrepreneurialism and adventure led to most employees looking after their own interests rather than the company's. The second problem, that of knowing where it was making and losing money, was similarly never solved: management accounting was in its infancy, and accounts for some voyages were years late. Some commentators claim that lack of up-to-date financial data was the main reason for the company's demise. The issue of managing cultural diversity was partly solved by setting up a company college in London where local history, culture and languages were taught to those heading for the Far East.

The 18th century provides us with the first systematic analyses of the basis of modern organisational life, that of **division of labour**. The division of labour is the breaking down of tasks into simple components which can be undertaken on a repetitive basis by job specialists. Since antiquity, there had always been an element of division of labour. There were those who specialised in warfare, engineering, tax gathering and the like. But most were born into a station in life, such as peasant or labourer, and most grew their own food and led a self-sufficient life. Son followed father and daughter followed mother in occupation and activity.

Not surprisingly, productivity was low. Adam Smith, observing what was happening around him in an industrialising Britain, wrote in 1776 about the

division of labour
functional specialisation; job broken down into simple and repetitive tasks

economic advantages of the division of labour in the pin-manufacturing industry.[3] Smith noted that 10 individuals, each doing a specialised task, could produce about 48 000 pins a day among them. He proposed, however, that if each were working separately and independently, the 10 workers would be lucky to make 200 or even 10 pins between them in one day. Smith concluded then what most practising managers now accept as common sense: namely, that division of labour can bring about significant efficiencies.

The concept of the division of labour had widespread implications for organisations and their management. No longer was one person producing all his/her own needs according to his/her own wants. The division of labour implied that someone had to decide what to produce, how to produce it, provide the capital equipment and then staff what was, in effect, a small production line. These are all, of course, functions of management. The other implication was that a far more sophisticated system of exchange was required to trade the outputs of the division of labour. Adam Smith identified that market forces played this role, and he was the first to describe the role of markets as mediators in economic exchange.

The 19th century saw the development of two other industrial innovations with far-ranging implications for organisation theory. These were the emergence of mass production and the introduction of the railways.[4] These days we hardly give these two major innovations a second thought. But the organisational structures needed to make them work were the forerunners of the modern industrial undertaking.

First, mass production. Folk law has it that Henry Ford's model-T production line was the first example of mass production, but this is not the case. Ford was greatly influenced by previous attempts at mass production, including the Chicago abattoirs with their moving production line. The first modern use of mass production emerged in the United States around the 1840s. A large array of industrial and consumer goods, ranging from harvesters, sewing machines and locks to armaments, was built on production lines using specially constructed capital equipment. Components were accurately built to very fine tolerances, which enabled the interchanging of parts. This was in contrast to the craft method of production, where a craftsman built a complete item such as a lock using just sheet metal and basic tools as inputs. Needless to say, no two locks were the same, and no part was interchangeable with a lock made by another craftsman.

Using modern terminology, mass production 'dumbed down' labour, in that craftsmen disappeared to be replaced by low-skilled assembly-line workers. The system was, however, knowledge-intensive. The extent of engineering input, including product design, knowledge of metals, alloys and machining as well as tooling and capital equipment manufacturing, led to the production line as the 'high-tech' phenomenon of its day. One of the greatest achievements of mass production was at the Springfield armaments factory in the 1860s. So well known were the mass production techniques at this plant that the system used on the Ford production line was initially known as the Springfield system.

Out of the mass production system emerged the modern industrial structure, with workers, foremen, superintendents, works managers and general managers. We also see a type of line and staff arrangement, with the designers and administrators comprising the staff and the assembly-line workers forming the line. Socially, we see the widespread introduction of working for wages. Prior to the modern factory, most workers were self-employed either as farmers or contractors. The emergence of the wage earner as the urban proletariat had significant implications for the political activity and the structure of society.

The second major 19th-century innovation was the railway. Although still a transport backbone in most countries, the railways' neglect in some parts of the world gives them an air of run-down obsolescence. From today's perspective it is difficult to appreciate how innovative railways were, or to comprehend the many management challenges their administration posed. At the height of railway construction in the 1850s and 60s, railway companies were being floated at a rate hardly matched until the dot-com boom of the late 1990s. Railways were very knowledge-intensive. They posed significant engineering challenges, in both the construction of the railway and the engines and rolling stock. But matters were not easy when it came to their organisation. They had to be run profitably in order to pay dividends to those who subscribed capital to build them. Large numbers of people had to be employed with many different job specialisations. Extensive training in new skills was required. The railways were a 24-hour per day operation, and long distances and often different time zones had to be accommodated. Safety and profitability required the development of timetables and schedules. A workforce culture had to be developed to reinforce strict timekeeping.

It is not surprising that the army provided a basis for the management systems that were adopted. The railways were structured along departmental lines, with each department specialising in a particular task. Planning staff undertook the task of scheduling and timetabling. Uniforms with badges of rank reinforced strict hierarchical control. And in Prussia station staff even stood to attention as a train passed.

The structure that evolved promoted effective work effort and minimised complexity. Clear lines of authority were introduced and areas of responsibility spelt out. High levels of coordination were achieved through planning and scheduling and the division of labour was promoted through hiring and training. All of these will be familiar to most readers, even though the technologies we now use are radically different.

Turning to contributions made during the 20th century, we will begin with the organisational forms that emerged to exploit the new technological discoveries of the late 19th and early 20th centuries.

From 1900 to the 1930s—early management theories

1900–1930s
Need to reduce production costs leading to improving efficiency. Achievement of rational goals with closed system perspective. Focus of analysis was work practices

The main aim of theorists during the **1900–1930s** was to identify universal principles that could be applied to management. The challenges of management seemed to be the same everywhere, and technologies were not considered to be sufficiently different to justify different ways of managing. As this period saw the emergence of the first systematised approach to organisation theory, we call the output of the various theorists the classical school. In a sense it is misleading to call those whose work is described below 'theorists'. They were in fact practical people, generally successful practising managers, who drew on their experiences in publication and lecturing.

Managers faced considerable challenges in this period. They were responding to the challenge of how to manage the large-sized organisations that were emerging at the end of the 19th century. This was the beginning of the age of mass production, when the products of technological innovation had an extensive market if they could be produced in quantity at a low price. As a result, organisations that produced them had to be of a large size.

There were, however, additional social factors complicating the management of organisations. It was a period of great industrial unrest, with bitter strikes and continuous agitation by many workers in support of major political change. Both complicating and contributing to this were the tensions caused by wars and the Depression. Additionally, most governments were attempting to isolate their economies through high tariff barriers and other restrictions on trade. It is not surprising that most managers took a similar attitude and attempted to isolate their organisations from outside influence.

The classical theorists had in common the view that organisations were established, and managed, to achieve rational goals such as profit or return on assets. As we have seen, there was a very strong desire to reduce the costs of production in order to expand the market for their products. One of the main aims of the classical theorists was to improve productive efficiency of the organisations. They viewed the ideal organisation as a closed system created to achieve goals efficiently. Let's now examine the contributions of the main contributors to this approach.

Frederick Taylor and scientific management

The publication in 1911 of Frederick Winslow Taylor's *Principles of Scientific Management* marked the beginning of serious theory building in the field of management and organisations.[5] Taylor was a mechanical engineer by training, employed by the Midvale and Bethlehem Steel companies in Pennsylvania. He strongly believed, on the basis of his observation of work methods at the time, that worker output was only about one-third of what was possible. He set out to correct the situation by applying the scientific method to jobs on the shop floor. His desire to find the 'one best way' in which each job should be done would be part of what today we would call the issue of work design.

After years of conducting experiments with workers, he proposed four principles of **scientific management**, which, he argued, would result in significant increases in productivity: (a) the replacement of rule-of-thumb methods for determining each element of a worker's job with scientific determination; (b) the scientific selection and training of workers; (c) the cooperation of management and labour to accomplish work objectives, in accordance with the scientific method; and (d) a more equal division of responsibility between managers and workers, with the former doing the planning and supervising and the latter doing the execution.

This process, however, led to the workers' greatest criticism of Taylorism—that is, the shift in power from the worker to the manager. The deskilling of work took away much of the workers' pride in their jobs. It also took away their independence to determine how a job was to be done, and placed this decision with the management of the organisation. Under Taylorism, there was a distinct shift towards centralisation in organisations. Taylorism was also introduced when mass production could greatly reduce the cost of many products. The motor car, a whole range of domestic appliances, aircraft manufacture, and food preserving and packaging were just some of the industries in their infancy in the early days of Taylorism. They were to prove the most enthusiastic adopters of Taylor's principles.

In retrospect, we recognise that Taylor offered a limited focus on organisations. He was looking only at organising work at the lowest level of the organisation—

scientific management a movement, initiated by Frederick Taylor, to achieve production efficiencies by systematising and standardising jobs to achieve the 'one best way' they should be done appropriate to the managerial job of a foreman. If you were to take a course today in industrial engineering or production management, you would find that Taylor's work created the foundation for these disciplines. Yet in spite of the fact that he focused on a very limited segment of organisational activity, he revolutionised the manager's job. He explicitly demonstrated that managers should carefully assess the one best way for each job to be done to maximise efficiency. Then it was management's responsibility to explicitly select, train and motivate workers to ensure that the one best way was followed.

OT CLOSEUP

Scientific management and organisation theory

Most writings on scientific management concentrate on organising work on the factory floor. But Taylor and his colleagues made a major contribution to the management of the modern corporation. Large organisations are certainly not new: most civilisations have had to grapple with the problems of government and the need to organise armies and navies. Churches and other religious bodies are also large organisations that have had to develop the means of coping with large size and geographic spread. The growth of the large corporation, however, raised its own problems. From the beginning of the 20th century it became clear that the large corporation would become the pre-eminent organisation form, which would define industrialised life. Corporations did not become big because it was easy to manage large numbers of people; in fact, the opposite applied. Corporations became large because of the need for large-scale capital investment, the complexity of the product, such as with motor cars, or the economies arising from mass production. Large workforces had to be managed as a result of these other imperatives. The need to monitor costs and provide many of the clerical services necessary to run a complex business contributed to the growth of the workforce.

Taylor's organisational innovation was the functional foreman, who acted as a link between management and shop floor worker. But Russell Robb, of the newly formed Harvard Business School, attempted a compromise between the old military style and the new conditions of industry. He claimed that all organisations differ, depending on their methods and what they are trying to achieve. Robb noted that the modern corporation had much to learn from the military, particularly the military's stress on fixing responsibility and authority, clearly defining duties and channels of communication, and providing order and discipline.

However, in the military, order and discipline were stressed far more than was needed in the modern corporation. The industrial corporation was built on extensive division of labour and needed greater coordination of effort than did the military. Success in industry was not based on obedience but on economy of effort, and as a result the industrial corporation had to be different. There should be more stress placed on worker and management selection and training, processes had to be arranged to keep costs low, and the manager needed to be aware of the organisation as a system.

These problems rose in prominence as the corporation moved from the entrepreneurial stage, which was managed by its founder and owner, into the stage where ownership and management were distinctly separate.

Adapted from: Daniel A. Wren, The Evolution of Management Thought, 4th edn, New York: John Wiley, 1994.

Henri Fayol and principles of organisation

At about the time Taylor was writing up the results of his research on shop management in the United States, the Frenchman Henri Fayol was consolidating his **principles of organisation**.[6] Though they were writing at the same time, Fayol's and Taylor's focuses were considerably different. Taylor's ideas were based on improving the efficiency of factory work. Fayol was more concerned with the problems of management. Fayol sought to develop general principles applicable to all managers at all levels of the organisation and to describe the functions a manager should perform. Taylor, you will remember, focused on the lowest level in the organisation—floor-level management.

Fayol proposed 14 principles that he argued were universally applicable and could be taught in schools and universities. Many of these organising principles, though lacking in universality, are widely followed by managers today:

1 *Division of work.* This principle is the same as Adam Smith's 'division of labour'. Specialisation increases output by making employees more efficient.
2 *Authority.* Managers need to be able to give orders. Authority gives them this right. Along with authority, however, goes responsibility. Wherever authority is exercised, responsibility arises. To be effective, a manager's authority must equal his or her responsibility.
3 *Discipline.* Employees need to obey and respect the rules that govern the organisation. Good discipline is the result of effective leadership, a clear understanding between management and workers regarding the organisation's rules, and the judicious use of penalties for infractions of the rules.
4 *Unity of command.* Every employee should receive orders from only one superior.
5 *Unity of direction.* Each group of organisational activities that have the same objective should be directed by one manager using one plan.
6 *Subordination of individual interests to the general interests.* The interests of any one employee or group of employees should not take precedence over the interests of the organisation as a whole.
7 *Remuneration.* Workers must be paid a fair wage for their services.
8 *Centralisation.* This refers to the degree to which subordinates are involved in decision making. Whether decision making is centralised (to management) or decentralised (to subordinates) is a question of proper proportion. The problem is to find the optimum degree of centralisation for each situation.
9 *Scalar chain.* The line of authority from top management to the lowest ranks represents the scalar chain. Communications should follow this chain. However, if following the chain creates delays, cross-communication—a 'gangplank'—can be allowed if agreed to by all parties and if superiors are kept informed.
10 *Order.* People and materials should be in the right place at the right time.
11 *Equity.* Managers should be kind and fair to their subordinates.
12 *Stability of tenure of personnel.* High employee turnover is inefficient. Management should provide orderly personnel planning and ensure that replacements are available to fill vacancies.
13 *Initiative.* Employees who are allowed to originate and carry out plans will exert high levels of effort.
14 *Esprit de corps.* Promoting team spirit will build harmony and unity within the organisation.

principles of organisation
developed by Fayol to identify the functions which a manager should perform

Max Weber and bureaucracy

The third major contribution made at this time was the 'ideal-type' organisation structure proposed by the German sociologist Max Weber.[7] Writing in the early part of this century, Weber developed a structural model that, he argued, was the most efficient means by which organisations can achieve their ends. He called this ideal structure **bureaucracy**. It was characterised by division of labour, a clear authority hierarchy, formal selection procedures, detailed rules and regulations, and impersonal relationships. Weber's description of bureaucracy became the design prototype for most of today's large organisations.

Ralph Davis and rational planning

The final contribution of the classical theorists that we will introduce is the **rational-planning perspective**, which proposed that structure was the logical outcome of the organisation's objectives. This position was best expressed in the work of Ralph C. Davis.[8]

Davis stated that the primary objective of a business firm is economic service. No business can survive if it doesn't provide economic value. Economic value is generated by the activities members engage in to create the organisation's products or services. These activities then link the organisation's objectives to its results. It is management's job to group these activities together in such a way as to form the structure of the organisation. Davis concluded, therefore, that the structure of the organisation is contingent on the organisation's objectives.

The rational-planning perspective offered a simple and straightforward model for designing an organisation. Management's formal planning determines the organisation's objectives. These objectives, then, in logical fashion determine the development of structure, the flow of authority and other relationships.

Summarising the classical theorists

The classical theorists treated the organisation as having machine-like properties. They felt that the purposes of the organisation could be reduced to a few clearly defined goals, and that the way to achieve those goals was by optimising production processes through analysis and scientific thought. They considered that the task of management was capable of being expressed in a number of clearly articulated principles. They were not promoting organisational flexibility or proposing methods of adapting to change. They regarded labour as just another factor of production, and this perhaps was one of the weaknesses of the approach.

The classical theorists developed an approach to organisational theory that is very much alive today. For many organisations, particularly for those which seek to make a profit, costs are important. Continuous effort is put into attempts to produce goods more cheaply through the more efficient use of resources and selecting the right person for the task, and through formulating systems of management which are very similar to Fayol's. The motor vehicle production line is a 'classic' illustration of this.

From the 1930s to 1960—the behaviouralists

The theorists associated with this period coexisted with those from the classical school. Major events conspired to ensure that classical management theories still basically dominated management thought. In particular, World War II (1939–45),

bureaucracy an organisational form characterised by division of labour, a well-defined authority hierarchy, high formalisation, impersonality, employment decisions based on merit, career tracks for employees and distinct separation of members' organisational and personal lives

rational-planning perspective a model of organisation based upon the development of clear goals and plans to achieve those goals

with its need to recruit, train and lead large numbers of personnel, reinforced a 'military model' of management, with clearly defined goals and a tightly structured and disciplined management hierarchy. In particular, the concept of planning was given a great boost by the war. Many of the campaigns fought, such as those of D-Day in Europe and the Pacific landings, required the use of extensive coordination and planning. It was natural that the success of these campaigns would influence the thinking of the private sector. The transfer of military management techniques was facilitated by the return to business life of many of those who took part in the military campaigns as part of their war service. However, experience in the 20 years succeeding the end of the war showed that only a limited parallel could be drawn between war and business, and the role of drawing up strategic plans that looked like military campaigns diminished.

So in what way were the theorists who emerged in the 1930s different? Perhaps the best way to answer this is to look at their background and what influenced them. The early theorists such as Taylor and Fayol were primarily practical people, who were closely associated with the operation of the companies they worked for or advised. In contrast, the background of many of those who emerged in the 1930s was in the behavioural sciences. The 20th century saw the emergence of disciplines such as psychology and anthropology and their application to the workplace. It became clear to this group, which we will call the human relations school, that one of the major impacts on organisational effectiveness was the motivations and actions of the workforce. One of the characteristics of this period was the recognition of the social nature of organisations. These theorists, who are often referred to as forming the human relations school, view organisations as made up of both tasks and people. Below we discuss the contribution of a number of influential thinkers.

Elton Mayo and the Hawthorne studies

Elton Mayo probably does not deserve his prominent place in the pantheon of management history. He was an academic researcher called in to explain some unusual findings which emerged from some quite simple experiments being undertaken between 1924 and 1927 at an electrical manufacturing plant in the United States. His research became known as the **Hawthorne studies**. These studies, which would eventually be widely expanded and would carry on through the early 1930s, emerged from work being undertaken by Western Electric industrial engineers at the Hawthorne plant to examine the effect of various lighting levels on worker productivity. Control and experimental groups were established. Lighting for the experimental group was raised and lowered in intensity, while the control group worked under unchanging illumination levels. The engineers had expected individual output to be directly related to the intensity of light. However, there were contradictions in their findings. As the light level was raised in the experimental unit, output rose for both the experimental and control group. To the surprise of the engineers, as the light level was lowered in the experimental group, productivity continued to rise in both groups. In fact, a productivity decrease was observed in the experimental group only when the light intensity had been reduced to that of moonlight. The engineers concluded that illumination intensity clearly was not directly related to group productivity, but they could not explain the behaviour they had witnessed.

The Western Electric engineers asked the Harvard psychologist Elton Mayo and his associates to join the study as consultants. This began a relationship that would last until the end of 1932 and encompass numerous experiments covering the

1930–1960
Accommodating human needs in work practices. Achievement of social goals with a closed system perspective. Focus of analysis was individual worker and work group

Hawthorne studies
a series of studies which identified the behavioural basis of organisational outcomes

redesign of jobs, changes in the length of the workday and workweek, introduction of rest periods, and individual versus group wage plans.[9] For example, in one experiment the researchers sought to evaluate the effect of a piecework incentive pay system on group productivity. The results indicated that the wage-incentive plan was a less determining factor for a worker's output than were group pressure and acceptance and the feeling of security. Social norms of the group, therefore, were concluded to be the key determinants of individual work behaviour.

It is generally agreed by management scholars that the Hawthorne studies had a dramatic impact on the direction of management and organisation theory. It ushered in an era of organisational humanism. Managers would no longer consider the issue of organisation design without including effects on work groups, employee attitudes and manager–employee relationships.

Chester Barnard and cooperative systems

Merging the ideas of Taylor, Fayol and Weber with the results from the Hawthorne studies led to the conclusion that organisations were cooperative systems. They are composed of tasks and people that have to be maintained at an equilibrium state. Attention only to technical jobs or to the needs of people who do the jobs suboptimises the system. Therefore, managers need to organise around the requirements of the tasks to be performed and the needs of the people who will perform them.

The notion that an organisation is a cooperative system is generally credited to Chester Barnard. He presented his ideas in *The Functions of the Executive*, in which he drew on his years of experience with American Telephone and Telegraph, including senior management positions.[10]

In addition to being one of the first to treat organisations as systems, Barnard offered other important insights. He challenged the classical view that authority flowed from the top down by arguing that authority should be defined in terms of the response of the subordinate; he introduced to organisation theory the role of the informal organisation; and he proposed that the manager's major roles were to facilitate communication and to stimulate subordinates to high levels of effort.

Douglas McGregor: Theory X and Theory Y

One of the most often mentioned contributions from Type 2 theorists is Douglas McGregor's thesis that there are two distinct views of human beings: one basically negative—Theory X—and the other basically positive—Theory Y.[11] After reviewing the way managers dealt with employees, McGregor concluded that a manager's view of the nature of human beings is based on a certain grouping of assumptions and on the fact that he or she tends to mould his or her behaviour towards subordinates according to those assumptions.

Under Theory X, the four assumptions held by managers are:

1 Employees inherently dislike work and, whenever possible, will attempt to avoid it.
2 As employees dislike work, they must be coerced, controlled or threatened with punishment to achieve desired goals.
3 Employees will shirk responsibilities and seek formal direction whenever possible.
4 Most workers place security above all other factors associated with work and will display little ambition.

In contrast to these negative views of human beings, McGregor listed four other assumptions that he called Theory Y:

1 Employees can view work as being as natural as rest or play.
2 Human beings will exercise self-direction and self-control if they are committed to the objectives.
3 The average person can learn to accept, even seek, responsibility.
4 Creativity—that is, the ability to make good decisions—is widely dispersed throughout the population and is not necessarily the sole province of those in managerial functions.

What are the implications of McGregor's Theory X and Theory Y for organisation theory? McGregor argued that Theory Y assumptions were preferable and that they should guide managers in the way they designed their organisations and motivated their employees. Much of the enthusiasm, beginning in the 1960s, for participative decision making, the creation of responsible and challenging jobs for employees and developing good group relations can be traced to McGregor's advocacy that managers follow Theory Y assumptions.

OT CLOSEUP
The organisation man

The growth of the large corporation, particularly in the United States, led to a large section of the workforce being known as 'organisation men', a concept popularised in the 1950s. These were seen as faceless individuals foregoing all their individuality to the numbing conformity of the organisation. This conformity extended beyond the workplace: organisation men shared similar values, family life and ways of living. Indeed, the suburbs they lived in and the cars they drove all suffered from the same uniformity. This raised particular concern in the USA, where the mythology of the rugged individual was seen to be giving way to a collectivism that subjugated the individual to the group.

The writings on the organisation men were sociological in origin. The 'men' part obviously excluded women who were generally invisible in the organisation, as least as far as promotion and careers were concerned. The writings also had a white-collar

orientation, omitting reference to those who might be termed working-class from the shop floor. And with the notable exception of Frederick Taylor, few of the other theorists we discuss have much to say about work on the factory floor.

Although the era of the organisation man may have passed, along with the social contract that underpinned the role, the impact of the organisation on its workers is as current as it was in the 1950s. Rather than worrying about numbing uniformity, we are now concerned about overwork, lack of security, and the impact of travel and work demands on family life. To many of those caught between career and family demands, the role of the 1950s organisation man must seem extremely comfortable.

Adapted from: Anthony Sampson, *The Company Man: The Rise and Fall of Corporate Life*, London: HarperCollins, 1995.

Warren Bennis and the death of bureaucracy

The strong humanistic theme of this period culminated with a eulogy on the passing of bureaucracy.[12] Warren Bennis, for example, claimed that bureaucracy's centralised decision making, impersonal submission to authority and narrow division of labour were being replaced by decentralised and democratic structures organised around flexible groups. Influence based on authority was giving way to influence derived from expertise. In the same way as Weber argued that bureaucracy was the ideal organisation, Warren Bennis argued the other extreme: conditions now pointed to flexible adhocracies as the ideal organisational form.

Contribution of the human relations school

In 50 years we had essentially moved from one extreme position to another. The human relations school still regarded organisations as closed systems, but they stressed the social aspects of the system rather than the nuts and bolts of production. By the 1960s, most managers were aware of the influence that human behaviour had on organisational outcomes. One of the problems facing them was how to classify this behaviour and to incorporate the more humanistic attitude in organisational structures and practices. This had to be achieved in such a way that did not compromise efficiency. Both Barnard and McGregor proposed classifications which advanced the understanding of workplace behaviour and permitted managers to incorporate these understandings into organisational practices. This process did not end with the 1960s. Although the period under review was a productive time in theory development and practical understanding, the task of balancing organisational and human needs is ongoing. Given that the pressures of globalisation on organisations appear to be leading to longer work hours and less job security, we may in the future see a re-emergence of the human relations school.

From 1960 to 1980—the age of contingency

1960–1980
Determining the most appropriate structural form.
Achieving rational goals with an open systems perspective. Focus of analysis was the total organisation and its structural form

There was a gap in the various approaches so far considered. What was missing was consideration of organisational structure. Was there a structure that was right for all occasions? Or did different circumstances give rise to the need for different structures? The contingency approach views the structure of organisations as contingent— that is, dependent on—pressures that can be identified and analysed. As a result, organisations do not have an infinite number of forms. Their structures are predictable depending on the contingency factors. Researchers at this time used the methodology of sampling large numbers of organisations and then looking for cause-and-effect relationships between structures and environmental relationships. They therefore viewed the organisation as an open system. Their research had the purpose of improving organisational effectiveness by providing managers with guidance as to the most appropriate structure, given the contingency factors. This has sometimes been described as building a general theory of management.

This period was a very productive one for organisational research. Many of the theories and studies described in subsequent chapters derive from this time. The contingency approach was facilitated by the more stable social and political conditions of the period. Technological change was slow and there were high levels of government ownership of business and regulation of industry. Globalisation had yet to make its presence felt. The most influential researchers of this period are described below.

Herbert Simon and the principles backlash

Herbert Simon foreshadowed the rise of the contingency movement in the 1940s, and developed the intellectual template for others to follow. Simon noted that most classical principles were nothing more than proverbs, and many contradicted each other. He argued that organisation theory needed to go beyond superficial and over-simplified principles to a study of the conditions under which competing principles were applicable.[13] Nevertheless, the 1950s and 60s tended to be dominated by simplistic principles—of both the mechanistic and humanistic variety. It took approximately 20 years for organisation theorists to respond effectively to Simon's challenge.

Katz and Kahn's environmental perspective

Daniel Katz and Robert Kahn's *The Social Psychology of Organizations* was a major impetus towards promoting the open-systems perspective on organisation theory.[14] Their book provided a convincing description of the advantages of an open-systems perspective for examining the important relations of an organisation with its environment and the need for organisations to adapt to a changing environment if they are to survive.

Since Katz and Kahn's work, numerous theorists have investigated the environment–structure relationship. Various types of environments have been identified, and much research has been conducted to evaluate which structures mesh best with the various environments. The classic studies of Burns and Stalker and Lawrence and Lorsch, described in later chapters, stand out as leaders in the field. No current discussion of organisation theory would be complete without a thorough assessment of environment as a major contingency factor influencing the preferred form of structure.

The case for technology

Research in the 1960s by Joan Woodward and Charles Perrow, as well as the conceptual framework offered by James Thompson, have made an impressive case for the importance of technology in determining the appropriate structure for an organisation.[15] As with environment, no contemporary discussion of organisation theory would be complete without consideration of technology and the need for managers to match structure with technology. This period largely predated the expanding influence of information technology and the rise of the service industries. Research on these influences necessarily belongs to a later period but is influenced by such as those by Perrow and Thompson.

The Aston Group and organisation size

In addition to advocates of environment and technology, theorists from this period include those who advocate organisation size as an important factor influencing structure. This position has been most zealously argued by researchers associated with the University of Aston in England.[16] Large organisations have been shown to have many common structural components. So, too, have small organisations. Most important perhaps, the evidence suggests that certain of these components follow an established pattern as organisations expand in size. Such evidence has proven valuable to managers in helping them make organisation design decisions as their organisations have grown.

Miles and Snow and the strategic imperative

The study of corporate strategy gathered pace in the 1970s, and in 1978 an influential book written by Raymond Miles and Charles Snow was published which categorised strategy.[17] They then proposed that successful implementation of the chosen strategy required an appropriate structure to be adopted. They were arguing in support of the strategic imperative: that is, that one of the determinants of structure is the strategy which an organisation adopts. The study of strategy has expanded over the past 20 years, with the research of Michael Porter being widely disseminated and influencing how the organisation can profitably exist within its environment.[18]

OT CLOSEUP

Is there an Australian organisational form?

There is probably little that is unique in Australia's business structures. We have been heavily influenced by the writings of management theorists in the United Kingdom and the United States, and their ideas on management reach Australian shores very quickly after they are released overseas. Moreover, those Australian organisations that are subsidiaries of companies based in those countries tend to take on a structure dictated from the head office. The management of Australian multinationals is influenced in turn by the practices they see in overseas countries. And there is no reason to believe that a steel mill in Australia would have a structure that was radically different from a steel mill in most parts of the world: the skills and knowledge to run it are much the same as steel mills everywhere. This is the concept of mimetic isomorphism—that is, firms faced with similar environments and using similar technologies could be expected to develop similar structures.

The scale and scope of business have a great influence on the structural form it adopts, and it is here that Australia differs from many countries. Neither Australia nor New Zealand can hope to compete in highly complex manufacturing areas which have dense networks of interdependent suppliers such as occur in parts of Japan, the United States and Europe. However, networks are developing in certain areas, as can be seen in the wine industry in South Australia, fast ferry development around Fremantle, and finance in Sydney. New Zealand and

Australia are also developing downstream processing of natural resources, such as minerals and food, which is leading to horizontally linked companies and industries. Owing to our small population base we cannot expect to support large-scale, capital-intensive and risky manufacturing such as commercial jet aircraft design along the lines of Boeing or Airbus. Capital equipment projects would be similarly limited. And Australia, because of its small population base, is just managing to hold onto its car industry.

So what could pass as typical of an Australian structure? To do that we need to look at what areas of the Australian economy are world competitive. We can take three examples: local manufacturing companies investing overseas, arts and entertainment, and mining. There are a large number of successful Australian manufacturing companies investing overseas, including BHP Billiton, CSR, Pacific BBA and Coca-Cola Amatil. They all have one thing in common: they invest only in areas they are familiar with. They take their core skills, which they have generally developed in the Australian market, and apply them in their overseas investments. This is called a multi-domestic strategy, where the firm sets up a subsidiary to be an inside producer in an overseas market. To support this strategy they often take a joint venture partner who knows the local market. In this case, the overseas subsidiary is run as a separate entity with its own structure and management.

The arts and entertainment industry has grown rapidly over the past 20 years. Its output includes such well-known movies as *Moulin Rouge*, *Babe* and *Shine*, the writings of authors such as Thomas Keneally, and the worldwide reach of soap operas such as 'Neighbours', all of which have had international acclaim. And Australia has a significant presence in areas ranging from television commercial to animated films. The industry is very fragmented and subject to wide swings in demand for labour, depending on what is being produced and when. To allow for the variations in demand, the industry draws heavily on a host of subcontractors and specialists, who are hired as required. Each group of specialists have their skills, which they use as they move from project to project. These specialists range from financiers to postproduction editing studios and even to location caterers. One of the features which makes the industry competitive is the structure it has adopted. The flexibility that the extensive contracting network permits allows each person and group to concentrate on their own skills, and provides the necessary capital equipment to support their specialty. Scarce talented labour is used productively over a range of projects. In this way overheads are kept low, making Australia a competitive place in which to undertake production.

The mining industry has been at the forefront of Australian overseas business expansion. It has achieved this partly by skill and partly by default. There are not a lot of nations that have well-developed mining skills, but Australia is one of them. The skills in the industry are not confined to digging holes in the ground. They range from exploration to financing and through to final marketing. It is in order to undertake this diverse range of activities that mining companies such as BHP Billiton or Western Mining can grow to a very large size. The mining industry has no alternative but to go where the minerals are, and consequently its reach is worldwide. However, other functions are located where they make the most sense: finance in a financial centre, refining which balances proximity to an industrial area with the access to cheap energy, and marketing which requires links to the various metals and futures exchanges and customers. The different economies has led to the development of a hybrid, dual-listed financial structure. In order to capture the economies of large-scale finance, companies are often dual-listed on both the London and Australian stock exchanges, while dividing their head office between Australia and the UK.

The comparison with many US companies' overseas expansion is revealing. Many US IT companies manage their worldwide operations as one integrated organisation, with a very powerful head office. Common cultures are promoted and accounts integrated. During downturns, when layoffs occur, they are made on a worldwide basis, with individual countries having to contribute to the total numbers required. It is not as common for US companies to adopt a multi-domestic strategy.

No matter what the country of origin, overseas operations raise the risk profile of an organisation and place additional burdens on management. Often strategies are poorly thought out and management skills not up to the job. There is always the problem of insiders in a market having better knowledge than outsiders. This can lead to companies paying too much for second-rate assets. Australian companies that have lost large amounts overseas range from all the big banks and building material companies to some of the top mining houses. Within Australia, companies as diverse as Air New Zealand and Vodafone have lost out to stronger local competitors.

The political nature of organisations— from 1980 to the present

It is in the nature of academic research to be continually exploring new areas of inquiry. The most recent approach to organisation theory focuses on the political nature of organisations. In part this emerged from the limitations of the contingency

1980–2000+
Influence of power
and politics on
management
decisions and
organisational
structures.
Explanation of social
actions with an open
systems perspective.
Focus of analysis is
the exercise of power
and political plays
within organisations.
The symbolic-
interpretive nature of
organisations.
The organisation as a
social construct

theory approach. While having its merits, and providing significant insight into organisations, the search for a general theory of management proved elusive. The contingency factors could explain part of what was happening in organisations, but there were significant variations in structures that seemed to defy easy explanation. From the 1980s, the influence of power and politics was promoted as being able to account for many of the unexplained areas. It further became apparent that, with the growth of large organisations, there were limitations on the ability of managers to cognitively, that is mentally, process all that was going on about them. This prompted various researchers to develop theories as to how managers coped with the limitations on their ability to process information. An early formulation of this position was made by James March and Herbert Simon, but it has been extensively refined by Jeffrey Pfeffer.

In many ways it is surprising that organisation researchers took so long to incorporate the realities of power in their theories. In one way it is understandable: power is difficult to understand, elusive and almost impossible to measure. But its influence in all human interactions, including formal organisations, has been well documented for as long as humans have been recording their history. Classical theorists attempted to ignore power issues by the scientific structuring of jobs and organisational structures. The behaviour theorists thought that power issues could be bypassed by creating more people-friendly organisations. The contingency theorists did not take power into account in their research. By the 1980s, it was clear that issues relating to power could not be ignored and that any study of organisations must include consideration of power.

March and Simon's cognitive limits to rationality

March and Simon challenged the classical notion of rational or optimal decisions.[19] They argued that most decision makers selected satisfactory alternatives—ones that were good enough. Only in exceptional cases would they be concerned with the discovery and selection of optimal alternatives. March and Simon called for a revised model of organisation theory—one very different from the rational cooperative systems view. This revised model would recognise the limits of a decision maker's rationality and acknowledge the presence of conflicting goals. It also provided the theoretical foundation for power and politics to play a part in the way in which organisations are structured and managed.

Pfeffer's organisations as political arenas

Jeffrey Pfeffer has built on March and Simon's work to create a model of organisation theory that encompasses power coalitions, inherent conflict over goals, and organisational-design decisions that favour the self-interest of those in power.[20] Pfeffer proposes that control in organisations becomes an end rather than merely a means to rational goals, such as the efficient production of output. Organisations are coalitions composed of varying groups and individuals with different demands. An organisation's design represents the result of the power struggles by these diverse coalitions. Pfeffer argues that if we want to understand how and why organisations are designed the way they are, we need to assess the preferences and interests of those in the organisations who have influence over the design decisions. This view is currently very much in vogue.

Critical theory and postmodernism

We discussed critical theory and postmodernism in Chapter 1. We are including them here because chronologically this is where they fit. Also they are concerned with issues of power, although not perhaps in the sense considered by most organisational writers. Critical theory and postmodernism are often considered together as they share the basic feature of acting as a counterpoint to the business and organisational structures with which we are familiar. Critical theory seeks to describe organisations not as mechanisms of production and exchange but as arenas of exploitation and of marginalisation. This exploitation may be of lower-level workers in the organisation or of minorities. The perception that business organisations destroy Third World cultures and values through their global operations, and the undesirability of this, form part of critical theory. So do many of the gender studies we will discuss in Chapter 15.

Postmodernism is a more difficult construct. Not surprisingly, postmodernism reflects a world which is held to exist after modernism. Modernism grew out of the enlightenment in Europe, in which science and reason replaced superstition and intuition as the way towards progress. Our society and the organisations in it are based on modernistic ideas. Postmodernism would consider that these are now in decay, and that a new concept of progress will result. This new way to progress largely rests on redefining equality, reordering power relationships, and a reduced role for science in relation to symbolism and meaning.[21]

Both critical theory and postmodernism consider that what industrialised societies define as progress is in reality a means of exploitation and marginalisation. To build a new and better world, the existing order needs to be deconstructed—that is, pulled apart—before a new and more equitable order can be built. However, apart from generalised statements regarding the rights of the individual and the promotion of equality, no concrete proposals have been made which represent a new order that can be debated.

In researching organisations from a critical or postmodern perspective, stress is placed on power systems; the use of language or dialectics, which define knowledge and relationships; and the multiple roles and loss of meanings associated with organisational life.

You may wonder why organisations figure so prominently in the writings of the critical and postmodern school. The reason is that organisations are inherently more powerful than individuals, and by their nature have hierarchies in which not all are, or can be, of equal status. Similarly, organisations consume resources from their environment, as well as producing products and services for consumption by those in the environment. They therefore have a major influence in shaping the societies of which they are a part.

Symbolic-interpretive perspectives— from the 1980s

Nominating the 1980s as the beginning of the symbolic-interpretive perspective is to a certain extent misleading. Anthropologists and sociologists have long realised that organisations provide a sense of meaning and belonging to members. The role of symbols as means of identifying organisations and their members predates the

Roman Empire. The cross of the Christian Church is probably the pre-eminent example of an organisational symbol. Myths, legends and stories have also been extensively studied as a means of interpreting a culture and for their role in transmitting a culture from one generation of members to another.

Anthropological techniques are still used to study organisations and provide valuable insight into their operation. But the movement of the symbolic-interpretive perspective to a central focus in organisation theory developed as a result of two emerging observations. The first was by Karl Weick, who claimed that an organisation is a social construct—that is, it is enacted by its members. The second was the publication of *In Search of Excellence* in 1980, which popularised the idea that organisations had an identifiable culture and that the appropriateness of this culture was a major contributor to organisational effectiveness. Since these observations, the symbolic-interpretive approaches have taken a central place within organisational theory.

Karl Weick and enactment theory

Karl Weick's *The Social Psychology of Organizing* was influential in directing researchers' attention to the intangible nature of organisations.[22] Prior to Weick's work, organisations had tended to be viewed as something tangible and solid, and hence capable of easy interpretation and study. Weick claimed that this reification of organisations—that is, attributing real properties to an intangible body—was a process where the phenomenon was created by the observer. He called this enactment; we can make a culture, an environment or an organisation appear, but it is then difficult to identify the difference between that creation and reality.

Berger and Luckman's social construction of reality

Two German sociologists, Peter Berger and Thomas Luckman, in their book *The Social Construction of Reality*, proposed that human relationships were built up through a process of negotiations between people and a common interpretation of shared history and experience.[23] What sustains social order is at least a minimum agreement as to how events are to be perceived and the meanings that are attached to them. These interpretations take on a life beyond that of abstract occurrences, but nevertheless remain socially constructed. Although aimed at societies, Berger and Luckman's insights also apply to the way business organisations create and interpret their reality.

Peters and Waterman's *In Search of Excellence*

Peters and Waterman popularised the idea that organisational culture had a significant impact on effectiveness.[24] Although only one of a number of factors identified as characteristic of excellent companies, their observations popularised the notion of the culture of business organisations and redirected the research attention of management and business researchers. Also popularising the importance of culture was the extensive literature relating to the culture of Japanese companies. Such books as *The Art of Japanese Management* by Pascale and Athos dwelt heavily on the way in which culture was the key to the strength of Japanese companies.[25]

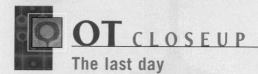

OT CLOSEUP
The last day

In the normal day-to-day operation of organisations, the emotional ties that permeate organisational life are rarely felt; the significance of the symbols, relationships, and the sense of belonging and place are subsumed within the routines of daily work life. It generally takes a major crisis, such as a corporate failure, to highlight the meanings of these taken-for-granted phenomena. This is one of the reasons why the symbolic-interpretive approach presents difficulties in research methodology.

The collapse of Ansett in 2001 provides a good illustration of the deeper meanings associated with organisational life. Ansett had been established for over 70 years when it unexpectedly ceased trading and was put into the hands of administrators. It was Australia's second-largest airline, with over 16 000 employees and a fleet in excess of 100 aircraft. Many employees had worked with Ansett all their lives, and the average length of service was over 20 years. It seemed solid and, although its financial difficulties were well known, impervious to failure. There was also a sense of belonging to a family, no doubt reinforced by the difficulties the airline had faced over the previous few years.

When the announcement was made that the airline had no cash left to pay its bills and would cease trading within a few hours, employees entered a state of disbelief. Rumours started to circulate about all manner of things: someone heard from someone's secretary that there was no fuel left, someone else heard from a truck driver that there was plenty of fuel and people should stop worrying.

The sense of camaraderie saw rank and status diminish, and people drew together to seek comfort and solace. Little knots of employees gathered with blank looks, discussing in hushed tones any scrap of information they had and wondering what significance it had for them. It seemed as if hard news couldn't be talked about loudly. In the face of the progressive withdrawal of services by subcontractors and suppliers, taken-for-granted services such as cleaning and even the coffee shops started to take on added importance. Pilots of the last flights reported that simple things such as landmarks took on heightened significance, particularly as it was not known if they would ever be seen again.

Employees felt that they had been badly let down by management and it took little time for them to vent their frustration. Ansett had been running an advertising campaign that gave prominence to the managing director of Ansett's owner, Air New Zealand. His photograph was posted on many billboards around the airport and the terminal. His images were stripped from their frames, the shredded paper standing in stark contrast to otherwise tidy terminals. One former employee wrote 'You shiver in stark vulnerability as the corporate catch-cries of "Synergy", "Value Added", "Business Plan", "Win Win", "Corporate Vision", and "Team Building", chase one another as mirthless echoes through the grey steel rafters'.

Adapted from: 'That Last Day', *Australian Aviation*, November 2001, p. 30.

Recently developed perspectives

A number of other approaches to organisation theory have been developed over the past 20 years. These approaches have little in common, although researchers in future may find common threads between them. We will describe each of them briefly in turn.

Organisational economics

The link between organisations and economics was first proposed in 1937 by the economist Ronald Coase.[26] In addressing the basic problem of why organisations exist, he proposed that organisations can sometimes mediate exchanges between members more easily and cheaply than markets can. If the price system was used to determine what each worker was to do, it would involve a complex round of negotiations in relation to discovering what comparable prices are elsewhere, negotiating and renegotiating contracts, monitoring performance and settling disputes. These costs are called transaction costs and they are incurred in determining the scale, scope and price of a task. In contrast, an employee, within reason, can be told what task to carry out, thus minimising transaction costs.

Williamson has developed organisational economics further by taking Coase's analysis and building it into an exploration of the relationships between hierarchies and markets.[27] Hierarchies are well known to most of us as the chain of command in organisations that instructs lower-level employees what to do. Markets in turn are a social construct, with ongoing participants who contract with each other to provide goods and services. The form that dominates will reflect what is cheapest to run in any given situation. This will be a reflection of the costs of each transaction between individuals and groups. Also, markets compared with hierarchies are often poor at handling uncertainty and risk. Consequently, in many cases, the cost of running hierarchical organisations is lower than that for organising performance through markets.

Another application of economics to organisation theory is that of agency theory.[28] A manager in an organisation has a number of subordinates, who are considered to be the manager's agents. The manager has the natural motivation to obtain as much benefit from his or her agents as possible, and the agents in turn have the incentive to shirk or otherwise cheat on the contract. The resulting behaviour is an outcome of the bargaining process. Another common application of agency theory is where the managers of a company are the agents of the shareholders. Agency theory examines these relationships, particularly where there is asymmetrical knowledge—that is, where more is known about the transaction by one party than the other.

The picture painted of managers by those who study organisational economics is not particularly flattering. The assumptions made are that it is human nature for managers and workers to act in selfish and opportunistic ways. For this reason, organisational economics has been called an anti-management theory.[29]

Institutional theory

Up to this point we have considered organisations as having rational, almost machine-like properties and that organisational members are well informed and act in rational ways in response to the world they see around them. Institutional theory, however, claims that organisational responses are often repetitive and products of past actions and practices. That is, over time, responses become institutionalised. These institutionalised practices are often the result of social pressures to conform to convention. As a result, we find that many organisational actions and management decisions are imitations of past practices. And as institutional theory tends to look at groups of organisations, many management decisions are seen to be cloning the practices of other successful organisations.[30]

Gender in organisations

Until 30 years ago, few questioned the gender segregation obvious in most organisations. Men and women had their respective jobs, and men were dominant in management. However, women increasingly objected to their exclusion from key parts of the organisation and, even when the obvious barriers were removed, women were still underrepresented in many areas. This started a field of research that has as its foundation the role of gender in organisations. This has developed into feminist approaches to organisational structuring and research.

There are many subgroups of feminist thought.[31] Most will be familiar with the women in management literature, which seeks to research and promote the interests of women within existing organisational structures. But many may not be so well known, including the socialist, psychoanalytic and Third World/postcolonial viewpoints.

Most feminist literature takes the view that organisations are run as patriarchies which marginalise women's participation. Some theories extend to challenging our businesses and organisations as constructs of exploitation. Their research methods have extended beyond normal survey and statistical processing into the analysis of language, called dialectics, non-verbal communication patterns, and the use of empathic case studies where the researcher adopts a partial and sympathetic approach to the subject. The result of such research is mixed and, not surprisingly, outcomes are closely related to the positions of those undertaking the research. In complex organisations and social systems it is difficult to identify the mechanisms through which social forces and processes operate. As with power, these mechanisms are largely invisible.

The research into gender in organisations is part of the wider analysis of the role that gender plays in the functioning of society. (We discuss gender in organisations in Chapter 15.)

Popular management writers

Management thinkers writing for a mass market adopt a different approach to academic researchers. Most of course are writing for a living, so they must grab the attention of potential readers. These writers rarely emerge from the intellectual background of universities; they have largely built on industry experience, particularly in management consulting.

Many management thinkers and writers have an extensive following. Most use the written word as well as seminars and even television to communicate their message. In contrast to the postmodernists, they seek to make organisations more productive by helping them use their resources, including human ones, more innovatively and effectively. We will discuss the ideas of a few of the better-known management gurus.

Tom Peters

Tom Peters came to prominence through his co-authorship with Bob Waterman of the modern management book *In Search of Excellence*. There they describe the characteristics of America's most successful large corporations. Since that time, Tom Peters has continued to develop the theme of the most appropriate organisational form for modern organisations.[32] He claims that the environment in which business operates is becoming more unpredictable and competitive. In response, organisations need to improve communications, become more innovative and nimble, and respond to environmental changes in shorter time frames that in the past.

Peters sees organisational structure as having an important role in business becoming more responsive. He claims that crazy times call for crazy organisations. He advocates the reduction of management layers and the widening of the span of control, even to the extent of each supervisor having up to 70 subordinates. Middle managers should become boundary spanners and facilitators rather than experts and guardians of functional units. Lower-level employees should form self-managing teams, unhindered by restrictive bureaucracy. The result of these moves would be a far more decentralised and responsive organisation.

Charles Handy

Charles Handy is a British management theorist who also stresses the need for innovation and flexibility in organisations.[33] But he advocates a far softer role for organisations and management through stressing the human side of the organisation. Whereas Peters was seeking to create organisations with a harsh edge which could be fiercely competitive, Handy promotes the idea of organisations as places where people would like to work as well as competitive entities.

Handy's main contribution was to identify, in terms understandable to most, what he called the tribes and gods who make up the corporate world. Tribes reflect the corporate culture, and gods, the attributes of individuals within the culture. No one tribe or god is more important than the other, but both within and between organisations the various tribes and gods interact to produce productive and innovative companies. He also claims that employees should identify what type of person they are and seek organisations that complement their talents. Handy seeks to improve the way organisations are managed by advocating a greater understanding of organisational behaviour. In this he is an educator rather than an innovative management thinker.

Ricardo Semler

Ricardo Semler is a Brazilian industrialist who inherited a metals manufacturing company from his parents.[34] Becoming disillusioned with traditional management practices, which emphasised command and control, he turned much of the management of the company over to his employees. They determined the rates of pay for each worker, working hours, how the work was to be organised, who was responsible for what task, what to produce and who to hire and fire. In order to accommodate this, most of the workforce operated as teams of no more than 10 people. So far the experiment seems to have been successful.

Semler's contribution was to devolve decision-making power onto his employees, eliminating most of the input from the management hierarchy. He also set up many employees as subcontractors, who supplied goods to his main plants. It is still too early to determine the extent of the success of Semler's work, as long-term decisions such as financing and adapting to technological change still have to be faced. But it does indicate that many management tasks can be undertaken by lower-level workers.

Michael Hammer and re-engineering

Although there are a number of theorists who have promoted re-engineering, Hammer is the person commonly associated with it.[35] The proponents of re-engineering claim that traditional organisational structures are hierarchies that are constructed around role specialisations. Re-engineering seeks to build the structure of the organisation around multidisciplinary processes, which can then be grouped together to create the totality of the organisation's effort. The structure of the organisation therefore represents a series of largely self-contained tasks, rather than a hierarchy built around occupational specialists.

Summary

Modern organisation theory began with the scientific management approach, which emerged at the beginning of the 20th century. This approach relied heavily on simplistic and universal principles, developing models of organisation that were excessively rational and mechanistic. Subsequent approaches in the 1930s, to a large degree, represented a counterpoint to the rational-mechanistic view. The focus moved away from the division of labour and centralised authority towards democratic organisations. The human factor, which tended to be treated as a predictable 'given' by the scientific management approach, moved to centre stage as the core of organisation theory in the years between 1930 and 1960.

The current state of organisation theory more fully reflects subsequent schools of thought.

Contingency advocates have taken the insights provided by the earlier theorists and reframed them in a situational context. The contingency view, in addition to underlining the point that there is not 'one best way', has made significant strides in identifying those contingency variables that are most important for determining the right structure. The political perspective, which emerged in the 1970s, builds on our knowledge of behavioural decision making and political science, and has significantly improved our ability to explain organisational phenomena that the contingency advocates' rational assumptions overlooked.

Contemporary approaches to organisational theory may be divided into two groups. The first comes from an intellectual analysis of features of organisational operations. These investigations include organisational economics, institutional theory and gender in organisations. Critical theory and postmodernism create a new paradigm, or basic set of assumptions, in the way that organisations are viewed. Researchers who approach their tasks from these perspectives would emphasise the inequalities of organisations, in both the sense of power and rewards. They would also stress the coercive nature of organisations.

The second contemporary approach to organisations is to make them more efficient and to improve their use of resources, particularly people. Ever since organisations started to grow large, managers and theorists have been grappling with the need to balance control with decentralising decision making. They are also constantly challenged by the problems of organisational change. Much of the modern thinking regarding organisations approaches these old problems in ways applicable to today's workforces and levels of technology.

For review and discussion

1 In what way may classical and contingency approaches be considered to be related to each other?

2 Explain how the behaviourist and power approaches to organisations share a social perspective.

3   Why have the various approaches to organisation theory emerged as a series of groups rather than randomly?

4   How might theory guide practice in organisational studies?

5   'Adam Smith could be labelled a classical theorist.' Do you agree or disagree? Discuss.

6   Contrast Taylor's and Fayol's levels of organisational analysis.

7   How valid are Fayol's principles today?

8   'As most large organisations today are bureaucracies, Weber views could be considered the most influential.' Do you agree or disagree? Discuss.

9   What are the implications of the Hawthorne studies for contemporary organisation theory?

10 Do you think most managers have Theory X or Theory Y views of people? How might this view affect their organisation design decisions?

11 What are the key contingency variables that researchers identified in the 1960s and 70s?

12 Are the four main approaches described independent of each other? Defend your position.

13 Why is it difficult to classify modern approaches to organisational theory as one coherent type?

14 Why have the modern theories regarding organisations been called anti-management?

15 How applicable is critical theory and postmodernism to managers of organisations?

16 Contrast the approach to organisations of postmodernists with that of the popular management writers.

17 Of the recently developed perspectives, including the modern management writers, which do you think will have the greatest long-term impact? Why?

CASE FOR CLASS DISCUSSION
The Japanese transplant car factory

The Japanese have an enviable reputation for building quality cars.[36] Although not to everyone's taste (even the managing director of Toyota Australia has been known to refer to his products as refrigerators on wheels), Japanese cars are rarely rivalled in the fields of build quality and durability. Once solely built in Japan, from the 1980s the Japanese manufacturers started to establish transplant factories around the world. This presented them with a major management problem. The capital equipment of the factory was easy to establish in foreign fields; the unique Japanese production system

proved much harder. To maintain quality, and keep production costs low, the Japanese relied on teamwork and quality circles. Their management system, at least on the factory floor, was very flat, with little in the way of hierarchy. The problem was how to instil this way of working in a foreign workforce.

The setting up of a greenfields factory in the United States (i.e. one completely new and built on a 'green field') provides a good example of how Toyota has tackled the problem. Toyota selected staff who had never worked in a factory before. It had no shortage of applicants: 58 000 applied for 1200 jobs. To select those it wanted, Toyota put all applicants through an extensive series of tests. These included measurements of reading and maths skills, group exercises, and an extensive interview aimed at identifying certain personality and attitudinal traits and communication skills. This process took 20–25 hours.

From this process, team leaders were selected. (Teams form the basis of Toyota's production system, and so the role of the team leader is critical.) The team leaders were sent to Japan for up to four weeks for training. They spent nine hours a day on the shop floor, learning the processes they would be using back home. They also spent their leisure time together, thus developing a camaraderie they would be expected to take back to their own factory. Team leaders have managerial responsibilities for immediate production activities. They play a crucial role in the organisation, design and allocation of work on a daily basis.

The training of 'new hires' is extensive. The first week is given over to training activities both in the classroom and on the production line. This process is called assimilation. It includes extensive safety and quality training. There are just a few job classifications, and everyone in the team is capable of undertaking all tasks allocated to the team. Jobs are rotated in order to avoid repetitive strain injuries. The team members themselves largely determine how tasks will be undertaken and who will undertake them. As the vehicle moves down the assembly line, each team is encouraged to regard the next team as its customers. There are meetings at the start of each workday to review the previous day's work and plan for the current one. At this time the team also discusses any problems that may have arisen.

Suggestions aimed at improving quality and reducing costs are encouraged and expected. In many cases they are rewarded with monetary payments. This is part of the management philosophy of delegating managerial authority and responsibility to shop floor workers.

The attempts at building a common bond between workers and encouraging community of spirit are further enhanced by the dining arrangements. All personnel, from management to cleaners, eat in the same cafeteria. Dress standards encourage uniformity of outlook. Similarly, managers do not have walled-in offices but sit at desks in large, open areas adjacent to the production facility.

Adapted from: Greg Gardner, *Tracking Toyota's Tundra Ward's AutoWorld*, 34(10), pp. 42–44, 1998.

QUESTIONS

1 Identify and describe the similarities and differences between scientific management and the Toyota manufacturing system.

2 Does the evidence of the use of power in the above case make Pfeffer's ideas relevant only to Western cultures? Discuss.

3 What evidence is provided in the case of the other approaches to organisation theory discussed in this chapter?

FURTHER READING

Thomas Clarke & Stewart Clegg, *Changing Paradigms: The Transformation of Management Knowledge in the 21st Century*, London: HarperCollins, 1998.

Lex Donaldson, *American Anti-Management Theories Organization: Critique of Paradigm Proliferation*, Cambridge: Cambridge University Press, 1995.

Charles Handy, *Inside Organisations: 21 Ideas for Managers*, London: BBC Books, 1990.

Daniel Katz & Robert Khan, *The Social Psychology of Organizations*, New York: John Wiley, 1966.

Tom Peters, *Thriving on Chaos*, New York: Knopf, 1988.

Anthony Sampson, *Company Man: The Rise and Fall of Company Life*, London: HarperCollins, 1995.

W. Richard Scott, 'Theoretical Perspectives' in Marshall W. Meyer, ed., *Environments and Organizations*, San Francisco: Jossey-Bass, 1978.

Ricardo Semler, *Maverick: The Success Story Behind the World's Most Unusual Workplace*, New York: Warner, 1993.

Oliver Williamson, Markets and Hierarchies: *Analysis and Unit Trust Implications*, New York: Free Press, 1975.

Daniel Wren, *The Evolution of Management Thought*, 4th edn, New York: John Wiley, 1994.

NOTES

1   This selection is based on W. Richard Scott, 'Theoretical Perspectives', in Marshall W. Meyer, ed., *Environments and Organizations*, San Francisco: Jossey-Bass, 1978, pp. 21–8.

2   John Keay, *The Honourable Company: A History of the English East India Company*, London: HarperCollins, 1993.

3   Adam Smith, *An Inquiry into the Nature and Causes of the Wealth of Nations*, New York: Modern Library, 1937. Originally published in 1776.

4   Daniel Wren, *The Evolution of Management Thought*, 4th edn, New York: John Wiley, 1994.

5   Frederick W. Taylor, *The Principles of Scientific Management*, New York: Harper & Row, 1911.

6   Henri Fayol, *Administration Industrielle et Générale*, Paris: Dunod, 1916.

7   Max Weber, *The Theory of Social and Economic Organizations*, ed. Talcott Parsons, trans. A.M. Henderson & Talcott Parsons, New York: Free Press, 1947.

8   See, for example, Ralph C. Davis, *The Principles of Factory Organization and Management*, New York: Harper & Row, 1928; and *The Fundamentals of Top Management*, New York: Harper & Row, 1951.

9   Elton Mayo, *The Human Problems of Industrial Civilization*, New York: Macmillan, 1933; and Fritz J. Roethlisberger & William J. Dickson, *Management and the Worker*, Cambridge: Harvard University Press, 1939.

10   Chester I. Barnard, *The Functions of the Executive*, Cambridge: Harvard University Press, 1938.

11   Douglas McGregor, *The Human Side of Enterprise*, New York: McGraw-Hill, 1960.

12   Warren G. Bennis, 'The Coming Death of Bureaucracy', *Think*, November–December 1966, pp. 30–5.

13   Herbert A. Simon, *Administrative Behavior: A Study of Decision-Making Processes in Administrative Organizations*, New York: Macmillan, 1947.

14   Daniel Katz & Robert L. Kahn, *The Social Psychology of Organizations*, New York: John Wiley, 1966.

15   Joan Woodward, *Industrial Organization: Theory and Practice*, London: Oxford University Press, 1965; Charles Perrow, 'A Framework for the Comparative Analysis of Organizations', *American Sociological Review*, April 1967, pp. 194–208; and James D. Thompson, *Organizations in Action*, New York: McGraw-Hill, 1967.

16   See, for example, Derek S. Pugh, David J. Hickson, C.R. Hinings & C. Turner, 'The Context of Organization Structures', *Administrative Science Quarterly*, March 1969, pp. 91–114.

17   Raymond Miles & Charles Snow, *Organizational Strategy, Structure and Process*, New York: McGraw Hill, 1978.

18   Michael Porter, *Competitive Strategy*, New York: The Free Press, 1980.

19   James G. March & Herbert Simon, *Organizations*, New York: John Wiley, 1958.

20   Jeffrey Pfeffer, *Organizational Design*, Arlington Heights, IL: AHM Publishing, 1978; and *Power in Organizations*, Marshfield, MA: Pitman Publishing, 1981.

21   See S. Clegg, C. Hardy & W. Nord, *Handbook of Organisation Studies*, London: Sage, 1996. See also M. Foucault, *Power/Knowledge*, New York: Pantheon, 1980, and R. Cooper, 'Modernism, Postmodernism and Organization Analysis: The Contribution of Jaques Derrida', *Organization Studies*, 10(4), 1989, pp. 479–602.

22   Karl Weick, *The Social Psychology of Organizing*, Reading MA: Addison Wesley, 1969.

23 Peter Berger & Thomas Luckman, *The Social Construction of Reality: A Treatise in the Sociology of Knowledge*, Garden City, NY: Doubleday, 1966.

24 Thomas Peters & Robert Waterman, *In Search of Excellence: Lessons From America's Best-Run Companies*, New York: Harper & Row, 1982.

25 Richard Pascale & Anthony Athos, *The Art of Japanese Management*, New York: Simon & Schuster, 1981.

26 Robert Coase, 'The Nature of the Firm', *Economics*, 4, 1937, pp. 386–405.

27 E. Williamson, *Markets and Hierarchies: Analysis and Antitrust Implications*, New York: New York Free Press, 1975.

28 Agency theory literature derives from that concerning property rights. See, for instance, A.A. Alchian & H. Demsetz, 'Production, Information Costs and Economic Organization', *American Economic Review*, 62, 1972, pp. 777–95.

29 Lex Donaldson, *American Anti-Management Theories. Organization: a Critique of Paradigm Proliferation*, Cambridge: Cambridge University Press, 1995.

30 See Walter W. Powell & Paul DiMaggio, eds, *The New Institutionalism in Organizational Analysis*, Chicago: Chicago University Press, 1991; and Lynne G. Zuker, *Institutional Patterns and Organisations: Culture and Environments*, Cambridge: Balinger, 1988.

31 Clegg, Hardy & Nord, op cit.

32 Tom Peters, *Thriving on Chaos*, New York: Knopf, 1988.

33 Charles Handy, *Inside Organisations: 21 Ideas for Managers*, London: BBC Books, 1990.

34 Ricardo Semler, *Maverick: The Success Story Behind the World's Most Unusual Workplace*, New York: Warner, 1993.

35 Michael Hammer, *Re-engineering the Corporation: A Manifesto for Business Revolution*, London: Nicholas Brealey, 1993.

36 This section is drawn from Martin Kennly & Richard Florida 'The Transfer of Japanese Management Styles in Two US Transplant Industries: Autos and Electronics', *Journal of Management Studies*, 32(6), 1995, pp. 789–802; Greg Gardner, 'Tracking Toyota's Tundra', *Ward's Auto World*, 34(10), 1998, pp. 42–4; and Terry Besser, 'Rewards and Organizational Goal Achievement: A Case Study of Toyota Motor Manufacturing in Kentucky', *Journal of Management Studies*, 32(3), 1995, pp. 383–99.

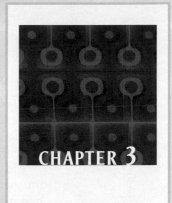

CHAPTER 3

Organisational effectiveness

After reading this chapter you should be able to:

1 define four approaches to organisational effectiveness;

2 list the assumptions of each of the organisational effectiveness approaches;

3 describe how managers can operationalise each approach;

4 identify key problems with each approach;

5 explain the value of each approach to practising managers;

6 compare the conditions under which each is useful for managers.

Introduction

Are you sure you know what effectiveness is?

The class looked a little confused. The lecturer had asked a simple question: each student was to nominate an organisation they considered to be effective and give reasons as to their choice. Initially no-one said much, but then a few students came up with ideas and others followed. Eventually everyone had made a nomination.

The nominations included a wide range of organisations, with many reasons given for their choice. One student thought Macquarie Bank was the most effective as he had just had a job there during the vacation and would like to join the bank after graduating. He thought it provided good careers for those who worked hard. Another thought supermarkets such as Coles and Woolworths were because they kept the population supplied with food and other essentials. There was general consensus that those companies that made large profits such as the National Australia Bank and Telstra must be effective, otherwise they would not have made profits. Holiday resorts, five-star hotels and airlines were favourably looked on, but mainly because of the desirability of their product.

Some non-commercial companies were nominated as well. Amnesty International was considered effective largely because of its goals: no-one in the class was informed enough to make a judgement as to whether it used its resources well. Similar comments were made about organisations such as the Smith Family and the Salvation Army and various green groups.

What was also revealing was what was left out of the students' consideration. Battling manufacturing companies such as Ford Australia were not considered effective. The various state railway undertakings were universally held as poorly performing. The oil companies were not rated as being effective because of their environmental record. This was in spite of everyone using the products of the industry daily. Electricity-generating companies fell within the same category. For the same reason most students did not consider mining companies effective. There was also general agreement that government organisations didn't rate highly on effectiveness; they seemed too inefficient and bureaucratic, with a general aura of being too slow to change.

The examples above are meant to introduce the problems inherent in defining and measuring organisational effectiveness. As you will see, researchers have had considerable difficulty in trying to agree on what the term means. Yet almost all these same researchers are quick to acknowledge that this term is the central theme in organisational theory: what we are trying to do is develop the capacity to generate more effective organisations. In fact, it is difficult to conceive of a theory of organisations that does not include the concept of effectiveness.[1]

Importance of organisational effectiveness

Every discipline in the administrative sciences contributes in some way to helping managers make organisations more effective. Marketing, for instance, guides managers in identifying market needs and promoting and selling products. Financial concepts assist managers in making the optimum use of funds invested in the organisation. Production and operations management concepts offer guidance in designing efficient production processes and controlling supply chains. Accounting principles assist managers by providing information that can enhance the quality of the decisions they make.

Organisation theory presents another answer to the question of what makes an organisation effective. That answer is: the proper organisation structure! This book will demonstrate that the way we put people and jobs together and define their roles and relationships is an important determinant in whether an organisation is successful. As we will demonstrate in later chapters, some structures work better under certain conditions than do others. Importantly, those managers who understand their structural options and the conditions under which each is preferred will have a definite advantage over their less informed counterparts. Organisation theory, as a discipline, clarifies which organisation structure will lead to, or improve, organisational effectiveness.

In addition to studying the structure of an organisation, organisation theory also studies issues that arise when we view the organisation as a collective of people. Organisation behaviour examines the actions of individuals through such fields of study as leadership, motivation and teamwork. In contrast, organisation theory is concerned with such organisation-wide features as culture and organisational change. We also consider the interaction of the organisation with its environment, and how organisations transform themselves over time in response to environmental and technological change and the process of growth and decline.

The issue of organisational effectiveness has taken on greater importance over recent years in response to changes in financial markets, government policy and community expectations. Funds managers, looking to invest large amounts of savings, are seeking sound investments with good growth prospects. Those companies that can provide this need never be short of capital. However, the opposite is also true. Many organisations have found that their lack of access to funds has crimped growth prospects and in some cases forced them into liquidation. Major shifts in government policy over the past 20 years, including deregulation and privatisation, has led to new demands being placed on organisations to respond to emerging environmental pressures. Improving quality has led to a reappraisal of many established practices and technological innovation has been rapid, altering the way organisations relate to their environment. As well, globalisation has greatly increased the level of competition under which companies operate. Finally, all organisations, from churches and the taxation department through to consumer products firms, are under close scrutiny from a community concerned about breaches of trust and ethical standards.

All this has meant that issues relating to organisational effectiveness are very much of concern to the community. But what is effectiveness, and how do we measure it?

In search of a definition

If you had been a student of organisational theory in the 1950s you would have had a deceptively simple way of assessing organisational effectiveness. At that time effectiveness was considered to be related to whether an organisation achieved its goals or not.[2] Although simple in concept, when it came to putting the goal attainment approach into practice, many ambiguities became apparent that limited research into the topic, as well as its application by managers. For example: Whose goals? Short-term goals or long-term goals? The organisation's official goals or actual goals?

Another simple approach to measuring effectiveness is to consider *survival* a necessary precondition for success.[3] If there is anything an organisation seeks to do, it is to survive. But the use of survival as a criterion presumes the ability to identify the death of an organisation. Unfortunately, the death of an organisation is nowhere as clear as a biological death. Some organisations clearly do die. They become insolvent, their remaining assets are sold and employees are laid off. But, in fact, most organisations don't die—they're remade. They merge, reorganise, sell off major parts or move into totally new areas of endeavour. The business pages of newspapers carry daily reports of mergers, acquisitions and takeovers, which often occur in the name of organisational effectiveness. Although it is less common, even churches merge. Charities evolve from catering to one sector of the community to another as needs change. For example Legacy, which was set up to cater for the needs of deceased servicemen who had served overseas, now sees itself as promoting the interests of youth generally. Other organisations can survive long periods of time while not being considered effective. For some organisations—and common targets for most people include government departments and large corporations—death practically never occurs.[4] They seem to have a life beyond any evaluation as to whether they are doing a good job. The airline industry is notorious for consuming large amounts of capital while making remarkably little profit. But somehow airlines are still in business. Other companies are started by entrepreneurs with the intention of building them to a certain size in order to 'flip' them to someone else (i.e. sell them to another buyer). So survival, and indeed corporate death, is a far more difficult concept to operationalise than appears at first glance

The 1960s and early 70s saw a proliferation of organisational effectiveness studies. A review of these studies identified 30 different criteria—all purporting to measure 'organisational effectiveness'. These are listed in Table 3.1. The fact that few studies used multiple criteria, and that the criteria themselves ranged from general measures such as quality and morale to more specific factors such as accident rates and absenteeism, certainly leads to the conclusion that organisational effectiveness means different things to different people. Some of the items in Table 3.1 are even contradictory. Efficiency, for instance, is achieved by using resources to their maximum. It is characterised by an *absence* of slack. In contrast, flexibility/adaptation can be achieved only by having a surplus: that is, by the *availability* of slack. If absence of slack is a measure of effectiveness, how can a surplus of slack also be a measure of effectiveness?

No doubt the large number of items in Table 3.1 is partly due to the diversity of organisations being evaluated. It also reflects the different interests of the evaluators. As we argue later in this chapter, when we consider more specifically how values affect organisational effectiveness, the criteria chosen to define effectiveness may tell us more about the person doing the evaluation than about the organisation being evaluated. But all 30 criteria cannot be relevant to every organisation, and certainly some are more important than others. The researcher who tabulated these 30 criteria concluded that as an organisation can be effective or ineffective on the basis of a number of different facets that may be relatively independent of one another, organisational effectiveness has no 'operational definition'.[5]

TABLE 3.1 Organisational effectiveness criteria

1 Overall effectiveness	16 Planning and goal setting
2 Productivity	17 Goal consensus
3 Efficiency	18 Internalisation of organisational goals
4 Profit	19 Role and norm congruence
5 Quality	20 Managerial interpersonal skills
6 Accidents	21 Managerial task skills
7 Growth	22 Information management and communication
8 Absenteeism	23 Readiness
9 Turnover	24 Utilisation of environment
10 Job satisfaction	25 Evaluations by external entities
11 Motivation	26 Stability
12 Morale	27 Value of human resources
13 Control	28 Participation and shared influence
14 Conflict/cohesion	29 Training and development emphasis
15 Flexibility/adaptation	30 Achievement emphasis

Source: Adapted from John P. Campbell, 'On the Nature of Organizational Effectiveness', in P.S. Goodman, J.M. Pennings & Associates, eds, *New Perspectives on Organizational Effectiveness*, San Francisco: Jossey-Bass, 1977, pp. 36–41.

This belief that organisation effectiveness defies definition has been widely accepted. From a research perspective, it may be true. On the other hand, a close look at the recent effectiveness literature does reveal movement towards agreement. Even more important, from a practical standpoint: all of us have and use some operational definition of organisational effectiveness on a regular basis, even if it is only a mental concept of what an effective organisation is. That is so in spite of the supposed problem researchers have in defining it.[6]

A close examination of the organisational effectiveness literature, however, indicates that there are some commonalities that may have been overlooked.[7] As will become evident by the time you finish reading this chapter, there is almost unanimous agreement today that assessment of organisational effectiveness requires multiple criteria, that different organisational functions have to be evaluated using different characteristics, and that effectiveness must consider both means (processes) and ends (outcomes). The implication is that it is difficult for us to develop a single and universal criterion of effectiveness. In addition, because organisations do many things and their success depends on adequate performance in a number of areas, the definition of effectiveness must reflect this complexity. It also means of course that organisations may be effective in some things they do but not effective in others. Because of this complexity, we will have to reserve our statement of a formal definition until the end of this chapter, after a number of effectiveness concepts have been discussed.

While researchers may debate whether organisational effectiveness can be defined, the fact is that all of us have a working definition of the term. We all make effectiveness judgements regularly, whenever we buy shares, choose a university, select a bank or garage, evaluate job offers, decide which charities will get our donations or make other, similar decisions. Managers and administrators, of course, also make regular effectiveness determinations when they appraise and compare units or allocate budgets to these units. The point is that evaluating the effectiveness of an organisation is a widespread and ongoing activity. From a managerial perspective alone, effectiveness judgements are going to be made with or without agreement on a formal definition.

The remainder of this chapter is devoted to presenting the diverse approaches that the study of organisational effectiveness has taken. It concludes with an integrative framework that acknowledges the earlier approaches, deals explicitly with their differences, and provides a complex but clear definition of organisational effectiveness.

 OT CLOSEUP

The effectiveness of the 'green' movement

It seems churlish to even think about criticising the green movement. International organisations such as Greenpeace and locally based environmental groups such as the Wilderness Society and the Nature Conservation Council have long been at the forefront of attempting to raise environmental awareness. In doing this they have generally concentrated on a few high-profile issues, such as mining at Kakadu and logging in various state forests, particularly in Tasmania and northern New South Wales.

These programs have been successful in putting green issues on the public agenda, and in most cases legislation has been passed that went some way towards meeting the environmentalists' demands. However, some in the movement are re-evaluating the effectiveness of this type of approach. Their main concern is that concentrating on a few high-profile issues does not address the most significant environmental issues facing Australia. These are logging and the clearing of privately owned land, the buildup of salinity in the Murray–Darling basin and the increase in the number of feral pests, such as rabbits, foxes and fire ants. The problem for organisations active in the green movement is that these issues do not have the headline-grabbing attention of rainforests or wetlands. But compared to a very small mine in Kakadu, or the insignificant amount of logging in national forests, they are of infinitely great importance.

One of the difficulties for the green movement has been that it has been slow to identify the use of economic incentives in eliciting environmentally sound practices. In part this is ideological: many in the green movement were anti-economics, and incorrectly linked economics with exploitation rather than conservation. Certainly governments provided economic disincentives to conserve natural resources. For instance, governments provided water to irrigators at almost no cost, leading to overuse and rising water tables. Farmers received major tax concessions to clear land, not conserve it. The greens now realise that economic incentives will need to play a major role in future environmental efforts.

So could we say that the various green movements have been effective? Answering this question highlights the difficulties of the goal-attainment approach. They have met their goals on a few high-profile issues such as rainforest logging. But these goals neglected what were far more significant environmental problems. Additionally, measuring goal attainment is difficult in relation to issues such as salinity, feral pests and raising general environmental awareness. The political nature of the conservation movement is also an issue. The anti-economics and pro-economics approaches would set themselves different goals in relation to what they were trying to achieve.

Drawn from: James Woodford, 'A Load of Hot Air', *Sydney Morning Herald*, 29 September 2001, Spectrum pp. 4–5.

The goal-attainment approach

An organisation is, by definition, created deliberately to achieve one or more specific goals.[8] It should come as no surprise then to find that goal attainment is probably the most widely used criterion of effectiveness.

The **goal-attainment approach** states that an organisation's effectiveness must be appraised in terms of the accomplishment of *ends* rather than means. Put another way, it should be judged by whether it has achieved what it set out to achieve, rather than how it got there. Popular goal-attainment criteria include achieving profit objectives or meeting budgets, achieving certain quality outcomes, helping a certain number of disadvantaged people, attaining health objectives or winning a sports competition. Their common denominator is that they consider the ends that the organisation was created to achieve.

goal-attainment approach an organisation's effectiveness is appraised in terms of the accomplishment of its goals

Assumptions

The goal-attainment approach assumes that organisations are deliberate, rational, goal-seeking entities. Therefore, successful goal accomplishment becomes an appropriate measure of effectiveness. But the use of goals implies other assumptions that must be valid if goal accomplishment is to be a viable measure. First, organisations must have ultimate goals. Second, these goals must be identified and defined clearly enough to be understood. Third, these goals must be few enough to be manageable. Fourth, there must be general consensus or agreement on these goals. Finally, progress towards these goals must be measurable.

Making goals operative

Given that the assumptions cited are valid, how would managers operationalise the goal-attainment approach? The key decision makers would be the group from which the goals were obtained. This group would be asked to state the organisation's specific goals. Once they had been identified, it would be necessary to develop some measurement device to see how well they were being met. If, for instance, the consensus goal was profit maximisation, measures such as return on investment, return on sales or some similar computation would be selected.

The goal-attainment approach is probably most explicit in **management by objectives (MBO)**. MBO is a well-known philosophy of management that assesses an organisation and its members by how well they achieve specific goals that superiors and subordinates have jointly established. Tangible, verifiable and measurable goals are developed, cascading down the organisation through levels of management. Each layer of goals is derived from those above. Actual performance is then measured and compared with the goals. If each manager reaches his/her individual and departmental goals then it is assumed that the organisation must reach its goals. MBO represents the ultimate in a goal-oriented approach to effectiveness.[9]

management by objectives (MBO) a philosophy of management that assesses an organisation and its members by how well they achieve specific goals that have been jointly established

Problems

The goal-attainment approach is fraught with a number of problems that make its exclusive use highly questionable. Many of these problems relate directly to the assumptions that we noted earlier.

It is one thing to talk about goals in general, but when you operationalise the goal-attainment approach you have to ask: Whose goals? Top management's? If so, who is

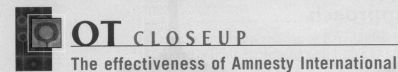

OT CLOSEUP

The effectiveness of Amnesty International

While academics debate issues of effectiveness, for business organisations effectiveness is often fairly straightforward to determine: normally, assessment concentrates on whether the organisation is satisfying the owner's needs. For shareholders, this means profitability and rising share prices. For private companies, whose owners' needs are more complex, it may be employment for family members or lifestyle issues. Greater difficulties arise in assessing the effectiveness of non-profit and charitable organisations. Often these undertake work that has political implications and may involve value judgements as to what poverty is or what constitutes a good education.

One organisation which on the surface would seem to have an unassailable claim to effectiveness is Amnesty International. Established just over 40 years ago in the shadow of the Berlin Wall, its aims were ending torture and the death penalty, prompt and fair trial for political prisoners, and the release of all prisoners of conscience who had not condoned violence. It works through publicity, 'naming and shaming', and various reports, including its annual report.

Over the past few years, however, Amnesty has been the subject of a number of adverse comments. For instance, the nations that attract the most criticism are Western democracies, such as Australia and the USA. Indeed, the more democratic a country, the more likely it is to be criticised by Amnesty. South Korea gets more mention as a transgressor than North Korea, Iraq receives little criticism and Syria and Vietnam virtually none. Any number of African countries where strongmen rule by the gun receive no mention. Amnesty also has been criticised for the size of its bureaucracy, with the London head office having over 325 employees.

Amnesty justifies its bias towards naming Western countries as transgressors by saying that it relies only on independent and verifiable information. Hence the lack of criticism of countries that are oppressive: the more tightly controlled a country is, the less likely it is to be criticised. Critics have claimed that it has strayed from its original charter and is now keen to play to Western audiences in order to expand its membership base and fee income.

Amnesty rejects such criticism. But the market for ideas and commitment is fundamentally different from the market for cars. The market soon punishes an ineffective car manufacturer. For non-profit organisations such as Amnesty there is no similar market, and political opinion and emotion can soon overwhelm reason.

Drawn from: Peter Phelps, 'Bloated Amnesty a Travesty of its Charter', *The Australian Financial Review*, 6 January 2001.

---

included and who is excluded? In some large corporations, just surveying general managers and above can include dozens of respondents. It's also possible that some of the decision makers with real power and influence in the organisation are not members of senior management. There are cases in which individuals with a number of years of experience or particular expertise in an important area have a significant influence on determining their organisation's goals (they are part of the dominant coalition), even though they are not among the senior executive cadre. Yet again, workers lower in the organisation's structure will no doubt have goals for the organisation, which might bear little relationship to top management's goals.

What an organisation states officially as its goals does not always reflect its actual goals.[10] Official goals tend to be influenced strongly by standards of social desirability. This includes responding to fashions and fads and politically active social groups. Representative statements such as 'to produce quality products at competitive prices', 'to be a responsible member of the community', 'to ensure that our productive efforts do nothing to damage the environment', 'to maintain our reputation for integrity', and 'to be the employer of choice' are common organisational goals. These vague 'motherhood' official statements may sound good, but rarely do they make any contribution to an understanding of what the organisation is actually trying to accomplish. Given the likelihood that official and actual goals will be different, an assessment of an organisation's actual goals should probably include the statements made by the dominant coalition plus an additional listing derived from observations of what members in the organisation are actually doing.

An organisation's short-term goals are often different from its long-term goals. For instance, a firm's primary short-term goal may be financial—to raise $20 million of working capital within the next 12 months. Its five-year goal, however, may be to increase its market share from 4% to 10%. It may even have a longer-term goal of selling itself to someone else at a profit for shareholders. In applying the goal-attainment approach, which goals—short-term or long-term—should be used?

The fact that organisations have multiple goals also creates difficulties. They can compete with each other and sometimes are even incompatible. The aims of 'high product quality' and 'low unit cost', for example, may be directly at odds with each other. The goal-attainment approach assumes consensus on goals. Given that there are multiple goals and diverse interests within the organisation, consensus may not be possible unless goals are stated in such ambiguous and vague terms as to allow the varying interest groups to interpret them in a way favourable to their self-interests. This may, in fact, explain why most official goals in large organisations are traditionally broad and intangible. They act to placate the many different interest groups within the organisation.

The interpretation of whether a goal has been achieved may not be easy. Protecting the environment, for instance, means different things tó different people, depending on their attitudes and orientation. The best way to render assistance to various disadvantaged groups may be highly politicised, particularly if outcomes are not clear. Even providing employment may create disputes over goals. McDonald's has continual conflict with its critics over the type of work it offers its young restaurant staff. McDonald's claims to be proud of the job opportunities offered and the fact that it provides a valuable mode of entry into the world of work. Its critics dismiss the work as mere 'hamburger flipping', and the word 'McJobs' has been coined to describe work lacking challenge and interest.

Where multiple goals exist, they must be ordered according to importance if they are to have meaning to members. But how do you allocate relative importance to goals that may be incompatible and represent diverse interests? Additionally, one of the main sources of disagreement within the top management team of an organisation arises from the determination of which goals should be important for the organisation. This may be particularly so in charitable and not-for-profit organisations, where the goals may be intangible statements of purpose. These difficulties make us appreciate the problems that operationalising the goal-attainment approach poses.

A final insight should be mentioned before we conclude this section on problems. It just may be that for many organisations, goals do not direct behaviour: 'The common assertion that goal consensus must occur prior to action obscures the fact that consensus is impossible unless there is something tangible around which it can occur. And this "something tangible" may well turn out to be actions *already completed.*[11] In some cases, official goals may be merely statements of past actions rather than guides to future attainment. Organisations may act first, then later create a 'goal' to justify what has happened. If this is true, measuring organisational effectiveness by surveying the dominant coalition should result not in benchmarks against which actual performance can be compared but rather in formal descriptions of the dominant coalition's perceptions of prior performance.

What does all this mean? It would appear that we should treat goals identified by senior management as guiding the organisation with caution. Only the naive would accept the formal statements made by senior management to represent the organisation's goals. As one author concluded after finding that corporations issue one set of goals to shareholders, another to customers, a third set to employees, a fourth to the public and a fifth for management itself, formal statements of goals should be treated 'as fiction produced by an organization to account for, explain, or rationalize its existence to particular audiences rather than as valid and reliable indications of purpose'.[12]

Value to managers

These problems should not be construed as a blanket indictment of goals. Some goals are clearly measurable and relevant to an organisation. Examples of such goals may be to remain independent, to attain certain returns on capital, to bring a project on stream within a certain time frame and budget, or to attain certain medical or charitable goals.

This reminds us that organisations exist to achieve goals—the problems lie in their identification and measurement. The validity of those goals identified can probably be increased significantly by:

- ensuring that input is received from all those who have a major influence on formulating the official goals, even if they are not part of senior management;
- including actual goals obtained by observing the behaviour of organisation members;
- recognising that organisations pursue both short- and long-term goals;
- insisting on tangible, verifiable and measurable goals rather than relying on vague statements that merely mirror societal expectations;
- viewing goals as dynamic entities that change over time rather than as rigid or fixed statements of purpose.

If managers are willing to confront the complexities inherent in the goal-attainment approach, they *can* obtain reasonably valid information for assessing an organisation's effectiveness. But there is more to organisational effectiveness than identifying and measuring specific ends.

The systems approach

In Chapter 1, we described organisations in a systems framework. Organisations acquire inputs, engage in transformation processes and generate outputs. It has been argued that defining effectiveness solely in terms of goal attainment results in only a partial measure of effectiveness. Goals focus on outputs. But an organisation should also be judged on its ability to acquire inputs, process them, channel the outputs, and maintain stability and balance. This means that the organisation can maintain itself through a repetitive cycle of activities. Another way to look at organisational effectiveness, therefore, is through a **systems approach**.[13]

In the systems approach, end goals are not ignored, but they are only one element in a more complex set of criteria. Systems models emphasise criteria that will increase the long-term survival of the organisation, such as the organisation's ability to *acquire* resources, *maintain* itself internally as a social organisation and *interact* successfully with its external environment. So the systems approach focuses not so much on specific ends as on the means needed for the achievement of those ends.

systems approach
evaluating an organisation's effectiveness by its ability to acquire inputs, process the inputs, channel the outputs and maintain stability and balance

Assumptions

The assumptions underlying a systems approach to organisational effectiveness are the same as those that applied in our discussion of systems in Chapter 1. We can elaborate on a few of the more evident ones.

A systems approach to effectiveness implies that organisations are made up of interrelated subparts. If any one of these subparts performs poorly, it will negatively affect the performance of the whole system.

Effectiveness requires awareness and successful interactions with environmental constituencies. Management cannot fail to maintain good relations with customers, suppliers, government agencies, unions, the community and other constituencies that have the power to disrupt the stable operation of the organisation.

Survival requires a steady replenishment of resources consumed. Raw materials and other inputs must be secured, vacancies created by employee resignations and retirements must be filled, declining product lines must be replaced, changes in the economy and the tastes of customers or clients need to be anticipated and reacted to, and so on. The resources of the system are not just productive machinery and physical assets. They include such intangibles as ideas, inventions and patents, brand names, customer goodwill and the skills of the management team. Failure to replenish these as they decay will result in the organisation's decline and, possibly, death.

Making systems operative

Let us turn now to the issue of how managers can apply the systems approach. First, we look at a sampling of criteria that systems advocates consider relevant; then we consider the various ways in which managers measure these criteria.

The systems view looks at factors such as relations with the environment to ensure continued receipt of inputs and favourable acceptance of outputs, flexibility of response to environmental changes, the efficiency with which the organisation transforms inputs to outputs, the clarity of internal communications, the level of conflict among groups and the degree of employee job satisfaction. These measures may be benchmarked against other organisations doing similar things. In contrast to the goal-attainment approach, the systems approach focuses on the means necessary to ensure the organisation's continued survival. And it should be noted that systems advocates do not neglect the importance of specific end goals as a determinant of organisational effectiveness. Rather, they question the validity of the goals selected and the measures used for assessing the progress towards these goals.

It has been suggested that the critical systems interrelationships can be converted into organisational effectiveness variables or ratios.[14] These could include output/

input, transformations/input, transformations/output, changes in input/input, and so on. Table 3.2 gives some examples of measurement criteria that could be used together with these variables in a business firm, a hospital and a university.

Operations managers and management accountants use many of these measures when they assess the effectiveness of the transformation process. In keeping with the systems idea of environmental interaction, many organisations, including charities and government departments, benchmark many of their measures, often called critical ratios, against their competitors and industry standards.

TABLE 3.2 Examples of effectiveness measures of systems for different types of organisations

System variables	Business firm	Hospital	University
Output/input	Return on investment	Average length of patient stay	Number of publications per staff member
Transformations/ input	Inventory turnover	Staff per patient	Staff/student ratio
Transformations/ output	Sales volume	Total number of patients treated	Number of students graduated
Changes input/ input	Change in working capital	Change in number of patients treated	Change in student enrolment

Source: Adapted from William M. Evan, 'Organization Theory and Organizational Effectiveness: An Exploratory Analysis', in S. Lee Spray, ed., *Organizational Effectiveness: Theory, Research, Utilization,* Kent, OH: Kent State University Press, 1976, pp. 22–3. Reproduced with permission.

OT CLOSEUP

The systems approach and world's best practice

The concepts of world's best practice have spread throughout the business community as a result of the progressive lowering of tariff barriers. When high tariffs and other forms of protection and regulation were in force, a business producing solely for the Australian or New Zealand market had only to worry about competition within the relevant country. Now, however, the comparison point is the lowest-cost producers in the world.

Comparisons of effectiveness under these conditions are largely made using the systems approach. Businesses operating in a market economy acquire inputs, transform them in some way and sell the outputs in a repetitive cycle. For any activity, a monetary value can be attributed and a comparison with those undertaking similar business activity made. The market is very unforgiving of those companies which don't use their resources productively.

Another type of comparison not using a monetary base can be made by benchmarking. This is a process where comparisons of such factors as hours to undertake a process, absenteeism rates and ratios of inputs to outputs are made using units of production rather than money. Most companies operating in the market sector are now undertaking such comparisons as a measure of effectiveness.

Yet another systems application of organisational effectiveness is the concept of added value popularised by a professor at the London Business School, John Kay.[15] The cycle of absorbing inputs from the environment, turning them into usable products and services and then marketing these should leave a surplus of cash over and above that needed to maintain the system in its repetitive cycle. This surplus is called the value added, and the larger it is the more successful the company. Kay considers that a commercial organisation that adds no value (i.e. one that contributes no more than the value of its inputs) cannot justify its existence in the long run.

The determination of added value starts with money received from sales to customers. From this are deducted salaries and wages, capital costs and payments to suppliers. These groups are called stakeholders, and payment to them ensures their future cooperation. What is left is the added value. This is less than the operating profit of the firm, because return to shareholders is included in the capital costs. But it represents the effectiveness with which resources are used in the organisation, including shareholders' funds. This approach concentrates on profit-making organisations, so it has little applicability to government or charitable organisations.

Problems

The two most telling shortcomings of the systems approach relate to measurement and the issue of whether means really matter.

While some process variables may be specific and easy to measure, such as hours to build a motor vehicle, or coal consumption per kilowatt hour, other critical ratios are not so easy to quantify. Rates of innovation, quality of the management team and community goodwill, all necessary for organisational strength, defy easy measurement. Environments may also change very quickly, rendering one set of measures superfluous and raising the importance of what previously seemed to be not significant. The entry of cut-price airlines into Australia, for instance, very quickly changed the environmental landscape for the established airlines.

A second problem derives from the concentration on processes rather than end goals. It makes little sense to be a great producer of steam locomotives if they are technologically obsolescent—or a cost-effective microchip producer if there is glut of product. The problem with the systems approach, at least according to its critics, is that its focus is on the means necessary to achieve effectiveness rather than on organisational effectiveness itself.

This criticism may take on more substance if we conceptualise both goal-attainment and systems approaches as goal-oriented. The first uses *end* goals; the second uses *means* goals. If we do not reach our *end* goals, such as certain levels of market share or profitability ratios, then management should establish a process to find out why this may be so. In this they would be focusing on *means* goals. So, in a sense, both measures of effectiveness complement each other.

However, the systems approach leaves us with the impression that it is better at measuring the efficiency of the system rather than the effectiveness of the organisation. We will take up this point later in the chapter.

Value to managers

Managers who use a systems approach to organisational effectiveness are less inclined to look for immediate results. They are less likely to make decisions that trade off the organisation's long-term health and survival for ones that will make

OT CLOSEUP

General Electric and organisational effectiveness

For over 20 years, until he retired in 2001, Jack Welch was the CEO of General Electric. During that time he developed legendary status as a successful manager and contributed to the belief that the CEO was critical to a firm's success. His unusually long tenure allowed him to develop and implement his ideas on how large organisations should be structured and managed. And General Electric was certainly large: with over 250 000 employees and worldwide operations it was, and is, one of the largest organisations in the world. It also has a very large product range, extending from medical imaging equipment through to electrical generators and aircraft engines. This makes Jack Welch's achievements all the more noteworthy; such companies, known as conglomerates, are out of fashion with current strategic thinking. Most companies now try to concentrate on just a few core competencies. So what are Jack Welch's ideas on how a CEO can contribute to organisational effectiveness? These many be summarised as follows:

- Integrity is critical. It sets the tone for the organisation and helps build better relations with customers, suppliers and analysts.
- Intensity and passion are critical. Without passion there is not motivation and without motivation performance will be suboptimal. The biggest enemy of passion is bureaucracy.
- An organisation must maximise its intellect. Everyone's mind must be on the game and their ideas should be transferred to others.

- Getting the right people in the right jobs is far more important than developing a strategy. You may have the greatest strategy in the world, but without the right people to deliver you will get only so-so results.
- Bureaucracy strangles while informality liberates. Bureaucracy can be the ultimate insulator from reality. But informality is not about first names and unassigned car-parking spaces: it is about making everybody count and making everybody know they count.
- Stretch goals are important. Mediocre goals lead to mediocre effort.
- The bottom 10% of managers should be let go; it is the best antidote for bureaucracy.
- The CEO should spend as much time away from the corner office and in the field as possible.
- Don't attempt to do everything. Don't try to run a cafeteria and a canteen when your business is turbines. It only distracts time and effort from what you are good at. Get a company to do it that specialises in doing it.
- Business success is less a function of grandiose strategies than it is a result of being able to respond rapidly to real changes. Consequently, strategy needs to be dynamic and anticipatory.
- Never underestimate your competition. One of the most common errors business people make is thinking that the competition is going to act in a way in which they would like them to act.

Adapted from: Jack Welch, 'Jack', New York: Hodder Headline, 2001.

them look good in the near term. They are aware of the need for continuous improvement and that it takes time. Moreover, the systems approach increases the managers' awareness of the interdependence of organisational activities. For instance, if management fails to have inputs on hand when they are needed or if the quality of those inputs is poor, this will restrict the organisation's ability to achieve its end goals.

A final plus for the systems approach is its applicability where end goals either are very vague or defy measurement. Managers of public organisations, for example, often use 'ability to acquire budget increases' as a measure of effectiveness—substituting an input criterion for an output criterion.

The strategic-constituencies approach

A more recent perspective on organisational effectiveness—the **strategic-constituencies approach**—proposes that an effective organisation is one that satisfies the demands of those constituencies in its environment from which it requires support for its continued existence.[16]

This approach is similar to the systems view, yet it has a different emphasis. Both consider interdependencies, but the strategic-constituencies view is not concerned with all the organisation's environment. It seeks to appease only those in the environment who can threaten the organisation's survival—that is, the strategic constituencies. As an example, let's take the case of three motor vehicle companies: one a public company listed on the stock exchange, the second a family-owned company, and the third owned by the government. Although undertaking the same task, part of the strategic constituencies are radically different. The first must concentrate on satisfying shareholders looking for a return on their assets. The second may be more concerned with such issues as family succession and bankers, who provide most of the working capital. The last has government as a critical constituency, so maintaining good relationships with politicians is very important. What is critical varies with the circumstances of the company.

Assumptions

The goal-attainment approach views organisations as deliberate, rational and goal-seeking entities. The strategic-constituencies approach views organisations very differently. They are assumed to exist within an environment where demands are placed on the organisation by various important constituencies and, as a result, the organisation becomes a political arena where vested interests compete for control over resources in order to satisfy the environmental demands. In such a context, organisational effectiveness becomes an assessment of how successful the organisation has been in satisfying those strategic constituencies on which the survival of the organisation depends.

The 'political arena' metaphor further assumes that the organisation has a number of constituencies, with different degrees of power, each trying to satisfy its demands. But as each constituency also has a unique set of values, it is unlikely that their preferences will be in agreement. For example, a study of the major tobacco companies found that the public evaluated them in terms of the harmful effects of tobacco smoking, while shareholders evaluated their ability to produce cigarettes efficiently and profitably. Not surprisingly—using such diverse criteria—the public rated the tobacco firms as ineffective, and shareholders rated the same firms as highly effective.[17] The effectiveness of a tobacco company, therefore, can be said to be determined by its ability to identify its critical constituencies, assess their preference patterns and satisfy their demands. Shareholders and smokers might be satisfied with tobacco companies, but if the public, through its legislative representatives, outlaws the sale of cigarettes, then the companies face large losses.

Finally, the strategic-constituencies approach assumes that managers pursue a number of goals and that the ones selected represent a response to those interest

strategic-constituencies approach
an organisations effectiveness is determined by how successfully it satisfies the demands of those constituencies in its environment from which it requires support for its continued existence

groups that control the resources necessary for the organisation to survive. No goal, or set of goals, that management selects is value-free. Each implicitly, if not explicitly, will favour some constituency over others. When management give profits

OT CLOSEUP
Nike and sweatshops

For businesses, some critical constituencies are fairly predictable; shareholders, key suppliers and distributors and customers spring to mind. But sometimes a surprise occurs, and the environment throws up a completely unexpected critical constituency. Nike provides a good example of this process. Nike is what is called a virtual organisation. Notwithstanding the financial size of the company, few are employed by Nike; those that are, work in areas such as design and marketing. All manufacturing is outsourced to contractors, who primarily work in the Asian region. The contractors themselves contract part of the work to subcontractors, and so it goes on through an extended supply chain.

The problem is that many of the employment practices of the subcontractors are questionable. The publicity given to this has been so extensive that 'Nike' and 'sweatshop' have become almost synonymous. Employees overcome by the smell of glues and chemicals, long working weeks of up to 72 hours, unpaid overtime, low wages and the use of underage labour are all criticisms Nike has had to endure. Nike is not, of course, the only firm that has been the subject of such criticism. Most high-profile firms which have their goods made in Asia by subcontractors, particularly in Indonesia and Vietnam, have come in for their share of bad publicity.

This issue was in the public domain for most of the 1990s, and most of the issues raised by activists were valid. But regardless of Nike's best efforts to improve employment practices, the problem is still very much current for it. Small things also have a habit of attracting poor publicity to the issue. For instance, Nike runs a service that personalises sneakers with the purchaser's name. One purchaser wanted 'sweatshop' embroidered onto the sneaker, but Nike refused. The resultant publicity was something Nike could have done without.

Nike has attempted to eliminate unacceptable conditions. It employs independent consultants to inspect its factories to identify any unethical practices. It has formed a group with 10 other sporting-goods manufacturers to form an anti-sweatshop taskforce which generates a 'No-Sweat' label for clothing. It has an extensive ethical charter for its contractors to follow. The pressure is so great that the US government has established a taskforce on sweatshops. But the problem never seems to go away. Perceptions are important, and Nike has lost the perceptions war. Even companies that thought they were immune to criticism have been on the receiving end of embarrassing publicity. Chocolate makers, such as Cadbury, Nestlé and Mars, which are major processors of cocoa, were identified as purchasing most of their cocoa from the Ivory Coast, where 90% of the plantation workers are reported to work in a form of slavery.

But it seems unlikely that the issues raised by protesters can be solved simply. In poorer countries, the desperate will always queue for any job, and there is no shortage of employers willing to take advantage of them. There are also definitional issues and differences in customs and practices which provide fertile ground for different perceptions to be exploited. For instance, is slavery the same as indentured labour? Is a 14-year-old girl, married with two children, still a child and unable to work in a factory? Considering these issues highlights variations in the way that they are perceived by different cultures.

Adapted from: Anonymous, 'The Global Sweatshop', *Far Eastern Economic Review*, 19 September 1996, p. 5; Aaron Bernstein, 'A Potent Weapon in the War against Sweatshops', *Business Week*, 1 December 1997, p. 40; Tania Mason, 'Nike Axes "Sweatshop" after BBC Investigation', *Marketing* 19 October 2000, p. 5.

highest priority, for instance, they make the interests of owners paramount. Similarly, adaptability to the environment, customer satisfaction and a supportive work climate favour the interests of society, clients and employees, respectively.

Making strategic constituencies operative

The manager wishing to apply this perspective might begin by asking members of the dominant coalition to identify the constituencies they consider to be critical to the organisation's survival. This input can be combined and synthesised to arrive at a list of strategic constituencies.

As an example, Caltex, which refines and markets petroleum products, may have as its strategic constituencies the suppliers of crude oil, state and local governments concerned with pollution and safety issues, and unions representing workers at the plant. It would also include shareholders and banks at which the company may have short-term loans. Finally, wholesalers and retailers who distribute the product are critical to the company's success.

The above list could then be evaluated to determine the relative power of each constituency. Basically, this means looking at each one in terms of how dependent on it the organisation is. Does it have considerable power over the organisation? Are there alternatives to what this constituency provides? How do these constituencies compare in the impact they have on the organisation's operations?

The third step requires identifying the expectations that these constituencies hold for the organisation. What do they want of it? Given that each constituency has its own set of special interests, what goals does each seek to impose on the organisation? Shareholders' goals may be in terms of profit or appreciation in share prices, and the union's may be in terms of acquiring job security and high wages for its members, whereas the Environmental Protection Authority will want the firm's manufacturing plants to meet all minimum air-, water- and noise-pollution requirements. Table 3.3 contains a list of strategic constituencies which a business firm might confront and the typical organisational-effectiveness criteria each is likely to use.

TABLE 3.3 Typical organisational effectiveness criteria of selected strategic constituencies

Constituency	Typical OE criteria
Owners	Return on investment; growth in earnings
Employees	Pay; benefits; satisfaction with working conditions and career prospects
Customers	Satisfaction with price; quality; service
Suppliers	Satisfaction with payments; future sales potential
Creditors	Ability to pay debts
Unions	Competitive wages and benefits; satisfactory working conditions; willingness to bargain fairly
Local community officials	Involvement of organisation's members in local affairs; lack of damage to the community's environment, provision of employment
Government agencies	Compliance with laws; avoidance of penalties and reprimands

The strategic-constituencies approach would conclude by comparing the various expectations, determining common expectations and those that are incompatible, assigning relative weights to the various constituencies and formulating a preference ordering of these various goals for the organisation as a whole. This preference order, in effect, represents the relative power of the various strategic constituencies. The organisation's effectiveness then would be assessed in terms of its ability to satisfy these goals.

The stakeholder approach to effectiveness

As we have seen, the strategic-constituencies approach is an overtly political way of assessing effectiveness. The stakeholder approach recognises not only the importance of the strategic constituencies but also those who may not have the political power to influence the existence of the organisation or even its direction. To the list in Table 3.3 we could add such groups as families of workers, environmentalists, residents near the plant and those generally concerned to see that ethical decision making is maintained. All of these groups, even though they may not be formally organised as a pressure group, are considered to be affected by the organisation and should therefore be taken into account when important decisions are made.

The stakeholder approach has been developed by theorists such as Archie Carroll[18] as a counterpoint to the view that business organisations exist only to maximise profits for their shareholders. Carroll considers that this not only leads to a narrow focus in decision making but also neglects the community of which the organisation is a part. The stakeholder approach considers that an organisation is effective only if it takes into account the wider community that has an interest in the decisions of the organisation, even if this is at the cost of profits.

The advocates of the stakeholder approach see its advantage as taking the harsh edge from organisational decision making and civilising what may seem to be a system purely focused on profit. However, most organisations are aware of at least some of their wider responsibilities. And the interests of shareholders and other stakeholders may coincide when profits are increased because customers are satisfied, or when superior employment conditions attract the best staff.

Problems

Like the previous approaches, the strategic-constituencies approach is not without problems. The task of separating the strategic constituencies from the larger environment is easy to talk about but difficult to carry out. Because the environment changes rapidly, what was critical to the organisation yesterday may not be today. For example, the privatisation of government enterprises introduced a whole new set of constituencies for organisations. An example of an even quicker change in strategic constituencies is provided by banks, which exist on the goodwill and confidence of their depositors. If word is spread that a bank is insolvent, the resulting run on the bank by depositors can put it out of business in an afternoon. This highlights that strategic constituencies are not static but are constantly shifting as circumstances change.

Even if the constituencies in the environment can be identified and are assumed to be relatively stable, what separates the strategic constituencies from the 'almost' strategic constituencies? Where do you draw the line? And won't the interests of each member in the dominant coalition strongly affect what he or she perceives as strategic? An executive in finance is unlikely to see the world—or the organisation's strategic constituencies—in the same way as an executive in the supply chain management function. Finally, identifying the expectations that the strategic constituencies hold for the organisation presents a problem. How do you tap that information accurately?

The strategic-constituencies approach also assumes that an organisation's basic goal is survival. This may not be the case in many instances. Organisations are often established with the idea of selling them to someone else once they reach a certain size. Many businesses realise that they must merge with another in order to achieve some form of economies of scale, and management then negotiates the best deal that it can. Even charities and not-for-profit organisations such as hospitals or recreation clubs realise that that independence may not be the best policy for their strategic constituents. Amalgamations and mergers then follow.

Value to managers

If survival is important for an organisation, it is incumbent on managers to understand just who it is (in terms of constituencies) that survival is contingent on. By operationalising the strategic-constituencies approach, managers decrease the chance that they might ignore or severely upset a group whose power could significantly hinder the organisation's operations. If management knows whose support it needs if the organisation is to maintain its health, it can modify its preference ordering of goals as necessary to reflect the changing power relationships with its strategic constituencies.

The balanced scorecard approach

Organisations can be very confusing and difficult to comprehend. Notwithstanding advances in management techniques and the ability to process information, the complexity associated with the activities and interactions of large numbers of people defies easy analysis and understanding. The technologies of even a medium-sized organisation are beyond the grasp of one person. Areas of waste and inefficiency are often difficult to identify in a large organisation. Environments are constantly changing, and the demands on the organisation for performance, and indeed to justify its existence, never seem to diminish. Whether an organisation is performing well or poorly may not even be obvious to senior management. Given this complexity, it is easy for those managing and working in an organisation to concentrate their energies on a few, easy-to-grasp measures that are readily available.

So far in this chapter we have identified the importance of ends, means and processes in measuring organisational effectiveness. We have also identified that responding innovatively to environmental pressures contributes to the effectiveness of an organisation. The **balanced scorecard** attempts to integrate all of these approaches.[19]

In generating the various measures used in the balanced scorecard, one seeks to balance (hence the name) the various demands on the organisation with its capabilities. As a result, developing the measures becomes a diagnostic tool—a management technique to align the organisation with its environment and a measurement system to identify whether goals are being met. It is also seen as a means of developing and implementing strategy.

balanced scorecard
the balanced scorecard seeks to balance the various demands on the organisation with its capabilities

The balanced scorecard, developed by Kaplan and Norton, is an attempt to provide an integrated measure of organisational effectiveness. As with the approaches previously discussed, it proposes that there is no one measure which can assess an organisation's performance or which can focus attention on critical areas of the business. Financial measures are historical rather than future-oriented and are limited as to what can be measured in monetary terms. Operational measures, such as cycle times and defect rates, often lack the ability to differentiate between items of greater and lesser importance. The balanced scorecard attempts to view performance in several areas simultaneously and identify not just results but how the results were achieved.

Making the balanced scorecard operative

The various components of the balanced scorecard are illustrated in Figures 3.1a–b. The various performance measures are linked, highlighting that they are inter-related. The components attempt to identify four basic questions facing any organisation. These are:

- How do shareholders perceive us? (*Financial Perspective*) All organisations have financial demands and constraints. Financial measures enable an organisation to determine how profitable it is and the rate of return on assets. In short, the financial measures indicate whether an organisation's strategy and its execution are contributing to profitability.
- How do customers see us? (*Customer Perspective*) Goals and measures under this heading typically include assessment of time to delivery, product utility, and performance and service which, when combined, show how the product or service contributes to creating value for customers.
- What must we excel at? (*Internal Perspective*) These measures must concentrate on what the company must do internally to meet the customers' expectations. This is a process-driven measure, examples of which may include on-time running, quality measures, availability of equipment, cycle times for introduction of new product, after-sales service and costs of production.
- Can we continue to improve and create value? (*Innovation and Learning Perspective*) This goal is associated with the ability to develop and introduce new products of value to customers. It also includes measures of continuous improvement and production efficiencies.

Kaplan and Norton stress that it is possible to have too many measures of organisational performance. Management should identify just a few goals for each of the four perspectives. The measures developed for each goal should be easy to understand and contribute to deciding whether the goal has been achieved or not. The goals and measures will of course vary between organisations. In one way, the balanced scorecard is similar to the goal-attainment approach. Where it differs is that it formalises the way in which goals are determined. It also proposes that there are multiple goals, which exist within a network of interrelationships. Choosing what to measure is very important, as measurements guide actions, but it is difficult to avoid subjectivity. An example of goals and measures for a city-based rail system is shown in Figure 3.1b.

The first benefit attributed by Kaplan and Norton to the balanced scorecard is that it brings together in a single report many areas of importance to a organisation's competitiveness. These include both short-term efficiency issues and those relating

FIGURE 3.1A Representation of the balanced scorecard

The Balanced Scorecard Links Performance Measures

Financial Perspective — How do we look to shareholders?
Goals | Measures

How do customers see us?

Customer Perspective
Goals | Measures

What must we excel at?

Internal Business Perspective
Goals | Measures

Innovation and Learning Perspective
Goals | Measures

Can we continue to improve and create value?

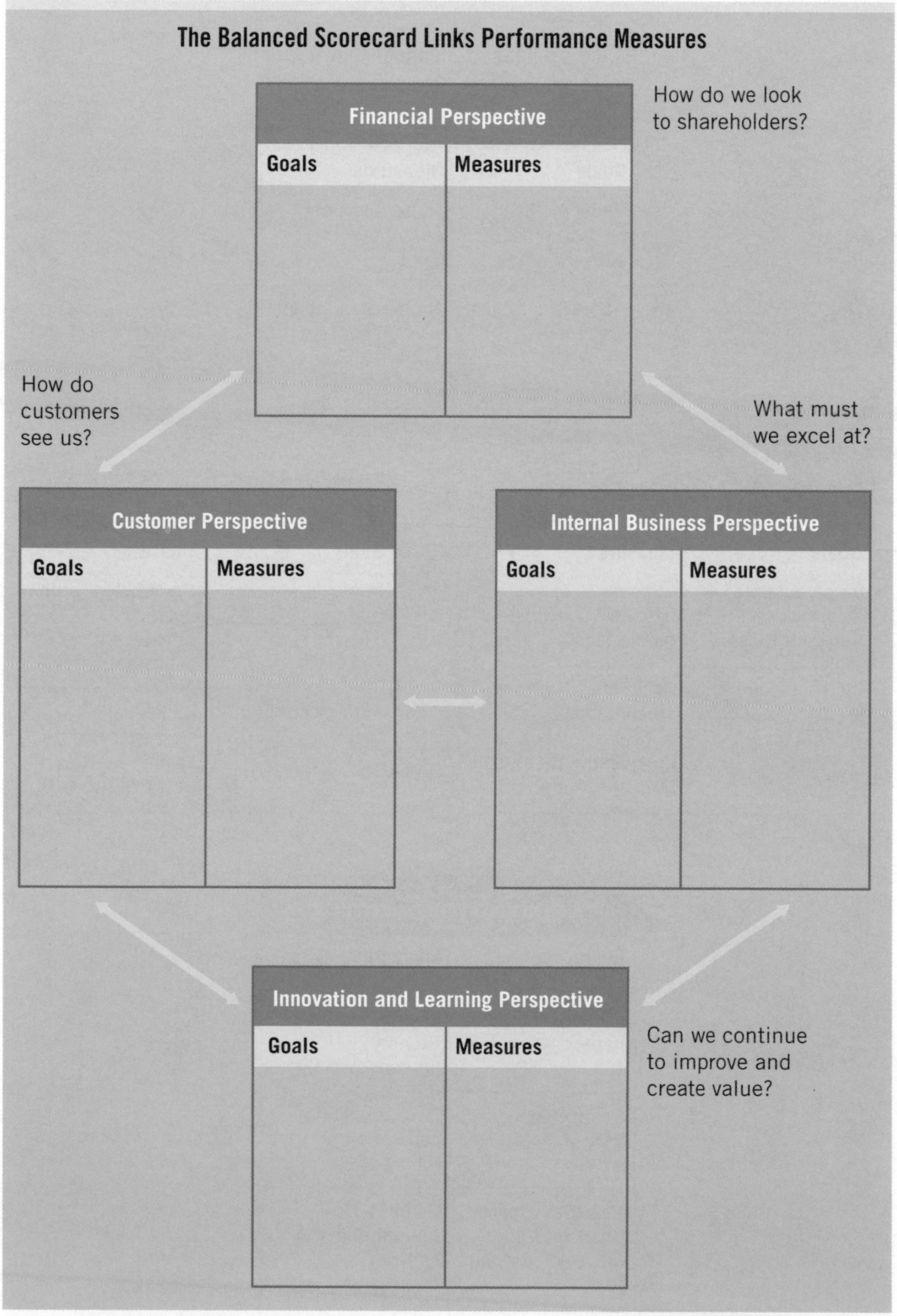

Source: Robert Kaplan & David Norton, 'The Balanced Scorecard—Measures that Drive Performance', *Harvard Business Review*, Jan/Feb 1992, pp. 71–9.

FIGURE 3.1B Application of the balanced scorecard to a city rail system

Railco's Balanced Business Scorecard

Financial Perspective

Goals	Measures
Reduce reliance on government subsidy	Increase % of revenue from fares
Accelerate system upgrade	Increase number of joint venture undertakings

Customer Perspective

Goals	Measures
Be an accepted means of transportation	Increase % of travellers choosing rail transport
Increase comfort levels	Complete air-conditioning of fleet Clean carriages at terminus stops

Internal Business Perspective

Goals	Measures
Improve on time running	Undertake signals upgrade Introduce planned maintenance
Reduce staffing costs	Benchmark staffing levels against world's best practice

Innovation and Learning Perspective

Goals	Measures
Reduce environmental impact	Instal environmentally friendly air-conditioning
Reduce energy usage	Develop new generation of rolling stock
Improve response times to unexpected events	Computerise timetabling and station information boards

to the long-term adaptability of the organisation. Second, the scorecard acts to guard against suboptimisation. By forcing senior managers to consider all important operational issues together, they are compelled to evaluate whether improvement in one area may have been achieved at the expense of creating problems in another. For instance, there is always the temptation within organisations to achieve superior short-term performance at the expense of long-term viability. A good example is that equipment maintenance can be curtailed, improving short-term cash flows but leading to unreliable plant and higher costs in the future. The balanced scorecard should be able to identify where unwise compromises have been made.

The balanced scorecard also puts into perspective the use of financial measures as a means of information to managers. Financial measures tend to be backward-looking, as they provide information only on what has occurred in the past. They fail to reflect contemporary value-creating actions. Money is a symbolic measure which lacks the diagnostic ability of those which, for example, use time, defects or consumption rates as their unit of measure. Financial measures are important, but must be considered in combination with other sources of information in order to allow a comprehensive picture of the organisation to emerge.

Although it may appear that the balanced scorecard is applicable only to business organisations, it can be of use to organisations in the non-profit sector. No organisation can ignore resource constraints; organisations must derive their funds from somewhere. Likewise, all organisations have some form of consumer group that must be serviced. And in the not-for-profit sector, these groups can be difficult to define. Should charities, for instance, regard donors as customers? However they are regarded, they must be satisfied that their donations are being put to good use, or they will take their donations elsewhere. The balanced scorecard allows all of these competing interests to be assessed and incorporated in decision making.

Problems

The utility of the balanced scorecard may be limited if what is chosen to be measured is not important. Kaplan and Norton recommend that the top management team and major stakeholders be involved in identifying the goals. But, as we have seen with the goal-attainment approach, the identification and ranking of goals by importance is often a subjective process, which is influenced by political agendas. Additionally, what is important often changes over time. These changes may be obvious and easily incorporated by changes in goals or measures. But they may be subtle and difficult to identify or quantify. Customers are also a difficult-to-satisfy group, with the habit of constantly requesting unrealistic performance from suppliers. Similarly, identifying genuine technological innovation as distinct from continuous improvement is easier in theory than it is in practice.

Value to managers

Notwithstanding its problems, the balanced scorecard is a useful framework, which enables managers to assess effectiveness. It also aids in the development and implementation of strategy. Organisations are rarely easy to understand, and this problem increases with size. The balanced scorecard is an attempt to identify what is important to the organisation and to develop measures for these. It brings together in a single management report the different elements of a company's competitive agenda. In our city rail example, for instance, on-time running is linked to expenditure on capital equipment; and the more reliable the system is perceived to be, the easier it would be for the rail system to raise fares to cover costs. A further benefit of the balanced scorecard is that it guards against suboptimisation. As all important operational decisions are considered together, it enables managers to see whether improvements in one area have been made at the expense of another.

The balanced scorecard also has the advantage of involving a reasonably wide range of managers and stakeholders in the process of nominating what is important for the organisation. In moving away from a top-down imposition of values, it has the capacity to be a mechanism in which the collective ownership of goals and performance is promoted. But of course this does not necessarily follow: much depends on the attitudes of senior managers as to how it is implemented.

Comparing the four approaches

In this chapter we have presented four different approaches to assessing organisational effectiveness. Each, in its own way, provides useful insight, and may be of benefit when applied under appropriate circumstances. But what are the circumstances when each is preferred? Table 3.4 summarises each approach, identifies what it uses to define effectiveness, and then notes the conditions under which each is most useful.

TABLE 3.4 Comparing the four organisational effectiveness approaches

Approach	Definition	When useful
	An organisation is effective to the extent that . . .	*The approach is preferred when . . .*
Goal attainment	it accomplishes its stated goals	goals are clear, time-bound and measurable
Systems	it acquires needed resources	a clear connection exists between inputs and outputs
Strategic constituencies	all strategic constituencies are at least minimally satisfied	constituencies have a powerful influence on the organisation, and the organisation must respond to demands
Balanced scorecard	the identification and measurement of areas critical to the business	the organisation is complex and is operating in a demanding environment

Source: The first three approaches were adapted from Kim S. Cameron, 'The Effectiveness of Ineffectiveness', in B.M. Staw & L.L. Cummings, eds, *Research in Organizational Behavior*, vol. 6, Greenwich, Con.: JAI Press, 1984, p. 276. Reproduced with permission.

Summary

Organisational effectiveness has proven difficult, some even say impossible, to define. Yet, as the central theme in organisation theory, its meaning and measurement must be confronted. Four approaches have been offered as guides out of the organisational effectiveness 'jungle'.

The two dominant positions, and frequent antagonists, are the goal-attainment and systems approaches. The former defines organisational effectiveness as the accomplishment of ends. The latter focuses on means, defining effectiveness as the ability to acquire inputs, process them, channel the outputs, and maintain stability and balance in the system.

A more recent offering is the strategic-constituencies approach. It defines organisational effectiveness as satisfying the demands of those constituencies in the environment from which the organisation requires support for its continued existence. Success, then, is the ability to placate those individuals, groups and institutions on which the organisation depends for its continued operation.

The final perspective is one based on the balanced scorecard. It has sought to accommodate organisational complexity and environmental demands by promoting a framework in which the key goals that the organisation must achieve for survival are identified and measures developed for them. The scorecard is 'balanced' because the measures are aimed at identifying areas where unwise compromises have been made. Hence the aim is to ensure that areas that are important to the organisation are accommodated within decision making.

To those who desire a simple definition of organisational effectiveness, this chapter will have proven a disappointment. Effectiveness is conceptually complex and, therefore, so must be its definition. **Organisational effectiveness** can be defined as *the degree to which an organisation attains its short- (ends) and long-term (means) goals, the selection of which reflects strategic constituencies, the self-interest of the evaluator and the life stage of the organisation.*

organisational effectiveness the degree to which an organisation attains its short- and long-term goals, the selection of which reflects strategic constituencies, the self-interests of the evaluator and the life stage of the organisation

For review and discussion

1   Why is organisational effectiveness relevant in the study of organisation theory?

2   On what factors do almost all definitions of organisational effectiveness agree?

3   'The final test of an organisation's effectiveness is survival.' Construct an argument to support this statement. Then construct one to refute it.

4   Give three examples of effectiveness criteria that are consistent with the goal-attainment approach.

5   'For a business firm, the bottom line is profit. You don't need any other measures of effectiveness.' Construct an argument to support this statement. Then construct one to refute it.

6   MBO was presented as a goal-attainment approach. Could it also be part of the systems approach? Explain.

7   'Goals are a viable standard against which effectiveness can be measured.' Construct an argument to support this statement. Then construct one to refute it.

8   Are organisational efficiency and flexibility conflicting goals?

9   'Organisations like Amnesty International and the Wilderness Society manage to avoid issues relating to effectiveness because of the type of work that they do.' Evaluate this statement.

10 Why might the administrator of a public service or department use 'ability to acquire budget increases' as a measure of effectiveness? Could such a measure be dysfunctional?

11 Why are stakeholders considered part of the strategic constituencies?

12 Compare the strategic-constituencies and balanced-scorecard approaches. How are they similar? How are they different?

13 Identify how the balanced scorecard is intended to promote 'balance' in organisational activities.

14 How would the size of an organisation affect the criteria used to evaluate its effectiveness?

15 Select three or four organisations familiar to you and to members of your class. How have you, in the past, evaluated their effectiveness? How would you now assess their effectiveness using the goal-attainment, systems and strategic-constituencies approaches?

CASE FOR CLASS DISCUSSION
How effective is The Body Shop?

There would be few who had not at least heard of The Body Shop, the retail chain specialising in body-care products. It boasts that everything has been manufactured from natural ingredients, preferably sourced and processed in Third World countries by indigenous communities, and sold with the minimum of packaging. It particularly stresses that none of its products are tested on animals and all are environmentally friendly.

The Body Shop is synonymous with Anita Roddick, the founder and former managing director of the company. Now in her early 60s, Roddick opened her first shop in Brighton, England in 1976, as something to do when her husband Gordon took an extended holiday in South America. By 1996 The Body Shop had expanded to a chain of 1400 stores operating in 45 countries around the world. The chain relies heavily on franchisees, all of whom subscribe to its values and ideals and who are considered part of the Body Shop family. Rather than take franchise fees and royalties, The Body Shop makes its money from selling its products to the franchisee. The ideas struck a chord with the newly affluent in the 1980s, and new products and franchisees were added at a breakneck rate. The company was floated in 1984, and for more than a decade sales and profits grew at over 50% per year.

Anita Roddick can always be relied on to be controversial and, depending on your point of view, she is either a breath of fresh air in the staid world of business or a disaster. Assessing her contribution is difficult. The idea to set up The Body Shop and the ideals that underpinned it were hers. But increasingly her chaotic management style affected The Body Shop as a business. She conducted no market research, paid scant attention to advertising and marketing, and gave little thought to the location of shops. New products were developed quickly without adequate research. Testing on animals was strictly off-limits and she even objected to bristle hairbrushes. There was no strategic plan, and most decisions were based on emotions and impulse rather than analysis. Poorly thought out expansion into the United States bled the company of money. Mundane but essential areas such as inventory control and supply-chain management were neglected. Ms Roddick even boasted about being financially illiterate, and espoused an active dislike for the business community, particularly the faceless 'suits' of the financial world.

But all has not been well at The Body Shop over the past few years. It was initially half-funded with a £4000 loan from a garage proprietor in return for a half-share in the company. It was floated in 1984 and the shares rose to $US6.55 in 1992 before settling back to $US2.29 in 1996. Even at the lower share price, this rise made Anita Roddick and her husband a couple of considerable wealth, along with the low-profile garage owner. Profits have been erratic, but in most of the 1990s they trended downwards. They are now low enough for shareholders to be concerned about its future. One of the issues that the company has found difficult to counteract is that its initial success has spawned a host of imitators. Not only are there independent chains such as Lush, which do much the same thing as The Body Shop, but traditional retailers and cosmetic manufacturers now have their own 'green' range of products, which are often better marketed and provide superior value for money than The Body Shop's products. Faced with increasingly vocal demands from shareholders for improved financial performance, the Roddicks brought in outside management and in 1998 stepped aside from day-to-day involvement in the company. More lately, the low share price and poor performance has seen a number of takeover offers, none of which have so far come to fruition.

The company finds itself in a bind; it is a public company with shareholders and profits to worry about, but it has the ideals and attitudes of a not-for-profit business. Although Ms Roddick is no longer involved in day-to-day management, she, along with her husband, still owns a significant number of shares. They are a continuous high-profile presence, and indeed provide the best marketing pitch that The Body Shop has. But contradictions abound. Ms Roddick's left-of-centre views sees her taking a vocal stand against globalisation, free trade and multinational corporations. But The Body Shop is the quintessential multinational enterprise. She is against consumerism, sweatshops and environmental damage.

But by its nature The Body Shop promotes consumerism, with most of the products sold being luxury items rather than necessities. She also wanted to use her franchisees to run a campaign against the World Trade Organization, but they refused. Ms Roddick laments that the passion is fading from the company.

Based on: Deborah Baird, 'Return of the Green Goddess', *The Independent*, 8 October 2001; Anonymous, 'A Deeper Shade of Green', *Financial Times*, 7 June 2001; Sarah Ellison, 'Body Shop Seeks a Makeover', *The Wall Street Journal Europe*, 8 June 2001.

QUESTIONS

1 Using the goal-attainment approach, the systems approach and the strategic-constituencies approach, evaluate the effectiveness of The Body Shop.

2 Using the balanced scorecard approach, draw up goals and measures for The Body Shop.

3 How effective would you consider The Body Shop to be if you were a franchisee, a customer, a shareholder, a senior manager, or Anita Roddick?

4 From the above observations, is it possible to come to a consensus about organisational effectiveness? What other possible measures of organisational effectiveness can you think of that may be universally applicable?

FURTHER READING

Kim Cameron & Dave Whetton, eds, *Organizational Effectiveness: A Comparison of Multiple Models*, New York: Academic Press, 1983.

Kim Cameron, 'Effectiveness as Paradox: Consensus and Conflict in Conceptions of Organizational Effectiveness', *Management Science*, 32(5), 1986, pp. 539–53.

Michael Hitt, 'The Measuring of Organizational Effectiveness: Multiple Domains and Constituencies Management', *International Review*, 28(2), 1988, pp. 28–40.

Robert Kaplan & David Norton, *The Balanced Scorecard: Translating Strategy into Action*, New York: McGraw Hill, 1996.

Arie Lewin & John Minton, 'Determining Organizational Effectiveness: Another Look and an Agenda for Research', *Management Science*, 32(5), 1986, pp. 538.

Jeffrey Pfeffer & Gerald Salancik, *The External Control of Organizations*, New York: Harper & Row, 1978.

NOTES

1 Paul S. Goodman & Johannes M. Pennings, 'Perspectives and Issues: An Introduction', in P.S. Goodman, J.M. Pennings & Associates, eds, *New Perspectives on Organizational Effectiveness*, San Francisco: Jossey-Bass, 1977, p. 2.
2 Amitai Etzioni, *Modern Organizations*, Englewood Cliffs, NJ: Prentice Hall, 1964, p. 8.
3 John R. Kimberly, 'Issues in the Creation of Organizations: Initiation, Innovation, and Institutionalization', *Academy of Management Journal*, September 1979, p. 438.
4 Jeffrey Pfeffer, 'Usefulness of the Concept', in Goodman et al., *New Perspectives on Organizational Effectiveness*, p. 139; and H. Kaufman, *Are Government Organizations Immortal?*, Washington, DC: Brookings Institution, 1976.
5 John P. Campbell, 'On the Nature of Organizational Effectiveness', in Goodman et al., *New Perspectives on Organizational Effectiveness*, p. 15.
6 Kim S. Cameron, 'A Study of Organizational Effectiveness and its Predictors', *Management Science*, January 1986, p. 88.
7 Kim S. Cameron, 'Effectiveness as Paradox: Consensus and Conflict in Conceptions of Organizational Effectiveness', *Management Science*, 32(5), 1986, pp. 539–53.
8 Charles Perrow, 'The Analysis of Goals in Complex Organizations', *American Sociological Review*, December 1961, pp. 854–66.
9 Campbell, 'On the Nature of Organizational Effectiveness', p. 26.
10 Charles K. Warriner, 'The Problem of Organizational Purpose', *Sociological Quarterly*, Spring 1965, pp. 139–46.
11 Karl Weick, *The Social Psychology of Organizing*, Reading, MA: Addison-Wesley, 1969, p. 8 (author's emphasis).
12 Warriner, 'The Problem of Organizational Purpose', p. 140.
13 Ephraim Yuchtman & Stanley E. Seashore, 'A Systems Resource Approach to Organizational Effectiveness', *American Sociological Review*, December 1967, pp. 891–903.
14 William M. Evan, 'Organization Theory and Organizational Effectiveness: An Exploratory Analysis', in S. Lee Spray, ed., *Organizational Effectiveness: Theory, Research, Utilization*, Kent, OH: Kent State University Press, 1976, pp. 21–4.
15 John Kay, *Foundation of Corporate Success: How Business Strategies add Value*, Oxford: University Press Oxford, 1993.
16 Jeffrey Pfeffer & Gerald Salancik, *The External Control of Organizations*, New York: Harper & Row, 1978.
17 Robert H. Miles, *Coffin Nails and Corporate Strategies*, Englewood Cliffs, NJ: Prentice Hall, 1982.
18 Archie Carrol, *Business and Society: Ethics and Stakeholder Management,* 3rd edn, Cincinnati, OH: South Western College Publishing, 1996; and Ian March, *Stakeholder Capitalism and Australian Business, Politics and Public Policy*, Sydney: AGSM, 1996.
19 Drawn from Robert Kaplan & David Norton, 'The Balanced Scorecard—Measures that Drive Performance', *Harvard Business Review*, January–February 1992, pp. 71–9 and Robert Kaplan & David Norton, *The Balanced Scorecard: Translating Strategy into Action*, New York: McGraw Hill, 1996.

PART

2

Comparing
Organisations

part 2

CHAPTER 4

Dimensions of organisation structure

After reading this chapter you should be able to:

1 describe the three components comprising complexity;

2 identify the benefits that accrue from formalisation;

3 list the common formalisation techniques;

4 discuss why the centralisation debate is important;

5 identify the importance of coordination;

6 describe the five basic structural configurations;

7 explain the benefit of metaphors to describe organisations.

Introduction

Australia is restructuring

In response to static profits and declining sales in the department store division, Coles Myer, Australia's largest retailer, launched 'Operation Right Now'. It was a major restructuring of the business, aimed at cutting costs and responding to the changes in consumer demand.[1] But Coles Myer isn't alone. In the past couple of years, as competition has increased and globalisation and technological innovation has thrown up new challenges and opportunities, almost all firms have had to restructure. AMP, National Australia Bank, ANZ Bank, Consolidated Press Holdings, Orica, Goodman Fielder, and such government undertakings as Pacific Power, Newcastle University, the Department of Foreign Affairs and Trade and the Industries Commission. Even charities such as the Smith Family and World Vision find it necessary to restructure from time to time. In fact, it is difficult to find a well-managed organisation now which has not recently restructured to cut costs, become more responsive to customers or competitors, or achieved some similar aim. But what is it that these organisations are restructuring?

We often read of references to the structure of an organisation. And, of course, when changes are made to an organisation's structure we call it restructuring. The structure of an organisation refers to its overall dimensions, characteristics and areas of responsibility. We need terms to describe these as we often need to compare organisations and describe them to others. But as organisations are intangible—that is, as they lack physical properties—conventional measurement is not possible. For instance, we can describe the dimensions of a room by its length, breadth and height. We cannot 'measure' an organisation in a similar manner. And measures such as number of employees or financial indicators provide us with little guidance as to the nature of the organisation. So what measures are available to us? We are largely reduced to identifying characteristics and then describing where organisations 'fit' in relation to the measures chosen. This chapter introduces and describes what those measures are. We will draw on the dimensions described in later chapters.

Needless to say, not everyone would agree with the dimensions we have chosen; some may feel that they reflect a dated way of looking at organisations.[2] They may also feel that the measures reflect a tangibility which it is not possible to achieve when researching organisations. However, discussion of the nominated dimensions provides us with the basic vocabulary that observers and researchers commonly use. We will start by looking at the various components of complexity.

Complexity

What do we mean by the term *complexity*? Why is complexity important? The purpose of this section is to answer those two questions.

Definition

Complexity refers to the degree of differentiation that exists within an organisation.[3] *Horizontal differentiation* considers the degree of horizontal separation between units. *Vertical differentiation* refers to the depth of the organisational hierarchy. *Spatial differentiation* encompasses the degree to which the location of an organisation's facilities and personnel is dispersed geographically. An increase in any one of these three factors will increase an organisation's complexity.

complexity the degree of horizontal, vertical and spatial differentiation in an organisation

Horizontal differentiation

Horizontal differentiation refers to the degree of differentiation between units on the basis of the orientation of members, the nature of the tasks they perform, and their education and training. We can state that the larger the number of different occupations within an organisation that require specialised knowledge and skills, the more complex the organisation is. Why? Because diverse orientations make it more difficult for organisational members to communicate and more difficult for management to coordinate their activities. For instance, when managers create specialised groups or departments, they differentiate each one from the other, making interactions between them more complex. If the organisation is staffed by people who have similar backgrounds, skills and training, they are likely to see the world in similar terms. Conversely, diversity increases the likelihood that they will have different goal emphases, time orientations and even a different work vocabulary. *Job specialisation*, sometimes called the division of labour, reinforces differences: the chemical engineer's job is clearly different from that of a recruitment specialist. Their training and skills are different. The vocabulary that they use on their respective jobs is different, and they are typically assigned to different departments which are based in different locations.

horizontal differentiation the degree of differentiation among units based on the orientation of members, the nature of the tasks they perform and their education and training

Almost all organisations, whether they be profit- or community-based, rely on job specialisation. It is so common that very few of us question why this should be so. So it is worthwhile briefly identifying why it is so common in organisations. First, in highly sophisticated and complex operations, physical limitations mean that no one person can perform all required tasks. If one person had to build a complete motor car alone, even possessing the hundreds of skills necessary, it would take months of full-time effort. Second, limitations of knowledge act as a constraint. Some tasks require highly developed skills; others can be performed by the untrained. If many of the tasks require a large amount of skill, it may be impossible to find people capable of performing all the tasks involved. Additionally, to have highly trained workers undertaking tasks requiring lower-level skills is a waste to the organisation. In additional to skill levels, special knowledge may be required in order to respond to local conditions or the needs of particular groups of customers.

Another element in favour of division of labour is efficiency. One's skill and knowledge of a task increases through repetition and concentration on a particular specialised area. Moreover, training for functional specialisation is more efficient from the organisation's perspective. It is easier and less costly to train workers to undertake a specific and repetitive task than to train them for difficult and complex activities. In addition, all workers have unique talents and abilities. It makes sense to workers to concentrate on what they are good at rather than to undertake a whole range of tasks, few of which they have any talent for.

Division of labour creates groups of specialists which are normally organised into departments. Departments can be created on the basis of simple numbers, function, product or service, client, geography or process. Most large corporations will use all six. On the other hand, in a very small organisation simple numbers represent an informal and highly effective method by which people can be grouped.

Job specialisation leads to the organisation defining areas of responsibility. This is often spelt out in a job description. Most job descriptions are formalised and agreed to by each party, but in some cases contain general statements or are verbal agreements. In the case of lower-level workers, they may be part of an industrial enterprise agreement. Through defining the areas of responsibility, management attempts to ensure that all important areas and tasks have someone responsible for them and that coordination and cooperation is promoted.

The areas of responsibility reflect the complexity of the organisation. A small manufacturing organisation may make a verbal agreement with the production

OT CLOSEUP

What are we restructuring and what are we aiming to achieve?

To put restructuring into perspective, the following examples of restructuring by prominent Australian institutions provide us with a glimpse of what senior managers are attempting to achieve.

Goodman Fielder. An attempt to simplify the structure by integrating the various business units into a smaller number of more focused units. The aim is to increase focus on Australian retail brands, simplify the business, reduce complexity and use assets more efficiently. Smaller overseas operations have been sold to enable management to concentrate more on the strengths of the business. Shared service units such as purchasing and logistics have been created to reduce costs.[4]

Coles Myer. 'Operation Right Now', referred to in the introduction, brought together general merchandising and apparel under one management. This was in order to create clear differentiation between Myer-Grace Bros, Target and Kmart and to minimise their cannibalising each other's sales. Merchandising (selecting and buying what is to be sold in stores) is to be centralised for some items such as shoes and manchester. One thousand head office positions

were abolished to reduce costs and increase flexibility. Clear roles and accountabilities were defined to enable staff to concentrate on improving performance.[5]

ANZ Bank. The branch network is to be restructured in order to raise its strategic effectiveness. This will involve closing poorly located branches and opening others in high traffic areas. Others will be merged. The aim is to make more intensive use of the branch network.[6]

Newcastle University. Eleven faculties are to be reduced to five and administration departments are to be combined. The aim is to produce a one-stop approach for students and staff.[7]

Pacific Dunlop's South Pacific Tyre division. Rationalisation of three Victorian manufacturing plants is reducing both costs and the range of tyres produced.[8]

PMP. PMP is a magazine publisher faced with falling demand. Magazine sorting and delivery to retailers is to be subcontracted to freight forwarders. Warehouses in Adelaide, Brisbane and Perth are to close. About 440 staff will be laid off. The aim is to reduce the cost base.[9]

manager in relation to his or her tasks. On the other hand, a large multinational organisation may define in close detail the responsibility and authority of the holder of a particular position. It is fair to say that the greater the complexity of the organisation, the more likely it is that the areas of responsibility of incumbents will be more highly defined. Top management do not escape these restrictions. Often included in their responsibilities are targets and goals for the organisation to achieve within certain time frames.

As specialisation increases, so does complexity. This is because an increase in specialisation requires more sophisticated and expensive methods of coordination and control. Later in this chapter we'll analyse the techniques available to organisations to coordinate their specialists.

Vertical differentiation

Vertical differentiation refers to the depth of the structure of an organisation, and is often referred to as the number of *layers of management* from the operatives to the chief executive officer. The greater the number of layers of management, the more complex an organisation is to manage. The more levels that exist between top management and operatives, the greater the potential for communication distortion, the more difficult it is to coordinate the decisions of managerial personnel, and the more difficult it is for top management to oversee the actions of operatives.

Organisations with the same number of employees need not have the same degrees of vertical differentiation. Organisations can be tall, with many layers of hierarchy, or flat, with few levels. The determining factor is the span of control.

The **span of control** defines the number of subordinates that a manager can direct effectively. If this span is wide, managers will have a number of subordinates reporting to them. If it is narrow, managers will have few subordinates. All things being equal, the smaller the span, the taller the organisation. This point is important and requires elaboration. Simple arithmetic will show that the difference between an average management span of, say, four, and one of eight in a company of 4000 non-managerial employees can make a difference of two entire levels of management and of nearly 800 managers.

This statement is illustrated in Figure 4.1. You will note that each of the operative (lowest) levels contains 4096 employees. All the other levels represent management positions: 1365 managers (levels 1–6) with a span of 4, and 585 managers (levels 1–4) with a span of 8. The narrower span of four creates high vertical differentiation and a tall organisation. The wider span creates a flatter organisation.

The various layers of management may broadly be classified into three main areas. The first is top management, whose main responsibility is setting the strategic direction of the organisation. This normally comprises the top layer or two of management. Then comes middle management, which consists of those layers in the middle of the organisation. A strict definition of middle management is that they implement the plans of senior managers. But in addition they supervise lower-level managers and provide input into the decisions made by top management. In many ways middle managers are an information conduit for information flowing up and down the organisation. Lower-level management is primarily concerned with the day-to-day tasks of supervising the production of goods and services.

Information technology has had an impact on both the span of control and the extent of vertical differentiation in organisations.[10] The use of computers and

vertical differentiation the number of hierarchical levels between top management and operatives. Sometimes referred to as layers of management

span of control the number of subordinates that a manager can supervise effectively

FIGURE 4.1 Contrasting spans of control

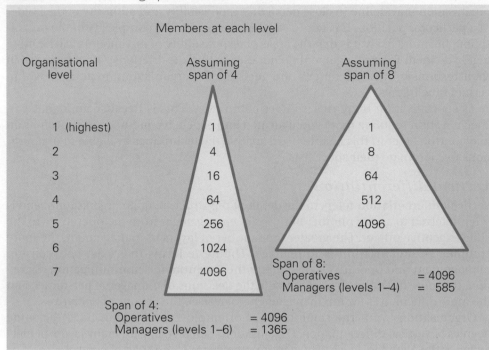

Span of 4:
Operatives   = 4096
Managers (levels 1–6)   = 1365

Span of 8:
Operatives   = 4096
Managers (levels 1–4)   = 585

computer-based communication technologies, such as e-mail, has facilitated the flow of communication across and up and down the organisation. This has removed the need for large numbers of managers who previously acted as communication channels. It has also made it easier for managers to gather and process information.

There has also been a shift in management attitudes over the past 10 years towards giving greater responsibility to lower-level employees. Computers have again helped by allowing employees as diverse as production workers and accounts clerks to access a far greater range of information than in previous generations of workers. Combined with higher levels of education in the workforce and better selection of employees, this has allowed many tasks previously undertaken by management to be undertaken by the workers themselves.

Spatial differentiation

spatial differentiation the degree to which the location of an organisation's facilities and personnel are dispersed geographically

The third element in complexity is spatial differentiation. **Spatial differentiation** refers to the degree to which the location of an organisation's offices, plant and personnel are dispersed.

Spatial differentiation arises when the operations of an organisation are geographically widely spread. This separation includes dispersion by both number and distance. For instance, a manufacturing company differentiates horizontally when it separates marketing functions from production. Yet if essentially identical marketing activities are carried on in six geographically dispersed sales offices—Melbourne, Sydney, Perth, Brisbane, Singapore and London—while all production is done in a large factory in Adelaide, this organisation is more complex than if both the marketing and production activities were performed at the same facility in Adelaide.

OT CLOSEUP

Are organisations becoming flatter?

Although there is not a great deal of evidence to support the fact that flatter organisations are either cheaper or more effective to run, most organisation restructuring in recent years has involved the flattening of the organisation. For instance Boral, which has operations in Australia, Europe and the USA, has only five layers of management from the shop floor to the managing director. Many large organisations and government departments have a legendary number of management layers. Sydney Water and its predecessor reduced its management structure from 14 to seven layers. Indeed, most consultants will recommend that the number of layers of management in most organisations should be reduced. If the numbers at the bottom of the organisation remain unchanged, this in effect means that the span of control should be increased.

Tom Peters, one of the authors of *In Search of Excellence*, claims that there is great scope in Western organisations to increase spans of control.[11] He notes that in Japan spans of control are often 100 and in some cases, 200. In Western organisations, spans of control are often only 10 although it

should be noted that different methods of counting are often used.[12] Comparisons of this nature are also often complicated by cultural factors. Peters claims that no organisation needs any more than five layers as a maximum. ASEA-Brown Boveri, the Swiss-Swedish company heavily involved in the electromechanical industry, has 215 000 employees in 140 countries and still manages to operate with only five layers of management.[13] Flight Centre, which we discuss in the closing case, operates in five countries and has only three layers of management.

Peters proposes that all organisations should aim for three layers of management, with a span of control at the supervisory level of 25–75. He admits that his solution is a radical response to making organisations more flexible and responsive, but it is a point of view that all companies should consider. Certainly, when restructuring, unless some limits are placed on the number of layers of management, or goals set and progress towards them monitored, then layers of management can continue to grow without check.

Similarly, consider two banks. Both may have a similar asset base. However, one promotes itself as a regional bank, concentrating its operations in one state, say Victoria. The other sees itself as a national bank, with operations covering all of Australia and parts of New Zealand. The state-based bank may have only one-sixth of the number of branches that the national bank has, and it may do most of its business out of only a few of those branches. It is only logical that communication, coordination and control are made easier for management in the state-based bank, where spatial differentiation is low.

The rise in the number of organisations with overseas operations has increased the complexity level. This also applies to charities and not-for-profit organisations, which now often have a worldwide constituency. If senior executives reside in one city, middle managers in half a dozen cities and lower-level managers in a hundred different offices around the world, complexity is increased. This also increases the amount of information the organisation must process.

In summary, spatial differentiation is the third element in defining complexity. It tells us that even if horizontal and vertical differentiation were to remain the same across spatially separated units, the physical separation itself would increase complexity.

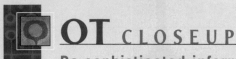

OT CLOSEUP

Do sophisticated information systems change the basic organisation dimensions?

In this chapter we have described the ways in which we compare organisations. Although we have referred to the impact of information technology in different parts of the chapter, we are left with the question as to whether information technology will render the measures we have discussed obsolete.

There is no doubt that information technology will alter the way in which organisations are structured and managed. But we can say that the basic organisational dimensions described in this chapter will still be those which are used for organisational comparison. Why? No matter what their technology, organisations will still conform to our basic definition given in Chapter 1, namely that each will still be a consciously coordinated social entity with an identifiable boundary which aims to meet certain goals. Part of the need for an identifiable boundary

arises from the legal requirement to incorporate an organisation, and the need to hire employees and to have managers responsible for the operation of the company. Furthermore, most organisations produce complex products, which is one of the reasons why organisations, as opposed to single traders, exist. This implies a division of labour, the need for supervision and coordination, and the need for managers to determine the strategic direction of the company. All of these mean that there is a need to determine where decisions are made and how formalised and complex the organisation will be.

Even though each of these dimensions of organisation structure may be affected by changes in the way an organisation gathers and processes information, we will still use the measures of organisational structure discussed in this chapter.

Why is complexity important?

Why is the issue of complexity important for managers? The various specialised subsystems of organisations require communication, coordination and control if they are to be effective. The more complex an organisation, the greater the need for effective communication, coordination and control devices. In other words, as complexity increases, so do the demands on management to ensure that differentiated and dispersed activities are working smoothly and together towards achieving the organisation's goals. The need for devices such as committees, computerised information systems and formal policy manuals is reduced for organisations that are low in complexity. So one way of answering the 'What does complexity mean to managers?' question is to say that it creates different management tasks and influences the way in which managers use their time. The higher the complexity, the greater the amount of attention they must pay to dealing with problems of communication, coordination and control. Increased complexity also contributes to greater difficulties in managing organisational change.

This has been described as a paradox in the analysis of organisations.[14] Management's decision to increase differentiation is made typically in the interests of economy and efficiency. But these decisions create pressure to add managerial personnel to facilitate control, coordination and manage conflict. Thus the economies that complexity creates may be counterbalanced by the increased burden of keeping the organisation together. Rarely are large organisations effective or efficient simply because they are large. The benefits of large size emerge from efficiencies in other areas, such as production or financial economies. Managers must balance economies from these areas from the diseconomies of having to manage large, complex organisations.

Formalisation

The second component of organisation structure is formalisation. In this section we define the term, explain its importance, introduce the two general ways in which management can achieve it, demonstrate the more popular formalisation techniques and compare formalisation with complexity.

Definition

Formalisation refers to the degree to which jobs and procedures within the organisation are standardized.[15] If a job is highly formalised, the job incumbent has a minimum amount of discretion over what is to be done, when it is to be done, and how he or she should do it. Employees can be expected always to handle the same input in exactly the same way; this results in a consistent and uniform output. Where there is high formalisation, there are explicit job descriptions, many organisational rules and clearly defined procedures covering work processes in organisations. Where formalisation is low, employees' behaviour would be relatively non-programmed. Such jobs would offer employees a great deal of freedom to exercise discretion in their work. Thus formalisation is a measure of standardisation. Formalisation may exist both in written form and in the attitudes and values of employees and managers. While the existence of extensive policy manuals and highly defined job descriptions may be evidence of written formalisation, similarities in the ways of thinking by organisational members may impose similar constraints on the organisation. The familiar McDonald's restaurant chain is an example of an organisation high in formalisation.

formalisation the degree to which jobs within the organisation are standarised

Range of formalisation

It's important to recognise that the degree of formalisation can vary widely among and within organisations. It is well known that certain jobs have high formalisation. Counter sales staff at McDonald's have little discretion in how they go about their work. Additionally, their hours of work are closely monitored and any deviation from predetermined schedules immediately identified and corrected. Alternatively, head office staff have far more freedom in how they do their job, including their hours of work. It is generally true that the narrowest of unskilled jobs—those that are simplest and most repetitive—are most amenable to high degrees of formalisation. The greater the professionalisation of a job, the less likely it is to be highly formalised. Yet there are obvious exceptions. Public accountants and consultants, for instance, are required to keep detailed records of their minute-by-minute activities so that their companies can bill clients appropriately for their services, and lawyers need to follow strict procedures in dealing with legal matters. In general, however, the relationship holds. The jobs of lawyers, engineers, social workers, librarians and professionals tend to rate low on formalisation.

For any given organisation, formalisation also differs with the level and functional department in the organisation. Employees higher in the organisation are increasingly involved in activities that are less repetitive and require innovative solutions. The discretion that managers have increases as they move up the hierarchy. So formalisation tends to be inversely related to level in the organisation. Moreover, the kind of work in which people are engaged influences the degree of formalisation. Jobs in production are typically more formalised than are those in sales or research. That is because production tends to be concerned with stable and repetitive activities. Such jobs lend themselves to standardisation. In contrast, the sales department must be flexible in order to respond to the changing needs of customers, while research must be flexible if it is to be innovative.[16]

Why is formalisation important?

Organisations use formalisation because of the benefits that accrue from regulating employees' behaviour. Standardising behaviour reduces variability. Retailers such as David Jones and Woolworths ensure that their store presentation and standards of service are the same regardless of where they are located. Formalisation allows cars to flow smoothly down the assembly line, as each worker on the line performs highly standardised and coordinated activities. Formalisation also permits all members of the organisation to anticipate how others will act in certain situations and lays down guides to follow. For instance, it prevents members of a paramedic unit or fire-fighting team from standing around at the scene of an accident and arguing about who is to do what.

The economics of formalisation also should not be overlooked. The greater the formalisation, such as procedures to be followed at a supermarket checkout, the less discretion is required from a job incumbent. This is relevant because discretion costs money. Jobs that are low on formalisation demand greater judgement, and organisations must pay for the skill and knowledge to exercise that judgement. Typically, hiring employees with a professional background is far more expensive than hiring those with little formal training.

Formalisation may also be used to manage risks. Airline pilots follow strictly enforced procedures. Most managers have limitations placed on them in relation to expenditures of money and other major decisions. Foreign exchange dealers are limited in the trades they can make and banks strictly control the clients they lend money to. The aim of these restrictions is to reduce the amount of damage any one person can do to an organisation.

Formalisation techniques

Managers have at their disposal a number of techniques by which they can bring about the standardisation of employee behaviour. However, not all formalisation techniques are internal to the organisation. When professional employees are hired, they come with extensive formalisation acquired through years of study in their chosen profession. Membership of a professional body commits a member to certain values and standards of behaviour. In hiring such employees, the organisation can be reasonably confident that these standards will become part of formalised behaviour patterns of employees. We call this external formalisation, as it has been acquired external to the organisation.

OT CLOSEUP
The bourgeois bohemians

It is not surprising that stateless corporations are developing a class of stateless managers. In previous generations of business, multinationals had a clear place of domicile and their culture and management style reflected that country. But as multinational firms have shed many of their national ties, a group of managers has emerged with shared characteristics which people the various regional and head offices of the companies. It is no longer fashionable to speak of classes in society, but the bourgeois bohemians, or Bobos as they are sometimes called, form an identifiable managerial group.

So what are their characteristics? They are generally male and work in global corporations. They prefer to work with each other, shunning the parochialism of more nationally anchored management. They are mobile, and often move from country to country and corporation to corporation. They are well educated and often speak a second language. Their family arrangements support the global lifestyle, which is a polite way of saying that their wives, and in some cases husbands, don't complain. They are not from any particular nationality, but those from English-speaking countries dominate. Many have been to the

more prestigious business schools. They communicate in the language of business: references to return on assets, market positioning, strategy and cash flow pepper their talk. In their social life they prefer to spend time with other Bobos, leading to most Bobos being culturally indistinct.

An example of how Bobos bring a common standard of management to most multinationals is in the teams formed by executives from BHP Billiton, Asea-Brown Boveri, ABN Amor and Boeing to look at strategic options. In a form of 'action learning', real work problems are used as lessons. Given the dominance of the Bobos in management of multinationals, how can a corporation build a unique culture? Analysts consider that the chief executive has the greatest influence on the corporate culture, not the other way around. This provides an insight into how Bobos can move so freely between companies: they can clone their behaviour on the leadership of the company.

Adapted from: David James, 'Citizens of Boboland Unite', *Business Review Weekly*, 6 July 2001, pp. 56–7.

Most formalisation occurs, however, as a result of direct action on the part of management and others in the organisation. In this section, we review the most common formalisation techniques used by organisations.

Selection

Organisations do not choose employees at random. Even though there is a comprehensive body of laws to eliminate discrimination against target groups in hiring, this still leaves companies a fair amount of discretion as to who to hire. And even though the ability to do the job is the main criterion for selection, there are still generally a number of employees from whom to select. As a consequence, interviewers will always be looking at the ability of a person to fit into the organisation as one of the prime requirements for selection.[17]

Role requirements

Individuals in organisations fulfil roles. Every job carries with it task requirements and expectations about how the incumbent is supposed to behave. Role requirements may be explicit and defined in great detail. In such cases, the degree of formalisation is high. Other roles allow employees freedom to react to situations in unique ways. Minimum constraints are placed on the person doing the job. So organisations that develop exacting and complicated job descriptions go a long way towards making clear the abilities expected of a person undertaking a task. Formalisation is thus increased.

Rules, procedures and policies

rules explicit statements that tell an employee what he or she ought or ought not to do

Rules are explicit statements that tell an employee what he or she ought or ought not to do. Examples of rules are limits on credit card sales approvals, specified hours of work, limitations on managers approving expenditure, and forms for annual and sick leave approval. Rules generally leave no room for employee judgement or discretion. They state a particular and specific required behaviour pattern.

procedures specific standardised sequences of steps that result in a uniform output

Procedures are a series of interrelated sequential steps that employees follow in the accomplishment of their job tasks. These are established to ensure standardisation of work processes. The same input is processed in the same way, and the output is the same each day. Procedures are aimed at establishing a specific standardised sequence that results in a uniform output.

policies statements that guide employees, providing discretion within limited boundaries

Policies are guidelines that set constraints on decisions that employees make. Each of these represents techniques that organisations use to regulate the behaviour of members. Policies leave greater discretion for decision makers than do rules. Rather than specifying a particular and specific behaviour, policies allow employees more alternatives but within limited boundaries. The discretion is created by including judgemental terms (e.g. 'best', 'satisfied', 'competitive'), which the employee is left to interpret. Policies need not be written to control discretion. Employees may absorb an organisation's implied policies merely by observing the actions of members around them. This is part of the process of socialisation.

Socialisation

socialisation an adaptation process by which individuals learn the values, norms and expected behaviour patterns for the job and the organisation of which they will be a part

Socialisation refers to an adaptation process by which individuals learn the values, norms and expected behaviour patterns for the job and the organisation of which they will be a part. This may be likened to learning the organisation's culture. All employees will receive at least some moulding and shaping on the job, but for certain members the socialisation process will be substantially accomplished *before* they join the organisation. This is specifically true of professionals.

Training

Many organisations provide training for employees. This includes the on-the-job variety, where cadetship development programs and apprenticeship methods are used to teach employees preferred job skills, knowledge and attitudes. It also includes off-the-job training, such as classroom lectures, films, demonstrations, simulation exercises and programmed instruction. Again, the intention is to instil in employees preferred work behaviour and attitudes.

New employees are often required to undergo a brief orientation program in which they are familiarised with the organisation's objectives, history, philosophy and rules, as well as with relevant personnel policies such as hours of work, pay procedures, overtime requirements and benefit programs. In many cases, this is followed by specific job training. The aim of such training is to reduce the variability in the behaviour of organisational members.

Rituals

We are all familiar with **rituals** in organisations. Churches and the armed forces are the best-known examples of organisations that regularly require members to show their loyalty by taking part in ceremonies in which all members participate. Business organisations also have their rituals, which all those who aspire to higher management positions must attend. Even lower-level employees and those who do not want promotion must often take part.

rituals a process in which members prove their trustworthiness and loyalty to the organisation by participating in various behaviours in which predetermined responses are expected

Typical rituals are attending Christmas parties, sales or other departmental conferences, informal lunches, after-dinner drinks and taking part in outdoor and other training exercises. Rituals can also extend to the style of clothes that are the accepted form of dress. Merchant bankers with their power dressing are clad differently from workers in the Toyota factory, with their monogrammed work shirts and zip-up jackets. But each group is uniformly clad, thus showing a common bond between them and the organisation. Taking part in rituals is a way for a manager, and those aspiring to management, to show loyalty to the organisation and adherence to established practices and attitudes. They thereby show that they can be trusted to reflect the organisation's norms and values.[18]

Centralisation

Where are decisions made in the organisation: at the top by senior management, or down low where the decision makers are closest to the action? This question introduces the last of the components making up organisation structure. The subject of this section is centralisation and its counterpart, decentralisation.

Definition

Centralisation is the most difficult to define of the three components. Most theorists agree that the term refers to the degree to which decision making is concentrated at a single point in the organisation. When applied in common usage, the 'single point' in the organisation is normally the top decision makers. Alternatively, where decision making is widely dispersed within the organisation, the term *decentralisation* is normally used. There is also agreement that it is distinctly different from spatial differentiation. Centralisation is concerned with the dispersion of authority to make decisions within the organisation, not geographical dispersion. However, beyond these points it is difficult to pin the concept of centralisation down. Yet our pragmatic approach demands that we develop a definition that can resolve these issues. Towards that end, centralisation is the degree to which the formal authority to make discretionary choices is concentrated in an individual, a unit or a level (usually high in the organisation), thus permitting employees (usually low in the organisation) minimum input into their work.

centralisation the degree to which decision making is concentrated in a single point in the organisation usually top management

This elaborate definition highlights the following points in relation to centralisation:

1 Centralisation is concerned only with the formal structure, not the informal organisation. It applies only to formal authority.

2 Centralisation looks at decision discretion. Where decisions are delegated downwards but extensive policies exist to constrain the discretion of lower-level members, there is increased centralisation. Policies can therefore act to override decentralisation.

3 Concentration at a single point can refer to an individual, a unit or a level, but the single point *implies* concentration at a high level.

4 Information processing can improve top management control, but the decision choice is still with the low-level member. Thus, an information-processing system that closely monitors decentralised decisions does not maintain centralised control.

5 The transference of all information requires interpretation. The filtering that occurs as information passes through vertical levels is a fact of life. The top managers are free to verify the information they receive and to hold subordinates accountable in their choices of what they filter out, but control of information input is a form of de-facto decentralisation. Management decisions are centralised if concentrated at the top, but the more the information input to those decisions is filtered through others, the less concentrated and controlled the decision is.

Why is centralisation important?

The heading of this section may mislead you, because it implies that centralisation, in contrast to decentralisation, is important. The term *centralisation* in this context is meant to be viewed in the same way as complexity and formalisation are viewed in this chapter. It represents a range—from high to low. It may be clearer, therefore, if we ask: why is the centralisation–decentralisation issue important?

As described, in addition to being collections of people, organisations are decision-making and information-processing systems. They facilitate the achievement of goals through coordination of group effort; decision making and information processing are central to the coordination process. Yet information itself is not a scarce resource in organisations. The scarce resource is the processing capacity and knowledge to make the best use of the information.[19]

Every manager has some limit to the amount of information that he or she can process appropriately; after that limit, further input results in information overload. To avoid reaching the point where a manager's capacity is exceeded, some of the decisions can be given to others. This dispersion or transfer of decision making is called decentralisation.

There are other reasons why organisations might decentralise. Organisations need to respond rapidly to changing conditions. Decentralisation facilitates speedy action because it avoids the need to process the information through the vertical hierarchy. Problems may be acted on by those closest to the issue. This explains why marketing activities tend to be decentralised. Marketing personnel must be able to react quickly to the needs of customers and actions of competitors. Of course, major organisational change is still the preserve of senior managers.

In addition to speed, decentralisation can provide more detailed input into the decision. If those most familiar with an issue make a decision, they are more likely to discriminate between relevant and irrelevant information. The sales people at a company's facility in Tokyo are much more likely to know the relevant facts for making pricing decisions on the company's products in Japan than would a sales executive 8000 kilometres away in Sydney.

Decentralised decision making can act as a motivator to employees by allowing them to participate in the decision-making process. Professionals and skilled employees are particularly sensitive to contributing to those decisions that will affect how they do their jobs. If management has autocratic values and centralises authority, employee motivation can be predicted to be low.

A final plus for decentralisation is the training opportunity that it creates for low-level managers. By delegating authority, top management permits less experienced managers to learn by doing. By making decisions in areas where impact is less critical, low-level managers develop decision-making skills with the potential for

OT CLOSEUP
The centralisation dilemma

One of the most telling examples of the risks of centralised decision making was to be found in Australia during the boom of the late 1980s, when entrepreneurs such as Alan Bond and Christopher Skase were at the height of their influence. The entrepreneurs of the time specialised in asset trading and company takeovers. They had few assets of their own and consequently were dependent on banks and other financial institutions to lend them the money for their activities.

There was no shortage of lenders in the banking community, and the relationship between the entrepreneurs and the banks became one of mutual dependence. The entrepreneurs needed the money to continue their deal making, and the banks needed to lend money to continually expand their assets. The banks not only financed the well-known entrepreneurs: they also lent heavily on property speculation to a host of lesser-known developers.

The banks were in intense competition with one another. Each was trying to expand and become dominant in what was now a deregulated market. To chase business, they waived their normal checks and balances on lending. In order to minimise the possibility of non-performing loans to business, banks normally separate a number of functions. The person who negotiates a loan is not the person who is responsible for checking that the security for the loan is in order. There are also limits in place as to how much can be lent on any project and to any

particular lender. The size of the loan is then important, as loans to any party should not be so great as to put the bank at risk in the event of a default. All of this adds up to a fairly decentralised loan approval system, where no one person has the capacity to put the bank at risk.

In the race to expand their loan books, these requirements were largely dispensed with. The authorisation to make loans was centralised, so that often only one person was needed to approve sizeable loans. The two worst offenders were the State Bank of South Australia (SBSA) and Tricontinental Bank in Victoria, both government-owned banks. The managing directors of these two banks made loans totalling billions of dollars over the telephone with no approval or check on the capacity of the borrower to repay. No independent assessment of risk was undertaken, and security was rarely checked by an impartial bank officer. It was the ultimate in centralisation.

When property prices crashed and interest rates reached 20%, the inevitable bankruptcies among borrowers occurred. SBSA and Tricontinental became insolvent and the resulting debts brought the South Australian and Victorian governments down. Westpac went within weeks of insolvency. The lesson for the banks was 'Do not centralise decision making'.

Adapted from: Trevor Sykes, *The Bold Riders*, Sydney: Allen & Unwin, 1996.

minimum damage. This prepares them for assuming greater authority as they rise in the organisation.

Of course, the goal of decentralisation is not always desirable. There are conditions under which centralisation is preferred. When a comprehensive perspective is needed in a decision or where concentration provides significant economies, centralisation offers distinct advantages. Top-level managers are obviously in a better position to make strategic decisions. This provides them with advantages in choosing actions that will be consistent with the best interests of the whole organisation rather than merely benefiting some special-interest group. Furthermore, certain activities are clearly carried out more efficiently when centralised. This explains, for instance, why financial and legal decisions tend to be centralised. Both functions permeate activities throughout the organisation, and there are distinct economies to centralising this expertise.

This discussion leads to the conclusion that either high or low centralisation may be desirable. Situational factors will determine the 'right' amount. But *all* organisations process information so that managers can make decisions. Therefore, attention must be given to identifying the most effective way in which to organise where those decisions should be made.

OT CLOSEUP

Responsibility is deciding where the buck stops

Decentralisation may be a current management mantra, but it is not without its problems. One of the disadvantages is having to know where the buck stops. One of the benefits of the traditional hierarchical style of management is that it is easy to identify where responsibility lies. The bosses are responsible for the overall output, the workers are responsible for their specific tasks, and there is always a senior manager in overall charge.

When there is a flatter management structure, determining where responsibility lies is often an elusive task. Many senior and middle managers are being placed in a difficult position. On the one hand, they are asked to delegate more and 'empower' those below them. On the other, they are asked to be more responsible for the results, even though they can exert less control.

Not all decentralisation of decision making and participative approaches to management are as rosy as they first seem. Employees will naturally be happy to accept more power, and that is likely to lead to better performance if the business's output is dependent on employee satisfaction. But it is human nature to be reluctant to accept the blame when something goes wrong. If too much reliance has been placed on employees' accepting new responsibilities, the result may simply be a frantic passing of the buck.

The greater amount of delegation may mean that a given group, rather than an individual, must give its general agreement on the way things are done and then take responsibility for performance. Doing so will have major implications for the way organisations are run. It seems that the old management principle of balancing responsibility and accountability will need to be taken out of retirement and relearned.

Source: Adapted from David James, 'Responsibility is Deciding Where the Buck Stops', *Business Review Weekly*, 1 November 1991.

Coordination

Coordination is the process of integrating the objectives and activities of the separate units of an organisation in order to achieve organisational goals efficiently.[20] All organisations require coordination between the various individuals and groups. Even small isolated groups must consult with each other and observe what each is doing to avoid getting in each other's way. Coordination becomes even more important in larger organisations. Common sense tells us that as complexity increases, so does the need to coordinate the activities of the various organisational members. Where adequate coordination is absent, efficiency is lost as staff duplicate work, lose time while they are waiting for the work of others to finish, or are idle wondering what is required of them next.

Needless to say, most organisations use a number of different coordination devices. We can group these under three main readings.

coordination the process of integrating the objectives and activities of the separate units of an organisation in order to achieve organisational goals efficiently

Programmed coordination

Most of us are familiar with the rules and regulations characterising a bureaucracy. These are examples of programmed coordination. But programmed coordination also includes such common management techniques as planning, goal setting, scheduling, timetabling, sequencing and developing various types of standard operating procedures. These techniques have been developed to cope with familiar or anticipated situations. Their use ensures that everyone knows the responsibilities and actions of each party and when each activity needs to be undertaken. We can see programmed coordination at work in tasks ranging from enrolling in courses to scheduling trains on a rail system.

Programmed coordination also includes those actions arising from the use of goals and targets. A goal may be to commission a new piece of capital equipment by a certain time at a specified cost. Movement towards this goal may be planned in detail with tasks and responsibilities being allocated in order to meet the goal requirements.

Individual coordination

Where situations cannot be fully anticipated or where unusual circumstances demand a unique solution to a problem, individual coordination is often used. This generally involves the appointment of a person whose main task is to coordinate the work of others. Typical roles undertaken by individual coordinators are project managers, brand managers, and various types of system and activity integrators. These coordinators are, however, expensive: their tasks are typically time-consuming and they need to possess sophisticated communication and technical skills to undertake their work. As a consequence they tend to command high salaries.

Coordination by hierarchy is also part of individual coordination. When lower-level employees experience an unusual circumstance, they often refer the matter to their supervisor or manager. That person can then undertake whatever action is necessary to solve the difficulties that have been experienced.

Informal coordination

A large amount of coordination that takes place in an organisation results from the voluntary action of those who need to cooperate with others. This is sometimes called mutual adjustment. It is not possible to anticipate everything that is likely to be encountered in order to get jobs done, so there is a need for employees to coordinate among themselves on a day-to-day basis. This may be achieved by face-to-face discussion, formal and informal meetings, e-mails, telephone calls and even casual encounters around water coolers and coffee machines. Without such coordination among members, the work of the organisation would be greatly hampered.

Organisation design options

In this second part of the chapter we look at the ways in which whole organisations may be structured. In one respect, organisations are like fingerprints. Each has its own unique structure. Unilever and Colgate-Palmolive, for instance, are both large corporations that derive most of their income from domestic consumer goods. But a careful review finds that their organisational structures are not clones of each other. Yet, again like fingerprints, no structure is *truly* unique. All fingerprints have common properties that allow them to be classified around common elements. If we look at the organisations that currently exist, it's immediately obvious that they too have common elements. To make our point, BHP Billiton, ANZ Bank, Fletcher Challenge and Nestlé are all in very different industries. However, a close look at their structures reveals that they have at least two things in common—they are all high in complexity and high in formalisation. So while there may be hundreds of thousands of organisations today in Australia and New Zealand, there certainly aren't hundreds of thousands of *different* forms or configurations. There are a number of common elements that, once identified, allow the development of a classification framework.

In this section we introduce a classification framework that will enable us to identify the main organisational configurations.[21] There are five basic organisational forms, which we shall introduce and describe. We shall also identify when each is most likely to be the most appropriate. The choice of a basic set of configurations is to a certain extent arbitrary. We have already noted that all organisations have unique elements, so grouping organisations together requires compromises to be made. We therefore need a categorisation in which those organisations that have a set of common elements may be grouped but in which the groups differ from each other in some way. We call each grouping a **configuration**. To be useful, the number of configurations should not be too large but should contain most organisations within a given population. For instance, 20 configurations would be too large to be useful, while two configurations would lead to insufficient sensitivity in measurement. In describing the basic configurations we concentrate on structural elements. Structure refers to the reporting relationships within the organisation, the way in which departments relate to each other, and the way in which authority and responsibility is allocated.

Organisations are constantly evolving. Changes in technologies, environments, productive processes and management fashions are leading to the emergence of new organisational innovations. Incorporating these into standard configurations presents difficulties that are not easily overcome. However, little has emerged over the past 20 years to challenge the existence of the basic configurations we shall describe. We discuss the emergent forms that rely on new technologies and management styles in subsequent chapters.

configuration
a complex clustering of elements that are internally cohesive and where the presence of some elements suggests the reliable occurence of others

Common elements in organisations

While there is no universally agreed-on framework for classifying organisations, Henry Mintzberg's work is the one that is most widely used.[22] Mintzberg argues that there are five basic parts to any organisation. They are shown in Figure 4.2, and are defined as follows:

1 The **operating core**—employees, who perform the basic work related to the production of products and services.
2 The **strategic apex**—top-level managers, who are charged with the overall responsibility for the organisation.
3 The **middle line**—managers, who connect the operating core to the strategic apex.
4 The **technostructure**—analysts, who have the responsibility for effecting certain forms of standardisation in the organisation.
5 The **support staff**—people who fill the staff units that provide indirect support services for the organisation.

Any one of these five parts can dominate an organisation and where each dominates, a different organisational form emerges. Moreover, a given structural configuration is likely to be used depending on which part is in control. As a result, there are five distinct design configurations and each one is associated with the domination by one of the five basic parts. If control lies with the operating core, decisions are decentralised. This creates the *professional bureaucracy*. When the strategic apex is dominant, control is centralised and the organisation is a *simple structure*. If middle management is in control, you will find groups of essentially autonomous units operating in a *divisional structure*. Where the analysts in the technostructure are

operating core the part of an organisation encompassing employees who perform the basic work related to the production of products and services

strategic apex the part of an organisation encompassing top-level managers, who are charged with the overall responsibility for the organisation

middle line the part of an organisation that encompasses managers that connect the operating core to the strategic apex

technostructure the part of an organisation that encompasses analysts who have the responsibility for effecting forms of standardisation in the organisation

support staff the part of an organisation that encompasses people who fill the staff units that provide indirect support services for the organisation

FIGURE 4.2 Five basic elements of an organisation

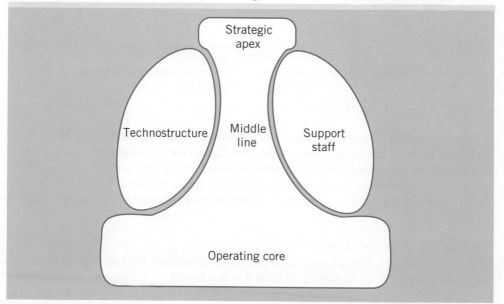

Source: Henry Mintzberg, *Structure in Fives: Designing Effective Organizations*, © 1983, p. 262. Reprinted by permission of Prentice-Hall, Englewood Cliffs, NJ.

dominant, control will be through standardisation and the resultant structure will be a *machine bureaucracy*. Finally, in those situations where the support staff dominates, control will be via mutual adjustment, and *adhocracy* arises.

Each of these design configurations has its own unique set of pluses and minuses. Consistent with the contingency philosophy, each is the preferred configuration under certain conditions. In the remainder of this chapter, we will describe each configuration, its strengths and weaknesses, and the conditions that make it the preferred option.

The simple structure

What do a small retail store, an electronics firm run by a hard-driving entrepreneur, and a family-owned manufacturing company have in common? They probably all use the simple structure.

simple structure a structure that is low in complexity, low in formalisation, and which authority is centralised in a single person

The **simple structure** is low in complexity, has little formalisation, and has authority centralised in a single person. It is typical of a small business. As shown in Figure 4.3, the simple structure is best depicted as a flat organisation, with an organic operating core and almost everyone reporting to a one-person strategic apex where the decision-making power is centralised.

FIGURE 4.3 The simple structure

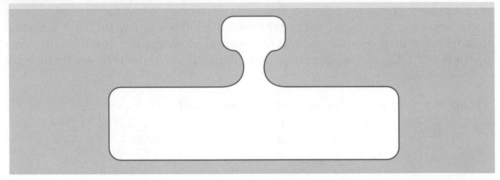

Source: Henry Mintzberg, *Structure in Fives: Designing Effective Organizations*, © 1983, p. 11. Reprinted by permission of Prentice-Hall, Englewood Cliffs, NJ.

Figure 4.4 illustrates an application of the simple structure. Notice that this organisation, Fashion Flair retail stores, is flat. All important decisions are centralised in the hands of the senior executive, who because of the low complexity is able to obtain key information readily and to act rapidly when required. It also implies that few people are involved in substantial decision making apart from the one-person strategic apex.

Strengths and weaknesses

The strength of the simple structure lies in its simplicity. It's fast and flexible and requires little cost to maintain. There are no layers of cumbersome structure. Accountability is clear. There is a minimum amount of goal ambiguity because the goals are closely associated with those of top management, and it is fairly easy to see how one's actions contribute to the organisation's goals.

FIGURE 4.4 Fashion Flair stores

The simple structure's predominant weakness is that it is applicable only to small organisations. When confronted with larger size, this structure generally proves inadequate. Additionally, the simple structure concentrates power in one person. Rarely does the structure provide countervailing forces to balance the chief executive's power. Therefore, the simple structure can easily succumb to the abuse of authority or lack of managerial skills by the person in power. This concentration of power, of course, can work against the organisation's effectiveness and survival. The simple structure, in fact, has been described as the 'riskiest of structures hinging on the health and whims of one individual'.[23] One heart attack can literally destroy the organisation's decision-making centre. Similarly, if the person at the top of the organisation is a poor manager, the whole organisation will be poorly run.

When should you use it?

The simple structure is effective when the number of employees is small. Informal communication is convenient. And as long as the structure remains small, one person can effectively oversee all activities, be knowledgeable about key problems and make all important decisions.

The simple structure also meets the needs of organisations when they are in their formative years. New organisations need clear directions and a drive and vision from the top of the organisation if they are to grow. The simple structure provides this. Almost all organisations, therefore, pass through the simple-structure stage. For those that remain small in size, the simple structure may be permanent rather than transitory.

Regardless of size, when an organisation suddenly confronts a hostile environment, management is likely to resort to at least some features of the simple structure. The reason for this is that when survival is threatened, top management wants control. Furthermore, as the hostility disrupts the standard operating procedures, these are likely to be suspended. The result is a temporary flattening out of the organisation.

Those managers who want to acquire maximum power will gravitate towards the simple structure as it is an excellent vehicle for concentrating power in a single place. While large size generally excludes the possibility of a permanent simple structure, this configuration may be used by medium- and small-sized organisations whose power is consolidated at the top. As organisations grow, they are often too large for one person to manage effectively. Operations must be decentralised and rules and regulations put in place to control the day-to-day management of tasks. The number of managers typically grows to cope with the complexity of expanded operations. The simple structure then grows into what is called the machine bureaucracy.

The machine bureaucracy

Standardisation is the key concept that underlies all machine bureaucracies. Take a look at the bank where you keep your account; the department store where you buy your clothes; the company that built your car; or the government offices that collect your taxes, operate the health system, issue drivers' licences and register your car. They all rely on standardised work processes for coordination and control. It is this standardisation that gives rise to the machine bureaucracy.

machine bureaucracy an organisation with very routine and formalised operating tasks, rules and regulations and which is highly centralised

The **machine bureaucracy** has highly routine operating tasks, formalised rules and regulations, tasks that are grouped into functional departments, centralised authority and a decision making that follows the chain of command. It also has large numbers of people whose task is to standardise the work of the organisation. Figure 4.5 depicts this configuration, using Mintzberg's framework. Rules and regulations are characteristic of the entire structure. While not explicitly evident from Figure 4.5, the key part of this design is the technostructure. That's because this is where the staff analysts who do the standardising—the production engineers, job-description designers, schedulers, planners, budgeters, systems analysts and operations management personnel—are clustered.

Figure 4.6 illustrates the machine-bureaucracy form as utilised at the IAG Insurance. Note the reliance on functional departmentation, with similar and related occupational specialties grouped together. In a manufacturing company, activities such as operations, research and development, production and personnel are typically grouped under functional executives. These executives oversee their occupa-

FIGURE 4.5 The machine bureaucracy

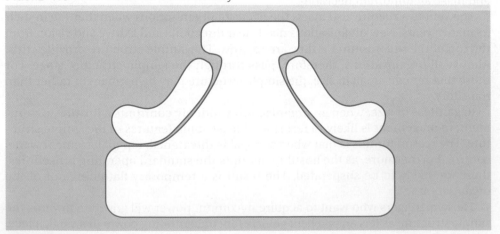

Source: Henry Mintzberg, *Structure in Fives: Designing Effective Organizations*, © 1983, p. 170. Reprinted by permission of Prentice-Hall, Englewood Cliffs, NJ.

FIGURE 4.6 Abbreviated organisational chart of IAG Insurance

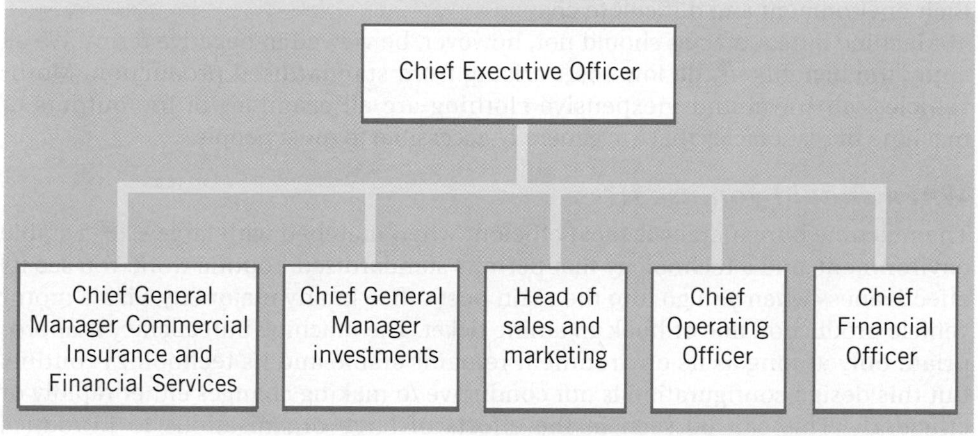

Source: Annual Report 2001.

tional specialties but are, in turn, responsible to a general manager, who acts as overall coordinator.

Strengths and weaknesses

The primary strength of the machine bureaucracy lies in its ability to perform standardised activities in a highly efficient manner. Putting like specialties together results in economies of scale, minimisation of duplication of personnel and equipment, and permits employees with similar occupational backgrounds to talk 'the same language' among their peers. It also permits the generation and transfer of knowledge within the specialties. Furthermore, machine bureaucracies can get by with less talented—and hence less costly—middle- and lower-level managers and operatives. The pervasiveness of rules and regulations substitutes for managerial discretion. Standardised operations, coupled with high formalisation, allow the parameters of major decisions to be centralised. Managers below the level of senior executive become enforcers of rules and regulations rather than managers of innovation. This contributes to machine bureaucracies being generally poor at adapting to change.

One of the major weaknesses of the machine bureaucracy is that specialisation creates subunit conflicts. Functional unit goals can override the overall goals of the organisation. Production departments, for instance, become production-focused, marketing becomes marketing-focused and so on, leading to the goals of the department overriding those of the organisation. This also inhibits the transfer of knowledge between specialties.

The other major weakness of the machine bureaucracy is something we have all experienced at one time or another when having to deal with people who work in these organisations: obsessive concern with following the rules. When cases arise that don't precisely fit the rules, there is no room for modification. The machine bureaucracy is efficient only as long as employees confront problems that they have previously encountered and for which programmed decision rules have already been established. This tendency leads to machine bureaucracies being unresponsive to their environment and difficult to change.

Machine bureaucracies should not, however, be viewed in negative terms. We all enjoy the benefits of the low costs arising from standardised production. Motor vehicles, air travel and inexpensive clothing are all examples of the outputs of machine bureaucracies that are generally accessible to most people.

When should you use it?

The machine bureaucracy is most efficient when matched with large size, a stable environment, and a technology that permits standardised, routine work. You see its effectiveness when you go into the main post office in any major city, visit a motor vehicle production line or book an airline ticket. The machine bureaucracy is appropriate only as long as its environment remains stable and its technology routine. But this design configuration is not conducive to making changes either rapidly or efficiently. This can be seen in the efforts of large organisations to introduce programs of change. Such processes may take decades and, in many cases, fail to meet the expectations held of them.

Given these strengths and weaknesses, where are you likely to find machine bureaucracies? In mass-production firms, such as those in the car and steel industries; service organisations with simple, repetitive activities, such as banks or insurance and telephone companies; government agencies with routine work, such as post offices and the taxation department; and organisations that have special safety needs, such as airlines and railways. All these organisations have routine and highly standardised activities. Most of their contingencies have occurred many times before and are therefore predictable and amenable to formalised procedures. Such formalised procedures are also critical for safety and maintenance of quality.

The divisional structure

divisional structure
a structure characterised by a set of self-contained, autonomous units coordinated by a central headquarters

The **divisional structure** is a set of autonomous self-contained units, each typically configured as a machine bureaucracy. CSR, ANZ Bank, Boral, Wesfarmers and Goodman Fielder are examples of organisations that use the divisional structure. As Figure 4.7 illustrates, the dominant part of the divisional structure lies with middle management. They report to, and are administered by, a central headquarters. As the divisions are autonomous, this allows middle management—the division managers—a great deal of control over their individual businesses.[24]

FIGURE 4.7 The divisional structure

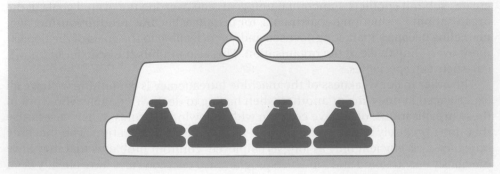

The use of the term middle managers needs some clarification in this context. Chief executives of large businesses (i.e. the divisions) are not normally described as being middle managers. But in the context of divisionalisation they are middle managers. They are answerable to the senior managers in the headquarters and they supervise lower-level managers. Thus they meet the role requirements normally associated with middle managers.

Figure 4.8 shows how the divisional form is utilised at Wesfarmers. Each of its major areas of responsibility—groups headed by a senior executive—represents a separate division. As with most divisional structures, each division is generally autonomous, with the divisional managers responsible for its performance. The divisional general managers generally hold major strategic and operating decision-making authority in relation to their businesses. This form also has a central head-quarters that provides support services to the divisions. This typically includes financial, legal and tax services. Additionally, of course, the headquarters acts as an external overseer, evaluating the performance of each division and deciding which receives capital for investment. This task is facilitated by the divisions being run as profit centres. That means each division is run as a separate business, showing a profit or loss. Divisions, therefore, are autonomous within given parameters. Given its dominance in the world of business, it is surprising that the divisional structure is relatively new. It was introduced by Alfred Sloan in the early part of the last century when he put together General Motors from a group of previously independent car manufacturers.

FIGURE 4.8 Modified organisational chart of Wesfarmers Limited

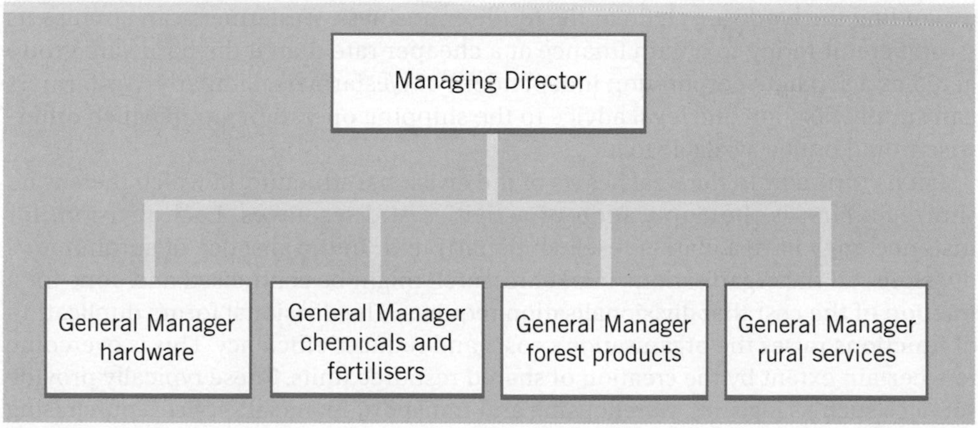

Source: www.wesfarmers.com

Strengths and weaknesses

One of the strengths of the divisional structure is that it provides clear accountability and responsibility for the performance of each division. The divisional manager is more focused on outcomes—that is, the profit or loss of his/her division—than on internal processes.

Another strength of the divisional structure is that it frees the headquarters staff from being concerned with day-to-day operating details so that they can pay attention to the long term. Big-picture, strategic decision making is done at head-quarters. At Wesfarmers, for instance, senior executives can wrestle with the strategic problems of the total organisation while the division managers can concentrate on producing fertilisers and distributing building material products as effectively as possible.

It should be obvious that the autonomy and business focus of the divisional form make it an excellent vehicle for training and developing general managers. For instance, a large corporation with 15 divisions has 15 division managers, who are developing the kind of generalist perspective that is needed in the organisation's top spot.

Another strength of the divisional form is that as each division is autonomous, it can be sold or disposed of with minimal effect on the entire organisation. It follows that businesses may be added with little disturbance to existing businesses. Also, ineffective performance in one division has little effect on the other divisions. Consequently, the divisional structure spreads risk by reducing the chance that a poorly performing part of the organisation will take down other parts of the organisation with it.

It is evident that the real strengths of the divisional form come from the creation of self-contained businesses 'within a business'. The divisions are responsive to their environment, are accountable, derive the benefits of specialisation, and are able to process information as if they were organisations unto themselves.

In the divisional form, the headquarters are generally responsible for the allocation of capital and making major investment decisions. Returning to our example of Wesfarmers, the board of Wesfarmers itself will decide whether to invest in expanding the hardware chain or the fertiliser business. Wesfarmers can also use its strong credit rating to obtain finance at a cheaper rate than if the hardware group acted as a separate corporation independent of Wesfarmers. Similarly, Wesfarmers can supply taxation and legal advice to the shipping operation group which otherwise would not be available to it.

Let us turn now to the weaknesses of the divisional structure, of which there is no shortage. First is the duplication of activities and resources. Each division, for instance, may have a market research department. In the absence of autonomous divisions, all the organisation's market research might be centralised and done for a fraction of the cost that divisionalisation requires. The divisional form's duplication of functions raises the organisation's costs and reduces efficiency. This is overcome to a certain extent by the creation of shared resource units. These typically provide services such as logistics, warehousing and transport, financial services, purchasing and buying of advertising space for each division.

Another disadvantage is the propensity of the divisional form to stimulate conflict. There is little incentive with this structural design to encourage cooperation among divisions. Conflict is created as divisions and headquarters argue about where to locate support services. The more the divisions succeed in having these services decentralised to their level, the less dependent they are on headquarters and, hence, the less power headquarters personnel can wield over them.

The autonomy of the divisions, to the degree that it is more theory than practice, can breed resentment in the division managers. While the structure gives autonomy to the divisions, this autonomy is exercised within constraints. The division manager is being held fully accountable for results in the unit, but because the manager must operate within the uniform policies imposed from headquarters there is likely to be resentment and for his/her authority to be less than his/her responsibility.

Finally, the divisional form creates coordination problems. Personnel are often unable to transfer between divisions, especially when the divisions operate in highly diverse product or service markets. Personnel in Wesfarmers Bunnings hardware stores would find it difficult to transfer to the fertiliser division. This reduces the flexibility of headquarters executives to allocate and coordinate personnel. Additionally, the divisional form may make coordination of customer relations and product development a problem. If the divisions are in competing or closely adjoining markets, they may compete with each other for the same sale. To many prospective shoppers, Kmart and Target are different chains, selling similar merchandise to discount shoppers. However, as both are owned by Coles Myer, they both compete for the same dollar as if they were owned by separate companies.

Similarly, the competition between divisions over product development can be dysfunctional. The classic illustration is the NDH (not developed here) syndrome. An innovation developed by one division and then authorised by headquarters to be instituted in all divisions often fails because it was NDH. This rivalry and territorial protectionism by the individual divisions can make coordination by headquarters extremely difficult.

When should you use it?

The primary reason for using the divisional structure is product or market diversity. When an organisation chooses a diversification strategy—to become a multiproduct or multimarket organisation—the divisional form becomes preferable to a machine bureaucracy. When an organisation diversifies, conflict along the horizontal dimension between functions becomes too great and a change in structural design becomes necessary.

Other contingency factors include size, technology and environment. As size increases, it becomes more difficult to coordinate functional units and to keep members' attention focused on the organisation's goals. Organisational size and goal displacement appear to be highly correlated. With growing size, communication channels become strained and unable to handle the greater complexity. Growth in size encourages movement to the divisional structure.

Not all technologies are compatible with the division form. To be applicable, the organisation's technology must be divisible: 'Divisionalization is possible only when the organization's technical system can be efficiently separated into segments, one for each division'.[25] It is difficult, for instance, for IAG Insurance to divisionalise because economies of scale and the commitment of hundreds of millions of dollars to very high fixed-cost technical systems basically preclude divisibility. Finally, the environment affects preference for the divisional form. The divisional structure works best where the environment is neither very complex nor very dynamic. This is because highly complex and dynamic environments are associated with non-standardised processes and outputs, yet the divisional form is a lot like the machine bureaucracy in its emphasis on standardisation. The divisional form, therefore, tends to have an environment that is more simple than complex and more stable than dynamic.

The professional bureaucracy

professional bureaucracy a structural form that has highly skilled professionals, high complexity, decentralisation and the use of internalised professional standards in place of external formalisation

The past quarter of a century has seen the emergence of a new structural configuration, called the professional bureaucracy. The **professional bureaucracy** is a decentralised configuration in which highly trained specialists form the operating core but where the benefits of standardisation and decentralisation are still achieved.

The jobs that people do today increasingly require a high level of specialised expertise. Hospitals, schools, universities, museums, libraries, engineering design firms, management consultancies, social service agencies and public accounting and legal firms are just some of the types of organisations that employ staff with professional expertise. The employment of professionals has created the need for an organisational design that permits high levels of expertise to be applied to unique problems.

Figure 4.9 illustrates the configuration for professional bureaucracies. The power in this design rests with the operating core because they have the critical skills that the organisation needs and they have the autonomy—provided through decentralisation—to apply their expertise. The only other part of the professional bureaucracy that has a large complement of employees is the support staff, but their activities are focused on serving the operating core.[26]

FIGURE 4.9 The professional bureaucracy

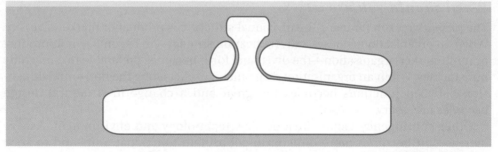

Source: Henry Mintzberg, *Structure in Fives: Designing Effective Organizations*, © 1983, p. 159. Reprinted by permission of Prentice-Hall, Englewood Cliffs, NJ.

You can see what a professional bureaucracy looks like in Figure 4.10. The Legal Aid Commission of New South Wales relies on the skills of lawyers in various specialties as well as other professionals in such areas as social work and child support. These professionals acquired their skills through years of study, leading to their admission to professional bodies. They perform their activities relatively autonomously, but the structure is high in complexity and there are many rules and regulations; however, the formalisation is internalised rather than imposed by the organisation itself. The Legal Aid example also illustrates a fact about most professional bureaucracies, which is that they also typically include machine bureaucracies within them. In Legal Aid, for example, the support staff that assist the professionals—secretaries, clerks, computer services, library, human resources and so on—will not have decentralised authority, and their formalisation will be externally imposed by the rules and regulations surrounding their work.

FIGURE 4.10 Abbreviated organisational chart of the Legal Aid Commission of New South Wales

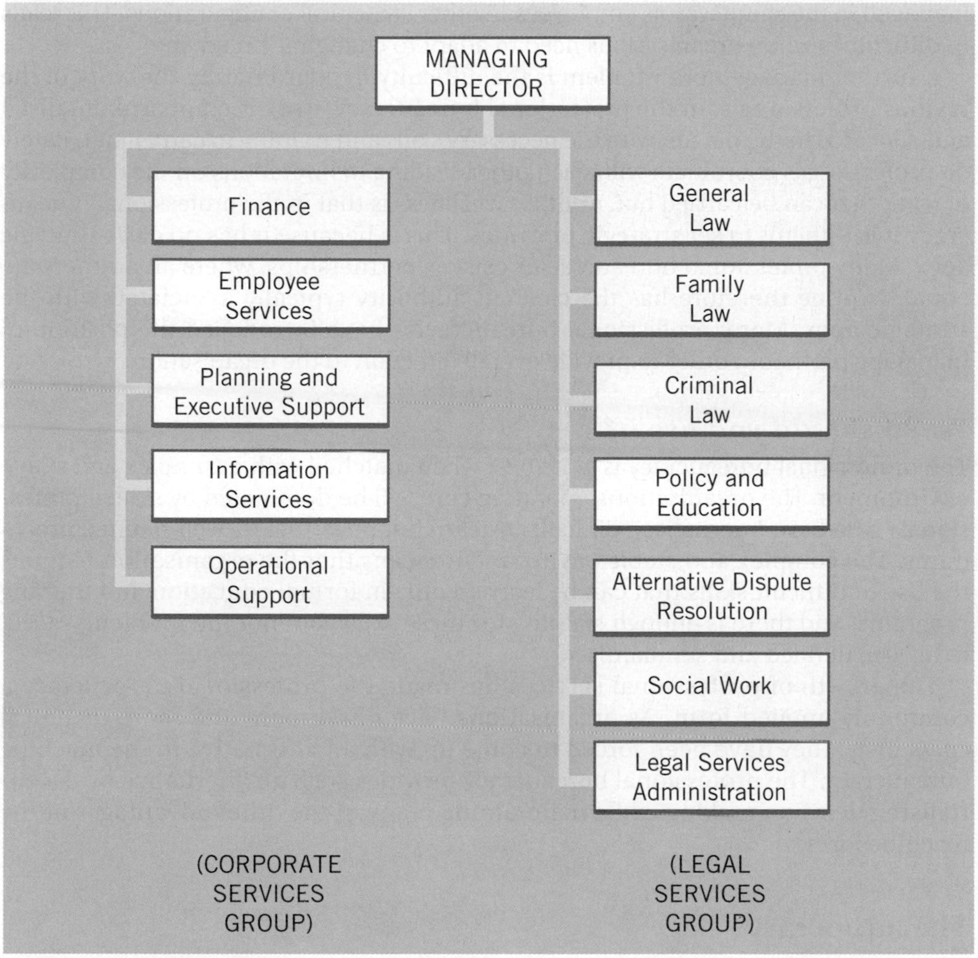

```
                    MANAGING
                    DIRECTOR

    Finance                         General
                                    Law

    Employee                        Family
    Services                        Law

    Planning and                    Criminal
    Executive Support               Law

    Information                     Policy and
    Services                        Education

    Operational                     Alternative Dispute
    Support                         Resolution

                                    Social Work

                                    Legal Services
                                    Administration

    (CORPORATE                      (LEGAL
     SERVICES                        SERVICES
     GROUP)                          GROUP)
```

Source: Annual Report, 1996.

Strengths and weaknesses

The strength of the professional bureaucracy is that it can perform specialised tasks—ones that require the skills of highly trained professionals—with the same relative efficiency as the machine bureaucracy. One of the characteristics of tasks undertaken by professionals is that few of the problems faced are the same. The professional bureaucracy allows high levels of expertise to be brought to bear on a continuous series of unique problems. In this environment, professionals need the autonomy to do their jobs effectively.

The professional bureaucracy has its weaknesses. First, there is the tendency for subunit conflicts to develop. The various professional functions seek to pursue their own narrow objectives, often placing their own self-interest over that of the organisation. Second, the specialists in the professional bureaucracy are often constrained by the rules of their profession: standards of professional conduct and codes of ethical practices have been socialised into the employees during their training and through membership of professional bodies. This means that they cannot be managed in the same way as employees in other structural configurations. This leads to difficulties when organisations need to adapt to changing circumstances.

A further management problem is the difficulty in coordinating the work of the various professionals. In the professional bureaucracy, work is compartmentalised and allocated to the person with the necessary skills and training to carry it out. Rarely do professionals coordinate with each other, leading to limitations on the complexity of work that can be carried out. Another weakness is that in the professional bureaucracy it is difficult to set strategic priorities. This is because it has no clear strategic apex. Many professional bureaucracies exist as partnerships, where all partners are equal. No-one therefore has the clearcut authority typically associated with the strategic apex. Many professional bureaucracies have introduced the position of managing partner in order to provide overall direction to the organisation.

When should you use it?

The professional bureaucracy is at its best when matched with a complex and stable environment. The organisation's operating core will be dominated by skilled professionals who have internalised difficult-to-learn but nevertheless well-defined procedures. The complex and stable environment means that the organisation requires the use of difficult skills that can be learned only in formal education and training programs, and there is enough stability for these skills, but not the problems faced, to be well defined and standardised.

The growth of professional services has made the professional bureaucracy a commonly applied form. As organisations have hired more and more technical specialists, they have been forced to come up with an alternative to the machine bureaucracy. The professional bureaucracy provides such an alternative by decentralising decision making while maintaining many of the other advantages of the machine form.

The adhocracy

When Peter Weir or George Lucas make a film, they bring together a diverse group of professionals. This team—composed of producers, scriptwriters, film editors, set designers and hundreds of other specialists—exists for the one purpose of making a single film. They may be called back by Weir or Lucas when either of these directors begins another film, but that is irrelevant when the current project begins. These professionals often find themselves with overlapping activities because no formal rules or regulations have been provided to guide members of the team. While there is a production schedule, it must often be modified to take into consideration unforeseen contingencies. The film's production team may be together for a few months or, in some unusual cases, for several years, but the organisation is temporary. In contrast to bureaucracies or divisional structures, these film-making organisations have no entrenched hierarchy, no permanent departments, no formalised rules, and no standardised procedures for dealing with routine problems. This leads to our last design configuration. The **adhocracy** is a decentralised form which is characterised by high horizontal differentiation, low vertical differentiation, low formalisation, intensive coordination, and great flexibility and responsiveness.

adhocracy an organisational form characterised by high horizontal differentiation, low vertical differentiation decentralisation and great flexibility and responsiveness

Horizontal differentiation is significant because adhocracies are staffed predominantly by professionals with a high level of expertise. Vertical differentiation is low because the many levels of administration would restrict the organisation's ability to adapt. Also, the need for supervision is reduced because professionals have internalised the behaviours that management wants. However, coordination is quite extensive as it is important for tasks to be carried out in the correct sequence.

We have already found professionalisation and formalisation to be inversely related. The adhocracy is no exception. There are few rules and regulations. Those that exist tend to be loose and unwritten. Again, the objective of flexibility demands an absence of formalisation. Rules and regulations are effective only where standardisation of behaviour is sought. However, the adhocracy is far more intensively coordinated than the professional bureaucracy, often having specific individuals whose only role is to coordinate the activities of others.

Decision making in adhocracies is decentralised. This is necessary for speed and flexibility and because senior management cannot be expected to possess the expertise needed to make all decisions. So the adhocracy depends on decentralised teams of professionals and highly skilled employees for decision making.

The adhocracy is a very different design from those we encountered earlier. This can be seen in Figure 4.11. Because the adhocracy has little standardisation or formalisation, the technostructure is almost non-existent. Because middle managers, the support staff and operatives are typically all professionals in orientation, the traditional distinctions between supervisor and employee and line and staff become blurred. The result is a central pool of expert talent that can be drawn on to innovate, to solve unique problems and to perform flexible activities. Power flows to anyone in the adhocracy with expertise, regardless of his or her position.[27]

Adhocracies are best conceptualised as groups of teams. Specialists are grouped together into flexible teams that have few rules, regulations or standardised routines. Coordination between team members is through mutual adjustment, but often a team member's main role is to coordinate the efforts of others. As conditions change,

FIGURE 4.11 The adhocracy

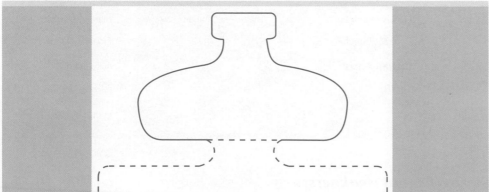

Source: Henry Mintzberg, *Structure in Fives: Designing Effective Organizations*, © 1983, p. 262. Reprinted by permission of Prentice-Hall, Englewood Cliffs, NJ.

so do the activities of the members. However, adhocracies do not have to be devoid of horizontally differentiated departments. Departments may be used for clarity and then department members deployed into small teams—which cut across functional units—to perform their tasks.

The Sydney Theatre Company is a typical example of an adhocracy (see Figure 4.12). Developed around the concept of mounting a continuously changing range of productions, it relies heavily on the flexibility inherent in the adhocratic form. Most of its employees and contract staff work in teams built around productions. Each team is composed of experts who are under the coordination of the director for each production. The distinction between managers and workers is minimised, as the organisation is essentially staffed by professionals. All employees enjoy a great deal of autonomy, within the limits of having to coordinate with other employees. The Sydney Theatre Company's structure is based on the constant need to change and update its repertoire, rather than on narrow functional specialties. Instead of being permanently part of a team, employees have tenure on a specific team, depending on how long it takes for that team to accomplish its task.

FIGURE 4.12 Modified organisational chart of the Sydney Theatre Company, 2002

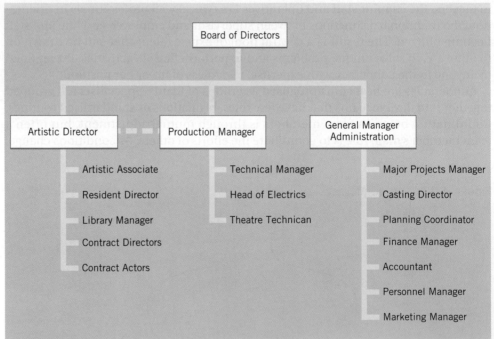

Strengths and weaknesses

The history of adhocracy can be traced to the development of taskforces during World War II, when the military created ad-hoc teams that were disbanded after completion of their missions. There was no rigid time span for their existence: teams

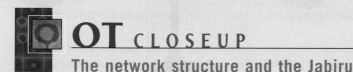

OT CLOSEUP

The network structure and the Jabiru

Unless you are a light aircraft aficionado, it is unlikely that you have heard of the Jabiru. It is a small training and sports utility aircraft built in Bundaberg, Queensland. It is the brainchild of Phil Ainsworth and Rod Stiff, two sugar cane harvester manufacturers who thought of the idea of producing a light aircraft in 1987. Their ideas proved so successful that up to 500 have been delivered and over 100 are on order. Most of the aircraft are sold in kit form: that is, the various parts are put into a shipping container with the customer being responsible for final assembly. Some, however, are fabricated in Bundaberg and flown to final customers.

The aircraft has been so successful that Ainsworth and Stiff soon realised that they did not have the space to manufacture the numbers being ordered. As most of the parts were not large (the Jabiru is no jumbo jet), they made their employees an offer to set up their own businesses fabricating the parts of the aircraft that they were already trained for. This mainly involved fibreglassing and light metal work. Local families have found new skills, with some parts being made by 'Gran and Grandad' in the shed while the more sophisticated parts are made by teams of five or six workers who lease a hangar at the airport. The engine is made in Bundaberg by another subcontractor, CAMit. The parts are machined from solid blocks of metal. This allows design changes to be easily incorporated through a simple change to the computer program controlling the machine. Over 35 engines are produced per month.

Ainsworth and Stiff derive considerable advantage from using their network of suppliers. They don't have to worry about day-to-day management of a workforce. They can concentrate their efforts on design and marketing. They have no layers of middle management. The system has the flexibility of being able to expand and contract the production schedule with minimum disruption to the company; most of Ainsworth's and Stiff's costs are variable and dependent on the number of aircraft ordered. The subcontractors themselves are free to seek other work commensurate with their skills and interests. CAMit supplies engines for many different types of small aircraft.

The network structure used to manufacture the Jabiru offers considerable advantages in flexibility and workforce management. It comes as no surprise that networks are becoming more common in industry.

Adapted from: Tony Arbon, 'Australia's Jabiru Flies High', *Australian Aviation*, September 2001, pp. 34–6.

could last a day, a month or a year. Roles performed in the teams were interchangeable and, depending on the nature and complexity of the mission, the group could be divided into subunits, each responsible for different facets of the job to be done. The advantages of these ad-hoc teams included their ability to respond rapidly to change and innovation and to facilitate the coordination of diverse specialists. Over 50 years have passed since the end of World War II, but the advantage of ad-hoc teams, or what we call adhocracy, continues today. When it is important that the organisation be adaptable and creative, when individual specialists from diverse disciplines are required to collaborate to achieve a common goal and when tasks are technical, non-programmed and too complex for any one person to handle, the adhocracy represents a viable alternative.

On the negative side, conflict is a natural part of adhocracy. There are no clear boss–subordinate relationships. Ambiguities exist over authority and responsibilities.

Activities cannot be compartmentalised. In short, adhocracy lacks the advantages of standardised work.

Adhocracy can create social stress and psychological tensions for members. It is not easy to set up and quickly dismantle work relationships on a perpetual basis. Some employees find it difficult to cope with rapid change, living in temporary work systems and having to share responsibilities with other team members.

In contrast to bureaucracy, adhocracy is clearly an inefficient configuration. It is also a vulnerable design. As one author noted, 'Many of them either die early or else shift to bureaucratic configurations to escape the uncertainty'.[28] So why, you might ask, would it ever be used? Because its inefficiencies, in certain circumstances, are more than offset by the need for flexibility and innovation.

When should you use it?

Given the limitations of the adhocracy, it is obviously applicable only under certain circumstances. The factors that determine when adhocracy will be effective are the organisation's strategy, technology, environment and life stage.[29]

The adhocracy is associated with strategies of diversity, change, complexity and/or high risk. Such strategies demand the flexibility inherent in adhocracy. The adhocracy is mostly used to solve non-routine problems, such as mounting an advertising campaign or designing a jet engine. As a consequence, the technology that an adhocracy uses will be non-routine. The technology will contain little formalisation, relying on the expertise of professionals to provide an appropriate input. Moreover, the technology will be complex, in that it will draw on the talents of diverse specialties. This, in turn, requires coordination and integration of specialised and heterogeneous skills. The adhocracy is the preferred mechanism for facilitating this integration.

The adhocracy's environment will be dynamic and complex. That is because dynamic environments constantly require unique solutions to difficult and unforeseen problems, often within a short time frame. It is also because complex environments are often difficult to interpret and understand.[30]

Small, innovative firms are often adhocracies. This is because they need flexibility as they attempt to identify a market niche and determine precisely how goals are to be attained. Innovation is high in an organisation's formative years, as it struggles to survive. Of course, the lack of precedents and entrenched vested interests fosters experimentation with new and different approaches. It has been argued that adhocracy is most evident in those industries that are relatively young—ones that have developed since World War II.[31] These would include organisations engaged in the manufacture of computers and electronics as well as consulting and research.

A final point regarding the adhocracy is its trendiness. During the 1970s and 80s, this design was particularly susceptible to managers' propensity to follow fashion. It fits well with the notion, held by many managers today, that environments are dynamic and complex. It also conforms to ideas that employees are more creative and satisfied when they have a high degree of autonomy over their work. Add to this the fact that organisations are increasingly being staffed by well-educated employees and it becomes fashionable for management to choose work designs that emphasise decentralised teams and taskforces.

Summary of the basic configurations

While our society is populated by millions of organisations, these can essentially be reduced to one of five general configurations: the simple structure, the machine bureaucracy, the divisional structure, the professional bureaucracy, and the adhocracy.

As Table 4.1 demonstrates, the simple structure and adhocracy are essentially flexible structures, while the other three are more formalised. Yet each is unique and preferable to the other four under certain conditions.

The simple structure is recommended for small organisations, for those in their formative stage of development, for those in environments that are simple and dynamic, as a response to times of crisis or when those in control desire power to be centralised.

The machine bureaucracy is designed to effectively handle large size, a simple and stable environment, and a technology that is composed of routine and standardised work. Parts of the divisional structure look a lot like a machine bureaucracy. However, it has been designed to respond to a strategy that emphasises market or product diversity, where the organisation is large, technologies are divisible, and the environment tends to be simple and stable.

The professional bureaucracy is also designed for large organisations with a routine technology. However, the professional bureaucracy's members are technical specialists confronting a complex environment. To operate effectively with these professionals and a complex environment, a decentralised bureaucratic design is necessary.

The adhocracy requires top management to give up the most control. In power-control terms, therefore, it is the least desirable of the five configurations.

When will management select the adhocracy? With diverse, changing or high-risk strategies or when the technology is non-routine and the environment is both dynamic and complex. It is also effective in dealing with the problems that are typically encountered when an organisation is in the formative years of its life cycle.

TABLE 4.1 Summary of the five configurations

Characteristic	Simple Structure	Machine Bureaucracy	Professional Bureaucracy	Divisional Structure	Adhocracy
Specialisation	Low	High functional	High social	High functional	High social
Formalisation	Low	High	Low	High within divisions	Low
Centralisation	High	High	Low	Limited de-centralisation	Low
Environment	Simple and dynamic	Simple and stable	Complex and stable	Simple and stable	Complex and dynamic
General structural classification	Organic	Mechanistic	Mechanistic	Mechanistic	Organic

However, as the simple structure is also well designed to deal with the problems in an organisation's formative period—while maintaining centralised control—the simple structure is likely to be more widely adopted in an organisation's early years.

Metaphors and organisations

So far in this chapter we have discussed ways in which organisations may be measured, compared and classified. As useful as the measures we have introduced may be, organisations have many ways of confounding us. They are confusing, mystifying and surprising. They are often difficult to comprehend and tax our powers of understanding, They surround us and dominate our lives, but exist only as abstractions and as relationships between people. No two are the same, but the differences are often of degree rather than of substance.

Given the intangible and confusing nature of organisations, it is not surprising that we often revert to informal ways to describe them. In doing this we often draw on language and symbols familiar to us in other contexts. When we do this we are using metaphors.[32] Metaphors are words that are familiar to us but do not literally apply in the circumstances in which they are used. We used a metaphor in Chapter 1 when we talked of the life-cycle perspective of organisations. We also use metaphors when we describe organisations as an octopus, a family or a well-oiled machine. The term bureaucracy is used to denote a specific organisational form in this book. But it has another more widely used meaning, as representing an organisation that is rule-bound, unresponsive and staffed by unimaginative employees.

Needless to say, what metaphor we use depends on who we are in relation to an organisation. The Commonwealth Bank used to promote itself as being big, safe and friendly—all desirable attributes to have in relation to a bank. To support this image, it used an elephant in promotional material. However, customers faced with closed bank branches might not have regarded the Commonwealth Bank in the same manner as the promotional material. Neither might career employees faced with unanticipated redundancy.

In addition to using metaphors, we often feel the need to attribute to organisations either human or familiar form. This is not surprising, given that organisations are made up of people and form a central part of our life. Thus, Qantas is often referred to as the Flying Kangaroo, in a clear reference to the widely identified kangaroo on the tail of its planes. Although the origins of the term are lost in history, the ABC is sometimes called Aunty by its aficionados. Most are also familiar with the term bloodsuckers when referring to the taxation department. Sporting teams often use the names of aggressive animals or natural characteristics to describe themselves: Lions, Tigers, Hawks, Bombers and Broncos are just some of the terms used. Rarely are terms such as mice, sloths, cowards or rats used, except perhaps informally by competing teams or coaches trying to motivate teams after poor performances.

Viewing organisations as metaphors also helps us make sense of the places where we work and helps us to understand our environment. Herbert Simon introduced the term 'bounded rationality' when talking of organisations.[33] By this he meant that, because of limitations in our mental processing capacities, it was not possible to fully comprehend all that was occurring in organisations such as large businesses. Because of the confusion and complexity of our environment, and our limited capacity to understand it, we build mental or cognitive maps as representations of reality. Just like road maps, which represent the road system and in reality look nothing like a road or the houses along it, mental maps help us navigate around confusing and difficult-to-comprehend organisational environments. No two people's cognitive maps are the same; we all experience the world a little differently. But tapping into these cognitive maps is important when introducing change programs. Likewise, the substitute of one metaphor for another can assist in re-orienting attitudes and values at work.

Summary

This chapter has discussed the ways in which organisations may be described and compared. We have introduced the concepts of complexity, formalisation and centralisation as well as the basic organisational configurations.

Complexity refers to the degree of differentiation that exists within an organisation. Horizontal differentiation considers the degree to which jobs differ based on the nature of tasks being undertaken. Vertical differentiation refers to the depth of the organisation and is normally measured by counting the number of layers of managers separating the chief executive from the lowest-level employees. Spatial differentiation encompasses the degree to which jobs are dispersed geographically.

The greater the horizontal differentiation, holding the span of control constant, the taller the hierarchy; the more geographically dispersed the organisational units, the more complex the organisation. And the more complex the organisation, the greater the difficulties of communication, coordination and control.

Formalisation refers to the degree to which jobs within the organisation are standardised. The higher the formalisation, the more regulated the behaviour of the employee. Formalisation can be achieved on the job. In such cases, the organisation would make use of rules and procedures to regulate what employees do. But a pseudo-formalisation process can occur off the job in the training the employees receive before joining the organisation. This characterises professional employees. They have acquired a formalised response to problems through training in their profession.

The most popular formalisation techniques are the selection process (for identifying individuals who will fit into the organisation); role requirements; rules, procedures and policies; training; and having employees undergo rituals to prove their loyalty and commitment to the organisation.

Centralisation is the most problematic of the three components. It is defined as the degree to which the formal authority to make discretionary choices is concentrated in an individual, a unit or a level (usually high in the organisation), thus permitting employees (usually low in the organisation) minimum input into their work. The degree of control that an individual has over the full decision-making process can be used as a measure of centralisation. Decision making is most centralised when the decision maker controls all these steps.

Decentralisation reduces the probability of information overload, facilitates rapid response to new information, provides more detailed input into a decision, instils motivation and represents a potential vehicle for training managers in developing good judgement. Centralisation, in contrast, adds a comprehensive perspective to decisions and can provide significant efficiencies.

Organisations conform to five basic configurations. The first of these is the simple structure, which is typically adopted by small business. It is highly centralised, with low formalisation but an inability to handle high complexity. The second form, the machine bureaucracy, handles complexity well through the ability to standardise processes and practices. The divisionalised structure is a decentralised form which accommodates product and geographic diversity. The fourth form, the professional bureaucracy, allows professional staff to bring their expertise to bear on complex but well-defined problems. The adhocracy is the final form. This configuration has high levels of coordination, which permits the undertaking of complex, one-off undertakings.

There are other, informal ways in which organisations may be described. One of these is the use of metaphors, as when we use something familiar to us to describe an organisation. While metaphors may provide a powerful and rich description of an organisation, they lack the precision to permit organisational comparison.

For review and discussion

1   Identify and briefly describe the measures of complexity. Are the three measures intercorrelated? Discuss.

2   Identify and briefly describe the common formalisation techniques.

3   What are the benefits and disadvantages of formalisation to an organisation?

4   Compare the formalisation of unskilled workers with that of professionals.

5   Why is the issue of centralisation important to an organisation?

6   In what way would working in a centralised organisation be different from working in a decentralised one?

7   Discuss how job satisfaction could be maintained in a highly formalised and centralised organisation.

8   Identify and describe the different types of coordination used in organisations.

9   Identify and briefly describe an organisation you are familiar with which is likely to have (a) high formalisation and centralisation, (b) low formalisation and centralisation, (c) high formalisation and decentralisation.

10   What is authority? How is it related to centralisation?

11   How may metaphors be used to better understand people's perceptions of organisations?

12   Identify and describe the five component parts of most organisations.

13   Identify and describe the five basic structural configurations.

14   Discuss how it is possible for a large organisation to possess the characteristics of a number of the basic structural configurations.

15   Which of the structural configurations would be most attractive to a potential graduate? Why?

CASE FOR CLASS DISCUSSION
Flight Centre's families, villages and tribes

Flight Centre travel agencies with their red and white signs are a familiar sight in most shopping centres in Australia and increasingly overseas. Headquartered in Brisbane. Flight Centre has over 800 shops in six countries (Australia, New Zealand, South Africa, Canada, Britain and the USA). Having grown at over 20% compound per year for the past decade, it is one of Australia's fastest-growing companies, and its fourth-largest retailer, with a share price to match. At first glance, you might consider that Flight Centre would be managed in much the same way as any other large organisation. But a quick look at the spread of the shops indicates that this may not be the case. They are all small, with only a few staff in each, and there are often two or three shops in the one city shopping block. No economies of scale or centralised bureaucratic control here. But that is not the only thing that makes Flight Centre different.

The structure of Flight Centre emanates from the beliefs of the founder, Graham Turner. He claims that after 200 years of industrialisation, people are still hard-wired to work in small groups within larger groups. Flight Centre's basic structure is built on the 'family' of three to seven people who form a retail shop. A family can also be an administrative or head office team, providing services such as HR, IT or marketing. Next comes the 'village' of seven to ten families. This is roughly a department or an area. Further on is 'tribal' country, which is roughly equivalent to a regional office of three or four villages from the same tribe. 'Tribes' are also the different brands within the company, such as Corporate Traveller, Flight Centre and Student Flights.

The 'country' is the business unit that buys the services, such as training, recruitment, holiday packages and marketing for the families and villages. When 'countries' become too big, they are split into smaller countries. 'Countries' don't have to buy the service from another Flight Centre business unit. Travel consultants can buy products from any wholesaler, and are free to negotiate with whomever they want if they can get a better deal. Flight Centre wholesale products are run as profit centres. Innovation and new business development is handled through national and global SWOT teams (strengths, weaknesses, opportunities and threats), which try out new ideas.

This results in a flat structure with no more than three levels from the bottom to the top of the company. It also allows for expansion to be accommodated within the structure without too much of a problem. But operationally the company must change quite dramatically every two or three years, as it adds about 150 shops per year.

The company discovered one of its basic management ideas early in its existence, when a shop in Melbourne made $200 000 in its first year with six staff, the same profit the next year with 14 staff and $120 000 in the third year with 18 staff. That's when the benefits of keeping the shops small became apparent. With six staff the manager knew everyone and had regular contact with the staff. With 18 staff this was not possible; administration work piled up, morale and motivation slumped, and staff turnover rose. Graham Turner realised that, to be successful, units needed to be small and dynamic.

The company goes to great lengths to foster communication between staff and develop a community of feeling. 'Buzz nights' are held once a month as well as other less formal get-togethers. Turner feels that 100 people are about the maximum that staff can know and interact with.

The managers of Flight Centre shops take 10% of the shop's profit and may own up to 20% of their shop. Travel consultants, those staff dealing with the customers, are paid a guaranteed base salary plus a share of the shop's profit. Team managers normally stay at their job for 10 years and then move on, often to other tasks within the company. Women make up 60%–65% of staff, and most staff are aged between 25 and 35. Entry age is normally about 25 years.

Adapted from: Elizabeth Johnson, 'Fly Boys', *The Australian Financial Review*, Boss Magazine, 8 June 2001, p 26; and Darryl Blake, *Skroo the Rules*, Brisbane: Information Australia, 2001.

QUESTIONS

1 Relate the organisational structure at Flight Centre to as many relevant aspects as you can identify in this chapter.

2 Using Mintzberg's classification scheme, how would you classify Flight Centre's structure? Nominate points of similarity with and difference from the classification you have identified.

3 From the case, provide evidence of the roles of functional and social specialisation. Show how both are necessary for Flight Centre to function effectively.

4 Discuss how Flight Centre has resolved the problem of what to centralise and what to decentralise.

5 With what advantages does the use of metaphors provide the managers and workers at Flight Centre?

FURTHER READING

Jay Galbraith, *Designing Organizations: An Executive Briefing on Strategy, Structure and Process*, San Francisco: Jossey-Bass, 1995.

Richard H. Hall, *Organizations: Structure and Process*, 3rd edn, Englewood Cliffs, NJ: Prentice-Hall, 1982, p. 84.

Henry Mintzberg, *The Structuring of Organizations*, Englewood Cliffs, NJ: Prentice-Hall, 1979, pp. 91–2.

Charles Perrow, *Complex Organizations: A Critical Essay*, 3rd edn, New York: Random House, 1986.

D.S. Pugh, D.J. Hickson, C.R. Hinings & C. Turner, 'Dimensions of Organization Structure', *Administrative Science Quarterly*, June 1968, p. 75.

NOTES

1 Coles Myer Ltd press release, 25 September 2001.

2 For a critique of the methodology by which complexity, formalisation and centralisation have come to dominate the definitions of major structural dimensions, and for presentation of an alternative approach, see Richard Blackburn & Larry L. Cummings, 'Cognitions of Work Unit Structure', *Academy of Management Journal*, December 1982, pp. 836–54.

3 See, for example, James L. Price & Charles W. Mueller, *Handbook of Organizational Measurement*, Marshfield, MA: Pitman Publishing, 1986, pp. 100–5.

4 Goodman Fielder, Annual Report, 2001.

5 Coles Myer, op. cit.

6 Anthony Hughes, 'ANZ Bank to Restructure Branch Network', *Sydney Morning Herald*, 25 August 2001, p. 47.

7 Anonymous, 'Uni Plans to Restructure No Answer', *Newcastle Herald*, 8 May 2001, p. 12.

8 Ian Porter, 'SPT Factory revamps to Boost PacDun Shares', *The Age*, 28 September 2001, p. 1.

9 Annie Lawson, 'PMP to Trim 120 Jobs to Cut Gordon and Gotch Losses', *The Age*, 7 September 2001.

10 H. Gleckman et al., 'The Technology Payoff', *Business Week*, 14 June 1993, p. 57–68; M. Liu, H. Denis, H. Kolodny, & B. Stymne, 'Organization and Design for Technological Change', *Human Relations*, 43, January 1990, pp. 7–22; Huber, George, 'A Theory of the Effects of Advanced Information Technologies on Organizational Design, Intelligence and Decision Making', *Academy of Management Review*, 14, 1990, p. 47–71.

11 Tom Peters, *Thriving on Chaos*, New York: Knopf, 1988, pp. 354–65.

12 ibid.

13 'Preaching the Euro-Gospel', *Business Week*, 23 July 1990, pp. 30–8.

14 Richard H. Hall, *Organizations: Structure and Process*, 3rd ed., Englewood Cliffs, N.J.: Prentice-Hall, 1982, p. 84.

15 D. S. Pugh, D. J. Hickson, C. R. Hinings & C. Turner, 'Dimensions of Organization Structure', *Administrative Science Quarterly*, June 1968, p. 75.

16 Henry Mintzberg, *The Structuring of Organizations*, Englewood Cliffs, N.J.: Prentice-Hall, 1979, pp. 91–2.

17 Benjamin Schneider, 'The People Make the Place', *Personnel Psychology*, Autumn 1987, pp. 437–52.

18 Charles Perrow, *Complex Organizations: A Critical Essay*, Glenview, Ill.: Scott, Foresman, 1972, p. 100.

19 Herbert A. Simon, *Administrative Behavior*, 3rd edn, New York: Free Press, 1976, p. 294.

20 James Stoner, Roger Collins & Philip Yetton, *Management in Australia*, Sydney: Prentice-Hall, 1985.

21 See, e.g., Henry Mintzberg, *Structure in Fives: Designing Effective Organizations*, Englewood Clifts, NJ: Prentice Hall, 1983.

22 All the information in relation to the five basic structural configurations is drawn from Henry Mintzberg, *Structuring in Fives: Designing Effective Organisations*, Englewood Cliffs, NJ: Prentice-Hall, 1983.

23 Mintzberg, *Structure in Fives: Designing Effective Organisations*, p. 217.

24 Mintzberg, *Structuring of Organisations*, pp. 397–8.

25 Mintzberg, *Structure in Fives: Designing Effective Organisations*, p. 194.

26 ibid, p. 261.

27 Henry Mintzberg, *Structure in Fives: Designing Effective Organisations*, p. 261.

28 Danny Miller and Peter H. Friesen, *Organizations: A Quantum View*, Englewood Cliffs, N.J.: Prentice Hall, 1984, p. 85.

29 Henry Mintzberg, 'Structuring in 5's: A Synthesis of the Research on Organization Design,' *Management Science*, March 1980, pp. 336–8.

30 Mintzberg, *The Structuring of Organizations*, p. 449.

31 Mintzberg, *Structure in Fives: Designing Effective Organisations*, p. 338.

32 See for instance Ian Palmer & Richard Dunford. 'Conceptualising Metaphors: Reconceptualising Their Use in the Field of Organizational Change', *Academy of Management Review*, 21(3), 1996, pp. 691–717.

33 Simon, *Administrative Behaviour*.

PART

3

Contingencies

part 3

CHAPTER 5

Strategy

After reading this chapter you should be able to:

1 define strategy;

2 compare business-level with corporate-level strategy;

3 describe Chandler's 'structure-follows-strategy' thesis;

4 list and define Miles and Snow's four strategic types;

5 explain the structural implications of Porter's competitive strategies;

6 describe how globalisation strategies lead to different structures;

7 explain the industry–structure relationship.

Introduction

Uncle Toby's—strategy and structure

The brand name Uncle Toby's is one of Australia's icons, with its reputation based on the healthy nature of its products.[1] Like most consumer brands, Uncle Toby's is part of a much larger group, in this case the trans-Tasman food company Goodman Fielder. Goodman Fielder can date its origins back to 1909, when George Fielder started a bakery in Sydney. Its current form was established in 1986 through the merger of Allied Mills of Australia and the Goodman Group of New Zealand. The idea behind the merger was to establish a trans-Tasman food company to challenge the dominance of foreign food processors. Through various acquisitions the company grew at a reasonable rate during the 1980s. It owned major bakeries in Europe and Australia, significant gelatine and starch businesses, and had interests in Asia. In 1992 it bought Uncle Toby's with its range of healthy foods and in 1997, the consumer products business of Burns Philp. But Goodman Fielder found it difficult to turn this range of business into a profitable operation. Continuous underperformance and low profitability led to a languishing share price and three years ago the senior board and management of Goodman Fielder embarked on a new strategy. This was to sell poorly performing businesses and most of those operating in overseas countries and to develop the business as a focused Australasian food company with an emphasis on those products with a strong retail presence in the local market. This meant the disposal of businesses such as the European baking operations, the gelatine business and its Germantown ingredients business in the USA. Renewed focus was given to what Goodman Fielder called its power brands, those such as Uncle Toby's, Buttercup, Meadow Lea, White Wings, Helga's, and Bluebird in New Zealand.

But to put this new strategy into effect, Goodman Fielder needed a new structure. Disposing of the overseas operations was relatively easy; the staff went with them. But in Australia and New Zealand major structural changes were made to focus people around the brands. The number of departments was reduced in order to simplify reporting relationships and clarify responsibilities. Shared service units, such as those providing logistics and purchasing of key products for the various divisions, were formed to reduce costs. Even a quick glance at the new structure identified that developing the key brands was the main focus of the company. In other words, Goodman Fielder's new structure was heavily influenced by the strategy it adopted.

Over the next five chapters we will be examining in some detail what determines an organisation's structure. In this chapter we look at the way that strategy can *cause* an organisation's structure to take a certain form. We consider strategy as being an **imperative** (an imperative *dictates* something; in our usage that 'something' is structure). Of the imperatives we consider, strategy is probably the oldest. The study of strategy goes back to the early days of modern organisations, and an awareness of how strategy influences structure gradually developed over subsequent years. Up to 40 years ago, strategy was considered to be the only cause of organisational structure. Since then it has became clear that other imperatives influence structure, but strategy remains as one of the fundamental influences on the way organisations are managed.

imperative a variable that dictates structure

The early study of organisations did not differentiate clearly between goals and strategy. Organisations were considered to be machine-like in nature. Clear and identifiable goals were determined, and the organisation's structure subsequently evolved to attain the goals. This process reflected the assumptions inherent in classical economic theory. These assumptions included the following:[2]

- The organisation has a goal or goals towards which it strives.
- It moves towards its goals in a 'rational' manner.
- The organisation exists to transform economic inputs to outputs.
- The environment within which the organisation operates is a given.

There were times when such assumptions were valid. For much of the 20th century economies were isolated, and firms attempted to control their environments in such a way that they almost existed as a closed system. The growth of globalisation and the promotion of competition by governments have altered the environments in which organisations operate. Research has also thrown more light on how goals and strategies are determined. As discussed in Chapter 3, they are no longer considered as the rational outcome of a purposeful, deliberative process.

Regardless of these limitations, we can still identify how strategy influences structure. We are fortunate that strategy lends itself to easy classification. As a result, a number of useful models have been developed that may be applied to any organisation which has choices. Basically this refers to those organisations operating in a market economy, which precludes such organisations as the police and the taxation department. But the models can be used to explain the link between strategy and structure for charities such as the Smith Family or services such as a private hospital. However, first we need to identify what strategy is.

What is strategy?

Whenever management is discussed, *strategy* and *strategic* suffer from being the two most overused and ill-defined words. As a result, they have lost much of their specific meaning and relevance to the study of organisations. But for our purposes, strategy can be defined in such a way that it is possible to give it an exact meaning. We need to do this in order to undertake a systematic study of its impact on organisation structures. According to Chandler,[3]

> **Strategy** can be defined as the determination of the basic long-term goals and objectives of an enterprise, and the adoption of courses of action and the allocation of resources necessary for carrying out these goals. Decisions to expand the volume of activities, to set up distant plants and offices, to move into new economic functions or to become diversified among many lines of business involve the defining of new basic goals. New courses of action must be devised and resources allocated and reallocated in order to achieve these goals and to maintain and expand the firm's activities in the new areas in response to shifting demands, changing sources of supply, fluctuating economic conditions, new technological developments, and the actions of competitors.

strategy the adoption of courses of action and the allocation of resources necessary to achieve the organisation's goals

It can be seen from the above definition that *goals* and *strategy* are not the same thing. Goals refer to ends. Strategy refers to both means and ends. As such, goals are part of an organisation's strategy. Of course, not all goals refer to strategy. Many relate to performance, financial or other measures, and as a result are not relevant when the structural implications of goals are being considered.

Our definition does not tell us how an organisation determines its strategy. With anything as important and as complex as strategy it is not surprising that there are different approaches as to how it may best be determined. Two approaches emerge: the first views strategy as the outcome of a rational deliberation process; the other sees strategy as emerging from a string of minor incremental decisions.[4]

planning mode
strategy as an explicit and systematic set of guidelines developed in advance

The first view can be called a **planning mode**. Planning mode views strategy as a plan or explicit set of guidelines developed in advance. Managers identify where they want to go; then they develop a systematic and structured plan to get there. This approach may be viewed as almost scientific in its practice. It reduces the determination of strategy to a well-thought-out process where rationality plays a significant role. Proponents would regard the planning mode as the ideal form of strategy determination, and until recently this viewpoint dominated the organisation theory literature.

The planning mode is still widely practised. Virtually all large firms have a strategic plan that sets out what the organisation is attempting to achieve and how it intends to get there. This applies particularly to those firms listed on the stock exchange, where external analysts are continually assessing their performance and prospects with a view to making investment decisions. But environments are never stable, competitors rarely predicable, and strategy can change with the fortunes of the various factions constantly jostling for influence within the organisation.

evolutionary mode
a strategy that evolves over time as a pattern in a stream of significant decisions

A perspective that acknowledges the complex processes involved in strategy formation is what we call an **evolutionary mode**. Evolutionary mode views strategy as a stream of significant decisions evolving over time. The evolutionary mode does not necessarily view strategy as a well-thought-out and systematic plan. The strategies of many organisations follow the evolutionary mode. This may arise because of the opening of an unexpected opportunity, the changing perceptions of the board of directors and senior management, or the unanticipated actions of competitors. It may also include realisation that changes in technologies and tastes led to products becoming mature and not providing the growth companies aspire to. The organisation may have outgrown its initial market niche. Technological and environmental change can create opportunities in one area while closing them in another. Organisations have no alternative but to evolve with these changes or cease to exist. Any firm that has been in existence for more than a few years has faced situations in which its original strategy has been overtaken by events. For those established over 100 years, changes in strategy often have led to companies changing their entire line of business. CSR, for instance, started out as a sugar refiner but now is basically a building material manufacturer, with most of its business in the USA. BHP Billiton has long since ceased to have any association with Broken Hill. In many cases, both the buying and the selling of the assets were made opportunistically rather than being the result of long-range planning. Figure 5.1 illustrates the difference between the planning and evolutionary mode.

Organisational behaviour gives us another insight into how strategy may evolve in ways other than as a well-thought-out process. The actions of people in organisations even call into question whether some decisions in the strategy area may be called rational at all. Simon introduced the concept of bounded rationality to

FIGURE 5.1 Comparison of planning and evolutionary mode of decision making

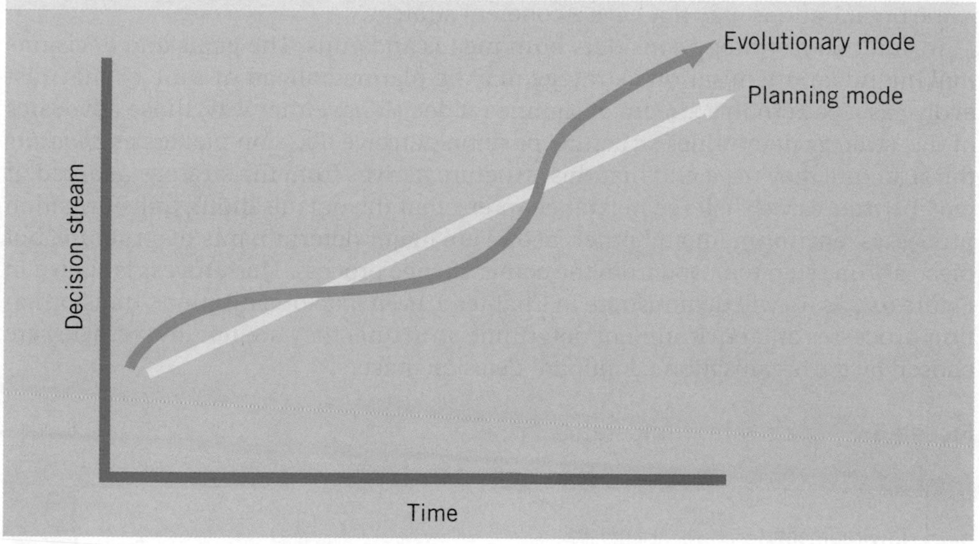

describe the situation where the human mind has difficulty in grasping a situation because of its complexity.[5] In other words, the decision maker does not have perfect knowledge of all variables. Decisions are therefore made under a number of psychological and external constraints that lead to a decision maker 'satisficing': that is, they will stop searching for an alternative as soon as the minimum requirements for a decision have been met. We can see that these limitations may lead to a strategy formulation that simply evolves from one state to the other. Lindblom has called this the science of muddling through, which highlights the fact that planning and decision execution are seldom orderly and sequential but the victims of chance and the internal workings of the firm.[6]

The planning and evolutionary modes, however, need not be viewed as exclusive categories. All successful organisations must take a rational approach to determining strategy; they cannot leave themselves entirely at the mercy of short-term incrementalism. This particularly applies to organisations that must commit large amounts to capital spending and that have a 10-year time frame. But environments are continuously changing, and within the overall strategy there is room for opportunistic changes. So one way of viewing the determination of strategy is that the overall direction of the organisation is set by the planning mode but the evolutionary mode is often used in response to short-term opportunities and threats.

Some firms confound us by not having an identifiable strategy. Needless to say, we do not consider these firms to be leaders in their field, or hold them up as examples for others to follow. Such organisations are drifting and making incremental changes without any overall plan. While this situation may emerge because of poor management, it is mainly a result of environmental changes and external shocks, which render the current strategy inapplicable. Some firms may find that their products are no longer accepted in the marketplace, their plant may be too small to be economical and they have no recourse to ready finance, or changes in government regulations have altered the competitive landscape. These firms tend not to have a long life. They remind us that the basic proposition we raise in this chapter—that strategy influences structure—may not hold for all organisations; some organisations may not have a coherent strategy.

In summary, strategy considers both means and ends. The goals and decisions making up an organisation's strategy may be planned ahead of time or may just evolve as a pattern in a stream of significant decisions. Either way, those advocates of the 'strategy determines structure' position perceive decision makers as *choosing* the structure they have and that this structure derives from the strategy adopted. It may be true, as we shall see in later chapters, that the organisation's transformation processes, environment and other factors are major determinants of structure, but these are one step removed from the actual change process. This process is shown in Figure 5.2. As we will demonstrate in Chapter 9, even if an organisation's transformation processes and environment determine structure, they are not givens. They are chosen by the organisation's dominant decision makers.

FIGURE 5.2 The strategy imperative

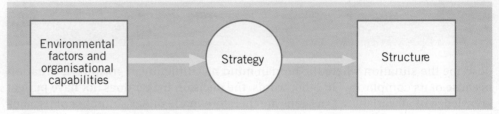

Levels of strategy

If all organisations produced a single product or service, the management of any organisation could develop a single strategy that encompassed everything it did. But many organisations are in diverse lines of businesses, most of which are only vaguely related. Wesfarmers, for instance, has lines of businesses ranging from fertilisers to hardware distribution. Each of these faces different environments and different conditions. Organisations that are in multiple businesses, therefore, need to develop different strategies for different levels of activities. Thus, it is necessary to differentiate between corporate-level and business-level strategies (see Figure 5.3).

corporate-level strategy attempts to define the nature of the businesses in which the firm seeks to operate

If an organisation is in more than one line of business, it will need a **corporate-level strategy**. This strategy seeks to answer the question 'In what set of businesses should we be?'. It determines the roles that each business in the organisation will play. At a company like Wesfarmers, top management's corporate-level strategy integrates the business-level strategies for its fertiliser, hardware and agriculture and other divisions. For a multinational corporation, corporate-level strategy may revolve around which country to invest in.

business-level strategy refers to those strategies adapted by business units of the organisation

Business-level strategy seeks to answer the question 'How should we compete in each of our businesses?'. For the small organisation in only one line of business or the large organisation that has avoided diversification, business-level strategy is typically the same as corporate strategy. But for organisations in multiple businesses, each division will have its own strategy that defines the products or services it will offer, the customers it wants to reach and so on. For example, Wesfarmer's Bunnings hardware business has its own unique business strategy that encompasses expansion of stores and merchandising operations.

FIGURE 5.3 Levels of strategy

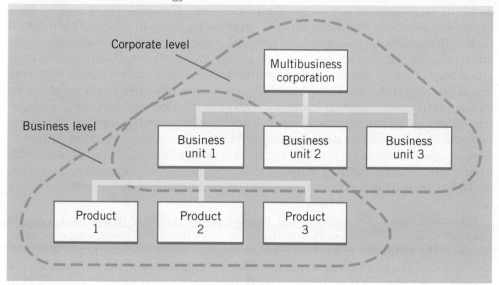

Most contemporary strategy–structure theories we discuss focus on the business-level strategies of each division. But the original research into this topic began by looking at the corporate-level strategies of large, multi-product organisations. To the degree that strategy actually determines structure, the strategy level is an important point to keep in mind. Why? For small organisations in only one line of business or for non-diversified large organisations, business and corporate strategy will be the same, and the organisation should have a relatively uniform organisation structure. But organisations with diverse business strategies should be expected to have a variety of structural configurations: that is, management will design structures to fit with different strategies for each division.

The beginnings—Chandler's strategy–structure thesis

The classic work on the relationship between an organisation's strategy and its structure was done by the American business historian Alfred Chandler, who published a series of works commencing in the early 1960s.[7] All the current work on the strategy–structure relationship has been clearly influenced by Chandler's research.

Chandler studied nearly 100 of America's largest firms between the period 1900–1950. Using a technique based on extensive case studies, he concluded that changes in corporate strategy preceded and led to changes in an organisation's structure. As he put it, 'A new strategy required a new or at least refashioned structure if the enlarged enterprise was to be operated efficiently . . . unless structure follows strategy, inefficiency results'.[8]

Chandler found that the companies he studied began as centralised structures with characteristics very close to those of a machine bureaucracy. This reflected the fact that they offered limited product lines. As demand for their products grew, the companies expanded. They expanded their product lines and had to develop different structures to cope with their changing strategies. For instance, they integrated vertically by buying many of their own sources of supply. This reduced their dependence on suppliers. To produce a greater variety of products more efficiently, they created separate product groups within the organisation, with each group focusing on a similar group of products. The result was structures that were fundamentally different. Growth and diversification gave rise to the need for an autonomous multidivisional structure, with each division having its own management. The highly centralised structure became inefficient and impractical for dealing with the significantly greater complexity. As Chandler summarised the situation, 'Unless new structures are developed to meet new administrative needs which result from an expansion of a firm's activities into new areas, functions, or product lines, the technological, financial, and personnel economies of growth and size cannot be realized'.[9]

Chandler essentially argued that organisations typically begin with a single product or line. They do only one thing, such as manufacturing, sales or warehousing. The simplicity of this strategy is compatible with a loose or simple structure. Decisions can be centralised in the hands of a single senior manager. Because the organisation's strategy is narrowly focused, the structure to execute it can be low in both complexity and formalisation. So, Chandler concluded, the efficient structure for an organisation with a single-product strategy is one that is simple—high centralisation, low formalisation and low complexity.

Chandler's research indicated that as the firm moves to a multi-product strategy, the firm adopts a divisionalised structure. As organisations seek to grow, their strategies become more ambitious and elaborate. From the single-product line, companies typically expand activities along the supply and distribution chain. This vertical integration strategy makes for increased interdependence among organisational units and creates the need for a more complex coordinating device. This desired complexity is achieved by redesigning the structure to form specialised units based on the functions performed.

Finally, if growth proceeds further into product diversification, structure must again be adjusted if efficiency is to be achieved. A product-diversification strategy demands a structural form that allows the efficient allocation of resources, accountability for performance and coordination between units. This can best be achieved through the creation of a multiple set of independent divisions, each responsible for a specified product line. This evolution is depicted in Figure 5.4.

According to Chandler's theory, successful organisations that diversify should have a different structure from that of successful firms that follow a single-product strategy. Boral, for instance, adopted a product-diversification strategy and followed

FIGURE 5.4 Chandler's thesis

Time	t	t + 1	t + 2
Product-diversification strategy	Low		High
Structure	Simple	Functional	Divisional

OT CLOSEUP

BHP Billiton and Chandler's thesis

BHP Billiton, one of Australia's largest private-sector companies, can be seen as fitting Chandler's thesis. Incorporated in 1885 to exploit the rich silver, lead and zinc lode at Broken Hill in New South Wales, the company built its smelters at Port Pirie in South Australia to convert the ore to purified metal. In the smelting process ironstone was used as a flux, and this was obtained from the nearby Iron Monarch deposit.

Iron Monarch and its nearby neighbour Iron Knob were rich deposits, and a trial smelting in 1905 convinced the company that it could profitably make iron from the deposit. In 1915 the company set up its first iron-making facility at Newcastle, carrying the ironstone around the Australian coast by ship. Further expansion occurred in the steel industry when it bought the Port Kembla-based Australian Iron and Steel in 1935. Using its basic steel-making capacity, BHP, as it then was, expanded into downstream activities such as wire drawing, sheet steel rolling and tube and pipe making. The company also became involved in coal mining, initially to service the steel industry. In 1936 it joined a number of other companies in establishing the Commonwealth Aircraft Corporation and in 1941 began to build ships at Whyalla, in South Australia. During World War II it was involved in the manufacture of various types of munitions and in the substituting of local material for imports unavailable because of the war. In addition to opening new iron ore mines in Western Australia, BHP opened a manganese mine at Groote Eylandt in 1966.

In 1967 BHP, in partnership with Esso, discovered commercial quantities of oil in the Bass Strait. This led to a major expansion of interest in an area with little connection to its steel-making activities. Later, in 1976, BHP joined Shell in proving the enormous North West Shelf natural gas deposits.

During the 1970s, BHP continued its expansion in the mineral area with the opening of coal and iron mines, aimed at the export market, and with the OK Tedi project in New Guinea. In 1983, BHP bought Utah International, the mining subsidiary of General Electric. Utah has mining interests in the United States, Canada, Brazil, Chile and other countries, as well as in Australia. BHP has also bought a number of oil exploration companies, the main one being the US-based Energy Resources Group.

But BHP also illustrates the flaws in Chandler's analysis. During the 1990s BHP fell on hard times, with a string of poor decisions which weakened the company. New management was appointed to set the company back on a growth path. But the world situation had changed. The mantra for mining companies was get big or get out, and so a merger with Billiton, the former Shell mining interest was executed. All of the companies studied by Chandler have had chequered histories as they have struggled to adapt to technological change, inbred management and innovative actions of competitors. Perhaps new historical analysis would provide more light on the strategy–structure nexus.

---

with a multidivisional form. In contrast, Comalco maintained a vertical integration strategy and has matched it with a functional structure. Both Boral and Comalco have been successful with different structures—but, Chandler would argue, that is because they are following different strategies.

The research

Is Chandler right? Does structure follow strategy? Limitations inherent in Chandler's research plus additional studies that have tried to duplicate and extend his work suggest that the theory has some validity but also some distinct restrictions.

First, let's look at Chandler's sample of organisations. His companies were not a cross-section of organisations in general. He looked only at very large and powerful industrial business firms which dominated their industries. Whether his findings would be applicable to small- and medium-sized organisations, service companies or those in the public sector could not be answered from this sample.

Second, Chandler's sample was composed of companies that were prominent in the new technological waves developing in the first part of the 20th century. The motor vehicle, electrical and chemical industries figured prominently, for instance. Further, the companies in the emerging technologies lent themselves to large size, partly to achieve economies of scale.

Third, a careful review of Chandler's work reveals that when he used the term 'strategy', he really meant *growth* strategy. Growth was his major concern, not profitability or even survival. Chandler paid no attention to companies that were being displaced by technological change, such as horse carriage manufacturers or sailing ship-builders. In organisational-effectiveness terms, a proper strategy–structure fit according to Chandler is more likely to lead to growth than increased profitability.[10]

Lastly, as with all historical research, there is always the problem of generalising from one point in time to another. Chandler's sample was drawn from firms exhibiting strong growth in the early part of the 20th century. Further research is required to determine whether his thesis holds for those firms established at different times or in different countries.

These caveats should not be taken as sufficient to reject Chandler's work. Within the parameters set by Chandler, several studies have confirmed his conclusions, specifically relating to a strong relationship between product diversification and the multidivisional form.[11] One researcher essentially supported Chandler's findings, although he used a different classification scheme for defining strategy.[12] Organisational strategies were labelled as single business (no diversification), dominant business (70–95% of sales coming from one business or a vertically integrated chain), related business (diversified in related areas, with no one business accounting for more than 70% of sales) and unrelated business (diversified in unrelated areas, with no one business accounting for more than 70% of sales). The researcher found that the related and unrelated business strategies were linked to functional structures. No single structure was found consistently in the dominant-business category.

Conclusions

Chandler's claim that strategy influences structure seems well supported, but this generalisation is constrained by the limitations and definitions inherent in Chandler's work. He looked only at large, profit-making organisations. He focused on growth as a measure of effectiveness rather than profitability. Moreover, his definition of strategy, based on product differentiation, is far from all-inclusive. Strategy can, for instance, include concern with market segmentation, financial strengths and leverage opportunities, actions of competitors, assessment of the organisation's comparative advantage vis-à-vis its competition, and the like. There is also the problem of generalisation inherent in all historical analysis: Chandler's analysis refers only to one phase of industrial expansion, and its applicability to current industrial experience and technologies may be limited. Nevertheless, 'there appears to be little question that strategy influences structure at the top levels of business firms. The evidence on this point is overwhelming'.[13]

Contemporary strategy–structure theory

As we noted previously, strategy is a broad concept and can be described along a number of dimensions. Since Chandler's work in the early 1960s, the most important research on the strategy–structure relationship has been undertaken by Miles and Snow. In addition, the landmark work of Michael Porter on competitive strategies has direct relevance to the strategy–structure relationship. Finally, Bartlett and Ghoshal's study includes the applicability of the strategy–structure relationship as it refers to companies operating in the international environment. Below we review each of those three contributions.

Miles and Snow's four strategic types

Raymond Miles and Charles Snow classify organisations into one of four strategic types based on the rate at which they change their products or markets. They call these types defenders, prospectors, analysers and reactors.[14] While their discussion centres on business firms, the categories they use probably have their counterpart in non-profit organisations.

Defenders seek stability by producing only a limited set of products directed at a narrow segment of the total potential market. Within this limited niche, or domain, defenders strive aggressively to prevent competitors from entering their 'turf'. Organisations do this through standard economic actions, such as competitive pricing or production of high-quality products. But defenders tend to ignore developments and trends outside their domains, choosing instead to grow through market penetration and perhaps some limited product development. There is little or no scanning of the environment to find new areas of opportunity, but there is intensive planning oriented towards cost and other efficiency issues. The result is a structure made up of high horizontal differentiation, centralised control and an elaborate formal hierarchy for communications and coordination. Over time, true defenders are able to carve out and maintain small niches within their industries that are difficult for competitors to penetrate.

An example of a defender strategy is the grocery chain Woolworths. Although it is not exclusively a grocery retailer (it owns Big W and the Dick Smith electronic chain), the company maintains its focus on grocery retailing. It is aggressive in protecting its market share and loses little opportunity to expand within its narrow sector of food retailing. It maintains is competitiveness through constant pressure on supplier's prices and economies of scale in areas such as warehousing and purchasing. Any firm seeking to challenge the dominance of Woolworths would face a formidable task.

There are more defenders around than initially meet the eye. Many of the more complex manufactured goods whose brand names are well known have as components the output of many smaller, specialised firms. These firms, which are unknown outside a small industry circle, specialise in areas as diverse as motor vehicle brake shoes, railway signalling equipment, air compressor valves and fast ferry construction. They dominate one small, clearly defined area through being at the leading edge of both knowledge and manufacturing techniques, making it difficult for others to displace them. They have adopted a classic defender strategy.

Prospectors are almost the opposite of defenders. The prospector's strength lies in finding and exploiting new product and market opportunities. Innovation may be

defenders
organisations whose strategy is to produce a limited set of products directed at a narrow segment of the total potential market

prospectors
organisations whose strategy is to find and exploit new product and market opportunities

more important than high profitability. When thinking of prospectors, Internet and biotechnology companies immediately spring to mind. But they also include firms in more mundane areas, such as magazine publishers that introduce new magazine titles almost monthly, constantly attempting to identify new market segments. Fashion companies, such as Mambo and Billabong, grew to prominence on their reputation as innovators. As befits the name, prospectors also include mining companies anxious for a significant discovery that will propel them into the major mining league.

The prospector's success depends on developing and maintaining the capacity to survey a wide range of environmental conditions, trends and events and then introduce new products based on that research. Therefore, prospectors invest heavily in personnel who seek potential opportunities. As flexibility is critical to prospectors, the structure will also be flexible. It will rely on multiple technologies that have a low degree of routinisation and mechanisation. There will be numerous decentralised units. The structure will be low in formalisation and have decentralised control, with lateral as well as vertical communications: 'In short, the prospector is effective—it can respond to the demands of tomorrow's world. To the extent that the world of tomorrow is similar to that of today, the prospector cannot maximise profitability because of its inherent inefficiency'.[15]

analysers
organisations whose strategy is to move into new products or markets only after their viability has been proven

Analysers attempt to minimise risk by adopting innovations after they have been proven by others. They try to capitalise on the best of both of the preceding types. They seek to minimise risk and maximise opportunity for profit. Their strategy is to move into new products or new markets only after viability has been proven by prospectors. Analysers live by imitation. They take the successful ideas of prospectors and copy them or, as happens in some cases, take them over and greatly expand their production. Manufacturers of mass-marketed fashion goods that are copies of designer styles follow the analyser strategy. This label also probably characterises such well-known firms as Unilever, Pacific Dunlop and Goodman Fielder. They essentially follow their smaller and more innovative competitors with imitation products, but only after their competitors have demonstrated that the market is there.

Analysers must have the ability to respond to the lead of key prospectors, yet at the same time maintain operating efficiency in their stable product and market areas. They will tend to have smaller profit margins in the products and services that they sell than will prospectors, but they are more efficient as they are generally better financed. Prospectors have to have high margins to justify the risks that they take and to cover their productive inefficiencies.

Analysers seek both flexibility and stability. They respond to these supposedly contradictory goals by developing a structure made up of dual components. Parts of these organisations, such as manufacturing and distribution, have high levels of standardisation, routinisation and mechanisation for efficiency. Other parts, such as marketing and product development, are adaptive in order to enhance flexibility. In this way, they seek structures that can accommodate both stable and dynamic areas of operation. But in this compromise there can be costs. If situations change rapidly, demanding that organisations move fully in either direction, their ability to take such action is severely limited.

reactors a residual strategy that describes organisations that follow inconsistent and unstable patterns

Reactors represent a residual strategy. The label is meant to describe the inconsistent and unstable patterns that arise when one of the other three strategies is pursued improperly. In general, reactors respond inappropriately, perform poorly and, as a result, are reluctant to commit themselves aggressively to a specific strategy for the future. What can cause this? Top management may have failed to make the organisation's strategy clear. Management may not have fully shaped the organisation's structure to fit the chosen strategy. Management may have maintained its current strategy–structure relationship despite overwhelming changes in environmental conditions or despite the fact that its products or services may be obsolescent. Whatever the reason, however, the outcome is the same. The organisation lacks a set of response mechanisms with which to face a challenging environment. Decline and extinction is often the outcome of this strategy.

Table 5.1 summarises Miles and Snow's strategic typologies. It shows the goal(s) of each, the type of environment that each faces, and the structural mechanisms that management would choose to achieve the goal(s). The reactor strategy is omitted for the obvious reason that it results in ineffective performance.

The key element in Miles and Snow's strategy–structure theory is management's assessment of environmental uncertainty. If management selects a defender strategy, for instance, this suggests that it perceives the environment as stable. Of course, perceptions of environmental uncertainty vary from manager to manager. Managers in two organisations can face exactly the same environment and perceive it very differently.

The dropping of tariffs in the clothing industry has revealed that there are significant differences in opinion about what this will mean for the industry. On the one hand, some clothing companies such as Mambo and Billabong are closing down local manufacturing operations completely and moving them to low-wage countries. Their reasoning is that it is virtually impossible to compete against the dollar-a-day labour used in parts of Asia. They see their strength in innovative design. This group of clothing manufacturers may be viewed as prospectors. Other designers and manufacturers see the length of time from order to delivery for overseas-made goods providing them with an edge in manufacturing short production runs of high-fashion goods. This group conforms more to analysers. Others, such as R.M. Williams, conform more to a defender strategy, by focusing on a narrow range

TABLE 5.1 Miles and Snow's strategic typologies

Strategy	Goals	Environment	Structural characteristics
Defender	Stability and efficiency	Stable	Tight control; extensive division of labour; high degree of formalisation; centralised
Analyser	Stability and flexibility	Changing	Moderately centralised controls; tight control over current activities; looser controls for new undertakings
Prospector	Flexibility	Dynamic	Loose structure; low division of labour; low degree of formalisation; decentralised

Source: Adapted from Raymond E. Miles, Charles C. Snow, Alan D. Meyer & Henry J. Coleman, Jr, 'Organizational Strategy, Structure, and Process', *Academy of Management Review*, July 1978, pp. 552–6.

OT CLOSEUP

Applying Miles and Snow's strategy to Australian retailing

Not every industry is large enough to provide examples of defenders, analysers and prospectors, but as retailing has such a dominant presence in modern business systems and as most of us are familiar with the main players in the industry, it provides us with examples we can relate to. The defenders of the industry are the discount sellers of food and clothing. Men's clothing retailers such as Gowings in Sydney and Lowes around the country make no pretence of defining fashion, or of charging high prices for designer-label quality. Their attitudes are best summed up by the slogan often attributed to Gowings of 'Make it well, pile it high and sell it cheap'. Anyone wanting a garment that is passable and at the lower end of the price range would shop at shops such as these. The same applies to shops such as Aldi and Bi-Lo in the grocery retailing area. Few people set out to patronise these shops because of the pleasure of the shopping experience. The shops stock basic necessities which are bought in a repetitive cycle at a low price. They are the standard against which new entrants to the industry must measure their prices.

The analysers would be stores such as Target and Harvey Norman. They will add a new range or department only after the market has been proven by someone else. Once they enter a market, however, they use their superior retailing skills and financial strength to offer advantages over the initial entrants. Harvey Norman, for instance, is now one of Australia's largest computer retailers, but it entered the field only a few years ago. Woolworths also acts as an analyser by adding petrol retailing to some of its supermarkets. Rather than this being a chancy venture, the linking of supermarkets and petrol retailing is common in Britain and France and has occurred in the reverse in Australia, with petrol stations offering groceries.

Examples of prospectors can be found in the small boutiques and chain stores that dot malls and shopping centres around the country. Such stores as Jeans West and Colaraso constantly change their product range, searching for new lines that will provide the greatest profit. The boutiques often have cutting-edge fashion which the larger and more conservative stores will not sell. Being a fashion leader can be very profitable if it strikes a chord in the market. Alternatively it can be rejected by buyers and the retailers left with a large amount of unsold stock.

The large department stores such as David Jones, Grace Bros and Myers are the reactors of the industry. They attained their position by dominating a previous generation of retailing. But changing spending patterns, which have seen the amount spent on clothing rapidly drop over the past 20 years, and the rise of self-service and discount chains have left the large stores in a quandary over how to react. They don't have the image to support moves into computer and whitegoods retailing, and the community standard on a reasonable price to pay for clothing is constantly being lowered by the action of discount retailers. Like all retailers they are affected by the trend for consumers to spend more of their disposable income on holidays, dining out, home cleaning and other domestic services, all purchases made in non-traditional retail outlets. They are left reacting to the initiatives of others by constantly changing stock lines and service levels in an attempt to find a profitable combination.

of products and fending off imitations. They achieve this by maintenance of high quality and promoting nation-of-origin advantages.

Figure 5.5 describes Miles and Snow's four strategies as falling along a continuum that ranges from low to high in terms of environmental change and uncertainty. Following the logic of this theory, the more uncertainty and change that

FIGURE 5.5 Environment strategy continuum

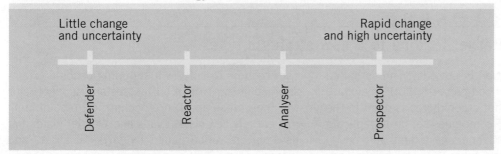

management forecasts, the more it will move to the right along the continuum in Figure 5.5. Similarly, as strategies move to the right along the continuum, the organisation's structure should be modified or redesigned to be increasingly flexible and adaptive.

Management perceives little or no change and uncertainty in the environment under the defender strategy. The successful structure, under such conditions, should be designed for optimum efficiency. This efficiency can best be achieved through high division of labour, standardisation of operations, high formalisation and centralised decision making.

Organisations following a reactor strategy respond to change reluctantly. Management perceives some change and uncertainty but is not likely to make any substantial adjustments until forced to by environmental pressures. So this structure is apt to look very like the one described for defenders; it is difficult to see a reactor adopting a prospector strategy.

Managers pursuing an analyser strategy perceive a considerable degree of change and uncertainty but wait until competitors develop a viable response, and then quickly adopt it. As for structure, analysers try to combine the best of both worlds by tightly structuring their current and more stable activities while developing flexible structures for new activities that face greater uncertainty.

Finally, prospector strategies require the greatest degree of structural flexibility. There is a lot of change and uncertainty, so structures should be highly adaptive. This would translate into low complexity, low formalisation, high levels of coordination and decentralised decision making.

Porter's competitive strategies

Michael Porter of the Harvard School of Business is one of the current leaders in the study of business strategy. He argues that no firm can successfully perform at an above-average level by trying to be all things to all people. He proposes that management must select a strategy that will give its organisation a competitive advantage. Management can choose from among three strategies: cost leadership, differentiation, and focus.[16] The one management chooses depends on the organisation's strengths and the competitor's weaknesses. Management should avoid a position in which it has to slug it out with everybody in the industry. Rather, the organisation should put its strength where the competition isn't.

A **cost-leadership strategy** is adopted when an organisation sets out to be the low-cost producer in its industry. Success with this strategy requires that the

cost-leadership strategy aims to achieve the lowest cost within an industry

OT CLOSEUP

Is the Internet leading to a new strategic type?

Answering this question is not easy. The so-called tech wreck of Internet companies in 2000 may have left the impression that e-commerce is dead in the water. Certainly, most companies set up to replicate existing distribution channels have fared very poorly and have mostly been taken over by bricks-and-mortar retailers and other established companies. But while the potential of Internet technology is too great to dismiss, its long-term impact is difficult to predict. Two authors, Philip Evans and Thomas Wurster, have identified a number of likely impacts in their book *Blown to Bits*. They claim that information can be characterised by its richness and reach. Rich information is that which contains a lot of detail; an encyclopaedia would be an example. Reach is how many people have access to this information; a billboard advertising campaign represents information that has extensive reach but little richness. The printed version of the *Encyclopaedia Britannica* is an example of information with great richness and little reach. Evans and Wurster claim that the Internet completely renders redundant the old trade-offs between richness and reach.

The business model of the *Encyclopaedia Britannica*, with its extensive and expensive sales force, was turned on its head by CD-ROM, and more lately the Internet. The authors claim that this process will happen in many different industries. Across the economy, information is the glue that holds supply chains, value chains, consumer franchises and organisations together. As the ability to access richer information grows, it will lead to a breakdown in the connectivity of the chains, radically transforming economic relationships. Organisational functions such as a sales force, a system of branches, a chain of stores, a printing press, which provided signifi-

cant barriers to entry will suddenly become expensive liabilities. Parts of businesses and supply chains will then break apart, or deconstruct, recombining into entirely new ways. Evans and Wurster claim that new players, unburdened by physical assets and legacy systems, will emerge from nowhere to cherry-pick the most profitable parts of the business. These are the parts that an incumbent business can least afford to lose. They also claim that the new disinter-mediation—that is, the elimination of business from its role as mediators between parts of the supply chain—will resegment markets and possibly make redundant some businesses whose role it is to mediate.

How does this affect the strategy–structure relationship? The strategy imperative states that the structure chosen must be appropriate to the strategy that is adopted. *Blown to Bits* does not propose that the information revolution is leading to a new strategy, at least not in the way in which we have categorised it in this chapter. From the arguments, however, we can identify that organisations are likely to become smaller and more innovative, hence a prospector or or differentiation strategy is likely to become more common. But there is still room for defenders and those with a focus strategy. But a focus or defender strategy will depend less on economies of scale and more on information as to customer needs. So, overall, e-commerce appears to have a greater impact on the relationships between firms than within an organisation itself.

Adapted from: Philip Evans & Thomas Wurster, *Blown to Bits: How the New Economics of Information Transforms Strategy*, Cambridge: MA: Harvard Business School Press, 2000.

organisation be *the* cost leader and not merely one of the contenders for that position. Additionally, the product or service being offered must be perceived as comparable to that offered by rivals, or at least acceptable to buyers. How does a firm gain such a cost advantage? Typical means include efficiency of operations, economies of scale, technological innovation, low-cost labour and preferential access to raw materials. Examples of firms that have used this strategy are the airline Virgin Blue, Aldi supermarkets, Rio garments and Hyundai cars.

A **differentiation strategy** is one where a firm seeks to be unique in its industry in ways that are widely valued by buyers. It might emphasise high-quality, extraordinary service, innovative design, technological capability or an unusual, positive brand image. The key is that the attribute chosen must be different from those offered by rivals and significant enough to justify a price premium that exceeds the cost of differentiation. There is no shortage of firms that have found at least one attribute that allows them to differentiate themselves from competitors: Mercedes-Benz (status), Herbon (environmentally sensitive products), David Jones (quality and service), 7-Eleven stores (convenience) and Akubra hats (nationalism).

The above two strategies seek a competitive advantage in a broad range of industry segments. A **focus strategy** aims at a cost advantage or differentiation advantage in a narrow segment. That is, management will select a segment or group of segments in an industry (e.g. product variety, type of end buyer, distribution channel, geographical location of buyer) and tailor the strategy to serve this segment to the exclusion of others. The goal is to exploit a narrow segment of a market. Of course, whether a focus strategy is feasible or not depends on the size of a segment and whether it can support the additional cost of focusing. Black Stump restaurants use a cost focus strategy to reach customers who do not want to pay the higher prices of traditional restaurants but who want a dining experience superior to that provided by a fast-food chain. The Range Rover, with its superior handling and ride and more comfortable interior, follows a differentiation focus strategy to gain an advantage over the Toyota Landcruiser and the Nissan Patrol.

Porter uses the term **stuck in the middle** to describe organisations that are unable to gain a competitive advantage by one of the previous strategies. Such organisations will have great difficulty achieving long-term success. When they do, according to Porter, it is usually a result of competing in a highly favourable industry or having all their rivals similarly stuck in the middle. Porter notes that successful organisations often get themselves into trouble by reaching beyond their competitive advantage and ending up stuck in the middle. Kmart, part of the Coles Myer retail chain, became stuck in the middle during the 1990s. Traditionally a discount store, with all the discount store attributes of basic store fittings and self-service, it allowed its cost structures and prices to rise to those of department stores, which offer far higher levels of service and comfort. Furthermore, it relied for much of its clothing sales on imported products. Imported garments, however, had long lead times before delivery and could be bought only in large quantities. Many of its buying decisions were incorrect and it ended up with large quantities of unsold merchandise. The subsequent discounting of poorly chosen products did nothing for Kmart's image. In an attempt to convince customers that it had returned to its discount roots, it introduced store-brand household products called Australia's Choice. This included products, such as AC Cola, which were priced at the discount end of the product range. However, this proved to be a poor merchandising decision because the products required a large amount of floor space but had a very small profit margin. Sales were up, but margins suffered. The AC brand products were then de-emphasised, leading to further confusion among customers as to where Kmart was positioned in the market.

differentiation strategy aims to achieve a unique position in an industry in ways that are widely valued by buyers

focus strategy aims at cost advantage or differentiation advantage in a narrow segment

stuck in the middle organisations are those unable to gain a competitive advantage through one of various strategies

TABLE 5.2 Skills, resources and structural requirements of Porter's strategic types

Generic strategy	Commonly required skills and resources	Common organisational requirements
Overall cost leadership	Sustained capital investment and access to capital Process engineering skills Intense supervision of labour Products designed for ease in manufacture Low-cost distribution system	Tight cost control Frequent, detailed control reports Structured organisation and responsibilities Incentives based on meeting strict quantitative targets
Differentiation	Strong marketing abilities Product engineering Creative flair Strong capability in basic research Corporate reputation for quality or technological leadership Long tradition in the industry or unique combination of skills drawn from other businesses Strong cooperation from channels	Strong coordination among functions in R&D, product development and marketing Subjective measurement and incentives instead of quantitative measures Amenities to attract highly skilled labour, scientists or creative people
Focus	Combination of the above policies directed at the particular strategic target	Combination of the above policies directed at the particular strategic target

What are the structural requirements of these four strategies? These are summarised in Table 5.2. First, no predictions are made for the stuck-in-the-middle strategy. Like the reactor strategy described by Miles and Snow, it is not recommended as a desirable route to success. Second, predictions have generally excluded the focus strategy for the simple reason that it is merely a derivative of one of the other two. So let's look at the two that are left: cost leadership and differentiation.

The goal of cost leadership is to achieve efficiencies through tight controls, minimisation of overheads and economies of scale. The best structure for achieving this end would be one that is high in complexity, high in formalisation and centralised. In contrast, a differentiation strategy relies essentially on the development of unique products. This demands a high degree of flexibility, which can best be achieved through low complexity, low formalisation and decentralised decision making.[17]

Strategy and globalisation

A glance at the strategy–structure relationships so far discussed reveals that they concentrate on operations in one country. One of the features of business over the past 20 years has been the rise of globalisation. This has been driven by a reduction in barriers to the flow of goods, services and capital between countries. What makes globalisation a challenge for those companies entering overseas markets is that it introduces a whole new set of complexities to their operations. Different countries exhibit variations in tastes, customs, practices, legal systems, as well as industry structures and technical sophistication. The challenges arising from globalisation permit us to further our investigation into the relationships between strategy and structure.

Two researchers, Bartlett and Ghoshal,[18] proposed a theory linking global strategy and structure. They claim that the strategy adopted when entering overseas markets depends on the interaction of cost pressures found in the market and the pressures for local responsiveness. Responding to cost pressures means that firms must work hard at reducing costs, while local responsiveness implies that products must be altered in some way to suit local tastes. Price-sensitive markets include those for mass-market cars, basic grocery products and economy air travel. Markets that are not so price-sensitive include those for luxury consumer goods, such as Louis Vuitton luggage or French perfume, specialist capital goods and defence equipment. Examples of products for which there is a high need for local responsiveness are banking and insurance, some clothing and food items, and retailing activities. Those products with a low need for local responsiveness include aircraft, commodities such as metals and paper, and petroleum products.

Barlett and Ghoshal propose that each of these quadrants requires a different entry strategy for a firm to be successful. The strategies are shown in Table 5.3. An

TABLE 5.3 Relationship between Bartlett and Ghoshal's strategic types and the corresponding structural elements

Strategy	Structural characteristics
International	Centralisation of core competencies, other tasks decentralised. Knowledge and strategy developed at the centre and transferred to local units. Local operations aimed at adapting and leveraging parent company competencies. Moderate need for coordination with few integrating mechanisms. Moderate need for culture control. Predominant structural form is worldwide divisionalisation based on product.
Mutidomestic	Decentralised and nationally self-sufficient units which sense and exploit local opportunities. Knowledge is developed and contained within each unit. Low need for coordination with almost no integrating mechanisms. Low need for a common culture. Predominant structural form is divisionalisation based on geographic area.
Global	Centralisation of most operating decisions. Knowledge developed and retained at the centre. Global scale of operations leads to requirement for intensive coordination and integration mechanisms. Extensive effort to promote a common culture. Predominant structural form based on worldwide product divisions.
Transnational	Mixed centralised and decentralised form with integrated worldwide operations. Knowledge jointly shared and developed worldwide. Units are dispersed, interdependent and specialised. Very high need for coordination and extensive coordinating mechanisms. Predominant structural form is a worldwide matrix.

international strategy to transfer valuable skills and product knowledge to overseas markets

multidomestic strategy aims to achieve maximum local responsiveness with products customised to meet local conditions

global strategy lowering costs by selling a common product on a global basis

transnational strategy attempts to achieve maximum local responsiveness while achieving worldwide economies of scale.

international strategy requires firms to transfer valuable skills and product knowledge to overseas markets. Some customisation may take place for local markets. Research and development is centralised in the home market, but manufacturing, distribution and marketing is carried out locally. Generally, however, the head office maintains tight control. Firms such as McDonald's, Unilever, Nestlé, IBM and Microsoft are examples of companies with international strategies. A **multidomestic strategy**, aims to achieve maximum local responsiveness with products customised to meet local conditions. In support of this firms tend to establish complete value chains in each of the major markets they serve. Achieving economies of scale and spreading experience around the firm is difficult using this strategy. Many Australian firms use multidomestic strategies, but not necessarily for the reasons identified by Bartlett and Ghoshal. Building materials companies must locate close to their customers as the cost of transport is high, and mining companies must go where the minerals are to be found. Service industries such as banking must also be located close to customers.

A **global strategy** is adopted where a product can be sold in most markets with very little modification. Firms using this strategy work very hard at lowering costs by locating activities where they make the most sense and through extensively engaging in practices that spread knowledge throughout the company. Firms are not spread too thinly; their activities are normally located in a few key centres, which provide cost and other benefits. Examples of this strategy are the major motor vehicle manufacturers like Toyota and General Motors and oil companies such as Shell and Mobil. The **transnational strategy** is very rare in practice. A transnational strategy attempts to achieve maximum local responsiveness while achieving worldwide economies of scale. Experience is spread throughout the organisation regardless of its origins, and firms are considered stateless with no obvious county of location. ABB, the Swiss–Swedish engineering company, is often considered to be one of the few transnational companies in existence.

Bartlett and Ghoshal proposed that each of these strategies required specific organisational structural characteristics to be effective. The structure appropriate to each strategy is shown in Table 5.3. Attempting to implement a strategy with an inappropriate structure would lead to underperformance and failure.

Bartlett and Ghoshal base their model on extensive research. In studying the attempts at overseas expansion by a number of companies, they determined that many failures arose not from lack of technological competence or inadequate product offering but from the lack of organisational capability. To be successful, they not only had to have an appropriate strategy for their product but they also needed a structure that fitted the strategy. Achieving this is not easy. Internationalisation puts many strains on established practices and managerial systems. New organisational control mechanisms take time to develop and implement and are subject to considerable political lobbying. This is particularly so for the behavioural aspects of control, such as organisational culture. Perhaps this is one of the reasons that so few truly global companies have emerged over the past 30 years.

The strategic types of Barlett and Ghoshal, and those of Miles and Snow and Porter, bear little relationship to each other. They are not, however, mutually exclusive. Miles and Snow and Porter concentrate on a strategy aimed at a single market. Barlett and Ghoshal develop strategies appropriate to internationalising firms. The theories do have in common the proposition that once a strategy is determined on,

OT CLOSEUP

ASEA-Brown Boveri—a transnational corporation?

When transnational strategies are spoken of, ASEA-Brown Boveri (ABB) is generally the company that springs to mind as being one of the few examples in existence. It was formed in 1987 with the merger of ASEA, a Swedish company, and Brown Boveri, based in Switzerland. The merger was overseen by the chief executive of the joint company, Percy Barnevick, and the structure he implemented remains the template for transnational corporations. To make integration matters more complex, over 70 more companies with over 100 000 employees have been added to the company since the original merger.

The structure introduced by Barnevick attempted to achieve what is one of the most difficult tasks in business—achieving global scale and world class technology while maintaining deep roots in the local community. In order to attain this he introduced a master matrix, in which one dimension consists of product-area managers, such as those responsible for electricity-generating equipment or locomotives within a certain geographic area. They make decisions on product strategy and performance without regard to national boundaries. The second dimension of the matrix are a large number of traditionally organised national companies run as profit centres and having close contact with their home markets. A typical profit centre at ABB is made up of only 50 people. A group of 250 global executives leads some 210 000 employees. Barnevick's own head office team of eight, based in Zurich, controls over 1300 companies, divided into 5000 profit centres located in 140 countries.

Barnevick, who has since retired, was a firm believer that decentralisation was the only way to make his structure work. Prior to the merger, Brown Boveri had 4000 people in its head office while ASEA had 2000. Barnevick had a poor opinion of head offices: the stultifying effect of bureaucracy, the distance between head office and customers, the lack of engagement and the absence of entrepreneurial spirit they engender were counterproductive to his aims. Needless to say, the head offices in their traditional sense were largely disbanded. Through the structure, ABB has tried to create small

business dynamism while being a big business. There are only five layers of management from the chief executive to the worker on the shop floor. No workshop is permitted to be bigger than 250 workers.

A string of locally focused companies would not make a great deal of sense, nor would it generate much in the way of return on assets. ABB achieves its economies by building into the structure synergies in research and development, economies of scale and distribution, and the sharing of information. Achieving these places a premium on communication and shared values. The shared values are promoted by the 'policy bible', which lays down the desired behaviours from all in the corporation. The second glue is the customer focus philosophy.

The structure at ABB has come in for its share of criticism. It is very reliant on the skills and ability of the 250 business area managers; if they do not understand the system or lack communication skills, it can have extensive repercussions for profitability. Another criticism is that the top eight executives are severely overstretched in having to reconcile so many business areas, countries and functions. There is also a tendency for responsibility for strategic decision making to be pushed to the highest levels in the organisation. In part this arises because of difficulties in allocating profits and making major investment decisions. There are also serious contradictions between the need for central control and the desire for entrepreneurial behaviour. And as local managers report to both a country manager and a business area manager, there is the danger of conflicting signals between the parties. Further problems arise in communicating with such a widespread and decentralised workforce. Critics argue that all this adds up to an unwieldy structure.

Shell, another archetypal multinational company, has had a form of matrix similar to ABB since the 1930s. It recently abandoned it to concentrate on clearly defined product lines.

Adapted from: Manfred Kets de Vries, 'Making a Giant Dance', *Across the Board*, 31(9), 1994, pp. 27–32.

it will be ineffective without an appropriate organisational structure. In other words, strategy causes structure.

Limitations to the strategy imperative

We have presented the positive case for strategy determining structure. Not surprisingly, as with many issues in organisation theory, there is another side to the debate.

No-one argues that strategy *cannot* determine structure. Attacks on the strategy imperative lie in questioning the degree of discretionary latitude that managers actually have. For instance, it seems logical that the impact of strategy would be greater in the early development period of an organisation. Once personnel have been hired, capital equipment has been purchased, and procedures and policies have been established, they are much more difficult to change. When the organisation is in its infancy, vested interests have yet to be solidified. But once a firm becomes established, managers may be severely restricted in their discretion. Organisations cannot change their technology very easily. Similarly, it is logical that the capital-to-labour ratio in an organisation will affect the impact of strategy on structure. If the ratio is low—that is, it is labour-intensive—managers have much more flexibility, and hence discretion, to effect change and influence structure. Clothing manufacturers, for instance, can easily change the cut, style and colour of clothing. In contrast, cement manufacturers have little alternative but to make cement.

Another challenge to the strategy imperative deals with the lag factor. When management implements a new strategy, there is often no immediate change in structure. Does this suggest that structure does not follow strategy? Advocates of a strong strategy–structure relationship say no. They point out that there is often a lag: structures respond to changes in strategy, but slowly. At the extreme, this lag argument can almost be considered an apology for the strategy-structure relationship.[19] If researchers fail to find a strategy–structure relationship in the study of an organisation, they can always claim that there is a lag and that structure just hasn't caught up yet. More realistically, however, we find that this lag is not a purely random phenomenon. Some organisations are slower to adapt their structures to changes in strategy than are others. The major factor affecting response is the degree of competitive pressure. The less competition an organisation faces, the less rapid its structural response.[20] Without competition, the concern for efficiency is reduced. So we would conclude that where an organisation faces minimal competition, there is likely to be a significant lag between changes in strategy and modifications in structure.

A further factor to consider is that although we talk about strategy as a stand-alone topic, it does not exist independently of other impacts on organisational structure such as technology and environment. Motor vehicle manufacturers, for instance, are in the business of mass production regardless of the preferences of senior management. This implies that their strategic options are limited; the technology of mass production limits the extent to which cars can be customised. Those firms producing commodities similarly face restrictions on their strategic choice. Producers of minerals, electricity, cement, basic building materials and agricultural products find it difficult to differentiate their product. The only strategy open to them is one based on cost containment and price leadership.

Could strategy follow structure?

Is it possible that strategy and structure are positively related but that the causal arrow is the opposite from what we've assumed? Perhaps structure determines strategy! One author acknowledges at least the logical possibility, 'as when a multi-divisional structure is installed because everyone else is doing it and then an acquisitions strategy is developed to make the structure viable'.[21] Structure may limit strategic choices and channel strategy in certain directions.

A little thought would certainly suggest that structure could influence strategy. Structure can motivate or impede strategic activity as well as simply constrain strategic choices. For instance, strategic decisions made in a centralised structure are typically going to have less diversity of ideas and are more likely to be consistent

OT CLOSEUP

Cemex's structure leads its strategy

When thinking of multinational companies, Mexico and cement don't immediately spring to mind. But one of the most successful cement manufacturers in the world is Cemex, a Mexican cement manufacturer. It is managed by Lorenzo Zambrano, the grandson of the founder who happens to be a great believer in the benefits of using information technology to manage his business better. Cement is basically a commodity, so the greatest returns go to the cheapest producer. Zambrano has used information technology to relentlessly reduce costs of operations in his Mexican plants. On taking up the CEO's position in 1985, he chafed at the lack of ready data to identify how well his plants were performing. He set up an IT department to devise programs to provide him with automated plant reports. Over time, a system was set up to transmit performance data from satellite plants to the head office in Monterey in northern Mexico. Automation has not only reduced staffing—it has permitted ongoing functions such as quality control, kiln temperatures and even sales to be constantly monitored from a central location. Cemex was an early user of e-mail, constantly keeping touch with managers in the plants and asking them to explain any deviation from optimal operations or sales targets.

Once the cement is mixed and loaded onto one of the ready-mixed concrete trucks it must be poured within 90 minutes. Cemex has developed a program to improve the logistics of its delivery system to meet the tight time frames. By putting a computer and global positioner in each truck, Cemex has been able to introduce a system that not only calculates which truck should go where but enables dispatchers to redirect trucks as the need arises.

Until Mr Zambrano took over the running of the company, Cemex was a typical conglomerate with interests not only in cement but also in hotels, petrochemicals and mining. These latter interests were disposed of very early in Mr Zambrano's term to allow the concentration on cement. But by 1990 Mr Zambrano realised that the structure he had developed was an excellent platform for expanding overseas, particularly into Third World countries. Since that time he has bought cement plants in Asia, Egypt and Central and South America. He has also expanded into Spain and the United States. Whenever Cemex makes an acquisition it imposes its IT system and the organisational structure that has worked so well in Mexico.

Cemex is now the third-largest cement manufacturer in the world, and it has got there by strategy following its structure.

Adapted from: Business: The Cemex Way, *The Economist*, London, June 16, 2001.

over time than in a decentralised organisation, where input is likely to be diverse and the people providing that input change, depending on the situation.

A further pointer to structure influencing strategy is the existence of what are called legacy systems (see Figure 5.6). Any company of long standing has legacy systems; these are the established ways of doing things, often reflected in rules and regulations and standard operating procedures. These take time to establish and once in place channel thinking into predetermined patterns. Problems are defined and interpreted in ways that make sense to the organisation. Solutions are based on what the organisation can put in place through its standard practices. As a result, strategy becomes a projection of past actions based on what the organisation can structurally achieve. Of course, organisations can change their structure, but this is not undertaken without difficulty, as we will see in later chapters.

FIGURE 5.6 Structure–strategy relationship

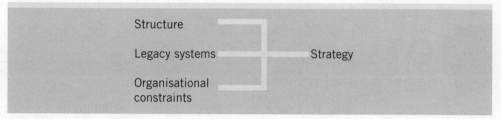

What is the research indicating that structure determines strategy? A study of 110 large manufacturing firms found that strategy followed structure.[22] Another study of 54 large firms found that structure influences and constrains strategy, rather than the other way round.[23] If further research were to support these conclusions, we could state that as a structural determinant, strategy is of limited importance.

The industry–structure relationship

Closely related to the issue of strategy's impact on structure is the role of industry as a determinant of structure. There are distinguishing characteristics of industries that affect the strategies they will choose.[24] Therefore, as shown in Figure 5.7, strategy may be merely an intermediate step between the unique characteristics of the industry in which the organisation operates and the structure it implements to achieve alignment.

Industries differ in terms of growth possibilities, regulatory constraints, barriers to entry, capital requirements and numerous other factors: 'Simply knowing the industry in which an organization operates allows one to know something about product life cycles, required capital investments, long-term prospects, types of production technologies, regulatory requirements, and so forth'.[25] Public utilities, for example, face little competition, normally produce a single product such as water or

FIGURE 5.7 Industry–structure relationship

electricity, and so can have more tightly controlled structures. Similarly, if a firm is in the motor vehicle industry and seeks to competitively produce cars to sell in the $15 000–$20 000 range, it will need to be extremely large in size and use standardised operations—in other words, probably a global firm. In some industries, strategic options are relatively few. The home computer industry, as a case in point, is rapidly becoming the exclusive province of companies that compete on a high-volume, low-cost basis. The alcoholic beverage industry supports a much broader range of strategic options—competing on manufacturing, marketing or product-innovation bases.

To illustrate how industry can affect structure, let us take two variables that tend to differ by industry category—capital requirements for entry, and product-innovation rates. Figure 5.8 shows four industry categories with examples for each. Type A industries rate high on both variables, while type C industries are high on capital requirements and low on product innovation. The high capital requirements tend to result in large organisations and a limited number of competitors. Firms in type A and C industries will be highly structured and standardised, with the type Cs being more decentralised to facilitate rapid response to innovations introduced by competitors. Type B and D industries, because of low capital requirements, tend to be made up of a large number of small firms. Type D, however, is likely to have more division of labour and more formalisation than type B, because low product innovation allows greater standardisation. In the same way as capital requirements influence organisational size and number of competitors, we should expect high product-innovation rates to result in less formalisation and more decentralisation of decision making.

The preceding analysis argues that industry categories *do* influence structure. While there are certainly intraindustry differences—Colgate-Palmolive and Avon are both in personal-care products but use very different marketing channels—there is a high degree of similarity within industry categories. These similarities lead to strategies that tend to have largely common elements, and this results in structural characteristics that are very similar.

FIGURE 5.8 Two variable analyses of industries

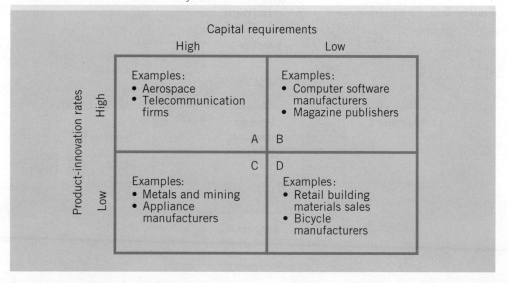

The power of combinations—the strategy of industrial networks

This chapter has concentrated on the strategies, and the corresponding structures, of individual companies. It infers that individual companies have sole responsibility for choosing a strategy. However, recent years have seen the growth of interfirm structures, which pool their resources through strategic alliances and other forms of cooperation.[26] This means that in many cases **networks** of companies, as well as individual companies, implement strategies. It also means that the strategies of individual companies are both shaped and constrained by other companies with which they have commercial relationships. The network's strategy can influence individual firms' strategy.

networks groups of companies that pool their resources in various ways

We can identify a number of different forms of networks and strategic alliances. The first is where there is a dominant company which clearly leads a group of subcontractors.[27] The motor car companies such as Ford, General Motors and Toyota, and aircraft manufacturers such as Boeing and Airbus, are typical examples. Take the example of Ford building a new Falcon. Motor cars are composed of many different systems such as brakes, gearboxes, engines, fuel systems and computerised engine management. Ford, as project manager, defines broadly what it wants from, say, the brake manufacturer and then lets the brake manufacturer design and manufacture the brake system. As a result, a Falcon is composed of the cooperative efforts of the brake manufacturer and a large number of different specialist suppliers, all working together as a *network*. The aircraft manufacturers such as Boeing take the sharing of research and development and manufacturing a step further. Hawker De Haviland in Australia may undertake to design part of the wing for the Boeing 777. But it does this for a share in the 777 project. If the aircraft is successful, Hawker shares the profits with Boeing: if it fails; Hawker may be lucky to make money from the venture. The attraction for Boeing is that the risks associated with introducing a new aircraft, which are always high, are shared among many different designers and manufacturers. Should the aircraft not prove to be commercially successful, Boeing's survival is not threatened. An example of an industrial network is given in Figure 5.9.

FIGURE 5.9 Example of an industrial network

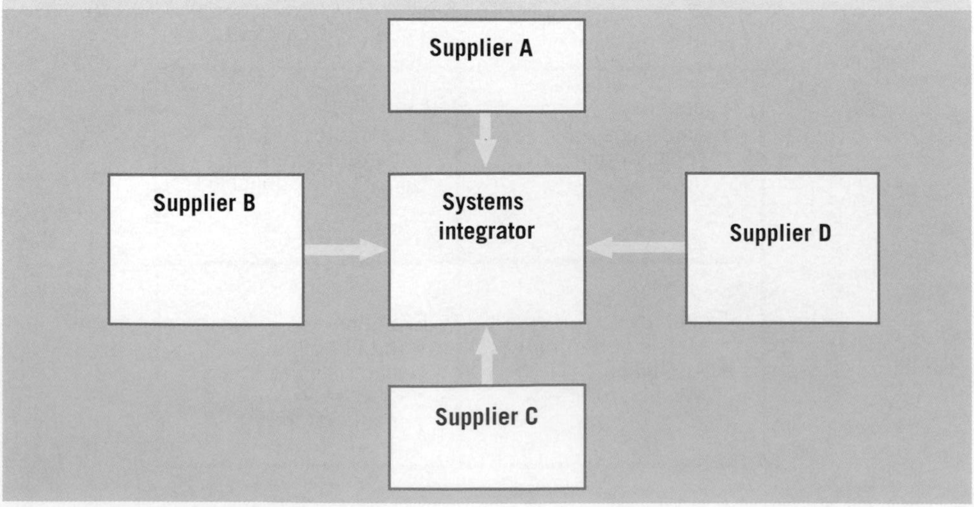

Another type of network arises when there is not a leading company or project manager to offer direction or control.[28] The personal computer industry provides us with a good example. The personal computer is made up of many different parts, such as the monitor, hard disc, power supply, microprocessors and motherboard. Designing and putting into production each of these requires extensive research and development and investment in manufacturing capacity. In an industry that is very dispersed and decentralised, it is clearly beyond the capability of any one company to develop all aspects of the personal computer by itself. So each company concentrates on what it is good at, selling its components to computer assemblers, who are generally close to the customer. There is even a futures market for the output of the specialist manufacturers.

OT CLOSEUP
Underground visionaries

It is becoming increasingly common for technologically leading-edge industries to exist as clusters. One of these clusters, based on mineral exploration technology, has developed in Perth around the Australian Resources Research Centre (ARRC). The ARRC is a purpose-built centre which houses the CSIRO divisions of exploration and mining, petroleum and mineral products research, as well as Curtin University's department of exploration geophysics. Rio Tinto's research laboratories are a short distance away.

Scattered around Perth are many independent, and sometimes informal, research efforts funded by mining companies and specialty research teams. These are undertaking research into mining industry-related fields such as airborne aeromagnetics, three-dimensional computer modelling of underground resources, and the use of bacteria to liberate nickel and other metals from low-grade ore.

The cluster has no formal membership or association; it does not exist as a legal entity. But each part supports the other with information, sharing of ideas and resources, and sometimes personnel. Top researchers are also attracted by the proximity of other researchers and potential employers. As each part of the cluster concentrates on a specialised area, collaborators are close by for the more complex research tasks. And, of course, the educational institutions, such as Curtin, benefit from drawing on the research capabilities close by, and the cluster benefits from the supply of skilled graduates produced by Curtin.

Adapted from: Tim Treadgold, 'Underground Visionaries', *Business Review Weekly*, 20 April 2001, p. 76.

Networks of these types are often called *clusters* and are generally coordinated by market forces.[29] Networks in the computer industry have developed in places such as Silicon Valley in California and on the coastal China–Hong Kong–Taiwan axis. Similar networks have developed in other industries. The entertainment industry has a cluster around Los Angeles. And New York and London form a cluster in banking and financial services. In Australia there are clusters of tourism and financial services around Sydney, a wine cluster in South Australia, and the motor vehicle industry is networked around the Melbourne-based car manufacturers (see Figure 5.10). There is also a cluster of fast-ferry manufacturers around Kwinana in Western Australia.

FIGURE 5.10 Example of an industrial cluster

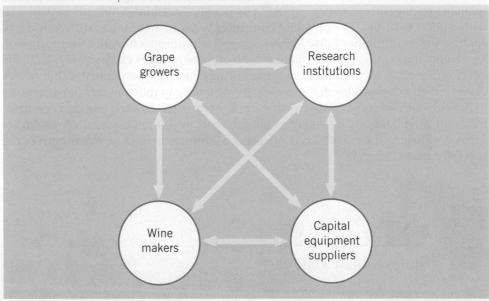

A third type of relationship is the *strategic alliance*. The strategic alliance is a management term for two or more companies which cooperate in a venture by each contributing their distinctive skills while maintaining their independence. Strategic alliances can exist in engineering design and construction, in the marrying of new technologies (e.g. computers and television) and in relationships between manufacturers and distributors. The relationship between the strategic alliance partners is often formalised through contracts and letters of agreement, although there is generally a high level of trust between the partners.

The various forms of relationships we have discussed indicate that looking at individual companies and their strategies in the networks or alliances gives us an incomplete picture of what is actually being produced. The success of any individual company largely depends on the success of the network or the grouping. And if a network leader fails, or the network loses its competitive edge, then the chances of the businesses in the network surviving are greatly diminished.

How does being in a strategic alliance, or being a specialist producer in a network of companies, affect the structure of the organisation? This depends partly on the size of the company and the role it plays in the network. Obviously Ford will have a different structure from that of the manufacturer of windscreen wipers, if only because of their different size. But all the relationships we have discussed have allowed the various participants to concentrate on what they do best. Brake manufacturers don't have to worry about designing engine management systems. Hard disk manufacturers are not concerned with motherboards. Developers of aircraft navigation systems don't need to concern themselves with landing equipment. But each in its own way contributes to the success of the final product. By specialising, companies can reduce their complexity by narrowing the range of products they produce. And they can get more out of their research and development efforts, and probably be more innovative, by knowing their product in greater detail. They can also generate economies from specialising their manufacturing on a narrower range of products. Consequently they enjoy the benefits of simpler, less complex structures with smaller investment in coordinating devices.

Many companies that are part of dense networks don't neatly fit any of the typologies we have mentioned. They are defenders, actively trying to protect their position against competitors and seeking cost advantages. As they do this by constantly being at the leading edge of their field, which is often very narrow, they also embody the characteristics of the prospector. They are not altogether analysers, however, because they are not seeking to copy other companies' inventions and innovations; they would rather generate their own.

In many ways the use of networks is growing. Most complex products are manufactured by networks of companies. It is also natural for expert companies in many fields to gather together to share resources and ideas while being in competition with each other. One of the means of doing this is trade fairs. A problem facing companies in Australia and New Zealand is their distance from most of the financial and manufacturing networks, with the consequent problems faced by suppliers in integrating with them.

Summary

The early position on 'what determines structure' was the organisation's goals and strategies. Structure was seen as just a rational means of facilitating the attainment of goals. More recently, strategy has been offered as but one of a number of variables vying for the crown of 'major determinant of structure'.

Strategy was defined as including both the long-term goals of an organisation plus a course of action that would provide the means towards their attainment. To some it is seen as planned in advance; others view it as evolving over time as a pattern in a stream of significant decisions.

Chandler studied nearly 100 of America's largest business firms and concluded that 'structure follows strategy'. While there is considerable support for this thesis, the limitations in his research restrict any wide generalisation of his findings. Miles and Snow offered a four-category strategy–structure typology that allowed for specific structural predictions. Analysis of major firms in the retailing industry confirmed this typology's predictive capability. Porter proposed that organisations can pursue one of four strategies: cost leadership, differentiation, focus, and stuck in the middle. Specific structural predictions could be made for the first two strategies. Bartlett and Ghoshal examined how the globalisation of a firm's operations may affect the structure it adopts.

Attacks on the strategy imperative have generally focused on three points: (a) managerial discretion over changes in strategy may be considerably less than suggested; (b) where competition is low, the lag may make the interaction between strategy and structure appear almost unrelated; and (c) structure may determine strategy rather than vice versa.

The industry in which organisations operate was introduced as an important factor influencing strategy and, hence, structure. Industries differ in terms of growth possibilities, regulatory constraints, barriers to entry and so forth. Most firms within a given industry share these characteristics. The result is that firms within industry categories tend to have similar organisation structures.

Another issue to be considered in relation to strategy is the influence of industry networks. Components for many complex products, such as motor cars and computers, are produced by a dense network of interlinked suppliers, each specialising in a particular component. The final product of the network may bear little relationship to its component parts. The challenge for the study of strategy and structure is to develop a theory that can link the actions of individual companies to the evolving strategy of the network, particularly as the strategy of many networks is not the result of planning or managerial decision making.

For review and discussion

1   What is an 'imperative'?

2   'The strategy imperative is based on classical economic assumptions.' Construct an argument to support this statement.

3   Contrast planning and evolutionary modes. Which dominates the management-theory literature?

4   What is Chandler's thesis? What evidence does he present to support this thesis?

5   What criticisms can you direct at Chandler's research?

6   Does Chandler's thesis have any application to small-business management?

7   If structures are relatively stable over time, does this imply that strategies don't change?

8   Using Miles and Snow's typology, describe the structure that would align with each strategy type.

9   How can Bartlett and Ghoshal's classification be reconciled with the strategies adopted in each individual country which a firm operates?

10 Under what conditions might you expect strategy to exert a significant influence on structure?

11 'Strategy follows structure rather than vice versa.' Construct an argument to support this statement. Then construct one to refute it.

12 Do you think there is any relationship between an organisation's life-cycle stage and organisational strategies? Explain.

13 How are strategy and industry categories related?

14 Using Figure 5.8 as a guide, select examples of firms that you believe fit into each of the four boxes. Do these firms' structures align with the predictions made for each box?

15 How might industry networks affect the strategy of those firms which are members of them?

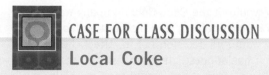

CASE FOR CLASS DISCUSSION
Local Coke

By any measure, Coca-Cola would appear high on anyone's list of globalised companies. It is one of the most recognisable brand names around the world and is sold in more markets than most other products. You would consider therefore that Coca-Cola, or 'Coke' as it is perhaps better known, would be the main exponent of the 'act global, think local' mantra often quoted as encapsulating the strategy to success in world markets. But Coca-Cola rejects such thought, and says that thinking global is not the way to go; its preferred mantra is 'think local, act local'.

What has drawn Coca-Cola to this way of thinking is a combination of the need to seek growth in what is a slow-growing market segment. As companies seek to have a dominant position in world markets they are finding themselves in a financial vice: their cost of capital is at least 10%, but world markets are growing at little more than 3%—hence, for Coca-Cola, the imperative to diversify into markets other than carbonated beverages. Coke, Fanta and Sprite are all Coca-Cola brands.

Coca-Cola has an unusual structure for a globalised company. The Coca-Cola Company has its head office in Atlanta, Georgia. It owns the brand and performs various administrative and coodinating activities. It also undertakes extensive market and product research and development and manufactures and sells the concentrate to bottlers around the world. The Coca-Cola Company has various subsidiary companies around the world, based on geographic area, reporting back to the head office. The companies that dilute the concentrate and then bottle and distribute the product are independent companies. They own a franchise to bottle and sell Coke products within a certain geographic area and have the responsibility to undertake local promotional activities for their product. The Coca-Cola Company often owns part of the bottlers. For instance, it owns 36% of Coca-Cola Amatil, the local Australian bottler.

Coca-Cola is consumed in radically differently ways around the world and has a varied market penetration. Carbonated drinks, like Coke and Fanta, themselves have different penetrations against non-carbonated drinks such as juice, coffee and bottled water. In Australia Coca-Cola is primarily consumed as a refresher, with sales being higher in the summer months. In other countries it is seen as drink to relax with. The attraction of Diet Coke varies with age and gender, even in markets as similar as Australia and New Zealand. In addition, different levels of economic development affect customer behaviour and product type. Distribution systems also vary from country to country, making local knowledge extremely important in trying to gain market share.

Although the relationship between the Coca-Cola Company and its bottlers is basically sound, their returns derive from different activities. The main company in Atlanta basically obtains its income from selling intangibles, with its main asset being brand names. It also derives profits from selling concentrate to bottlers. The bottlers, however, have sunk considerable capital into fixed plant and equipment and are seeking a return on the large amount of funds invested. As a result, much of the research into new product development is undertaken by the Coca-Cola Company's own subsidiaries around the world.

New product development is concentrated on extending the product range beyond carbonated drinks, into areas such as bottled water, juice-based drinks and in some countries products such as iced tea. Thinking local and acting local derives from Coca-Cola's experience that what works well in one country cannot be guaranteed to work well in another. As a consequence it needs the flexibility to react to local market needs. It is at the level of the bottler that the localisation strategy has the potential to create problems. Maintaining a competitive edge in what is essentially a commodity business of bottling and distributing is more difficult than maintaining a competitive edge based on intellectual property, which is the strength of the Coca-Cola company of Atlanta.

Adapted from: David James, 'Local Coke', *Business Review Weekly*, 26 September 2001, pp. 70–4.

QUESTIONS

1 Identify the different levels of strategy discussed in the case. Why would the different levels of strategy lead to different structural requirements?

2 Using Miles and Snow's and Porter's typologies, how would you describe the strategies of the Coca-Cola Company and Coca-Cola Amatil? How closely does the strategy fit the typology?

3 Why wouldn't the Coca-Cola Company want to own its own bottling and distribution facilities? How would its decision not to, affect the strategies it has adopted? If it did own the bottling facilities, in what way would the Coca-Cola Company's structure differ from its present one?

4 Identify how the structures of the Coca-Cola Company and Coca-Cola Amatil are likely to differ? Provide reasons for your answer.

FURTHER READING

Christopher Bartlett & Sumantra Ghoshal, *Managing Across Borders*, Boston MA: Harvard Business School Press, 1991.

Alfred D. Chandler, Jr, *Strategy and Structure: Chapters in the History of the Industrial Enterprise,* Cambridge, MA.: MIT Press, 1962, p. 13.

Raymond E. Miles & Charles C. Snow, *Organizational Strategy, Structure, and Process*, New York: McGraw-Hill, 1978.

Michael E. Porter, *Competitive Strategy: Techniques for Analyzing Industries and Competitors*, New York: Free Press, 1980; and *Competitive Advantage: Creating and Sustaining Superior Performance*, New York: Free Press, 1985.

Ralph Stacey, *Strategic Management and Organizational Dynamics,* 2nd edn, London: Pitman, 1996.

NOTES

1 This section is drawn from the Goodman Fielder Annual Report, 2001.

2 Joseph McGuire, *Theories of Business Behavior*, Englewood Cliffs, NJ: Prentice Hall, 1964, p. 47.

3 Alfred D. Chandler, Jr, *Strategy and Structure: Chapters in the History of the Industrial Enterprise,* Cambridge, MA: MIT Press, 1962, p. 13.

4 Henry Mintzberg, 'Research in Strategy-Making', *Proceedings of the Academy of Management,* 32nd meeting, Minneapolis, 1972, pp. 90–4.

5 H.A. Simon, *Models of Man: Rational and Irrational*, New York: Wiley, 1957.

6 C.E. Lindblom, 'The Science of Muddling Through', *Public Administration Review*, 19, 1959, pp. 78–88.

7 Chandler, *Strategy and Structure: Chapters in the History of the Industrial Enterprise*; Alfred D. Chandler, *The Visible Hand: The Managerial Revolution in American Business*, Cambridge, MA: The Belknap Press, 1977; Alfred D. Chandler, *Scale and Scope: the Dynamics of Industrial Capitalism*, Cambridge, MA: The Belknap Press, 1990.

8 Chandler, *Strategy and Structure: Chapters in the History of the Industrial Enterprise*, p. 15.

9 ibid., p. 16.

10 See, for instance, John M. Stopford, 'Growth and Organizational Change in the Multinational Firm', DBA dissertation, Harvard Business School, 1968; and Peter H. Grinyer, Masoud Yasai-Ardekani & Shawki Al-Bazzaz, 'Strategy, Structure, the Environment, and Financial Performance in 48 United Kingdom Companies', *Academy of Management Journal,* June 1980, pp. 193–226.

11 Stopford, 'Growth and Organizational Change in the Multinational Firm'; and Richard P. Rumelt, 'Strategy, Structure, and Economic Performance', Graduate School of Business Administration, Harvard University, 1974.

12 Leonard Wrigley, 'Divisional Autonomy and Diversification', DBA dissertation, Harvard Business School, 1970.

13 John B. Miner, *Theories of Organizational Structure and Process*, Chicago: Dryden Press, 1982, p. 315.

14 Raymond E. Miles & Charles C. Snow, *Organizational Strategy, Structure, and Process*, New York: McGraw-Hill, 1978.

15 Raymond E. Miles, Charles C. Snow, Alan D. Meyer & Henry J. Coleman, Jr, 'Organizational Strategy, Structure, and Process', *Academy of Management Review,* July 1978, p. 553.

16 Michael E. Porter, *Competitive Strategy: Techniques for Analyzing Industries and Competitors*, New York: Free Press, 1980; and *Competitive Advantage: Creating and Sustaining Superior Performance*, New York: Free Press, 1985.

17 See, for example, Vijay Govindarajan, 'Decentralization, Strategy, and Effectiveness of Strategic Business Units in Multibusiness Organizations', *Academy of Management Review*, October 1986, pp. 844–56; and Danny Miller, 'Relating Porter's Business Strategies to Environment and Structure: Analysis and Performance Implications', *Academy of Management Journal*, June 1988, pp. 280–308.

18 This section is drawn from Christopher Bartlett & Sumantra Ghoshal, *Managing Across Borders*, Boston MA: Harvard Business School Press, 1991.

19 Miner, *Theories of Organizational Structure and Process*, p. 316.

20 Gareth P. Dyas & Heinz T. Thanheiser, *The Emerging European Enterprise: Strategy and Structure in French and German Industry*, Boulder, CO: Westview Press, 1976; and Lawrence G. Franko, *The European Multinationals: A Renewed Challenge to American and British Big Business*, Stamford, CN: Greylock, 1976.

21 Miner, *Theories of Organizational Structure and Process*, p. 315.

22 Barbara W. Keats & Michael Hitt, 'A Causal Model of Linkages Among Environmental Dimensions, Macro Organizational Characteristics, and Performance', *Academy of Management Journal*, September 1988, pp. 570–98.

23 Robert A. Pitts, 'The Strategy-Structure Relationship: An Exploration into Causality', working paper, Pennsylvania State University, 1979.

24 Raymond E. Miles & Charles C. Snow, 'Toward a Synthesis in Organization Theory', in M. Jelinek, J.A. Litterer & R.E. Miles, eds, *Organizations by Design: Theory and Practice*, Plano, TX: Business Publications, 1981, pp. 548–50.

25 Peter Lorange & Johan Roos, 'Why Some Strategic Alliances Succeed and Others Fail', *Journal of Business Strategy*, January/February 1991, pp. 25–30.

26 'Contract Manufacturing: Make it Up', *The Economist*, 27 January 1996, p. 62.

27 For a description of such a network, see 'Silicon Valley', *The Economist*, 29 March 1997 (survey included in the issue).

28 Michael Porter, *The Competitive Advantage of Nations*, London: Macmillan, 1990.

29 ibid.

CHAPTER 6

Organisation size

After reading this chapter you should be able to:

1 define organisation size;

2 list the pros and cons of large size;

3 summarise the conclusions from the Aston Group's research;

4 describe the effect of size on complexity, formalisation and centralisation;

5 describe the special problems facing large organisations and how organisation theory can help solve them;

6 list which organisation theory issues are of greater and lesser importance to small-business managers;

7 discuss the trend towards organisational downsizing.

Introduction

A case of two oil companies

The oil company BP is one of the world's biggest companies. It is a British company with headquarters in London. It has a market capitalisation of $400 billion, 107 000 employees, and worldwide operations ranging from oil exploration and oilfield development through to retailing activities. Oil Search is another oil company. You have probably not heard of it. It is based in Papua New Guinea and was established in 1936 to search for oil in that country. It did not find any oil until the late 1980s and, owing to the small size of the findings and the difficult terrain in which it operates, has made little in the way of profits. It is, however, sitting on a large quantity of natural gas, which it hopes to sell onto the Queensland market by building a pipeline from Papua New Guinea down the Queensland coast. Difficulties in obtaining customers and political uncertainty have delayed the project. Oil Search has only a few hundred employees and a market capitalisation of $700 million. Just a glance at these two companies, which operate in the same industry, suggests that their structures would differ. BP has worldwide operations, while Oil Search operates in just one country; the complexity of Oil Search's operations is not as great, so we would expect fewer departments and would expect to find far fewer people involved in activities such as planning and coordination. By looking at these two organisations we might therefore conclude that size influences structure.

Even to a casual observer, the influence of organisational size on structure should be obvious. But the observation that size influences structure may be complemented by research into the nature of this influence. We know from the limitations on the span of control that as more operative employees are added there will be greater need for supervision, and as a result we will find more layers of management. We also know that as the number of employees increase there will be an expansion of job specialisation, with the result that there will be a greater range of skills and job orientations. While this may lead to increased effectiveness of a given group, the problems of intergroup coordination increase as each group focuses on its own activities. This will lead to increased layers of management and more sophisticated coordination devices. An expansion in size is also likely to result in spatial differentiation as the organisation operates over a wider geographic area. This increase in complexity will reduce top management's ability to directly supervise activities within the organisation. The control achieved through direct surveillance, therefore, will be replaced by the implementation of formal rules and regulations. This increase in formalisation may be accompanied by still greater horizontal differentiation as management creates new units to coordinate the expanding and diverse activities of organisational members. These may take the form of planning and coordinating teams. Finally, with top management further removed from the operating level, it becomes more difficult for senior executives to make rapid and informed decisions. The solution is to substitute decentralised decision making for centralisation. Following this reasoning, we see changes in size leading to major structural changes.

While the preceding description is logical enough, does it actually happen this way in practice? This chapter, after addressing the issue of defining size, reviews the evidence on the size–structure relationship and attempts to test the validity of our logical scenario.

Defining organisation size

There is wide agreement by organisation theory researchers on how an organisation's size is determined. **Organisation size** is generally accepted as referring to the total number of employees.[1] Over 80% of studies use this measure of size in their research. This is consistent with the assumption that as it is people and their interactions that are structured, their number should be more closely associated with structure than with any other size measure. However, substantial agreement among researchers on what constitutes an organisation's size is no assurance that they are right!

For example, the total number of employees may be an adequate measure for organisations composed solely of full-time employees. But what if the organisation has a large number of part-time workers? How are they to be counted? Or what if the business is seasonal? It's not unusual for retail stores to increase their sales staff by 50% during the Christmas holiday season. How should these seasonal workers be assessed? The issue of long-term subcontractors working within the organisation also needs to be considered. And counting the total number of employees doesn't distinguish among different types of industries. A small beauty parlour may have three employees, while one with 20 employees would be quite large. On the other hand, a university with 500 employees is small compared with most universities, which have several thousand employees. Should the measure of an organisation's size—and the subsequent assessment of whether it is small or large—be qualified to reflect industry norms? Finally, it has been noted that using a count of the total number of employees as the measure of organisational size inherently mixes size with efficiency.[2] If one organisation requires 100 people to carry out the same activities performed by 50 people in another organisation, is the first twice as large or merely half as efficient? The answers to these questions are not easy.

A further consideration is the nature of the business that an organisation is in. Retailers such as Coles Myer or Woolworths are basically composed of the same organisational units, namely stores and logistics operations, replicated numerous times. Although extremely large as measured by numbers of employees, their structure is not as complex as the basic number of employees suggests. Contrast this with an integrated steelworks, where there is almost no duplication of function. While the steelworks would have far fewer employees, it would have a more complex structure.

Although it can be argued that different measures of size are not interchangeable,[3] and as we have seen have limitations, most of the evidence suggests that counting the total number of employees is as good as many other measures. The reason for this is that total number is closely related to other measures of size. For instance, one study found the correlation between number of employees and the organisation's net assets to be 0.78.[4] Number of employees also appears valid in hospitals and educational institutions. The correlation between total hospital labour force and average daily patient load was found to exceed 0.96,[5] whereas size of full-time and part-time teaching and lecturing staff correlates with student enrolment at above 0.94.[6] One can conclude from these studies that the total number of employees is closely related to other popular gauges of size. As such, it should be a fairly accurate measure across organisations.

organisation size
the total number of employees in the organisation

Advocates of the size imperative

One of the strongest arguments for the importance of size as a determinant of structure has been made by Peter Blau. On the basis of studies of government agencies, universities and department stores, he concludes that 'size is the most important condition affecting the structure of organisations'.[7] In one of Blau's most-cited studies, he looked at 53 American employment-security agencies, whose responsibilities included administering unemployment insurance and providing employment services. His analysis included the structure of over 1200 local agency branches and 350 headquarters divisions.[8] What Blau found was that increasing size promotes structural differentiation but at a decreasing rate. Increases in organisation size are accompanied by initially rapid and subsequently more gradual increases in the number of local branches into which the agency is spatially dispersed, the number of official occupational positions expressing division of labour, the number of vertical levels in the hierarchy, the number of functional divisions at the headquarters, and the number of sections per division. This implied an increase in complexity with size, but only up to a point. Blau's conclusions are visually depicted in Figure 6.1: an increase of, say, 500 employees when an organisation has only 300 has a significantly larger impact on structural differentiation than an addition of 500 employees to an organisation that already employs 2300. That is, the difference between X´ and Y´ is smaller than the difference between X and Y.

FIGURE 6.1 Increases in organisation size affect differentiation at a decreasing rate

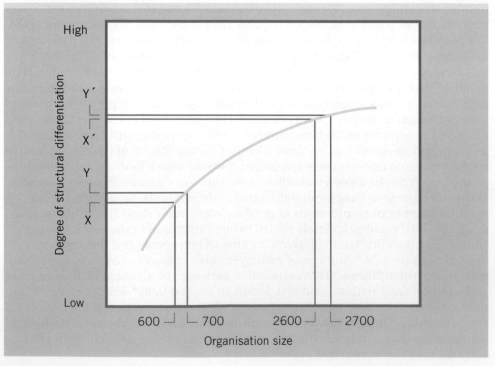

Research at the University of Aston in England also found size to be the major determinant of structure.[9] For example, the **Aston Group** looked at 46 organisations and found that increased size was associated with greater specialisation and formalisation. They concluded that 'an increased scale of operation increases the frequency of recurrent events and the repetition of decisions', which makes standardisation preferable.[10]

One researcher's efforts to replicate the Aston findings resulted in supportive evidence.[11] He found that organisational size was related positively to specialisation, formalisation and vertical span, and negatively to centralisation. In further comparing his results with Blau, he concluded that 'larger organizations are more specialized, have more rules, more documentation, more extended hierarchies and a greater decentralization of decision making further down such hierarchies'.[12] He also agreed with Blau that the impact of size on these dimensions expanded at a decreasing rate as size increased. That is, as size increased, specialisation, formalisation and vertical span also increased but at a declining rate, whereas centralisation decreased but at a declining rate as size increased.

One of the strongest cases for the size imperative has been made by Meyer.[13] Acknowledging that a relationship between size and structural dimensions does not imply causation, he designed a research project that allowed for causal inferences. He created a longitudinal study of 194 government departments of finance in the United States. He compared them over a five-year period. He argued that only by comparing organisations over time would it be possible to determine the time ordering of variables. That is, even if size and structure were found to be related among a set of organisations at a specific time, only a longitudinal analysis would permit the elimination of the counter-hypothesis that structure causes size. Meyer's findings led him to conclude that 'one cannot underestimate the impact of size on other characteristics of organizations'.[14] Specifically, he found that the effects of size showed everywhere; the relationship was unidirectional (i.e. size caused structure but not the reverse); and the impact of other variables that appeared to affect structure disappeared when size was controlled.

Other research has revealed insight into how size may affect organisation structure and operations. One study found that larger organisations were slower at adopting innovations than their smaller counterparts.[15] However, innovations adopted by larger organisations tended to be more complex in scope. Another study found that larger organisations put greater effort into socialising new employees compared to their smaller counterparts.[16] Larger firms were also found to rely more on information technology, with their greater need, combined with resource availability, leading to increased adoption.[17] All of these studies are supportive of the link between size and complexity.

Aston Group
researchers at the University of Aston in Great Britain who supported the theory that size was a major determinant of structure

Critics of the size imperative

There has been no shortage of critics of the size imperative. Attacks have been launched specifically against Blau's and the Aston Group's research. In addition, independent studies have demonstrated no impact, or minimal impact, of size on structure. Finally, there is some preliminary evidence indicating that size affects structure only in organisations that have professional managers—not among those that are owner-controlled.

Chris Argyris analysed Blau's data, questioned his measures and argued that civil-service organisations are unique.[18] On this last point, he noted that civil-service organisations have budget limitations, distinct geographical boundaries and pre-determined staff sizes, and are influenced primarily by regulations. He also acknowl-edged the role of managerial discretion. Managers in government bureaus follow traditional management theories regarding task specialisation, unity of command, span of control and so forth. Thus, you would expect to find that an increase in the number of employees was accompanied by an increase in differentiation, because managers believe in the appropriateness of management theories and are able to act on their beliefs. Size may be related to structure, Argyris concluded, but you cannot say that it causes it.

Blau's size imperative was also challenged by Mayhew and his associates.[19] Using a computer program that determined the degrees of differentiation possible for each level of size, they concluded that Blau's findings of a relationship between size and complexity were a mathematical certainty when equal probabilities were assigned to all possible structural combinations.

The Aston Group's research has had its share of critics, too. Aldrich reanalysed the Aston data and proposed several alternative and equally plausible interpretations.[20] For example, size is the *result*, not the cause: technology determines structure, which in turn determines size. Aldrich said that the firms that were high in complexity and formalisation simply needed to employ a larger workforce than did less structured firms.

Even some of the Aston researchers have questioned the group's original position after an abbreviated replication.[21] They used 14 of the organisations that had been included previously. As some time had gone by between the original study and the replication, there was an opportunity to do a partial longitudinal test of Aston's original findings. The data, however, showed that although size generally decreased over the period, the measure of structure dimension increased. This was contrary to the original findings.

A general attack on the size imperative has come from Hall and his associates. They studied 75 highly diverse organisations, ranging in size from six employees to over 9000 and including business, governmental, religious, educational and penal organisations. Hall believed that if size and the structural dimensions of complexity and formalisation were related, this diverse set of organisations would allow that relationship to appear. Their results were mixed. The researchers concluded that 'neither complexity nor formalization can be implied from organizational size'. Even though some relationships were statistically significant, enough deviant cases existed to question seriously the assumption that large organisations were neces-sarily more complex than small ones. Hall sided with Aldrich's structure-causes-size thesis when he concluded, 'If a decision is made to enlarge the number of functions or activities carried out in an organization, it then becomes necessary to add more members to staff the new functional areas'.[22] However, in terms of objectivity, it must be noted that the evidence was more inconsistent than rejecting the link between size and the other variables. Hall and associates, therefore, may question the size–structure relationship, but their research has certainly not demonstrated that the two are unrelated.

A final consideration relates to the status of the management in an organi-sation. A study of 142 small- and medium-sized businesses found that changes in size were related to changes in structure among those firms that were run by professional managers but that no such relationship appeared among the businesses that were controlled by owner-managers.[23] Specifically, it was found that increases in size were associated with more horizontal differentiation, more formalisation and more delegation of decision making only in firms controlled by professional managers. While it is dangerous to generalise from a single study, this research may help to explain some of the diverse findings in previous studies where there have been a large number of business firms in the sample but no control for the type of ownership. If, for example, owner-managers are unwilling to dilute their personal power over their organisations by decentralising decision making—even though this unwillingness reduces their organisation's effectiveness—we should expect the relationship between a business organisation's size and its structure to be moderated by the kind of management the firm has.

Is it possible to isolate size as a contingency?

The above discussion highlights the difficulties involved in isolating size as a contingency. The motor vehicle industry provides a good example of this problem. Let's look at a large manufacturer, say Ford. By any measure, Ford is a large organisation with all the complexity that one would expect of its size. But it also manufactures a complex product, requiring extensive design and planning capability. As a manufacturer catering to most sections of the market, it must keep its costs low. This leads to mass production. It also means spreading its fixed costs over a large number of units, leading to worldwide operations. Its suppliers are similarly scattered.

In summary, Ford does not have the luxury of being a small organisation. What is driving its size is its strategy of being a mass-market manufacturer. This leads to the technologies appropriate to mass production. Such strategy and production techniques are predicated on a stable environment; designs of cars change slowly and there is predictable demand. Therefore, if we study the forces leading to Ford's organisational structure, how do we isolate the influence of size from other variables?

Researchers have attempted to overcome this problem by undertaking longitudinal studies. These allow us to look at the same sample of organisations over a given period of time, typically during their growth phase. We have quoted a number of these in the previous section. But as we are looking at the effects of size, we do not need to be too exact as to what caused it: size itself is capable of being isolated. But it does mean that we must exercise caution in drawing conclusions as to cause and effect.

As with all organisational research, researchers are limited by their methodology and measuring instruments. Organisations defy easy measurement and analysis, and it is possible that the differences we intuitively expect to find between large and small organisations are difficult to discern using traditional research techniques. There is a bias throughout this book to rely on quantifiable measures, and it is recognised that these do not capture the subtleties of organisational life. However, the subtleties in turn defy easy measurement, and in some cases may be difficult for organisational members themselves to articulate and describe. We need to reiterate that this book concentrates on organisation-wide phenomena, particularly where these refer to the structure of the organisation and the relationships between people and departments. The behaviour of individuals and the teams and departments they form is covered in the discipline of organisational behaviour.

Conclusions on the size–structure relationship

In overview terms, the relationship between size and structure is not clear.[24] Although some have found a strong relationship and argue for its causal nature, others have challenged these findings on methodological grounds or have argued that size is a consequence, rather than a cause of structure. But when we look at the research in more specific terms, a clearer pattern seems to evolve. We will demonstrate that size certainly does not dictate all of an organisation's structure but that it is important in predicting some dimensions of structure.

Size and complexity

Blau found that the impact of size on complexity was at a decreasing rate. As noted by Argyris, this conclusion may apply only to government-type agencies with the unique characteristics of the unemployment offices studied. Meyer's findings, however, certainly cannot be ignored. Although they were also restricted to government offices, he demonstrated strong evidence in favour of the size imperative. We might conclude tentatively that size affects complexity, but at a decreasing rate, in government organisations. Whether this holds for business firms is questionable. It may well be that in business organisations, where managers have greater discretion, structure causes size. Consistent with the strategy imperative, if managers have discretion they may choose to make their structure more complex (consistent with management theory) as more activities and personnel are added. Neither can it be ruled out that the size–structure relationship is circular. There is evidence indicating that size generates differentiation and that increasing differentiation also generates increasing size.[25]

The strongest case can be made for the effect of size on vertical differentiation.[26] In fact, one study found that size alone was the dominant predictor of vertical differentiation, explaining between 50% and 59% of the variance.[27] A less strong but certainly solid case can be made for the relationship between size and horizontal differentiation. That is, the larger the organisation, the more pronounced (at declining rates) the division of labour within it, the same being true of the functional differentiation of the organisation into divisions.[28]

The relationship between size and spatial differentiation is problematic. Blau's high correlations are almost certainly attributable to the kind of organisations he studied. Other efforts to assess this relationship have failed to generate Blau's strong positive relationship; however, yet other investigations support Blau.[29] Further research covering diverse types of organisations is needed before conclusions of any substance can be drawn.

What about the criticism of the Aston Group's work and Hall's research? Our position is that they have not demonstrated the importance of size. More longitudinal studies are needed to clarify the size–structure causation. But in the interim, we propose that the critics have pointed out methodological problems with several of the important studies confirming the impact of size on complexity and have suggested potential alternative hypotheses, although they certainly have not demonstrated size to be irrelevant. Even Hall noted that six of his 11 measures of complexity were significantly related to size.[30]

Size and formalisation

The Aston findings supported the view that size affects formalisation. Hall's conclusion was that formalisation could not be implied from knowledge of organisation size, but he acknowledged that it could not be ignored either. A recent comprehensive review of 27 studies covering more than 1000 organisations concluded that the relationship between size and formalisation was high, positive and statistically significant.[31]

There would appear to be a logical connection between an increase in size and an increase in formalisation. Management seeks to control the behaviour of employees. Two popular methods are surveillance by the hierarchy of management and the use of formalised regulations. While not perfect substitutes for each other, as one increases, the need for the other should decrease. Because surveillance costs should increase very rapidly as organisations expand in size, it seems reasonable to propose that there would be economies if management substituted formalisation for direct surveillance as size increased. The evidence supports this contention.[32] Rules and surveillance are both aspects of control. The former are impersonal; the latter requires such activities as supervising work closely and inspecting the quantity and quality of work. In small organisations, control through surveillance may be achieved relatively easily through informal face-to-face relationships. But as the organisation grows there are more subordinates to supervise, so that it becomes increasingly efficient to rely more on rules and regulations for exerting control. Rules and regulations also provide for uniformity of control across a wide range of employees. We can expect, therefore, to find an increase in formal rules and regulations within an organisation as that organisation increases in size.

After reviewing the size–formalisation literature, one author proposed boldly that 'the larger the organization, the more formalized its behavior'.[33] His explanation, however, emphasised that larger organisations formalise those activities that tend to recur often. The larger the organisation, the more behaviours repeat themselves; hence management is motivated to handle them more efficiently through standardisation. With increased size comes greater internal confusion. Given managements' general desire to minimise this confusion, they seek means to make behaviour at lower levels in the hierarchy more predictable. Management turns to rules, procedures, job descriptions and other formalisation techniques to bring about this predictability.

A final point about the size–formalisation relationship should be noted: we cannot ignore whether the organisation is independent or is a subsidiary of a larger organisation.[34] Parent firms often impose rules and regulations to maintain financial and reporting consistencies that would be unnecessary if the small firm were independent. So a moderating factor in size's effect on formalisation would be whether the organisation was a subsidiary of a larger firm. If so, expect the former to have higher formalisation than its size alone would dictate.

Size and centralisation

'It is only common sense that it is impossible to control large organizations from the top: because much more is happening than an individual or set of individuals can comprehend, there is inevitable delegation.'[35] But what is the evidence in support of this statement? As we concluded, formalisation increases with size.

These rules and regulations *allow* top management to delegate decision making while at the same time ensuring that the decisions are made in accordance with the desires of top management. But the research is mixed in demonstrating that size leads to decentralisation.[36] In fact, one comprehensive review concluded that the relationship between size and centralisation is not significantly different from zero.[37] Precisely why this occurs is not clear. One possibility is that these studies combine professionally-managed and owner-managed business enterprises. The owner-manager's desire to maintain control is likely to override the loss in organisational effectiveness, with the result being no move towards decentralised decision making as size increases.

When does an organisation become large?

Throughout this chapter we have tried to assess what effect, if any, changes in an organisation's size have on its structure. One interesting finding has been that size's influence seems to dissipate as the number of employees expands. Once an organisation becomes large in size, it tends to be high in complexity, high in formalisation and decentralised. That is, once an organisation becomes big, increases in the number of employees have no noticeable further influence on structure. This conclusion, then, begs the question: how big is big? Put another way: at what point do additional employees become irrelevant in determining an organisation's structure?

Our answer can only be an approximation. However, most estimates tend to fall in the range of 1500–2000 employees.[38] Organisations with fewer than 1500 employees tend to be labelled as 'small'. Chances are that in an organisation up to this size, most people will have met, or at least know of, everyone else in the organisation. Employees may have greater understanding of the business as they are in contact with a greater number of activities that are undertaken. There may still be a fair amount of informal coordination, and the full range of formalisation techniques is probably not present. On the other hand, when an organisation or any of its subunits starts to exceed 2000 employees, it becomes increasingly difficult to coordinate without differentiating units, creating formalised rules and regulations, or delegating decision making downwards. So we'll define a large organisation as one having approximately 2000 or more employees.

The preceding definition now allows us to make two important statements. First, adding employees to an organisation once it has approximately 2000 members should have a minimal impact on its structure. Second, a change in size will have its greatest impact on structure when the organisation is small. The big organisation, with 5000–10 000 employees, can double its size and you're not likely to see any significant changes in its structure. But if an organisation with 500 employees doubles its size, you should expect this to be followed by significant structural changes.

Special issues relating to organisation size

In this section we address three issues related to size. First, how can organisation theory assist managers of large organisations? Second, is organisation theory applicable to small organisations? Lastly we will consider the issue of downsizing.

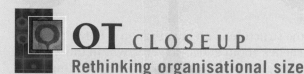

OT CLOSEUP
Rethinking organisational size

The relative benefits of being small and big continue to challenge managers of all types of organisations. One author has attempted to identify the benefits and disadvantages of being large. He identifies the benefits as follows:

Size provides the leverage for capturing significant market share. This leads to increased profitability. This is of considerable benefit in such consumer products as motor vehicles, pharmaceuticals and information technology. The increased profitability derives from economies of scale, better access to shelf space in shops, acquisition of cheaper inputs, price setting and establishing orderly markets.

Size improves access to low-cost capital. Many investors identify size with financial stability. The bigger the company, the more likely it is to be included in major investment indices and be covered by financial analysts. It is also likely to have a superior credit rating. Access to lower-cost capital reduces the cost of acquisitions and investment in new plant and equipment.

Size brings improved brand recognition and advertising benefits. A recognisable brand has its benefits. Firms like Nike, Sony and IBM can introduce new products without the perceived risks of an unknown brand.

Size permits greater investment in research and development. The advantages of investment in R&D, particularly in areas such as biotechnology and information technology, are obvious. New products are often developed by those who can afford to spend on R&D.

Size permits global reach. Accessing new markets is often risky and requires large amounts of capital—particularly in emerging markets such as China. Larger companies are more able to bear the high costs involved in establishing a market position.

Size facilitates expertise and systems development. Compared to their smaller counterparts, large firms can hire specialists in areas such as finance and human resources. They can also invest in corporate infrastructure such as information systems and financial control systems, investments that would often be prohibitively expensive for smaller companies.

But size does bring its disadvantages. These include:

Size leads to lower employee satisfaction. Larger organisations suffer from increased employee turnover, lowered job satisfaction, higher absenteeism. The link in the employees' mind between their actions and the company's success becomes blurred, leading to lower motivation and potentially weaker company performance.

Size leads to resistance to innovation. Large firms harbour individuals with a strong vested interest in the status quo and who actively resist change. As a result, innovation is lower and new products and services are not developed well or rapidly.

Size leads to coordination problems. Large firms need expensive and extensive infrastructure to coordinate actions. They develop layers of management and elaborate staff groups which can easily become insulated from the market. This results in a system biased towards measuring internal performance rather than external value to customers.

Size leads to high formalisation. High formalisation need not be a problem but when associated with bureaucracy can lead to poor customer service and uninspired products. Further, managers in such bureaucracies rarely see the need for change, and often block the initiatives of those who are more in touch with the market.

Large organisations are often highly scrutinised. Large organisations are particular targets for attention from governments and activist organisations such as Greenpeace. They are also more likely to be sued.

Adapted from: Edward Lawler III, 'Rethinking Organizational Size', *Organizational Dynamics*, 26(2), 1997, pp. 24–35.

The problems of large size

In this chapter we have seen that the structure of an organisation is fully elaborated when the number of employees reaches about 2000. However, within the world of business and government there are organisations of enormous size. For instance, IBM has 240 000 employees and Royal Dutch Shell 106 000. Coles Myer is Australia's largest employer with just over 152 000 employees, many of them part-time. But these all pale into insignificance with the armies of the United States, Russia and China, which each have well over one million members.

Needless to say, large size presents management with problems that may either not be present in a smaller organisation or may be more difficult to manage. In this section we consider what additional problems arise in managing large organisations, and how managers can use the structure of the organisation to assist them in alleviating the problems of size.

Given that managing large organisations consumes a significant amount of management time and effort, it is worth considering why large organisations exist. The reason is that there are other significant economies in their operations that outweigh the diseconomies of employing and managing large numbers of people. The large costs involved in designing a car and equipping a factory to manufacture it means that small car companies are not an option. The risks and capital involved in discovering, refining and distributing oil products indicate why there are few small, integrated oil companies. And in government services, such as social security and foreign affairs, the need to apply uniform standards and deliver services over a large area dictates the size of the organisation.

We can identify a number of problems that are common to most large organisations. These are listed below, and we have summarised them in Table 6.1.

1 *The growth of bureaucracy.* Bureaucracy, such as rules and regulations, tends to increase as managers try to maintain control over an increasingly unwieldy organisation. However, the extent of bureaucracy means that most large organisations have a tendency towards inertia. Top managers are often remote from workers and customers and incentives largely favour predicability. However, the environment often changes faster than the rules and regulations, leading to a misfit between what the organisation is actually doing and what the environment is demanding.[39]

2 *The need to gather and process information and turn it into knowledge.*[40] Data in themselves are of little use: the organisation must find a way to process data into useful information that the organisation can act on.

TABLE 6.1 Problems associated with large size and structural contributions to solutions

Growth of bureaucracy	Divisionalisation
Turning information to knowledge	Outsourcing
Adapting to changing technologies	Decentralisation
Long time frames for action	Structuring to facilitate change
Need for accurate costing information	Allocating responsibilities
Managing over a wide geographic spread	
Bounded rationality	

3 *The need to adapt to changing technologies and product life cycles.*[41] Most organisations grow large because they have exploited a given technology. Toyota and cars, Microsoft and personal computer software, CSR and sugar are examples. However, all of these technologies can be overtaken by new innovations. The challenge for companies is to adapt to new technologies as they develop.

4 *Extended time frames for action.*[42] In large organisations it can take a long time before realising that change is required. Stagnation may have set in for some time before management realises that action is necessary. During this time an organisation can 'live off its fat'—that is, run down its assets while maintaining its activities. Further, once remedial action has been taken, it can take a number of years to determine whether it is working or not.

5 *Knowing where profits are being made and costs incurred.*[43] In large organisations it is often difficult to allocate costs and revenues to individual products. For instance, how does Sony allocate overheads across its wide product range? How can the costs of information technology be allocated to each part of the organisation? And how does a large bank determine the costs and benefits of each customer or product?

6 *Difficulty in managing over a wide geographic spread.*[44] By their nature, most large organisations operate in different markets and regions. Indeed, the multinational corporation is the dominant form of business in our time. But managing such firms leads to problems of employing people from different cultures, adapting products and services to suit local conditions, and maintaining control over operations that are located far away from the head office.

7 *Bounded rationality.*[45] The scale and scope of operations of large organisations means that it is impossible for one person, or a even a group of people, to fully understand all that is going on. Procedures must therefore be introduced to reduce this complexity into bits of information that are capable of being grasped by the senior managers of the company.

Given these difficulties, how can structure contribute to the efficient management of large organisations? Remember that structure is the way we allocate responsibilities, the extent of formalisation and the location of decision making. The following structural solutions can be applied to problems we have identified above.

1 *Dividing the organisation into manageable parts.*[46] This is called divisionalisation. Each division operates largely as a separate business, with its own identifiable goals, management, staff and facilities. It enables a clearer identification of costs and revenues and places decision making close to where business is transacted. It also reduces the amount of communication needed for day-to-day operations.

2 *Outsourcing.*[47] Organisations can reduce many problems arising from size by not doing everything themselves. Airlines often outsource maintenance and baggage handling. Computer services are often bought in, and other companies have specialist firms undertake their cleaning, distribution, logistics or warehousing. Each of these actions removes the need for large staff numbers.

3 *Finding a balance between what decisions to centralise and decentralise.* Managers often tend to centralise decision making in order to maintain control. However, decision making should be made as close as possible to where the problem lies while controlling factors such as risk and access to information. Successful large companies have found the balance between centralisation and decentralisation.

4   *Structuring to facilitate change.*[48] There is no easy way to combat the bureaucratic tendency. However, part of the response involves adopting an appropriate organisational structure. In seeking to reduce the tendency towards bureaucracy, managers should aim to reduce power distances, develop means of facilitating communication, and support new ways of recognising and solving problems. Further, they should seek to reward actions that promote flexibility rather than adherence to fixed ways of responding to problems. The structure should also reflect the current and future needs of the organisation, rather than past practices.

5   *Ensuring that important tasks have someone responsible for them.* If important tasks have no-one responsible for them, chances are they will be neglected or overlooked. Managers must also be aware of how environmental changes create the need for new responsibilities. For instance, mining companies are finding that they now need environmental and local community liaison managers. Quality-control managers in manufacturing and the growth of human resource managers are all examples of responsibilities that have been generated to address important functions.

In summary, we see that organisation theory can assist in the management of large organisations. Although the set of structural options open to large organisations may be extensive, the consequences of choosing the wrong one can lead to significant problems. We have argued that successful large organisations manage best by actually becoming small—that is, by dividing themselves into units of such a size as to enable managers to understand the operations of their area and to respond accordingly. Formal mechanisms to promote adaptation to change are also necessary for large organisations.

Organisation theory and small businesses

We live in a society dominated by large organisations. Although 97% of all enterprises may be classified as small—that is, as having fewer than 10 employees—over 50% of the workforce can be found in the remaining 3% of organisations.[49] While there may be a great number of small organisations, large organisations have the greatest impact on our society.

These considerations have not been lost on those who study organisation theory. Studies are almost exclusively of medium-sized and large organisations, those with hundreds of employees or more. Even textbook authors fall prey to this bias: you'll find references in this book to large statutory authorities and government departments, or firms the size of BHP Billiton, Coles Myer and National Australia Bank, but rarely a mention of the small business, particularly the owner-managed firm. It may therefore be appropriate to ask whether the organisation theory being described in this book has any application to those who manage or expect to manage a small business?

The answer is a resounding yes! The right structural design is critical if a small business is to succeed. An important point, however, is that small businesses do not face the same problems as large organisations; therefore, we should expect a different priority to be assigned to organisation theory issues by the small-business manager.

The influence of the owner

Although many definitions of small business are based on number of employees (this varies, and definitions up to 500 employees in manufacturing have been used), a

OT CLOSEUP

Obtaining the benefits of being small while being big

The benefits of a small organisation are fairly well known: there are fewer impediments to communication, creativity is heightened, innovations can be introduced far more quickly and, as workers and management are closer to the customer, they are more responsive to customers' needs. These are the very attributes that large businesses often lack, and one of the great management challenges of the present day is to try to derive many of the benefits of being small while being a big business.

For the better part of the 20th century, large organisations advertised their power by the architecture of their head office. It was generally located in a fashionable area of the city and was large and imposing, with grand entrances and state-of-the-art materials. Inside there were thousands of head office employees overseeing the far-flung divisions. The large head office turned out to be an impediment to change, and one of the features of the past 20 years has been the downsizing of the head office, with most staff either being made redundant or moving to the divisions.

In the previous chapter we identified how ABB, a large transnational corporation, structures its operations in an attempt to overcome the problems associated with the head office syndrome. It has divided the organisation into 1300 separate companies which in turn comprise 5000 profit centres. The maximum size of a manufacturing plant has been kept at 250 persons, and many are no bigger than 50. However, ABB does not manufacture a simple product like Coca-Cola; its product range is at the cutting edge of mechanical and electrical engineering. In order to transfer research and development around the company, business-area managers for each product range and geographic area under-

take the coordination and communication function across businesses. The success of this structure relies on the abilities of the business-area managers, and the structure requires active and persistent management to keep it operating. Nevertheless, the idea of small operating units which are profit centres that agglomerate into a larger organisation is a popular way to capture the benefits of being small.

Another method used to improve creativity in large organisations is introducing a 'skunk-works'. This is a group of people isolated from the main, highly formalised processes of the organisation, charged with the task of creating an innovative product. Motor vehicle manufacturers often use skunk-works to generate concept cars or new means of motive power. A skunk-works of young people may be created, for instance, to generate ideas for a car aimed at the youth market. Many innovations in aerospace are undertaken in skunk-works. The layout of the skunk-works is extremely informal, with few offices and physical barriers in the workplace. Timekeeping is informal and there is little in the way of hierarchy. There is generally intensive use of IT for design and communication purposes.

The skunk-works highlights the long-standing practice of firms locating their operations where most benefit is to be derived. Research and development laboratories are located at some distance from production facilities, mining companies locate their main administrative offices in a financial centre, their operations where the mines are and their marketing staff where the customers are. The imposing head office may have impressed those on the outside looking in, but the organisational structure it was built to support proved to be unsuited to the modern, competitive world.

small business could more accurately be described as one where one person, generally the owner, makes all the major decisions. These would include where to locate, what to produce, the target market, the source of inputs, and who to hire and fire. This should give us the clue that a small business is often a reflection of the owner's personality and management style. So not all small businesses will be structured the same. Some may have decentralised decision making for operational decisions, while in other small businesses of a similar type nothing goes on without the owner's knowledge and permission. Other businesses may have created positions for relatives or friends. And many small start-up high-technology companies reflect the owner's passion for innovation and unstructured work hours.[50]

The world view of owner-managers—that is, their personality, attitudes and beliefs—influences the way that small businesses are structured and managed.[51] On the whole they tend to prefer a relatively unstructured workplace, where roles and responsibilities are not clearly defined. But decision making, including even day-to-day decisions, is highly centralised. Organisational structure tends to follow the decisions that have been made, rather than anticipating them. And when staff are recruited, they are chosen because of situational factors rather than a rational assessment of requirements.[52]

This does not mean that in a small business anything passes as a satisfactory design. There is the same need for the structure to suit the environment, the technology and strategy in a small organisation as in a big one. But following the principle of equifinality, discussed in Chapter 1, there is likely to be a large number of variations between the structures of organisations doing much the same thing. This does not prevent us from making generalisations about what structure small businesses are likely to adopt.

 ## OT CLOSEUP
Difficulties with small business research

One of the problems with small-business research is reaching agreement on what constitutes a small organisation.[53] Researchers have in the past used number of employees, but this measure is simply an administrative convenience. Some researchers claim the perceptions of size by those in the sample should be taken into account when determining whether a business is small or large. They claim that the parties involved will show general agreement as to what is small and large in their sector, and that this should guide research. So key participants perceptions and beliefs take precedence over a numerical measure.

Data on many small businesses remain hard to come by, which may account for the lack of organisational research. Generally, gathering data means speaking to the owner or manager or seeking his or her permission to interview or submit a questionnaire to employees. But owners are often busy people with little time, or sympathy, for research. They are generally practical people, with a strong distrust of abstract and theoretical constucts. Data gathering is also time-consuming, with each entry to a workplace having to be negotiated separately but yet, because of the size of the business, yielding relatively few data. It is hardly surprising that medium- and large-sized businesses are the main subject of research.

Issues of reduced importance

All the structural variables are less important to the small-business manager, because the range of variation in small businesses is typically limited. Small businesses tend to have a minimal degree of horizontal, vertical and spatial differentiation, and most are characterised by low formalisation and high centralisation. There is also less internal specialisation. When specialised expertise is needed, it is typically purchased from outside. For instance, instead of having full-time accountants and lawyers on staff, their services can be bought as needed. The reduced horizontal differentiation means that in occupations such as accounting, the accountant may do all the accounting work rather than specialise in one particular part of it. Vertical differentiation in small businesses is usually low for the obvious reason that these structures tend to be flat. Similarly, spatial differentiation is usually low because small businesses don't spread their activities widely. Even separate units, such as in a chain of small, retail women's wear shops, tend to be geographically close in small businesses. If they have overseas operations they largely work through agents rather than set up an overseas presence themselves. You will also find little formalisation in small businesses. The small-business manager achieves control, but not usually through high formalisation. Some of that control is achieved by holding on to the decision-making machinery: that is, you can expect most small businesses to be characterised by centralised decision making.

As the structure of small business is less elaborated, it means that there are fewer formal barriers to communication. The smaller number of departments, fewer layers of management and the fact that most people know each other creates an environment that facilitates improved communication. Lower barriers to communication should provide a competitive advantage to the small business by promoting the goals of the organisation, improving coordination and facilitating the flow of work. Time delays in communication should also be reduced. Of course, reaping the benefits of these advantages depends on supportive management and preventing conflict from becoming destructive.

In addition to these structural issues, there are other concerns that take on reduced importance in small business organisations. These include stimulating innovation, managing conflict and changing the organisation's culture. The topic of stimulating innovation, discussed in Chapter 12, has reduced importance to small business because the concern of organisation theorists with innovation is largely a response to the constraints that high complexity and formalisation impose on an organisation's creative juices. These constraints do not exist in most small businesses. Indeed, many small businesses are set up to be innovative; they don't have to worry about creativity being strangled by bureaucracy. Organisational culture (discussed in Chapter 13) presents less of a problem for small businesses. Small organisations tend to be young. As a result, they have less sense of history and fewer traditions. Because their cultures are younger and less entrenched, they are less likely to require change. And when change is required, it is easier to implement.

Issues of increased importance

The organisation theory issues that take on greater importance for small business include control and accountability, efficiency and environmental dependence.

The small-business owner is often willing to settle for a smaller monetary reward in return for personal control and accountability. In place of formalisation, he or she tends to control through direct supervision and observation. Small-business managers are strong advocates of 'management by walking around'.

Achieving high efficiency is typically more important in the small business than in the large, for the simple reason that large organisations have more slack resources. Large organisations typically have greater access to capital, control over sources of supply and leverage over customers and distributors. Slack resources such as these act as shock absorbers to reduce the impact of mistakes. The fact that small organisations have less tolerance for inefficiency than do better-funded organisations places an increased importance on ensuring that the right structural design is chosen. The structural-design problem, discussed in Chapter 4, may thus be more critical to the small-business manager.

We also suggest that the environment that confronts the small business is often very different from the one facing its larger counterpart. The larger an organisation, the more able it is to use its power to manage its environment and reduce its dependence on such constituencies as material suppliers, competitors and financial sources. Small businesses rarely have much influence over their environment. This places more importance on the organisation's environmental monitoring system. The effective small business must have a structural design that facilitates rapid and accurate assessment of its environment and allows this information to be acted on promptly.

Finally, management issues can have a major impact on the effectiveness of small business. Most small businesses fail because of shortcomings in management. As a result of smaller size, one poorly performing manager can have a significant impact on business performance. An associated issue is management succession. Often top management jobs are reserved for relatives of the owners, regardless of their management capabilities. This can generate resentment among those who feel that they are better qualified, or who must serve under incompetent managers.

In summary, we can see that small businesses are different from their larger counterparts. They have different concerns and priorities. Some issues presented in this book have limited relevance to the small organisation; others have much greater importance.

In addition to the fact that small businesses have a different organisational theory agenda, their managers, so we have argued, have a more limited set of structural options. If there is any message in this section, it may be for the small-business manager to guard against what can be called BHPitis—the desire to build a complex and sophisticated organisation design regardless of whether it is appropriate. The small business has unique problems that require unique structural solutions. The appropriate structural design for a small business is not merely a scaled-down version of the design used by its industry's giants.

Downsizing

Most of us have heard of downsizing and some of the effects it has had on both individuals and communities. Although downsizing is not new, the issue has come to greater prominence over the past 10 years. Hardly a week goes by without reports of a prominent company cutting the number of its workers or managers. This includes organisations such as banks, insurance companies and government departments, which used to pride themselves on the job security they offered their employees.

There has been considerable debate about the causes and effects of downsizing, but first let us define what downsizing is. Downsizing may be defined as the planned elimination of positions or jobs.[54] Downsizing differs from retrenchments and layoffs, which arise from downturns in the trade cycle. In this case, when demand recovers, people are rehired to replace those laid off.

Downsizing also has the implication that it affects more than lower-level employees and factory workers. In recent times, managers and other white-collar workers have been at the forefront of those who have lost their jobs through downsizing. The favourite target of downsizing efforts have been middle managers, who have borne the brunt of management hierarchies being reduced from in excess of 12 layers of management to five layers or even fewer. Even the most senior of managers have lost their jobs in downsizing efforts.

Those companies that are downsizing, however, were not always overstaffed or under pressure to downsize. And most downsizing has not been the result of a company crisis or impending bankruptcy. Some of the most successful companies in Australia have been among the most aggressive downsizers. The following environmental factors have led to the need for companies to reduce their payroll. Table 6.2 summarises the need for downsizing and its benefits.

1 *Increased competition*. This is the result of government policy, the progressive lowering of tariffs and the low growth rates of most markets. Competitive conditions mean that all in an industry must strive to match the lowest-cost producer.

2 *Computerisation and automation*. The widespread use of computers and automation in factories and offices means that fewer people can do an equivalent amount of work. However, there is typically a long time lag between the introduction of labour-saving devices and the laying off of staff.

3 *Technological obsolescence*. New processes and inventions reduce the need for those associated with redundant technologies. Thousands of workers in railway workshops and shipyards were made redundant with the introduction of diesel locomotives and container shipping. Telstra found that it had a surplus of over 20 000 technicians when old technology was superseded in telephone exchanges.

4 *Declining profitablity*. Declining profitability and return on assets leads management to consider shedding staff. The arithmetic sounds good: every laid-off worker and manager saves the company money, which should immediately go to the bottom line. But rarely do the outcomes meet the expectations.

5 *Information technology and management*. Many of the roles of middle management, such as controlling, coordination and decision making, are being pushed

TABLE 6.2 The reasons leading to downsizing and some of the resulting benefits

Increased competition	Lowered overheads
Computerisation and automation	Less bureaucracy
Technological obsolescence	Faster decision making
Changes in strategy	Smoother communications
Limitation of size advantages	Greater entrepreneurship
Rise of outsourcing	Increased productivity

Source: Adapted from Wayne F. Cascio, 'Downsizing: What Do We Know? What Have We Learned?', *Academy of Management Executive*, 7(1), 1993, pp. 95–104.

down the organisation structure by the increasing use of IT. As a result many middle management layers, and middle management, no longer have meaningful work.

6   *The realisation that size of itself does not bring advantages.* Some of the most successful firms over the past decade have been small and medium-sized. By contrast, some of the largest companies have experienced low growth and poor adaptation to change.

7   *Changes in strategy.* Rather than diversifying, which was common in the 1970s, companies are now reducing their businesses to a few core skills. Because businesses are less diverse, fewer managers are needed to run them.

8   *The rise of outsourcing.* Companies are finding that it is often easier and cheaper to purchase goods and services as they are required rather than produce them in house.

The following six reasons have been proposed as the benefits companies seek from downsizing.[55]

1   *Lowered overheads.* Companies often find themselves with cost structures that are out of line with those of their competitors. They find they have little alternative but to reduce numbers to lower their costs and improve their competitive positions. In this case, downsizing is often undertaken according to a formula: costs need to be reduced by a certain amount and this amount is divided by the cost of each employee, leading to a reduction in the headcount of a certain number.

2   *Less bureaucracy.* As the number of employees are reduced, there should be fewer complications arising from paper processing and general overheads.

3   *Faster decision making.* Fewer management layers should mean that decision making can be made by a smaller number of better-informed people, thus leading to faster decisions.

4   *Smoother communications.* Again, with fewer employees, the possible barriers to communication are reduced.

5   *Greater entrepreneurship.* Downsizing should lead to greater decentralisation of functions, which should lead to more innovative behaviour on the part of management.

6   *Increased productivity.* Downsizing rarely leads to less work being undertaken. Those who are left are expected to do much the same amount of work with fewer people.

A favourite target of downsizing has been the large head offices organisations built up over many years. In some companies, managers in the field had control over only 30% of their costs, so they had little incentive to search for economies or instigate change. By reducing the number of head office staff and making the business managers responsible for a greater proportion of their costs, managers are more likely to be more careful in spending money. As well, the impact of information technology allows many of the functions of head office to be undertaken at a decentralised location.

The effects of downsizing

Downsizing rarely achieves all of the benefits attributed to it. A number of studies have shown that the benefits of downsizing have fallen short of the set objectives. In a survey in the USA of 1005 firms, only 46% felt that they had reduced costs in accordance with expectations, fewer than one in three felt that profits grew as much as expected, and only 20% reported satisfactory improvement in shareholders' return on investment.[56]

Not only are the financial returns of downsizing often not as great as anticipated, but companies often poorly handle the problem of how to make the best use of those who remain. Studies consistently show that after a downsizing has occurred, the surviving employees become narrow-minded, self-absorbed and risk-averse. There is a lowering of commitment and morale, more job insecurity, productivity often drops and, needless to say, management fails to maintain the trust of other employees.[57] These symptoms are so common that they are called survivor's syndrome.

Most companies start downsizing programs with few policies or programs to minimise the negative effect of cutting back. Senior managers easily forget that organisations rely on a complex web of communication channels and interrelationships to get things done. Once these relationships are severed, new ones must be established, and this can take time. The remaining managers and lower-level employees can feel misused and alienated, and rather than productivity increasing it can actually drop. The reserve of trust that organisations need to operate effectively takes a long time to be re-established.

Further problems with downsizing can arise because the skills of those remaining in the organisation are not able to replace those who have been dispensed with. Part of the collective memory of the organisation walks out of the door with the employees who leave the firm. Because of this, many companies that have downsized have found that they have had to re-employ managers and lower-level workers either as consultants or other part-time help at a higher cost than having them on the payroll. This has contributed to the cost savings of downsizing being lower than most companies anticipated.[58]

The way that downsizing is implemented can also have an influence on its success. Downsizing is often attempted in a random manner, with the intention of reducing headcounts rather than considering the ongoing needs of the organisation. Table 6.3 lists a number of ineffective downsizing practices. Poorly thought out downsizing practices can see those with considerable experience leaving the organisation, without anyone to take their place. This is a typical effect of the voluntary redundancy and early retirement schemes open to all employees. Another counter-productive way of implementing downsizing is to phase it in over time: productivity and morale plummets as everyone wonders who will be next to go.

TABLE 6.3 Ineffective downsizing practices

The use of voluntary early retirement practices
Making across-the-board layoffs
Eliminating training and development programs
Cutting too deeply into the numbers of personnel
Placing remaining employees into jobs for which they have insufficient skills
Emphasising employee accountability over employee involvement
Expecting survivors to 'row harder'
Implementing layoffs slowly in phases over time
Promising high monetary rewards rather than careers

Source: Adapted from M.A. Hitt, B.W. Keats, H.F. Harback and R.D. Nixon 'Rightsizing: Building and Maintaining Strategic Leadership and Long-Term Competitiveness', *Organizational Dynamics*, Autumn 1994, p. 25.

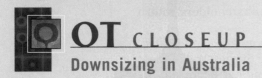

OT CLOSEUP

Downsizing in Australia

Australian industry has experienced its fair share of downsizings. Public corporations, such as water supply and electricity authorities, and the finance industry, especially banking, have shed large numbers of employees over the past 10 years. One of the reasons that downsizing has attracted so much media publicity is that, while reducing work-forces because of economic downturn has been common in the past, current downsizing owes little to economic decline. It has created enormous social stress as families have lost income and workers career prospects. It has also led to many workers taking retirement earlier than they would have wanted owing to their inability to find other employment. Identifying the reasons for downsizing is difficult, but technological change, heightened levels of competition and a desire to increase productivity have played their part.

Two Australian researchers, Peter Dawkins and Craig Littler, have undertaken a major study into the effects of downsizing. They studied data from over 4000 large Australian firms over the period 1990–1998. Over 80% of the firms they studied downsized during that time, and downsizing appears to have permeated Australian business organisations.

Their study revealed that downsizing almost always led to a loss of skills and knowledge within the organisation. Laying people off to reduce numbers is a random exercise which often leads to what has been termed 'cesspool syndrome' where less qualified employees rise to the top.

Downsizing firms are far more likely than their non-downsizing peers to substitute temporary or part-time staff than non-downsizing firms. In some cases, employees who have been made redundant through downsizing return soon afterwards as contractors. The use of temporary staff, however, does not stem the loss of skills from the organisation.

In relation to individual exposure to downsizing, Dawkins and Littler found that:

- men were more likely than women to experience downsizing;
- older workers were significantly more exposed to downsizing than younger workers;
- education and skill levels provided no protection against downsizing;
- primary industry workers and those in regional areas were less likely to experience downsizing than were urban dwellers.

Older workers are more likely than younger workers to be affected by downsizing. They are more likely to be employed by downsizing firms and, when laid off, their chances of finding comparable employment opportunities are slim. Most downsized workers experience a loss of job satisfaction in their new jobs.

Downsizing appears to have little effect on rates of unemployment generally. An expanding economy generates as many jobs as have been lost. But downsizing firms don't appear to increase their profitability as a result of laying off staff. Indeed, most report that the aims of downsizing are rarely met.

Drawn from: Peter Dawkins & Craig Littler, eds, *Downsizing: Is it Working for Australia?*, Melbourne: Institute of Applied Economic and Social Research, University of Melbourne, 2001.

One of the problems of downsizing is that managers are often neither well informed nor experienced in implementing it. Unfortunately, managers do not enjoy perfect knowledge of how the organisation works or the detailed roles of those in the organisation. The larger the organisation, the more remote senior management will be from the day-to-day running of it. Under these conditions, their judgements in relation to downsizing are often only best guesses. And those who are expert in downsizing often cannot perform in any other role. The American manager Al

Dunlap has earned the nickname 'Chainsaw' for his attack on corporate staffing and overheads. But his tenure is typically only 18 months in a company before he moves on. He was employed by Kerry Packer in the early 1990s to reduce the costs and staffing levels of Consolidated Press.[59]

The need to maintain investment in the future

One factor that is easy to forget during the downsizing phase is that the future of the organisation should be as high in management's mind as the present. New products need to be brought to market, distribution channels and product image maintained, management development undertaken, and the general entropy associated with organisations as open systems constantly resisted. This cannot be achieved if an organisation is staffed and structured to produce only for the present range of tasks, with no resources allocated to preparing for the future. Cuts in staff, systems and equipment that are too hard and too deep are generally counterproductive. In times of declining profit, research staff may seem to be a luxury, maintenance engineers easy to cut, investment in new processes and skills unnecessary and market development a waste. However, it is from these areas that future profitability springs. And even though there may be a short-term gain, the long-term future of the company will be put at risk if areas such as these are neglected for too long.

Summary

Organisational size is defined as the total number of employees. Strong arguments have been proposed indicating that size is the major determinant of structure, but there has been no shortage of critics of this position.

A review of the evidence indicates that size has a significant influence on vertical differentiation. The effect of size on spatial differentiation is unclear. Increases in formalisation appear to be related closely to increases in organisational size. Finally, although common sense suggests that size and centralisation would be inversely related, research reveals mixed findings.

Large organisations present managers with a range of significant problems to solve. These include the tendency towards bureaucracy, the need to adapt to changing technologies and product cycles, identifying the sources of revenues and costs, and the difficulty of managing over a wide geographic area. Structure was found to contribute to the successful management of large organisations by reducing complexity to manageable parts, locating decisions at the right place in the organisation and ensuring that important tasks have someone responsible for them.

We noted that organisation theory is based on studies almost exclusively of medium- and large-sized organisations. Small businesses face different problems and have different priorities in terms of important organisation theory concepts. In addition to the fact that small businesses have a different organisation theory agenda, their managers have a more limited set of structural options.

Finally we looked at the issue of downsizing. Almost all large organisations have downsized at some time during the past few years. However, few have achieved the goals they set themselves. We examined the aims of downsizing and found that there were many reasons for it apart from reducing costs. Other reasons included attempting to make a more nimble and responsive organisation. All downsizing had a negative impact on those left in the organisation, but the effects could be far worse than they need be if it was implemented inappropriately.

For review and discussion

1   Alpha College has 100 full-time teachers, 10 part-time teachers and 1500 full-time students. National College has 30 full-time teachers, 150 part-time teachers and 2000 full-time students. Beta College has 50 full-time teachers, 30 part-time teachers and 2500 students. Assuming that each has a support staff of 75 and no part-time students, which organisation is the largest in size? Explain.

2   'One of the strongest cases for the size imperative has been made by Meyer.' What is the support for this statement?

3   'Size is the major determinant of structure.' Construct an argument to support this statement. Then construct one to refute it.

4   How does ownership moderate the size–structure relationship?

5   What is the relationship between size and complexity?

6   What is the relationship between size and formalisation?

7   What is the relationship between size and centralisation?

8   At what point in an organisation's growth do additions to size have relatively little further impact on structure?

9   When will size have its greatest impact on structure?

10 What are the main problems management faces when running large organisations?

11 Nominate the ways in which the structure can assist managers in running large organisations.

12 What are some of the problems unique to the small-business manager?

13 Which organisation theory issue takes on increased importance for the small-business manager? Which take on decreased importance?

14 What are the main benefits managers seek to gain from downsizing?

15 What are some of the effects of downsizing on those remaining in the organisation?

CASE FOR CLASS DISCUSSION
Billabong rides the fashion wave

The surf culture of the 1960s and 70s gave birth to more than just a lifestyle aimed at finding the perfect wave—it also spawned a number of prominent clothing companies. One of these is Billabong, which was started by Gordon Merchant and his former wife Rena in 1973. At the beginning it was a small-scale family affair. Gordon Merchant thought that board shorts that reached below the knee would be a good idea, so he and his wife made 500 pairs, using their kitchen table as a cutting board. They were sold out of the back of his station wagon at local open-air markets around the Gold Coast.

Business was slow at first, with the first batch of 500 shorts taking a long time to move. But eventually a market was established, which provided a living of sorts for the Merchants. It remained a husband and wife business for some time but gradually markets expanded and other clothing items, such as T-shirts and tops, were added. Early on it was decided to only sell through surf shops, to maintain the integrity of the brand. Further expansion was made to the product range to include accessories such as sunglasses and equipment for snowboarders, skaters and surfers, all capturing the image behind the Billabong brand. Further growth depends on diversification, both in expanding into new geographical areas and in introducing new products.

Growth did not come with enormous expansion in those employed in the company. Billabong is basically a designer and wholesaler, with manufacturing undertaken by subcontractors, mainly in Asia. Goods are not made until an order from a retailer is received. Overseas distribution was handled by agents, who paid Billabong a 5% royalty on sales. The range was also expanded to target women. During this growth phase, Merchant worked hard at keeping the image of the label close to the surf culture. He was, and remains, a sponsor of surf competitions and individual surfers. This keeps the brand alive and keeps it close to the culture it seeks to serve. All members of the company are hired for their identification with the surf culture, including the mandatory surf break during lunchtime, at least when the surf is up. Even the chairman, the 60-year-old Garry Pemberton, turns up for board and other meetings in casual beach clothing.

In the early days of the company, Merchant was happy to use agents to distribute his products in overseas markets; any sale was better than none. But profit margins were low, and sometimes the products were not distributed as Billabong would have wished. Matters came to head in 1998, when all the employees of the US agent left to start their own company. After much soul-searching Merchant decided that the best strategy was to dispense with the agency arrangement and for Billabong to undertake its own distribution. This means that more control could be exerted and margins would be bigger. Billabong has progressively bought out all its overseas agents. It set up a wholly owned subsidiary in Japan in 2001, to capture some of the lucrative Japanese market. Billabong brand goods are now sold in 64 countries around the world, with the USA accounting for 50% of sales.

A major milestone in Billabong's growth was the floating of the company on the stock exchange in 2000. The float raised $250 million and the shares have performed strongly since the float. It was quite a journey from kitchen table to stock exchange. In the process, Merchant had become a man of considerable wealth.

Adapted from: Alex Kennedy, 'Bad Boy Wade Just Keeps on Winning', *Business Review Weekly*, 17 March 1997, pp. 51–3.

QUESTIONS

1 In what way could we expect the management of Billabong to have changed as the organisation has grown?

2 Identify the ways in which Billabong attempts to maintain the benefits of being small with selling its product in 64 different countries.

3 If Billabong grew to have a turnover of $1 billion and over 1000 employees, how might its culture and management style change as it expanded?

FURTHER READING

Peter Blau & Richard Schoenherr, *The Structure of Organizations*, New York: Basic Books, 1971.
Wayne Cascio, 'Downsizing: What Do We Know, What Have We Learned?', *Academy of Management Executive*, 7(1), 1993, pp. 95–104.
Peter Dawkins & Craig Littler, eds, *Downsizing: Is it Working for Australia?*, Melbourne: Institute for Applied Economic and Social Research, University of Melbourne, 2001.
Michael Hitt, Barbara Keats, Herbert Harback & Robert Nixon, 'Rightsizing: Building and Maintaining Strategic Leadership and Long-Term Competitiveness', *Organizational Dynamics*, 23(2), 1994, pp. 18–32.
Edward Lawler III, 'Rethinking Organizational Size', *Organizational Dynamics*, 26(2), 1997, pp. 24–35.
M.G. Scott, ed., *Small Firms: Growth and Development*, Aldershot: Gower, 1986.

NOTES

1   J.R. Kimberly, 'Organizational Size and the Structuralist Perspective: A Review, Critique, and Proposal', *Administrative Science Quarterly*, December 1976, pp. 571–97.

2   Nina Gupta, 'Some Alternative Definitions of Size', *Academy of Management Journal*, December 1980, p. 761.

3   ibid., pp. 759–66; and Richard Z. Gooding & John A. Wagner III, 'A Meta-Analytic Review of the Relationship between Size and Performance: The Productivity and Efficiency of Organizations and Their Subunits', *Administrative Science Quarterly*, December 1985, pp. 462–81.

4   D.S. Pugh, D.J. Hickson, C.R. Hinings & C. Turner, 'The Context of Organization Structures', *Administrative Science Quarterly*, March 1969, pp. 91–114.

5   Theodore Anderson & Seymour Warkov, 'Organization Size and Functional Complexity: A Study of Administration in Hospitals', *American Sociological Review*, February 1961, p. 25.

6   Amos Hawley, Walter Boland & Margaret Boland, 'Population Size and Administration in Institutions of Higher Education', *American Sociological Review*, April 1965, p. 253.

7   Peter M. Blau & Richard A. Schoenherr, *The Structure of Organizations*, New York: Basic Books, 1971.

8   Peter M. Blau, 'A Formal Theory of Differentiation in Organizations', *American Sociological Review*, April 1970, pp. 201–18.

9   See, for example, Pugh et al., 'The Context of Organization Structures'; and D.J. Hickson, D.S. Pugh & D.C. Pheysey, 'Operations Technology and Organization Structure: An Empirical Reappraisal', *Administrative Science Quarterly*, September 1969, pp. 378–97.

10 Pugh et al., 'The Context of Organization Structures', p. 112.

11 John Child & Roger Mansfield, 'Technology, Size, and Organization Structure', *Sociology*, September 1972, pp. 369–93.

12 John Child, 'Predicting and Understanding Organization Structure', *Administrative Science Quarterly*, June 1973, p. 171.

13 Marshall W. Meyer, 'Size and the Structure of Organizations: A Causal Analysis', *American Sociological Review*, August 1972, pp. 434–41.

14 ibid., p. 440.

15 Shanthi Gopalakrishnan & Fariborz Damanpour, 'The Impact of Organizational Context on Innovation Adoption in Commercial Banks', *IEEE Transactions of Engineering Management*, 47(1), 2000, pp. 14–25.

16 Blake Ashforth, Alan Saks & Raymond Lee, 'Socialization and Newcomer Adjustment: The Role of Organizational Context', *Human Relations*, 51(7), 1998, pp. 897–926.

17 Matthew McGowan & Gregory Madley, 'The Influence of Organizational Structure and Organizational Learning Factors on the Extent of EDI Implementation in US Firms', *Information Resources Management Journal*, 11(3), 1998, pp. 17–27.

18 Chris Argyris, *The Applicability of Organizational Sociology*, London: Cambridge University Press, 1972, pp. 1–19.

19 B.H. Mayhew, R.L. Levinger, J.M. McPherson & T.F. James, 'System Size and Structural Differentiation in Formal Organizations: A Baseline Generator for Two Major Theoretical Propositions', *American Sociological Review*, October 1972, pp. 629–33.

20 Howard E. Aldrich, 'Technology and Organization Structure: A Reexamination of the Findings of the Aston Group', *Administrative Science Quarterly*, March 1972, pp. 26–43.

21 J.H.K. Inkson, D.S. Pugh & D.J. Hickson, 'Organizational Context and Structure: An Abbreviated Replication', *Administrative Science Quarterly*, September 1970, pp. 318–29.

22 Quotations in this paragraph are from Richard H. Hall, J. Eugene Haas & Norman J. Johnson, 'Organizational Size, Complexity, and Formalization', *American Sociological Review*, December 1967, pp. 903–12.

23 Guy Geeraerts, 'The Effect of Ownership on the Organization Structure in Small Firms', *Administrative Science Quarterly*, June 1984, pp. 232–7.

24 Jeffrey D. Ford & John W. Slocum, Jr, 'Size, Technology, Environment and the Structure of Organizations', *Academy of Management Review*, October 1977, p. 566.

25 N.P. Hummon, P. Doriean & K. Teuter, 'A Structural Control Model of Organizational Change', *American Sociological Review*, December 1975, pp. 813–24.

26 Dennis S. Mileti, David F. Gillespie & J. Eugene Haas, 'Size and Structure in Complex Organizations', *Social Forces*, September 1977, pp. 208–17; and Lex Donaldson & J. Angus Robertson, 'A Meta-Analysis of Size and Hierarchy: Universal Generalization Moderated by Routineness and Managerial Capitalism', paper presented at Annual Academy of Management Conference, Chicago, August 1986.

27 John R. Montanari, *An Expanded Theory of Structural Determination: An Empirical Investigation of the Impact of Managerial Discretion on Organization Structure*, unpublished doctoral dissertation, University of Colorado, Boulder, 1976.

28 See, for example, Mileti, Gillespie & Haas, 'Size and Structure in Complex Organizations', pp. 213–14; George A. Miller & Joseph Conaty, 'Differentiation in Organizations: Replication and Cumulation', *Social Forces*, September 1980, pp. 265–74; and George A. Miller, 'Meta-Analysis and the Culture-Free Hypothesis', *Organizational Studies*, No. 4, 1987, pp. 309–25.

29 Mileti, Gillespie & Haas, 'Size and Structure of Complex Organizations', p. 214.

30 Hall, Haas & Johnson, 'Organizational Size, Complexity, and Formalization', pp. 903–12.

31 George A. Miller, 'Meta-Analysis and the Culture-Free Hypothesis'.

32 William A. Rushing, 'Organizational Size, Rules, and Surveillance', in Joseph A. Litterer, ed., *Organizations: Structure and Behavior*, 3rd edn, New York: John Wiley, 1980, pp. 396–405; and Y. Samuel & B.F. Mannheim, 'A Multidimensional Approach Toward a Typology of Bureaucracy', *Administrative Science Quarterly*, June 1970, pp. 216–28.

33 Henry Mintzberg, *The Structuring of Organizations*, Englewood Cliffs, NJ: Prentice Hall, 1979, p. 233.

34 Lex Donaldson, *In Defence of Organisation Theory: A Reply to the Critics*, Cambridge: Cambridge University Press, 1985, p. 158.

35 Richard H. Hall, *Organizations: Structure and Process*, 2nd edn, Englewood Cliffs, NJ: Prentice Hall, 1977, p. 184.

36 Blau and Schoenherr, *The Structure of Organizations*; Child & Mansfield, 'Technology, Size and Organization Structure'; Pradip N. Khandwalla, 'Mass Output Orientation of Operations Technology and Organization Structure', *Administrative Science Quarterly*, March 1974, pp. 74–97; and George A. Miller, 'Meta-Analysis and the Culture-Free Hypothesis'.

37 George A. Miller, 'Meta-Analysis and the Culture-Free Hypothesis'.

38 See, for example, Daniel Robey, *Designing Organizations*, 2nd edn, Homewood, IL: Richard D. Irwin, 1986, p. 121; and Richard L. Daft, *Organization Theory and Design*, 2nd edn, St Paul: West Publishing, 1986, p. 196.

39 Victor Thompson, *Bureaucracy and Innovation*, Alabama: University of Alabama Press, Alabama, 1969.

40 'In Praise of Knowledge', *The Economist*, 27 May 1995, p. 19.

41 Danny Miller & Peter Friesen, 'A Longitudinal Study of the Corporate Lifecycle', *Management Science*, 30, 1984, pp. 1161–83; and Raymond Zammuto & Kim Cameron, 'Environmental Decline and Organisational Response', in L.L. Cummings & B.L. Staw, *Research in Organisational Behaviour*, 7, 1985, pp. 223–62.

42 John P. Kotter & James Heskett, *Corporate Culture and Performance*, New York: Free Press, 1992.

43 C.T. Horngren, G. Foster & S. Dator, *Cost Accounting: A Managerial Emphasis*, 2nd edn, Englewood Cliffs: Prentice Hall, 1994.

44 Kenichi Ohmae, 'Managing in a Borderless World', *Harvard Business Review*, May–June 1989, pp. 152–61.

45 H.A. Simon, *Administrative Behavior*, New York: Macmillan, 1961.

46 See Chapter 4 for more details on divisionalisation.

47 Donna Brown, 'Outsourcing: How Corporations Take Their Business Elsewhere', *Management Review*, February 1992, p. 16–19.

48 B.J. Hodge, W.P. Anthony & C.M. Gales, *Organizational Theory: A Strategic Approach*, Englewood Cliffs, NJ: Prentice Hall, 1996.

49 Australian Bureau of Statistics, *Small Business in Australia 1995*, No. 1321.

50 Stephen Ackroyd, 'On the Structure and Dynamics of Some Small UK Based Information Technology Firms', *Journal of Management Studies*, 32(2), 1995, pp. 141–61.

51 James Curran & John Stanworth, 'Small Firms, Large Firms: Theoretical and Research Strategies for the Comparative Analysis of Small and Large Firms in the Wider Environment', in Michael Scott et al., eds, *Small Firm Growth and Development*, Aldershot: Gower, 1986.

52 Curran & Stanworth, ibid.

53 Curran & Stanworth, 'Small Firms, Large Firms'.

54 Wayne F. Cascio, 'Downsizing: What Do We Know? What Have We Learned?', *Academy of Management Executive*, 7(1), 1993, pp. 95–104.

55 Cascio, ibid.

56 See, for example, F. Lalli, 'Learn from My Mistake', *Money*, February 1992; E.R. Greenburg, 'The Latest AMA Figures on Downsizing', *Compensation and Benefits Review*, 22, 1990, pp. 66–71; and J.R. Dorfman, 'Stocks of Companies Announcing Layoffs Fire Up Investors, but Prices Often Wilt', *The Wall Street Journal*, 10 December 1991. The figures are quoted from Lalli.

57 J. Brokner, 'The Effects of Work Layoffs on Survivors: Research, Theory and Practice', in L.L. Cummings & B.L. Staw, *Research in Organisational Behaviour*, 7, 1985.

58 Cascio, 'Downsizing: What Do We Know? What have we Learned?', and 'Making Companies Efficient: The Year Downsizing Grew Up', *The Economist*, 21 December 1996, p. 93–5.

59 Al Dunlap, *Mean Business*, Singapore: Butterworth Heinemann Asia, 1996.

CHAPTER 7

Technology

After reading this chapter you should be able to:

1 define technology;

2 describe the contributions of Woodward, Perrow, Thompson and Galbraith;

3 explain the moderating influence of industry and size on the technology–structure relationship;

4 summarise how the concept of routineness runs through most studies on technology;

5 identify the influence of level of analysis on the technology–structure relationship;

6 identify the differences between manufacturing and service technologies;

7 discuss the impact of information technologies and computer-integrated manufacturing on the way firms are structured;

8 describe the effect of technology on complexity, formalisation and centralisation.

7

Introduction

Holden and Rolls-Royce—a contrast in technology

If you are in the market for a new car you may consider buying a Rolls-Royce or a Holden Commodore. Chances are that you are not going to spend too much time debating your choice. The Rolls-Royce is probably far too expensive for most of us. And those who have the means of buying Rolls-Royce would not consider buying a Commodore—or any other mass-market car, for that matter. The Commodore and the Rolls differ in many respects. Customers can specify any number of changes they want to make to their Rolls, including the type of cocktail bar. The Commodore comes with limited choice, a few basic decisions as to colour, whether or not you want an automatic and selection of trim items almost exhausts the list of options. When we look at how the cars are made we begin to appreciate the differences in cost and options. Holden has an extensive production line, assembling over 100 000 cars per year. Workers perform repetitive tasks, and in order to reduce costs variations are kept to a minimum. The Rolls is virtually hand-built, with extensive use of craft skills, particularly in the area of upholstery and other internal finish items. Only a few thousand are built each year, almost all to individual order. Although both the Rolls and the Commodore get you from place to place, they are the outputs of radically different productive systems.

Both Rolls-Royce and Holden produce motor cars. But it is clear from the above that they do so in radically different ways. One uses the well-known production line, made famous by the motor industry. The other individually assembles cars to customer preferences. In achieving their goals, both Holden and Rolls-Royce use a technology. Further, we would expect that as the way they produce cars is different, their organisational structure would be different. This would be reflected in the different work experiences of those producing Commodores and Rolls-Royces.

Both Rolls-Royce and Holden convert inputs into outputs. The way they do this has some bearing on structure. Is it *the* dominant determinant of a structure, or is it merely *a* determinant? By the time you finish reading this chapter, you will find that it can be both. As usual, however, let us begin by clarifying what we mean by the term. As with so many concepts in organisational theory, the way in which it is defined and measured has a great deal to do with the consistency of the research surrounding it and the confidence we have in generalising from this research. There is probably no construct in organisational technology where diversity of measurement has produced more incompatible findings and confusion than the research into technology.

Defining technology

Although intuitively we accept that technology must have an influence on the way organisations are structured, it is extremely difficult to develop a definition of technology that is capable of guiding research. As long as we adopt a generalised approach, there is general agreement among organisational theory researchers that **technology** refers to the information, equipment, techniques and processes required

technology
the information, equipment, techniques and processes required to transform inputs into outputs

to transform inputs into outputs in an organisation. This definition permits us to include within the technology construct not just physical processes but also mental concepts. That is, technology looks at *how* the inputs are converted to outputs. There is also agreement that the concept of technology, despite its IT or manufacturing connotation, is applicable to all types and kinds of organisations. As discussed in Chapter 1, all organisations turn inputs into outputs. Regardless of whether the organisation is a manufacturing firm, a bank, a hospital, a social service agency, a research laboratory, a newspaper or a military unit, it will use a technology of some sort to produce its product.

The problems begin when we move from the generalised level to something which is more specific. At issue is basically the question: how does one measure technology? Researchers have used a number of technology classifications. A partial list would include operations techniques used in work-flow activities; characteristics of the materials used in the work flow; varying complexities in the knowledge system used in the work flow; the degree of continuous, fixed-sequence operations; the extent of automation; and the degree of independence between work systems. Each of these measures of technology is slightly different, and you would expect them to obtain different results even if they were applied to the same organisation.

But this introduces several additional problems—that is, accommodating varying types and sizes of organisations and different levels of analysis. Some studies have been limited to manufacturing firms. Others have included only very large organisations. Still others have been directed to the total organisation, yet the researchers attempt to compare their findings with studies conducted at the work-unit or job level. Not surprisingly, the breadth of these efforts, and the attempt to generalise to all organisations from samples that are highly limited, might be expected to end up producing inconsistent results. And that is exactly what has happened.

In summary, we lack the precision to measure technology accurately. So where does this leave us? There have been a number of landmark contributions linking technology to various aspects of organisational structure. We let these studies put forward their own arguments, and we will then evaluate them to see whether we can identify any linkages between them. To minimise confusion, we will restrict our discussion to the landmark contributions to the technology–structure debate. The four studies we describe take very different perspectives on technology, but they will give you the basics for understanding what we know about how technology affects structure. After reviewing these four positions, we tie them together, ascertain where we stand today on the technological imperative, and determine what specific statements we can accurately make about the impact of technology on structure.

The initial thrust: Woodward's research

The initial interest in technology as a determinant of structure can be traced to the mid-1960s and the work of Joan Woodward.[1] Her research, which focused on production technology, was the first major attempt to view organisation structure from a technological perspective. But first we need a word of caution in interpreting Woodward's findings. Woodward's study does not pretend to be applicable to all organisations. It applies only to manufacturing industries located in the south of England. As relevant to us as the findings is the methodology she used and whether this methodology is worth replicating in other similar studies. Woodward was searching for the most appropriate structure, which if it could be identified might then be incorporated into management practice and teaching. Subsequent studies have used the same methodology, although in recent times not on such a broad scale as Woodward. As we can see from Chapter 1, those more influenced by post-modernist thinking would eschew a survey-type methodology.

Background

Woodward chose approximately 100 manufacturing firms in the south of England. These ranged in size from fewer than 250 employees to over 1000. The data she gathered were quite extensive, but we will concentrate our discussion on the structural variables. The data allowed her to compute various measures of structure: the number of hierarchical levels, the span of control, the administrative component, the extent of formalisation and the like. She also gathered financial data on each firm (e.g. profitability, sales, market share), which allowed her to classify the companies as above-average or below-average in terms of success or organisational effectiveness. Her objective was straightforward: is there a correlation between structural form and effectiveness? Her hypothesis, derived from the classical prescriptions of management theorists, was that there is one optimum form of organisational structure that leads to organisational effectiveness.

Her efforts to link common structures to effectiveness were unsuccessful. The structural diversity among the firms in each of her effectiveness categories was so great that it was impossible to establish any relationship or draw any valid conclusions between what was regarded as sound organisational structure and effectiveness. It was only after Woodward had grouped the firms according to their typical mode of production technology that relationships between structure and effectiveness became apparent.

Woodward categorised the firms into one of three types of technologies: **unit**, **mass** or **process production**. She treated these categories as a scale with increasing degrees of technological complexity, unit being the least complex and process the most complex. Unit producers would manufacture custom-made products such as locomotives, turbines for hydroelectric dams or special-purpose vehicles. Mass producers would make large-batch or mass-produced products such as refrigerators or motor cars. The third category, process production, included heavily automated continuous-process producers such as oil and chemical refiners.

Conclusions

Woodward found that there were distinct relationships between these technology classifications and the subsequent structure of the firms, and that the effectiveness of the organisations was related to the 'fit' between technology and structure.

For example, the degree of vertical differentiation increased with technical complexity. The median number of management levels for firms in the unit, mass and process categories were three, four and six respectively. More important, from an effectiveness standpoint, the above-average firms in each category tended to cluster around the median for their production group.

Woodward also found that the administrative component varied directly with the type of technology: that is, as technological complexity increased, so did the proportion of administrative and support staff personnel. However, not all the relationships were linear. For instance, the mass-production firms had the smallest proportion of

unit production
technology wherein units are custom-made and work is non-routine

mass production
large-batch or mass-produced technology

process production
highly controlled, standardised and continuous processing technology

skilled workers and scored high in terms of overall complexity and formalisation, whereas the unit and process firms tended to rate low on these structural dimensions.

A careful analysis of her findings led Woodward to conclude that for each category on the technology scale (unit, mass, process) and for each structural component, there was an optimal range around the median point that encompassed the positions of the more effective firms. That is, within each technological category, the firms that conformed most nearly to the median figures for each structural component were the most effective (see Table 7.1). The mass-production technology firms were highly differentiated, relied on extensive formalisation, and did relatively little to delegate authority. Both the unit and process technologies, in contrast, were structured more loosely. Flexibility was achieved through less vertical differentiation, less division of labour and more group activities, more widely defined role responsibilities and decentralised decision making. High formalisation and centralised control apparently were not feasible with unit production's custom-made, non-routine technology and not necessary in the heavily automated, inherently tightly controlled continuous-process technology.

Woodward's investigation demonstrated a link between technology, structure and effectiveness. Firms that most nearly approximated the typical structure for their technology were the most effective. Firms that deviated in either direction from their ideal structure were less successful. Therefore, Woodward argued that effectiveness was a function of an appropriate technology–structure fit. Organisations that developed structures that conformed to their technologies were more successful than those that did not.

Woodward was also able to explain the disparity between her findings and the classical prescriptions of management theorists: these prescriptions must have been based on the theorists' experiences with organisations that used mass-production technologies. The mass-production firms had clear lines of authority, high formalisation, a low proportion of skilled workers achieved through a high division of labour, wide spans of control at the supervisory level and centralised decision making. But as not all organisations use mass-production technology, these

TABLE 7.1 Summary of Woodward's findings on the relationship between technological complexity and structure

	Low		High
		Technology	
Structural characteristic	**Unit production**	**Mass production**	**Process production**
Number of vertical levels	3	4	6
Supervisor's span of control	24	48	14
Manager/total employee ratio	1:23	1:16	1:8
Proportion of skilled workers	High	Low	High
Overall complexity	Low	High	Low
Formalisation	Low	High	Low
Centralisation	Low	High	Low

prescriptions lacked generalisability. Thus Woodward's research spelt the beginning of the end for the view that there were universal principles of management and organisation. Her work was to represent the initial transition by organisation theory scholars from a principles perspective to a contingency theory of organisations.

Evaluation

Several follow-up studies have supported Woodward's findings, but she has also had her share of criticism. Let us review what others have had to say about Woodward's research.

Edward Harvey was an early advocate of Woodward.[2] He believed that the underlying foundation of Woodward's scale was technical specificity. That is, he assumed that more specific technologies present fewer problems requiring new or innovative solutions than do more diffuse or complex technologies. So he took 43 different industrial organisations and rated them as technically diffuse (which closely paralleled Woodward's unit production), technically intermediate (akin to mass production) and technically specific (similar to Woodward's process production). These categories were based on the number of major product changes that the sample firms had experienced in the 10 years before the study. Harvey found, consistent with Woodward's technological imperative, a relationship between technical specificity and structure. Basically, organisations with specific technologies had more specialised subunits, more authority levels and higher ratios of managers to total personnel than did those with diffuse technologies.

Woodward's findings were also supported in another study of manufacturing firms.[3] The researcher, like Woodward, found no evidence of such a thing as a universally optimum structural form. His data constituted strong evidence to confirm Woodward's claim that unit, mass and process production result in different structural forms and that proper fit within categories increases the likelihood that the organisation will be successful.

Woodward's research and analysis by no means developed a tightly sealed argument for the technological imperative. Attacks have been made at a number of levels.[4] Her measure of technology has been criticised as unreliable. Her methodology, as it relied primarily on subjective observations and interviews, is open to interpretational bias. Woodward implies causation, yet her methodology can allow her to claim only association. Her measures of organisational success are open to attack as lacking rigour. Finally, as her firms were all British companies engaged almost exclusively in manufacturing, any generalisations to all organisations, or even to manufacturing firms outside Great Britain, must be guarded.

Knowledge-based technology: Perrow's contribution

One of the major limitations of Woodward's perspective on technology was its manufacturing base. As manufacturing firms represent less than half of all organisations, technology needs to be operationalised in a more general way if the concept is to have meaning across all organisations. Charles Perrow proposed such an alternative.[5]

Background

Perrow looked at knowledge technology rather than at production technology. He defined technology as 'the action that an individual performs upon an object, with or without the aid of tools or mechanical devices, in order to make some change in that object'.[6] He then proceeded to identify what he believed to be the two underlying dimensions of knowledge technology.

The first dimension, labelled **task variability**, considers the number of exceptions encountered in one's work. These exceptions will be few in number if the job is high in routineness. Jobs that normally have few exceptions in their day-to-day practice include those on a motor vehicle assembly line or a cook at McDonald's. At the other end of the spectrum, if a job has a great deal of variety a large number of exceptions can be expected. Typically, this characterises top management positions, consulting jobs or the work of professionals. So task variability appraises work by evaluating it along a variety–routineness continuum.

The second dimension assesses the type of search procedures followed to find successful methods for responding adequately to task exceptions. The search may, at one extreme, be described as well defined. If your car does not start, the mechanic works through a series of well-defined procedures to identify the cause—is the battery flat, is there petrol in the tank, is there a fuel blockage and so on. Using this kind of logic, you can find the source of the problem and rectify it.

The other extreme would be ill-defined problems. If you are an architect with a brief to design a building which 'reflects its environment but whose style will be noteworthy', then you will have no previous models to work from. You will not use a formal search technique. You will have to rely on your prior experience, judgement and intuition to find a solution. Through guesswork and trial and error you might find an acceptable choice. Perrow called this second dimension **problem analysability**, ranging from well-defined to ill-defined. Table 7.2 represents a 10-item questionnaire that measures these two dimensions.

These two dimensions—task variability and problem analysability—can be used to construct a two-by-two matrix. This is shown in Figure 7.1. The four cells in this matrix represent four types of technology: routine, engineering, craft, and non-routine.

- **Routine technologies** (cell 1) have few exceptions and easy-to-analyse problems. The mass-production processes used to make steel or motor cars or to refine petroleum belong in this category. A bank teller's job is also an example of activities subsumed under routine technology.
- **Engineering technologies** (cell 2) have a large number of exceptions, but they can be handled in a rational and systematic manner. The construction of office buildings would fall into this cell, as would the activities performed by tax accountants.
- **Craft technologies** (cell 3) deal with relatively difficult problems but with a limited set of exceptions. This would include shoe making, furniture restoring or the work of performing artists.
- **Non-routine technologies** (cell 4) are characterised by many exceptions and difficult-to-analyse problems. Examples of non-routine technologies would be strategic planning and basic research activities.

In summary, Perrow argued that if problems can be studied systematically, using logical and rational analysis, cells 1 or 2 will be appropriate. Problems that can be

---

task variability the number of exceptions encountered in performing a task

problem analysability the type of search procedures followed to find successful methods for adequately responding to task exceptions from well-defined and analysable to ill-defined and unalalysable

routine technology containing few exceptions and easy-to-analyse problems

engineering technology containing a large number of exceptions, but can be handled in a rational and systematic manner

craft technology containing relatively difficult problems but with a limited set of exceptions

non-routine technology containing many exceptions and difficult-to-analyse problems

TABLE 7.2 Measuring technology

Task variability and problem analysability can be measured in an organisational unit by having employees answer the following 10 questions. Scores are normally derived from responses scored on a 1–7 scale for each question.

Task variability
1. How many of these tasks are the same from day to day?
2. To what extent would you say your work is routine?
3. People in this unit do about the same job in the same way most of the time.
4. Basically, unit members perform repetitive activities in doing their jobs.
5. How repetitious are your duties?

Problem analysability
1. To what extent is there a clearly known way to do the major types of work you normally encounter?
2. To what extent is there a clearly defined body of knowledge of subject matter that can guide you in doing your work?
3. To what extent is there an understandable sequence of steps that can be followed in doing your work?
4. To do your work, to what extent can you rely on established procedures and practices?
5. To what extent is there an understandable sequence of steps that can be followed in carrying out your work?

Source: Michael Withey, Richard L. Daft & William H. Cooper, 'Measures of Perrow's Work Unit Technology: An Empirical Assessment and a New Scale', *Academy of Management Journal*, March 1983, p. 59.

FIGURE 7.1 Perrow's technology classification

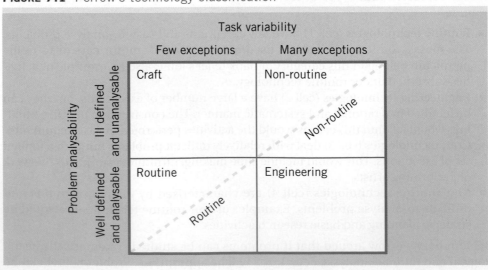

handled only by intuition, guesswork or unanalysed experience require the technology of cells 3 or 4. Similarly, if new, unusual or unfamiliar problems appear regularly, they will be in either cells 2 or 4. If problems are familiar, then cells 1 or 3 are appropriate.

Perrow also proposed that task variability and problem analysability were positively correlated. By that he meant that it would be unusual to find instances where tasks had very few exceptions and search was clearly unanalysable or where tasks had a great many exceptions and search was well defined and easily analysable. Thus the four technologies can be combined into a single routine–non-routine dimension. This is shown in Figure 7.1 as a diagonal line.

Perrow argued that control and coordination methods should vary with technology type. The more routine the technology, the more highly structured the organisation should be. Conversely, non-routine technologies require greater structural flexibility. Perrow then identified the key aspects of structure that could be modified to the technology:

- the amount of *discretion* that can be exercised for completing tasks;
- the *power* of groups to control the unit's goals and basic strategies;
- the extent of *interdependence* between these groups;
- the extent to which these groups engage in *coordination* of their work, using either feedback or the planning of others.

Conclusions

What does all this mean? Simply that the most routine technology (cell 1) can be accomplished best through standardised coordination and control. These technologies should be aligned with structures that are high in both formalisation and centralisation. At the other extreme, non-routine technologies (cell 4) demand flexibility. Basically, they would be decentralised, have high interaction among all members and be characterised as having a minimum degree of formalisation. In between, craft technology (cell 3) requires that problem solving be done by those with the greatest knowledge and experience. That means decentralisation. Engineering technology (cell 2), because it has many exceptions but analysable search processes, should have decisions centralised but should maintain flexibility through low formalisation. Table 7.3 summarises Perrow's predictions.

TABLE 7.3 Perrow's technology–structure predictions

Cell technology	Structural characteristic			
	Formalisation	Centralisation	Span of control	Coordination and control
1 Routine	High	High	Wide	Planning and rigid rules
2 Engineering	Low	High	Moderate	Reports and meetings
3 Craft	Moderate	Low	Moderate—wide	Training and meetings
4 Non-routine	Low	Low	Moderate—narrow	Group norms and group meetings

Evaluation

The two-by-two matrix of technologies and the predictions of what structural dimensions are most compatible with these technologies were not examined empirically by Perrow. But others have tested the theory.

One study of 14 medium-sized manufacturing firms that looked only at the two extreme cells—routine and non-routine technologies—found support for Perrow's predictions.[7] Another, covering 16 health and welfare agencies, confirmed that organisations do have diverse technologies and that the more routine the work, the more likely it is that decision making will be centralised.[8]

State employment-service agencies were the set of organisations analysed in yet another test of Perrow's theory.[9] In this study, technology was operationalised at the unit rather than the organisational level, in the belief that if routineness of technology actually affects structure, this effect should be greatest at the unit level. Again, the results proved consistent with Perrow's predictions: work that was high in routineness was associated with high formalisation.

Unlike Woodward, Perrow did not intend that his typology should be applied to the total organisation. He viewed technology as being best measured at the work-group or individual level. Hence Perrow's model is applicable to all types of work in all nature of industries. This was because he viewed technology as a mental process, rather than a physical output. So no matter whether we are a clerk in the public service, a motor mechanic or the managing director of a large public corporation, the technology we use may be classified according to Perrow's typology.

In summary, there appears to be considerable support for Perrow's conclusions. Organisations and organisational subunits with routine technologies tend to have greater formalisation and centralisation than do their counterparts with non-routine technologies.

One note of caution before we move on. Perrow's original theory went somewhat beyond what we have presented here. He predicted, for instance, relationships between the type of technology and structural aspects such as hierarchical discretion levels and types of coordination. These other relationships have found limited support by way of empirical studies.[10] We point this out to acknowledge that Perrow has his critics and that there is ammunition available for attacking his matrix theory. But at the general level—and by that we mean the issues of whether technologies can be differentiated on the basis of routineness and whether more routine technologies are associated with higher degrees of formalisation and centralisation—the evidence is largely supportive.

Technological uncertainty: Thompson's contribution

The third major contribution to the technology–structure literature has been made by James Thompson.[11] In contrast to Woodward and Perrow, Thompson is not a member of the technological-imperative school. Rather, as will be shown, Thompson's contribution lies in demonstrating that technology determines the selection of a strategy for reducing uncertainty and that specific structural arrangements can facilitate uncertainty reduction.

Background

Thompson sought to create a classification scheme that was general enough to deal with the range of technologies found in complex organisations. He proposed three types that are differentiated by the tasks an organisational unit performs.

Long-linked technology

If tasks or operations were sequentially interdependent, Thompson called them long-linked. This technology is characterised by a fixed sequence of connected steps, as shown in Figure 7.2A. That is, activity A must be performed before activity B, activity B before activity C and so forth. Examples of **long-linked technology** include mass production assembly lines and taking a trip on a train.

long-linked technology a fixed sequence of connected steps: sequentially interdependent tasks

Owing to sequential interdependence, efficiency requires a high level of coordination among activities. This leads to the major uncertainties facing management lying on the input and output sides of the organisation. Acquiring raw materials, for instance, and disposing of finished goods become major areas of concern. As a result, management tends to respond to this uncertainty by controlling inputs and outputs. One of the best means of achieving this is to integrate vertically—forwards,

FIGURE 7.2 Thompson's technology classification

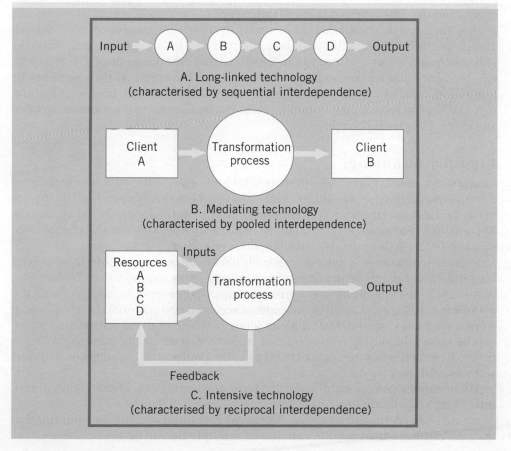

backwards, or both. This allows the organisation to encompass important sources of uncertainty within its boundaries. Comalco, for example, has large plants for manufacturing aluminium foil. It integrates backwards by controlling its input, operating aluminium smelters and refineries that provide the raw materials to the foil plants. It integrates forwards by controlling its output, marketing much of its foil through supermarkets under its own name.

Mediating technology

mediating technology the process of linking together different clients in need of each other's services; pooled interdependence

Thompson identified **mediating technology** as one that links clients on both the input and output side of the organisation. Banks, telephone companies, retail stores, insurance companies, employment and welfare agencies, and post offices are examples. As shown in Figure 7.2B mediators perform an interchange function, linking units that are otherwise independent. The linking unit responds by standardising the organisation's transactions and establishing conformity in clients' behaviour. Banks, for instance, bring together those who want to save (depositors) with those who want to borrow. Neither of the groups know each other, but the bank's success depends on attracting both. A bank with money and no borrowers cannot succeed. Failure can also occur when borrowers are plentiful but no-one wants to leave his or her money with the bank. As a result, the managers of mediating technologies face uncertainty as a result of the organisation's potential dependence on clients and the risks inherent in client transactions.

How does one deal with this uncertainty? By increasing the populations served. The more clients one has, the less dependent one is on any single client. So banks seek many depositors and attempt to develop a diversified loan portfolio. Similarly, employment agencies seek to fill jobs for many employers so that the loss of one or two major accounts will not jeopardise the organisation's survival. Insurance companies also seek to reduce their overall levels of risk by increasing the numbers insured and diversifying their portfolio.

Intensive technology

intensive technology the utilisation of a wide range of customised responses, depending on the nature and variety of the problems; reciprocal interdependence

Thompson's third category—**intensive technology**—represents a customised response to a diverse set of contingencies. The exact response depends on the nature of the problem and the variety of problems, which cannot be predicted accurately. This includes technologies dominant in hospitals, universities, research laboratories, full-service management consulting firms or military combat teams.

Intensive technology is most dramatically illustrated by the work of a large general hospital. At any moment an emergency admission may require some combination of dietary, X-ray, laboratory and housekeeping or hotel services, together with the various medical specialties, pharmaceutical services, occupational therapies, social work services, and spiritual or religious services. Which of these is used, and when, can be determined only from evidence about the state of the patient.[12] What is preprogrammed is not the treatment given to the patient, but the range of skills and services available.

Thompson's typology identified three technological classifications—long-linked, mediating, and intensive technology.

Figure 7.2C demonstrates that intensive technology achieves coordination through mutual adjustment. A number of multiple resources are available to the organisation, but only a limited combination is used at a given time depending on the situation. The selection, combination and ordering of these resources are determined by feedback from the object itself. Because of this need for flexibility of response, the major uncertainty that managers confront is the problem itself. They respond by ensuring the availability of a variety of resources to prepare for any contingency. As in our hospital example, the organisation has a wealth of specialised services and skills available with which it can respond to a variety of situations.

Conclusions

The structural implications from Thompson's framework are less straightforward than those derived from the work of Woodward and Perrow. Basically, each technology creates a type of interdependence. Long-linked technology is accompanied by *sequential interdependence*—the procedures are highly standardised and must be performed in a specified serial order. Mediating technology has *pooled interdependence*—two or more units each contribute separately to a larger unit. Intensive technology creates *reciprocal interdependence*—the outputs of units influence each other in a reciprocal fashion. Each of these interdependences, in turn, demands a certain type of coordination that will facilitate organisational effectiveness yet minimise costs.

In general terms, we can translate Thompson's insights into structural terminology. He argued that the demands placed on decision making and communication as a result of technology increased from mediating (low) to long-linked (medium) to intensive (high). Mediating technology is coordinated most effectively through rules and procedures. Long-linked should be accompanied by planning and scheduling. Intensive technology requires mutual adjustment. This suggests that:

- mediating technology   = low complexity and high formalisation;
- long-linked technology   = moderate complexity and formalisation;
- intensive technology   = high complexity and low formalisation.

Let us look at the research to evaluate empirically the validity of Thompson's predictions.

Evaluation

There is, unfortunately, a shortage of data against which Thompson's predictions can be judged. The only study of consequence using Thompson's dimensions measured not structure but the relationship between technology and organisational effectiveness.[13] Analysing 297 subunits from 17 business and industrial firms, investigators were able to support part of Thompson's model. Long-linked and mediating technologies were associated closely with the use of standardisation, rules and advanced planning, whereas intensive technologies were characterised by mutual adjustments to other units. The investigators concluded that the criterion of effectiveness varies with the type of technology used by the organisational unit.

The lack of data makes it impossible to conclude whether Thompson's framework is empirically supported, but it does have face validity: that is, it appears to be a comprehensive model that explains the behaviour of organisations. It certainly permits a wide range of varying organisations to be compared. Its value, however, may lie far more in offering a rich and descriptive technology classification than in providing insight into the relationship between technology and structure.

Task uncertainty: Galbraith's contribution

We have seen that organisational technology involves transforming inputs into outputs. This process of transformation has different levels of uncertainties.[14] Jay Galbraith defined uncertainty as '. . . the difference between the amount of information required to perform a task and the amount of information already possessed by the organisation'.[15] An example of a certain task with a high level of existing knowledge would be that undertaken by a checkout operator at a supermarket. An example of an uncertain task with smaller levels of existing knowledge would be designing a new type of jet aircraft, such as the 'stealth' bomber.

Background

The extent of uncertainty of the task itself was not of primary importance to Galbraith. Rather, he considered that as task uncertainty increased, so did the amount of information that had to be processed among decision makers in order to achieve the desired level of organisational performance. The amount of information, and how this information was processed, became the major determinant of the structure of the organisation.

Figure 7.3 shows how Galbraith has identified different organisation design strategies to accommodate different levels of uncertainty and information processing. In a straightforward routine task, such as the checkout operator mentioned above, rules and programs that reflect the existing knowledge of the organisation may be used. Any exception encountered is referred to a manager further up the hierarchy. Another method used to deal with uncertainty is the use of goals or targets. In this case, a complex task such as reconditioning a locomotive is not undertaken as one piece of work. Instead it is divided into a number of activities, such as electrical system maintenance and work on the brakes. These tasks can progress independently of each other. The goal in this case would be to have all systems completed at the same time.

Once these systems of handling uncertainty are no longer effective, the organisation can do one of two things: it can reduce the need for information processing, or

FIGURE 7.3 Galbraith's organisation design strategies

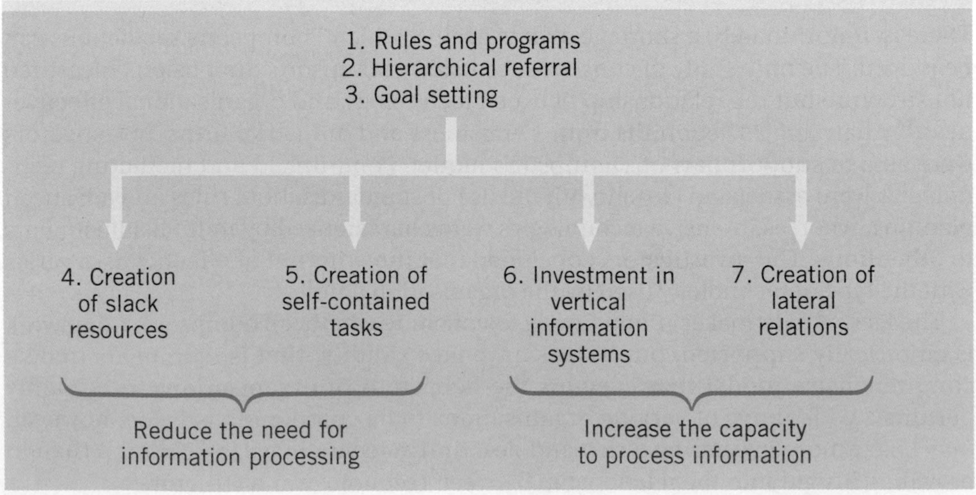

increase its capacity to handle information. Slack resources are additional resources over and above the minimum required to complete the task. The most common use of slack resources is to increase the time, or reduce the performance levels, necessary to achieve a goal. This means that the likelihood of a target being missed is lower and therefore there is less possibility that the management hierarchy of the organisation will become overloaded. The creation of self-contained tasks involves altering the work design so that it moves from a functional design controlled by managers to one where each group has all the resources it needs to complete its task. For instance, in designing an aircraft, work proceeds on the navigation systems, engines and hydraulic systems independently of each other. All that those designing these systems need is sufficient information to coordinate with the other design teams.

The final group of design responses is to increase the capacity to process information. This may be through the use of sophisticated computer systems or application of other advanced operations management techniques. Finally, the creation of lateral relations sees greater management involvement in providing and improving communication across the organisation, through such positions as project managers and coordinators of various types. This means that those actually doing the work can better integrate with others who are working on interdependent coordinating tasks.

Conclusions

Galbraith argued that the key determinant of organisational structure was the amount of information that had to be processed in order to turn inputs into outputs. In organisations where there was a repetitive cycle of events, such as a retail chain, rules and regulations could be used to handle most tasks. These reflected the collective experience of the organisation. Exceptions to events covered by formalisation methods were few in number and could be handled by hierarchical referral. However, as exceptions became more common, so uncertainty and the need to process information grew. This resulted in changes to the organisation's structure.

Galbraith's model has similarities to Perrow's typology in that both deal with the routineness of tasks. But whereas Perrow looks at the impact of routineness on the level of those carrying out the task, Galbraith considers the effect of routineness on the structure of the whole organisation, or at least those parts dealing with uncertainty. We can also identify similarities with Thompson's typology. Mediating technology categorises information which allows the use of rules and regulations. This reduces the need to process information. Long-linked technology proposes the use of goals to coordinate the various parts of the chain, and intensive technology adopts a structure which increases the capacity to process information.

Underlying Galbraith's model is the idea that organisations become more complex as the need to process information increases. But none of the options introduced by Galbraith are mutually exclusive: that is, they can all exist in different parts of the organisation at the same time. And neither do they form an hierarchy in which there is a logical progression from one level to the next. It is common, for instance, for rules and regulations to be used in conjunction with hierarchical referral and computerisation, which both increase the capacity to process information.

Evaluation

Galbraith's typology did not grow out of an empirical investigation into how organisations processed information. It was more the result of theorising from the premise of how organisations deal with uncertainty. There is also not a great deal in the model to prove or disprove. Each of the seven methods of dealing with information, with its consequent structures, demonstrably exists. What Galbraith has done is bring them together as interconnected parts of a model which has as its base the assertion that the need to process information is the main determinant of organisation structure.

Finally, Galbraith's categories also allow for an element of routineness. Work that is routine in nature has low uncertainty, and there is not a great requirement to process information. Alternatively, non-routine work tends to have high uncertainty, with far more need to process information.

Tying it together: what does it all mean?

Is it possible to isolate technology as a contingency?

We have already highlighted the difficulty in arriving at a useful definition of technology. In this section we discuss a further difficulty, namely whether it is possible to isolate technology from the other influences on organisational structure. Technology and structure are both multidimensional concepts. As a result, it is possible that technology is related to structure, although not in any simple, straightforward manner. There are, in fact, some logical arguments to support the idea that the industry sector within which the organisation operates and the organisation's size influence the relationship between technology and structure. This increases the difficulty in determining causal relationships.

Our introduction, which discussed the different production technologies of Rolls-Royce and Holden, highlights the influence of the industry on structure. Rolls-Royce has chosen to compete in a market that demands individuality and craft production. This leads to non-routine technologies being used. Holden competes in an area characterised by price competition: what it charges for a motor vehicle is limited by what people can afford to pay. As a result, Holden is forced to rely on the cost benefits of standardisation and mass production. Both manufacturers use different production technologies. But the technology is largely dictated by market demands.

This highlights the difficulty in isolating the influence of technology from other variables. If we interviewed the managing director of Rolls-Royce about the company structure, we might find that he (or she) identified strategy or industry demands as being the main determinant of structure. Technology might not rate a mention. Similarly, the demands of mass production are probably so internalised within Holden that other alternatives are not even considered.[16]

Separating the influence of size and technology also presents difficulties. A number of researchers suggest that organisational size is the critical determinant of structure, not technology.[17] For instance, several of the Aston Group studies failed to find an association between technology and organisation structure.[18] Rather, size was found to have a more dominant influence on structure. The researchers reason that the larger organisations become, the more they are likely to differentiate their operations into smaller units relying on formalised processes. This diminishes the impact of technology as a variable. However, in one case the Aston Group was able to support Woodward's conclusions concerning technology and structure, but again the explanation for the association was based on size.[19] If technology has an influence on structure, the Aston Group reasoned, it is most likely to affect those activities closest to the technology itself. Therefore, the larger the organisation, the smaller the role technology is likely to play. Conversely, the smaller the organisation, the more likely it is that the whole organisation will be impinged on by the production work flow or operating core. The Aston Group then noted that the firms Woodward sampled were basically small in size and thus more likely to be influenced by their technology. Their conclusion: in smaller organisations the structure of operations is likely to be dominated by the primary transformation process, but in large organisations the impact of technology is not likely to be so powerful. And where is technology's influence the greatest? In those organisational units immediately impinged on by the operating core.

The preceding discussion suggests that an organisation's size moderates the impact of technology on structure. In small organisations, divisions of large organisations or organisational activities most closely related to the operating core, technology should explain more of the resultant structure. It does appear, however, that there is a symbiotic relationship between size and technology; increasing size and routinisation of work are closely related, and the influence of each is difficult to separate.

Summary

Figure 7.4 illustrates an integration of the relationship between industry, size, technology and structure. Industry constrains technology options. But organisations need to reach a particular size before advantages can be obtained from the benefits offered by the more complex technologies. The decision to adopt a complex technology is unlikely to be made until the organisation has reached a large enough size to capitalise on economies of scale. So size determines technology. Yet, as Figure 7.4 demonstrates, the causal arrow can also go the other way—from technology to size. The decision, for example, to use mass-production technology may lead to the decision to increase the organisation's size to enable it to utilise the technology more efficiently. Discount stock brokerage firms use a routine technology but require a sizeable operation with reasonably high volume in order to operate profitably.

The common denominator: routineness

The common theme throughout this chapter, sometimes more evident than at other times, is that the processes or methods that transform inputs into outputs differ by their degree of routineness.[20]

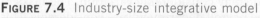

FIGURE 7.4 Industry-size integrative model

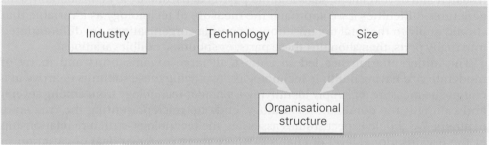

TABLE 7.4 Cataloguing technologies as routine or non-routine

	Technology	
Contributor	Routine	Non-routine
Woodward	Mass, process	Unit
Perrow	Routine, engineering	Craft, non-routine
Thompson	Long-linked, mediating	Intensive
Galbraith	Low uncertainty	High uncertainty
	Low information-processing needs	High information-processing needs

Woodward identified three types of technology—unit, mass, and process—each representing, respectively, an increased degree of technological complexity. At the extremes, unit technology deals with custom or non-routine activities, while process technology describes automated and standardised activities. Woodward describes mass technology as basically routine in nature. Perrow, too, presented two extremes—routine and non-routine technologies. His 'in-between' technologies—engineering and craft—also differ on routineness, the former more standardised than the latter. Thompson's categories include two technologies that are relatively routine (long-linked and mediating) and one that is non-routine (intensive). Finally, Galbraith's categories also contain an element of routineness in them. Work that is routine in nature has low uncertainty and there is not a great need to process information. Alternatively, non-routine work tends to have high uncertainty with far more need to process information. Table 7.4 summarises these observations.

The research into technology has proceeded in a number of different directions, yet there is a common underlying theme. Of course, the technology paradigms of Woodward, Perrow, Thompson, Galbraith and others cannot be substituted for each other. But this is not a book for researchers. Our intention is to provide some insight into organisation theory for use by managers. Given this less demanding objective, conceptualising technology as differing by degrees of routineness should be adequate for our analysis included at the end of this chapter, which evaluates technology's impact on our three structural components.

Work-unit level versus organisational level

Organisations and their components display considerable variation. The tasks of research and development, sales and the payroll department vary considerably. This generates difficulties if we approach the measure of technology as a variable that should apply to the total organisation. If complex organisations are differentiated into many parts, then shouldn't these parts, or subunits, exhibit variations?

This differentiation has led to almost all large organisations and many of moderate size having multiple technologies. Averaging these subunits to arrive at a composite measure, or simply identifying a singular technology from among several and calling it the dominant technology, ends up misrepresenting the true state of affairs. We should expect studies assessing the technology–structure relationship at the organisational level of analysis, where there is a great deal of variation in technology between subunits, to result in aggregate measures that are likely to be meaningless. As we will see, this is precisely what happens.

Technology research has been undertaken at the organisational and work unit levels. Both view technology as the means by which tasks are accomplished, but one considers the organisation as the unit of analysis and the other considers the work unit as the primary unit. Organisational-level analysis starts with the major product or service offered, which leads it to focus on the dominant conversion technology. Work unit-level analysis starts with the tasks performed by the individual employees, and is thus led to consider the methods by which they are accomplished.

When these two types of studies are combined, it is difficult if not impossible to draw useful conclusions. However, when they are separated, a clear pattern emerges. The organisational-level studies are still mixed, with few consistent relationships appearing between technology and structure. But the work unit-level studies provide a completely different picture. In evaluating the relationship between technology and a set of structural variables in eight work unit-level studies, at least half the correlations were found to be significant and all were in the same direction.[21]

Why do work unit-level studies support the technological imperative, whereas those at the organisational level do not? Several explanations have been offered.[22] First, work unit-level studies have far fewer conceptual and methodological problems. They have a unified concept of technology, and homogeneity is greater. The other reason for the high correlation between technology and structure at the work unit level is undoubtedly related to size. Work unit-level studies are looking at technology at the operating core. If there is a technological imperative, this is where it should be most evident because technology's impact should be greatest closest to the core. The fact that organisational-level studies are conceptually and methodologically heterogeneous, plus the realisation that technology at this level should have a lesser effect on structure, suggest that a reasonable doubt must remain concerning the demise of the technological imperative. If there is such an imperative, it may exist only with small organisations or those with homogeneous technologies throughout.

Special issues in organisational technology

Manufacturing versus service technologies

A complicating factor in assessing the impact of technology on organisation structure is that most studies that have been carried out have been on manufacturing organisations. However, more and more of the workforce is involved in providing services. There is also a third group, which can be called combined product and service firms. Figure 7.5 shows how service and manufacturing firms form a continuum and the typical industries in each category.

We are all familiar with the typical manufacturing firm, but what are the features of the service industries that make them different?[23] First, there is simultaneous production and consumption. Examples are a hairdresser cutting our hair, the journey to work on the train, and services provided by a doctor. This also means that the customer is part of the production process and that the output is customised to the consumer's needs. Even mass-transit journeys are customised, to the extent that passengers are getting on the train or bus all the time at places to suit their requirements.

FIGURE 7.5 Examples of service and manufacturing technologies

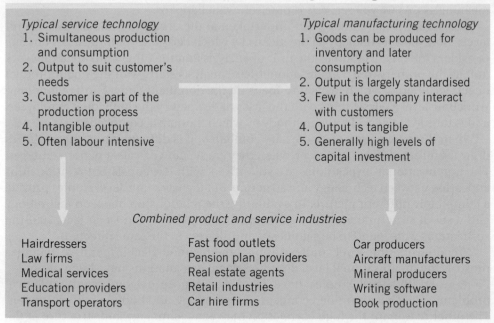

Typical service technology
1. Simultaneous production and consumption
2. Output to suit customer's needs
3. Customer is part of the production process
4. Intangible output
5. Often labour intensive

Typical manufacturing technology
1. Goods can be produced for inventory and later consumption
2. Output is largely standardised
3. Few in the company interact with customers
4. Output is tangible
5. Generally high levels of capital investment

Combined product and service industries

Hairdressers
Law firms
Medical services
Education providers
Transport operators

Fast food outlets
Pension plan providers
Real estate agents
Retail industries
Car hire firms

Car producers
Aircraft manufacturers
Mineral producers
Writing software
Book production

Source: Adapted from David E. Bowen, Caren Siehl & Benjamin Schneider, 'A Framework for Analysing Customer Service Organizations in Manufacturing', *Academy of Management Review*, 14, 1989, pp. 75–95.

Another major difference is that the output of the service industries is often intangible: that is, it cannot be inventoried. Watching a movie, undertaking a journey and attending a concert are all activities that cannot be inventoried to be drawn on in the future. Lastly, many services are labour-intensive. Hairdressing, medical services and personal fitness training all involve a labour intensity that is difficult to automate.

Do the characteristics of the service industries have an impact on their structure? Research shows that they do. One of the features of the service industries is that those providing the service come into direct contact with the customers of the organisation.[24] We continuously interact with transport, banking and retail employees. This means that service providers must stress interpersonal skills, which in turn indicates higher levels of training in the service industries, at least in communication and customer interface skills. It would make little difference to us if our car was assembled by grumpy workers, but irritable flight attendants can put an airline out of business.

Because of the need for customer interaction, decision making in service industries tends to be more decentralised than in manufacturing. This applies not only in the professions, such as law and medicine: it extends to those in lesser-skilled occupations such as hairdressers and taxi drivers, who must customise their output.

Another feature of service industries that influences their structure is that they tend to be both smaller and more geographically dispersed than manufacturing companies. In many service operations it is difficult to achieve economies of scale. And most services must be taken to where the customers are. This means that most service organisations are segregated into smaller operating units.

How do manufacturing industries interact with their customers? They have what are termed boundary spanners, whose main task it is to interact with customers.[25] The boundary spanners have the effect of protecting the operating core from intrusions by customers, thus allowing work to proceed without interruptions. If we buy a new car and want to make an inquiry about the car's performance, we will not speak to a production-line worker who built the car, or to one of the engineers who designed it. Rather, we will speak to a boundary spanner such a salesperson or distributor, who can generally handle our inquiry.

Technology and information processing

One of the greatest changes in production technologies for both the manufacturing and service industries that has occurred over the past 30 years has been the application of microprocessors to various organisational tasks. Often called the 'computer revolution', 'information technology' or 'high-tech', the new technologies apply computer-based controls and problem-solving techniques to traditional tasks such as scheduling, coordination and routine information manipulation and processing. Our interest in this technology arises from the impact that these changes have had on organisational structure. To identify what impacts have occurred, it is necessary to examine the forms that the new technologies take.

Before we do this, a word of warning. Research in this area has been greatly hampered by the difficulty in generating an operationalised definition of information technology.[26] As well, while the impact of computerisation can be found in just about every business activity, devising a unit of measurement for it is extremely difficult. Likewise, separating computerisation from other variables that can influence structure is a complex task. Further, many of these variables complement each other. For instance, e-mails do not displace face-to-face or voice communication but rather change the nature of both. Like much new technology, its influence is both subtle and long-term as people learn to incorporate it into their working practices. Notwithstanding these difficulties, researchers have identified certain influences, which form the basis for our discussion.

The first technologies we shall consider may be grouped together under the heading of **information technologies** (IT). IT is a general term covering five different categories of information processing.[27] The first is the one most usually associated with computers, that of undertaking tasks associated with the *day-to-day operations* of the organisation. Examples are routine accounting tasks, inventory control and payroll calculations. The second grouping comprises *technologies that improve communication*. These technologies help bring people together by reducing the restraints imposed by geography and time. Examples include fax machines, e-mail, the Internet and teleconferencing. The third grouping comprises *control systems*. These monitor and evaluate the performance of the organisation. They are often designed to conform to the control mechanisms of the organisation, and undertake much of the routine work associated with control. Such tasks as stock management, monitoring bank balances, maintaining budgets and keeping track of the costs of a vehicle fleet are typical control functions. The fourth application of IT is that of acting as a *decision support system*. In this role it supports the intellectual process of planning and decision making but cannot replace the intuitive insight of the decision maker. Functions such as calculating potential rates of return, generating spreadsheets, the analysis of various financial projections and the use of computers to

information technology (IT) a generic term covering the application of computerised information-processing techniques to organisational operations

undertake quality-control evaluation are examples of this function. The last grouping is that which supports *interorganisational systems*. This facilitates the movement of information from one organisation to another. We have previously mentioned e-mail and the Internet, but many organisational networks have a need for their computer-based systems to communicate with one another. These may be based on business-to-business Internet linkages but may also include electronic data interchange. The links between airlines and travel agencies and between retailers and wholesalers, interbank transfers and graphical and data interchanges between organisations producing different parts of a product are examples of interorganisational systems.

The influence of IT on structure

Most organisations use some form of information technology; even the humblest of businesses generally have a computer for routine tasks. But we also know intuitively that some organisations use IT far more extensively than others. Banks come to mind as extensive users of information technology, with agricultural organisations using IT less extensively. We can, however, make useful generalisations as to the intensity of IT usage. Given this limitation, we can identify a number of ways in which IT has influenced the structure of organisations. The main ones will be considered in turn (see Table 7.5).

Extent of IT usage

Can we expect that those organisations which use IT intensively to have different structural properties to those which do not? The answer is yes. One study determined that firms which are extensive users of IT tend to have decentralised decision making, a greater reliance on workforce skills, and provide incentives that are subjective (rather than quantitative) in nature.[28] Another theorist has proposed that there

TABLE 7.5 Summary of the influence of information technology usage on organisational structure

- **Extent of IT usage.** Most organisations use some form of IT. But those with dynamic and less routine work tend to use IT more intensively.
- **Impact on communication and coordination.** IT's ability to facilitate communication and coordination has permitted more complex work to be undertaken.
- **Impact on middle managers.** IT usage has led to a reduction in the number of middle managers in centralised organisations. In decentralised organisations, middle managers have tended to increase.
- **Impact on decision making.** IT tends to support lower-level, routine decision making rather than higher-level, conceptual decision making.
- **Impact of communication technologies.** IT has facilitated the dispersion of organisational activities and the formation of networks and clusters. It has reduced the cost of coordination and integration.
- **Structure of IT departments.** These tend to reflect the structure of the organisation. If the organisation is centralised, so too will the IT department be centralised. The opposite also holds.

are conditions which would predict the extent of IT usage. He proposed that the more dynamic and less routine the work of an organisation, the more likely it is that extensive IT will be used.[29] This is supported by our OT Closeup discussing the design of the B2 'stealth' bomber. In designing the aircraft the complex tasks, intense communication and the geographic dispersion of the design teams are only made possible by extensive use of IT.[30] One study also concluded that as investment in IT increased, organisations tended to become smaller. This decrease in size did not occur as the investment in IT was made, but was most pronounced two to three years after the investment was made.[31] This introduces one of the problems of studying the influence of IT on organisations—that is, the long time frame from the introduction of the technology until its use has settled into a stable pattern.

Impact on communication and coordination

IT has greatly increased the capacity to improve coordination both within and between units. This has permitted an increase in the complexity of the work being undertaken (see the OT Closeup on the B2 'stealth' bomber) and reduced the amount of time needed to accomplish a given task. Such operation management techniques as PERT networks and critical path analysis may be easily undertaken by computer. On a more general level, communication programs such as Lotus notes help break down barriers between departments, geographic areas and even organisations. It is therefore not surprising that increased IT investment has been associated with greater task complexity. This raises the problem of cause and effect: does IT facilitate tasks that require significant communication intensity, or are the tasks that require high levels of communication intensity natural users of IT-based communication and coordination mechanisms? The evidence indicates that the answer is probably both.

Impact on middle managers

One of the most talked-about effects of computerisation is the impact of IT on middle managers. Hardly a week goes by without a headline appearing regarding the effects of downsizing on organisations (see Chapter 6). But to what extent is this a product of IT, or is it influenced by other factors? The result of research is mixed with evidence supporting both an increase and decrease in the numbers of middle managers as a result of IT usage.[32] The key variable is the extent to which decision making in the organisation is centralised. Where both computing decisions and organisational decisions are centralised, top management tends to use IT to reduce the numbers of middle managers. This would affect those middle managers who are involved in making routine operating decisions. However, where both decisions regarding the use of IT and decisions made by middle managers are decentralised, then typically middle management numbers increase. This is made possible because IT provides the tools that permit middle managers to make decisions and supports lateral mechanisms of communication and coodination. We can see that IT, in this case, supports decentralisation and hence the influence of middle managers.[33]

Impact on decision making

There is evidence that IT is assisting lower-level decision making rather than executive decision making. IT is used more intensively by those at the operating levels of the organisation rather than occupying the executive suite.[34] There are inevitable limitations in the ability of IT to undertake higher-level decisions. IT systems

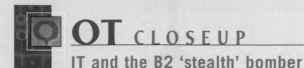

OT CLOSEUP

IT and the B2 'stealth' bomber

Some of the most complex engineering and organisational tasks are undertaken by military organisations. The design of the 'stealth' bomber provides ample evidence of this. It was developed in considerable secrecy in the 1980s, and its existence came to widespread public attention only in the Gulf War. It is not an aircraft with great performance, and its speed, range and manoeuvrability are not impressive; its main asset is its ability to fly undetected by radar. This is achieved by the aircraft's overall shape, complex surface, use of advanced radar-absorbent material and the fitting of engines free of acoustic and thermal 'signatures'. Much of the design was at the cutting edge of knowledge and was beyond the capacity of any one company to carry out. As a result four companies, Northrop, Boeing, Vought and General Electric, undertook the design work. They split the work, with each company concentrating on a different aspect of the design.

Normally this would lead to a high level of costs to administer the project. These costs are called transaction costs by organisational economists, and they refer to the expense related to the large numbers of liaison personnel, project managers and various administrators whose sole task is to provide coordination services. In effect they are human information processors. As the design work was being carried out at a number of different locations, these costs would have been extremely heavy, made worse by the need to travel between locations.

The project, however, demonstrated one of the strengths of information technology, namely that of reducing the cost of information processing. Information technology is a very economical means of coordinating; the cost of transmitting data is very low and simple computer programs can do many scheduling and data-manipulation tasks far cheaper than humans can. In order to derive these benefits from such a diverse range of contractors, the head contractor, Northrop, insisted on a common information-processing protocol. That means that the computers of all the contractors and subcontractors should use the same software and operating systems. Once this was in place, the engineers involved developed a common 'technical grammar', a terminology, jargon and idiom to be used by all contractors. This in itself removed many of the traditional coordination tasks involved in complex design. Costs were also saved in generating the comprehensive and voluminous technical manuals that accompany complex engineering projects. This was achieved by tapping into the common database on a progressive basis, rather than starting work once the design had been completed. Coordination was also facilitated by greatly increasing the number of messages that could be sent between those working on the project.

The information-processing system also permitted faster assessment of the contribution and performance of each of the design teams. What they were doing, and whether they were doing it on time, could be easily assessed on an ongoing basis by the project managers with little recourse to lengthy meetings and subjective evaluation of performance.

The stealth bomber involved an incredibly complex design effort. It was completed in five years without major coordination or design problems. Using more traditional coordination and design approaches would have raised costs significantly and extended time frames. The experiences in designing the bomber have implications for non-military situations. The lower cost of processing information has made organic and adhocratic structures feasible in many situations. Managers may have thought twice before introducing more complex designs because of the high costs involved in having to control and administer them. These costs are progressively dropping as the cost of information technology falls. As a result we can see that information technology is favouring the more organic over the more mechanistic structures.

Adapted from: Nicholas Argyres, 'The Impact of Information Technology upon Coordination: Evidence from the B2 "Stealth" Bomber', *Organization Science*, 10(2), 1999, pp. 162–80.

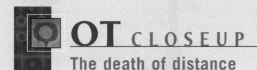

OT CLOSEUP
The death of distance

One of the great innovations of our time has been the development of technology to transmit information over vast distances at relatively little cost. How is this likely to affect the organisations we work for and manage? Frances Cairncross proposes that organisations will be affected in a number of ways. She identifies the following as being likely outcomes of the so called information revolution.

The death of distance. Distance will no longer determine the cost of communicating electronically. Some types of work, such as share and futures trading, financial services and call centres will work three shifts a day across the world's three main time zones.
Location will become unimportant. Companies will locate any screen-based activity wherever the best combination of skills and cost can be found.
Size will become irrelevant. Small companies will be able to offer services that previously could be offered only by large companies. Individuals anywhere with great ideas will attract global capital.

More customised content. Improved networks will allow individuals to order customised products.
A deluge of information. As information becomes plentiful and cheap, there will be a significant role for those who can filter, sift, process and edit it.
The loose-knit corporation. Many companies will become networks of independent specialists, leading to more employees working in smaller units or alone.
More minnows, more giants. On the one hand, the costs of starting a new business will decline and some barriers to entry will fall. Companies are also more likely to outsource to smaller companies. On the other, communication will amplify the strengths of brands and the power of networks.
Increased power of the brand. Whatever is fashionable—whether it be music, a clothing label or sports stars—will greatly increase its exposure, thus magnifying profits.

Adapted from: Frances Cairncross, *The Death of Distance*, London: Orion Publishing, 1997.

generally provide cheap data, but the data require human intervention to analyse and interpret them.[35] The lower the level of manager, the more likely it is that decision making is routine and hence supported by IT. Higher-level management is involved in decisions requiring more intuitive judgement, which is poorly supported by IT. As a result IT may be seen as permitting the decentralisation of some decision making. However, we need to qualify this. The ability to process and consolidate information allows senior management to monitor decisions made lower in the organisations. So decentralised decision making may be an illusion; the only decision which senior managers have delegated may be those relating to routine operating matters.

Impact of communication technologies

The ability to transmit large amounts of information and to communicate with those who may be half a world away inevitably has an impact on the way organisations are managed. As well, we can expect relationships between organisations to take a different form. Electronic mail, for instance, links those who may not otherwise communicate, thus enabling coordination over a wider area. It also has the effect of flattening hierarchies by encouraging less social inhibition about communications.[36]

One study showed that computer conferencing centralised decision making and reduced the number of middle managers concerned with production. However, it increased the number of staff specialists higher in the organisation.[37] The lower costs of communicating will also increase the likelihood of there being more widely dispersed units, each specialising in what they do best.

Relations between organisations have also undergone a significant change with the new forms of communication. Electronic linkages allow information to flow between vendors, suppliers and customers, creating what has been termed a virtual organisation. Companies can often turn these electronic linkages into new ways of doing business. This has led to a much more fluid relationship between companies, with teaming arrangements becoming possible in response to market opportunities.[38] It has also led to spatially dispersed organisations, where certain functions are often carried out in different parts of the world.

The structure of IT departments

There has been considerable research on the structure of IT departments. This is not surprising, as many IT departments are large and effectiveness depends on the structure reflecting the key tasks which they undertake. IT departments are now significant parts of most organisations, and the loss of middle managers from production and accounting functions has been made up by many new managers being hired to administer the IT function.[39] Not all IT departments are structured the same way.[40] Not surprisingly, the structure of IT departments reflects that of the organisation it serves. Where decision making within the organisation is centralised, the IT departments tend to be centralised as well. However, where organisations are decentralised, the IT function also tends to be decentralised.[41] Functions that are centralised include application decisions, telecommunications and communication protocols. Those which are decentralised include the specific needs of user departments. This sees the IT function divided into groups, some working closely with the operating units of the organisation, others working at remote locations. This separation of functions has led to the introduction of a liaison person to link the two. Essentially this person acts as a coordinator between the users and providers of IT, helping to reconcile needs and capabilities. He or she is sometimes called an account manager, but the actual job title varies from organisation to organisation.

A further influence on IT departments is the increasing trend to outsource.[42] IT lends itself to outsourcing, as it can be bundled into self-contained operations which are capable of being undertaken by those outside the organisation, often at a lower price than undertaking the function in-house. This has led to subcontractors undertaking long-term assignments within an organisation, blurring the boundaries of the organisation. It has also led to the introduction of various liaison and coordination roles to link the contractor with the organisation. The role of this person is much the same as that between the IT and user departments.

One of the changes in organisational structure that has occurred in recent times is the creation of the position of Chief Information Officer (CIO). This person normally sits on the highest decision-making committees of the organisation. His/her high-level position reflects the importance of the integration of IT with the goals, strategies and production processes of the organisation. This requires an appreciation of the business and its interaction with its environment. A successful CIO is must be technically competent and able to converse with technical specialists but also possess business acumen in order to understand how IT can assist the organisation.

The structure of IT companies

Many companies have been set up to provide various forms of IT and e-commerce services. Although there are many large IT companies, such as Microsoft and SAP, small companies tend to dominate. The staff in such companies are almost all multi-skilled knowledge workers. Research has identified that the small companies tend to share common structural and management characteristics.[43] Because skills and knowledge are fairly widespread, there is little in the way of hierarchy. The basic work group is the team and there is much movement of staff between teams. The structural form adopted is always a variation on the matrix, with the specific form and roles depending on staff competencies. There is high adaptability and mobility in terms of size, number of teams and geography. The companies are heavily oriented towards the customer, but the customer has been specifically selected to fit the company's skill profile. And even the boundaries of the company itself are permeable, with staff moving from assignment to assignment and contract to contract.

The nature of the work and the resultant structure supports the observations we have made linking technology and structure.

Computerisation and manufacturing systems

A specific category of computerisation can broadly be called **computer-integrated manufacturing** (CIM). This category applies computerisation to manufacturing tasks. It allows the linking of design, production systems, inventory control, planning, scheduling and distribution into virtually one function. This has had a major impact on both the control of operations and the type of work people do. It has also led to manufacturing companies changing their basic structure over the past 10 years or so.

computer-integrated manufacturing
a manufacturing process controlled by computers and which brings together all aspects of the production process

CIM permits the speeding up of product innovation by parallel design and development of various components, reduced time for product testing, and the simultaneous development of manufacturing processes and tooling as a product is being designed. Prior to computerisation these procedures were all carried out in sequence, leading to slow rates of product development. Once the item is in production, information technology can monitor inventories and replenish them through automatically placing an order with suppliers, coordinate the delivery of parts to a production line, allow the production of a number of variations to a basic product to be scheduled, and plan future material requirements. It also allows the production of a range of different styles and types of goods down the same production line.

CIM has also led to a change of strategy for many manufacturing companies. For much of the 20th century manufacturing companies sought to achieve economies of scale—that is, large production runs of standard products leading to lower costs of production. Whereas economies of scale are still applicable, computer-based control of manufacturing has led to companies being able to achieve economies of scope. Economies of scope are derived from the ability to change production quickly to any one of a set of products. This enables organisations to respond flexibly to changing demands and market conditions. These developments have made time, along with labour, capital, management and entrepreneurial skill, one of the factors of production.

A further contribution to strategy is that advanced manufacturing technologies, including CIM and computer-based design (CAD/CAM), enables the firm to work selectively with external designers, suppliers, customers and other firms. This permits the rapid reduction in product development times and the commercialisation process. These communication linkages also enable the firm to reduce uncertainty.

Not surprisingly, CIM has led to a requirement for organisations to adapt their structure to derive the most from the new technology. Even though new patterns of work have developed and the nature of jobs has changed, we can still use existing classification schemes to relate technology to structure. Whereas the technological categories derived by Woodward still apply, and small batch and continuous process industries can still be identified, the capacity of industries to perform efficiently in them is greatly enhanced. For instance, some companies that were previously large-batch and mass-production firms may now be classified as small-batch and unit-production firms. Perrow's typology, concentrating as it does on an individual's and department's task, may still be used to predict structural features that can be derived from a person's job. However, we can expect that the numbers of people falling into each category has changed. For example, there will be fewer people performing routine work and more in the other categories.

Research has identified that certain predicable structural changes will occur if computer-aided manufacturing firms are to get the most from their investment.[44] First there will be less job specialisation, as there will be a greater use of self-managing teams. People will be required to learn new skills and undertake a wider variety of work. Continuous training will become part of their employment. They will need to become computer-literate, at least to the level of being a competent user of the new technology. They will also need to accept control by computer, which will determine much of the scheduling of their daily work. In Australia, the term multi-skilling has been used to describe these phenomena. It has also led to changes in the industrial relations system. As the boundaries of jobs have expanded, traditional union coverage and award classifications no longer describe the type of work people do, and new unions and enterprise agreements have evolved.

As in the service industries, we can see changes in centralisation and decentralisation. Whereas operational decisions are decentralised to the plant or even lower, major strategic decisions will continue to be determined more effectively from a centralised location. Implementation of decisions is also likely to be faster, as computerisation has eliminated many jobs and delays associated with the gathering, processing and dissemination of information.

Table 7.6 summarises the differences in organisational characteristics that can be expected between traditional manufacturing organisations and those which have adopted computer-integrated manufacturing. It can be seen that to derive the advantages of the new technology, changes in most areas of organisational operations are necessary. The potential of the system is such that its full benefits cannot be derived from using the technology to conform to the existing structure. From this observation, we can therefore claim that there is a technological imperative determining structure.

Does IT cause structure or does structure cause IT?

We are left with the question as to the extent to which information technology has influenced organisational structure. We can answer this by saying that IT reinforces the existing structure, as well as allowing new structures to evolve. Although IT can replace much of the routine work in organisations, it need not change the basic

TABLE 7.6 Comparison of the characteristics of mass-production and computer-integrated manufacturing (CIM) organisations

Organisational characteristics	Mass-production technology organisations	CIM organisations
Environment	Stable, little change, low complexity	Turbulent, dynamic change, complex
Strategy	Economies of scale, control environment, cost leadership	Economies of scope, adapt to environment, product quality, low cost, dependability, flexibility
Product life cycle	Long	Short
Products	Simple or complex, low differentiation	Complex, changing, high differentiation
Structure	Mechanistic	Organic
Span of control (first-level)	Wide	Narrow
Vertical levels	Many	Few
Tasks	Routine, repetitive	Responsive, craft-like
Specialisation (production)	High	Low
Integration	Low	High
Decision making	Centralised	Decentralised
Information flow	Vertical	Horizontal
Power base	Position	Knowledge
Behaviour	Standardised	Adaptive
Management skills	Specific, detailed	Integrative
Rewards	Individual/production	Group/innovation
Control	Bureaucratic	Self-regulatory

Source: Patricia L. Nemetz & Louis W. Fry, 'Flexible Manufacturing Organizations: Implications for Strategy Formulation and Organization Design', *Academy of Management Review*, October 1988, p. 632.

reporting relationships of the organisation. IT is often implemented to make existing structures work better. A food company still produces food, for instance, with departments such as production, accounting, sales and marketing. But IT allows superior market research, more efficient use of resources, and greatly streamlines the accounting function. But these departments still undertake the same tasks they always have.

On the other hand, IT has seen the evolution of some radically new structures and ways of working. Motor vehicle producers can design the shape of a car in Los Angeles, the engine in Germany, the suspension in Britain and the manufacturing system in Japan, with all the tasks being carried out simultaneously. The creation of networks of separately owned companies each producing individual parts of a complex product, such as those for television or computer production, are permitted by electronic data interchange. And the use of decentralised structures where formalisation is low and tasks loosely defined is made easier by dense IT networks. Our

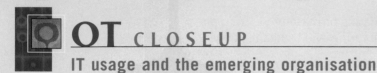

OT CLOSEUP

IT usage and the emerging organisation

Is there a link between the ability to process information and certain organisational forms? As with so much else in organisational theory, our explorations are limited by our ability to measure what we are discussing. Our measurement of IT usage provides a good example of the difficulties. One study attempted to identify whether there was a link between the use of IT and emerging organisational forms. Both of these are difficult to measure. IT usage was measured by the number of transactions via a computer during a typical day, with a second measure of the number of transactions during a given time period.

The emerging organisational form is not difficult to identify in the literature, although there has been little attempt to determine how common it is actually becoming. It is seen to place less emphasis on hierarchy and bureaucracy, have low levels of formalisation, be more decentralised than its bureaucratic forebears and more spatially dispersed. This type of structure has been identified as being organic, or 'informatic'.

In a study of public accounting firms, it was found that the emerging organisation was a greater user of IT than the more traditional bureaucratic form. Use of IT was negatively associated with centralisation and formalisation. There was no relationship between hierarchy and IT usage, indicating that hierarchy is a fairly resilient aspect of organisational structure. IT usage was also positively associated with the extent of interteam communication.

What is difficult for researchers is separating out cause and effect. Are the emerging forms of organisational structure only made possible by IT or did they exist prior to IT but have absorbed IT faster as it supports their structure? Intuition would indicate that some managers are appreciating the benefits of IT faster than others and are introducing an organisational form that makes the most of its advantages.

Adapted from: Bob Travica, 'Information Aspects of New Organizational Designs: Exploring the Non-Traditional Organization', *Journal of the American Society for Information Science*, 49(13), 1998, pp. 1224–44.

discussion above regarding CIM is a typical illustration of how the new technology is permitting new structures.

Technology and structure

As we did with strategy and size, we will now review the literature to determine the relationship of technology to the three structural dimensions of complexity, formalisation, and centralisation. Despite all the qualifications stated in the previous section, there are some important findings.

Technology and complexity

The evidence, while not overwhelming, indicates that routine technology is positively associated with low complexity. The greater the routineness, the fewer the number of occupational groups and the less training possessed by professionals.[45] This relationship is more likely to hold for the structural activities in or near the operating core, such as the proportion of maintenance employees and the span of control of first-line supervisors.

The reverse also holds: that is, non-routine technology is likely to lead to high complexity. As the work becomes more sophisticated and customised, the span of control narrows and vertical differentiation increases.[46] Teamwork and intensive coordination becomes more common. This, of course, is intuitively logical. Customised responses require a greater use of specialists, and managers require a smaller span of control because the problems that they confront are mostly of the non-programmed variety.

Technology and formalisation

A review of five major technology studies found routine technology to be positively related to formalisation. While only one of the sample correlations was statistically significant, all were positive, which has a 1 in 1000 occurrence due to chance.[47] However, when size was controlled for, the relationship vanished. Another study also supported the routineness–formalisation relationship.[48] Routineness was significantly associated with the presence of a rules manual, presence of job descriptions and the degree to which job descriptions were specified. Routine technologies enable management to implement rules and other formalised regulations because how to do the job is well understood, and the job is repetitive enough to justify the cost of developing such formalised systems. Non-routine technologies require control systems that permit greater discretion and flexibility.

These studies suggest that care must be taken in generalising about technology's impact on formalisation. That they are related is undoubtedly true. But when controlled for size, most of this association disappears. We propose, therefore, that the relationship holds for small organisations and activities at or near the operating core. As the operating core becomes more routine, work becomes more predictable. In such situations, high formalisation is an efficient coordination device. But these conditions are also those associated with large size.

Technology and centralisation

The technology–centralisation relationship generates inconsistent results. The logical argument would be that routine technologies would be associated with a centralised structure, whereas the non-routine technology, which would rely more heavily on the knowledge of the specialist, would be characterised by delegated decision authority. This position has met with some support.[49]

A more generalisable conclusion is that the technology–centralisation relationship is moderated by the degree of formalisation. Both formal regulations and centralised decision making are control mechanisms, and management can substitute them for one another. Routine technologies should be associated with centralised control if there is a minimum of rules and regulations. However, if formalisation is high, routine technology can be accompanied by decentralisation. We would, therefore, predict routine technology to lead to centralisation, but only if formalisation is low.

Summary

Technology refers to the processes and methods that transform inputs into outputs in the organisation. The four landmark contributions to understanding technology were made by Joan Woodward, Charles Perrow, James Thompson and Jay Galbraith.

Woodward proposed three types of production technology: unit, mass, and process. Her major contribution lay in identifying distinct relationships among these technology classes and the subsequent structure of the firms, and in indicating that the effectiveness of the firms was related to the 'fit' between technology and structure.

Perrow proposed a broader view of technology by looking at knowledge. He identified two underlying dimensions of knowledge technology: task variability, and problem analysability. These combine to create four types of technology: routine, engineering, craft, and non-routine. Perrow concluded that the more routine the technology, the more highly structured the organisation should be.

Thompson demonstrated that the interdependence created by a technology is important in determining an organisation's structure. Specifically, he identified long-linked, mediating, and intensive technologies; noted the unique interdependence of each; determined how each dealt with the uncertainty it faced; and predicted the structural coordination devices that were most economical for each.

Galbraith proposed that the structure adopted by an organisation depended on the extent to which it had to process information. The need to process information derived from the degree of task uncertainty. The greater the degree of task uncertainty, the greater the amount of information that had to be processed. An organisation would adopt a structure that allowed it to process information appropriate to its needs at an acceptable level of organisational performance. Galbraith identified seven major organisational design strategies associated with different capacities to process information.

We concluded that the technological imperative, if it exists, is supported best by job-level research and is most likely to apply only to small organisations and to those structural arrangements at or near the operating core, and that 'routineness' is the common denominator underlying most of the research into technology. The evidence indicates that routine technology is positively associated with low complexity and high formalisation. Routine technology is positively correlated with centralisation, but only if formalisation is low.

Another category of technology is the contrast between manufacturing and service industries. In service industries, there is simultaneous production and consumption of the product. As well, the product is intangible and cannot be inventoried. This leads to far higher numbers of people in the service industries interacting with customers.

The evidence of the influence of information technology on structure is inconclusive. It is an enabling device that facilitates both centralisation and decentralisation. It is also to be used to reduce layers of middle managers. It seems to be more widely used by those involved in routine data processing and design work.

For review and discussion

1   What does the term *technology* mean?
2   What are the main contributions to organisational theory made by Joan Woodward, Charles Perrow, James Thompson and Jay Galbraith?
3   Describe the various technologies that might be used in:
   a   a plumbing-repair firm;
   b   the admissions office at a highly selective college;
   c   a firm that manufactures wristwatches.

4   Clarify how 'routineness' reconciles the more specific technology classifications.

5   How are technology and interdependence related, if at all?

6   Differentiate between work unit-level and organisation-level analyses of technology. Which has proven more valuable in explaining organisation structures? Why?

7   'Technology is really part of strategy.' What does this mean?

8   Under what conditions is technology likely to be a major determinant of structure?

9   What is the relationship between technology, size, industry and structure?

10 How does technology influence a classroom's structure? Is size a stronger determinant? Explain.

11 In what way do service and manufacturing technologies differ? How does this influence structure?

12 What is an organisation's *dominant* technology?

13 What are the characteristics of information technologies? How do these affect an organisation's structure?

14 What characteristics do IT departments and firms take? Relate these to one of the technology classifications discussed in the chapter.

15 How does the structure of a firm using computer-integrated manufacturing differ from that of a traditional mass-production firm?

CASE FOR CLASS DISCUSSION
It's sink or swim for the textile king

Most Australians have heard of King Gee, the brand name typically associated with heavy-duty workwear, such as overalls and industrial-weight shirts and trousers. King Gee, which is now owned by the American company Sara Lee, is among Australia's better-performing textile and clothing companies, with a turnover of $77 million. In addition to industrial workwear, it produces the famous 'Stubbies' shorts as well as an extensive range of lighter-weight industrial clothing and uniforms. These are worn by airline and bank staff as well as police and other government employees. In addition, King Gee supplies uniforms to McDonald's, Australia Post and five-star hotels.

King Gee has 650 employees, most of whom are unionised production workers. Most of King Gee's manufacturing is carried out in Australia at factories in Wollongong, Kempsey and Rutherford. Most sales consist of standardised products, which are retailed through mass merchandisers or are ordered from listings in a catalogue. King Gee, however, has higher

aspirations than mass-produced uniforms. It recently established a strategic alliance with Neat N' Trim, which will give it access to uniforms in the corporate wardrobe market including tailored suits and women's uniforms.

As a typical manufacturing company, King Gee takes in raw materials, mostly fabric, and converts them into ready-to-wear clothing. It is also involved in distribution. Orders are sought either by catalogue sales or, in the case of uniforms for organisations such as the police, through tendering. Sales to the general public are made through conventional retailers. The catalogue, and standardised designs for items such as Stubbies and overalls, allows standardisation of production. There is extensive computerisation of inventory, patterns and flow of products in the factories. The factories are shining examples of modern production facilities and technology.

Modern production facilities can do only so much to raise productivity. In order to derive the most from the new machinery, the cooperation of the workforce must be obtained and the appropriate abilities, values and attitudes brought to the job. In 1994 King Gee introduced radical changes to match the skills of its workforce with a new program of capital investment and the updating and modernisation of its product range. This involved a program of multi-skilling to ensure that the machinery was being effectively used and that the staff could work on a wider range of products. It also involved training people to work in small teams and allowed teams to choose new members, with managerial approval needed only at the final stage. Production decisions are now made at factory level rather than at head office. Piecework, the linking of pay to output, has been replaced by a straight salary. The company has also moved to two shifts, with a minimum of penalty rates.

All this has meant that inventory has been cut by 15% and that throughput of orders has been reduced to days rather than the weeks typical before reorganisation. Managers are now more concerned with seeking orders and making strategic decisions than continuously becoming involved in matters concerning the factory floor.

Adapted from: Alex Kennedy, 'It's Sink Or Swim for the Textile King', *Business Review Weekly,* 24 June 1996, pp. 60–1.

QUESTIONS

1 How can King Gee's technology be explained by Perrow's and Thompson's typologies? How closely does King Gee fit the two models? Support your answer.

2 King Gee improved its ability to handle information by raising the proficiency level of its workforce and by computerisation. How closely does this fit Galbraith's model?

3 How could advanced information technology be applied to improve King Gee's effectiveness? How would this be likely to change the structural dimensions in King Gee?

FURTHER READING

Louis W. Fry, 'Technology–Structure Research: Three Critical Issues', *Academy of Management Journal,* September 1982, pp. 532–52.

Jay Galbraith, *Designing Effective Organizations,* Reading, MA: Addison Wesley, 1973.

Charles Perrow, 'A Framework for the Comparative Analysis of Organizations', *American Sociological Review,* April 1967, pp. 194–208.

Alain Pinsonneault & Kenneth L. Kraemer, 'The Impact of Information Technology on Middle Managers', *MIS Quarterly,* 17(3), 1993, pp. 271–92.

James D. Thompson, *Organizations in Action,* New York: McGraw-Hill, 1967.

Bob Travica, 'Information Aspects of New Organizational Designs: Exploring the Non-Traditional Organization', *Journal of the American Society for Information Sciences,* 49(13), 1998, pp. 1224–44.

Joan Woodward, *Industrial Organization: Theory and Practice,* London: Oxford University Press, 1965.

NOTES

1 Joan Woodward, *Industrial Organization: Theory and Practice,* London: Oxford University Press, 1965.

2 Edward Harvey, 'Technology and the Structure of Organizations', *American Sociological Review,* April 1968, pp. 247–59.

3 William L. Zwerman, *New Perspectives on Organization Theory,* Westport, CN: Greenwood Publishing, 1970.

4 See, for example, Lex Donaldson, 'Woodward Technology, Organizational Structure, and Performance—A Critique of the Universal Generalization', *Journal of Management Studies,* October 1976, pp. 255–73.

5 Charles Perrow, 'A Framework for the Comparative Analysis of Organizations', *American Sociological Review,* April 1967, pp. 194–208.

6 ibid.

7 Karl Magnusen, 'Technology and Organizational Differentiation: A Field Study of Manufacturing Corporations', Doctoral dissertation, University of Wisconsin, Madison, 1970.

8 Jerald Hage & Michael Aiken, 'Routine Technology, Social Structure, and Organizational Goals', *Administrative Science Quarterly*, September 1969, pp. 366–77.

9 Andrew H. Van de Ven & Andre L. Delbecq, 'A Task Contingent Model of Work-Unit Structure', *Administrative Science Quarterly*, June 1974, pp. 183–97.

10 See, for example, Lawrence Mohr, 'Operations Technology and Organizational Structure', *Administrative Science Quarterly*, December 1971, pp. 444–59.

11 James D. Thompson, *Organizations in Action*, New York: McGraw-Hill, 1967.

12 ibid, p. 17.

13 Thomas A. Mahoney & Peter J. Frost, 'The Role of Technology in Models of Organizational Effectiveness', *Organizational Behavior and Human Performance*, February 1974, pp. 122–38.

14 Jay Galbraith, *Designing Effective Organizations*, Reading MA: Addison Wesley, 1973.

15 ibid, p. 5.

16 Raymond E. Miles & Charles C. Snow, 'Toward a Synthesis in Organization Theory', in M. Jelinek, J.A. Litterer & R.E. Miles, *Organizations by Design: Theory and Practice*, Plano, TX: Business Publications, 1981, pp. 549–51.

17 It is interesting that a careful review of a recent study that proposes to give renewed support to the technological imperative (see Robert M. Marsh & Hiroshi Mannari, 'Technology and Size as Determinants of the Organizational Structure of Japanese Factories', *Administrative Science Quarterly*, March 1981, pp. 33–57) finds that complexity and formalisation are a function of size and that centralisation varies randomly in relation to both technology and size.

18 See, for example, David J. Hickson, D.S. Pugh & Diana C. Pheysey, 'Operations Technology and Organization Structure: An Empirical Reappraisal', *Administrative Science Quarterly*, September 1979, pp. 378–97; and D.S. Pugh, D.J. Hickson, C.R. Hinings & C. Turner, 'The Context of Organization Structures', *Administrative Science Quarterly*, March 1969, pp. 91–114.

19 Hickson et al., 'Operations Technology and Organisation Structure: An Empirical Reappraisal'.

20 Donald Gerwin, 'Relationships between Structure and Technology at the Organizational and Job Levels', *Journal of Management Studies*, February 1979, p. 71; and James L. Price & Charles W. Mueller, *Handbook of Organizational Measurement*, Marshfield, MA: Pitman, 1986, pp. 209–14.

21 Donald Gerwin, 'Relationships between Structure and Technology at the Organizational and Job Levels'.

22 ibid; and Louis W. Fry, 'Technology-Structure Research: Three Critical Issues', *Academy of Management Journal*, September 1982, pp. 532–52.

23 David E. Bowen, Caren Siehl & Benjamin Schneider, 'A Framework for Analysing Customer Service Organisations in Manufacturing', *Academy of Management Review*, 14, 1989, pp. 79–85; Peter K. Mills & Newton Margulies, 'Towards a Core Typology of Service Organisations', *Academy of Management Review*, 5, 1980, pp. 225–65; Peter K. Mills & Dennis J. Moberg, 'Perspectives on the Technology of Service Operations', *Academy of Management Review*, 7, 1982, pp. 467–78.

24 Richard B. Chase & David A. Tansik, 'The Customer Contact Model for Organization Design', *Management Science*, 29, 1983, pp. 1037–50.

25 ibid.

26 Karlene H. Roberts & Martha Grabowski, 'Organizations, Technology and Structuring', in Stewart Clegg, Cynthia Hardy & Walter Nord, eds, *Handbook of Organization Studies*, London: Sage, 1996.

27 This classification is derived from Daniel Robey, *Designing Organizations*, 2nd Ed. Homewood, Ill., Irwin, 1986.

28 Lorin Hitt & Erik Brynjolfsson, 'Information Technology and Internal Firm Organization: An Exploratory Analysis', *Journal of Management Information Systems*, 14(2), 1997, pp. 81–101.

29 Bob Travica, 'Information Aspects of New Organizational Designs: Exploring the Non-Traditional Organization', *Journal of the American Society for Information Sciences*, 49(13), 1998, pp. 1224–44.

30 Nicholas Argyres, 'The Impact of Information Technology on Coordination: Evidence from the B2 "Stealth" Bomber', *Organization Science*, 10(2), 1999, pp. 162–80.

31 Erik Brynjolfsson, 'Information Assets, Technology and Organization', *Management Science*, 40(12), 1994, pp. 1645–62.

32 Alain Pinsonneault & Kenneth L. Kraemer, 'The Impact of Information Technology on Middle Managers', *MIS Quarterly*, 17(3), 1993, pp. 271–92; and Daniel Robey, 'Computers and Management Structure: Some Empirical Findings Re-examined', *Human Relations*, 30, 1977, pp. 963–76.

33 C. Ferioli & P. Migliarese 'Supporting Organizational Relations through Information Technology in Innovative Organizational Forms', *European Journal of Information Systems*, 5(3), 1996, pp. 196–207.

34 Andrew Stein, 'Re-engineering the Executive: The 4th generation of EIS', *Information Management*, 29(1), 1995, pp. 55–62.

35 H. Simon, 'Applying Information Technology to Organization Design', *Public Administration Review*, 1973, pp. 268–78.

36 Roberts & Grabowski, 'Organizations, Technology and Structuring'.

37 Pinsonneault & Kraemer, 'The Impact of Information Technology on Middle Managers'.

38 Roberts & Grabowski, 'Organizations, Technology and Structuring'.

39 Michael J. Mandel, 'The New Business Cycle', *Business Week*, 31 March 1997, pp. 48–54.

40 Kirk Fiedler, Varun Grover & James T.C. Teng, 'An Empirically Derived Taxonomy of Information Technology Structure and its Relationship to Organization Structure', *Journal of Management Information Systems*, 13(1), Summer 1996, pp. 9–34.

41 ibid; William King & Vikram Sethi 'An Empirical Assessment of the Organization of Transnational Information Systems', *Journal of Management Information Systems*, 15(4), 1999, pp. 7–28.

42 Joan Graef, 'Getting the Most from R and D Information Services', *Research-Technology Management*, 41(4), 1998, pp. 44–7.

43 Stephen Ackroyd, 'On the Structure and Dynamics of Some Small, UK Based Information Technology Firms', *Journal of Management Studies*, 32(2), 1995.

44 Patricia L. Nemetz & Louis W. Fry, 'Flexible Manufacturing Organizations: Implications for Strategy Formulation and Organization Design', *Academy of Management Review*, October 1988; and Wayne F. Cascio & Raymond F. Zammuto, 'Societal Trends and Staffing Policies', in Wayne F. Cascio, ed., *Human Resource Planning, Employment and Placement*, Washington DC: BNA/ASPA, 1989.

45 See, for example, Stanley H. Udy, Jr, *Organization of Work*, New Haven, CN: HRAF Press, 1959; Hickson et al., op. cit., and Raymond G. Hunt, 'Technology and Organization', *Academy of Management Journal*, September 1970, pp. 235–52.

46 Gerwin, 'Relationships between Structure and Technology at the Organizational and Job Levels'.

47 Hage & Aiken, 'Routine Technology, Social Structure, and Organizational Goals'.

48 Andrew Van de Ven, André Delbecq & Richard Koenig Jr, 'Determinants of Coordination Modes within Organizations', *American Sociological Review*, April 1976, pp. 322–38.

49 Jerald Hage & Michael Aiken, 'Relationship of Centralization to Other Structural Properties', *Administrative Science Quarterly*, June 1967, pp. 72–92.

CHAPTER 8

Environment

After reading this chapter you should be able to:

1 define environment;

2 differentiate between the specific and the general environment;

3 explain the key dimensions of environmental uncertainty;

4 describe the contributions of Burns and Stalker, Lawrence and Lorsch, and Duncan;

5 contrast mechanistic and organic structures;

6 review the contributions of population ecology, institutional theory and resource dependency;

7 describe the effect of environmental uncertainty on complexity, formalisation and centralisation.

Introduction

Things are changing at Boral

Boral is one of Australia's leading companies.[1] Most people have seen the yellow and dark-green rectangles of Boral's logo on the side of trucks and stacks of building materials. Boral started as an oil refiner and bitumen producer in 1948 in the heady days of postwar reconstruction and expansion. The environment was kind to Boral: there was a great demand for fuel and bitumen for roads, so a good cash flow was generated. It used this cash to expand into other areas. First it purchased businesses in the gas industry which could use the outputs of the oil-refining activities. In 1963 it purchased its first gas supply company and in 1973 the company that supplied the large Brisbane market. In between times it invested in ships and started to distribute gas to the Pacific Islands.

The two main ingredients in road base are bitumen and crushed rock, which is called aggregate. Given that Boral was already in bitumen it was logical that it move into quarrying, which it did progressively from 1965. Also acquired were companies associated with sand, premixed concrete and other forms of road surfacing.

Given the buoyant mood of the economy in the 1960s, Boral had a lot of spare cash, and it sought to invest this in building materials. The need to expand into other industries was reinforced by the expectations of financiers and shareholders regarding strategy. This was the age of the conglomerate—a whole series of businesses, often in unrelated areas, held together by a large head office. Successful companies were expected to conform to this pattern. Another expectation starting to emerge in the 1970s was that companies would have overseas operations. Boral responded to both of these needs by a rapid expansion into building materials. The move seemed like a good idea, and indeed it was. Australia had a large backlog of housing and infrastructure to catch up on. The population was growing strongly, and the expectations were that the postwar baby boomers would greatly increase the need for housing stock.

In quick succession from 1969 Boral made major acquisitions in bricks, masonry, roof tiles, windows and doors. It also continued to expand in premixed concrete, buying the large cement works at Marulan in New South Wales in 1987. Businesses in timber were acquired, as well as in general engineering.

North American expansion started in 1979 with the purchase of a roof tile plant in California and a brick plant in Georgia in 1980. North American expansion has been rapid, with Boral now being the largest manufacturer of clay bricks in the United States. Similar expansion in Europe started in 1990, including moves into Eastern Europe. Asia followed in 1992.

As the number of different businesses owned by Boral grew it was clear that management of them was becoming increasingly time-consuming. Not only did each business operate in a different market with its own environmental demands, but many businesses were small-scale and would be unlikely to achieve any form of market leadership. In accordance with the austere 1990s, and the changed expectations of financial analysts and shareholders, Boral undertook a series of divestments of many of its smaller businesses, such as lifts and engineering products.

However, Boral's acquisitions of the previous 20 years was coming back to haunt it. Even with the divestments, return on assets was low. Further, Boral's share price was considerably less that the sum of its assets. In 2000 it split the company into two, forming a building materials company and a company concentrating on gas and energy. One of the motives for doing this was pressure from the investment community to unlock some of the hidden value in the company.

Boral also has had its fair share of criticism from environmentalists. By their nature, activities such as quarrying and cement manufacturing carry environmental hazards, which must be carefully monitored. But the biggest problem has come from Boral's timber activities, which log old growth forests and also include wood chipping. Balancing the demands of the environmentalists and the needs of continuing activity in the sector has been a juggle for management and has damaged Boral's reputation. But Boral's greatest problem, at least in Australia, has been the maturity of the Australian market. Population growth is slowing, the population is well housed, and most roads and infrastructure have been built. These environmental constraints mean that Boral is no longer a high-growth company and its strategic options are limited.

In Chapter 1 we discussed organisations in an open-systems framework. We identified that the key to understanding organisations as open systems was the recognition that organisations interact with their environment. But since that introduction we have said little about the environment and its impact on the organisation. In this chapter, that omission will be rectified.

A common theme in organisation theory is that organisations must adapt to their environments if they are to maintain or increase their effectiveness. In open-system terms, we can think of organisations as developing monitoring and feedback mechanisms to identify and follow their environments, sense changes in those environments and make appropriate adjustments as necessary. At Boral, management first found that the environment was supportive of its activities and prospered with high demand for its products. However, its environment slowly changed. The markets it operated in matured and no longer offered high growth. The spread of businesses was criticised by financial analysts as being too wide and difficult to manage, and many of these businesses were subsequently divested. Overseas expansion meant that new demands were placed on management as environments became more complex.

In this chapter we clarify what we mean by the term *environment* and assess the relationship between environment and structure. A central point throughout is that different organisations face different degrees of environmental uncertainty. As managers do not like uncertainty, they try to eliminate it or at least minimise its impact on their organisation. We demonstrate that structural design is a major tool that managers have for controlling environmental uncertainty.

Defining environment

There is no shortage of definitions of environment. Their common thread is consideration of factors outside the organisation itself. For instance, the most popular definition identifies the environment as everything outside an organisation's boundaries. Another author has proposed that ascertaining an organisation's environment appears simple enough: 'Just take the universe, subtract from it the subset that represents the organisation, and the remainder is environment'.[2] We agree with this writer when he adds that, unfortunately, it isn't that simple. First, let us differentiate between an organisation's general environment and its specific environment.

General versus specific environment

An organisation's environment and general environment are essentially the same. The latter includes everything, such as economic factors, political conditions, the social milieu, the legal structure, the ecological situation and cultural conditions. The **general environment** encompasses conditions that *may* have an impact on the organisation, but their relevance is not particularly clear. Consider the price and availability of petrol in the general environment of cinema chains such as Greater Union. At first glance it may appear that Greater Union has little to worry about in relation to petrol supply, as it is not a consumer of the commodity in its normal course of business. But should there be a significant increase in the price of petrol, or a shortage either through strikes or some other interruption, then Greater Union is likely to be hard-hit. This is because many cinema patrons travel by car, and if petrol is either unavailable or expensive, they are likely to be more careful as to what trips they make. But for Greater Union, the price and availability of petrol is a distant concern: most of its attention is paid to the specific environment.

general environment conditions that potentially have an impact on the organisation

The **specific environment** is the part of the environment that is directly relevant to the organisation in achieving its goals. At any given moment, it is that part of the environment with which management will be concerned, because it is made up of the critical constituencies that can positively or negatively influence the organisation's effectiveness. It is unique to each organisation and it changes with conditions. Typically, it will include clients or customers, suppliers of inputs, competitors, governments, unions, trade associations and public pressure groups. The operator of Sydney airport is in the specific environment of Air New Zealand but in the general environment of Woolworths. On the other hand, the bakers of Tip Top bread are in the specific environment of Woolworths but in the general environment of Air New Zealand. Figure 8.1 shows the general and specific environments of a refrigerator manufacturer.

specific environment the part of the environment that is directly relevant to the organisation in achieving its goals

An organisation's specific environment will vary depending on the domain it has chosen. **Domain** refers to the claim that the organisation stakes out for itself with respect to the range of products or services offered and markets served. It identifies the organisation's niche. Volkswagen and Mercedes-Benz are both German firms that manufacture motor vehicles, but they operate in distinctly different domains. Similarly, Queensland TAFE and James Cook University are both higher-education institutions in Queensland, but they do substantially different things and appeal to different segments of the higher-education market. These two institutions have identified different domains.

domain an organisation's niche that it has staked out for itself with respect to products or services offered and markets served

Why is the concept of domain important? It is because the domain of an organisation determines the points at which it is dependent on its specific environment.[3] Change the domain and you will change the specific environment. And it is from the specific environment that most of the pressure on organisations is initially felt.

FIGURE 8.1 The general and specific environment of a refrigerator manufacturer

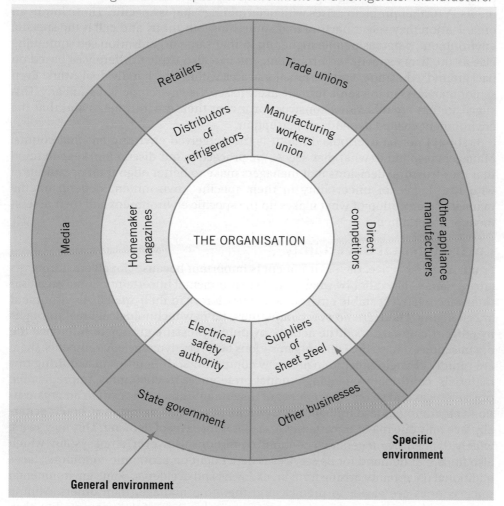

Actual versus perceived environment

Any attempt to define environment requires making a distinction between the objective or actual environment and the one that managers perceive. Evidence indicates that measures of the actual characteristics of the environment and measures of perceived characteristics are not highly correlated.[4] What you see depends on where you sit! Furthermore, it is perceptions—not reality—that lead to the decisions that managers make regarding organisation design.

Unfortunately, we lack the ready means of measuring how fast an environment is changing or how stable it might be. There may be general agreement that new technologies in telecommunications lead to rapid environmental change and that manufacturers of basic foods, such as noodles and breakfast cereals, face a stable environment. But the same environment that one organisation perceives as unpredictable and complex may be seen as static and easily understood by another organisation.[5] The bakers of Tip Top bread may feel that their environment is unstable, but compared to a fire-fighting organisation Tip Top enjoys the most stable of environments. A further problem arises with determining what is specific. Those low in an organisation may select parts of that something 'out there' and call it the specific environment, whereas people higher up in that same organisation see something else as the firm's specific environment. You can also expect differences based on background, education, and the functional area within which individuals work. Even senior managers in the same firm are likely to see the environment dissimilarly. This suggests that organisations construct or invent their environments and that the environment created depends on perception.

It should not be overlooked that it is the perceived environment that counts. Managers respond to what they see. As we proceed in our discussion, keep in mind that the structural decisions that managers make to better align their organisation with the degree of uncertainty in their specific environment depend on the managers' perception of what makes up the specific environment and their assessment of uncertainty.

Environmental uncertainty

From our perspective, the environment is important because not all environments are the same. They differ by what we call environmental uncertainty. Some organisations face relatively stable environments: few forces in their specific environment are changing. There are no new competitors, no new technological breakthroughs by current competitors, little activity by public pressure groups to influence the organisations, and so on. Other organisations face very dynamic environments: there are rapidly changing technologies, new competitors, difficulties in acquiring raw materials, continually changing product preferences by customers, unpredictable price changes and so on. The number of uncertainties that may exist in an organisation's environment also influences management action. For instance, hotels generally face only one major uncertainty, and that is the level of demand. This may swing widely depending on general economic conditions. However, a rail system, which also finds that demand for its services is dependent on economic conditions, faces additional uncertainty arising from breakdowns and accidents. Some environmental uncertainties are easier to predict, and therefore manage, than others. Mining companies know that their main uncertainty is the price of their commodity; they can thus manage this uncertainty by hedging, being prudent with expenditure and constantly monitoring costs. Retail stores know that the level of economic growth affects their sales; low growth leads to low sales. As they have been through this cycle many times before, they have a set of responses they have learned from experience to handle the situation (e.g. sales, discounting and various forms of promotion). But most importantly they know that there is little alternative but to wait until growth rates improve. Alternatively, some environmental change is difficult to understand. This particularly applies to technological change. The introduction of the Internet and e-commerce saw many managers facing difficult decisions. Managers felt that unless they embraced the new technologies their companies would be disadvantaged. Their confusion was compounded by the considerable overselling of many of the benefits of e-commerce by early-adopting proponents. But its impact was poorly understood, difficult to predict, and at least in the short term not as great as expected. As most managers had no experience of a similar technology to fall back on, their environmental uncertainty was very high.

OT CLOSEUP

How easy is it to read the environment?

Reading this chapter may give the impression that understanding the environment and responding to it is a fairly easy task. Certainly, in some ways it is. A transport company, for instance, knows the relationship between how much fuel it uses, its price and the profitability of the company. But major technological innovations are more difficult to identify and respond to. Most major technological innovations have taken time to disseminate throughout the business world, and managers have had to ride the experience curve to determine how innovations can best be used. The steamship, aircraft, motor transport, computerisation and the telephone are just a few innovations that have had a slow introduction but which, when the technology was fully developed, pushed aside all competing technologies.

So how do you know when one of these major innovations has been made and, more importantly, how do you know how to respond? Andy Grove provides some useful insight. Andy Grove is a co-founder of Intel, one of the icons of the microprocessor age. His observations derive from the impact of computerisation on organisations. He sees the Internet as having a similar, if not greater, long-term impact, even though many of the benefits were overhyped by e-commerce proponents in the late 1990s. (Remember that the Internet was no overnight introduction: its use dates back to the 1970s.)

Grove calls major technological innovations strategic inflection points. So how do you know you are at a strategic inflection point? Most of the time, recognition takes place in stages. First is the subtle uneasiness that something is different. Customers' attitudes change and new competitors emerge from out of nowhere armed with the new technology. Second, there is a dissonance between what your company thinks it is doing and what is actually happening within the organisation. This type of chaos always exists, but at strategic inflection points it is quantitatively different. Eventually a new set of actions emerges, which is more like a rebirth than the normal adaptation process. Often this occurs under a new management with a fundamentally different understanding of how the new technology affects the business.

So when is the right moment to take appropriate action? Unfortunately you don't know, but you cannot afford to be late. The company must change while it is still healthy and generating cash, and that implies acting when not everything is known. This places a premium on judgement, intuition and instinct; nothing else will get you through. Grove is ever-hopeful. He claims that it is possible to pick the strategic inflection points by looking at them using a different frame, or mindset, from the one we have been used to. The signals are out there and capable of being read by those with the appropriate perception.

Of course, the strategic inflection points may put you out of business if you are right where they are operating. Intuition and judgement did not save sailing ship owners or horse-drawn carriage manufacturers.

Adapted from: Andy Grove, *Only the Paranoid Survive: How to Exploit the Crisis Points which Challenge every Company and Career*, New York: HarperBusiness, 1996.

Stable environments and those that are easier to predict create significantly less uncertainty for managers than do dynamic ones, and as uncertainty is a threat to an organisation's effectiveness management will try to minimise it.[6] In this chapter we show that management's concern is with reducing environmental uncertainty, and that this can be accomplished through the adoption of an appropriate organisation structure. We discuss how environmental uncertainty influences structure later in the chapter.

The enacted environment

The way in which the actual and perceived environment interacts with environmental uncertainty has been explored in an interpretation called the enacted environment.[7] Proponents of the enacted environment claim that uncertainty and the environment exist simultaneously within the decision maker's head. There then commences a cycle of searching for information in order to reduce uncertainty, leading to a perception of more uncertainty because of the information gathered. This feeds into a need to gather more information, and so the uncertainty environment becomes enacted within the decision maker's mind. Uncertainty is not reduced by more information, but rather the amount of information increases uncertainty. Because this approach highlights how environments are enacted in the decision maker's mind, it is sometimes called the social constructionist view of environments.

Environmental enactment explains how the introduction of computers may have increased uncertainty. Take our example of a breakfast cereal manufacturer. Whereas 30 years ago the manufacturer may have simply produced the cereal, put it on the supermarket shelves and received quarterly sales reports, the same manufacturer is now able to process information as to who is buying the product and why, how competing products are selling, and how sales vary between different geographic regions. Computers also allow the retailers to gather data on how fast the cereal is selling and compare revenues with those achieved by other brands. Pressure to improve performance can therefore be exerted on poorly performing brands. With all this considered, it would not be surprising if the cereal manufacturer considered that the environment had become far more uncertain.

As much as enactment theory helps explain how environments are perceived, for most of this chapter we will take what may be called a rational view of environments. That is, that is it possible, at least for our purposes, to consider environments along certain dimensions, and that managers perceive these environments in fairly predictable ways. Further, the response to these perceptions, particularly the structural responses, can be categorised. The next section introduces landmark studies which inform the environmental imperative.

Landmark contributions

There is no shortage of research on the influence of environments on organisations. But much of the research can be summarised in the work of just a few researchers who have made landmark contributions. Here we have summarised the work of Burns and Stalker, Lawrence and Lorsch, and Duncan.

Burns and Stalker

Tom Burns and G.M. Stalker studied 20 English and Scottish industrial firms to determine how their organisational structure and managerial practice might differ depending on different environmental conditions.[8] Using interviews with managers and their own observations, they evaluated the firms' environmental conditions in terms of the rate of change in their scientific technology and their relevant product markets. What they found was that the type of structure that existed in rapidly changing and dynamic environments was significantly different from that in organisations with stable environments. Burns and Stalker labelled the two structures organic and mechanistic, respectively.

TABLE 8.1 Comparing mechanistic and organic structures

Characteristic	Mechanistic	Organic
Task definition	Rigid	Flexible
Communication	Vertical	Lateral
Formalisation	High	Low
Influence	Authority	Expertise
Control	Centralised	Diverse

Mechanistic structures were characterised by high complexity, formalisation and centralisation. These performed routine tasks, relied heavily on programmed behaviours, and were relatively slow in responding to the unfamiliar. **Organic structures** were relatively flexible and adaptive, with emphasis on lateral rather than vertical communication, influence based on expertise and knowledge rather than authority of position, loosely defined responsibilities rather than rigid job definitions, and emphasis on exchanging information rather than giving directions (see Table 8.1).

Burns and Stalker believed that the most effective structure is one that adjusts to the requirements of the environment, which means using a mechanistic design in a stable, certain environment and an organic form in a turbulent environment. However, they recognised that the mechanistic and organic forms were ideal types defining two ends of a continuum. No organisation is purely mechanistic or purely organic but rather moves towards one or the other. Moreover, they emphasised that one was not preferred over the other. The nature of the organisation's environment determined which structure was superior.

Efforts to test Burns and Stalker's conclusions have met with general support.[9] For instance, engineering consultants must deal with an endless series of unpredictable problems.[10] They require a structure that can allow the organisation to respond and adapt to continual change. It should not be surprising, therefore, to find that their structure closely follows the characteristics of an organic form.

Lawrence and Lorsch

Paul Lawrence and Jay Lorsch, both of the Harvard Business School, went beyond the work of Burns and Stalker in search of more information about the relationship between environmental differences and effective organisation structures.[11] They chose 10 firms in three industries—plastics, food, and containers—in which to carry out their research.

Lawrence and Lorsch deliberately chose these three industries because they appeared to be the most diverse (in terms of environmental uncertainty) they could find. Bear in mind that they undertook their research in the 1960s. The plastics industry was highly competitive: the life cycle of any product was historically short, and firms were characterised by considerable new-product and process development. The container industry, on the other hand, was quite different. There had been no significant new products in two decades. Sales growth had kept pace with population growth but nothing more. Lawrence and Lorsch described the container firms as operating in a relatively certain environment, with no real threats to consider. The food industry was midway between the two. There had been heavy innovation, but

mechanistic structure a structure characterised by high complexity, formalisation and centralisation

organic structure flexible and adaptive structures, with emphasis on lateral communication, non-authority-based influence and loosely defined responsibilities

new-product generation and sales growth had been lower than in the plastics industry and higher than in the container industry.

Lawrence and Lorsch sought to match the internal environments of these firms with their respective external environments. They hypothesised that the more successful firms within each industry would have better matches than the less successful firms. Their measure of the *external* environment sought to tap the degree of uncertainty. This measurement included the rate of change in product innovation over time, the clarity of information that management had about the environment, and the length of time it took for management to get feedback from the environment on actions taken by the organisation. But what constituted an organisation's *internal* environment? Lawrence and Lorsch looked at two separate dimensions: *differentiation* and *integration*.

differentiation task segmentation and attitudinal differences held by individuals in various departments

The term **differentiation** as used by Lawrence and Lorsch closely parallels our definition of horizontal differentiation. However, Lawrence and Lorsch argued that in addition to task segmentation, managers in various departments can be expected to have different attitudes and behave differently in terms of their goal perspective, time frame and interpersonal orientation. Different interests and differing points of view mean that members of each department often find it difficult to see things the same way or to agree on integrated plans of action. Therefore, the degree of differentiation becomes a measure of complexity and indicates greater complications and more rapid changes. The other dimension that interested Lawrence and Lorsch was **integration**, the quality of collaboration that exists among interdependent units or departments that are required to achieve unity of effort. Integration devices that organisations typically use include rules and procedures, formal plans, the authority hierarchy and decision-making committees.

integration the quality of collaboration that exists among interdependent units

The unique, and probably the most important, part of Lawrence and Lorsch's study was that they did not assume the organisation or the environment to be uniform and singular. In contrast to previous researchers, they perceived both the organisation and the environment as having subsets: that is, that *parts* of the organisation deal with *parts* of the environment. They were proposing that an organisation's internal structure could be expected to differ from department to department, reflecting the characteristics of the sub-environment with which it interacts. They postulated that a basic reason for differentiating into departments or subsystems was to deal more effectively with sub-environments. For example, in each of the 10 organisations that Lawrence and Lorsch studied, they were able to identify market, technical-economic and scientific sub-environments. These three sub-environments corresponded to the sales, production and research-and-development functions within the organisations.

Lawrence and Lorsch postulated that the more turbulent, complex and diverse the external environment facing an organisation, the greater the degree of differentiation among its sub-parts. If the external environment was very diverse and the internal environment was highly differentiated, they further reasoned, there would be a need for an elaborate internal integration mechanism to avoid having units going in different directions. The need for increased integration to accommodate increases in differentiation related to the different goals of departmental managers. In all three industries, the researchers found manufacturing people to be most concerned with cost-efficiency and production matters. Research and engineering people emphasised scientific matters. Marketing people's orientation was towards the marketplace.

In reference to their three industries, Lawrence and Lorsch hypothesised that the plastics firms would be the most differentiated, followed by food firms and container firms, in that order. And this is precisely what they found. When they divided the firms within each industry into high, moderate and low performers, they found that the high-performing firms had a structure that best fitted their environmental demands. In diverse environments, subunits were more differentiated than in homogeneous environments. In the turbulent plastics industry, this meant high differentiation. The production units had relatively routine activities, in contrast to sales and research and engineering. Where the greatest standardisation existed, in the container industry, there was the least differentiation. Departments within the container firms generally had similar structures. The food firms, as postulated, were in the middle ground. Furthermore, the most successful firms in all three industries had a higher degree of integration than their low-performing counterparts.

What does all this mean? First, there are multiple specific environments with different degrees of uncertainty. Second, successful organisations' subunits meet the demands of their sub-environments. As differentiation and integration represent opposing forces, the key is to match the two appropriately, creating differentiation between departments to deal with specific problems and tasks facing the organisation and getting people to integrate and work as a cohesive team towards the organisation's goals. Successful organisations have more nearly solved the dilemma of providing both differentiation and integration by matching their internal subunits to the demands of the sub-environment. Finally, Lawrence and Lorsch present evidence to confirm that the environment in which an organisation functions—specifically in terms of the level of uncertainty present—is of foremost importance in selecting the structure appropriate for achieving organisational effectiveness.

Before we leave Lawrence and Lorsch, it should be mentioned that they have been sharply criticised for their use of perceptual measures of environmental uncertainty.[12] As noted earlier, actual and perceived degrees of uncertainty are likely to differ. Attempts to replicate Lawrence and Lorsch's work using objective measures of uncertainty have often failed, which suggests that their results may be a function of their measure.[13] From a research standpoint, this criticism is valid. However, from the practising manager's perspective, it is his or her perceptions that count. So while you should recognise that Lawrence and Lorsch have used perceptual measures and that defining the environment in terms of certainty/uncertainty criteria is by no means simple, you should also recognise that the findings of Lawrence and Lorsch represent an important contribution to our understanding of the impact of the environment on organisational structure.

Duncan's complexity and change framework

Robert Duncan classified environments along two dimensions.[14] The first is the *rate of change* of environments. Some environments change only slowly. The environments of brewers, cement manufacturers and banks change only gradually over time. Alternatively, the fashion and telecommunications industries are characterised by rapid change. The second dimension identified by Duncan is that of *environmental complexity*. The greater the number of elements there are in an environment, the more complex the environment. Airlines face a complex environment because of the large number of environmental elements they face. But companies making toys and baking bread face a small number of environmental elements. The interaction of environmental complexity and stability forms a matrix, where different levels of uncertainty may be identified. Each of these levels of uncertainty leads to the adoption of different structural responses. Although Duncan did not expand on these, it is not difficult to identify what they are likely to be (see Figure 8.2).

The combination of a stable environment and low complexity leads to *low uncertainty* for organisations. Breweries, bakeries and soft-drink manufacturers all face this type of environment. The nature of the environment they face permits them

FIGURE 8.2 Duncan's environmental framework

Simple	Complex
High uncertainty	**Moderate to high uncertainty**
Large number of unpredictable external elements	Few environmental elements but each element changes often and unpredictably
Examples:	*Examples:*
Telecommunication companies	Fashion clothing
Aerospace firms	Music industry
Biotechnology companies	Computer games
Structural elements:	Television programming
• Decentralised, organic structure	*Structural elements:*
• Many different departments, extensive use of boundary spanners	• Decentralised with an emphasis on teamwork
• Extensive integration mechanisms and use of coordination and liaison roles	• Constant environmental monitoring by boundary spanners
• Extensive planning and forecasting	• High levels of coordination in order to promote imitation and innovation
	• Production facilities often mechanistic
Low to moderate uncertainty	**Low uncertainty**
Large number of dissimilar external elements which change only slowly	Small number of easily understood environmental elements which change slowly
Examples:	*Examples:*
Motor vehicle manufacturers	Cement manufacturers
Banks	Soft-drink bottlers
Oil companies	Breweries
Retail chains	Bakeries
Structural elements:	*Structural elements:*
• Centralised, formalised and mechanistic structure	• Centralised with high formalisation, mechanistic
• Differentiated into many departments to meet environmental elements	• Few departments
• Large numbers of boundary spanners	• Coordination by programs and planning
• Programmed coordination and use of planning for integration	

Adapted from: Robert Duncan, 'Characteristics of Perceived Environments and Perceived Environmental Uncertainty', *Administrative Science Quarterly*, 17, 1972, pp. 313–27.

to centralise their operations, as there is a low level of need to gather and process information. The small amount of change in their productive activities permits high levels of formalisation. There are few departments, as there are not a large number of environmental elements to respond to. Because there is little change in the way goods or services are produced, production processes are highly formalised. Coordination is by program and planning, with few roles for coordinators. In summary, the structure is mechanistic in operation.

A stable environment combined with a high level of complexity leads to *low to moderate uncertainty*. In this environment, there are many different elements but each changes only slowly, if at all. This describes the environment of educational institutions, motor vehicle manufacturers, banks and large retail chains. The stability of the environment leads to centralisation and high formalisation. Operations are mechanistic in nature. But the organisation differentiates itself into many different departments to meet the environmental elements. Because of the complexity of the environment, there are a large number of boundary spanners. But as there is little change in day-to-day operations, programmed coordination dominates.

An unstable environment combined with low levels of complexity leads to *moderate to high uncertainty*. In this environment, there are only a few elements but each element changes in an unpredictable manner. Examples include fashion clothing, the music industry, computer games and television broadcasters. As there is a heightened need to process information and respond to it, management is decentralised. Teamwork is emphasised in order to facilitate communication. There is extensive use of boundary spanners and intensive coordination devices are used to enable the organisation to respond to environmental pressures. However, production processes are more stable and tend towards being mechanistic.

When organisations are both complex and unstable, *high uncertainty* ensues. This is the most demanding environment for management, and it places great demands on the organisation's structure. Industries in which we are likely to find high uncertainty are in telecommunications, biotechnology and aerospace. In highly uncertain environments, firms are decentralised as it is not possible for one person to grasp the full nature of the challenges facing the company. Structures have many different departments and are organic in nature. Extensive and expensive coordination and integration devices are used, including coordinators and liaison staff. There is also extensive use of planning and forecasting.

Duncan's framework did not emerge from an empirical study, but it does encapsulate most of the variables that have been identified as defining organisational environments. It draws on Lawrence and Lorsch's findings that environments are not single elements but are composed of a number of elements. The greater the number of elements, the greater the complexity. The rate of change of these elements determines the stability of the environment. Stability enables decision making to be centralised and permits high levels of formalisation; it is not possible to formalise something that is constantly changing. But complexity comes with the need to gather, process and respond to numerous environmental elements, each with their own demands. This leads to decentralisation and a greater need for coordination.

As with other environmental classifications, Duncan's framework can be criticised because of its inability to actually measure stability and complexity: perceptual differences will lead to differing interpretations.[15] But notwithstanding this, it stands as a powerful reminder of the influence of environment on structure.

A synthesis: defining the environment and environmental uncertainty

In this section, we look for common threads among the studies on the environment. As our goal is integration and clarity rather than merely the presentation of many diverse research findings, we think it is important to seek some common ground in the environmental literature. Recent research suggests that there are three key dimensions to any organisation's environment—capacity, volatility, and complexity.[16] As you will see, these three dimensions synthesise much of the literature previously discussed.

capacity the degree to which an environment can support growth

The **capacity** of an environment refers to the degree to which it can support growth. Rich and growing environments generate excess resources, which can buffer the organisation in times of relative scarcity. They also provide the sustenance for organisations to grow. Scarce environments, in contrast, provide little sustenance for organisations and struggle to survive. In the late 1990s for instance, dot.com companies experienced an abundant supply of finance, leading to the formation of many new companies. Those companies in the petroleum-refining industry faced relative scarcity of capital and struggled to raise capital for modernisation.

stability the extent to which there is little change in the environment

The degree of instability in an environment is captured in the **stability** dimension. Where there is a high degree of unpredictable change, the environment is dynamic. At the other extreme is a stable environment. Financial markets are often dynamic, while the environment surrounding cement manufacture is an example of a stable market.

environmental complexity the degree to which the environment is concentrated on just a few elements

Finally, the environment needs to be assessed in terms of **environmental complexity**—that is, the degree to which the environment is concentrated on just a few elements. Simple environments have a few, concentrated elements. This might describe the tobacco industry, as there are relatively few players. It's easy for firms in this industry to keep a close eye on the competition. And the threats are largely associated with government legislation and court action. In contrast, environments characterised by heterogeneity and dispersion are called complex, as there are many elements in the environment to accommodate. A shipping company faces a complex environment. It must deal with various port authorities, freight forwarders, shipbuilders, suppliers and so on. A mining company, in contrast, may have only a few inputs and produce only one product. In this case the mining company exists in a simple environment.

Figure 8.3 summarises our definition of the environment along its three dimensions. The arrows in this figure are meant to indicate movement towards higher uncertainty. Thus organisations that operate in environments characterised as scarce, dynamic and complex face the greatest degree of uncertainty. Why? Because they have little room for error, high unpredictability, and a diverse set of elements in the environment to constantly monitor.

Given this three-dimensional definition of environment, we can offer some general conclusions. There is evidence that relates the degrees of environmental uncertainty to different structural arrangements. Specifically, the more scarce, dynamic and complex the environment, the more organic a structure should be. The more abundant, stable and simple the environment, the more the mechanistic structure will be preferred. Note how the preceding conclusions align with our discussion

FIGURE 8.3 Three-dimensional model of the environment

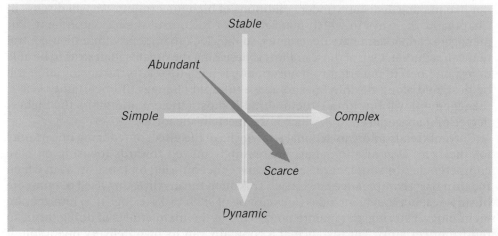

of technology and structure in the previous chapter. Routine technologies operate in relative certainty, whereas non-routine technologies imply relative uncertainty. High environmental uncertainty and technology of a non-routine nature both require organic-type structures. Similarly, low environmental uncertainty and routine technology can be managed more effectively in mechanistic structures.

The environmental imperative

As a result of our previous analysis, you should now have a reasonable understanding of what environment is and what some scholars have found in their efforts to better understand the environment–structure relationship. You now have the background to interpret more fully the cases for and against the environmental imperative.

The case for

The case for the theory that environment determines structure has been made by Burns and Stalker, Lawrence and Lorsch, and Duncan. Basically, they believe that environmental pressures generate task demands that are met by appropriate organisational structures. A more elaborate defence can be built using the systems perspective.

Organisations are dependent on acquiring inputs and disposing of outputs if they are to operate and survive. These inputs and outputs flow from and to the environment. Because of this dependency, organisations cannot ignore their environments. It is true that some organisations need to pay much closer attention than others and that some subunits within an organisation must monitor their sub-environments more closely than other subunits, but no organisation is so autonomous that it can insulate itself completely from its environment.

Further, not all of these environments behave in the same way. Some cannot be predicted with any degree of confidence. Some behave in random ways while yet others vary along predictable dimensions. Further, new elements in the environment are constantly emerging while other unpredictable elements progressively come under greater control. All told, environmental dependence creates uncertainty for managers. Environments are not amenable to easy control. The less management can control its environment, the greater the uncertainty for managers. Managers do not like making decisions under conditions of high uncertainty. We will discuss in Chapter 11 the ways in which managers seek to control their environment. But managers cannot eliminate uncertainty, so they look to options within their control that can reduce it. One of those options is designing the organisation so as to be able to respond best to uncertainty. If uncertainty is high, therefore, the organisation will be designed along flexible lines to adapt to rapid changes. If uncertainty is low, management will opt for a structure that is most efficient and offers the highest degree of managerial control, which is the mechanistic form.

Current trends in organisational strategy have the effect of reducing uncertainty for the firm. Organisations have increasingly moved towards focusing on core competencies. In simple terms this means concentrating on those areas in which the firm has a comparative advantage. This often means divesting itself of non-core businesses, but it also includes outsourcing of such tasks as logistics, information technology, catering and maintenance. One of the main effects of doing this is to reduce uncertainty. For instance, if a company ran its own delivery operation, it would have to deal with the complexities and uncertainties associated with fuel and capital equipment supplies, labour unions, insurance and reliability of delivery. Through outsourcing this function, it transfers much of this responsibility to another company, hence reducing its uncertainty.

The case against

If there is an environmental imperative, it may be limited to those subunits at the boundary of the organisation—those that interact directly with the environment. For instance, the structure of purchasing and marketing functions may be a direct response to their dependence on the environment. Yet it may have little or no impact on production, research and development, accounting and similarly insulated activities. It may also be that, as environments are perceived from within the organisation, what is perceived reflects the structure of the organisation.[17] If environments are creations, it is possible that structures differentiated into many different parts will perceive a heterogeneous environment or that decentralised structures will perceive more environmental uncertainty because of their structural arrangement. This reflects the social constructionist view of environments and may, in fact, explain Lawrence and Lorsch's findings.

A major contention of the environmental imperative supporters is that organisations structure themselves to minimise the impact of uncertainty—that is, environmental changes that organisations cannot forecast. As noted earlier in our discussion of the specific environment, not all uncertainty in the environment may have consequences for the organisation. Uncertainty, therefore, is relevant only when it occurs along with dependence.[18] Moreover, uncertainty is *unplanned* variation. For a retailer a drop in demand because of a downturn in the economy would not constitute uncertainty; it has been experienced before and will be experienced again. Further, if there is constant rate of change, such as constant improvements in motor vehicles, there is no guarantee that the situation is uncertain. Indeed it is possible to argue that as constant technological innovation has characterised the past 150 years, such change represents stability rather than unpredictibility.

It is, however, not possible to ignore the mantra of most management writers, who advocate continuous change as a characteristic of our age. Of course, from a different perspective we might argue that instead of reflecting increasing change, what may be occurring is only management's reduced ability to forecast. Change may well be occurring in areas that were previously not part of the firm's environment. When economies were essentially closed and protected by high tariffs, the direction and degree of change were easier to predict. Often this was simply coping with changes in demand with the rise and fall of economic activity. As firms have globalised, they have introduced more complex and dynamic elements into their environments. Many of these elements are more difficult for managers to understand and predict. Even those firms which 'stay at home' and have no overseas operations are more exposed to dynamic environments. The diffusion and introduction of technological change is also occurring faster than in previous generations. We have entered an age of discontinuity, which makes our forecasts highly prone to error, in both overestimating and underestimating the rate of change. So change may be a constant; it is only our reduced ability to predict it that may have *created* turbulent environments.

Finally, it has been said that the environmental imperative is just not in agreement with observed reality.[19] Not only do organisations that operate in ostensibly similar environments have different structures—they often show no significant difference in effectiveness. Furthermore, many organisations have similar structures and very diverse environments. This latter point is consistent with our observation that there is no shortage of the mechanistic form of structure in Australia today. Businesses of all kinds, government departments and even charities, possess many of the structural elements of the mechanistic form. This suggests that the environmental imperative has been overstated.

Knowledge, information economy and environmental complexity

Most writers and commentators are in agreement that environments are becoming less predictable.[20] Using the classifications and terminology we have introduced in this chapter we can say that environments are becoming more complex: that is, there are more elements in the environment impinging on the organisation. Each of these elements is also becoming less stable and more difficult to predict. At the same time, environments are becoming more abundant. There is considerable venture capital to fund new start-ups, there is almost no shortage of physical resources, and skilled labour is not too difficult to find. Barriers to entry in most markets are falling and goods are freely traded around the world. Consumers, be they companies and individuals, are also not reticent in trying new products and services as long as they meet their needs. This leads to expanding opportunities for organisations.

The combination of these factors has contributed to the emphasis on knowledge as being the key to competitiveness. Where environments were predominantly simple and stable, they could be understood by just a few people within the organisation. Understanding environments was also made easier by the extensive market rigging and anti-competitive practices that were common prior to the introduction of the *Trade Practices Act 1974*. With an increase in competition and the move towards globalisation, environments became more complex, and the necessary knowledge to cope with resulting complexity dispersed within the organisation.

Gathering this knowledge into a coordinated response is one of the greatest challenges facing organisations. It is of course possible to hire staff with the appropriate knowledge and training. But there are a number of structural answers to this problem. The first is promoting *greater coordination and integration*. One of the ways of achieving this is by the use of interdisciplinary teams. Coordinators with the responsibility for integrating the different functions of the organisations are also becoming more common. And communication technologies contribute. Most large companies now have an *intranet*, which operates as an in-house Internet. The functions vary from company to company, but most employees have their own home page listing their skills and interests. There are chat rooms for staff with common interests but who may be dispersed over a wide geographical area, and there is a search engine to permit the intranet to be searched for key terms and people.

On a more local scale, *office layouts* have been designed to promote information sharing. Favourite among information technology companies is the converted warehouse. Most large cities have former industrial and warehouse sites that are no longer needed by industry. Often in desirable locations close to cafes and inner-city attractions, these were derelict for some time until they were found to be ideal for open workspaces. Their large size has enabled them to be easily wired for computers and there is sufficient space for lounge areas, informal meeting rooms and large,

OT CLOSEUP
From tea to high-tech

The conversion of the old Bushells' Tea building, in Sydney's CBD, into the offices of communications company Com Tech provides a good example of how former industrial sites provide opportunities to generate workspaces not possible in more conventional buildings. The Bushells' building provided particular problems. Although ideally sited close to Circular Quay, it was purpose-built for blending tea. Chutes connected various floors and tea silos were widely scattered. The lifts, although large in size, could no longer be used because of safety regulations. The large size and scattered workspaces were attractive to Com Tech. The old tea silos were turned into meeting rooms, furnished with bean bags and disco-style curtains. The old timber lift shaft was sealed at each floor and turned into more formal meeting rooms. Each of the meeting rooms was named after tea ships that used to deliver tea from Ceylon (now Sri Lanka). The design allows for a mix of open spaces, formal and informal meeting rooms, chill-out rooms and quiet withdrawal areas. The high ceilings allowed the installation of artificial flooring,

essential to the extensive communication cabling. The building is not all old: the lifts were fitted in an old open lightwell, each floor being connected to the lifts by a glass-covered walkway. The lightwell itself has been turned into a dramatic six-storey entrance atrium.

The old Bushells' building meets Com Tech's requirements to be close to the CBD, but at the same time avoids the blandness of standard office space. It makes a statement about what the company is about and the nature of its product. It also creates the ideal conditions for knowledge work and communicates to customers an appropriate image for the company. But being located in the building of a company that has long since ceased to exist (Bushells was taken over by Unilever over 25 years ago) and whose technology has long since been superseded is a constant reminder of the rigours of staying in business.

Adapted from: David Maher, 'From Tea to High Tech', *The Australian Financial Review*, 27 July 2001, p. 38.

communal 'chill-out' spaces. These have promoted informal communication and information sharing. As many of the companies in the software and Internet industries are small, all members can fit in the one location. Other creative industries, such as advertising and fashion designers, have moved to a similar office layout.

The contrast between the imposing multistoreyed head office of previous generations and the open-planned space with chill-out areas provides ample evidence of how management and organisations have changed over the past 50 years.

Special issues relating to organisational environments

So far in this chapter we have considered the ways in which an organisation may be structured in order to respond to its environment. We have mainly discussed the structural responses that managers may adopt in order to reduce uncertainty. However, scholars have developed other perspectives on the environment–organisation interface. These help explain how organisations survive and, in some cases, the structures they adopt. We will consider the three most important of these perspectives: population ecology, institutional theory, and resource dependency theory.

The population-ecology view

In Chapter 1, we used the biological metaphor to assist in understanding the life of an organisation. We discussed how organisations are born, grow and then reach maturity and die. The population-ecology view is somewhat like the biological metaphor, but it looks at whole populations rather than an individual organisation. It seeks to explain what happened, and what is happening, rather than to make predictions as to which particular organisation is likely to survive. Those organisations that survive would, according to population ecologists, be the best adapted to their environments. As a result, examining successful and surviving organisations should provide us with a good guide to an appropriate structure. But population ecology has no predictive power: it cannot provide managers in advance with actions that should be taken in order to improve the chances of an organisation's survival.

In drawing an analogy between population ecology and biology, we need to look more towards Darwinism than the life-cycle perspective. In any given population of organisations there are variations in such characteristics as structure, management skills and attitudes, and access to resources. Not all organisations will survive. Population ecologists argue that certain organisations survive based on the fit between the organisation and its environment. Those which are selected to survive are those which are best adapted to their environment. Another way of looking at this process is that the environment selects certain organisations to survive based on their environmental fit.

The past decade has seen the growth and development of what certainly stands as an extreme environmental-imperative position. This position, which has been labelled the natural selection or **population-ecology** view,[21] argues that the environment selects certain types of organisations to survive and others to perish on the basis of the fit between their structural characteristics and the characteristics of their environment. Population ecologists argue that organisational forms must either fit their environmental niches or fail.

population-ecology view the environment selects certain types of organisations to survive and others to perish based on the fit between their structural characteristics and the characteristics of their environment

Population ecology relies heavily on biology's survival-of-the-fittest doctrine. This doctrine argues that there is a natural selection process that allows the strongest and most adaptable species to survive over time. Population ecology applies the same kind of thinking to organisations. The environment 'naturally' selects 'in' some organisations and selects 'out' others. Those selected 'in' are the survivors, while those selected 'out' perish. More specifically, population ecologists would argue that organisations that survive have resources, management advantages and structural dimensions that the casualties didn't have.

Assumptions of population ecology

In order to understand population ecology better, we should be familiar with the assumptions underlying its approach. First, the population-ecology perspective operates at a different level of analysis from many of the studies in this book. It focuses on groups or populations of organisations, not on individual organisations. You would use a population-ecology approach to explain why, from thousands of producers of motor cars in 1900, only a handful now remain. It also helps explain why start-up airlines regularly fail in Australia and New Zealand, and why just a few companies dominate personal computer manufacturing. Second, population ecology defines organisational effectiveness as simply survival. At any time, the organisations that operate in any industry are defined as effective because they are among the survivors. Third, population ecologists assume that the environment is totally determining. In direct contrast to the theme in Chapter 5, where strategy is described as determining structure, the population-ecology view assumes that management—at least in the short or intermediate term—has little impact on an organisation's survival. Managers are not seen as proactively managing the organisation's interactions with its environment. Success, therefore, is a result of events beyond management's control.

A fourth assumption of population ecology is that the carrying capacity of the environment is limited. There are only so many hospitals, for instance, that a given community's size can absorb. This sets up a competitive arena, where some organisations will succeed and others will fail. Finally, population ecology assumes the existence of a three-stage process that explains how organisations, operating in similar environmental niches, end up having common structural dimensions. The process proposes that forces of change are generated in the environment rather than from managerial action. This three-stage process is described in the next section.

Organisational change process

How do organisations change to better fit with the environment they face? The answer can be found in a three-stage process of change that recognises *variations* within and between organisations, the *selection* of those variations that are best suited to their environments, and a *retention* mechanism that sustains and reproduces those variations that are positively selected (see Figure 8.4).

FIGURE 8.4 Population-ecology view of the change process

OT CLOSEUP

Population ecology and the whitegoods industry

Whitegoods are household appliances that are generally white, such as refrigerators, washing machines, cooking appliances and dishwashers. Although taken for granted now, they were once every householder's dream, and possession of them marked entrée to the modern world. Their manufacture was also at the cutting edge of production technology, and appliance manufacturing was an attractive and popular investment.

Australia now does not have any locally owned appliance manufacturers. The last one was Email, which was bought by the Swedish manufacturer Electrolux in 2000. The only other local manufacturer is Fisher and Paykel, a New Zealand company. But there was a time when there was no shortage of whitegoods manufacturers in Australia: there were more than 30 independent manufacturers in the 1950s, supplying what was then an ever-expanding market. Local manufacture was protected by high tariffs, and agreements among manufacturers set prices and territories for each manufacturer to sell into.

By the 1980s the environment had begun to change. Trade practices legislation outlawed agreements among manufacturers and promoted competition. High tariffs were progressively falling, with a resulting increase in price competition. Markets had also matured, with customers buying products only when old ones wore out or when a new household was established.

So what happened to the 30 manufacturers of whitegoods? One by one they merged, or went out of business, as their management realised that they could not all survive. The weakest went first. Brand names Malleys, Pope, Hallstrom, Silent Knight and Electrice disappeared. By the 1990s only a few manufacturers were left. Eventually Email emerged as the only Australian-owned manufacturer, it having become clear that the local market could support only one manufacturer. Its stable of brands, ranging from Simpson, Kelvinator, Westinghouse, Hoover through to Dishlex and Vulcan, revealed the path of its takeovers.

But the scale of the Australian market was against even Email. Its manufacturing facilities were up-to-date and low-cost, but it needed better access to overseas markets than it alone could forge. It also needed engineering and design input from better-financed design labs. In the event, Email did not so much fail as suffer from lack of shareholder interest. In order to diversify, Email had acquired a profitable metals-distribution business. This was of great interest to other metals businesses and they acquired Email and put the appliance part of the business back on the market. The only company that could extract sufficient economies from Email was Electrolux, which duly acquired full control. There were few other interested parties.

Within any population of organisations (e.g. fast-food restaurants, chemical firms, hospitals and private schools) there will be variations in organisational forms. These can be planned or random variations; but the key point is that there will be diversity. Some of these variations, however, are better suited to their environments than others. Those that are well suited survive, while the others fall out of the set and perish. Organisations that have a form that fits their environment are positively selected and survive, while others either fail or change to match their environmental requirements. This finally leads to the retention of those variations that are positively selected. Over time, selected organisational forms tend to develop in populations that share common size requirements for efficiency, technologies and control systems.

Following the above process, we should expect to find common organisational practices and structural characteristics within the same population. The reason is that those organisations that were different were less able to compete. There are not enough resources in any environment to support an unlimited number of organisations, so there is a natural selection process that reproduces organisational structures that best fit with their environment. Over the very long run, of course, even the positively selected variations are likely to be selected 'out' because environments change and, in so doing, favour a different set of variations.

Every industry is made up of sets of organisations that can be divided into populations with common resources and technologies. But there is only so much money and so many people, market segments and other resources available in the environment. Organisations can define a niche for themselves—emphasising low cost, quality, convenience of location, hours of service or the like—but there is still competition. The survivors will be those that have best adjusted their internal resources to their environment.

The recent history of the grocery industry in Australia provides a good illustration of how environments can select out even successful firms. Grocery retailing was dominated by four main groups, Woolworths, Coles, Franklins and a group of independents. Franklins was considered to be the most competitive as far as price was concerned, but a series of poor decisions left it with a declining market share and mounting losses. The overseas owners of Franklins decided to cut their losses and break the chain up. Woolworths, considered to be the most successful of the grocery retailers, was the main beneficiary. Coles, beset with management problems, gained little from Franklins' demise. A number of independents however, greatly expanded their market share.

We can also see support for the population-ecology viewpoint in the actions of venture capitalists in places such as Silicon Valley.[22] Venture capitalists specialise in funding start-ups whose only asset is a good idea. All venture capitalists are hoping to back the next Microsoft, but as there is no security for the loans that they give these loans are inherently risky. In addition, it is virtually impossible to pick in advance which investments will pay off handsomely and which will lose money. Venture capitalists, therefore, spread their investments over a wide range of promising options, knowing that only one or two will be outstanding successes and just a few more will pay their way. They are reduced to allowing the environment to do the selection.

Limitations to the population-ecology view

Population ecology is not a general theory to explain why and how organisations survive. As its critics have shown, it has clear limitations.[23]

The theory ignores managerial motives and abilities. But management can often manage their environment to their advantage. It may not be all-powerful, as it is often depicted in management textbooks; however, neither is it irrelevant. Management can choose the domains or niches it wants to compete in and, especially in the long term, change its domain.

Population ecology appears to have limited application to large and powerful organisations. The reason is that these organisations can often insulate themselves against failure. They have strong constituencies in government that will protect them. Moreover, as we show in Chapter 11, large organisations can control their environments because many elements in their environments—suppliers, customers, unions and the like—are dependent on them and accede to their demands. The coal industry provides us with a good example of how firms can manipulate their environments. Coal is used as the major energy source for generating electricity. Twenty years ago, the coal industry was characterised by a large number of small producers, which were price-takers in the market. Few were profitable, as the consumers of coal largely dictated the price. The subsequent 20 years were characterised by considerable industry consolidation, so much so that by 2000 four companies, Rio Tinto, BHP Billiton, Anglo–American and Enex dominated world seaborne trade in coal. In doing this, they wrested from the power utilities the ability to set prices. As a result of management action, the environment of the industry was completely changed.

A further limitation of population ecology is that among public-sector organisations efficiency and adaptation are not effectiveness criteria—we simply do not let police forces, treasuries and law courts go out of business.[24] So population ecology may best be described as a special theory, applicable to small and powerless organisations. Reality tells us that most large organisations, as well as almost all those organisations in the public sector such as the police force, tend to be relatively immune to threats to their existence from the environment and as a consequence are rarely selected 'out'.

Implications

Population ecology provides an explanation for why organisations in common populations tend to have common structural characteristics and why certain types of organisations survive while others die. It can explain why small organisations so often fail, why the divisional structure became popular in the 1960s and why organic structures flourished as environments become less stable. Perhaps most important of all, it can explain the rise and proliferation of the bureaucratic form.[25]

Population ecology also tells us that survival will be significantly influenced by the capacity and stability of the organisation's environment. Is the capacity of the environment rich or lean? The richer the environment, the more organisations that will survive. In the mid-1980s, the environment facing the farm-equipment industry was considerably leaner than that in which manufacturers of personal computers operated. It is not surprising that we saw considerable consolidation among farm equipment manufacturers and a proliferation of personal computer manufacturers. Furthermore, the more stable the environment, the harder it is for new organisations to enter and compete. This is because stable, certain environments tend to retain large organisations that have achieved significant economies with high market shares.

Population ecologists challenge the research methodologies often used in organisation theory. Organisation theory researchers have traditionally looked at different structural relationships and sought to relate them to varying degrees of organisational effectiveness. Population ecologists have correctly noted that such research is biased: it doesn't survey *all* organisations, merely the survivors. The truly 'ineffective' organisations are not studied because they died too soon. Thus the value of organisational research is likely to improve if researchers look at organisations that have failed as well as those that have survived.

Acceptance of population ecology as a mainstream theory, at least among students of management and business, is not likely to occur, because it runs counter to the doctrine of rational attribution. Outcomes that are random—which can be attributed to luck or chance—cannot, by definition, be managed. A view that organisational success is pure chance is not likely to be widely accepted in schools of business and management, whose survival is based on a proactive view of managers and their ability to influence an organisation's survival and growth.

Institutional theory

Institutional theory is difficult to pin down because of the large number of meanings we can attribute to the word institution. Another name for an organisation is an institution; and many organisations have 'Institute' as part of their name. But we can also use the word to describe a situation where outside pressures induce repetitive behaviours in organisations. These repetitive behaviours then become accepted practice. When this occurs we call it institutionalising behaviour, and it is from this use of the word that institutional theory derives. But there is yet another meaning. Pressures upon organisations can be random or they may emerge from a formalised pressure group or from groups acting in combination. Where pressures emerge as a result of combined action by groups or through legal bodies such as government, we call them institutional pressures. Generally, institutional pressures are more powerful than the pressures exerted by individuals. Where these external pressures have a significant impact on an organisation we call it an institutionalised environment. Provided that the institutional pressures in an environment are similar for most organisations, it is not surprising that we would expect most organisations to look somewhat alike, with similar structures and practices.[26]

institutional theory
an approach which integrates an organisation's past actions and the social and environmental pressures on it to explain organisational practices

Institutional theory proposes that organisations are influenced not only by their internal processes but also by the need to adapt to the institutional pressures in the external environment. This need for adaptation then leads to behaviours being repeated and becoming 'institutionalised'. We can divide these institutional demands into two broad types. The first is economic and technical demands, which can be seen most clearly in demands on profit-seeking organisations to show a profit, innovate and respond to change. Management must develop organisational structures to meet these demands. Another group of institutionalised demands derive from government regulations and laws. For instance, equal opportunity laws require organisations of a certain size to have an equal opportunity officer, and this person must report to a senior person in the organisation. Hence, it is not surprising that all large companies have such a position. Also, defence departments often require certain organisational structures of their contractors.

The second is social demands, which reward organisations for conforming to societal values, norms and expectations. These are basically cultural expectations. Organisations tend to reflect the cultural values of the society in which they exist. Further social demands arise from the pressure to conform to the practices of other organisations—that is, to mimic them. The third source of environmental pressure to conform comes from other companies. Managers are consistently studying other organisations and copying innovations they feel may be of use to them. This sometimes leads to organisations following the ideas of the latest fashion or fad in management thinking, often with inadequate consideration as to whether it would be of benefit to them.

Although all firms must respond to both demands, for many organisations one group clearly dominates. Firms in the commercial sector may place the commercial and technical demands uppermost in their consideration. For instance, Franklins did not go out of business because it was engaged in some form of antisocial behaviour or did not conform to societal values, but because it made a series of bad business decisions which led to significant losses being incurred. Alternatively, Amnesty International and Greenpeace, among similar organisations, rely heavily for their existence on the values, norms and beliefs of important groups of supporters, regardless of how efficiently they may be using resources.

Evaluation of institutional theory

One of the more useful contributions of institutional theory is the explanation of the way in which social, economic and legal pressures influence organisational structures and practices. An organisation's ability to adapt to these play a part in favouring organisational survival. Greenpeace and Amnesty International, for instance, have been greatly favoured by the appeal they have for many sections of the population. Many large and supposedly powerful corporations have been humbled by the social pressures exerted by critics or other constituencies. The oil company Shell was greatly embarrassed by public reaction to its operations in Nigeria, even though a strong case could be made that Shell had little influence on the course of events.

We can see cultural and social pressures operating at another level. Most multinational companies are clearly far from being stateless. It does not take long to identify the practices of the home country in their operations. Toyota is clearly Japanese, Siemens is clearly German, and McDonald's is considered to be the ultimate embodiment of American culture. While the influences of the home country may be identified, most of the overseas operations of the companies mentioned have been significantly modified by the local culture. Indeed, their overseas success depends on adapting to local conditions and expectations.

Overall, the claim that organisations must conform to the institutionalised environment is not very different from our observations in Chapter 3 regarding strategic constituencies. We noted in that discussion that certain groups in the organisation's environment had to be satisfied in order for the organisation to survive. What institutional theorists have done is provide a useful elaboration and understanding of how this occurs.

Resource dependence theory

In Chapter 1 we introduced the concept of the open system. This theory highlights the interaction of the organisation and its environment. Resource dependence theory draws on the concept of the open system to promote the ways in which the organisation depends on the environment for its resources—hence the name resource dependence theory.[27] However, resource dependence brings with it the capacity of suppliers to exert power on organisations, and as a result makes them vulnerable to the exercise of this power. The dependent organisation will in turn take various actions to minimise the impact of its resource dependence. The actions that the organisation takes depends on the criticality of the resource. Typical resource dependencies are the dependence of steel mills on the supply of raw materials, airlines on jet fuel, manufacturers of grocery items on the demands of supermarket chains, universities on government funding, bakeries on flour supplies and oil refineries on supplies of crude oil. High-profile management consultancies are also dependent on hiring the limited pool of talented and well-informed consultants.

One of the ways of looking at resource dependence theory is that dependence on resources increases uncertainty for the organisation. As we have seen, managers do not like uncertainty and will act to reduce it. Lawrence and Lorsch's theory indicates that organisations are likely to differentiate themselves to meet each environmental threat. But this does not reduce the threat so much as making it easier to focus management's attention on the problem. Most active responses must be external to the organisation. These include taking an equity stake in a supplier or distributor, long-term contracts, buffering (i.e. building up emergency supplies), diversifying suppliers, lobbying and building personal relationships. We discuss these more fully in Chapter 11, when we consider the ways in which an organisation manages its environment.

Resource dependence theory is a useful way for us to analyse threats to the organisation. Dependency creates uncertainty but while the direction of the uncertainty is generally predicable, its magnitude is not. For instance, an outbreak of war in the Middle East is likely to interrupt crude oil supplies. Airlines can easily predict that this will affect both the supply and price of jet fuel. The uncertainty arises from not knowing how much the supply and the price will change. As airlines are heavily dependent on fuel as a resource, we would expect to find that their organisational structure has been differentiated to meet this dependency. We would also expect airlines to take action external to the organisation, to minimise interruptions to supply.

The environment–structure relationship

It is time to attempt some specific formulations on the environment–structure relationship. As in the previous chapters, we look at the effect on complexity, formalisation and centralisation. However, before we make these formulations, several general predictions about the environment–structure relationship are offered.

Every organisation depends on its environment to some degree, but we cannot ignore the obvious: namely, that some organisations are much more dependent on the environment and certain sub-environments than are others. The environment's effect on an organisation, therefore, is a function of its vulnerability, which in turn is a function of dependence.[28] In the late 1980s, Ford was less vulnerable to economic fluctuations than Mercedes-Benz. Firms such as Ingham's chickens and Revlon cosmetics are more vulnerable to consumer advocate groups than, say, manufacturers of clocks. Organisations whose employees are unionised are more vulnerable to union activity, and their effectiveness is more dependent on maintaining good relations with the union's leadership than that of non-unionised organisations.

The evidence demonstrates that a dynamic environment has more influence on structure than a static environment does.[29] A dynamic environment will push an organisation towards an organic form, even if large size or routine technology suggests a mechanistic structure. But not all parts of the environment change at the same rate. When operating in a dynamic environment, firms differentiate themselves into various parts based on the needs of each environmental segment. Arising from this, we would expect more intensive coordination in a dynamic environment. We would also expect organisations actively to devise ways to reduce their dependency when facing dynamic environments.

Environment and complexity

Environmental uncertainty and complexity are directly related. That is, high environmental uncertainty tends to lead to greater complexity. In order to respond to a dynamic and more complex environment, organisations become more differentiated. An organisation faced with a volatile environment will need to monitor that environment more closely than one that is stable. This is typically accomplished by creating differentiated units. Similarly, a complex environment requires the organisation to buffer itself with a greater number of departments and specialists.

Environment and formalisation

We predict that stable environments should lead to high formalisation because stable environments create a minimal need for rapid response, and economies exist for organisations that standardise their activities. But we caution against assuming that a dynamic environment must lead to low formalisation throughout the organisation. Management's preference will undoubtedly be for insulating operating activities from uncertainty. If successful, a dynamic environment is likely to lead to low formalisation of boundary activities while maintaining relatively high formalisation within other functions.

Environment and centralisation

The more complex the environment, the more decentralised the structure.[30] Regardless of the static–dynamic dimension, if a large number of dissimilar factors and components exist in the environment, the organisation can best meet the uncertainties that this causes through decentralisation. It is difficult for management to understand a highly complex *environment* (note that this is different from a complex *structure*). Management information-processing capacity becomes overloaded, so decisions are carved up into subsets and are delegated to others.

Disparities in the environment are responded to through decentralisation.[31] When different responses are needed to different sub-environments, the organisation creates decentralised subunits to deal with them, so we can expect organisations to decentralise selectively. This can explain why, even in organisations that are generally highly centralised, marketing activities are typically decentralised. This is a response to a disparity in the environment: that is, even though the environment is generally static, the market sub-environment tends to be dynamic.

Finally, the evidence confirms that extreme hostility in the environment drives organisations, at least temporarily, to centralise their structures.[32] A wildcat strike by the union, an interruption of supplies or the sudden loss of a major customer all represent severe threats to the organisation, and top management responds by centralising control. When survival is in question, top management wants to oversee decision making directly. Of course, you may note that this appears to contradict an earlier prediction. You would expect this dynamic environment to meet with decentralisation. What appears to happen is that two opposing forces are at work, with centralisation the winner. The need for innovation and responsiveness (via decentralisation) is overpowered by top management's fear that the wrong decisions may be made.

Summary

The theme of this chapter has been that different organisations face different degrees of environmental uncertainty and that structural design is a major tool that managers can use to eliminate or minimise the impact of environmental uncertainty.

The environment was defined as everything outside an organisation's boundaries. Our concern, however, is with the specific environment—that part most relevant to the organisation. Management desires to reduce uncertainty created by this specific environment.

Three landmark contributions were cited. Burns and Stalker argued that an organisation's structure should be mechanistic in a stable, certain environment and organic when the environment is turbulent. Lawrence and Lorsch's major contributions included the recognition that there are multiple specific environments with different degrees of uncertainty, that successful organisations' subunits meet the demands of their sub-environments and that the degree of environmental uncertainty is of the utmost importance in the selection of the right structure. Duncan identified four different structural types drawn from the interaction of environmental complexity and environmental change. We synthesised the studies into three dimensions: capacity (abundant–scarce), volatility (stable–dynamic), and complexity (simple–complex).

The environment–structure relationship is complicated, but we concluded that:

1 The environment's effect on an organisation is a function of dependence.
2 A dynamic environment has more influence on structure than does a stable one.
3 Complexity and environmental uncertainty are inversely related.
4 Formalisation and environmental uncertainty are inversely related.
5 The more complex the environment, the greater the decentralisation.
6 Extreme hostility in the environment leads to temporary centralisation.

The summary so far approaches the influence of the environment from the perspective of managerial action. But there are a number of other approaches, which study environmental influence from a different perspective. Population ecologists view the environment as having limited carrying capacity. Environments select those organisations to survive that are best adapted to their environment. Population ecologists therefore seek to identify the processes through which the environment selects organisations to succeed or fail. Institutional theory helps explain how forces in the environment, including formal and informal ones, help influence organisational structure and practices. And resource dependence theory helps explain how dependence on scarce resources influences organisational actions to increase the chance of organisational survival.

For review and discussion

1 'Environmental states are objective.' Do you agree or disagree with this statement? Discuss.
2 What is the difference between an organisation's general environment and its specific environment?
3 Why do managers dislike environmental uncertainty? What can they do to reduce it?

4   Describe the technology and environment that fit best with (a) mechanistic and (b) organic structures.

5   Why would an organic structure be inefficient in a stable environment?

6   Discuss whether Duncan's typology oversimplifies the impact of the environment upon an organisation.

7   What was Lawrence and Lorsch's main contribution to organisational theory?

8   'Differentiation and integration are opposing forces.' Do you agree or disagree? Discuss.

9   Define each of the following environmental dimensions:

    (a) capacity;   (b) volatility;   (c) complexity.

10 Under what conditions is environment likely to be a major determinant of structure?

11 According to the population-ecology view, how do organisations change?

12 Why is a limited carrying capacity within the environment critical to the population-ecology view?

13 If the population ecologists are right, what can management do to make their organisations more effective?

14 Describe how institutional theory helps explain the structure and practices of an organisation you are familiar with.

15 Select an organisation with which you are familiar and identify its key resource dependencies. How does it seek to reduce uncertainty arising from the resource dependencies?

CASE FOR CLASS DISCUSSION
Qantas faces its environment

There is only one word to describe the airline industry, and that is brutal; it is not an industry for the faint-hearted. Capital costs are high, with one jumbo jet costing over $250 million dollars. Add to that the cost of terminals, maintenance facilities and a significant investment in IT, and a billion dollars hardly gets you started. But finding finance is only the first of your problems. One of the greatest difficulties is the cyclical nature of the industry. Air travel for most is a luxury; even business can get by with greatly reduced travel if need be. Holidays requiring air travel can be put off indefinitely; it is not like food, which is an everyday necessity no matter what your wealth. All this adds up to an industry with high fixed costs but wildly swinging levels of demand.

It is not surprising that the downturns take a toll on the financially weakest, as seen in aftermath of the terrorist attacks in 2001.

But there are ways in which uncertainty can be managed, and Qantas provides a good example. In 1992 Qantas, which flew only to overseas destinations, merged with Australian Airlines, a purely domestic carrier. Both were owned by the federal government and the merger formed what was the 12th-largest airline in the world in terms of passenger-kilometres flown. The merger between the two airlines was in preparation for the federal government privatising the airline in 1995. As part of the privatisation, British Airways bought 25% of the airline. This move cemented an alliance between the two carriers which enabled the sharing of a number of functions.

Although air transport is high in glamour, Qantas' operations can basically be classified as mechanistic. Its activities are undertaken in a repetitive cycle, which dominate the working life of most employees. Its operations conform to a timetable that it updates approximately every six months, and aircraft maintenance is performed in accordance with fixed schedules.

Planning to reduce uncertainty is a major function at Qantas, ensuring that for the time horizon being considered all major eventualities are covered. A constant brief must be kept on political factors affecting the airline and its competitors, and a politically savvy chief executive is almost a must. International air routes are governed by agreements between countries as to landing rights. Although this form of international cartel is coming under pressure, governments still intervene far more often in this than in most other industries. Factors affecting political instability in the countries in which the airline operates must be constantly monitored.

All industries have critical functions that can affect profitability. One of the keys to success in transport is to keep capital equipment earning revenue all the time. To do this, Qantas has developed advanced management information systems which allow it instant updates on the level of booking for each flight in any part of the world. It has a function that airlines call yield management and which could loosely be called pricing. This function is to fill an aircraft with passengers paying the maximum fare that can be extracted from them. Yield management plays demand off against availability, using the price of a ticket as the variable in keeping the planes full. Hence, there are such variables as seasonal fares, discounts for times of day, holiday excursions and so on. The business person who must travel at short notice, however, pays the full fare. Out of the 400 people in a jumbo jet, few will be paying the standard fare for their travel. They range from first class full-fare passengers to tourists on super-apex excursions and staff going on holidays at greatly discounted rates.

The range of skills at Qantas to cope with the environment are extensive. From fuel supply futures to juggling currency in hedging operations, just about every modern skill is used. Each skill is grouped into departments, which concentrate on their defined area of responsibility. These departments form larger groupings for management purposes. For instance, all maintenance functions combine to form a larger department. Some departments exist to form an interface with outside suppliers of services, such as airport authorities, advertising agencies and regulatory government departments. Now that shareholders are part of Qantas' critical constituencies, keeping shareholders informed of the financial position of the company is an important function.

The wide range of skills means that communication and coordination within the organisation is a necessity. This is not just to develop and maintain a common culture and good relations among staff. It is also necessary for a coordinated response to problems and to any changes to the published schedule. Heavy reliance is placed on the computerised information system, which acts as a glue to bind the organisation together. It also stores information on such things as bookings of passengers and cargo, performance of aircraft, availability of spares and crew schedules.

There is constant downward pressure on prices in the airline industry. Basically, air travel is a commodity, with all airlines offering the same services. Most of the travelling public are price-sensitive, and seek the cheapest deals commensurate with their needs. Qantas has one of the higher cost structures in the industry, particularly when ranked against its Asian competitors, and it is faced with the need to trim staff and lower operating costs. It has decided that whatever it does it must show a profit, and so has not moved to increase the number of destinations it flies to. Rather it has concentrated on making more use of its capital equipment and improving in-flight services. It has also undertaken a major program to raise productivity and force costs down.

The year 2001 was one of significant environmental turmoil. Ansett, its main competitor in the domestic market, went into liquidation, from which it never emerged. Qantas took over one of its domestic competitors, Impulse, and Virgin Blue, with its far lower cost base, snapped at Qantas' heels. Air New Zealand avoided failure only because

New Zealand refused to let it fail and renationalised the airline. With the terrorist attacks of 11 September, international traffic plummeted, forcing a number of well-known overseas carriers into bankruptcy. The burden on Qantas was not as great as it otherwise would have been, as it could redeploy excess overseas capacity onto the domestic market to take advantage of Ansett's failure. All told, the industry seems to be consolidating into fewer number of larger units. Provided Qantas keeps its cool, and its costs down, it should be one of the survivors.

QUESTIONS

1 How closely does Qantas' structure conform to the theories of Lawrence and Lorsch? Support your position showing areas of similarity and difference.

2 Identify how changes in Qantas' environment have affected important tasks in the organisation. How have these affected Qantas' strategy?

3 To what extent does the nature of the task that Qantas is engaged in determine its structure? Given your answer to question 1, what do you consider has a greater impact, technology or environment?

4 How could you apply the population-ecology view to the airline industry? In the Qantas case, what indicates a practical limitation to the population-ecology viewpoint?

5 How does Qantas seek to control uncertainty? How has it incorporated this into its structure?

FURTHER READING

Howard Aldrich, *Organizations and Environments*, Englewood Cliffs, NJ: Prentice Hall, 1970.
Tom Burns & G.M. Stalker, *The Management of Innovation*, London: Tavistock, 1961.
Robert Duncan, 'Characteristics of Perceived Environments and Perceived Environmental Uncertainty', *Administrative Science Quarterly*, 17, 1972, pp. 313–17.
Paul Lawrence & Jay W. Lorsch, *Organization and Environment: Managing Differentiation and Integration*, Boston: Division of Research, Harvard Business School, 1967.
Walter Powell & Paul DiMaggio (eds), *The New Institutionalism in Organizational Analysis*, Chicago, IL: University of Chicago Press, 1991.

NOTES

1 Adapted from Boral's *Annual Reports 1996, 1998, 2000.*
2 Robert H. Miles, *Macro Organizational Behavior*, Santa Monica, CA: Goodyear Publishing, 1980, p. 195.
3 James D. Thompson, *Organizations in Action*, New York: McGraw-Hill, 1967, p. 27.
4 H. Kirk Downey, Don Hellriegel & John W. Slocum, Jr, 'Environmental Uncertainty: The Construct and Its Application', *Administrative Science Quarterly*, December 1975, pp. 613–29.
5 William H. Starbuck, 'Organizations and Their Environments', in Marvin D. Dunette, ed., *Handbook of Industrial and Organizational Psychology*, Chicago: Rand McNally, 1976, p. 1080.
6 William R. Dill, 'Environment as an Influence on Managerial Autonomy', *Administrative Science Quarterly*, March 1958, pp. 409–43.
7 Karl Weick, *The Social Psychology of Organizing*, Reading, MA: Addison Wesley, 1979; Robert Duncan, 'Characteristics of Organization Environments and Perceived Environmental Uncertainty', *Administrative Science Quarterly*, 17, 1972, pp. 313–27.
8 Tom Burns & G.M. Stalker, *The Management of Innovation*, London: Tavistock, 1961.
9 See Henry Mintzberg, *The Structuring of Organizations*, Englewood Cliffs, NJ: Prentice Hall, 1979, pp. 270–2.

10   Margaret K. Chandler & Leonard R. Sayles, *Managing Large Systems*, New York: Harper & Row, 1971, p. 180.

11   Paul Lawrence & Jay W. Lorsch, *Organization and Environment: Managing Differentiation and Integration*, Boston: Division of Research, Harvard Business School, 1967.

12   See, for example, Henry L. Tosi, Ramon J. Aldag & Ronald G. Storey, 'On the Measurement of the Environment: An Assessment of the Lawrence and Lorsch Environmental Subscale', *Administrative Science Quarterly*, March 1973, pp. 27–36; and H. Kirk Downey & John W. Slocum, Jr, 'Uncertainty: Measures, Research, and Sources of Variation', *Academy of Management Journal*, September 1975, pp. 562–78.

13   Ramon J. Aldag & Ronald G. Storey, 'Environmental Uncertainty: Comments on Objective and Perceptual Indices', in Arthur G. Bedeian, A.A. Armenakis, W.H. Holley, Jr & H.S. Field, Jr, eds, *Proceedings of the Annual Meeting of the Academy of Management*, Auburn, AL: Academy of Management, 1975, pp. 203–5.

14   Robert Duncan, 'Characteristics of Perceived Environments and Perceived Environmental Uncertainty', *Administrative Science Quarterly*, 17, 1972, pp. 313–27.

15   Weick, op. cit.

16   Gregory G. Dess & Donald W. Beard, 'Dimensions of Organisational Task Environments', *Administrative Science Quarterly*, March 1984, pp. 52–73.

17   Weick, op. cit., 1969.

18   Jeffrey Pfeffer, *Organizational Design*, Arlington Heights, IL: AHM Publishing, 1978, p. 133.

19   John Child, 'Organizational Structure, Environment, and Performance: The Role of Strategic Choice', *Sociology*, January 1972, pp. 1–22.

20   Thomas Clarke & Stewart Clegg, *Changing Paradigms: The Transformation of Management Knowledge in the 21st Century*, London: HarperCollins Business, 1998.

21   Michael T. Hannan & John H. Freeman, 'The Population Ecology of Organizations', *American Journal of Sociology*, March 1977, pp. 929–64; Howard E. Aldrich, *Organizations and Environments*, Englewood Cliffs, NJ: Prentice Hall, 1970; Douglas R. Wholey & Jack W. Brittain, 'Organizational Ecology: Findings and Implications', *Academy of Management Review*, July 1986, pp. 513–33; Dave Ulrich, 'The Population Perspective: Review, Critique and Relevance', *Human Relations*, March 1987, pp. 137–52; John Betton & Gregory Dess, 'The Application of Population Ecology Models to the Study of Organizations', *Academy of Management Review*, 10(4), 1985, pp. 750–7; and Alessandro Lomi, 'The Population Ecology of Organizational Founding: Location Dependence and Unobserved Heterogeneity', *Administrative Science Quarterly*, 40(1), 1995, pp. 111–14.

22   See, for instance, J. Alay, 'The Heart of Silicon Valley', *Fortune*, 136(1), 1997, p. 66; and L.H. Dobkins, 'Regional Advantage, Culture and Competition in Silicon Valley and Route 128', *Journal of Economic Behaviour and Organisation*, 32(1), 1997, pp. 161–3.

23   Charles Perrow, *Complex Organizations: A Critical Essay*, 3rd edn, Glenview, IL: Scott, Foresman, 1986, pp. 211–16; Andrew H. Van de Ven, 'Review of Organizations and Environments by H.E. Aldrich', *Administrative Science Quarterly*, June 1979, pp. 320–6; Wai Fong Foo, John C. Oliga & Anthony G. Puxty, 'The Population Ecology Model and Management Action', *Journal of Enterprise Management*, June 1981, pp. 317–25; and Amos H. Hawley, 'Human Ecology: Persistence and Change', *American Behavioral Scientist*, January/February 1981, pp. 423–44.

24   ibid.

25   John Langston, 'The Ecological Theory of Bureaucracy: The Case of Josiah Wedgwood and the British Pottery Industry', *Administrative Science Quarterly*, September 1984, pp. 330–54.

26   Paul DiMaggio & Walter Powell, 'The Iron Cage Revisited: Institutional Isomorphism and Collective Rationality in Organizational Fields', *American Sociological Review*, 48, 1983, pp. 147–60; Walter Powell & Paul DiMaggio, eds, *The New Institutionalism in Organizational Analysis*, Chicago, IL: University of Chicago Press, 1991; Richard Scott,

'The Adolescence of Institutional Theory', *Administrative Science Quarterly*, 32, 1987, pp. 493–511; Lynn Zucker, ed., *Institutional Patterns and Organizations: Culture and Environment*, Cambridge, MA: Ballinger, 1988.

27 This section is mainly drawn from Jeffrey Pfeffer & Gerald Salancik, 'The External Control of Organizations: A Resource Dependence Perspective', New York: Harper & Row, 1978.

28 David Jacobs, 'Dependency and Vulnerability: An Exchange Approach to the Control of Organizations', *Administrative Science Quarterly*, March 1974, pp. 45–59.

29 Mintzberg, *The Structuring of Organizations*, p. 272.

30 ibid., pp. 273–6.

31 ibid., pp. 282–5; and Edward F. McDonough III & Richard Leifer, 'Using Simultaneous Structures to Cope with Uncertainty', *Academy of Management Journal*, December 1983, pp. 727–35.

32 Mintzberg, *The Structuring of Organizations*, pp. 281–2.

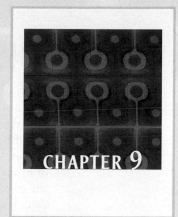

CHAPTER 9

Power-control

After reading this chapter you should be able to:

1   describe the strategic choice argument;

2   present the case against strategic choice;

3   identify the power-control assumptions about organisational decision making;

4   distinguish between power and authority;

5   describe how an individual or group gains power;

6   define politics;

7   explain the power-control model of how structures emerge;

8   describe the power-control interpretation of technology and environment's role in structure;

9   explain the power-control view of structural change;

10   examine how power and politics interact within organisations;

11   predict the degree of complexity, formalisation and centralisation that those in power prefer.

9

Introduction

The 'car guys' take charge at General Motors

General Motors in the USA has a reputation for producing stodgy cars.[1] It was traditionally an engineering-dominated company with an emphasis on what could be produced at reasonable cost. But starting in the 1980s, it watched as its market share slowly but continuously eroded, first to the Japanese and then to a host of other imports and smarter local producers. The only cars it made money on were the pick-up trucks, favoured by Americans, and a few four-wheel-drives and luxury vehicles. The main reason the GM cars were not selling was that they were just plain boring and indistinguishable from one another.

This reflected the combination of an emphasis on brand management and cost cutting. The marketers, who had gained the upper hand at GM, promised that by astute marketing and brand management they could arrest the decline in sales. They pushed consistent brand imagery and strong marketing, rather than innovative styling, to sell cars. Many rigid design rules were in place that resulted in boring cars. Stylists had to consult lengthy design manuals for each division, including up 40 pages describing the crest for each brand. Adding to these problems were the powerful engineers, who were more interested in cost cutting than producing attractive cars.

To try to overcome these problems, GM appointed Robert Lutz as vice chairman for product development. He is a classic 'car guy' with a passion for product and a flair for design. He is obsessed with producing cars not to a formula or a price but to a design that will grab customers and become a must-have product. His is a powerful position. He reigns supreme over every aspect of vehicle operations, from the design studio to the factory floor. He is trying to convince executives that unless the design is right, no marketing in the world will sell the product. He has thrown away the instruction book and told designers to be innovative. He approves all designs and has rejected some out of hand as being too stodgy.

Lutz has help. He has found allies in the organisation and has with key positions reporting to him. The resistance of the engineers and manufacturers has crumbled; the past history of poor market performance has left them without a power base to challenge Lutz's authority.

The 'car guys' story introduces another perspective on how organisation structures evolve. Organisation members, looking to satisfy their self-interest or point of view, seek to gain power and then use it to create structures that work to their benefit.

In the previous four chapters we have looked at strategy, size, technology and environment as independent determinants of structure. We found that while each of these contingency variables could explain some of the variations to be found in organisational structures, none could explain all of the variations identified. Each contributed by explaining a part, but only a part. Is it possible that the variables interrelate? That is, by combining them, could we get a whole greater than the sum of the parts? For instance, do large size, routine technology, stable environment and analyser strategy go together? Efforts in this direction suggest that there is an inter-action among the variables so that by combining them we can explain more of the variance,[2] but at best these four factors explain only 50%–60% of the variability in structure.[3] It may be that these contingency variables, either individually or in combination, are not as powerful as originally thought. Another possibility is that they are more potent than the evidence indicates, but the fault resides in the weaknesses of the research techniques used to measure them. After all, we are dealing with intangibles, and organisational research is fraught with measurement problems.

The power-control viewpoint proposes another answer: namely, that a major piece of the puzzle is still missing and that power and control can explain a good portion of the residual variance.

In this chapter, we will step outside the confines of rationality and maximising organisational effectiveness into the world of organisational power and politics. We will introduce the **power-control** view. The power-control view states that an organisation's structure at any given time reflects the interests of those in power, who select a structure that will, to the maximum degree possible, maintain and enhance their influence and control and permit them to implement their policies.

We will also use this chapter to briefly examine other challenges to contingency theory. Other researchers have raised questions suggesting that there are other influences on organisational structure in addition to those we have identified. Consideration of these expands our understanding of how organisational structures evolve.

> **power-control** an organisation's structure, at any given time, is to a large extent the result of those in power selecting a structure that will, to the maximum degree possible, maintain and enhance their control

A major attack: strategic choice

A substantive attack on those arguing for the dominance of technological, environmental or other forces as structural imperatives was developed by John Child in the early 1970s.[4] Child's work, which essentially is an expansion of the strategy–structure thesis presented in Chapter 5, sought to demonstrate that managers have considerable latitude in making strategic choices. Interest in Child's original work has expanded, and Child himself has expanded on his initial ideas in more recent times.[5]

The logic of strategic choice

Child's **strategic choice** argument is that while there are constraints on the discretion that managers have to make decisions, they still have significant latitude for making choices. Just as they choose objectives, personnel or control techniques, managers also choose the organisation's structural design. Environmental factors such as competitors, unions and government agencies are part of the constraints, but rather than impinging directly on an organisation's structure these factors are mediated by managerial choice. Similarly, technology can control structure only to the degree that managers choose a technology that leads to certain structural dimensions. So environment and technology are *constraints* on managers rather than imperatives. In other words, they do not oblige managers to implement certain structures. Rather, they limit the choices that managers have. Child's argument can be condensed into four basic points.[6]

> **strategic choice** managers have considerable discretion in which to choose their organisation's structural design

1 *Decision makers have more autonomy than that implied by those arguing for the dominance of environmental, technological or other forces.* Managers can select from among a wide range of viable alternatives compatible with the domain they occupy. Take motor vehicle manufacturing as an example. Both Toyota and Ford mass-produce motor vehicles for the same customer base using basically the same technology. But Toyota's management has chosen a radically different

structure from that used by Ford. Further, managers are constantly restructuring organisations even though there has been little change in such factors as size, technology or environment. Alternatively, managers can choose to enter a new domain. Businesses enter and leave markets regularly. The most obvious case is when they enter an overseas market. But they are also adding and divesting themselves of businesses. BHP Billiton is divesting itself of its steel-making operations and CSR is anxious to leave the sugar industry. Universities and TAFEs make decisions about what curricula to offer, charities cater for certain sections of the disadvantaged, and so forth. In choosing a given domain, management simultaneously determines its pattern of interdependence with its environment. Organisations are *not* constrained to do what they have done in the past. Given the fact that environmental domains are fairly broad, there may be a variety of organisational forms that are viable, rather than a single one.

The same logic holds true for technology. The selection of a domain determines the activities the organisation will engage in, and hence technology is also chosen. If an organisation decides to offer consulting advice tailored to the unique needs of its clients, it is not likely to use long-linked technology. Similarly, Aldi, the German supermarket chain that has established stores in Australia, has chosen to concentrate on a small range of highly discounted groceries sold under its own brand name. This implies a low-service operation with a tightly controlled supply chain. In contrast, David Jones' gourmet food halls promote variety and exclusiveness. The emphasis is more on obtaining suitable supplies and creating an appropriate ambience than on their cost. The point is that the choice of domain and its complementary activities and tasks is made by management. Technology does not dictate structure. Management dictates structure by its choice of domain.

This argument may also be applied to charities. The Smith Family, a charity set up to provide help to the needy, has identified one of the main indicators of adult poverty as poor education and life chances as a child. As a consequence it has reoriented much of its activity to supporting children in schools and providing home environments conducive to educational attainment.

2   *Organisational effectiveness should be construed as a range instead of a point.* Organisational effectiveness is not an optimum point of achievement. It is a range. This is important because managers do not optimise their decision making. They 'satisfice', seeking outcomes that are satisfactory and sufficient.[7] In other words, they make choices that meet the minimum criteria. Rather than seeking a structure that would result in *high* effectiveness, managers select structures that merely satisfy the minimal requirements of effectiveness. They might, for instance, trade off an optimum profit for greater power or autonomy, stability or other objectives. This means that decision makers may be content with varying levels of organisational effectiveness, so long as they all meet or exceed the minimum satisfactory level. The range between maximising and 'acceptable' creates an area in which managers can use their discretion.

3   *Organisations often have the power to manipulate and control their environments.* Organisations are not always pawns being acted on by their environments. Managers of large companies are able to create demand for their products and control their competitive environments. We discuss some of the measures used in Chapter 11. Other actions can include mergers, joint ventures, vertical integration or even lobbying for government regulation. The merger of Esso and Mobil in

Australia produced a new organisation, more powerful in controlling its environment. The vertical integration of many industries provides an illustration of how organisations expand control. For instance, Boral controls concrete supply from the quarries and the cement plant through to delivery to the final customer.

4 *Perceptions and evaluations of events are an important intervening link between environments and the actions of organisations.* There is a difference between objective characteristics of the environment and the perception and evaluation of these characteristics by organisation members. People do not always perceive environmental characteristics the same way. Their interpretations will show themselves in the decisions they choose. Their strategic choices, in other words, are likely to exert a significant influence on structural design, regardless of the actual characteristics of the environment. Decision makers evaluate the organisation's environment, make interpretations based on their experience, and use this information to influence the design of the internal structure.

A good illustration of differences in perception of environments was the dot.com Internet boom of the late 1990s, particularly in its relation to the retail industry. A large number of dot.com company promoters took the view that the Internet had changed the face of retailing and that in future most retail transactions would be carried out on-line. They spoke of retailing dinosaurs, which relied on 'bricks and mortar' to sell their product. Established retailers, however, looked on the Internet as just another distribution channel, which would complement rather than replace their existing operations. While both groups acknowledged the importance of the Internet, the perceptions of its impact were radically different.

The case against strategic choice

The generalisability of the strategic-choice argument is restricted by two facts: commitments often lock an organisation into a limited environmental segment, and there are barriers to entry in many markets. Both these forces can constrain managers from doing much with their discretionary latitude.

Physical and human-resource commitments often lock organisations into a narrow domain for a long time. Once management has spent $200 million in constructing a state-of-the-art plant to build television sets, its only option apart from running the plant is to close it or sell it. It cannot use the capital equipment to enter magazine publishing. Similarly, personnel are not totally variable costs. If an organisation's personnel were hired and trained to operate a soft-drink-bottling plant, management just cannot—with the wave of a magic wand—make its employees electrical engineers and move into the computer memory-disk business.

Barriers to market entry include economies of scale, absolute costs and product differentiation.[8] Economies of scale favour those organisations that are already in a market and command substantial market share. The high concentration in industries that produce cars, steel and major appliances is not accidental. It is a reflection of the economies of scale and the difficulties that new firms—with small market shares—would have in competing against the established companies. There are also absolute cost advantages that may be lower for existing organisations because of knowledge or technology not available to new entrants. For example, Onesteel's knowledge of coated-steel products allows it to produce roofing and similar materials at a cost and quality that would be difficult for new entrants to compete with. Finally, product differentiation clearly favours existing organisations that have achieved high visibility and whose brands have gained wide recognition. In 1975, for instance, it was fairly easy for someone with a little money and a few good ideas to get into the athletic shoe-manufacturing business. That is no longer true, as Reebok, Nike and Adidas have grown to dominate the market.

These constraints imply that strategic choice is most applicable in domains where entry is relatively easy. That means that managerial latitude is going to be greater in industries such as consulting or residential real estate sales. On the other hand, strategic choice is not likely to have much relevance in the breakfast cereal business, where competitors would have to compete against the likes of Kellogg's, Uncle Toby's and Sanitarium.

Summary

Strategic choice reaffirms that organisational decision makers have a degree of discretionary latitude in choosing their strategies and market domains. Even though critics have argued that discretion may be limited, the strategic-choice position nevertheless opened the door to thinking in terms of discretion on the part of the decision maker to *choose* an organisation's structure. Furthermore, it called into question the assumption that decision makers would seek an organisational structure that would optimise organisational effectiveness. The ideas presented in

OT CLOSEUP

The influence of the CEO's personality on structure

Would you be surprised to find out that chief executive officers (CEOs) with a thirst for power delegate very little authority, that CEOs who are suspicious of others establish elaborate information systems so that they can closely monitor what's going on, or that CEOs with strong creative and technical interests often set up substantial research departments? Probably not! This has led to the conclusion, consistent with the strategic-choice perspective, that the personality of an organisation's CEO might be a decisive influence on determining structure.

Recent research offers confirming evidence.[9] Specifically, it has been found that a CEO's need to achieve (*nAch*)—that is, the degree to which he or she strives to continually do things better—strongly influences structure. In what way? The more achievement-oriented the CEO, the more he or she centralises power and imposes high formalisation. This structural form allows the CEO to take major credit for, and to carefully monitor and control, the performance of his or her organisation.

Does this conclusion apply to all organisations? The evidence indicates that the relationship between *nAch* and formalisation is significantly stronger in small organisations than in large ones, and in young ones than in old ones. However, the preference for centralisation by high achievers seems to be evident regardless of the size or age of the organisation.

A final question: is the CEO's personality a more powerful determinant than the traditional contingency variables of size, technology and environmental uncertainty? Yes and no! On the no side, size was found to be a significant determinant. Consistent with the research studies discussed in Chapter 6, large organisations tend to be more decentralised and formalised. On the yes side, however, is the evidence that the *nAch* of the CEO seems to be a more powerful determinant of structure than the organisation's technology or its environment. But, according to this research, this impact of the CEO's preference is probably more potent in small organisations than in large ones.

the remainder of this chapter owe a debt to the insights offered by John Child in his strategic-choice thesis.

Contingency and the challenge to rationality

The contingency perspective—which states that structure will change to reflect changes in strategy, size, technology and environment—makes a number of implicit assumptions about organisational decision making. It implies, for instance, that managers have followed a structured decision-making process in arriving at their decision. This decision-making process assumes that there is agreement between decision makers as to the nature of the problem, that a comprehensive search for alternative solutions has been made, the most appropriate solution has been arrived at, and the solution has been able to be implemented in its entirety. We will argue from the power-control viewpoint that this process does not accurately describe how real decision makers in organisations make choices. The decision-making process we have described assumes that decision makers are rational with a commitment to **rationality**, and that in organisations it is possible to be rational. It assumes that rational decisions are consistent with the organisation's goals and directed towards maximising them. The assumption of rationality includes perfect knowledge of the problem, adequate information to assess possible alternative solutions, and no emotional attachment to any particular outcome on the part of the decision maker.

Rational decision making also assumes that decisions regarding structure are made by those responsible for decision making—that is, the **dominant coalition**. The dominant coalition refers to that group within an organisation with the power to influence the outcomes of decisions. In the contingency perspective, the dominant coalition and top management are assumed to be one and the same. This is important because it ignores the possibility that others in the organisation, besides management, might have the power to influence structural decisions.

A final assumption of the contingency perspective is that decision makers share a common purpose and that that purpose is to serve the interests of the organisation. Self-interests are ignored by decision makers for the good of the organisation. Should a decision maker find difficulty in choosing between alternatives that would benefit the organisation and those that would benefit him or her personally, the contingency perspective implies that the interests of the organisation would predominate.

If these four assumptions were accurate, we should expect contingency variables—such as technology and environment—to fully explain why structures are designed the way they are in the real world. But, power-control advocates argue, these assumptions *are not* accurate! Decision makers don't follow the traditional decision-making process. Their decisions are neither consistent nor value-maximising; hence, they don't meet the definition of rational. The actual structural decision in an organisation will be made by those members with power—that is, the dominant coalition. This group may or may not be synonymous with those who hold formal authority in top management positions. Lastly, the dominant coalition is typically made up of individuals with divergent interests, thus making goal consensus difficult, if not impossible.

Power-control supporters offer another set of assumptions about organisational decision making. They propose a process characterised by non-rationality, divergent interests, dominant coalitions and power. These challenge the idea of the rational

rationality the belief that decisions are goal-directed and consistent

dominant coalition the group within an organisation with the power to influence the outcomes of decisions

organisation and require some elaboration. The following attempts to provide evidence and explanation in support of the power-control position.

Non-rationality

Decision makers are human beings and thus have human frailties. They are driven by a multitude of motivations, some of which may be identified and some of which reside deep within their psyche. They seldom have a consistent ordering of goals; they do not always pursue systematically the goals they hold; they make choices with incomplete information; and they seldom conduct an exhaustive search for alternatives.[10] Even defining the nature of many problems facing an organisation is often difficult. Realistically, given the complexity of large organisations, decision makers reduce options to few decision criteria. Their choice of criteria and the selection of alternatives will reflect their self-interests, the culture of the organisation and outcomes of previous decisions. The result, as we described earlier in our discussion of strategic choice, is that a decision maker's selection of the best solution is not an optimum choice but one that meets the minimum decision criteria. Actual decision making, therefore, is not a comprehensive process of searching for an optimum solution. It is an incremental process, whereby the decision maker assesses choices until one is found that meets the minimum acceptable level. Once this level has been attained, the choice is made and the search stops. **Non-rationality** is a process of decision making that does not follow the principles of logical deduction.

Non-rationality a process of decision making that does not follow the principles of logical deduction

But the argument that organisations aren't rational carries with it the assumption that organisations cannot be managed. We know that organisations do respond to the actions of management. They achieve goals, select strategies, react to changes in the environment, downsize, innovate and introduce new production techniques. They may not always do these successfully or in accordance with the way top management and other interest groups would like. But organisations are the result of human intervention, not the chance outcome of random and unaccountable events. Non-rationality derives from the observation that organisations are only to a small extent like machines, and that, no matter how hard we try to bring discipline to decision making, decisions are always subject to a wide range of influences and unexpected outcomes. And most decisions look good when they are made; it is subsequent events that prove them to be appropriate or not.

In order to clarify this section, we should draw the distinction between non-rational and irrational decision making. Non-rationality means that appropriate decisions appear to be made, but they are made by a process other than deductive reasoning and appropriate search processes. By contrast, irrationality means that the decision appears to be inappropriate in the circumstances. Remember, an organisation's structure is only one of the mechanisms that may be used to move an organisation towards its goals. Other management processes, such as motivation and leadership techniques, reward mechanisms and management style, complement the structure of the organisation. This leaves managers scope to implement the same structure in different ways.

Divergent interests

The realities of organisational decision making tell us that the interests of the decision maker and the interests of the organisation are rarely one and the same. Rational decision making, however, assumes them to be. Figure 9.1 depicts reality.

FIGURE 9.1 Interplay of the decision maker's and the organisation's interests

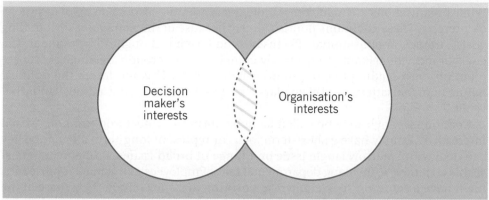

Organisations are composed of groups with divergent interests. Although it would be highly desirable, in terms of organisational effectiveness, for the two circles (representing the individual's interests and the organisation's interests) to align perfectly, that is far more likely to be the exception rather than the rule. Given that the two circles do not align, what can we predict, and what does it mean to decision making?

It is unreasonable for us to expect that decision makers will not act in their self-interest. As a result, their decision choices will reflect the criteria and preferences compatible with the shaded area. That is, for much of the time, the decision maker is likely to let his or her own interests influence decision making. Moreover, if confronted with a set of choices, all of which meet the 'good enough' criterion, the decision maker would obviously choose the one most beneficial personally. In Figure 9.1, the overlapping area of the circles represents the region in which the decision maker acts consistently with organisational-effectiveness criteria. In this area, for instance, we can expect managers to be concerned with economic efficiencies and to prefer an organisation structure that would facilitate them. This area also represents the discretionary range in which—given the constraints of size, technology and environment—managers still have room for making choices that can be self-serving. The shaded area outside the overlap represents situations in which the decision maker has chosen criteria or preferences that are not compatible with the best interests of the organisation but are beneficial to the decision maker.

For instance, phasing out one's department may be in the best interest of the organisation, but rarely is it in the best interest of the decision maker. As a result, we rarely expect managers to make that selection. But *expanding* one's department usually means greater responsibilities, status and remuneration. Those are rewards that managers value. As a result, we can expect managers to try to increase the size and domain of their units regardless of the effect on the organisation. It should be noted that the reward system can be designed to encourage managers to phase out their departments, but it rarely is. And if a manager wants to expand his or her department, the arguments will be couched in non-political terms. Overt politics are frowned on in organisations, so self-serving decisions will always be packaged in terms of improving organisational effectiveness.

Dominant coalitions

While organisations are made up of individuals, they are also made up of coalitions of interests. These coalitions flourish largely because of the ambiguity surrounding goals, strategy, organisational effectiveness and what is thought to be rational. The goals of individuals and groups rarely coincide, and decision-making criteria are often obscure, leading to compromises being made. This reinforces the political nature of organisations, and even plays a part in deciding what is rational and what is not.[11]

Coalitions, which may be called factions, form to protect and promote vested interests. They may have a short-term focus or represent long-term alliances. They can deal with a narrow single issue or a range of broad issues. Probably the most visible coalitions form along departmental lines. Employees in the marketing department have a common special interest, ensuring that they obtain their share of the organisation's resources and rewards. They also have a common interest in defining the organisation's problems in marketing terms. But they are not alone. Members of accounting, finance, purchasing and every other department will have their coalitions. Coalitions, of course, are not limited to horizontally differentiated units. Divisional and plant managers will have their coalitions, as will different levels of middle managers and even the top management cadre. And we should also not forget that coalitions may form around personalities, relationships and shared interests as well as ethnic and gender groups. Coalitions are able to exert influence through collective decision making, such as by membership of committees and boards, and through problem definition and manipulation of data gathering and information flows.

Although coalitions may form around any number of issues, the dominant coalition is the one that has the power to affect structure. In a small company, the dominant coalition and the owners are typically one and the same. In large organisations, top management usually dominates—but not always; politics is a constantly shifting arena based on opportunism and circumstance. Any coalition that can control the resources on which the organisation depends can become dominant, and of course uncertainty means that what is uncertain is constantly changing.[12] A group with critical information, expertise or any other resource that is essential to the organisation's operation can acquire the power to influence the outcome of structural decisions and thus become the dominant coalition. A fuller explanation of the sources of such power appears later in this chapter.

Power

The existence of divergent interests and dominant coalitions leads naturally to the discussion of the role of power in organisations. Simply put, because there is rarely agreement among organisational members on preferred outcomes, coalitions are in a power struggle. The power of the various coalitions determines the final outcome of the decision process. Note that this power struggle comes about because of differences concerning preferences or the definition of what constitutes a problem.[13] Without these differences, there would be no room for judgement, negotiation and the eventual politicking that occurs.

As power and authority are often confused by students of management and organisation theory, let us clarify the two terms. As you will see, the differences between them are important because they differentiate the power-control perspective from that of strategic choice.

In Chapter 4, we defined authority as the right to act, or to command others to act, towards the attainment of organisational goals. Its unique characteristic, we said, was that this right had legitimacy based on the authority figure's position in the organisation. Authority goes with the job. You leave your managerial job and you give up the authority that goes with that position. When we use the term **power** we mean an individual's capacity to influence decisions. As such, authority is actually part of the larger concept of power; that is, the ability to influence based on an individual's legitimate position can affect decisions, but one does not require authority to have such influence.

power an individual's capacity to influence decisions

Figure 9.2 depicts the difference between authority and power. The two-dimensional hierarchical arrangement of boxes in Figure 9.2A indicates that there are levels in an organisation and that the rights to make decisions increase as one moves up the hierarchy. Power, on the other hand, is conceptualised best as a three-dimensional cone. The power of individuals in an organisation depends on their vertical position in the cone and their distance from the centre of the cone.

Think of the cone in Figure 9.2B as an organisation. The centre of the cone will be called the power core. The closer one is to the power core, the more influence one has to affect decisions. The existence of a power core is the only difference between A and B in Figure 9.2. The vertical hierarchy dimension in A is merely one's level on the outer edge of the cone. The top of the cone is equal to the top of the hierarchy, the middle of the cone is equal to the middle of the hierarchy, and so on. Similarly, the functional groupings in A become wedges in the cone. This is seen in Figure 9.3, which depicts the same cone in Figure 9.2B, except that it is now shown from above. Each wedge of the cone represents a functional area. Thus, if the second level of Figure 9.2A contains the marketing, production and administrative functions of the organisation, the three wedges of Figure 9.3 are the same functional departments.

The cone analogy allows us to consider the following two facts:

1   The higher one moves in an organisation (an increase in authority), the closer one automatically moves towards the power core.
2   It is not necessary to have authority to wield power, because one can move horizontally inward towards the power core without moving up.

FIGURE 9.2 Authority versus power

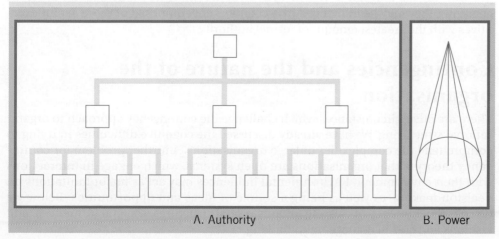

A. Authority   B. Power

FIGURE 9.3 Bird's-eye view of the organisation conceptualised as a cone

Centrally placed unions, whose members have little authority in the organisation, are often very powerful because of their ability to stop production. Secretaries to high-place managers traditionally wield a lot of power, even though their formal position gives them little authority. Alternatively, some senior managers may have considerable authority but not much power. An example of this situation may be the in-house company lawyer. The lawyer may have few staff if any, understand little about the company's core business, respond to a very narrow environmental segment, and have extensive access to the managing director. But the lawyer's capacity to influence key decisions in the organisation may be very limited.

The separation of authority and power is obviously important for understanding the power-control perspective and for differentiating it from strategic choice. It reminds us that those with formal authority may have the influence but, then again, that others in the organisation may have created strong power bases that allow them to have even greater influence over decisions. Moreover, because those with the capacity to influence decisions will select criteria and preferences that are consistent with their own self-interests, choices are likely to be highly divergent from those that would occur under strategic-choice conditions. In other words, the power-control position argues that not only will structural decisions be made against different goals, but they may be influenced by a coalition not composed of those senior executives with the greatest amount of formal authority.

Contingencies and the nature of the organisation

There are other circumstances which challenge the contingency approach to organisational structuring. We have already discussed the cognitive difficulties in trying to comprehend the complexities of large organisations. A further problem for contingency theory is that organisations are open systems, which engage in interactions with their environment. Environmental influences may act as major limitations on decision making, as well as being a source of ideas and opportunities. Below we discuss the influence of existing organisational structures, societal influences, and fashions and fads in management thinking.

Legacy systems and large size

Legacy systems are the existing rules, procedures, roles, responsibilities and ways of doing things that are accepted practice within an organisation. The word *legacy* is used to describe them because they have emerged as the product of a stream of past decisions. Organisational members become familiar with reporting relationships, ways of relating to each other, the manner in which technology is used, and how to interpret and interact with the environment. As a result, organisational structures often reflect past practices rather than current needs. They rarely reflect the future needs of the organisation. Once these practices are established and have proven successful, it takes a major management effort to change them.[14]

While legacy systems often contribute to the smooth operation of the organisation, there is a negative side. Established ways can predetermine courses of action. They can also orient managers to address problems using certain mindsets, even going so far as to define the nature of the problem. The existence of legacy systems also leads to the slowness of large organisations to react to change. Major organisational change normally takes years, and is not undertaken lightly.[15]

The combined effect of legacy systems and large size presents a challenge to the rationality assumption of contingency theory. Organisations clearly have structures, but these structures may reflect past circumstances rather than current needs or future requirements. The fact that the organisation is probably getting by satisfactorily with its existing structure again indicates that the most appropriate structure is not a point but one of a range of possibilities.

Institutional and external pressures

In Chapter 8, we discussed institutional forces in the environment and how they can influence an organisation to adopt certain structural characteristics. These forces may be legislative in origin, such as the need to have EEO officers reporting to a senior manager. But they may arise from the needs of customers or expectations of other stakeholders. For instance, the defence department often insists that its contractors adopt a matrix structure.[16] The customers of construction and civil engineering companies often require one point of contact, such as a project manager, within the organisation with sufficient executive authority to respond to issues raised. Organisations undertaking identical tasks, one a subsidiary of an overseas firm and one locally owned, may have different structural forms because of their different ownership patterns. A further example of institutional forces is the need to obtain quality endorsement (e.g. ISO9000) with its resultant influence on organisational practices. The challenge that these external forces present to contingency theory is that the resulting structure may not reflect the imperatives we have discussed in previous chapters.

Designing around people

The attitudes and capabilities of existing management and staff influence design outcomes. In a purely rational world, we might ignore who is at present in what position, and what their capabilities, strengths and weaknesses are. But in most cases these factors are taken into account when designing organisations. For instance, a chief finance officer with skills and interest in IT may find him- or herself with responsibility for the IT function. Another equally capable finance manager with little interest in IT would rarely be given responsibility for it. The subtle interplay of personality, skills, interests, experience, age, coalition membership and power and politics lead to tasks being allocated that may not be optimal but which suit the skill set of management staff. Some companies, particularly in the public sector, attempt to overcome this problem by having what is called a 'spill and fill'. All positions are declared vacant. An organisation design is proposed with job descriptions for each area of responsibility. Those who feel that they have the skills and experience appropriate to a position may then apply for it.

Management fashions and fads

We could have included fashions and fads when we discussed institutional theory, as it is an environmental influence, but its importance justifies separate consideration. Hardly a year goes by without a new fashion or idea being promoted as the answer to management's problems. Examples are re-engineering, strategies for the Internet, Japanese management, lessons from Sun Tzu's 'Art of War', one-minute managing, change imperatives such as 'Who moved my cheese?' and so on. The reminiscences of prominent managers, such as those of Jack Welch, are widely read and often influence decision making.[17] Many of these books are persuasively written, often by consultants seeking to promote their own businesses. Whatever their utility, and we do not condemn these approaches as having no use, they do create pressure to conform to their prescriptives. For instance, re-engineering was tried by a large number of companies, with mixed success.[18] Many managers no doubt tried to re-engineer their organisations because they saw others attempting it and were reluctant to be seen to be ignoring its proposed benefits. Jack Welch's approach to running General Electric, a large conglomerate based in the United States, has had a major influence on approaches to strategy. In the 1970s the matrix structure was widely adopted, generally inappropriately, in the expectation that organisations structured along matrix lines would become responsive and proactive.[19]

The above examples highlight the influence of social trends on management. If managers felt confident that their organisations were effective, perhaps they would be more resistant to fashions in management thought. But, as we have noted, organisations are difficult to understand and manage. And as organisations are composed of people and operate within a social environment, it is not surprising that social pressures exert an influence on managers.

The roads to power

How does an individual or group gain power? The answer to this question is to keep in mind that power derives from the structure of the organisation.[20] It is created by division of labour and departmentalisation. Horizontal differentiation inevitably creates some tasks that are more important than others. Those individuals or departments performing the more critical tasks, or who are able to *convince* others within the organisation that their tasks are more critical, will have a natural advantage in the power-acquisition game. The authority given to those in senior management positions is also structural in origin. The evidence indicates that there are three roads to the acquisition of power: hierarchical authority, control of resources, and network centrality.[21] Let's take a look at each of them.

Hierarchical authority

In spite of our detailed effort earlier in the chapter to differentiate authority and power, we cannot ignore the obvious: formal authority is a source of power. It is not the *only* source of power, but individuals in managerial positions, especially those occupying senior management slots, can influence through formal decree. Subordinates accept this influence as a right inherent in the manager's position.

The manager's job comes with certain rights to reward and punish. Additionally, it comes with prerogatives to make certain decisions. But, as we'll see, many managers find their formal influence over people or decisions extremely limited because of their dependence on others within the organisation. Their power is also limited by restrictions placed on them by more senior managers. The power of a supervisor is obviously less than that of a general manager. Supervisors have limits on the amount of expenditure they can approve, on hiring and firing, and on the number of staff they supervise.

Control of resources and ability to reduce uncertainty

If you have something that others want, you can have power over them. In an organisational setting, you can also have a major influence on decisions. But the mere control of a resource is no guarantee that it will enhance your power. The resource must be both scarce and important to the organisation.[22] If a resource is scarce and important, its supply creates uncertainty for the organisation. As we have seen, organisations don't like uncertainty, so those who can reduce uncertainty by ensuring supply of a scarce resource gather power to themselves or their group.

Unless a resource is scarce within the organisation, it is unlikely to be a source of power. In most organisations, cleaners have little power. This is not because cleaners are not necessary; we would soon notice their absence. It is simply because cleaners are easy to replace. Alternatively, airline pilots have typically been able to exact significant benefits from airlines because their skills are scarce and difficult to replace. So the mere possession of a resource means nothing if that resource is not scarce.

If resource scarcity increases the power of the resource holder, then the proximity of relevant substitutes for the resource should also be considered. That is, a resource for which there is no close substitute has greater scarcity than one that has high substitutability. Skills provide an example. Organisations rely on individuals with a wide range of special skills to perform effectively. Those who possess a skill that the organisation needs, but that no-one else in the organisation has, will obviously be in a more influential position than one whose skills are duplicated by hundreds of other employees. Design engineers at aerospace firms provide a powerful coalition because it would be virtually impossible to replace their skills in the short term. Alternatively, those sewing covers for the aircraft seats would be relatively easy to replace and consequently have less power within the organisation. Skills scarcity explains why presenters such as John Laws and Ray Martin can command such high salaries. Their abilities can raise ratings to such high levels that large advertising fees can be charged. Media owners see radio and television personalities as scarce and critical resources responsible for generating high earnings for which there is no close substitute.

Similarly, union power relative to management's is largely a function of its members' ability to restrict management's options. The most powerful unions are those which control a choke point in a supply chain, such as waterside workers and

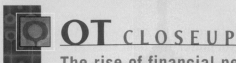

OT CLOSEUP

The rise of financial people to the top in large corporations

An understanding of power can help to explain the rise of financial personnel in recent years to positions of power in large corporations.[23]

Studies investigating the background of top managers of large companies have found that manufacturing personnel and entrepreneurs rose to the top in the early part of this century. From the late 1930s to the late 50s, sales and marketing personnel came to dominate large firms. The period 1960 to the mid-80s saw finance personnel increasingly rise to power.

This shift in the background of corporate managers largely reflects changes in the strategy and structure of organisations. These changes shifted the power of subunits within corporations, which resulted in new leaders coming out of those subunits who could best resolve the problems and uncertainties faced by the organisation.

The early years of the last century saw corporations run by entrepreneurial types and those promoted out of manufacturing. This reflected the product emphasis and single-product strategies of those firms. But over the next 30 years, large corporations began to develop multi-product strategies and adopt multi-divisional structures. This put a premium on sales and marketing expertise and increased promotion opportunities at the top for individuals with these kinds of backgrounds.

Over time, the business units of the multi-product firms became more independent. This, together with unrelated businesses, meant that top management required less knowledge of the goods and services sold. One of the few ways to evaluate the performance of the conglomerates was to use financial information. Hence financial personnel adept at interpreting this information rose to prominence in top corporate management. Similar skills were needed during the takeover boom in the 1980s, when decisions regarding the worth of companies were largely made on financial grounds.

The trends noted above illustrate an important point—that the person occupying the top job is normally the one who has the capacity to solve the biggest problem that the firm faces. If a firm is vulnerable to takeover, a takeover defence specialist is likely to be managing director; if the biggest problem is a production problem, a production person will be in the top job. Where return on assets is low, those who can identify where the costs are lying and institute an appropriate change program generally receive the nod for the executive suite. The research referred to above reflects the fact that corporate problems tend to run in waves and afflict all organisations in a similar manner.

those working in warehouses. Just a few workers can halt the delivery of petrol or idle motor vehicle production lines.

As environments become more competitive, and opportunities and threats more pronounced, those in the organisation who have the knowledge to manage the resultant uncertainty gain power for themselves. Staff such as those who trade in futures and hedge markets, control complex supply chains, or understand complicated marketing arrangements and customer needs, draw power to themselves. Knowledge in this case is a scarce resource because of its ability to reduce uncertainty. It consequently becomes a road to power.

The use of knowledge as a source of power provides insight into employee actions that are often seen as irrational. When placed in the context of controlling scarce and important resources, behaviour such as refusing to train people in your job or even to show others exactly what you do, creating specialised language and terminology that inhibit others' understanding of what you are doing, operating in secrecy so that the tasks you perform will appear more complex and difficult than they really are, or restricting entry to an occupation by a union or professional group, suddenly appear to be very rational actions.

Network centrality

Being in the right place in the organisation can be a source of power.[24] Those individuals or groups with **network centrality** gain power because their position allows them to integrate other functions or to reduce organisation dependencies. It also provides them with privileged access to information. Of course, being in 'the right place' is not a random phenomenon. Who has centrality depends on the organisation's strategy and the problems it faces at any given moment.[25] It is also very much a structural phenomenon. Functional departments within an organisation take on different degrees of importance relative to the strategy the organisation is pursuing and the critical problems that arise. This means that an organisation's primary strategic orientation is an influence on who has power. In an organisation that is market-oriented, such as Unilever, marketing personnel will be more powerful than, say, accountants or research and development people. Alternatively, we would expect accounting to be more powerful in organisations that rely heavily on financial data, such as banks and brokerage firms, or when the organisation faces critical financial or control problems.[26] When an organisation is financially healthy, the accounting function is generally not critical to the immediate needs of the organisation. But when the organisation is in a financial crisis, finding cash and getting financial data become the major concern of the entire organisation. Not surprisingly, when the financial crisis diminishes, accounting will become less critical and, thus, less powerful. The boom in the financial sector led to a large number of people being employed in recruitment, both directly by banks and in various consultancies. While there was a shortage of labour in this industry, those people who could identify and hire suitable employees could name their own terms. However, with the collapse of the boom and the contraction of the financial sector, these people very soon lost their influence.

The power of different functions can be seen in a study comparing hospitals with insurance firms.[27] The hospitals' strategies emphasised efficiency and cost control, while the insurance firms sought product and market innovation. Consistent with the role of centrality, the researcher found that the accounting, process-improvement and operations functions had the most power in the hospitals and the marketing and product-development functions had the most power in the insurance companies.

A study of a production plant in France gives us additional insight into how being in the right place in an organisation can be a source of power.[28] The researcher observed that the maintenance engineers in this plant exerted a great deal of influence although they were not particularly high in the organisational hierarchy. The researcher concluded that the breakdown of machinery was the only remaining uncertainty confronting the organisation. The maintenance engineers were the only personnel who could cope with machine stoppage, and they had taken the pains to reinforce their power through control of information. They avoided written procedures for dealing with breakdowns, they purposely disregarded all blueprints and

network centrality
the degree to which a position in an organisation allows an individual to integrate other functions or reduce organisation dependencies

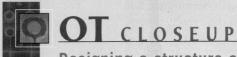

OT CLOSEUP
Designing a structure around a person

One example of how a person can influence the way in which a structure can evolve is that of General Electric (GE) Capital in Australia. GE has been in Australia for over 100 years, selling industrial products such as generators and lighting systems. GE Capital, which was initially established to finance the purchase of heavy industrial equipment, started to expand rapidly into consumer finance only five years ago. It is now Australia's largest provider of consumer finance and commercial lending.

The chief executive of GE Australia is Steve Bertamini, a German-born, Texas-educated manager.

Bertamini spent some time in Hong Kong with GE before moving to Melbourne five years ago. When he took charge of GE Australia, he was also appointed as the president of GE Capital Asia, the first time the position has been held by an Australian resident. Because GE wanted him in the job, reporting relationships were built around him.

Adapted from: Jan McCallum, 'GE Values Australia's Testbed for Growth', *Business Review Weekly*, 22 November 2001, p. 41.

maintenance directions and so on. Not even the supervisors in the plant had adequate knowledge to check on these engineers.

Structure can also confer network centrality by centralising flows of information through certain positions. Those people who fill these positions may be quite powerful in the organisation. For instance, consumer products companies, such as Nestlé and Procter and Gamble, have brand managers as part of their structure. Those holding this position collect and coordinate all information concerning a brand, including its position in the market, product improvements, changes in distribution channels, promotion and advertising. Although brand managers are not particularly high in the organisation structure, their power is considerable, as they collect and process the only coherent body of information about a firm's products. In other industries, project managers and coordinators of various types derive their power from being in a similar position in relation to the collection and dissemination of information.

Synthesising the power-control view

The previous discussions on non-rational decision making, dominant coalitions, divergent interests and power allow us now to synthesise the power-control view of how organisation structures are derived.

We can begin our synthesis by restating the power-control thesis: an organisation's structure, at any given time, is to a large extent the result of those in power selecting a structure that will maintain and enhance their control. As we will see, the power-control perspective does not ignore the impact of size, technology or other contingency variables. Rather, it treats them as constraints that must be met in what is otherwise a political process.

OT CLOSEUP
Ethics and the use of power

Are members of the dominant coalition acting unethically when they seek to use their power to enhance their control? In today's business environment—where unethical behaviour has become an increasing concern of executives, the media, academics, students of management and the general public—this question at least needs to be addressed.

Ethics refers to rules or principles that define right and wrong conduct.[29] This, then, begs the question: is the use of power, per se, wrong? Many contemporary behavioural scientists would argue that it isn't. They note that power is a natural part of human interactions—'we influence, or try to influence, other people every day under all sorts of conditions'—that carries over into organisational life.[30]

Power really has two faces—one negative and the other positive.[31] The negative side is associated with abuse—when, for example, power holders exploit others or use their power merely to accumulate status symbols. The positive side is characterised by a concern for group goals, helping the group to formulate its goals and providing group members with the support they need to achieve these goals.

If the dominant coalition chooses a structure that 'satisfices' rather than maximises goal attainment, has it acted unethically? Is 'satisficing' an abuse of the system? Does 'satisficing' exploit employees, shareholders or other relevant constituencies? Is any self-serving action by the dominant coalition that suboptimises the organisation's effectiveness an unethical act or has the dominant coalition acted ethically if the organisation's performance merely meets the 'good enough' standard? Undoubtedly, people will disagree on answers to these questions. But it is answers to questions such as these that will determine whether the power-control perspective describes unethical practice.

Structural decisions as a political process

In previous sections we have seen how structure can influence the way in which power can be acquired and exercised in the organisation. However, structural decisions are often the result of political activity. Organisational politics involves activities to acquire, develop and use power and other resources to obtain a preferred outcome when there is uncertainty or disagreement about choices.[32] When we discussed the role of dominant coalitions, we saw how groups of people were more effective at achieving goals than those who act alone. This gives us some indication of the role of politics in organisations.

The challenge to the concept of organisational rationality also indicates how areas of political activity can arise. In the rational organisation goals are clear, processes and customers are well understood, and choices are made in a logical, dispassionate way. However, organisations rarely conform to the rational model. Environments and technologies change, leading to different schools of thought as to how to respond. In addition, changes in senior management can lead to different approaches to defining what the problems facing the organisation are and how to solve them. Selecting between the different choices available to respond to problems gives rise to political activity in organisations. But organisations are not entirely political. The need to satisfy their various critical constituencies restricts the range of responses open to them and limits the possible options around which political activity can be carried on. Rationality therefore often constrains organisational choice.

Not everyone in the organisation is involved in political activity at any one time, although it is likely that everyone has engaged in it at some time in their career. Surveys show that the higher a person is in management, the more likely he/she is to use politics as part of their job.[33] This is not surprising, as the need to achieve consensus in uncertain situations is most common at this level. Those lower in the organisation are likely to face a more constrained set of options, which are more predictable and so can be guided by established procedures and practices.

The way we structure organisations can give rise to political activity. We can identify four areas in which structure creates political arenas in organisations:

1 *Resource allocation.* Typically resources are allocated to departments or divisions as part of a budget. The better funded the department, the more status it has and the more likely it is to achieve its goals. In addition, higher salaries can be paid, employees hired, and more influence can be exerted by the department and its head. It is therefore not surprising that resources such as budget allocations and funds for capital expenditure are subject to considerable political lobbying.

2 *Position in the hierarchy.* Status, and therefore influence, is closely attached to the position of a department head in the organisation's hierarchy. For instance, if the finance department head answers to the accounting manager, this signals that finance has a lower status in the organisation than accounting. However, if both the finance and accounting functions answer to the managing director, this signals that they are of equal status. Obviously, each department will want to report to the most senior person in the organisation.

3 *Interdepartmental coordination.* Relationships between departments are part of organisational life.[34] At the lower level, these relationships are often routine and characterised by established rules and practices. Further up the management hierarchy, relationships between departments are less well defined: conflict can easily arise, as there is a high level of uncertainty and many decisions are not routine. Precedents need to be set and areas of departmental responsibility and territory defined. Political activity is often involved in seeking an acceptable outcome.

4 *Structural change.* All structural change leads to managers and departments redefining their authority and power relationships. This inevitably creates those who gain and those who lose. In any structural change, intense political activity results as managers and departments seek to maximise their position after the change. This indicates why successful change programs are often difficult to implement.

We can also identify the ways in which power is likely to be exercised in a political arena. Often rational processes to solve problems cannot be used because of uncertainty or irreconcilable goals. Solutions depend on the willingness and ability of the participants to use power to solve the problem. The following describe the way that political tactics are used:

● *Building coalitions.* We have referred to the power of coalitions a number of times throughout this chapter. Coalition building relies on developing mutually strong relationships with other people.[35] These may be based on liking, trust and respect. But they may also be based on shared interests and desired outcomes. As organisational life involves people working with each other over a long period of time, it stands to reason that reliability and respect for others, rather than exploitation, are part of coalition building. But coalitions based on shared interests may be less stable; these are more likely to shift according to opportunity and changing circumstances

- *Defining the nature of the problem.* All decisions are aimed at solving problems.[36] But in many cases defining the problem is not easy. If a person, or coalition, can control the way the problem is defined, often they are well on the way to determining the likely solution For instance, David Jones, the upmarket retailer, experienced flat sales in the mid-1990s. The actual cause was difficult to define: was it economic downturn, poor mix of merchandise, prices too high, or the fact that department stores were no longer the preferred place to shop? Each of these problems required a different response, with different political implications for those involved. Defining the problem therefore became the main arena for political activity.

- *Enhancing legitimacy and expertise.* A manager's or department's power is greatly enhanced when they do their job well and when they have a good reputation for task knowledge and achievement.[37] Managers should seek to ensure that the reputation of their own department is enhanced, as this is their main base of power.

- *Make preferences explicit, but keep power implicit.* Politics requires that preferences be known to others.[38] Playing political games without revealing desired outcomes is an aimless, destructive exercise. The best political players are those who have the courage to reveal their preferred outcome, then try to convince others that their point of view is correct. But overt displays of power are counterproductive. Power is exercised most effectively when it is implied, rather than overtly exercised. This explains why many senior managers surround themselves with the trappings of power, such as well-furnished offices in the most desirable part of the building and the services of personal secretaries. It also explains why managers often become preoccupied with such trivialities as car-parking spaces and who travels what class when flying.

- *Expanding networks of influence.* Politics involves trying to boost the number of people who support you and minimise the number against you.[39] It stands to reason that increasing your support can involve two measures: bringing additional managers on side, and minimising the influence of those who may act against you. Alliances can be built or expanded by such means as hiring, transfers and promotions, as well as relationship building. One of the most common ways to minimise opposition is through the process of co-optation. Co-optation is bringing dissenters and opponents into the network of influence. Most committees have elements of co-optation in their make-up. Those opposed to the committee, for instance, are often asked to join, thus blunting their criticism. IT departments often have advisory committees made up of user departments. This allows the user departments to bring their complaints and comments direct to the IT department, rather than criticise the IT department behind its back. It also blunts any criticism that may be made of the IT department, as it is implied that problems should have been raised in the appropriate committee.

Contingency factors as constraints

It is important to keep in mind that power control acknowledges a role for technology, environment and the other contingency variables. But that role is not as imperatives: that is, they don't *determine* structure. Like strategic choice, the power-control view treats the contingency variables as constraints, or limitations, on what structure managers prefer.

Strategy, size, technology and environment act as general constraints on structure to narrow decision-making choices. They set the general parameters for organisational effectiveness. But within the parameters there is still a lot of room left for manoeuvring, especially as organisational effectiveness is a problematic state and the structural choice has only to 'satisfice'.

The power-control model

Figure 9.4 depicts how power-control advocates perceive the creation of an organisation's structure. The choice of a structure is constrained by the organisation's strategy, size, technology, environment and the required minimal level of effectiveness. These forces combine to establish the set of structural alternatives from which the decision will be made. The decisions are generally made by the dominant coalition. How will this dominant coalition make the decision? By imposing its self-interests on the criteria and preferences in the decision. The result is the organisation's emergent structure.

FIGURE 9.4 The power-control model

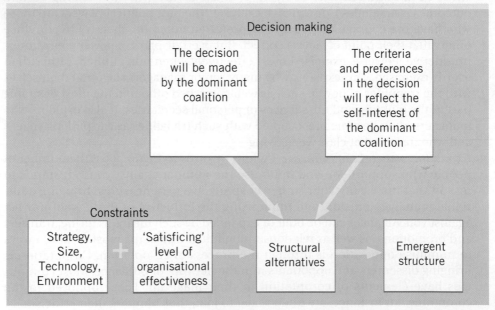

Implications based on the power-control view

It is now time to translate our insight from the power-control perspective into implications for the structuring of organisations. We begin by considering a power-control interpretation of the role of technology and environment in structure.

Technology and environment

'The picture of the organisation as an adaptive, responsive entity, proximately affected by the demands of technology or environment, is probably as misleading as the parallel portrait of the competitive organisation in classical economic theory.'[40] Power-control advocates argue that an organisation's structure, at any given time, will be one that allows those in power to maintain the control they have. In terms of technology and environment, therefore, the dominant coalition can be expected to seek routine technologies and attempt to manage their environment to reduce uncertainty. Let us expand briefly on each of these points.

Both the environmental domain and the technology an organisation adopts are chosen. The tendency of the dominant management group will be to adopt routine technologies. Routine technologies are associated with bureaucratic practices and centralised decision making, both of which concentrate power at the top of the organisation. Hence, routine technologies will be most prevalent because they enhance control.

Uncertainty is a problem for management; the greater the uncertainty, the more managers must rely on others for solutions, thus diluting their power. But all organisations manage their environment to reduce uncertainty. They enter legally binding contracts with others, form strategic alliances, and move up and down the supply chain. The view that structure is a response to the environment implies that changes in structure occur to improve organisational effectiveness. But when the organisation responds to external demands, it usually does so because it can no longer control its external environment: 'The organisation that appears to be innovative or responsive is so, we would argue, because such a course of action enhances the influence and resource position of those in control of the organisation's activities.'[41]

When is the environment likely to be an overpowering constraint in the structural decision? When opportunities in the organisation's environment are scarce or limited,[42] and when there is a minimal degree of organisational slack.[43]

Scarcity in the environment would include situations where there was intense competition or limited opportunities for growth. An abundant environment, on the other hand, would describe an industry that could adequately support all current competitors and where there were considerable opportunities for growth. In an abundant environment, there would be little incentive for management to change organisational practices. In the scarce environment, the organisation's options or strategic choices would be fewer, and less room would be available for the dominant coalition to manoeuvre. As a result, the environment would impose the need for the most appropriate structure on the organisation.

Organisational slack is that cushion of actual or potential resources that enables an organisation to adjust to environmental change.[44] These are the resources in excess of those required for the organisation to achieve a minimal level of effectiveness. They include things like extra cash, a large credit line, underutilised plant capacity, inventories of goods and materials, untapped management potential, discretionary funds for travel and entertainment, or earnings that far exceed the industry average. The less slack an organisation has, the tighter the parameters are within which the structural decision must be made and the more likely it is that structure will be dictated by external forces.

Organisational slack
a cushion of excess resources that enables an organisation to adjust to environmental change

Stability and mechanistic structures

These comments lead us to additional extensions. Because organisations seek routinisation and management of uncertainty, power-control advocates propose that structural change will probably be minimal. Those in power can be expected to try to maintain their control. If the current structure is effective in maintaining control, why should they want to change? They will not, except when forced. The argument made by power-control advocates is that significant changes represent, in effect, mini-revolutions.[45] They are likely to occur only as a result of a political struggle in which new power relationships evolve. This kind of political struggle is not common. When it does, it usually follows a major shake-up in top management or indicates that the organisation is facing obvious and direct threats to its survival. When changes in structure occur, they are more typically incremental.[46] Incrementalism maintains stability by keeping changes small and never deviating much from the previous structural arrangement. A look at the organisation structures of McDonald's, the RAAF or the University of Sydney shows each substantially unchanged over a 30-year period, and any change has been evolutionary rather than revolutionary.

The *power-control view of structure* predicts that not only will structural arrangements be relatively stable over time but mechanistic structures will be the most numerous. This is consistent with the conclusions drawn in Chapter 8. If stability, routinisation and centralised control are sought, it seems logical that mechanistic structures will rule. And observations of structures, as we noted in Chapter 8, concur with this prediction. Figure 9.5 expands the 'structural alternatives' box presented in Figure 9.4. Structural options range along an organic–mechanistic continuum. Those in power will choose structures that maintain their control. So given that organisational effectiveness is a range rather than a point, there will be some decision discretion available to the dominant coalition. Within its discretionary range, it will select the most mechanistic alternative (point A in Figure 9.5). This anti-contingency position is in direct opposition to the theme 'There is no one best way to organise'. The contingency advocates' theme of 'no one best way' uses performance as the standard. The mechanistic structure *is* the 'one best way' if *best* refers to 'maintenance of control' rather than performance.

Interestingly, there is even evidence that in dynamic environments, where there is rapid change, mechanistic structures emerge.[47] Contrary to the contingency view that dynamic environments would be matched with organic structures, decision makers appear to prefer control to increased effectiveness. Of course, this will be true only when a certain minimal level of organisational effectiveness has already been achieved.

FIGURE 9.5 Decision discretion in the power-control model

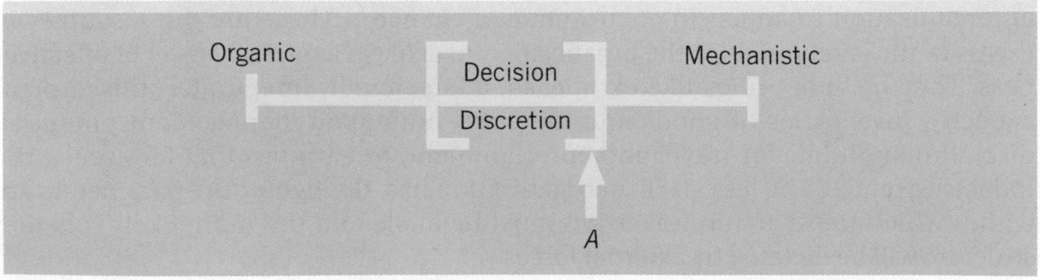

Complexity

Increased differentiation—horizontally, vertically or spatially—leads to difficulties in coordination and control. Management would prefer, therefore, all other things being equal, to have low complexity. But of course all other things are not equal. Size, technology and environmental factors lead to highly complex organisations, and so compromise is required. The 'imperatives' set the parameters. Management can then be expected to choose the lowest degree of complexity (to maximise control) consistent with the 'satisficing' criterion for organisational effectiveness.

It has been noted that information technology can permit the development of more elaborate and complex structures without necessarily forsaking management's control.[48] Sophisticated information systems using computer technology allow senior executives to receive continual communications. Management can monitor a large range of activities many levels down the hierarchy or thousands of kilometres away and still maintain close control over those activities. The fact that an executive in Brisbane can punch eight keys on the computer terminal at her desk and get an immediate readout on the current status of an inventory item in a company warehouse in Auckland means that this executive can monitor inventories more closely than managers in Auckland could 20 years ago.

Formalisation

Those in power will influence the degree of rules and regulations under which employees work. Because control is a desired end for those in power, organisations will have a high degree of formalisation.

If technology were non-routine or if environmental uncertainty could not be managed, we would expect that high formalisation, although desired by those in control, could not be implemented without disastrous effects on organisational performance. However, as we have concluded, management will make extensive efforts to routinise tasks and manage uncertainty. As technology and environments are chosen by those in power, we can expect them to select ones that are compatible with high levels of formalisation and maintenance of control. In those cases where factors require low formalisation—because of an extremely turbulent environment that cannot be managed or highly professionalised personnel—those in power can be expected to rely on sophisticated information technology as a control device that can be substituted for rules and regulations. They can also be expected to promote a strong culture as a form of control. In addition, we are more likely to see increased emphasis on teamwork as well as the cultivation of personal relationships, both non-written forms of formalisation.

Centralisation

From earlier discussions on centralisation, we know that it is preferred when mistakes are very costly, when temporary external threats exist or when it is important that decisions reflect an understanding of the strategic situation of the organisation. To these we can add: when those in control want to make the decisions. In fact, power-control advocates claim that decentralisation will occur infrequently. Even when it does, it may be pseudo-decentralisation. That is, top management will create the appearance of delegating decisions downwards but will use information technology for feedback. This feedback allows those in control to monitor lower-level decisions closely and to intercede and change at any time the decisions they do not like:[49]

> If persons are allowed discretion, but are permitted the opportunity to make decisions because their performance can be rapidly and accurately assessed, it seems that there has been no real sharing of control, influence, or power in the

organisation. It is conceivable, then, that the introduction of information technology can make possible the appearance of decentralisation while maintaining effective centralised control over organisational operations.

It can also be argued that those in power maintain control in decentralised situations by defining the parameters of decisions. For example, university lecturers perceive themselves as operating in a heavily decentralised environment. Important decisions, such as hiring, are made by lecturers at the department level. But the decision that a vacancy exists typically lies with the university-level administrators. The vice-chancellor decides which departments will be given new positions to staff and also decides the disposition of slots that open up as a result of resignations or retirements. While it is true that department members select their colleagues, top-level university administrators maintain considerable control through their power to allocate positions among campus units and their ultimate right to veto candidates of whom they do not approve.

Summary

Not much more than 50%–60% of the variability in structure can be explained by strategy, size, technology and environment. A substantial portion of the residual variance may be explained by the power-control view of structure, which states that an organisation's structure, at any given time, is largely the result of those in power selecting a structure that will, to the maximum degree possible, maintain and enhance their control.

The other determinants of structure assume rationality. However, for rationality to prevail, an organisation must have either a single goal or agreement over the multiple goals. Neither case exists in most organisations. As a result, structural decisions are not rational. The structural decision is a power struggle between special-interest groups or coalitions, each arguing for a structural arrangement that best meets their own needs. Strategy, size, technology and environment define the minimal level of effectiveness and set the parameters within which self-serving decision choices will be made.

Power is the central theme in the power-control perspective. Structural choices will be made by those who hold power—the group we have called the dominant coalition. This is usually the senior management, but it need not be. Power can be acquired by holding hierarchical authority, by controlling resources that are scarce and important in the organisation or by having a central position in the organisation.

The argument is made that both technology and environment are chosen. Thus, those in power will select technologies and environments that will facilitate their maintenance of control. Organisations, therefore, will be characterised by routine technologies and environments in which uncertainties are relatively low. To enhance control further, those in power will seek to choose structures that are low in complexity and high in both formalisation and centralisation.

For review and discussion

1   'Strategy, size, technology and environment are irrelevant in explaining an organisation's structure.' Do you agree or disagree? Discuss.

2   Contrast strategic choice and power control.

3   What flaws can you identify in the strategic-choice argument?

4   Describe the traditional decision-making process. What assumptions does it make?

5   Who makes up an organisation's dominant coalition?

6   Contrast power with authority.

7   How is it possible for someone low in the organisation to obtain power?

8   How does control over decision premises give power to a person?

9   Some positions in an organisation are essentially powerless. Why? Are certain functions in organisations typically more powerful? Less powerful?

10 What type of functional background do you think would be held by individuals running large corporations during the 1990s? Support your answer.

11 How is the structural decision a political process?

12 Using the power-control perspective, describe how most organisations are structured.

13 'Power is derived from the division of labour that occurs as task specialisation is implemented in organisations.' Construct an argument to support this statement.

14 How would advocates of the power-control view explain the existence of an organic structure?

15 The managing director of a large corporation hires an impartial consultant to analyse the organisation's structure. After a long and careful analysis, the consultant submits a report to the corporation's board of directors that suggests several small changes but leaves the current structure substantially in place. Explain the managing director's decision to use a consultant and the consultant's conclusions, from a power-control perspective.

CASE FOR CLASS DISCUSSION
Where to place MIS?

Where to place management information services, often abbreviated to MIS but more prosaically termed computing services, has always been a problem. And where there is problem, issues of power and politics are not far below the surface. In one medium-sized company, MIS was set up as a stand-alone department answering to the managing director. It allocated its services according to its own cost–benefit analysis on where the potential payoffs lay. (The problem with this approach is that, although it would appear to allocate resources fairly, it is not an exact science: there are always subjectivities involved.) As controlling costs became an increasing focus of the company, power started to swing towards the finance manager. Departments such as production

and human resources, as expenditure departments, found themselves constantly on the back foot, having to defend everything they did and constantly having to rework budgets. The finance manager used his new-found power to persuade the managing director to transfer full control of the MIS department to finance. Six months later the finance department had the best computer system in town and used it to monitor everything else that was going on in the company. Investment in MIS for the rest of the company started to lag behind.

The other department heads started meeting around water coolers and lingering behind after meetings had formally closed. They were discussing in confidence what could be done about the finance department. Finally they decided to 'roll' the finance manager at the six-monthly management committee meeting. They prepared their argument well, and against a well-prepared and united opposition neither the finance manager nor the managing director could provide much resistance. Finance never got any support from MIS, as the MIS manager would far rather answer to the managing director than to the finance manager.

At the conclusion of the meeting, MIS was an independent department again. At that meeting the finance manager ruminated on how he was rolled in what would have been in less health conscious times, smoke-filled rooms behind closed doors.

QUESTIONS

1 Why are issues of power and politics usually conducted in confidential tones and places?

2 Identify the sources of power in the case and relate them to those discussed in the text.

3 The managing director took the advice of the majority of the management committee. Why was the managing director likely to do this rather than exercise his/her own judgement?

4 What makes issues relating to power difficult to measure and to research?

FURTHER READING

Daniel J. Brass, 'Being in the Right Place: A Structural Analysis of Individual Influence in an Organization', *Administrative Science Quarterly*, December 1984, pp. 518–39.

John Child, 'Organization Structure, Environment and Performance: The Role of Strategic Choice', *Sociology*, January 1972.

Rosabeth Moss Kanter, 'Power Failure in Management Circuits', *Harvard Business Review*, July/August 1979, pp. 65–75.

Danny Miller & Cornelia Droge, 'Psychological and Traditional Determinants of Structure', *Administrative Science Quarterly*, December 1986, pp. 539–60.

Jeffrey Pfeffer, *Power in Organizations*, Marshfield, MA: Pitman, 1981.

Herbert Simon, *Administrative Behavior*, 3rd edn, New York: Free Press, 1976.

NOTES

1 Adapted from David Welch, 'The Car Guys Take Charge at General Motors', *Business Week*, 26th November 2001, p. 49.

2 Jeffrey D. Ford & John W. Slocum, Jr, 'Size, Technology, Environment and the Structure of Organisations', *Academy of Management Review*, October 1977, pp. 561–75.

3 John Child, 'Organization Structure, Environment and Performance: The Role of Strategic Choice', *Sociology*, January 1972, pp. 1–22; and Derek S. Pugh, 'The Management of Organization Structures: Does Context Determine Form?', *Organizational Dynamics*, Spring 1973, pp. 19–34.

4 ibid.

5 John Child, 'Strategic Choice in the Analysis of Action : Structure, Organizations and the Environment', *Organization Studies*, 18(1), 1997, pp. 43–76.

6 ibid.

7 Herbert A. Simon, *Administrative Behavior*, 3rd edn, New York: Free Press, 1976.

8 Howard E. Aldrich, *Organizations and Environments*, Englewood Cliffs, NJ: Prentice-Hall, 1979, pp. 149–59.

9 Danny Miller & Cornelia Droge, 'Psychological and Traditional Determinants of Structure', *Administrative Science Quarterly*, December 1986, pp. 539–60.

10 James G. March and Herbert A. Simon, *Organizations*, New York: John Wiley, 1958.

11 Jeffrey Pfeffer, *Organizational Design*, Arlington Heights, IL.: AHM Publishing, 1978, p. 8.

12 Eva C. Chu, 'Dominant Coalition as a Mediating Mechanism Between the Rational Model and the Political Model in Organization Theory', paper presented at Annual Academy of Management Conference, Anaheim, CA, August 1988.

13 Jeffrey Pfeffer, 'Power and Resource Allocation in Organizations', in Barry M. Staw & Gerald R. Salancik, eds, *New Directions in Organizational Behavior*, Chicago: St Clair Press, 1977, p. 240.

14 John Kotter & James Heskett, *Corporate Culture and Performance*, New York: Free Press, 1992.

15 ibid.

16 Stanley M. Davis & Paul R. Lawrence, *Matrix*, Reading, MA. Addison-Wesley.

17 Sun Tzu, *The Art of War*, Hodder and Stoughton, London, 1990; Spencer Johnson, 'Who Moved my Cheese', London: Vermillion, 2001; Jack Welch & John A. Byrne, *Jack: What I've Learned Leading a Great Company and Great People*, London, Headline, 2001.

18 See for instance Leonard L. Russell Jr, 'Reengineering: the Missing Links', *Human Resource Planning* 19(4), 1996, pp. 40–47.

19 Davis & Lawrence op. cit. and Stanley M. Davis & Paul R. Lawrence, 'Problems of Matrix Organization', *Harvard Business Review* 56 (May/June) 1978, pp. 131–142.

20 Jeffrey Pfeffer, *Power in Organizations*, Marshfield, MA: Pitman Publishing, 1981, p. 4.

21 W. Graham Astley & Paramjit S. Sachdeva, 'Structural Sources of Intraorganizational Power: A Theoretical Synthesis', *Academy of Management Review*, January 1984, pp. 104–13.

22 Pfeffer, 'Power and Resource Allocation in Organizations', pp. 248–9.

23 Neil Fligstein, 'The Intraorganizational Power Struggle: Rise of Finance Personnel to the Top Leadership in Large Corporations, 1919–1979', *American Sociological Review*, February 1987, pp. 44–58.

24 Daniel J. Brass, 'Being in the Right Place: A Structural Analysis of Individual Influence in an Organization', *Administrative Science Quarterly*, December 1984, pp. 518–39; and Judith D. Hackman, 'Power and Centrality in the Allocation of Resources in Colleges and Universities', *Administrative Science Quarterly*, March 1985, pp. 61–77.

25 Donald C. Hambrick, 'Environment, Strategy, and Power within Top Management Teams', *Administrative Science Quarterly*, June 1981, pp. 253–75; and M. A. Hitt, R.D. Ireland & K.A. Palia, 'Industrial Firms' Grand Strategy and Functional Importance: Moderating Effects of Technology and Uncertainty', *Academy of Management Journal*, June 1982, pp. 265–98.

26 Keith G. Provan & Germain Boer, 'Beyond Strategic Contingencies Theory: Understanding Departmental Power in Organizations', paper presented at the Annual Academy of Management Conference, Boston, MA, August 1984.

27 Hambrick, 'Environment, Strategy, and Power Within Top Management Teams'.

28 Michael Crozier, *The Bureaucratic Phenomenon*, Chicago: University of Chicago Press, 1964.

29 Keith Davis and William C. Fredrick, *Business and Society: Managment, Public Policy, Ethics*, 5th ed., New York: McGraw Hill, 1984, p. 76.

30 Harold J. Leavitt and Homa Bahrami, *Managerial Psychology: Managing Behavior in Organizations*, 5th ed., Chicago: University of Chicago Press, 1988, p. 121.

31 David C. McClelland, 'The Two Faces of Power', *Journal of International Affairs*, 24(1), 1970, pp. 29–47.

32 Jeffrey Pfeffer, *Power in Organizations*, Marshfield, MA: Pitman, 1981.

33 Jeffrey Gantz & Victor Murray, 'Experience of Workplace Politics', *Academy of Management Journal*, 23, 1980, pp. 237–51; Dan L. Madison, Robert W. Allen, Lyman Porter, Patricia Renwick & Bronston T. Mayes, 'Organizational Politics: An Exploration of Manager's Perception', *Human Relations*, 33, 1980, pp. 79–100.

34 Gantz & Murray, 'Experience of Workplace Politics'; Pfeffer, *Power in Organizations*, op. cit.

35 Pfeffer, *Power in Organizations*, op. cit.

36 ibid.

37 ibid.

38 Rosabeth Moss Kanter, 'Power Failure in Management Circuits', *Harvard Business Review*, July/August 1979, pp. 65–75; and Pfeffer, *Power in Organizations*, op. cit.

39 Donald J. Vredenburgh & John G. Maurer, 'A Process Framework of Organizational Politics', *Human Relations*, 37, 1984, pp. 47–66.

40 Pfeffer, *Organizational Design*, op. cit., p. 225.

41 ibid.

42 Barry M. Staw & E. Szwajkowski, 'The Scarcity-Munificence Component of Organizational Environments and the Commission of Illegal Acts', *Administrative Science Quarterly*, September 1975, pp. 345–54.

43 Richard M. Cyert & James G. March, *A Behavioral Theory of the Firm*, Englewood Cliffs, NJ: Prentice-Hall, 1963, p. 36.

44 L.J. Bourgeois III, 'On the Measurement of Organizational Slack', *Academy of Management Review*, January 1981, p. 30.

45 Pfeffer, *Organizational Design*, op. cit., p. 176.

46 ibid., p. 14.

47 L.J. Bourgeois III, Daniel W. McAllister & Terence R. Mitchell, 'The Effects of Different Organizational Environments upon Decisions about Organizational Structure', *Academy of Management Journal*, September 1978, pp. 508–14.

48 Pfeffer, *Organizational Design*, op. cit., pp. 73–5.

49 ibid., pp. 72–3.

PART

4

Organisations
in Action

part 4

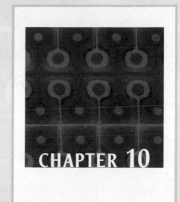

CHAPTER 10

The challenge of finding an appropriate structure

After reading this chapter you should be able to:

1 explain what is required of the organisation's structure;

2 identify how environmental changes have led to the demand for new structures;

3 discuss whether bureaucracy is dead;

4 discuss how traditional approaches to organisational structure are evolving;

5 describe emerging organisational forms.

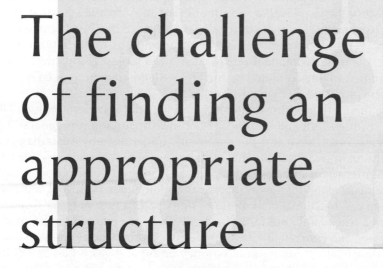

Introduction

CSR and the challenge of change

CSR, formerly the Colonial Sugar Refining Company Limited, should know a little about history: it has played a prominent part in Australia's business for over 120 years. As its name indicates, it started life as a sugar refiner and became marketer of Queensland's crop. It developed extensive sugar interests in the South Pacific and its dominant role in sugar made it one of Australia's largest companies. The sugar activities were first highly regulated by the Queensland government; later, its other businesses were protected by high tariff walls.

What were these other business interests, and why did it undertake them? By the 1950s, sugar required little more in the way of investment and was generating a lot of cash. Overseas investment was not commonly undertaken by Australian companies, one of the main reasons being that at that time there were considerable barriers raised by countries to inward flows of capital. So CSR diversified at home. Over the next 30 years it entered industries as diverse as building materials, coal and uranium mining, oil and gas, bauxite and aluminium, timber and a host of lesser investments. It even owned a macadamia nut farm. In the 1980s it also entered the US market by buying quarrying and concrete interests in Florida. Most of the attempts at diversification were disastrous. It lost so much money on oil and gas it had to sell its real estate holdings to cover the losses. By the late 1990s it had a billion dollars worth of timber assets that showed no return. Timber was not its only poor performer. In 1980 it was the fourth-largest company listed on the Australian Stock Exchange. By 2000 it was 26th, a sure indication of poor management. Over the past 25 years, CSR had created value—that is, earned returns above the cost of capital—only in the three years from 1998.

The actions taken by CSR to arrest its decline and return to growth provide a textbook example of the steps established companies have taken over the past 20 years. It cut bureaucracy, downsizing its head office from over 500 people to fewer than 50. It sold, merged or closed underperforming businesses (i.e. those showing little return). It concentrated its energies on just a few core areas such as sugar, building materials and the US businesses. It invested capital in businesses that were worth developing, which in CSR's case was primarily the North American building interests. Management decisions were decentralised. Responsibilities were focused on the divisions and each divisional manager was set performance targets to meet. Managers were then provided with the freedom to manage their businesses to reach the targets. Performance targets, mainly based on return on invested capital, reach deep into each divisional layer of management. All managers know how they will be assessed and that it will be on the performance of their business, not subjective bureaucratic evaluation. Rewards, such as pay and bonuses, are based on financial targets being met. And if a business looks as if it is not performing or there is little growth left in it, it is sold. Sugar, dear to the heart of CSR, is soon to be disposed of, because it fails to meet the investment criteria.

One of the themes of this book is that the structure of an organisation makes a major contribution to its effectiveness. The structure must reconcile many different demands, not the least of which is the power and political needs of top management. In this chapter we will discuss how environmental and technical changes have led to the modification of old structures and the emergence of new ones. But in order to understand how organisational structures have evolved, we need to identify the major environmental and technological changes to which most organisations have had to respond.

Before we do that, it is worthwhile considering the purposes of an organisation's structure (see Table 10.1). This issue is not commonly addressed in the literature on organisations; it is almost as if it is taken for granted and does not need elaboration. We do gain an insight into management's thinking when structural changes are made: these are normally accompanied by statements explaining what the changes are intended to achieve. Our discussion in this chapter applies to all organisations, including charities, government departments, profit-seeking businesses, and not-for-profit institutions such as schools and universities. Specifics will of course vary with each.

At its broadest level, structure must support the *implementation of strategy*. As we discussed in Chapter 5, strategy comprises the goals and plans of the organisation, which enable it to adapt to its environment. The structure must support the achievement of these plans; if it doesn't, then it indicates that the structure needs to change. For instance, if a company produces goods that are sensitive to consumer tastes but has no means of monitoring and disseminating changes in consumer preferences, we can say that there is a structural weakness in the company.

In creating a structure, we are clearly delineating *areas of responsibility*. A glance at an organisational chart easily identifies those areas which have someone responsible for them. Performance is evaluated and rewards allocated based on the areas of responsibility. Resources are also allocated along responsibility lines. Through identifying areas of responsibility, we are deciding what is important and, by default, what is not. We also focus the thoughts and efforts of office holders along the lines of their areas of responsibility. As a result, areas of responsibility must reflect those which are important for the organisation.

Another function of structure, and perhaps the one we are most familiar with, is that it provides *control mechanisms*. This maintains the unity of purpose of the organisation. Command and control often has a negative connotation, but without it organisations would soon become disorganised, important tasks would become

TABLE 10.1 The functions of structure

Implement strategy
Define areas of responsibility
Provide control mechanisms
Facilitate the flow of production
Promote coordination and information flows
Monitor and respond to environmental change
Maintain and promote organisational knowledge

neglected, and self-interest would overtake the organisation's interest as the primary focus of activity. The command and control mechanisms also establish the chain of reporting relationships within the organisation.

Structure is responsible for *facilitating the flow of production*. All organisations produce something—cars, charitable work, government administration, air travel and hospitality services and so on. These must be produced at a cost and quality acceptable to the consumer and competitive with others doing the same thing. By creating organisational forms that are adapted to the production technologies in use, we facilitate efficiency in the production process.

The structure should *promote coordination and information flows*. Modern organisations have often been referred to as 'silos'. We are all familiar with the large concrete silos that hold grain: they comprise separate vertical components that are linked to each other structurally. Each is self-contained and they are joined only by thin linkages. In organisations, most authority structures are vertical, like silos, running from the top to the bottom of the organisation. But as production tends to flow from one department to the other—that is, across the organisation—it is important that the structure support the necessary communication flows to support the production flow.

The structure must be able to *monitor and respond to environmental change*. Henry Ford, in the days of the Model-T in the 1920s, was typical of industrialists of his day. He tried to create a self-contained organisation which was insulated from its environment. He was unsuccessful, and no other organisation has managed to fully isolate itself from its environment. All organisations need to build within their structure the capacity to monitor environmental changes and demands and to respond appropriately to them. Without this capacity, and our argument is that it is a structural provision, there will be dissonance between the organisation and its environment, and its future existence will be put in jeopardy.

Structure finally plays a part in the *maintenance of organisational knowledge and learning*. Individuals are the repository of knowledge but their knowledge is specialised. Organisational knowledge occurs when the design and production of a product or service is too complex for one person to understand. Examples would be the manufacture of motor cars and aircraft and many aspects of information technology. In cases such as these, structure determines the way the specialised tasks are brought together and information and knowledge distributed. Without structure providing this facility, the full resources of the organisation would not be used.

The origins of organisational change

It seems that it is almost impossible to write a management book for a general audience without making breathless observations about the rate of change and apocalyptic claims about the future. Is there any substance for these statements or is it merely a means of grabbing the attention of readers? There is in fact an element of truth in the observations, although many are overstated for the purpose of selling books. Businesses, and organisations, have changed very rapidly over the past 20 years (see Table 10.2), probably as much as during the previous 80 years. The period after 1980 saw the accumulation of many changes, which created new management challenges and altered the world of work. In order for us to identify the way in which these changes are reconstructing organisations, we need to be

TABLE 10.2 Major sources of change over the past 20 years

Deregulation and privatisation
Promotion of competition
Growth of globalisation
Introduction of technological innovations
Demands for profitability
Commodification of markets
End of the public service mentality
Changes in expectations and society values

aware of what they are and how they have changed organisational environments. The changes have not affected all organisations equally, but there are few that have been unaffected by their influence. A number of changes have originated from government policies, others have had their origin in technological innovation and societal expectations. In particular, government decisions in relation to privatisation, deregulation and the promotion of competition have had a significant impact on all organisations.

Changes in government policy

During the 1970s, governments in Western countries began to introduce policies that were to have a far-reaching effect. Prior to that time, government was a major owner of companies, such as the Commonwealth Bank and Qantas. A number of industries, such as banking, transport, telecommunications and energy, were regulated: that is, the government determined who could enter the industry, what was to be charged and who was allowed to compete. Industry policies of self-sufficiency behind high tariff walls also started to be questioned as costs rose and economic growth slowed.[1]

During the 1980s these policies were progressively abandoned. Governments in most Western countries sold their trading enterprises. They deregulated industries by introducing market forces and moved to progressively lower tariff barriers. Globalisation started to accelerate, not as a product of technological change but as a result of government policy. Governments also started to question how they managed their own operations, such as schools, universities, hospitals and government departments. They generally concluded that these were neither particularly efficient nor effective and that the bureaucratic inertia and inefficiencies present in many would need to be addressed.

Competition

The result of government policies is that most organisations now experience high levels of competition. No longer do businesses have a guaranteed share of markets or the comfort of government protection. But while threats increased, so did opportunities. The dominant incumbent in many industries was a former government-owned monopoly with entrenched low productivity. These made an attractive target for sharp entrepreneurs attempting to establish new businesses. Manufacturers faced increased competition from imported goods, leading to significant changes in practices in the sector. This included the merger or exit of many companies while others sourced all or part of their product overseas. Industries found that their structure was inadequate to compete. The legacy of past policies and technologies led to too many small companies, which lacked economies of scale. Efficiency required the consolidation of smaller players into larger, better-capitalised units.

Globalisation

The reduction of tariff barriers is only one part of globalisation. Globalisation created many opportunities for companies to expand overseas as other countries lowered barriers to goods and capital flows.[2] Those companies wanting to grow now had access to larger overseas markets. But expansion demanded management skills and knowledge that companies in many cases did not possess. They not only had to assess business prospects in unfamiliar environments—they also then had to incorporate overseas businesses into the operations of the company, which in many cases involved making major structural changes. It also exposed companies to new risks, such as differing cultural standards, currency variations and unfamiliar legal systems.

Technological innovations

Technological innovation is normally high on most people's list of environmental changes.[3] Many of the innovations are obvious: mobile phones, the Internet and e-commerce, reduced cost of information processing, cheap telephone interconnectivity. All of these are electronic and are based on the microprocessor. And all are readily adaptable to business use. These innovations collectively mean that we can communicate faster and cheaper and transmit far more information than we could previously. The uniqueness of many innovations means that their impact is difficult to determine. Some, for instance mobile phones, may be easily and quickly incorporated into day-to-day activities. For others, such as e-commerce and electronic data interchange, new strategies and organisational practices must be developed before they can make their full contribution. Competitive advantage will go to those firms which make the right choices. Bill Gates, the founder of Microsoft, observed that we tend to overestimate technology's impact in the short term but to underestimate its long-term impact.

Demands for profitability

One of the key strategic constituencies of profit-making companies is shareholders.[4] An increasing proportion of companies are owned by professional investors such as superannuation and investment funds. These investors place heavy demands on performance; they are seeking increasing profitability and growth. They in turn require companies to perform or be starved of capital. As a result, management is under pressure to use resources productively and show an adequate return on assets. These demands have led to major changes in both management and the industrial relations system.

Commodification of markets

As a large number of product categories reach the mature phase of their life cycle, it is becoming increasingly difficult to differentiate products.[5] Products as diverse as motor cars, food, clothing and transport services have low rates of innovation and growth. This leads to price being the basis of most competition. In such markets, advantage goes to the producers with the lowest costs. Firms have little choice but to try to move down the cost curve by squeezing more performance out of the organisation.

End of the public service mentality

Government services, such as those of administration, health and education, although not required to show a profit, have seen the environment they operate in radically change.[6] Governments have cut budgets for education and told universities to become more entrepreneurial in raising funds. Many functions, such as IT, have been outsourced and others privatised. Governments now charge for many services that were previously provided at no cost to the consumer. This has led to many organisations being more aware of the need to provide value for money. New expressways are now toll roads built by private enterprise. Revised employment provisions have been introduced that remove jobs for life. And many services, such as metropolitan rail services, are set tight performance and financial targets to meet. Government organisations are having to do more with less and both workers and managers are having to focus on resource usage and efficiency issues.

Social changes and expectations

The social contract based on the male breadwinner being given a job for life in return for loyalty has ended, and new employment practices are emerging.[7] The competitive pressures we have identified in the previous sections have led to companies being far more likely to lay off surplus staff than in previous generations. Downsizing, redundancies and plant and office closures, even bankruptcies, are common. Organisations have also had to alter established practices in order to accommodate legislative changes in relation to women and the disabled. Other legislation covers harassment, antidiscrimination and occupational health and safety. Demographic changes, particularly the ageing of the workforce, are predicted to lead to skills shortages as older workers retire. Workforces are also becoming more diverse, leading to revised management practices. Accommodating the work needs of women with young families, family problems arising from overwork and expectations of excessive workforce commitment are issues that must be tackled. Society also expects high ethical standards, socially responsible attitudes and sustainable production methods, and managers must be prepared to provide these.

The changes we have identified are all the more challenging for having occurred simultaneously and within a short period of time. The rapidity and magnitude of the changes has no doubt contributed to the extensive 'paradigm shift' literature, which proposes continual and revolutionary changes in organisational structure.[8] But looking around us we can see that many traditional management practices have hardly passed from the scene. Motor vehicle production lines, banking back offices, call centres, government departments and transport companies all exhibit many of the characteristics of bureaucracy. So before we start to look at emerging organisational forms, we should ask 'Is bureaucracy dead?'.

Is bureaucracy dead?

Weber's bureaucracy

We have to answer the above question with a qualified, but firm, no! But before we pass judgement, we should first explain what bureaucracy is. *Bureau* means office in French, so bureaucracy roughly translates as rule by office. It was a term introduced by Max Weber, a German sociologist who wrote on a wide range of topics, extending from religion and capitalism through to Chinese social organisation. Although he wrote around the turn of the 20th century, his writings, originally in German, were not translated into English until 1947.[9] One of Weber's interests was in how to manage large industrial organisations. The modern corporation, with its large work-force and the separation of ownership and management, was one of the great organisational innovations of the second industrial revolution. Prior to its growth, most enterprises were owner-managed and business was conducted on a personal basis. The management of the modern corporation has fascinated observers, theorists, academics and practising managers for over 100 years; this book is one of many concerned with improving its effectiveness. Weber provided one of the first steps along this road. He proposed seven principles which, when applied, would lead to rational and efficient operations. There was little that was original in these; most had already been applied in one form or another. But Weber brought them together and highlighted the key elements. A number of his proposals are structural, others are behavioural. The seven principles are:

1 *Division of labour.* Each person's job is broken down into simple, routine and well-defined tasks. This is also called job specialisation.
2 *Well-defined authority hierarchy.* A multi-level formal structure, with a hierarchy of positions, ensures that each lower position is under the supervision and control of a higher one.
3 *High formalisation.* There is dependence on formal rules and procedures to ensure uniformity and to regulate the behaviour of job holders.
4 *Impersonal nature.* Sanctions are applied uniformly and impersonally to avoid involvement with individual personalities and personal preferences of members.
5 *Employment decisions based on merit.* Selection and promotion decisions are based on technical qualifications, competence and performance of the candidates.
6 *Career tracks for employees.* Members are expected to pursue a career in the organisation. In return for career commitment, employees have tenure: that is, they will be retained even if they 'burn out' or if their skills become obsolete.
7 *Distinct separation of members' organisational and personal lives.* The demands and interests of personal affairs and kinship ties are kept completely separate from work-related activities in order to prevent them from interfering with the rational impersonal conduct of the organisation's activities.

Positive qualities in Weber's 'ideal type'

Weber's bureaucracy had a number of desirable attributes. These include the focus on impartiality when selecting employees; security of employment to protect employees against arbitrary authority and changes in skill demands; rules and regulations to promote impartiality in decision making; and the establishment of clear lines of authority and responsibility.[10] Weber also sought to combat favouritism by bringing objectivity to employee selection and by reducing nepotism and other forms of favouritism by decision makers and replacing them with job-competence criteria.

The idea of tenure, or security of employment, has a positive and a negative side. The negative side is not difficult to identify: why work hard and apply yourself when your job is virtually guaranteed? Surely a guaranteed job leads to complacency? While this may be true in many cases, there is an upside to tenure. Many tasks are unique to an organisation and may take a long time to learn. Why would an employee take years to learn a highly specialised task if there was not a return obligation on the part of the organisation to provide some form of employment security? Also, security of employment allows employees to make a commitment to the organisation which is far deeper than if they are continually job-hopping. Tenure also protects the individual against arbitrary actions of management. Although 'jobs for life' is now an outdated management practice, most organisations still try to provide ongoing employment, although this is very much dependent on the organisation being able to afford it.

Weber's bureaucracy had its structural elements. These include division of labour, rules and regulations to cover all eventualities, and a management hierarchy with clearly defined areas of responsibility. Rules and regulations may be constraints on what you can and cannot do, but they do introduce predicability and increase uniformity of actions. Without a policy, for instance, how does a manager know when he or she can or cannot make a decision? Absence of policy, therefore, leaves managers open to reprimand for any decision made, however trivial. Similarly, if staff members do something wrong, they want to be assured that they will not be unduly penalised. Bureaucracy's high formalisation provides the mechanism with which to facilitate the standardisation of disciplinary practices.

The positive qualities of a hierarchy of management are often overlooked. Staff members know to whom to take problems, how much authority a manager has, as well as their areas of responsibility. The importance of these issues is revealed in a survey of managers in industrial firms. They were found to be decidedly 'in favour of more, rather than less, clarity in lines of authority, rules, duties, specification of procedures, and so on'.[11] These managers recognised that only when the structure and relationships are clear can authority be delegated and performance assessed.

Before we leave this section we should note that much of what passes as bureaucracy has not been adopted by organisations as an act of free choice. Institutional demands in the environment promote disciplined behaviour within the organisation that has the characteristics of bureaucracy. These include the need for quality control, the requirements of safety, to follow legal requirements in employment practices, and the need to protect assets. All of these require extensive paperwork and the maintenance of documentation, adherence to rules, regulations and systems and appropriate training.

Summarising Weber's contribution

The central theme in Weber's bureaucratic model is standardisation. In this we can see that many of its features are present in the machine bureaucracy we discussed in Chapter 4. The behaviour of people in bureaucracies is predetermined by the standardised structure and processes. The model itself can be dissected into three groups of characteristics: those that relate to the structure and function of the organisation, those that deal with means of rewarding effort, and those that deal with protection for individual members.[12]

Weber's model stipulates a hierarchy of offices, with each office under the direction of a higher one. Each of these offices is differentiated horizontally by division of labour. This division of labour creates units of expertise, defines areas of action consistent with the competence of unit members, assigns responsibilities for carrying out those actions and allocates commensurate authority to fulfil these responsibilities. All the while, written rules govern the performance of members' duties. This imposition of structure and functions provides a high level of specialised expertise, coordination of roles and control of members through standardisation.

The second group of characteristics in Weber's model relates to rewards. Members receive salaries in relation to their rank in the organisation. Promotions are based on objective criteria such as seniority or achievement. As members are not owners, it is important that there be a clear separation of their private affairs and property from the organisation's affairs and property. It is further expected that commitment to the organisation is paramount, the position in the organisation being the employee's sole or primary occupation.

Finally, Weber's model seeks to protect the rights of individuals. In return for a career commitment, members receive protection from arbitrary actions by superiors, clear knowledge of their responsibilities and the amount of authority their superior holds, and the ability to appeal against decisions that they see as unfair or outside the parameters of their superior's authority.

The downside of bureaucracy

In the previous section we identified the positive qualities of bureaucracy. It would be misleading to leave the impression that there was not a downside and, of course, you no doubt have experienced many of these either as an employee or as a customer (see Table 10.3). As a result, bureaucracies have received more than their share of unfavourable publicity. We review these criticisms below.

Goal displacement

goal displacement
the displacement of organisational goals by subunit or personal goals

Bureaucracy is attacked most often for encouraging **goal displacement**—that is, the displacement of organisational goals by subunit or personal goals. One critic

TABLE 10.3 The downside of bureaucracy

Goals displacement
Inappropriate application of rules and regulations
Employee alienation
Concentration of power
Inability to adapt to change
Overstaffing
Tendency towards large size and low productivity
Non-member frustration

identified that while rules, regulations and standard procedures introduced a high degree of reliability and predicability, the resultant conformity may be detrimental because it reduces flexibility.[13] Observation of rules and regulations becomes so entrenched that they take on a symbolic meaning of their own. The rules and procedures become more important than the ends they were designed to serve, the result being goal displacement and loss of organisational effectiveness. Another critic believed that means could displace ends as the goals of the organisation.[14] He emphasised that specialisation and differentiation create subunits with different goals. The goals of each separate subunit become the primary focus of the subunit members. This can lead to subunits trying to achieve their own goals, with consequent high levels of conflict and loss of organisational purpose. A third perspective on goal displacement proposed that rules and regulations not only define unacceptable behaviours but also define the level of acceptable performance, which is rarely exceeded.[15] That is, people will do just the bare minimum to get by.

Yet another criticism of bureaucracy proposes that high formalisation bureaucracy creates insecurities in those in authority that lead to what has been called **bureaupathic behaviour.**[16] Decision makers use adherence to rules to protect themselves from making errors. But such dependence in time becomes the main focus of behaviour, leading to unadaptive and unimaginative behaviour. A further aspect of bureaupathic behaviour suggests that as people in hierarchical positions become increasingly dependent on lower-level specialists for achievement of organisational goals, they tend to introduce more and more rules to protect themselves against this dependence. That is, they use rules to maintain centralised decision making.

bureaupathic behaviour adherence to rules and regulations by individuals to protect themselves from making errors

Inappropriate application of rules and regulations

Related closely to the problem of goal displacement is the undesirable effect of members' applying formalised rules and procedures in inappropriate situations— that is, attempting to force the needs of a unique situation into one of a range of standard problems. This results in suboptimal performance and dysfunctional consequences.[17] We can conclude that bureaucracies' high rates of formalisation make it difficult to respond to changing conditions.

Employee alienation

A major downside of bureaucracy is **employee alienation.** Members perceive the impersonality of the organisation as creating distance between them and their work. When one is just a 'cog in the wheel', it is often difficult to feel committed to the organisation. High specialisation further reinforces one's feeling of being irrelevant: routine activities can easily be learned by others, making employees feel interchangeable and powerless. Repetitive jobs with little challenge can also easily lead to loss of motivation and dysfunctional employee behaviour. In professional bureaucracies formalisation must be lessened, otherwise the risk of employee alienation is very high.[18]

employee alienation the distance an employee feels between themselves and their work

Concentration of power

The concentration of power in senior executives of bureaucracies has been targeted by some. Although this criticism is subjective—it depends on whether one considers the concentration of power undesirable—it undoubtedly flies in the face of those social scientists who want to equalise power in organisations.[19] It is a fact that bureaucracy generates an enormous degree of power in the hands of a very few.

If you perceive this as undesirable or counter to the values of a democratic society, as some do, you will find this attribute a negative consequence of the bureaucratic form.

Inability to adapt to change

Bureaucracies have a well-deserved reputation for being slow to change.[20] Environments can change around them, but bureaucracies tend to be always lagging in introducing new ways of doing things. This is because bureaucracies reward stability and adherence to the rules, both of which are reflected in the behaviour of workers and managers. They are rarely set up or managed to constantly monitor their environment and to respond quickly to changes. Change requires modification to the rules and regulations, which can often only be made after extensive consultations and committee meetings. Bureaucracies also have the tendency to maintain functions and services long after the need for them has passed.

Overstaffing

Because of the reluctance of bureaucracies to reduce workforces, at least in former years, many bureaucracies suffer a reputation for being overstaffed and for those employed by them being underworked.[21] This arises because technology does not stand still: new inventions and innovations are constantly reducing the numbers of people needed to undertake any given task. No organisation can go on forever without facing the need to adjust to market realities. But bureaucracies have developed a reputation for delaying the need for adjustment to their staff numbers as long as possible.

Tendency towards large size and low productivity

Until the waves of downsizing in the 1980s and 90s bureaucracies, in both business and government, had a reputation for being too big and costing too much to run. This was reflected in the size of the administrative component. The administrative component is comprised of those workers who are not actually producing the goods and services consumed by the customer. Large numbers of people were employed in support departments in seemingly ever-proliferating numbers. Researchers expended great effort on determining the rate at which administrative components were expanding. The growing administrative component was combined with low rates of productivity. Too many people were doing too many unnecessary things and there was enormous resistance to doing anything about it.

Non-member frustration

The last negative consequence that we address relates to those outside the organisation who must deal with the bureaucracy. Bureaucracies unfortunately have a reputation for slowness and inflexibility, which can frustrate those having to deal with them. But, as we see in the next section, it is possible for bureaucracies to breathe new life into the old form.

The greatly exaggerated death of bureaucracy

We should be fair to bureaucracy: many of the drawbacks to bureaucracy we have identified above are a result of the way in which bureaucracy has been operationalised rather than being inherent to the concept. In discussing bureaucracy we noted that it had both structural and behavioural components. We will look at each of these in turn and identify what parts of each are still relevant.

To help us answer the question 'Is bureaucracy dead?' we need only to look around us and, if we are employed, look at our place of work. We can find evidence of the structural components of bureaucracy, or at least parts of it, everywhere. The specialisation of labour is still fundamental to organised activity. Most goods and services are still mass produced in repetitive cycles. The demands of quality, efficient resource usage and safety ensure that high formalisation in the form of rules, regulations and procedures is fundamental to activity. There is still a hierarchy of management; there is little confusion as to whose boss is who and what their responsibilities are, and most employees leave voluntarily rather than through downsizing or redundancy. So viewing bureaucracy from a structural perspective would lead to the conclusion that it is far from being a dinosaur.

Let's move on to the behavioural aspects of bureaucracy. In some ways legal changes have forced the promotion-on-merit component on bureaucracy. The laws promoting equal opportunity oblige large organisations to select the best person for the job, but many smaller companies are exempt from the legislation. Although primarily aimed at gender equality, the provisions apply to all applicants. Obviously those 'in the know' or those who are well connected still have advantage in obtaining positions. This also highlights the impersonal nature of bureaucracy. It was an ambitious proposal on Weber's part that organisations could become impersonal. They are after all made up of people, with all their complexities of emotion, ambition and desires. It may be that few of us would want to work for an organisation that was devoid of the human touch.

There are still career tracks for employees. Most large companies have an internal labour market—that is, one where promotions are made from within the organisation. Where there is a suitably qualified candidate from within the management ranks, he/she will generally be offered any promotion positions. Imagine if that were not the case. Would you want to work for a company in which every management position was advertised on the open market for anyone to apply? Probably not. During periods of large-scale change, some companies have what is called a 'spill and fill': that is, every management position is declared vacant, and managers must then reapply for their old job and any other they consider they are qualified for. Even in periods as disruptive as this, most positions are filled from within the organisation. But while career tracks still exist, organisations are far from being the closed shops they used to be. Managers are regularly hired from outside the organisation, and mobility of labour is expected, especially from managers starting their career.

It is in the area of separation of members' organisational and personal lives that bureaucracies perhaps fall short of current expectations. In Chapter 15, we will discuss in detail the feminist view of bureaucracy. We can summarise that discussion by observing that bureaucracies are organised with the male career pattern as their basic building block—that is, continuous employment combined with the application of their undivided attention to work. Some sections of the workforce are obviously unsuited to this. In particular, women have discontinuous work patterns, arising from child-rearing and family responsibilities. This disadvantages women in areas such as career paths and the maintenance of knowledge of the organisation, which is necessary for advancement. So, of the characteristics of bureaucracy, this particular one stands criticised more for its existence than for the way it is applied.

Freshening up old approaches—bureaucracy revised

The significant changes in environment and technology to which organisations have had to adapt has led to modifications to traditional bureaucracies. Before we analyse these changes, let's clarify our terminology. Weber's bureaucracy, discussed above, was proposed about 100 years ago. It did not aim to describe a structural configuration but an approach to management. In Chapter 4, we introduced the five basic structural forms. Two of these had 'bureaucracy' in their names: the machine bureaucracy and the professional bureaucracy. They were called bureaucracy because a number of elements in the forms reflected Weber's components. For the purpose of giving us a starting point, we will treat the structural elements of Weber's bureaucracy and the machine bureaucracy as being very similar. These include job specialisation, high formalisation and a clear management hierarchy. So our use of bureaucracy basically refers to a machine bureaucracy.

The major structural innovations over the past 10–20 years have concentrated on responding to market needs, improving decision making, facilitating coordination and communication flows, focusing management's efforts on customers rather than internal processes, and using technology to lower costs (see Table 10.4). We will examine these and relate them to the environmental changes we noted earlier in the chapter.

Focusing management effort on key responsibilities

When we design a structure, the task of allocating responsibilities is important because it identifies the areas that will receive most management effort.[22] If we omit important areas, the chances are that they will be neglected and insufficient attention will be paid to them. The demands of competitiveness have led to the concentration of greater management responsibility on areas in the environment. This often means customers, but can include providers of inputs such as components and raw materials or other important environmental influences. In part, this does not require major structural change: we can always expand an existing function. But structural changes are emerging with the creation of new divisions and units which are oriented around specialised segments. So whereas we might have had a large machine bureaucracy, we now have a divisionalised form, with each division concentrating on a product or an area. For instance, a company may have produced a range of building products. It would now have divisions, each with their own manager,

TABLE 10.4 Emergent trends in organisational design

Focusing management effort on key responsibilities
Rethinking the centralisation–decentralisation balance
Moving focus from internal processes to external adaptation
Greater use of market controls
Improving communication flows
Working back from the customer
Concentrating effort on core competencies
Improving availability of information

responsible for bricks, cement and plasterboard. Each of the divisional managers would then be responsible, and accountable, for satisfying the customers of their particular division and for product innovation. So key management tasks have moved from being functional—that is, roles concerned with just production, accounting or sales; there is a layer of management that is now responsible for responding to customer needs. Of course functional managers are still present, but they in turn have had their focus turned outward rather than inward.

Rethinking the centralisation–decentralisation balance

Accompanying the change (identified in the previous section) has been a rethinking of the centralisation–decentralisation balance.[23] There is little point in holding managers accountable for a certain task if they have insufficient authority to operate in their role. There has thus been a move to decentralise decision making. This does not mean that all decisions are made and implemented by lower-level managers but that the ideas may be generated lower in the organisation for approval by more senior managers. In turn, it may be the responsibility of lower-level managers to implement them.

The combination of greater decentralisation and responsibility for customer satisfaction puts in place one of the structural elements that is important in rapidly changing, competitive environments. It allows for faster, more appropriate decision making; faster because the responsibility for decisions is clearly identified and more appropriate because they are made by those responsible for market performance.

Moving focus from internal processes to external adaptation

As we have seen, in a bureaucracy rules dominate. But one of the dysfunctions of many organisations in fast-changing environments is that their focus is far too firmly set on adhering to the rules rather than responding to the needs for change. In other words, management have an inward rather than an outward focus.[24] In part, adherence to the rules is a component of the organisation's culture. But it is also structural. If we structure management responsibilities in such a way that their performance is assessed against customer- or market-focused criteria, we are likely to find that the nature of formalisation changes in order to better serve the organisation's goals.

Greater use of market controls

One of the problems of bureaucracies is knowing what activities are making or losing money, what the return on capital is, and what activities should receive capital investment.[25] For a machine bureaucracy, we aggregate the cost of all activities and deduct it from revenue. Of course, management accounting techniques assist us in breaking down the cost of various activities, but assumptions must be made as to how fixed costs are to be allocated. In machine bureaucracies we have the further problem of aligning accountability with important organisational responsibilities. In the past the hierarchy of management has undertaken this function mainly on the basis of subjective assessment. Structural changes over the past 20 years have moved towards dividing the business into mini-businesses, each with its own financial and performance goals. Managers are made responsible for these. Where costs cannot be offset against revenue, such as for a specialised department, then budgets are set in place and managers are expected to achieve them.

We call this process moving from hierarchical control to market control. Simply put, we are using monetary performance as a substitute for subjective assessment by management. This process can also be seen operating in subcontracting and outsourcing, where parts of the operation are put out to open tender. Transport, logistics and information technology are functions that are often outsourced.

Improving communication flows

An emphasis on a clearly defined management hierarchy and high formalisation presupposes that little changes in an organisation; that once it is set up it can continue for a long time doing much the same as it has been doing. Few organisations have this luxury, but neither do they have the luxury of being able to dismiss the benefits of bureaucracy altogether. An emergent need therefore is to improve communication flows and adaptability without compromising the benefits that bureaucracy can provide. Most organisations have invested heavily in increasing their ability to process information. This may be achieved by using technology to improve information-processing capability. But it is also a structural feature; managers can be specifically allocated to the task of coordination. Their role may be broadly defined as being responsible for a task that crosses functional boundaries and integrates the work of specialists. For instance, a brand manager in a consumer products company is responsible for everything concerning the brand. IT coordinators liaise between the IT and user departments. Coordinators monitor progress of such disparate operations as goods in transit and material to be delivered to a city building site. These tasks could be handled in a bureaucracy, but it would be a very slow and inefficient process. The coordinators' main role is to speed up bureaucracy, not replace it.

We can further facilitate communication flows in the way we set out office.[26] The open-plan office is almost mandatory where good communication between staff is necessary. There are no partitions between offices, and the workspace has conveniently located 'chill-out' spaces with comfortable seating. There is a very high usage of IT. Communication around water coolers and tea- and coffee-making facilities is encouraged. If privacy is required for meetings or interviews, meeting rooms are available. Previously redundant warehousing in former industrial and dockland areas are proving popular for conversion to this type of facility.

Working back from the customer

While organisations cannot actually be built around customers, responding to customer needs can become one of the design focuses of the organisation. This involves monitoring customer needs and product perceptions, then designing the organisation to respond to these. This is in contrast to placing the main emphasis on production. Of course compromises must be made: customers can never be fully satisfied, their expectations may be fickle, and there are always cost and other restraints on what can be produced. But to stay in business basic customer needs must be satisfied.

Concentrating effort on core competencies

Concentrating on core competencies sounds more like a strategy than a structure, and of course it is. But, as we discussed in Chapter 5, strategy has structural implications. As the level of competition has increased, most businesses are finding that they can best maximise their returns by concentrating on just a few things.[27] This way they can achieve economies of scale, management can focus on just a few

OT CLOSEUP

The ethics of modern management

This chapter reflects the prevailing thoughts in relation to organisational structure. The changes we have identified here, and throughout this book, point to managers having to keep a close watch on costs and to be fairly ruthless when it comes to downsizing and pruning the products and services that are making insufficient return on capital. But this can come at an enormous social cost, which is not reflected in profit reports or corporate balance sheets. We can identify three areas of concern that have been discussed in public forums: overwork, particularly by professionals and rising managers; the social dislocation caused by layoffs and downsizing; and the removal of important customer services.

It is difficult to argue that overwork is a direct result of the way we manage organisations; workaholics have always been with us. But emerging technologies permit a person to be engaging in work-related activities 24 hours a day. E-mail, linkages to enable working from home and travel requirements can make work a constant activity. The potential of significant monetary rewards also contributes to a 'work must come first' attitude. The expectation of heroic efforts has become part of many management cultures rather than being an odd individual occurrence. As a result, Australian workers put in the longest hours of any industrialised country.

In previous generations, when bureaucratic rules laid down start and stop times and technology was entirely in-house, the eight-hour workday was common. There was also a balance between work and family life. But we have sighed with relief as bureaucratic controls have been reduced. It is now up to a new generation of workers to determine the extent to which the corporation dominates their life.

In Chapter 6 we discussed at some length the issue of downsizing. What was omitted in that discussion was the human costs associated with interrupted or terminated careers, unemployment and needing to look for other work, particularly for older employees. We are justified in doing this as the study of organisational theory precludes consideration of the micro-aspects of behaviour. But management studies generally are ill-equipped to examine such issues, because once he/she is unemployed a person is no longer a member of an organisation and hence not the subject of study. Most companies do try to handle downsizing humanely. Significant redundancy payments are generally made and help provided to find other employment. As we saw in Chapter 6, many do better on being laid off; others don't fare so well.

Critics of the large numbers of layoffs in recent years have not aimed their criticism just at companies but also at the economic and political system that has placed efficiency and resource usage issues as the goals to which organisations must strive if they are to survive.

The removal of important customer services is most clearly seen in the moves of the big banks to close branches and to charge for what was previously free to the customer. Country people often find that they no longer have a bank branch in their town. Not everyone wants to use an ATM or computer to do their banking. Account fees levied by the bank fall most heavily on the poorer section of society. Alternatively, many are paying far less for banking services, particularly those who borrow large sums of money.

All of these moves make good business sense, and follow from the changes in the environment we have discussed in this chapter. But they contribute to poor public relations. As banking services are essential for all, the matter has received wide publicity that generally paints the bank in a poor light. This issue remains one to be resolved by the various stakeholders of the organisations.

markets, and information-processing needs are reduced. We are therefore seeing the emergence of focused organisations. The old conglomerates that had a wide range of businesses are, with few exceptions, passing from the scene. The concentration may not just be on product but may also be on a geographic area. In order to reduce complexity, management may decide to concentrate its business on just one or a few countries.

Improving the availability of information

This topic is a little different from the section concerned with improving information flows, where we identify the ways in which structural positions may be introduced to improve information flows. The expanding use of IT is permitting information to be more widely spread throughout the organisation.[28] Not all information is available to everyone: most managers and workers have their access blocked to areas they are not authorised for. But sufficient information is available to counter power plays through hoarding information and to decrease management levels through reducing the need to gather and distribute information.

Emerging organisational innovations

The environmental and technological changes we have discussed cannot be accommodated simply by modifying bureaucratic structures. We can summarise the characteristics of the 'new age' organisations as follows: the organisations tend to specialise in a small number of things, they emphasise teamwork, promote coordination, and exist as part of a network of suppliers and distributors. Table 10.5 shows what is likely to become less important in the future and what is likely to become more common.

The shifts in emphasis we have identified in Table 10.5 have led to a number of structural innovations. These are an increasing use of boundary spanners, an expanding use of adhocracies, an emphasis on teamwork and, on a broader scale, increasing divisionalisation. We will consider each of these in turn.

TABLE 10.5 Trends in organisational orientation

Less of	More of
National focus	→ International focus
Internal orientation	→ External orientation
Customers and suppliers at arm's length	→ Integrating up and down the supply chain
Emphasis on hierarchy	→ Functional and cross-functional teams
Administrative control	→ Market control
Hoarding knowledge	→ Spreading knowledge
Inspecting quality in	→ Building quality in
Emphasis on physical assets	→ Emphasis on knowledge
Lifetime employment	→ Lifetime employability

Adapted from: Thomas Clarke & Stewart Clegg, *Changing Paradigms: The Transformation of Management Knowledge for the 21st Century*, London: HarperCollins Business, 1998.

Expanded use of boundary spanners

Boundary spanners have the task of linking the environment to the organisation.[29] They identify environmental changes that are occurring and, in turn, represent the organisation to the environment. Their increased use is linked to the rising level of competition, with its attendant uncertainties. Activities such as forming relationships with customers, managing the supply chain, monitoring the actions of competitors, seeking niches to exploit and expanding distribution channels do not occur unless there is someone responsible for them.

In the past, one of the main roles of boundary spanners was to buffer the organisation from environmental changes: that is, they protected the core operations from unwanted external shocks. Their role still includes this function, but increasingly they have the additional task of providing information to allow the organisation to adapt to external changes. To be effective, the boundary spanners must therefore be more involved in decision making of the organisation by their inclusion in important committees and decision-making teams.

The boundary spanning role may also be introduced by redefining role requirements. All managers have job descriptions, which identify their main areas of responsibility and the tasks associated with these. By giving these an outward orientation, we can incorporate part of the boundary spanning role in most managers' jobs.

Variations on adhocracies

Organisations have been very inventive in grafting some of the features of adhocracy onto traditional structures. These have the main effect of improving communication and facilitating innovation. We mentioned above the structural changes that have led to an increase in the ability to coordinate the various functions of the organisation. These are part of extending the use of adhocracies within organisations. The most widely spoken-of adhocracy is the matrix, but it is probably not the most common. The matrix stands as a counterpoint to the concept of unity of command and, where it is introduced in inappropriate situations or where inadequate preparations for its introduction are made, it can create major problems. A more common innovation are coordinators, who integrate the work of various functional groupings. Unfortunately for such coordinators, their responsibility normally exceeds the authority given to them. This leads to a heavy reliance on communication and management skills, rather than position power, to achieve results.

Other variations on adhocracies include the use of taskforces and various committees. These are formed on an as-required basis. Taskforces are temporary in nature and have a multidisciplinary membership. They have a single-purpose function and are disbanded once this is achieved. Examples of such roles are the installation of a software package, introduction of a quality control system or a major organisational change. Committees are generally more permanent and draw on a range of expertise relevant to their purpose. Examples include quality committees, audit committees and occupational health and safety committees.

An emphasis on teamwork

One of the characteristics of emerging organisations is that there has been an attempt to promote more cooperative ways of working.[30] In practice this normally means the use of teams and some form of collective responsibility. Theorists have extensively promoted the use of teams over the more common hierarchical management style. They do have practical advantages. Teams can promote effective coordination among themselves, and communication flows are often improved. Knowledge can be shared and experience more widely spread among members. As well, they remove some of the negativity associated with hierarchical management. Teams do have their drawbacks, however. They are often far from welcoming to members, and teams may be in conflict with each other. In practice, managers are happy to delegate responsibility to teams but give them limited authority. This way they still maintain a right of veto over team decisions.

Most quality control functions require the use of teams. The shift from inspecting quality, which was the function of an inspection department, to building quality in, which requires the input and involvement of those producing the product or service, predicates that teamwork will be involved.

Even where staff are not members of a formally constituted team, organisations often try to remove communication barriers between them by team-based activities. Executive or departmental retreats, outdoor exercises such as sailing or bushwalking, Friday night drinks and sporting activities are all efforts to bring a team approach to management.

A shift towards market control

The internationalisation of activities, high levels of competition and an increasing stress on performance have led to the need to know how each part of the organisation is performing and to focus management's attention on the organisation as a business.[31] This has seen the emergence of parts of the organisation being controlled by reference to markets. We are all familiar with hierarchical control: a manager subjectively assesses performance against a set of rules, regulations or performance criteria. In contrast, market control de-emphasises subjective assessment and continuous monitoring. In its place, performance is assessed by reference to the profit or loss of an activity or in comparison with a budget. Let's use as an example a medical centre, which may run a pharmacy for use by the general public. The centre management could monitor the effectiveness of the pharmacy by assessing the performance of the pharmacist, the opening hours, whether staff turn up for work, the number of times medicines are not available and so on. Alternatively, it could turn the pharmacy into a little business, put the pharmacist in charge, and assess performance by how much money the pharmacy makes or loses in a year. If we do this, we have replaced hierarchical performance with market-based performance. The pharmacist concentrates on building up the business and the medical centre management has greatly reduced its need to monitor performance by concentrating on a profit-and-loss statement.

The move to market controls is well underway in most organisations. Not all organisations are capable of being *divided* into *divisions* and run as separate businesses. But most have moved some way down the track. Qantas, for instance, isolated many of its functions, such as baggage handling and catering, and put them out to open tender. Existing employees were invited to tender for the work, and most were successful in retaining their jobs. What Qantas has in effect done is move to market control in those areas.

How does market control serve to promote greater environmental responsiveness and improved resource usage? It concentrates management's mind on environmental responsiveness and serving customers. It is only through doing this that profitability, or budgets, can be maintained. Using hierarchical controls, the incentive is to look good while adhering to existing practices and procedures. It also helps management know the costs of each task and compare these with what others are charging.

A new social contract

In Table 10.5 we identified the move from lifetime employment to lifetime employ-ability.[32] While the meaning of lifetime employment is fairly clear, lifetime employ-ability is extremely vague. The reality is that no-one can provide jobs for life any more. Changing environmental circumstances mean that organisations, except perhaps government ones, cannot guarantee their future existence. Companies fail, are taken over and merge with others. Almost all large organisations have had to downsize in order to stay in business; carrying all of their existing staff would have guaranteed insolvency.

So what replaces the social contract of loyalty in return for lifetime employment? Well, in reality no-one seems to know. But the idea of lifetime employability is that skills and knowledge should be kept current so that other employment may be sought as the need arises. But for a new social contract to emerge, organisations and their workforces must settle into the pattern of discontinuity and competitiveness that is emerging.

An emerging form—the virtual organisation

As its name implies, the virtual organisation has the characteristics of a formal organisation while not being one.[33] It comprises a complex network of smaller organisations which each contribute a part of the production process. Boundaries between the organisations are fuzzy; control is generally by market forces, reinforced with the legal certainty of long-term contracts. Nike is the most talked-about virtual organisation. Its headquarters in Oregon in the USA undertakes basic design and marketing functions. But all its manufacturing and logistics operations are sub-contracted through layers of contractors and subcontractors; Nike itself does not manufacture or distribute anything.

While Nike may be an extreme case, there would be few organisations today that attempt to do everything in-house. The Commonwealth Bank subcontracts out its extensive IT needs. Railway systems no longer own locomotives; they hire their loco-motives on a power-by-the-hour basis. Airlines do much the same with many of their aircraft and components. Billabong surfwear provides another example. Headquar-tered on the Gold Coast, like Nike it only designs and markets its products, with manufacturing and distribution being subcontracted to a range of suppliers. The personal computer industry provides another example of how firms are joined through networks. The personal computer comprises many discrete elements, each of which requires different manufacturing processes. No one company produces everything; there are specialist producers for components ranging from microchips through to knobs and switches and bent metal components. These are purchased by an assembler, who then retails the computer to the final purchaser. In this way hundreds of unrelated suppliers are linked through virtual linkages, which are in effect a combination of legal and market forces. The task of supply-chain manage-ment, a modern innovation which recognises the importance of managing the inputs into the organisation, responds to the need to manage the external linkages of the organisation.

The virtual organisation forms part of a network structure. The network structure does not exist as a configuration but as a set of linkages between independent companies. An organisation may be part of a number of networks.

The virtual organisation presents the difficulty for organisation analysis of deciding where the boundary of the organisation actually lies. We identified in Chapter 1 that organisations have identifiable boundaries, but how do we treat an IT subcontractor who turns up to work every day but does not work for the organisation? Is it valid to assess the environmental impact on the organisation when we should be looking at the impact on an industrial network of mutually supporting suppliers? The idea of looking at populations of organisations seems to have relevance in this situation.

Why have organisations moved to large-scale subcontracting? There are both economic and behavioural reasons. Often specialist subcontractors have greater expertise and knowledge in a particular area. The organisation letting the contract also has the advantage of moving part of its costs from fixed to variable, a big advantage in times of economic downturn. For instance, in a power-by-the-hour contract, if a locomotive is not used the state rail system does not incur the costs of paying for it. Also, behaviourally, it is easier and less costly to manage smaller specialised firms than large multidisciplinary ones.

Summary

As environments and technologies change, organisations must similarly change to enable them to adapt to their new circumstances. One of the great strengths of capitalist systems is the ability of businesses to adapt to change. The gales of 'creative destruction' that periodically blow through our economic system place enormous demands on organisations. In this chapter we have identified the major changes that have emerged over the past 20 years and related them to new organisational forms and practices. Not all organisations will adapt successfully; those with more enlightened management and more adaptable workforces will adjust successfully, while those that don't will in one way or the other fade from the scene. Entrepreneurs create new organisations, some of which are more suited to the emerging environment. These will overshadow those which cling to approaches and management methods more appropriate to another age.

One of our aims in this chapter has been to link environmental changes to specific structural responses. We propose that these responses are not random but may be grouped into a number of categories that highlight the major changes. The direction of organisational structural change has been towards greater coordination, improving responses to environmental change and the use of teams. We have also seen the emergence of the virtual organisation. This is an organisation which subcontracts many of the tasks which were previously undertaken inhouse. Even for those firms which are not virtual, organisations are now subcontracting an increasing range of tasks.

For review and discussion

1   What are the purposes of an organisation's structure?

2   How might the privatisation of the Commonwealth Bank have altered its environment? How is this likely to have affected its structure?

3   Discuss how increased competition may affect a manufacturer of refrigerators.

4   Identify the opportunities and threats of globalisation, and indicate how organisations may need to change their structure to meet these.

5   How have social changes and expectations led to changes in organisations?

6   Describe how technological changes have changed the way information is processed. How has this influenced structure?

7   Describe the characteristics of Weber's bureaucracy.

8   Identify the positive and negative aspects of bureaucracy.

9   'Bureaucracy is dead.' Evaluate this statement.

10 Why has management of large corporations grown to dominate the business literature?

11 Why has the use of market controls grown over the past 20 years?

12 What purpose do boundary spanners have in organisations? What has led to the greater use of boundary spanners in organisations?

13 Why are firms making greater use of coordinators?

14 Evaluate whether virtual organisations are likely to become more common.

15 What is likely to emerge as the new 'social contract' between employer and employee? What have you based your decision on?

16 Assess whether the material in this chapter is applicable to not-for-profit firms such as the Smith Family and Greenpeace.

CASE FOR CLASS DISCUSSION
Orica faces a brave, new world

Orica is one of those invented names for companies. The process of creating names became popular in the 1990s, but it depersonalises a company. The new name provides no indication of where a company has come from, where it is going to or what it produces. Orica could be a company producing anything from surfwear to cheese. In fact it produces plastics, vinyls, explosives, fertilisers and Dulux paint. And it has an origin and one that played a significant part in developing its culture: it is the former Australian subsidiary of ICI, the large British chemical company.

ICI was lured to invest in Australia in the 1920s by promises of high tariff protection. Behind tariff walls it produced basic chemicals, and over the years expanded into the newer areas of plastics and vinyls. It also was a major producer of pharmaceuticals and paint. ICI listed the company on the Australian Stock Exchange but kept 66% of the shares, hence control, for itself.

ICI Australia was a typical engineering-based company of its day. It had an extremely large head office of 600 people, leading to centralised decision making. This engineer-driven company put strong emphasis on values, safety and process. It emphasised analysis, perhaps to the detriment of action. It was also a company used to thinking long-term, and having the support of its parent it did not have to worry too much about the ups and downs of the cycles that characterised the industry. It also did not appear to be too concerned with return on assets or financial performance, which characterised the better-performing companies. Perhaps the best indicator of the culture of the company was the speed limit in the company's car park—4 kph.

In the late 1990s ICI, facing its own problems, decided to sell its Australian interests. In 1997 Orica was created, and ICI's 66% interests were sold to the Australian public. Orica contained most of what was formerly in ICI Australia minus pharmaceuticals, which arm was sold separately. But ICI transferred to Orica its explosives interests, making Orica a major worldwide player in this area.

Since its float Orica has performed poorly. Losses have mounted and its share price has halved. Simple mistakes have cost large sums of money. For instance, it signed long-term contracts for the supply of explosives but neglected to hedge the cost of the main input, natural gas. As the price of gas rose, so did losses. Constant minor adjustments by management to the structure and culture have had no impact. Eventually the board appointed a new managing director, with the brief to turn the company around.

Key parts of this case were drawn from: Stephen Bartholmeusz, 'Orica Needs More Speed to Outrun PacDun', *The Sydney Morning Herald*, 11 August 2001, p. 48.

QUESTIONS

1 Assuming that you have been appointed managing director, what actions would you take to help the company make a reasonable return on its assets?

2 How closely do your actions conform to those identified in this chapter?

3 To what extent have fashions in management thought influenced the course you have proposed?

4 Identify and discuss any social responsibility issues that may arise from your actions.

FURTHER READING

C. Bartlett & S. Ghoshall, *Transnational Management*, Chicago: Irwin, 1995.

Frances Cairncross, *The Death of Distance*, London: Orion Publishing, 1997.

Thomas Clarke & Stewart Clegg, *Changing, Paradigms: The Transformation of Management Knowledge for the 21st Century*, London: HarperCollins, 1998.

Philip Evans & Thomas Wurster, *Blown to Bits: How the New Economies of Information Transform Strategy*, Cambridge, MA: Harvard Business School Press, 2000.

Rosabeth Moss Kanter, *World Class: Thriving Locally in the Global Economy*, New York: Simon & Schuster, 1995.

Kenichi Ohmae, *The Borderless World*, London: Collins, 1990.

Michael Porter, *The Competitive Advantage of Nations*, Basingstoke: Macmillan, 1990.

NOTES

1 For details on the development of Australian industry policy see Alf Ratligan, 'Industry Assistance: The Inside Story', Melbourne University Press, Melbourne, 1986; and Department of Industry, Technology and Commerce, 'Australian industry new direction', AGPS, Canberra, 1987. For reference on the growth of globalisation, see for instance Charles Hill, *International Business: Competing in the Global Marketplace*, 2nd edn, Boston, MA: McGraw Hill, 1997.

2 See Thomas Clarke & Stewart Clegg, *Changing Paradigms: The Transformation of Management Knowledge for the 21st Century*, London: HarperCollins Business, 1998.

3 ibid.

4 Note 1 op. cit.

5 See for example, T. Vasko, R. Ayres and L. Fontvieille (eds), *Life Cycles and Long Waves*, New York: Springer, Verlag 1990.

6 See note 1 op. cit.

7 Peter Dawkins & Craig Littler, *Downsizing: Is it right for Australia?*, Melbourne: Melbourne Institute of Applied Economic and Social Research, 2001.

8 Clarke & Clegg, *Changing Paradigms: The Transformation of Management Knowledge for the 21st Century*.

9 Max Weber, *The Theory of Social and Economic Organizations*, Talcott Parsons, ed., A.M. Henderson & Talcott Parsons, trans. New York: Free Press, 1947.

10 The following discussion is adapted from Charles Perrow, *Complex Organizations: A Critical Essay*, Glenview, IL: Scott, Foresman, 1972, pp. 8–44.

11 ibid, p. 37.

12 Perrow, *Complex Organizations: A Critical Essay*.

13 Robert K. Merton, 'Bureaucratic Structure and Personality', *Social Forces*, May 1940, pp. 560–8.

14 Philip Selznick, *TVA and the Grass Roots: A Study in the Sociology of Formal Organizations*, Berkeley: University of California Press, 1949.

15 Alvin Gouldner, *Patterns of Industrial Bureaucracy*, New York: Free Press, 1954.

16 Victor Thompson, *Modern Organizations*, New York: Knopf, 1961.

17 Merton, 'Bureaucratic Structure and Personality'.

18 George A. Miller, 'Professionals in Bureaucracy: Alienation among Industrial Scientists and Engineers', *American Sociology Review*, October 1967, pp. 755–68.

19 See, for example, Chris Argyris, *Personality and Organization: The Conflict Between the System and the Individual*, New York: Harper & Rowe, 1957.

20 Victor Thompson, 'Bureaucracy and Innovation', *Administrative Science Quarterly*, 10, 1965, pp. 1–20.

21 William McKinley, 'Complexity and Administrative Intensity: The Case of Declining Organizations', *Administrative Science Quarterly*, March 1987, pp. 87–105.

22 See, for instance, the opening and closing case studies in this chapter and the case for class discussion in Chapter 4.

23 For a practical perspective on the centralisation–decentralisation dilemma, see Jack Welch, *Jack*, New York: Hodder Headline, 2001.

24 For examples, see the opening and closing cases in this chapter.

25 ibid.

26 Eric Substrom, *Workplaces: The Psychology of the Physical Environment in Offices and Factories*, Cambridge: Cambridge University Press, 1986.

27 G. Hamel & C.K. Prahalad, *Competing for the Future*, Boston: Harvard Business School Press, 1994.

28 Clark & Clegg, *Changing Paradigms: The Transformation of Management Knowledge for the 21st Century*.

29 Richard B. Chase & David Tansik, 'The Customer Contact Model of Organisational Design', *Management Science*, 29, 1983, pp. 1037–50.

30 Clarke & Clegg, *Changing Paradigms: The Transformation of Management Knowledge for the 21st Century*.

31 See opening and closing cases for examples of the application of market control.

32 Dawkins & Littler, *Downsizing: Is it right for Australia*.

33 W.H. Davidow & M.A. Malone, *The Virtual Corporation: Structuring and Revitalising the Corporation for the 21st Century*, New York: HarperCollins, 1992.

CHAPTER 11

Managing the environment

After reading this chapter you should be able to:

1 explain why management seeks to control its organisation's environment;

2 compare internal and external environment control strategies;

3 describe the most comprehensive action that management can take when faced with an unfavourable environment;

4 define environmental scanning;

5 identify several techniques for buffering the organisation from the input side;

6 explain how organisations smooth out fluctuations in the environment;

7 describe when an organisation would apply rationing;

8 differentiate between co-opting and coalescing;

Introduction

Western Metals ties up remote targets

Mining is a typically risky operation. Not only must minerals be found and mines developed and operated, but the price of minerals can vary widely depending on demand and supply. Western Metals is one of the many mid-sized Australian mining companies trying to make a living in a demanding environment such as this. At one point Western Metals decided it would no longer search for minerals: rather, it would develop its existing expertise in operating remote area mines and mineral-processing plants. This way it could form joint ventures or contractual arrangements with companies that had undertaken the risk of exploration while gaining the benefits of participating in the mining operation.

Although metals are a commodity, most mining companies sell to customers on an individual basis. Relationships with customers are therefore important in securing the best prices and reliable outlets for metal. Most of Western Metals customers are in Asia, so it has had to find a way to get behind the 'ASEAN wall'. It has done this by forming a joint venture with a Thai company, Padaeng Industry. Padaeng is a former government-owned mining company which has been privatised. Although Padaeng's mines were exhausted, it still operated a successful zinc smelter and was well connected with customers throughout the ASEAN region. Also, because of its former government ownership, Padaeng maintained close contacts with political decision makers in Thailand.

The tie-up with Padaeng offers benefits to Western Metals. It has an outlet for its metal concentrates, particularly zinc, in which it wants to be the dominant player in the ASEAN region. It has exposure to new mines in Thailand and its neighbours, which would not otherwise have been possible, and to these it can bring its expertise in remote area mining. Western Metals is working on similar deals in Indonesia and India. In each of these countries it has clear objectives: to secure markets, diversify operations, and expose itself to allied businesses in South-East Asia.[1]

Every organisation—regardless of the industry it is in or whether it is profit-seeking or not—faces some degree of environmental uncertainty. This is because no organisation is completely able to generate internally all the resources it needs to sustain itself.[2] Every organisation, for example, requires financial and human resources as inputs and clients or customers to absorb its outputs. But just because an organisation confronts environmental uncertainty does not mean that management must just accept what the environment has to offer. As the Western Metals case illustrates, there *are* things managers can do to lessen the impact of the environment on the organisation's operations. They can attempt to *manage* their environment![3]

Management's quest to control its environment

In Chapter 1 we acknowledged that organisations are open systems. Not only do they interact with their environment but this interaction is necessary for the organisation's viability and survival. But this environment is rarely static; it is constantly changing in unpredictable and uncertain ways. However, we know that managers don't like uncertainty.[4] They don't like being dependent on environments they have no influence over. This arises because if external threats actually come to pass, the existence of the organisation may be threatened. Steel mills without supplies of iron ore soon go out of business. Unstable customer bases provide uneven revenue streams, leading to financial risks. A charity without donations can no longer undertake its work. Major manufacturers who have invested heavily in production plant and employ large numbers of people are looking for stability in operations to meet their obligations. If management had its way, it would prefer to operate in a completely predictable and autonomous environment. In such a perfect world, there would be no need for contingency plans because there would be no surprises, and the organisation would be impervious to influences from other organisations and environmental threats. Yet all organisations face some uncertainty, and many environments are quite dynamic. It should not be surprising to find that managers want to reduce this uncertainty. But can the environment be managed?

The population-ecology perspective, presented in Chapter 8, argues that management cannot affect its environment. The environment is treated as a given and management is depicted as unable to influence it. But as we pointed out in our criticism of this theory, management does not accept environments as it finds them. Managers have discretion over the strategies they choose and the ways in which organisational resources are acquired and distributed. Also in a political sense, large and powerful organisations clearly have the means to shape major elements in their environment. Many of the actions of both unions and employer groups are aimed at uncertainty reduction. Further, markets have been developed that have enabled organisations to manage uncertainty. These include futures markets, for everything from metals to wool and computer chips, to hedging in financial markets.

This chapter stands as a counterpoint to the population-ecology view. Large organisations consistently demonstrate by their actions that they are not captives of their environments and that they do have the means to lessen their environmental dependence. They reduce labour uncertainty by locating their plant where there is an abundant supply of low-cost labour. They engage in joint ventures to lessen competition. They lobby politicians to support laws that benefit them and to defeat those that are perceived as detrimental. The larger an organisation is, the more resources, skills and influence it will typically have at its disposal. But environmental-management strategies are not available only to large and powerful organisations. Many of the techniques we will discuss can be, and are, used by small and uninfluential organisations. But keep in mind that large size is positively associated with increased power to reduce environmental uncertainty.[5]

Classifying strategies

In very simplistic terms, managers have two general strategies they can adopt in their attempt to lessen environmental uncertainty. They can respond by adapting and changing organisational practices to better fit the environment, or they can attempt to alter the environment to fit better with the organisation's capabilities. The former approach we call internal strategies and the latter external strategies.

Internal strategies are those which adapt and change organisational practices to better fit the environment. When management selectively cuts prices or recruits

internal strategies
managers adapt and change organisational practice to better fit the environment

TABLE 11.1 Internal and external strategies

Internal strategies	External strategies
Domain choice	Bridging
Recruitment	Advertising
Environmental scanning	Contracting
Buffering	Co-opting
Smoothing	Coalescing
Rationing	Lobbying
Improving information processing	Insuring
Geographic disperson	Hedging and futures markets

executives from its competitors, it is making internal adjustments to its environment. The environment does not change, but the fit between the organisation and the environment is improved. The result is that the organisation's dependence on the environment is reduced.

External strategies are efforts designed actually to *change* the environment. If competitive pressures are cutting an airline's profitability, it can merge with another airline to gain a more synergistic network of routes. If changes suggested in a tax reform proposal threaten a small life insurance company, it might use its membership of a trade association to lobby against the tax changes.

Using the internal–external dichotomy, we can categorise a number of uncertainty-reduction techniques. Table 11.1 summarises the internal and external strategies that we will now elaborate on.

external strategies
management alters the environment to fit better with the organisation's capabilities

Internal strategies

Management does not actually have to change the environment in order to lessen the organisation's dependence on it. The following internal strategies demonstrate that there are actions that almost any organisation—the small as well as the large—can take to match it better with its environment and, in so doing, lessen the impact of the environment on the organisation's operations.

Domain choice

Domain refers to that part of the environment in which the organisation operates. Organisations make deliberate choices as to which domain they operate in. The most comprehensive action that management can take when faced with an unfavourable environment is to change to a domain with less environmental uncertainty.[6] Management could, for instance, consider staking out a niche that has the advantages of fewer or less powerful competitors; barriers that keep other competitors out as a result of high entry costs, economies of scale or regulatory approval; little regulation; numerous suppliers; a single enterprise union; or less powerful public-pressure groups. Unfortunately, because there are not many opportunities for organisations to become unregulated monopolies, most domain-choice decisions substitute one set of environmental uncertainties for another.

Multidivisional companies have a greater ability to withstand changes in their environments than single-divisional companies. For instance, Wesfarmers operates in fertilisers, hardware distribution and agricultural services, among others. However, OPSM has chosen to stake its future existence on the provision of eyewear. Should powerful new entrants enter the market, or surgery reduce the need for eyewear, then OPSM will face a greatly reduced market for its products.

If management cannot change to a more favourable domain, it may choose to broaden its strategy to take a generalist format.[7] Both David Jones and Coles Myer are in the retail business. But whereas David Jones is focused on serving upmarket department store customers, Coles Myer caters to a far wider spread of shoppers and their needs. Both Coles Myer department store chains of Grace Bros and Myers compete directly with David Jones. But if the spending of this category of customers dropped, Coles Myer would be less affected than David Jones. This is because it has interests in discount stores, through Kmart and Target, and in Coles supermarkets. Because of this we would therefore expect Coles Myer to be less affected by changes in any one particular category of sales.

Alternatively, small professional firms with specific skills, such as IT companies or consultants of various types, specifically select an environmental domain that matches their knowledge and capabilities. One of the greatest threats they face is taking on a consultancy or task for which they lack the skills.

Recruitment

The recruitment of the right people can lessen the influence of the environment on the organisation. Corporations can hire executives with skills that the company does not already possess. Merchant banks entice foreign exchange dealers and those with specialist skills with offers of large salaries and fringe benefits. Senior public servants with experience in immigration are eagerly sought by immigration consultants because of their contacts within government. On their retirement from the armed forces, senior officers are often employed by defence contractors because of their knowledge of the operations of the defence establishment. High-tech firms entice scientists from other companies to gain the technical expertise possessed by their competitors. The idea behind such action is to provide the organisation with skills that can cope with environmental uncertainty.

Environmental scanning

Environmental scanning entails scrutinising the environment to identify actions by competitors, government, unions and the like that might impinge on the organisation's operations. Scanning activities also include predicting levels of economic activity and undertaking research to determine changes in fashions and demand patterns. To the extent that this scanning can lead to accurate forecasts of environmental fluctuations, it can reduce uncertainty. It allows management to anticipate changes and make internal adjustments rather than react after the fact. The manufacturing firm that can correctly anticipate changes in demand for its products can plan or schedule the operations of its technical core ahead of time and thereby minimise the impact of these changes. Similarly, the consulting firm that can forecast

environmental scanning scrutinising the environment to identify actions by factors that might impinge on the organisation's operations

accurately which contracts it will win during the next six months is better prepared, in having the right number and mix of consultants available to handle these projects.

Those employees who scan the environment are called boundary spanners. **Boundary spanners** are people whose specific jobs require them to act as conduits between the organisation and its environment.[8] Boundary spanners function, in effect, as exchange agents between the organisation and the environment. Examples of typical boundary-spanning jobs include sales representatives, market researchers, purchasing managers, lobbyists, public relations specialists and recruitment specialists. On a broader scale, multinational firms, particularly those with operations in politically unstable areas of the world, are continuously scanning the environment to monitor risks to their operations.

What do those who occupy boundary-spanning roles do? They handle the transactions an organisation makes with its environment, filter inputs and outputs into a form that can be understood, search and collect information, represent the organisation to the environment, and protect and buffer the organisation: 'It is through the reports of boundary agents that other organization members acquire their knowledge, perceptions and evaluations of organization environments. It is through the vigilance of boundary agents that the organization is able to monitor and screen important happenings in the environment.'[9]

Senior managers also regularly scan the environment to identify threats to and opportunities for their organisation. Every conversation they have with outsiders, often with insiders as well, concerns things that are happening or could happen to the organisation. Attendance at lunches, trade fairs, conferences and industry gatherings, and reading business journals, are other means of scanning the boundaries of the organisation. And for those firms operating internationally regional managers act as boundary spanners, feeding information to corporate headquarters.

Buffering

Buffering reduces the possibility that the organisation's operations will be disturbed by ensuring supplies and/or absorption of outputs. By buffering its operating core from environmental influences at the input or output side, management allows the organisation to operate as if it were a closed system.

On the input side, buffering is evident when organisations stockpile materials and supplies, use multiple suppliers, engage in preventive maintenance or recruit and train new employees. Each of these activities is designed to protect the operating function of the organisation from the unexpected. Oil refineries typically keep reserves of crude oil on hand to cover them in case of any interruptions to supply. The newspaper that buys newsprint from two or three different paper companies reduces its dependence on any one firm. Manufacturers stockpile parts in case of interruptions to supplies. Buffering can also be done with human resources. As organisations require trained personnel, their unavailability or lack of appropriate skills can mean a loss in productive efficiency. Management can meet this uncertainty through recruitment and training.

Buffering at the output level allows fewer options. The most obvious method is the use of inventories. If an organisation creates products that are not perishable, such as most manufacturers, then maintaining inventories in warehouses allows the organisation to produce its goods at a constant rate, regardless of fluctuations in sales demand. Toy manufacturers, for example, typically ship most of their products

boundary spanners people who operate at the periphery of the organisation, performing orgainsationally relevant tasks, and relating the organisation to elements outside it

buffering protecting the operating core from environmental variations in supply and demand

to retailers in early October for selling during the Christmas season. These manufacturers, of course, produce their toys year-round and merely stockpile them for shipping during the three months before Christmas.

The growth in the number of casuals in the workforce over the past few years is another form of buffering. It has enabled organisations to better match the supply of labour with peaks and troughs in demand. It would be highly inefficient to maintain a full-time catering workforce if the company's main business was providing food and beverages at weekend sporting events. The major supermarkets have casuals they can call on at peak times. Manufacturers often use labour hire firms to carry out their annual maintenance shutdowns or unanticipated breakdowns. By maintaining casuals in the workforce, an organisation can be more confident of being able to meet fluctuations in demand.

Buffering provides benefits by reducing environmental uncertainties. We would predict management's tendency to buffer to be related directly to the degree of routinisation in the organisation's technology. Where work is routine, such as manufacturing motor cars, it is possible to predict what the inputs into the system will be. As a result, we would expect buffering to be a popular strategy. However, the benefits must be appraised against the costs. The more obvious costs are those involved in warehousing the product and the risk of obsolescence inherent in stockpiling. Buffering is also of more use to those in manufacturing and those dealing in tangible products. It is difficult to buffer services; other uncertainty-reducing mechanisms may be used for this group of industries.

Smoothing

Smoothing seeks to level out the impact of fluctuations in the environment. This mechanism is commonly used in service industries, where the product cannot be placed into inventory. Organisations that use this technique include telecommunication companies, retail stores, car rental companies, magazines and sports clubs. The heaviest demand on intercity telephone equipment is by business between the weekday hours of 8.00 am and 5.00 pm. Telstra has to have enough equipment to meet peak demand during that period. But the equipment is still there during the rest of the time, with most of it under used. So Telstra smooths demand by charging its highest prices during the peak period and using low rates to encourage you to call relatives and friends during the evenings and at weekends. Airlines similarly use smoothing to charge more for travel during peak demand times. This is why you pay more to travel to Europe during July than when demand is lower during February and November, and why it is almost impossible to get a discount fare between Sydney and Melbourne at 8 o'clock on a weekday morning.

Retail clothing stores know that their slowest months are January (following the Christmas rush) and July (mid-winter). To reduce this 'trough' in the revenue curve, retail stores typically run their sales at these times of the year. Car rental companies make extensive use of smoothing. The same car that rents for $60 a day during the week is often half that price at the weekend. The reason is that business people are heavy users of rental cars during the week. Rather than have the cars sit idle at weekends, the rental companies smooth demand by cutting prices. Magazine publishers often give you a substantial discount—sometimes up to 50% off newsstand prices—if you take a subscription. This enables them to better predict their demand. Cut-price Tuesdays in cinemas is another example of buffering. Tuesday is

smoothing levelling out the impact of fluctuations in the environment by offering incentives to environmental units to regularise their interactions with the organisation

a very slow day in the entertainment business, so reducing prices gives patrons an incentive to visit the picture theatre in off-peak times.

Rationing

rationing the allocation of organisational products or services according to a priority system

When uncertainty is created by way of excess demand, management may consider **rationing** products or services—that is, allocating output according to some priority system. Examples of rationing can be found in hospitals, universities, post offices and restaurants. Hospitals often ration beds for non-emergency admissions. And when a disaster strikes— a major accident, fire or flood—beds are made available only to the most serious cases. University administrators often use rationing to allocate students to popular programs. In recent years, for instance, the demand for business courses has exceeded the supply of places available at many universities. In response, entrance requirements have often been raised as a way to limit demand. The post office resorts to rationing. Priority-paid mail takes precedence and lesser classes are handled on an 'as-available' basis. It is not unusual for better restaurants to require reservations. The use of reservations acts to both ration and smooth demand for tables.

Improving information processing

One of the main causes of uncertainty is lack of information. If it is possible to improve the flow of information, uncertainty will decrease. Modern information technologies allow us to gather large amounts of data and, using appropriate software, process it into a format that can assist managers to respond to environmental changes with minimum impact on the operating core. Airlines provide a good example of this. One of their key functions is yield management. This function constantly monitors forward bookings in order to know when to offer, or not offer, discounted flights, how many seats to allocate to each class of traveller, and whether timetables should be rearranged. Through identifying trends well before time, airlines can respond with minimum disruption to their schedules while maximising returns. Other examples are the monitoring of consumer goods sales in supermarkets and stores to immediately identify which lines are popular and which are slow-selling, software that allows shipments to be tracked so as to improve accuracy of delivery time, and inventory control software that reduces the likelihood of any particular item being out of stock.

Geographical dispersion

Environmental uncertainty sometimes varies with location. There is clearly more political uncertainty for a business firm operating in Port Moresby than for one operating in Townsville. To lessen location-induced uncertainty, organisations can move to a different community or lessen risk by operating in multiple locations.

Mining companies are an obvious example of spreading risk through geographic uncertainty. A mining company that had all of its operations in Indonesia, for instance, would be considered to have a higher risk profile than one that operated in any number of countries around the world.

Regional centres often promote themselves as being desirable places in which to locate manufacturing facilities because of their ability to reduce uncertainty. This ability is mainly due to the fact that the workforce there is more stable than that to be found in large cities, where there are more employment opportunities. Also, there are often lower rates of unionism in regional centres. And these centres promote their slower pace of living and shorter commuting times as leading to less workforce stress.

External strategies

We now turn to strategies that seek to change the environment directly to make it more favourable for an organisation. These include everything from the use of advertising to shape consumer tastes to illegal agreements with a rival to restrict competition.

Bridging

Bridging refers to the process by which managers endeavour to regulate their environments through negotiation, cooperation, exchange of information and other forms of mutual benefit.[10] It is the social actions undertaken by managers, and others, to create a supportive environment for the organisation, to sense threats and opportunities and to create obligations and favours, which can be called in when needed. Bridging may include such actions as building personal relationships with managers in supplying or distributing companies, sharing information, attendance at industry and chambers of commerce meetings, and being a member of golf or social clubs patronised by the well-connected. Bridging is essentially a political process, where the use of personal relationships is important for reducing uncertainty.

bridging the process by which managers endeavour to regulate their environments through negotiation, cooperation, exchange of information and other forms of mutual benefit

Advertising

Unilever spends tens of millions of dollars each year to promote Streets ice cream, Rexona products, Flora margarine, John West foods and dozens of other products. Through extensive advertising, Unilever's management seeks to reduce competitive pressures, stabilise demand, and allow itself the opportunity to set prices with less concern for the response of its competitors.

The organisation that can build brand loyalty has lessened its dependence on consumers. So regardless of the brand-name product or service—whether it's a Sony video recorder, the American Express card, Diet Coke, Ford motor vehicles, Gilette razors or Comet overnight delivery—when you see it actively promoted through advertising, keep in mind that this advertising is a device that management uses to reduce its dependence on fickle consumers and new alternatives offered by competitors.

Perhaps the classic example of advertising creating a following and sustaining demand for a product over time is Panadol. Panadol is paracetamol, a common analgesic sold under many brand names, and even under no brand in the case of generic products. Yet the manufacturer of Panadol has convinced a significant part of the paracetamol-buying public that Panadol is superior to its competitors and justifies a price considerably higher than that of generic brands.

Contracting

Contracting protects the organisation from changes in quantity or price on either the input or output side. For instance, management may agree to a long-term fixed contract to buy materials and supplies or to sell a certain part of the organisation's output. Brick manufacturers sign long-term contracts with gas suppliers in order to

contracting protects the organisation from changes on quantity or price on either input or output

secure supplies of gas at specified prices. A major detergent manufacturer may contract to sell to a large discount chain 2000 cases a month of its standard detergent, which will be marketed under the chain's private label. This assures the detergent manufacturer of a certain level of sales and reduces its dependence on the fluctuating preferences of consumers. An office block developer may sign a multi-million-dollar contract with a builder which (perhaps) provides legal certainty that the builder will complete the task. Banks and other lenders to resource developers want to see long-term sale contracts in place before they will finance a new mine or gas field.

Co-opting

co-opting the absorption of those individuals or organisations that threaten a given organisation's stablity

Organisations may resort to **co-opting** their uncertainties—that is, absorbing those individuals or organisations in the environment that threaten their stability. This is most often done in business firms through selective appointments to the organisation's board of directors.

Research demonstrates that the composition of a corporation's board can be explained by considering the organisation's requirements for various types of environmental support.[11] For example, it is common for firms with a need for finance to appoint a finance expert to the board. Those companies operating in overseas locations generally have a local board with representatives from the overseas country. This draws on people with local expertise and knowledge, and provides points of contact in the event of problems in the operation. The local directors often have strong political or business connections.

Boards of companies and statutory authorities can also reduce criticism of their operations by co-opting to the board representatives of various groups that may be critical of that organisation. In many cases this is done by setting up advisory committees which include, for instance, environmentalists and local community groups. Where the rights of indigenous people are likely to be affected by a mine, influential local people are appointed to advise the mining venture. This not only serves to provide valuable information to the company as to how it should conduct its affairs in the community's area—it also helps to blunt criticism that it is riding roughshod over the rights of local people. And education bodies use co-opting techniques when determining school curricula. Typically such bodies include representatives of all interest and lobby groups. The reason for this is that any criticism a particular lobby group may have is blunted because of their membership of the board.

interlocking directorate two or more organisations having one or more directors in common

The **interlocking directorate**, where two or more organisations share one or more directors, has been described as the most widely used environmental management strategy.[12] There is no shortage of studies that seek to explain the prevalence of interlocks and the benefits they can provide to management.[13] A study carried out in 1983, which investigated the extent of common directorships in the largest publicly listed companies on the Australian Stock Exchange, found that the holding of directorships in two or more companies was common.[14] A total of 73% of directors were permitted to sit on the boards of other companies, with 64% of directors holding positions on other boards. Some directors sat on the boards of over nine companies. On average, the chairmen of the boards sat on 4.3 other boards, with one chairman sitting on 54 other boards.

Why are interlocking directorates so popular? The general answer is that they co-opt market constraints. More specifically, it has been argued that they can facilitate coordination between and among organisations; provide useful expertise; and enhance the organisation's reputation.[15] Horizontally interlocked organisations— that is, those operating in the same industry—can gain advantages through pricing, advertising, and research and development. They can act as an informal means of coordinating plans between organisations. Such interlocks, however, can violate trade practices laws. Vertical coordination, such as often exists between a firm and one of its suppliers, increases the likelihood that needed resources will be available. Sometimes this interlocking is reinforced with shareholdings in each other's companies. Expertise is provided when outside directors hold information about other organisations or industry activities. This can help the focal organisation formulate its strategies more accurately. Finally, an organisation's reputation can be affected by whoever serves on its board and by those board members' organisational connections. Prestigious board members provide a more favourable image for the organisation and can attract sought-after customers, as well as avoid problems with financial institutions, government regulators and so on.

OT CLOSEUP
Sweet tooth appointment

A recent example of co-opting is the appointment of a dentist to head a group representing the Australian confectionery industry. Dr Stuart Spencer, a dentist, was appointed in 1988 to head the Confectionery Manufacturers of Australia, a Victorian-based lobby group.

The appointment was strongly criticised by the Australian Dental Association, which disputed the logic of having a dentist advocating confectionery. The president of the South Australian branch of the ADA stated that it was a fundamental belief among dentists that snack foods with a high sugar content were 'disastrous for teeth'. However, Dr Spencer claims that of greater importance for tooth decay is the time at which the snack is eaten, rather than the snack itself. He saw no conflict of interest, and has been so successful at his job that he has recently been appointed Asia-Pacific director for the international organisation of chocolate and confectionery manufacturers.

Source: Business Review Weekly, 16 April 1993, p. 53.

Coalescing

During the 1980s, hundreds of companies listed on Australian stock exchanges either merged or were taken over.[16] These mergers often brought about economies of scale by eliminating redundant administrative personnel and by providing opportunities for merging technical and managerial expertise. However, it would be naive to ignore the reality that many mergers reduce uncertainty by lessening interorganisational competition and dependence. Tooheys' merger with Castlemaine eliminated one player from the overcrowded beer market. The takeover of Blue Circle Southern Cement by Boral, its biggest customer, ensured that Boral was guaranteed supplies.

When an organisation combines with one or more other organisations for the purpose of joint action, this is called **coalescing**. Mergers and takeovers are an

coalescing the combining of an organisation with one or more organisations for the purpose of joint action

example. But so, too, are strategic alliances and joint ventures. Typical of joint ventures that are of benefit to both parties is the agreement between Ford and Mazda to produce the Ford Laser. The Ford Laser is basically a slightly modified Mazda 323. The agreement gives Mazda a wider spread of cars over which it can amortise its design costs, and certain economies in manufacture. Mazda can also capitalise on Ford's extensive marketing and distribution network. Ford in return obtains access to a proven dependable design, thus reducing the financial and engineering risk of introducing an entirely new model.

Mergers and strategic alliances are a legal means for an organisation to manage its environment, provided that it does not act as a restraint on trade. Strategic alliances are becoming increasingly common as companies seek to acquire skills and knowledge they do not have and which may be expensive or difficult to either buy or develop using internal resources. The small size of the Australian market means that no Australian manufacturer can produce a full range of cars. They therefore purchase lower-selling models from overseas affiliates and re-badge them under their own name. Opel in Germany and Holden take this even further. The Commodore is based on an Opel design which is adapted for Australian conditions. A further example can be seen in the airline industry. Airlines often code-share, which means that two airlines share the same flight with their own flight number, but only one airline makes the flight. This allows the airlines to offer greater frequency and a wider range of destinations without having to actually fly all the sectors. Often this arrangement is formalised through cross-shareholdings. Table 11.2 gives some examples of strategic alliances.

Another form of coalescing is moving up and down the supply chain. In doing this firms are able to control the supply chain from raw materials to customers (e.g. the former BHP-owned iron ore and coal mines, ships to transport raw materials, blast furnaces, rolling mills, divisions that transformed semi-finished product into such items as wire and building shapes, and steel merchants that distributed the final product). This process is called vertical integration, and its main aim is to reduce the uncertainty arising from other organisations controlling essential inputs or distribution facilities. While still practised to a certain extent, it greatest flaw was the inability to achieve best practice at each of the production stages. This often led to higher prices and lower rates of innovation.

TABLE 11.2 Examples of recent strategic alliances

Warner Bros/Village Roadshow	Cooperation in developing multiplexes worldwide
Qantas/British Airways	Flight sharing on Australia/UK Route
University of Technology, Sydney/ Taylor's College, Kuala Lumpur	Development of education facilities in Malaysia
Telstra/Pacific Century Cyber Works	Provision of mobile telephone services in Hong Kong
Shell/BHP/Woodside Petroleum	Development of gas deposits in the North West Shelf

Some coalescing acts are illegal. Agreements to fix prices, share markets, restrict entry or form monopolies are not permitted under the *Trade Practices Act*. All of these actions were common until the early-1970s laws were passed, making them illegal.

Lobbying

There are few industries that do not have their trade associations. These associations have a number of purposes, such as acting as a focal point for the dissemination of knowledge and negotiating in industrial relations matters. One of their main purposes, however, is to **lobby** members of parliament and other significant interest groups to ensure that the industry's voice is heard. The lobbying of members of parliament to ensure favourable legislation has become such an accepted practice that lobbyists in Canberra must now be registered and maintain records of the organisations for which they act. Lobbying—using influence to obtain a favourable outcome—is widely practised by organisations to manage their environment.

Whenever protection levels for the textile, clothing and footwear industry are being reviewed, the lobby group becomes active in presenting the industry's case with the Industry Commission and politicians. Other examples of lobby groups are the Tobacco Institute and the Australian Shooting Association, which seek to reduce the uncertainties that might affect the tobacco and gun interests respectively. Some organisations even use the power of government to stabilise relationships in an industry. Doctors, dentists, lawyers and other professional bodies lobby state licensing boards to restrict entry, regulate competition and enforce standards of conduct in order to keep their professions more stable. Educational institutions, hospitals, welfare associations, conservation coalitions and other single-interest groups regularly lobby parliamentarians and others to influence them to pass legislation, or to frame the budget, in their interest. Many employ specialist lobbying firms with inside information on the bureaucracy to give their lobbying efforts maximum impact.

> **lobbying** using influence on an external party to achieve favourable outcomes for an organisation

Insuring

Organisations face many risks which are unlikely to eventuate, but which may be catastrophic if they do. Such risks may arise from a building catching fire, accidents, acts of nature such as lightning strikes, hailstorms and cyclones, riots or insurgency in overseas countries, and oil or chemical spills. Organisations also run the risk of being sued for public liability, industrial accidents, health issues and negligence of various types. Most of these events, apart from floods, can be insured against. Insurance markets grew out of individuals and organisations pooling their risk so that any one occurrence did not result in a catastrophic loss. From this beginning developed the complex insurance markets which organisations find indispensable for managing their risk. Insurance companies even insure themselves against an excessive level of claims through the reinsurance market.

Hedging and futures markets

With the deregulation of industries and commodity markets and the free floating of currencies, the level of uncertainty of many businesses has risen. New markets have consequently been developed in order to permit companies to manage the risk. Futures exchanges allow miners and commodity producers to lock in a price in advance of production and consumption. Exchange markets allow hedging against currency shifts. And investment fund managers can buy or sell shares in major companies in advance to avoid fluctuations in share prices. There are futures markets for products as diverse as electricity, wool, crude oil, aviation fuel, coffee, gold and microchips. Without such mechanisms, many companies would be unable to plan with any degree of confidence. Additionally, a significant part of an organisation's management time would be allocated to crisis management, which would be aimed at trying to ensure the organisation's survival rather than being spent on strategic matters affecting the organisation.

The use of hedging and futures markets is, however, not without risk. Predicting future states is fraught with difficulty, and many companies have lost (and gained) large amounts of money by guessing that markets would move in certain directions. There is the further problem of 'rogue traders' making large, sometimes unauthorised bets on future product prices. Barings Bank was forced into bankruptcy by one such trader betting on moves in the Nikkei Index. Nevertheless, provided they are used to reduce uncertainty, rather than as a racecourse betting ring or a casino gambling table, futures and hedge markets are a valuable complement to living in an uncertain environment.

Guidelines for managing the environment

Success in managing the environment requires analysing the source of uncertainty and then selecting a strategy that the organisation can effectively implement. As we noted at the beginning of the chapter, large size facilitates environmental influence. Certainly, Telstra and Kodak are going to have more clout in controlling their relationships with suppliers than are a small telephone supplier or a local business offering one-hour film developing. Yet most of the strategies presented in this chapter have wide applicability.

Table 11.3 presents some actions that managers can take to reduce environmental uncertainty. The examples of strategic actions are only examples; they don't purport to be *all* or the *only* options available to management. But they all share the basic premise that organisations are not just passive receivers of environmental influence. The influence works both ways; organisations in turn manage their environments to reduce uncertainty.

In this chapter we can also see the influences at work that we identified in Chapter 9 in discussing power and politics in organisations. Through reducing uncertainty by the mechanisms we have identified, managers create a more stable internal environment. As a result they can maintain structures that are more mechanistic and centralised, thus reinforcing their power. Managers can also justify their claim to senior positions within the organisation by an ability to understand and control external environments. There would be few CEOs who did not claim to be able to understand and respond to environmental opportunities and threats.

Summary

Every organisation faces some degree of environmental uncertainty. However, in contrast with the population-ecology view that organisations are powerless to affect their environments, this chapter has sought to demonstrate that management can reduce the impact of environmental uncertainty on the organisation.

TABLE 11.3 Matching sources of uncertainty with strategic actions

Source	Examples of strategic actions
Government	Lobby for favourable treatment
	Recruit former government officials
	Commission research to influence government
	Relocate to a different state or country
Competition	Advertise to build brand loyalty
	Select a less competitive domain
	Merge with competition to gain larger market share
	Negotiate a cooperative agreement with competition
Unions	Negotiate a long-term enterprise agreement
	Develop a single-union plant
	Build facilities in countries with a large, low-cost labour supply
	Appoint prestigious union official to board of directors
Suppliers	Use multiple suppliers
	Inventory critical supplies
	Negotiate long-term contracts
	Vertically integrate through merger
Financial institutions	Appoint financial executives to board
	Establish a line of credit to draw on when needed
	Diversify by co-opting a financial institution
	Use multiple financial sources
Customers	Advertise
	Use a differentiated price structure
	Ration demand
	Change domain to where there are more customers
Public pressure groups	Appoint critics to board
	Recruit critics as employees
	Engage in visible activities that are socially conscious
	Use trade association to counter criticism

There are essentially two approaches available to management. The first is to adapt and change its actions to fit the environment. These are internal strategies and include changing domain, recruiting executives and technical specialists with links to the environment, scanning the environment to anticipate changes, buffering the operating core, smoothing out fluctuations in demand, rationing products or services, and geographical dispersion. The second approach is to alter the environment to fit better with the organisation's capabilities. These are external strategies such as advertising, contracting with suppliers or customers, co-opting individuals or organisations through absorption, coalescing with other organisations, and lobbying to achieve favourable outcomes. Organisations also use financial instruments and hedge markets in order to reduce uncertainty. While technically only external strategies change the environment, both types of strategies together create the techniques that we say are available for *managing the environment.*

For review and discussion

1   Contrast the population-ecology view of organisations with this chapter's theme.

2   Why do organisations seek to manage their environment?

3   Which strategies—internal or external—are more likely to involve interorganisational cooperation? Why?

4   Contrast the advantages of both specialist and generalist strategies.

5   Who are boundary spanners? What role do they play in managing environmental uncertainty?

6   How does smoothing reduce environmental uncertainty?

7   Is managing the environment illegal? Explain.

8   Is product differentiation a strategy for reducing environmental uncertainty? Explain.

9   Compare co-opting and coalescing.

10 What advantages accrue to an organisation whose board members are widely interlocked with other organisations?

11 Is it easier for a profit-making business to manage its environment than it is for a non-profit-making organisation?

12 Is it easier for a manufacturing organisation to manage its environment than it is for a service organisation?

13 What do you think are the major environmental uncertainties for each of the following organisations:

(a) a radio station?

(b) a car dealer?

(c) a university bookshop?

(d) a law firm?

(e) a large home-building firm?

14 Explain how the management of each of the previous organisations might attempt to manage its environment.

15 Why may it be more attractive to managers to manage their environment rather than adapt the organisation to the environment?

CASE FOR CLASS DISCUSSION
Westfield and its environment

Just about everyone would be familiar with Westfield shopping centres. The red Westfield signs are a common sight in Australian suburbia and most people would visit a Westfield shopping mall on a regular basis. The company has come to dominate the Australian shopping centre scene by a combination of canny management and street smart lobbying. The management of Westfield has developed a successful strategy of selecting top class retailers for their malls and then charging premium rents. Westfield can do this because in return it can offer retailers top quality space in well located and maintained centres with high levels of passing pedestrian trade. Part of the strategy is to ensure that there is a full range of retailers in the centre so that shoppers need only visit one mall to do all their shopping. In doing this, Westfield manages to earn more income per square metre of area than comparable shopping centres.

Westfield's formula has been successfully exported. Building upon the expertise built up in Australia, it has a major operation in the United States, and recently bought most of the portfolio of the Dutch shopping centre operator Rodamco. It is also expanding its operations in Europe. The overseas expansion allows it to spread its risks over a number of countries as well as permitting far higher rates of growth than could be wrung from the small Australian market. Because many of the unitholders in the property trust which owns the US centres are Australian based, Westfield has hedged its currency exposure in order to provide a more predicable flow of income. However, investing overseas is not without its own risk. Westfield was the main retail tenant in the basement of the World Trade Center in New York and suffered considerable loss in the terrorist bombing of the building. Most of its losses were covered by its insurance policies. Westfield has financed its overseas expansion mainly by drawing upon the Australian capital market. Its long run of rising share price and record profits has meant that there is no shortage of financiers willing to subscribe new capital or provide loans.

The company is no shrinking violet when it comes to protecting its own interests. Although the shopping malls are solid enough and loom over the surrounding areas as monuments to consumerism, the changing nature of business means that the location where people do their shopping is continuously evolving. Retailers at Westfield pay high rents for the benefits of location, but some retailers now want larger areas at cheaper rents than Westfield is prepared to offer. Examples are the large hardware stores and bulky goods warehouses which sell furniture and electrical appliances. Seconds stores and factory outlets are also looking for large, low cost retail areas. Most of

these types of operations set up in industrial areas which have been rezoned for retail activities.

Sensing the challenge that the new retail formats present to Westfield, the company has been actively lobbying politicians and public servants in an attempt to keep all retail activity close to public transport and prevent the rezoning of industrial land to retail activity. If successful, this would have the effect of forcing the bulky goods stores to set up in shopping malls such as Westfield's with resulting increases in prices and a restricted range of products.

Westfield also has its competitors in the shopping centre industry. The financial success of a shopping centre in many cases relies on having a monopoly in a certain geographic area. Often land shortages provide well located centres with a commanding position. But the zoning of land is a political decision and Westfield actively lobbies to keep direct competition to a minimum. Occasionally it crosses the boundary of legitimate lobbying to unethical behaviour. During 1999 it undertook an extensive campaign based on non-existent resident groups to successfully block a development in Sydney's Concord which would have posed a direct threat to Westfield's nearby Burwood development. The managing director of Westfield, Frank Lowy, subsequently apologised for the incident.

Some of the material for this case study was drawn from Robert Harley Kirela, 'Graduates From the School of Hard Knocks', *The Australian Financial Review*, 4 February 2000, p. 73 and Turi Condon, 'Westfield at Large', *Business Review Weekly*, 24 January 2002, p. 32.

QUESTIONS

1 Identify as many instances as you can of the ways in which Westfield controls its environment. Link them to the categories identified in this chapter.

2 Discuss the importance to Westfield of managing its environment.

3 Do you consider that when a firm engages in managing its environment it is contributing to its long-term effectiveness? Provide arguments to support your position.

FURTHER READING

Howard E. Aldrich, *Organizations and Environments*, Englewood Cliffs, NJ: Prentice-Hall, 1979.

Richard Leifer & André Delbecq, 'Organizational/Environmental Interchange: A Model of Boundary Spanning Activity', *Academy of Management Review*, January 1978, pp. 40–1.

Christine Oliver, 'Strategic Response to Institutional Processes', *Academy of Management Review*, 16, 1991, pp. 145–79.

Jeffrey Pfeffer & Gerald Salancik, *The External Control of Organizations: The Resource Dependence Perspective*, New York: Harper & Row, 1978.

NOTES

1 See Tim Treadgold, 'Thai Tie Tees Up Remote Targets', *Business Review Weekly*, 5 February 1996, pp. 22–30.

2 Howard E. Aldrich, *Organizations and Environments*, Englewood Cliffs, NJ: Prentice-Hall, 1979, p. 266.

3 Jeffrey Pfeffer, 'Beyond Management and the Worker: The Institutional Function of Management', *Academy of Management Review*, April 1976, pp. 36–46; and Jeffrey Pfeffer & Gerald R. Salancik, *The External Control of Organizations: The Resource Dependence Perspective*, New York: Harper & Row, 1978.

4 William R. Dill, 'Environment as an Influence on Managerial Autonomy', *Administrative Science Quarterly*, March 1958, pp. 409–43.

5 John Kenneth Galbraith, *The New Industrial State*, Boston: Houghton Mifflin, 1967.

6 See, for example, James D. Thompson & William J. McEwen, 'Organizational Goals and Environment: Goal-Setting as an Interaction Process', *American Sociological Review*, February 1958, pp. 23–31.

7 John H. Freeman & Michael T. Hannan, 'Niche Width and the Dynamics of Organizational Populations', *American Journal of Sociology*, May 1983, pp. 1116–45.

8 Richard Leifer & André Delbecq, 'Organizational/Environmental Interchange: A Model of Boundary Spanning Activity', *Academy of Management Review*, January 1978, pp. 40–1.

9 Dennis W. Organ, 'Linking Pins Between Organizations and Environments', *Business Horizons*, December 1971, p. 74.

10 P. Neegard, 'Environment, Strategy and Management', *Accounting Proceedings of the Second European Symposium on Information Systems*, Versailles: HEC.

11 See, for example, Jeffrey Pfeffer, 'Size and Composition of Corporate Boards of Directors: The Organization and Its Environment', *Administrative Science Quarterly*, March 1972, pp. 218–28; and Mark S. Mizruchi & Linda Brewster Stearns, 'A Longitudinal Study of the Formation of Interlocking Directorates', *Administrative Science Quarterly*, June 1988, pp. 194–210.

12 Max H. Bazerman & F. David Schoorman, 'A Limited Rationality Model of Interlocking Directorates', *Academy of Management Review*, April 1983, p. 206.

13 See, for example, Johannes M. Pennings, *Interlocking Directorates,* San Francisco: Jossey-Bass, 1980; Beth Mintz & Michael Schwartz, 'The Structure of Intercorporate Unity in American Business', *Social Problems*, December 1981, pp. 87–103; Mark Mizruchi, *The Structure of the American Corporate Network*, Beverly Hills, CA: Sage, 1981; and Michael Ornstein, 'Interlocking Directorates in Canada: Intercorporate or Class Alliance?', *Administrative Science Quarterly*, June 1984, pp. 210–31.

14 Blair Hunt, 'Australian Public Company Board of Directors—1983 Survey', *Australian Director*, 14(4); and Survey of Directors in *Australian Business Monthly*, January 1992.

15 David Schoorman, Max Bazerman & R.S. Atkin, 'Interlocking Directorates: A Strategy for Reducing Environmental Uncertainty', *Academy of Management Review*, April 1981, pp. 243–51.

16 Steven Bishop, Peter Dodd & R.R. Officer, *Australian Takeovers: The Evidence*, Centre for Independent Studies, Sydney, 1987.

CHAPTER 12

Managing organisational change

After reading this chapter you should be able to:

1 define planned change;

2 distinguish between revolutionary and evolutionary change;

3 list factors that might precipitate a structural change;

4 describe the four categories of intervention strategies;

5 explain the three-step change process;

6 describe organisational designs that foster innovation;

7 explain why stability, not change, characterises most organisations;

8 discuss how unplanned change may be managed.

Introduction

Kodak and the introduction of digital technology

The greatest challenge an organisation can face is that of the obsolescence of its basic technology. Photographic companies such as Kodak are now facing that with the growing popularity of digital photography. It's not that Kodak was caught unawares by the new technology: it was actually one of the earliest in the field.[1] But shifting the focus of the company from its traditional film and cameras to something radically new tested the powers and wisdom of management. Growth of the traditional film line of business was almost non-existent but it was extremely profitable. But although sales of the new technology was growing, it was only a very small part of the business and was losing large amounts of money. The profits from the old line of business were used to fund the new. This created two groups in the company—those who were associated with the old technology, and those who were hitching a ride on the new and were getting all the attention. Inevitably conflict developed, with each division having its own agenda.

There are some economies to be had from linking the old and new technology, so cooperation is necessary for digital to be a success. The CEO of Kodak, Daniel Carp, has set up a council of Kodak's six business heads and leaders of key staff groups to coordinate strategy. He has also formed a seven-member digital executive council, which regularly holds teleconferences to discuss strategy. Carp has had to address cultural issues. The old Kodak culture was called an 'entitlement culture': that is, one that is bureaucratic, with rewards depending on length of service and loyalty. Attempts are being made to change this to one that is performance-based in order to improve innovation and reduce resistance to change. Undertaking cultural change is never an easy task.

Kodak's transformation is painful. Not only must it take some big bets on new products, it must also manage a major organisational transformation. If Kodak can move from being a film dinosaur to a digital powerhouse it will be one of the few companies that have managed to successfully change their basic technology.

In the management literature, change has almost become an overworked cliché. It seems impossible to write a management book without the author exhorting us to dance the dance of change, adapt to a crazy world or envision a future that bears no resemblance to the present. It would be a brave writer who offered a prescription of the future based on stability and the established ways of doing things. It is not difficult to understand why change dominates management thinking. Most of us have lived through periods of significant environmental, regulatory and technological change, which have forced organisations radically to alter their structures and ways of doing things.

Effectiveness requires that organisations adapt appropriately to change. There is much that managers can do to facilitate change in their organisations; some of the most highly regarded managers are those who have instituted successful change programs. In this chapter we will look at how managers can actively promote change in their organisation. In keeping with the theme of this book, we will take an organisation-wide perspective rather than concentrating on individual responses.

An organisation-wide perspective means that we consider such factors as the environmental drivers of change, the allocation of tasks, and the processes adopted to promote change. The influence of change on an individual's behaviour is more appropriately considered in books dealing with organisational behaviour.

In this chapter, we will first consider the different types of organisational change. Then we will look at the environmental drivers of change, the indicators of an inappropriate structure, describe a model of change and how managers can promote innovation in organisations. We will also consider the issue of power and politics during the change process. It is not our intention to provide a comprehensive coverage of organisational change; that would take far more than one chapter to cover. Rather, we will concentrate on those issues which are relevant to the macro-approach we have adopted in this book.

The nature of change

Not all organisational change is the same. Some change alters the very nature of the organisation. Other changes may be minor and confined to one department or only part of a department. It follows that the way in which change is managed depends on the type, origin and magnitude of the drivers of change. So, in order for us to fully understand the nature of change, it assists us to clarify the various forms that change may take. We will first consider the difference between revolutionary and evolutionary change, then discuss planned and emergent change.

Revolutionary and evolutionary change

Sometimes, fortunately not too often, organisations are faced with a change that alters their very nature. We call change of this magnitude *revolutionary change*. Mostly, revolutionary change emerges as a response to significant technological and environmental changes. Some examples of revolutionary change emerging from technological changes are the replacement of hot metal with electronic typesetting in newspapers, the introduction of containerisation in shipping, and the computerisation of banking. Changes in environments can also lead to revolutionary change. Deregulation and privatisation have changed the nature of a number of industries, such as electricity generation, water supply and airlines. Globalisation has had a similar effect, with heightened threats and opportunities and greater levels of competition. A further source of revolutionary change often arises as a result of mergers and acquisitions. When two companies are merged into one entity, new relationships and management systems must be established and a common way of doing things developed. Such programs are never easy to implement, and the resultant change is often traumatic.

All of these events have forced management to introduce a comprehensive organisational change program. Usually the *rate of change*, in contrast to the *magnitude of change*, has been such that managers have been able to plan the change program and have had the luxury of a buffer of time to introduce it. But it has resulted in the organisation looking radically different. Revolutionary change is often accompanied by redundancies and downsizing, shifts in power, changes in strategy and a new organisational structure. As a result of such change, employees must relate to each other in different ways, get used to new management practices and learn to use new technologies. They may also need to relate to customers in different ways. The disruption and emotional trauma caused by revolutionary change is such that it occurs only on an occasional basis. Once the organisation settles into its new pattern and people adapt to their new roles, it does not mean that change has stopped. Change then becomes evolutionary.

Evolutionary change describes ongoing minor changes that are incorporated in the existing organisational structure. Examples would be adapting to a new computer program, moving to team rather than individual responsibility, introducing a new time-keeping system and upgrading the existing production process. These changes can often be introduced at the level of a department or individual and consequently do not have an organisation-wide impact. All employees are used to these changes—memos advising that a manager now has widened responsibilities, that a person has been appointed to take on certain tasks, the IT department will now have a representative at each user department, or that someone has resigned and their responsibilities are being transferred to someone else. None of these changes are particularly significant by themselves but they are the normal way in which organisations consistently adapt to the changes around them. Without such changes, an organisation would soon stagnate and lose its fit with its environment. Most change is evolutionary change: it involves minor adjustments in response to circumstantial and opportunistic events.

Revolutionary and evolutionary change are not self-contained categories; they are end-points of a continuum. While it is quite easy to identify examples of both types of change, there will always be changes that have characteristics of both. As a result they will fall somewhere between the two extreme cases. Examples of change between the two extremes are McDonald's extending its product range, a rail system introducing a new type of locomotive, and a company installing new accounting software. In each of these cases staff had to adapt to new ways of doing things, but the nature of the work remained basically the same.

Figure 12.1 shows the contrast between evolutionary and revolutionary change. We identified in Chapter 4 a set of five basic structural configurations. Each of these

Figure 12.1 Contrast between evolutionary and revolutionary organisational change

Evolutionary change	Revolutionary change
Evolution ⟷	Revolution
Maintain equilibrium ⟷	Seek a new equilibrium
Change individual parts or departments ⟷	Transform entire organisation
Optimise existing structure and management ⟷	Generate new structure and management
Incrementally change existing production technology ⟷	Adopt radically new production technology
Improve existing products ⟷	Introduce path breaking new products

Source: Based on Alan D. Meyer, James D. Goes & Geoffrey R. Brooks, *Organizations in Disequilibrium: Environmental Jolts and Industry Revolutions*, in George Huber & William H. Glick, eds, *Organizational Change and Redesign*, New York: Oxford University Press, 1992, pp. 66–111.

configurations have a common and consistent set of elements. Revolutionary change often involves moving from one basic configuration to another. It is unlikely that an organisation would adopt a sustainable form that was not one of our basic configurations, because a hybrid form would lose its internal consistency and balance. When a significant change does occur, it will probably be comprehensive.[2]

This suggests to us that management would prefer to avoid change, if possible, because of its cost, disruptive impact and threat to management's control. If the organisation faces a dynamic environment, we would expect management first to try to reduce its dependence on that environment. However, even the largest and most powerful organisations cannot completely manage their environment, and so management's options are essentially two.[3] It can change incrementally as environments change: this will achieve environmental fit but create internal inconsistencies. The other option is to delay change until it is absolutely necessary and then make it comprehensive: this maintains internal consistency but at the price of having a poor environment–structure fit for a period.

The choice between these two options might be a dilemma if it weren't for management's preference for making as few changes as possible and the reality that management does not seek to maximise organisational effectiveness. Existing structures can be adapted to new situations with a few changes in responsibilities and reporting relationships. If the choice were between 'change' and 'no change', management would be expected to prefer the status quo; but that option is not always available. Management is going to have to accept some changes in order to maintain a 'satisficing' level of organisational effectiveness. However, when the choice is between continual change and the infrequent variety, the decision is easy. It selects the latter. As a result, most organisations are characterised by long periods of inertia, punctuated by brief periods of dramatic and comprehensive change.

There are always, of course, exceptions to every observation. Some organisations are characterised by managers running change programs seeking the perfect structural form. As we have noted in Chapter 4, there are a range of structures that will provide a similar outcome. Therefore, seeking the perfect structure would be a never-ending task. Other managers feel that unless change is ongoing, the organisation will submit to bureaucratic inertia and lose its effectiveness. Everyone therefore needs to be 'on the move' in the fight against sluggishness. While many managers are no doubt motived by genuine ideals in their fight against bureaucracy, a cynic may take the view that rarely does a program of perpetual change threaten the senior managers responsible for introducing it. It may indeed assist in entrenching their own position at the top of the organisation. This is particularly so if the CEO or senior manager is newly appointed and wants to make an early impression on the organisation.

Planned and unplanned change

Another way in which we can classify change is as to whether it is planned or unplanned. Planned change refers to situations in which organisations have adequate time to formulate a response to the drivers of change. An example of planned change is the introduction of new equipment. In this case, management can draw up schedules for installation of the equipment, undertake job redesign and reallocate management tasks. Management may not, of course, do this entirely successfully, but at least the opportunity for planning for the introduction of new equipment is present. The objective of planned change is to maintain the viability of the organisation and respond with minimum disruption and cost.

In contrast, unplanned change emerges as a response to an unanticipated threat or event. The impact on airlines, broking houses, insurance companies and others as a result of the World Trade Center attack is an example of unplanned change. Most of these companies survived in one form or another, but their ability to adapt was sorely tested. Perhaps less spectacular examples of unplanned change are machinery and computer breakdowns, the collapse of a major supplier or customer, the impact of weather such as drought or cyclone, and even the resignation or death of a critical person in the organisation (e.g. the chief executive). The unanticipated actions of competitors and introduction of technical innovations that threaten core activities are also examples of unplanned change. These include the impact of TV news services on newspapers, e-commerce on existing distribution channels and the effect of competition from road transport on railways.

An unwelcome takeover or merger proposal generally also leads to planned change. The organisation undertaking the takeover normally wants to impose its way of doing things, and often has a different strategy from that of the company being taken over. This normally results in changes being introduced, which often include changes in top management.

The collapse of Ansett illustrates the ultimate in unplanned change—that of insolvency. Insolvency, or the threat of it, means that change in one form or another is unavoidable and will take a form that is unanticipated. Responses may range from the dissolution of the company through to parts being sold off as stand-alone companies or in a merger with other organisations.

Categorising change

Through combining the two dimensions of change we can develop a matrix which assists us in categorising the various forms of change. This is important because the way we manage the type of change in each category varies. The matrix is shown in Figure 12.2, along with examples of the change we can expect in each quadrant. *Adaptive change* is the least difficult change to manage. It generally does not affect everyone in the organisation, and presents management with choice as to how and when it will be implemented. Management also has discretion as to the timing and nature of change and has the time to undertake extensive negotiation with affected parties. Schedules can be drawn up which allow for the orderly introduction of change. *Systemic change* is the type of change we are most used to reading about. It forms the basis of most management writing on change. It is organisation-wide and touches on most areas of the organisation's operations. It is planned change, however; it does not emerge from a shock to the system, but as management's response to changes in the environment or competitive position. It is often undertaken only after extensive consultation among senior management and the board of directors. Outside consultants are also often involved in discussions. Because of the enormous amount of effort and disruption caused by systemic change, it is undertaken only as a matter of necessity. While *transitory change* is unplanned, it is not necessarily unanticipated. Most commodity producers, such as those of metals and agricultural products, know that the price of the product is going to rise and fall. Key managers can leave and new competitors emerge. All of these require a response that normally involves some type of organisational change. But the change is not radical:

FIGURE 12.2 Change classification scheme

Magnitude of change / Anticipation of change	PLANNED	UNPLANNED
REVOLUTIONARY	**Systemic** Introduction of a major new technology Privatisation or deregulation Entry into a major new market	**Chaotic** Terrorist attack Failure of major supplier or customer Unanticipated hostile takeover
EVOLUTIONARY	**Adaptive** Updating computer systems Change in distribution methods Modifications to existing products	**Transitory** Sudden strike Major change in commodity prices Loss of key management personnel

downsizing, reallocating responsibility, and concentrating on reducing costs or increasing flexibility are typical responses. These may be unplanned but manageable in the sense that they are easily grasped and implemented. The final type of change, *chaotic change*, is every manager's worst nightmare. It is unanticipated, threatens the organisation's existence, and arrives so fast that adequate planning is not possible. It includes the activities of terrorists, unanticipated hostile takeovers, financial collapse, sudden loss of critical input or customers and accident or misadventure involving critical assets. Handling the situation entails management going into crisis mode.

In this chapter we will concentrate on planned change. Because organisations are open systems—dependent on their environments—and because the environment does not stand still, organisations must develop internal mechanisms to facilitate planned change. Change efforts that are planned—that is proactive and purposeful—are what we mean by *managing* change. It is also the type of change in which managers normally have sufficient time to anticipate the nature of the change and what its effects are likely to be. It is aimed at keeping the organisation current and viable. In keeping with the focus of this book, we will further concentrate our attention on structural change. This means that we will not consider the effects of change on individuals or their response to it; this area is best considered under the topic of organisational behaviour. Structural change is a specific part of the change process, which we will discuss in the next section. We briefly consider unplanned change later in the chapter.

What is structural change?

The types of change that management seeks to create are varied and depend on the target. At the individual level, managers attempt to affect an employee's behaviour.

Training, socialisation and counselling represent examples of change strategies that organisations use when the target of change is the individual. Similarly, management may use interventions such as sensitivity training, survey feedback and process consultation when the goal is to change group behaviour. Individual and group change, which is typically studied in organisational-behaviour courses, is outside the province of this text.

Our concern is with structural change. In this chapter, we focus on techniques that have an impact on the organisation's structural system. This means that we will be looking at changing authority patterns, access to information, allocation of rewards, technology and the like. The fact that behavioural-change considerations are not discussed should in no way diminish their importance. Managers can, and should, use behavioural techniques, along with structural techniques, to bring about change. Together, the two represent a complete 'tool kit' for managing change. However, in this text we concern ourselves solely with the structural side.

OT CLOSEUP

How the environment forced the pace of change at BHP

All organisations face change, but the forces for the status quo are stronger in long-established companies than in those which are relatively new. BHP, now BHP Billiton, as one of Australia's largest and oldest companies, has had to cope with considerable change over its existence. Unfortunately, given that environments are not static, no sooner does one round of change end than another commences. During the 1990s the forces for change built up in BHP's environment. In analysing the reasons why the senior management of BHP has been forced to confront the need for radical change, we can identify the following factors. You will notice that most of these forces for change are not the result of sudden shocks but have built up over a period of time.

Obsolete plant and equipment. Many of BHP's investments, particularly in steel, had reached the end of their economic lives, and new investment using radically new technologies was required. However, the returns on this new investment were often small.

Lower rates of inflation. BHP had traditionally tried to expand by 15% per year. But this depended on a relatively high rate of inflation to underpin the figures. Trying to maintain this growth rate with virtually zero inflation meant taking higher risks. BHP was caught by paying too much for acquisitions, such as Magma Copper, in order to maintain its traditional expansion rate. Mistakes such as these led to a reassessment of the adequacy of the present management.

Falling commodity prices. BHP is basically a producer of such commodities as mineral and energy products. The price of these commodities has been consistently falling in real terms, forcing BHP to constantly seek to lower production costs in order to maintain profitability.

Inadequate corporate governance. BHP suffered from trying to centre too many of its operations in its Melbourne headquarters. This led to a 'Melbourne club' attitude developing which was increasingly out of phase with the demands of a global company. Additionally, BHP developed a narrowly focused culture because it rarely hired management talent from outside. Few of its managers had worked elsewhere, and its board of directors similarly lacked diversity in outlook and an international focus.

Poor investment fund allocation. BHP is a divisionalised company, with divisions based on steel, copper, minerals and petroleum. Because of its age and technology, the steel division required large amounts of investment. The amount of money consumed by the steel division, which gave only modest returns, was made at the expense of other divisions, particularly petroleum. This prevented the other divisions from reaching their potential.

Dated approach to industrial relations. The company was slow to realise that the industrial relations environment had changed. It remained committed to a centralised, union-focused workplace when its competitors, particularly Rio Tinto, had reaped the productivity gains from individual contracts and enterprise bargaining.

Internal revolution. It is not surprising that management of the petroleum division was discontented with the pace of change at BHP. It is also not coincidental that the head of the petroleum division, John O'Connor, formerly from Mobil, was one of the few outsiders in BHP's senior management. He started a process of change by lobbying analysts and fund managers to pressure the senior ranks of BHP to spin off the petroleum division into a separately listed company. He also started a wider campaign to reform management at the company. His strong track record of producing results gave his

criticisms credibility, and BHP's board had to take notice.

Poor investment decisions. A number of bad investments by BHP ending up losing shareholders over $4 billion. It was clear that the whole process of decision making was inadequate and that major changes in staff and systems were necessary to avoid a repetition.

The financial losses were the final straw for shareholders. An outsider, Paul Anderson, was appointed with the brief to bring the company more into line with its peers, such as Rio Tinto. This involved freshening up management practices. Most of the old management associated with the poor decisions was retired, the head office slimmed down, and a new culture with less stress on hierarchy was promoted. BHP also felt that it needed to get bigger in order to attract more investor interest, particularly from the northern hemisphere, and in 2001 it merged with Billiton to form BHP Billiton. In doing this, it passed most management control to the Billiton team.

Drawn from: Anne Hyland, 'Unrest Flares in BHP's Ranks', *The Sydney Morning Herald*, 7 August 1997, p. 27; and Elizabeth Knight, 'Top Performer Held in Check', *The Sydney Morning Herald*, 8 August 1997, p. 25.

What makes you think that you may need a new structure?

Many of the problems and challenges that beset organisations do not necessarily require a structural change. For problems such as poor morale, high absenteeism or inadequate skill levels, changing the structure may even make existing problems worse rather than better. So what are the indications that a new structure may be called for? We can summarise these in the following three areas.[4]

1 *Decision making is slow or inappropriate.* There may be a number of structural causes for this problem. One of the most common is that the appropriate information is not reaching the right person or group at the right time. Another cause may be that the wrong people may be making the decision, or it is being made at an incorrect level in the organisation. The input of important or knowledgeable people may not be sought, or there may be too many people who must agree on the decision. The extent of delegation may not suit the situation. Decision makers may be overloaded, not allowing them enough time to consider issues and gather

the appropriate information. Or decision makers may not have latitude to make the decision they feel is appropriate: they must abide by inflexible rules. Another decision-making problem experienced in many organisations is that too many managers are given the authority to say 'no' but not enough are permitted to say 'yes'. Decisions may therefore be easily blocked and inertia in decision making sets in. Overcoming this problem may involve changing reporting relationships, or the way that information is processed. It may involve hiring people with specific skills or removing superfluous people or departments. Job responsibilities may need rewriting.

However, if the problem is that of the inadequacies of an individual, then the structure should not be changed to adapt to that individual. People problems need people solutions.

2 *The organisation is not responding innovatively to environmental change.* Indications of this may be that the organisation's products may be out of date or technologically behind competing products. Other companies may be able to bring products to market faster or more cheaply. Important demographic changes may be overlooked. The company may not be keeping up with changing fashions or consumption patterns. Important changes, such as the low inflationary environment or the globalisation of business, may not be understood and consequently the organisation is unprepared for their impact. This indicates that the organisation's structure is not adequately monitoring these changes or that mechanisms do not exist to incorporate them in the decision-making process. Structural changes may therefore be called for to align responsibilities with important organisational needs, or to improve communication channels.

3 *All important tasks should have someone responsible for them.* Environments change over time, and each important segment of the environment should have someone responsible for dealing with it. The rise of environmental specialists and Aboriginal liaison officers in mining companies is relatively recent. Without constant monitoring of these sectors, mining companies would very soon find themselves dealing with major public relations disasters. Since privatisation, the nature of Qantas's relations with the federal government has changed. Instead of dealing with the government as owner, it now must continually place profitability first. This has necessitated structural change within Qantas as areas of responsibility have changed.

The tendency towards stability

Organisations, by their very nature, are conservative.[5] Once procedures and systems have been established, they actively resist change. You do not have to look far to see evidence of this phenomenon. Government agencies want to continue doing what they have been doing for years, whether the need for their service changes or remains the same. Organised religions are deeply entrenched in their history. Attempts to change church doctrine require great persistence and patience. Many charities and environmental groups find it difficult to alter their philosophies in the face of evolving circumstances. The majority of business firms, too, appear highly resistant to change.

Why do organisations resist change? There are at least four explanations. First, members fear losing what they already have. Those in power, who are in the best position to initiate change, typically have the most to lose. Second, most organisations are bureaucracies. Such structures have built-in systems and procedures that work against change. Third, many organisations can manage their environment and hence have buffered themselves against needing to change. For managers it is often easier to manage the environment than to introduce a change program. Finally, organisation cultures resist pressures for change. Let us elaborate on each of these points.

Any change can become a threat to employees' economic wellbeing, security, social affiliations or status. Change can result in the loss of money, friends, work group associates or even their jobs. As employees have a high investment in specific skills, change also threatens employee self-interest. Few people are prepared to throw away years of job preparation and experience. However, probably the greatest fear is loss of position and privilege by those in the managerial ranks. Top management can legitimately claim to have a great deal to lose from change. One author has noted why senior managers especially are prone both to resist change and to misinterpret signals that change is needed:[6]

> ... they have strong-vested interests; they will be blamed if current practices, strategies, and goals prove to be wrong; re-orientations threaten their dominance; their promotions and high statuses have persuaded them that they have more expertise than other people; their expertise tends to be out-of-date because their personal experiences with clients, customers, technologies, and low-level personnel lie in the past; they get much information through channels which conceal events that might displease them; and they associate with other top managers who face similar pressures.

Add to this the fact that major restructuring almost always includes wholesale replacement of the top managers and it is not surprising to find senior managers being critical impediments to change.

Bureaucracies endure as the most popular structural design in our society, with their popularity deriving from their ability to handle routine activities efficiently and their strong command and control emphasis. Even though writers and commentators promote the emergence of new organisational forms, most organisations, particularly large ones, exhibit many of the elements of bureaucracy. Large-scale change away from bureaucracy is unlikely to have a widespread following. Specifically, bureaucracy's standardised technologies, high formalisation and stability-based reward systems, which strongly penalise risk-taking and mistakes, discourage doing things differently.

Chapter 11 described how organisations manage their environment. Clearly, many large and powerful organisations use their strength to reduce dependence on their environment and so protect their core activities. In doing this, they reduce their need to adapt to changes in that environment.

The final force that we contend acts to impede change is the organisation's culture. As we will discuss in Chapter 13, every organisation has a culture that defines for employees what is appropriate and inappropriate behaviour. Once employees learn their organisation's culture—and this rarely takes more than a few months—they know the way things are supposed to be done. Although culture helps employees understand what is important and what is not, it also creates a consistency of behaviour that becomes entrenched and highly resistant to change.

In summary, it appears that planned organisational change gets much more attention in textbooks than it gets in practice. The forces against change, and the inertia surrounding existing practices, result in far more stability than the rational-change literature describes. Of course, inertia is not all bad. Organisations need some resistance qualities, otherwise they might respond to every perceived change in the environment. Every organisation needs stability to function. If an organisation was in a state of perpetual change, it would lose the consistent, goal-directed behaviour that makes a group of people into an organisation, and effectiveness would soon be lost.

A model for managing planned organisational change

Figure 12.3 represents a model for organisational change and shows how change can be broken down into a set of steps. Change is initiated by forces that generally originate in the environment. Occasionally, however, the forces for change may be internally generated, such as when an organisation seeks to commercialise an invention or discovery it has made itself. The forces for change must be identified and interpreted by management, which then decides the nature of the change that will take place. In some cases the responsibility for the change is delegated to a change agent, while in others a management team will take responsibility for the change. Either way there is someone, or some group, that is identified with introducing the change. The party responsible for the change determines the nature and type of change. The intervention requires that the change group must decide whether the change is a one-off occurrence or whether processes should be put in place to promote self-regeneration and continuous adaptation. Where it is only a one-off change, the process involves unfreezing the status quo, movement to a new state and refreezing the new state to make it permanent. Where continuous adaptation is involved, the change process omits the refreezing and attempts to make change an ongoing process. Implementation also includes the way in which the change agent or group chooses to put the change process into effect. The change itself, if successful, improves organisational effectiveness. Of course, changes do not take place in a vacuum. A change in one area of the organisation is likely to initiate new forces for other changes. The feedback loop in Figure 12.3 acknowledges that this model is dynamic. The need for change is presumed to be both inevitable and continual.

Determinants

All organisations change at some time during their life. This is particularly so for business organisations, which face a constantly changing environment. Opportunities arise, technologies evolve, competition becomes more pronounced and expectations of management and other critical constituencies change over time. These opportunities and problems may arise either from within the organisation or from outside it, or both.

The factors capable of initiating structural change are countless. While it is tempting to create several categories into which most of the factors can fall neatly, such efforts quickly show that the impetus for change can come from anywhere. Table 12.1 summarises a number of the more visible reasons for an organisation

FIGURE 12.3 A model for managing organisational change

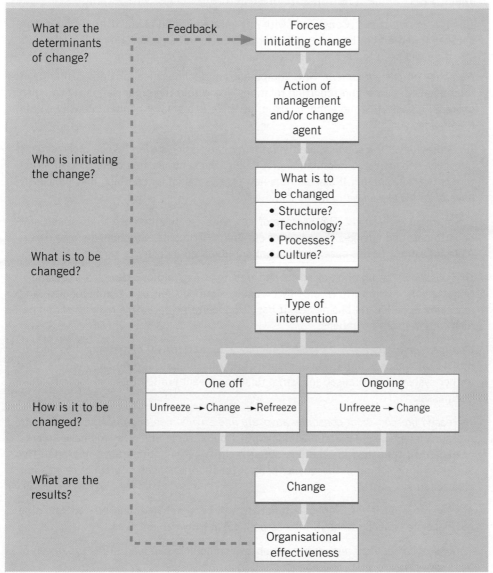

considering a change in structure. This list, of course, is far from comprehensive. The origins of structural change can come from an unlimited set of sources. But changes in strategy, size, technology, environment or power can be the source of structural change. It is part of the skills set of upper-level management to interpret what the changes are and how to respond to them.

It is at times when major changes are necessary that organisations are vulnerable to introducing inappropriate change. One of the problems with the issue of change is that markets and environments generally change faster than organisational members' ability to grasp what is actually happening. For instance, few managers

TABLE 12.1 Some determinants of structural change, with examples

Change in objectives. Consistent with the strategy imperative, if an organisation chooses to move from being an innovator to being a mass producer, it is likely that its structure will need to become more mechanistic.

Purchase of new equipment. New equipment and technological processes often lead to changes in power and reporting relationships within the organisation. It can also make an organisation more mechanistic, as there is a greater capital intensity within the organisation.

Implementation of a sophisticated information-processing system. When organisations introduce sophisticated information processing, the centralisation dimension of structure is typically altered. It also permits new organisational forms which may previously have been too expensive to introduce.

Government regulations. The passage of new laws creates the need to establish new departments and changes the power of current departments. Governments also deregulate industries. In this case, government control of an industry is removed.

Globalisation. The lowering of tariffs and freeing of capital flows have led to organisations seeking higher efficiencies by focusing more on their core competencies, and disposing of peripheral businesses. It has also greatly increased the number of companies with overseas operations.

Changes in industrial relations. The move to enterprise bargaining has led to individual business units taking responsibility for industrial relations matters. The former system of centralised industrial relations meant limited freedom for individual businesses.

Increased pressure from consumer-advocate and environmental groups. In response to pressure from consumer and environmental groups, some organisations have created or expanded their public relations department, whereas others have upgraded the authority of personnel in the quality-control function. Changes in product ranges has also occurred.

Mergers or acquisitions. Duplicate functions will be eliminated, and new coordinating positions are typically created. Intense political activity can emerge.

Actions of competitors. Aggressive action by competitors can lead to the expansion of boundary-spanning roles and an increased focus on costs.

Sudden internal or external hostility. Temporary crises are typically met by management's centralising decision making.

Decline in profits. When a corporation's profits fall, management often resorts to a structural shake-up. Personnel will be shuffled, departments added and/or deleted, new authority relationships defined and decision-making patterns significantly altered.

Reduction in layers of management. As organisations can offer few promotions to employees, they must consider changes in tasks and responsibilities in order to broaden employees' skills and keep them interested in their jobs.

understood the impact of low inflation on their organisations: they had to experience it for a number of years before its influence could be grasped. Similarly, technological change is typically either oversold as a panacea for all problems, or its introduction leads to unexpected consequences for the organisation. And the opportunities and threats of globalisation took some time to actually become apparent. Organisations whose managers interpreted the environment correctly had an advantage over their competitors.

The organisational initiator

Who initiates structural change? The person who introduces the change is called the change agent. Of course if there are more than one, which is common in large-scale organisational change, there is a group of change agents. But who are they? **Change agents** are those in power who want to implement change, and those who want either to replace or to constrain those in power.[7] This typically includes senior executives, managers of major units within the organisation, internal staff development specialists and powerful lower-level employees. It also includes consultants brought in from the outside. The definition of change agent provides insight into a central part of organisational change; it is a very political process.

Figure 12.3 depicts change agents as the intermediaries between the forces initiating change and the choice of an intervention strategy. They are important for who they are and the interests they represent. As our discussions of organisational effectiveness and the power-control perspective have demonstrated, decision making in organisations is *not* value-free. You should expect, therefore, that every change agent will bring along his or her own self-interests.

What one manager considers a situation 'in need of change' may be fully within the acceptable range for another. It is not unusual for employees in any given function to lobby actively for someone from their area to be selected for the organisation's top spot. If successful, they can typically expect favoured treatment—for instance, having problems defined in such a way that their department will be fundamental to solving them. A chief executive officer who has risen through the ranks of the marketing staff can be expected to be more receptive to marketing's problems. He or she is also more likely to recognise marketing's contribution to the organisation's effectiveness and more likely to see problems from a marketing perspective. As long as effectiveness is appraised in terms of who is doing the evaluating, the background and interests of the change agent are critical to the determination of what is perceived as a condition in need of change.

Managers do not have perfect knowledge of the organisation, and their perceptions may be influenced by their occupational background. Additionally, the organisation may be production-focused and lack sufficient knowledge in management ranks to be able to determine the most appropriate strategy. For this reason consultants may be hired to advise on and implement change. Consultants often have considerable experience in given industries, such as the tourist or motor vehicle industry, or technical specialties such as information technology or logistics management. This allows them to bring to the company a perspective that is better informed than that inside the company. Similarly, although organisational change tends to be ongoing, major change occurs less often, and senior managers may feel that there is a need for greater expertise in implementing change than currently exists in the organisation. Consultants may be able to provide this expertise.

change agents those in power, and those who wish either to replace or constrain those in power, who initiate structural change

However, not all consultants are perceived in this way. From the power-control perspective, the outside consultant may be hired by management to confirm and legitimise changes that might otherwise be perceived as self-serving.[8]

Another function of consultants is to work with senior management as facilitators. In this case senior management draw on the advice and expertise of consultants while maintaining responsibility for and ownership of the change. It is also important that when major change is introduced the CEO be closely identified with the change. It is difficult to sell the need for major change when a consultant is hired for a short-term appointment.

Some managers build their career around implementing major change, particularly downsizing and cost-cutting. This is never a popular task and it is difficult for those who have spent a long time in the organisation, with the associated political connections and obligations, to go about the task impartially. Similarly, when an organisation has been halved in size and put through wrenching structural change with the existing culture all but deconstructed, it is difficult for the manager responsible to expect long-term loyalty and respect. After introducing the change, managers in this position normally leave. One of the better-known cost-cutters is Al Dunlap, an American who downsized Kerry Packer's private company.[9] Most deregulated former government monopolies, such as Energy Australia and the various electricity and water supply authorities, have been through major organisational change under new management specifically appointed for the task. Once the major change program was completed, they left the organisation.

Intervention strategies

intervention strategies the choice of means by which the change process takes place

The term **intervention strategies** is used to describe the range of means by which the change process takes place. Strategies tend to fall into one of four categories: people, structure, technology, and organisational processes. As we are concerned with structural issues in this volume rather than with behaviour, we can omit from our discussion the topic of changing people.

Structure

The structure classification includes changes affecting the distribution of authority; areas of responsibility; allocation of rewards; alterations in the chain of command; degree of formalisation; and addition or elimination of positions, departments and divisions. As an illustration of structural change, the Adelaide-based company Baulderstone Hornibrook recognised in the late 1980s that engineering would offer better prospects in the 1990s than construction.[10] The company was split into two separate divisions, one to continue building and construction and the other to pursue opportunities in engineering. Each division was run as a profit centre, with its own management and day-to-day decision-making responsibilities. This allowed each division to concentrate on the area of its expertise and focused management's attention on a narrower range of activities, enabling these to be considered in greater depth. It also allowed greater assessment of the progress and success of each area of activity.

Structural change is easy to design but difficult to implement. At its simplest, it involves drawing up a new organisational chart and clarifying job descriptions. But not all staff may be supportive of the changes and may oppose, either actively or passively, the implementation of the change. Further, staff may not have the skills or

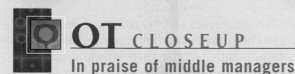

OT CLOSEUP

In praise of middle managers

Middle managers have attracted some adverse publicity over the past few years. They are generally portrayed in the popular press as unimaginative reactionaries doggedly defending the status quo. Twenty years' worth of change management consultants' writings have done little to dispel the stereotype. In contrast, a study by Quy Ngyuen Huy has in fact praised middle management and its role within the organisation. Quy defined middle managers as the two levels below the chief executive and one level above line workers and professionals. He found that their role was of great importance, particularly during times of radical organisational change. They performed four critical roles during change, that of entrepreneur, communicator, therapist, and what was termed tightrope artist.

Entrepreneur. Middle managers have the unique advantage of being close to day-to-day operations, front-line employees and customers. As a result, they are generally well informed as to what the problems are. But they are far enough away from frontline work that they can see the big picture. This allows them to see new possibilities both for solving problems and encouraging growth. As a group they are also more diverse, in terms of skills, occupational background, geography, gender and ethnicity, so they often have deeper insight than senior management. And they have a stronger track record in successful innovation than the highest level of management.

Communicator. The middle manager is ideally suited to communicating proposed changes across the organisation. Successful change programs require clear and compelling innovation. As middle managers have the best social networks in the company, they are usually better at getting the message across. They have close associations with lower-level workers and are in a position to know from where resistance to change is likely to emanate.

Therapist. Radical change generally stirs up high levels of fear. Uncertainty can deflate morale and trigger anxiety, which can degenerate into chaos within the organisation. Middle managers have no alternative but to address their employees' emotional wellbeing at times of radical change. If they ignore it, work will stall. Middle managers carry out this function even while battling their own demons of alienation and insecurity.

Tightrope artist. Successful change means balancing change and continuity. If there is too much change too soon, chaos ensues. Too little change results in inertia. Both extremes can result in underperformance. Middle managers have the difficult role of balancing the two. They generally have a good grasp of the core values and attributes of the organisation, while being problem solvers closely connected to the flow of work. They are the group that can translate the strategy to action, synthesise the various positions, and prevent the various work groups from degenerating into disorganisation and chaos.

Adapted from: Quy Nguyen Huy, 'In Praise of Middle Managers', *Harvard Business Review*, September 2001, pp. 72–9.

orientations for their new responsibilities. Additionally, when we change a structure we change reporting relationships and communication flows. These take time to re-establish as managers settle into their new role.

Technology

The technology classification encompasses modifications to the equipment that employees use, interdependencies of work activities among employees, and changes that affect the interrelationships between employees and the technical demands of their jobs. Any change must be supported by appropriate technology. For instance, if we expect more intensive communication among staff, then the technology must support this. This may mean improving electronic linkages, such as e-mails and intranets, and changing the spatial-physical characteristics of the workplace. The need to reduce the amount of time to design a motor vehicle provides a good illustration of how technology can drive change. Using traditional design methods, the length of time needed to design and produce a car from a clean sheet of paper to having the first model delivered to the showroom under the traditional sequential development system was approximately five years. New technology has allowed the use of development teams to cut this time to 30 months, with the expectation that it will be cut to two years in the near future. The new technology is based on the use of computers, undertaking what is called simultaneous engineering. Using this system, both design and production people can sit down and jointly develop the design and the manufacturing process for the product. Any likely manufacturing problems can be identified very early in the design process, so that any changes will not hold up production. The computer technology even allows the team to simulate such functions as crashing, test-driving the car, varying the body styling to see how minor variations affect the aesthetics, and wind testing. The adhocracy designing the car was made possible only by the technology used.

Organisational processes

The final strategy considers changing organisational processes, such as decision-making and communication patterns. If, for instance, a change agent introduces taskforces into a machine bureaucracy with the intention of improving the transmission of information between functional units and allowing representatives from each unit to participate in decisions that will affect each of them, he or she will have altered the organisation's decision-making processes.

Implementation

Referring again to Figure 12.3, once forces for initiating change exist, someone has assumed the change-agent role and it has been determined what is to be changed, we need to consider *how* to implement the change. Implementation depends on whether we want the changes to be permanent or part of an ongoing change process. Until recent years, rates of change in technology and the environment were slower and generally of a lesser magnitude that at present. The approach to change was that the new ways of doing things would be permanent. Hence we spoke of the process of unfreezing–moving–refreezing. To a certain extent this still holds true: effectiveness demands that established practices and procedures be adhered to. But most managers at the present time are reluctant to introduce a change program with a finite end; they look on change more as an ongoing process of adaptation. Hence, refreezing is not such a key part of the change process, although some degree of refreezing is normal. We begin by looking at the steps in the change process. Then we turn our attention to implementation tactics.

change process
the unfreezing of the status quo, moving to a new state and refreezing the new change

The change process

The **change process** consists of three steps: *unfreezing* the status quo, *moving* to a new state, and *refreezing* the change to make it permanent.[11] This three-step process is the recognition that change will not be successfully accomplished without unlearning the old ways, learning the new and then incorporating the new ways as part of established practice. Unlearning is the mental process involved in the realisation that the old ways of doing things are no longer applicable. They are not forgotten, but in changed circumstances they no longer apply.

Let us consider the case of a bank moving the back-office functions to a centralised processing facility. Banks formerly undertook most of their clerical and account-keeping tasks in each branch. The rising costs of the branch network and the increasing capability of information processing led to much of these tasks being centralised. Many employees moved to the new locations and the tasks they undertook, although having the same output, were significantly different from those in the branch. Existing patterns of work were broken, reporting relationships changed, and the camaraderie associated with working for the branch was lost. This process of organisational change will be used to illustrate the unfreezing–changing–refreezing process.

The status quo can be considered as the paper processing that took place in the branches. To move from this equilibrium—to overcome the pressures of both individual resistance and group conformity—**unfreezing** is necessary. This can be achieved in one of three ways. The *driving forces*, which direct behaviour away from the status quo, can be increased. The *restraining forces*, which hinder movement from the existing equilibrium, can be decreased. A third way is to *combine the first two approaches.*

unfreezing
overcoming resistence to change

Using the reorganisation example cited above, management can expect employee resistance to the relocations. To deal with that resistance, management can use positive incentives to encourage employees to accept the change. For instance, rises in pay or greater flexibility can be offered to those who accept the transfer. Improved working conditions may be used as an incentive. Management might also choose to unfreeze acceptance of the status quo by removing restraining forces. Employees could be counselled individually. Each employee's concerns and apprehensions could be heard and clarified specifically. Assuming that most of the fears are unjustified, the counsellor might assure the employees that there was nothing to fear and then demonstrate, through tangible evidence, that restraining forces were unwarranted. If resistance was extremely high, management might have to resort to both reducing resistance and increasing the attractiveness of the alternative for the unfreezing to be successful.

Of course, management may also use the threat of redundancies as a driving force. Increasingly, downsizing and staff redundancies are part of the unfreezing process. Because much resistance to change occurs in management ranks, it is not surprising that managers are often the first group within the organisation to feel the impact of this strategy. CEOs particularly must be aligned with the change process for it to be successful, and boards of directors generally ensure that a CEO is in place who both supports the proposed change and reflects in his or her actions what is intended to be achieved.

Once unfreezing has been accomplished, the change itself can be implemented. This is where the change agent introduces one or more intervention strategies. In reality, there is no clear line separating unfreezing and moving. Many of the efforts made to unfreeze the status quo may, in and of themselves, introduce change. Thus the tactics that the change agent uses for dealing with resistance may facilitate unfreezing and/or moving. Seven tactics that managers or change agents can use for dealing with resistance to change are described in Table 12.2.

Assuming that a change has been implemented, if it is to be successful the new situation needs to be refrozen so that it can be sustained over time. Unless this last step is attended to, there is a very high likelihood that the change will be short-lived and employees will attempt to revert to the previous equilibrium state. The objective of **refreezing**, then, is to stabilise the new situation by balancing the driving and restraining forces.

How is refreezing done? Basically, it requires systematic replacement of the temporary forces with permanent ones. In our illustration of the bank back office,

refreezing stabilising and sustaining a change action

TABLE 12.2 Tactics for dealing with resistance to change

Education and communication. Resistance can be reduced through communicating with employees to help them see the logic of a change. This tactic assumes basically that the source of resistance lies in misinformation or poor communication. If employees receive the full facts and get any misunderstandings cleared up, the resistance will subside. This can be achieved through one-on-one discussions, memos, group presentations or reports.

Participation. It's difficult for individuals to resist a change decision in which they have participated. Assuming that the participants have the expertise to make a useful contribution, their involvement can reduce resistance, obtain commitment and increase the quality of the change decision.

Facilitation and support. Change agents can offer a range of supportive efforts to reduce resistance. When employee fear and anxiety are high, counselling and therapy, new skills training or short, paid leaves of absence may facilitate adjustment.

Negotiation. This tactic requires the exchange of something of value for a lessening of the resistance. For instance, if the resistance is centred in a few powerful individuals, a specific reward package can be negotiated that will meet their individual needs.

Manipulation and co-optation. Manipulation refers to covert influence attempts. Twisting and distorting facts to make them appear more attractive, withholding undesirable information or creating false rumours to get employees to accept a change are all examples of manipulation. Co-optation is a form of both manipulation and participation. It seeks to 'buy off' the leaders of a resistance group by giving them a key role in the change decision. The advice of those who have been co-opted is sought only in order to get their endorsement, not to ensure a better decision.

Coercion. This tactic is the application of direct threats or force to the resisters. Examples include threats of transfer, loss of promotion, negative performance evaluation or a poor letter of recommendation.

Realigning staff profiles. This may involve both the dismissal of those who actively oppose the change and the hiring of new managers who support and reflect the values of the change.

Adapted from: John P. Kottler & Leonard A. Schlesinger, 'Choosing Strategies for Change', *Harvard Business Review*, March/April 1979, pp. 106–14.

refreezing will be relatively easy. Workers are faced with a new work location, probably a new work team, redesigned jobs and different supervisors. In this, there is nothing to revert to. But where none of these change, refreezing is far more difficult. It may mean formalising the driving or restraining forces: for instance, removal of time clocks or rearranging the physical work space to reinforce a climate of trust and confidence in employees. The formal rules and regulations governing the behaviour of those affected by the change should be revised to reinforce the new situation. Over time, of course, the group's own norms will evolve to sustain the new equilibrium, but until that point is reached the change agent will have to rely on more formal mechanisms.

Are there key factors that determine the degree to which a change will become permanent? The answer is yes. One review of change studies identified a number of relevant factors.[12] The *reward allocation system* is critical. For instance, if rewards fall short of expectations over time, the change is likely to be short-lived. If a change is to be sustained, it needs the *support of a sponsor.* This individual, typically high in the management hierarchy, provides the change with legitimacy. Evidence indicates that once sponsorship is withdrawn from a change project, there is strong pressure to return to the old equilibrium state. It is also important that managers close to the employees be seen to support the change. People need to know what is expected of them as a result of the change. Therefore, *failure to transmit information* about expectations should reduce the degree of refreezing. *Cultural change* and *group forces* are other important factors. As employees become aware that others in their group accept and sanction the change, they become more comfortable with it. *Commitment* to the change should lead to greater acceptance and permanence. As noted earlier, if employees participate in the change decision, they can be expected to be more committed to seeing that it is successful. Change is less likely to become permanent if it is implemented in a single unit of the organisation. Therefore, the more *diffusion* in the change effort, the more units that will be affected and the greater legitimacy the effort will carry.

These factors remind us that the organisation is a system, and that planned change will be most successful when all the parts in the system support the change effort. What is more, successful change requires careful balancing of the system. The consolidation of three divisional units into a single regional workshop obviously carries with it a wide range of reverberating effects. But the impact of even small changes (as when a multi-billion-dollar consumer products firm creates a new department of public affairs staffed with only a handful of personnel) can be expected to be widespread. Other departments and employees will be threatened. Still others will feel that a portion of their responsibility has been taken from them. All changes, regardless of how small, will have an impact outside the area in which they were implemented. No change can take place in a vacuum. A structural modification in unit A will affect other structural variables within unit A as well as structural variables in units B, C and so forth.

The systems perspective makes it imperative that change agents consider any and all interventions as having a potential impact on a far greater territory than the specific point where the change was initiated. Large-scale change projects often don't try to change the whole organisation simultaneously: change is introduced in one part, or subsystem, of the organisation which may be supportive of the change. The benefits are then disseminated throughout the organisation, with different parts picking up on the change as the benefits and problems are better understood. As a result, in large organisations change often proceeds at different rates, with some subsystems adopting change faster than others.

We mentioned earlier that refreezing may not always be a good idea. In many cases the aim of the change may be to create a more flexible and adaptable organisation. This may involve a greater reliance on teamwork, introducing improved coordination devices and pushing responsibility lower down the management hierarchy. Here the refreezing process will be aimed at reinforcing relationships and reducing barriers to communication flows rather than stressing formalisation and hierarchical relationships.

Implementation tactics

Appropriate tactics for implementing change are critical to success. Those responsible for the change must make decisions about how the planned change is to be brought about. Research has identified that four basic tactics summarise those that are most commonly used. One author has called these tactics intervention, participation, persuasion, and edict.[13]

The intervention tactic is characterised by change agents *selling* their change rationale to those who will be affected. They argue that current performance is inadquate and that new standards and procedures must be established. They cite comparable organisations or units with better performance to justify the need for change, then often explicitly describe how current practices can be improved. To assess more fully inefficient or poorly designed procedures, change agents using the intervention tactic often form taskforces made up of those subject to change. The taskforces can work backwards from a desired state, identifying the best means of achieving what is desired. This co-opting technique utilises the expertise of those who know the job best while reducing resistance to change. But change agents retain power to veto any of the taskforce's recommendations.

In participation, change agents *delegate* the implementation decision to those who will be affected. They stipulate the need for change or the opportunities change can provide, create a taskforce to do the job, assign members to the task force, and then delegate authority for the change process to the taskforce with a statement of expectations and constraints. Change agents who use this tactic give full responsibility to the taskforce for implementation and exercise no veto power over its decisions. This tactic is often used in large organisations, where the senior managers decide on the need for change while leaving the actual process to others.

Some change agents handle change by essentially *abdicating* the decision to experts. Change agents identify the need or opportunity for change. But because they are disinterested, lack knowledge or feel that others can handle the job better, they take a relatively passive role. What they do is to allow interested internal staff— or qualified outside experts—to present their ideas for bringing about change. The internal or external experts then use persuasion to sell their ideas. Change agents become active only after various ideas have been presented. They listen and often ask for supporting documentation. But those who will be affected choose the best ideas for implementing the change.

The final tactic is where top management makes the key decisions and uses hierarchical authority to implement them. This tactic is often used when implementing structural change. There is little or no participation and those affected are *told* what the change will be. This is called implementation by edict. When this tactic is used, change agents merely announce changes and use memos, formal presentations or the like to convey their decision. Edict is often used in mergers and acquisitions. Although politely sold as a merger between equals, in reality most mergers are a takeover of one company by another. The company doing the taking over gets to call the shots and imposes its will, and management team, on the other. Consultation in this situation is perfunctory, if it takes place at all. It is fairly typical for the senior managers in the company being taken over to vacate their positions in the year after the takeover.

In practice, how common is each of these implementation tactics? A study of 91 cases found persuasion to be the most widely used, occurring in 42% of the cases.[14] Edict was the next most popular with 23%, followed by intervention and participation with 19% and 17%, respectively.

Results

The model in Figure 12.3 culminates with change taking place and a resulting effect on organisational effectiveness. Whether that effect is positive, negative, temporary or permanent depends on each of the earlier steps.

Research into implementation tactics demonstrates that there are real differences in their success rates.[15] Change directives by managerial dictate are clearly inferior to other options. Edict was successful just 43% of the time. Participation and persuasion achieved success rates of 84% and 73%, respectively. Intervention, while used in only 19% of the cases, attained a perfect 100% success rate.

In many cases organisational change does not result in a measurable improvement in effectiveness. It may merely enable the organisation to survive or maintain its position in the industry. Competitors are often undertaking the same types of change, so in relative terms companies are not gaining on the competition. Also, major change programs consume large amounts of energy and commitment, often at the cost of focusing on producing goods and services. Productivity will fall until the workforce becomes familiar with new technology and ways of doing things and adapts to new reporting relationships. Until workers and management become confident in using a new technology, often the old and new systems are run in parallel. It takes time, often measured in years, for the impact of change to emerge.

Regardless of the outcome of the change, the model shown in Figure 12.3 is dynamic. The need for change is continuous, hence the need for the feedback loop. Organisations have little time to enjoy the benefits of stability and the benefits of a successful change program. New forces will already be working to make additional changes necessary. The change model we have proposed is therefore never at rest.

The innovative organisation

A business magazine cover story declared that innovating 'has become the most urgent concern of corporations everywhere'.[16] 'Innovate or die' is the new battle cry in industries as diverse as food processing, motor vehicles, home building, publishing and financial services. In industries such as these, where dynamic environments have become a fact of life, innovation has become closely linked to organisational effectiveness. But is *innovation* the same as *change*? And what type of organisation is best designed to stimulate innovation?

innovation the adoption of ideas that are new to the adopting organisation

technological innovation the use of new tools, techniques, devices or systems to produce changes in products or services or in the way those products are produced or services rendered

administrative innovation the implementation of changes in an organisation's structure or its administrative processes

product innovation designing, development, production and marketing of new products and services

Anything different represents a change. **Innovation**, however, is the adoption of ideas that are new to the adopting organisation.[17] All innovations therefore represent a change, but not all changes are innovative. The innovative change breaks new ground for the organisation and hence is more threatening and more likely to be resisted by the organisation's members.

Innovation typically takes one of three forms: technological, administrative or product.[18] **Technological innovation** is what most of us usually think about when we think about innovative change. These innovations encompass the use of new tools, techniques, devices or systems to produce changes in products or services or in the way those products are produced or services rendered. The introduction of fruit peeling and cutting machines at the Golden Circle processing facility in Brisbane, which reduces the amount of direct labour involved in preparing food for canning, is an example of technical innovation. For instance, it allowed for the economical canning of mangoes that were previously left to rot.

Administrative innovation is the implementation of changes in an organisation's structure or its administrative processes. This would include changes such as the introduction of flexitime work schedules or a matrix organisation design. It also includes changing the organisation's spatial-physical characteristics.

The third category is **product innovation**, which involves the designing, development, production and marketing of new products and services. It is this type of innovation that has captured the imagination of management theorists and commentators. The innovations of the information-processing industry are an obvious example. Other examples are the introduction of video recorders, home-delivered pizzas, self-assembled furniture and four-wheel-drive vehicles for urban areas. High rates of product innovation are often associated with the concept of an effective company.

The extent to which organisations seek to be innovative is determined by their strategy. Prospectors, for example, tend to foster more innovation. Reactors, by contrast, tend to be low innovators. But clearly certain structures are better than others for stimulating innovation.[19]

The machine bureaucracy is least likely to stimulate or accept innovation. Of course, one could argue that because it tends to be associated with stable environments, bureaucracy is least in need of innovation. Its value lies in efficiency through standardisation, not in initiating ideas. Innovation is most likely to flourish in adhocracies and simple structures. It is stimulated in adhocracies by its personnel, who tend to be professionals, by the lack of formalisation and by the active involvement of lower-level employees in decision making. The key to innovation in the simple structure, however, lies not in the structure but in its chief executive officer. The evidence indicates that the personality, power and knowledge of the CEO differentiates those simple structures that innovate from those that don't. Essentially, CEOs in innovative organisations have personality styles that demonstrate confidence in their abilities to control the environment, have centralised power for maximum control, and possess considerable knowledge about changes taking place in their organisation's environment.

Large organisations have found that they have had to differentiate their organisation to promote product innovation. Large sections of the motor vehicle and electrical manufacturers' and chemical companies' operations are bureaucratic. These include accounting and payroll functions, maintenance, human resources as well as production. Only part of the organisation is involved in generating new products. Those who do this are often located in research centres away from the day-to-day repetitive tasks. Innovation requires a flat structure with few barriers to horizontal communication and a supporting culture. It is often easier to achieve this at a separate location than to impose it on an otherwise bureaucratic structure.

Managing unplanned change

The heading of this section suggests a paradox: if something is unplanned there would appear to be very little management involvement. But even unplanned and unanticipated events require management, and a strong argument may be put that the demands on management are greater at times such as these than when organisations are going about their day-to-day work. But what types of situation lead to unplanned change? Turning to the model described in Figure 12.2, we can see that unplanned change may be either evolutionary or revolutionary—that is, small scale or sufficiently large to threaten the existence of the organisation. Unplanned change may come from an anticipated source or may be completely unexpected. If unplanned change is of sufficient magnitude there is an element of crisis, and the skills of crisis management are called for.

To put unplanned change into perspective we need some examples. Transitory change does not alter the nature of the organisation; it is generally short-term, and once the initiating forces have passed the organisation returns to much the same as it was before. Examples would be a sudden drop in economic activity, variations in commodity prices, machinery breakdowns, droughts and climatic change, and sudden changes in competition levels in industry. Each of these situations needs to be actively managed but, beyond local adaptation, the main work of the organisation proceeds without too much disruption. Chaotic change puts the whole organisation at risk unless appropriate corrective actions are taken. The impact of the terrorist attacks in New York on insurance companies, airlines and those who lost most of their staff is an example. Chaotic change also includes the threat of insolvency, the emergence of unwelcome takeovers, or a major health or environmental problem (e.g. poisoning tablets on supermarket shelves and large oil spills).

There is no one best way to manage unplanned change. Management often does not have the luxury of time to plan an adequate response or engage in wide consultation and coalition building. Nevertheless, there is a need to bring high levels of expertise to bear on the problem. As a guide we suggest the following actions as those which are the most appropriate to take. The extent to which they are applied depends on the nature and extent of the change.

Centralisation of management. In almost all cases we would expect some centralisation of management. There are two reasons for this. The first is that authority rests with the top of the organisation, so the CEO is normally the only person who can authorise an appropriate response. Second, information needs to be processed rapidly, and this is best undertaken in the mind of one person. Unplanned change by its nature requires a quick response, and there is insufficient time to have proposals passed from committee to committee for evaluation.

Establishment of special taskforces. Generally, crises have a multiple impact on the organisation. They may involve production and distribution problems, exposing the company to financial risk and causing rationing of resources within the organisation. A crisis normally requires a special taskforce to be established to deal with the complexities of the situation. The taskforce focuses the organisation's response. It gathers and processes information and issues instructions and edicts for the organisation to follow. It is composed of those managers who are sufficiently senior to commit the organisation to appropriate courses of action and who have expertise in the nature of the problem.

Active environmental management. In times of unanticipated change, the organisation needs to keep close touch with its critical constituencies. Depending on the nature of the threat, these may include banks and finance houses, shareholders, unions, key customers and suppliers, government and, if it is a high-profile company, the general public. Neglecting critical constituencies at this time may have fatal consequences.

Husbanding resources. Unplanned change by its nature comes at a cost. There may be loss of sales or revenue, shortages of inputs, extra expenditure for new plant or equipment, or loss of financial support. Management needs to develop a coordinated response to resource usage to minimise the impact on the organisation and maximise the chances of survival.

Need for active leadership. Unplanned occurrences place a great demand on leadership skills. Critical constituencies require the commitment and face-to-face presence of the chief executive. Substitutes, such as the actions of public relations departments and firms, cannot replace the CEO's up-front presence. He or she must be seen to be actively involved in managing whatever the problem is. Employees, customers and suppliers are also often confused and worried, and are seeking reassurance and direction from those with the capacity to respond to the problem. There is no substitute for the CEO being an active and high-profile presence to all concerned.

A power-control footnote

So far, there has been a sense of optimism about our discussion of organisational change. For instance, we have implied that managers are motivated to initiate change because they are concerned with effectiveness, and that change is a dynamic and continuous process driven by the organisation's need to adjust and match itself with the constant changes in its environment. We have also implied that senior managers, particularly CEOs, have perfect knowledge of the organisation and of which structure is most appropriate. We have assumed that they have identified how the environment affects the organisation and which structure is best for the technology in use. Further, we have assumed that all resistance to change occurs because of the poorly informed or self-seeking behaviour of lower-level managers and employees.

These assumptions treat change as a deductive rational process, amenable to management action. However, organisational change is an intensely political activity. This applies to determining whether change is necessary, what is to be achieved, and the manner in which change takes place. So the influence of organisational power and politics tends to render our assumptions, if not unworkable, at least subject to question.

In what way does the power-control approach to organisation design differ from that described in our rational model?[20] Power-control advocates recognise that those in power have little reason to change the current structure. The status quo maintains control and furthers the interests of the power holders. However, power-control advocates would ignore any concern for maintaining internal consistency among structural elements and, instead, emphasise the lack of planning in 'planned' change, arguing that change is more likely to represent a loss of control by the dominant power coalition than a response to the environment.

As effectiveness is defined in terms of those doing the evaluating, the rational assumption that 'changes in structure will be implemented as needed to ensure high performance' is unrealistic. The power-control position would argue that structural changes that do occur are neither planned nor occur in order to facilitate technical efficiency or to fulfil the demands of the environment. The following briefly summarises the power-control view.

Change is most likely a response to pressing demands created by internal and external parties interested in the organisation—that is, it is reactive rather than anticipatory. In practice, 'planned' change is typically a process of change, followed by the planning that legitimises and ratifies this change. As noted about goals in Chapter 9, meaning is attributed to an action, but usually *after* it has occurred. So while change is made in response to demands by powerful interest groups, it is packaged and sold in a more legitimate form: it is rationalised as being consistent with the goals of enhanced organisational effectiveness.

Pressure for change can come from anywhere outside the dominant coalition normally representative of the senior management group. If those in power are not able to keep this pressure in check, changes will be implemented. It may not be what the dominant coalition wants, but at that point it will have lost control. When these changes are implemented, in response to outside pressures, they will tend to be conveyed as planned and consistent with the organisation's goals of improved performance.

Summary

This chapter has discussed the management of planned structural change. Organisations need to change and adapt in order to be effective. A model was introduced in which change was described as being either evolutionary or revolutionary, and planned or unplanned, and we concentrated on planned change.

A wide range of forces can initiate change. The change agent is the individual (or individuals) who makes the structural changes. He or she chooses from structural, technological or organisation-process intervention strategies. The implementation of change requires unfreezing the status quo, moving to a new state, and refreezing the change to make it permanent. Implementation also requires a decision about the specific tactics to be used. In some cases there will be little attempt to refreeze the change, as the change agent may be seeking a more dynamic organisation.

The evidence indicates that innovating organisations are likely to have a prospector strategy and an adhocratic or simple structure.

Despite all the attention that change has received from organisation theorists, organisations are more stable than changing. Organisations can be characterised as having long periods of inertia, followed by brief periods of dramatic and comprehensive change that is over in a very short time. In other words, change is infrequent and revolutionary in nature. The power-control position further states that structural changes, when they occur, are neither planned nor in response to needs for technical efficiency or demands of the environment. Change indicates a loss of control by the organisation's dominant coalition.

For review and discussion

1   What is the traditional view of change in organisations?

2   What does 'managed' change mean?

3   Why do organisations resist change?

4   Describe five determinants of change.

5   Describe the three types of intervention strategies.

6   Contrast driving and restraining forces in unfreezing.

7   Is 'refreezing' of change necessary? Discuss.

8   Review the various tactics for dealing with resistance to change in power-control terms.

9   Explain why organisations have an inherent bias towards stability.

10 'Bureaucracies have survived because they have proved able to respond to change.' Do you agree or disagree? Discuss.

11 'Pressure for change originates in the environment, whereas pressure for stability originates within the organisation.' Do you agree or disagree? Discuss.

12 'Resistance to change is good for an organisation.' Do you agree or disagree? Discuss.

13 What type of organisations stimulate innovation? Why?

14 What could the management of a large bureaucracy do to stimulate innovation within their organisation?

15 How would you modify Figure 12.3 to reflect the descriptive and power-control views of organisational change?

CASE FOR CLASS DISCUSSION
Coles Myer's 'Operation right now'

Coles Myer is one of Australia's perennially under performing companies. Formed by the 1985 merger of Coles and Myer, the idea was to create a large retailing group which would benefit from significant economies of scale. A string of chief executives over the subsequent 15 years have always 'had a plan' to capture the economies but none has worked as anticipated. At least one of the major businesses has always had problems which has dragged down the performance of the group. Myer and Grace Bros have had endless troubles finding the right mix of merchandise and service, K-Mart allowed its costs to rise so that it was no longer a cheap shopping destination whilst Target tried to reinvent itself as a homeware store. These problems were compounded by overstocking and the subsequent disposal of excess merchandise impacted profits. About the only solid business in the group consisted of Coles supermarkets.

In order to overcome the performance shortfall, a new chief executive, John Fletcher, was appointed in 2001. A former respected chief executive of Brambles, he had no retailing experience; indeed one of his first statements on taking over the position was that he had not been in a shop for twenty years. However he felt that most of the problems facing Coles Myer were structural and that specialist retailing knowledge was not needed to address them. Fletcher's plan was called 'Operation Right Now'. This aimed to create a clear focus for each of the business groups. In order to achieve this, he aimed at breaking down the fiefdoms which had built up around each of the chains and which resisted central direction. Another major part of Fletcher's plan was to created shared service units in areas such as warehousing, logistics, buying and supply chain management and then forcing individual business units to use them. He is also trying to improve decision making by reducing the size of the head office bureaucracy and moving personnel into the operating divisions

In the longer term, Fletcher wants to recreate the corporate structure and culture in order to capture the synergies anticipated when the merger occurred. But he cannot turn his attention to this until the short term problems have been successfully tackled.

Adapted from: Stephen Bartholomeusz 'the Coles Myer Battle-ship Swinging Onto Its New Course', *The Age*, 15th March, 2002, p. 3.

QUESTIONS

1 What intervention strategies would you advise Fletcher to use in order to achieve the outcomes he desires?

2 How would your change program conform to the model in Figure 12.3?

3 What resistance to change might you expect, and how would you deal with it?

FURTHER READING

John Child, *Organization*, New York: Harper & Row, 1977.

Leonard Goodstein & Warner Burke, 'Creating Successful Organizational Change', *Organizational Dynamics*, Spring 1991, pp. 5–17.

Rosabeth Moss Kanter, *When Giants Learn to Dance*, London: Routledge, 1989.

Rosabeth Moss Kanter, Barry Stein & Todd Jick, *The Challenge of Organizational Change: How Companies Experience It and Leaders Guide It*, New York: Free Press, 1992.

NOTES

1 Bruce Urpin, 'Digital Dreams', *Business Review Weekly*, 1 September 2000, pp. 78–80 (originally published in *Forbes*).

2   Henry Mintzberg, *The Structuring of Organizations*, Englewood Cliffs, N.J.: Prentice-Hall, 1979.

3   William H. Starbuck and Paul C. Nystrom, 'Designing and Understanding Organizations', in P.C. Nystrom and W.H. Starbuck, eds, *Handbook of Organizational Design*, Vol. 1, New York: Oxford University Press, 1981.

4   John Child, *Organization*, New York: Harper & Row, 1977.

5   Richard H. Hall, *Organizations: Structure and Process*, 3rd edn, Englewood Cliffs, NJ: Prentice Hall, 1987, p. 29.

6   William H. Starbuck, 'Organizations as Action Generators', *American Sociological Review*, February 1983, p. 100.

7   Daniel Katz & Robert L. Kahn, *The Social Psychology of Organizations*, 2nd edn, New York: John Wiley, 1978, p. 679.

8   Jeffrey Pfeffer, *Power in Organizations*, Marshfield, MA: Pitman Publishing, 1981, pp. 142–6.

9   Albert Dunlap, *Mean Business*, Singapore: Butterworth Heinemann Asia, 1996.

10 Florence Chong, 'Hornibrook Divides and Conquers', *Business Review Weekly*, 22 March 1991, pp. 56–7.

11 Kurt Lewin, *Field Theory in Social Science*, New York: Harper & Row, 1951.

12 Paul S. Goodman, Max Bazerman & Edward Conlon, 'Institutionalization of Planned Organizational Change', in Barry M. Staw & Larry L. Cummings, eds, *Research in Organizational Behavior*, vol. 2, Greenwich, CN: JAI Press, 1980, pp. 231–42.

13 Paul C. Nutt, 'Tactics of Implementation', *Academy of Management Journal*, June 1986, pp. 230–61.

14 Nutt, op. cit.

15 Nutt, op. cit.

16 Kenneth Labich, 'The Innovators', *Fortune*, 6 June 1988, p. 50.

17 Richard L. Daft, 'Bureaucratic Versus Nonbureaucratic Structure and the Process of Innovation and Change', in Samuel B. Bacharach, ed., *Research in the Sociology of Organizations*, vol. 1, 1982, p. 132.

18 Fariborz Damanpour, 'The Adoption of Technological, Administrative, and Ancillary Innovations: Impact of Organizational Factors', *Journal of Management*, Winter 1987, p. 677.

19 This section is adapted from Danny Miller & Peter H. Friesen, *Organizations: A Quantum View*, Englewood Cliffs, NJ: Prentice Hall, 1984, pp. 176–201. See also James Brian Quinn, 'Managing Innovation', *Harvard Business Review*, May/June 1985, pp. 73–84; and Rosabeth Moss Kanter, 'When a Thousand Flowers Bloom: Structural, Collective, and Social Conditions for Innovation in Organization', in B.M. Staw & L.L. Cummings, eds, *Research in Organizational Behavior*, vol. 10. Greenwich, CN: JAI Press, 1988, pp. 169–211.

20 This section is based on Jeffrey Pfeffer, *Organizational Design*, Arlington Heights, IL: AHM Publishing, 1978, pp. 190–2.

CHAPTER 13

Managing organisational culture

After reading this chapter you should be able to:

1 define organisational culture;

2 list organisational culture's key characteristics;

3 differentiate between the dominant culture and subcultures;

4 identify the characteristics of a strong culture;

5 explain how a culture is sustained over time;

6 describe how employees learn an organisation's culture;

7 explain how culture affects the success of mergers and acquisitions;

8 list conditions that favour the successful changing of a culture.

Introduction

Mt Isa builds a new harmony

Mt Isa, located 900 kilometres inland from Townsville in Queensland, has never enjoyed either good profits or relations with its employees.[1] The mine, established over 60 years ago, had a typical adversarial industrial relations system, with managers trying to face down workers, and workers trying to exploit the complex industrial relations agreements to maximise their income by manipulating rosters and working hours. Absenteeism and labour turnover was high and the workers at the mine shared a strong solidarity, as is usual in an isolated mining environment.

Mt Isa had seen a number of long and bitter strikes in its history. But by the early 1990s it was becoming obvious to the directors of the company that unless changes were made to both management and work practices, the viability of the mine would be in question. A new manager was appointed with the task of reducing costs and improving productivity. But it was clear that this could not be achieved without a radical change to the way the mine was managed.

The new general manager of the Mount Isa operations, Phil Wright, started by making the unusual admission that management was primarily to blame for the problems, not the workers. The mine had been run by traditional command and control management practices with little input from the workers. Not that in many cases the workers could contribute much. In some parts of the mine labour turnover was up to 100% per year, and skills, mostly learned on the job, were lacking. The complex employment award, built up over decades of confrontation, was also a major barrier to reform. The mine workforce was divided into staff and unionised 'award' employees, who viewed each other with antagonism. It was essential that these barriers be removed for any major change to occur.

Wright began by negotiating a new enterprise agreement which moved most employees onto annualised salaries: that is, all allowances, including overtime, were combined into one predetermined payment. Then a major survey of the workforce was undertaken to find out what the employees liked and disliked about their job. This was used to identify what preferences were and match them with business needs. Management was also strengthened by adding management skills where they were needed.

The changes at Mt Isa led to a radical change in the culture of the mine. No longer are management and workers divided into two separate camps. Both have the incentive to improve the productivity of capital equipment and keep the mine operating at optimal levels. Labour turnover and absenteeism is down, indicating greater levels of work satisfaction. Managers cooperate with the workers rather than controlling them. And overtime, which was common under the old management structure, is now virtually unknown. What has taken place at Mount Isa is a change in the culture of the organisation. Conflict and suspicion have been replaced with cooperation and support, with significantly improved performance and employee satisfaction.

This chapter introduces the idea that organisations have personalities. We call them organisational cultures. We will show that culture has an important bearing on an organisation's effectiveness. We will also examine how cultures originate, and discuss the difficulties of managing cultures.

What is organisational culture?

There is no shortage of definitions of organisational culture. It has been described, for example, as 'the dominant values espoused by an organisation',[2] 'the philosophy that guides an organisation's policy toward employees and customers',[3] 'the way things are done around here',[4] and 'the basic assumptions and beliefs that are shared by members of an organization'.[5] A closer look at the wide array of definitions does uncover a central theme—**organisational culture** refers to a system of *shared meaning*. In every organisation there are patterns of beliefs, symbols, rituals, myths and practices that have evolved over time.[6] These, in turn, create common understandings among members as to what the organisation is and how its members should behave. Without such understanding, organisational life as we know it would not be possible.

organisational culture a system of shared meaning within an organisation

But there is more than this. Culture does not just refer to present actions: it is also one of the main mechanisms through which the behaviour and actions of new members of the organisation are shaped. A long-time researcher of organisation culture, Edgar Schein, has proposed the following definition:[7]

> Organisational culture is the pattern of basic assumptions that a given group has invented, discovered or developed in learning to cope with its problems of external adaptation and internal integration, and that have worked well enough to be considered valid, and, therefore, to be taught to new members as the new way to perceive, think and feel in relation to those problems.

A close study of Schein's definition enables us to highlight some key concepts of organisational culture. First it is composed of beliefs and assumptions. Beliefs and assumptions form our mental concepts of what we consider reality. This in turn affects how we perceive events around us and the interpretations we make in our daily lives. We take our beliefs and assumptions for granted, rarely if ever questioning or evaluating them. Indeed, so embedded are they that many of us may be unable to identify what our basic assumptions and beliefs are. In many cases we become aware of them only when we move to a different social system, such as a country or company, where our beliefs and assumptions are no longer the dominant ones.

Schein's definition also highlights that the beliefs and assumptions we apply at work are part of the social processes that have emerged from the way in which organisations adapt to their environment. In other words, cultures do not emerge as a random set of beliefs and thoughts. They have a purpose, and that purpose is to enable the organisation to survive in the environment in which it operates. It does this by providing a common set of values, which facilitates understanding among members. This provides members with a collective identity and enables them to work well together. Just as importantly, the culture of the organisation should be congruent—in other words it should fit—the external environment in which the organisation operates. Further, the emergent culture of the organisation is transmitted through a process of socialisation to new members.

Organisational cultures exist because the conditions that foster their creation are commonly found. These conditions may be identified from Schein's definition. These requirements are stability of membership and a repetitive cycle of events, leading to a stable pattern of interaction among members. Further, there is a need for at least some measure of organisational success, which indicates that the actions being taken are appropriate and should be transmitted to new members.

The culture of an organisation is carried in the values and behavioural norms of organisational members. There are two types of values: terminal and instrumental.[8] **Terminal values** refer to the desired end-state or outcome that people try to attain. Examples of terminal values may be achieving certain quality or performance levels, alleviating the effects of poverty, providing clean drinking water or providing aids for the disabled. **Instrumental values** refer to desired modes of behaviour. Examples are the standards of conduct of organisational members, professional standards, attitudes towards work, the extent of cooperation within an organisation, and values that support certain patterns of communication. 'Norms' are derived from the word 'normal', and that should provide us with a good idea as to what they are. *Norms* are behavioural and attitudinal standards that are taken as accepted for a given group.

This discussion indicates to us that culture exists at two levels. These are shown in Figure 13.1. The first is outward manifestations of the culture, which are observable and capable of some form of interpretation. We can identify the symbols of the organisation, the pattern of communications, the physical arrangement of work spaces and the ways in which power is expressed. We can also listen to the stories that are told and observe the ceremonies that members participate in. The second level of culture is composed of the deeply held values, beliefs, assumptions, attitudes and feelings that underlie behaviour. Beliefs and assumptions at this level are difficult to identify, interpret and understand. As a consequence they present complexities for managers and researchers alike. Even organisation members may be unable to identify what the values and beliefs of the organisation are. It is the visible level of culture that is more amenable to measurement and change, and consequently has been the focal point of management activity.

FIGURE 13.1 The different levels of culture, showing how interpretability varies with each level

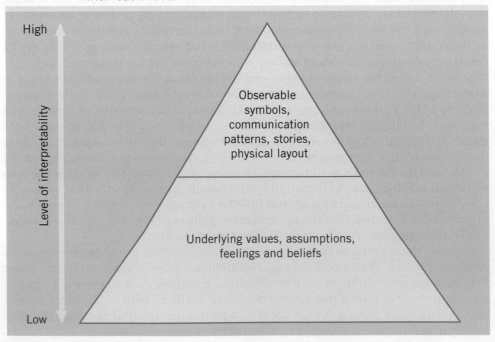

Researchers have identified that culture is not just an instrumental feature of an organisation whose sole purpose is to achieve environmental adaptation. It also satisfies a deeper human need by providing a sense of meaning and belonging to organisational members. This has been called the symbolic-interpretive approach to culture.[9] Membership of organisations provides more than just economic rewards. It also affords a source of identification on which people may build significance within their lives. Organisations that impart this for their members have been called social movements. The term 'clan' has been used to describe organisations which, in an industrial setting, exhibit many of the control and identification functions of self-sufficient preindustrial groups.[10] While many prominent businesses provide this identification for their members, it can be also clearly be seen in the non-profit sector. Religious organisations, those engaged in environmental lobbying such as Greenpeace, charities, overseas aid organisations and sporting bodies have a deep symbolic meaning for their members. In many cases, members of these organisations are happy to give their services free of charge because of their close identification with the basic purposes of the organisation. Needless to say, this presents challenges to the management of these organisations that are not encountered in profit-oriented businesses.

Is it possible to 'measure' culture?

Much of the discussion of culture, and the presentation of research, is of a descriptive nature: in other words, it describes in narrative form features that have been observed. However, there is a need for managers and others to describe culture in more concrete and measurable terms. This enables both diagnosis and comparisons between organisations to be made. So even though they may not tap the deeper meanings of culture, we propose that the following 10 characteristics, when taken together, reveal the visible features of an organisation's culture. While the whole of organisational culture may be somewhat different from the summation of its parts, the following represent the key characteristics where cultures differ:[11]

1 *Individual initiative.* The degree of responsibility, freedom and independence that individuals have.
2 *Risk tolerance.* The degree to which employees are encouraged to be aggressive, innovative and risk-seeking.
3 *Direction.* The degree to which the organisation creates clear objectives and performance expectations.
4 *Integration.* The degree to which units within the organisation are encouraged to operate in a coordinated manner.
5 *Management support.* The degree to which managers provide clear communication, assistance and support to their subordinates.
6 *Control.* The number of rules and regulations and the amount of direct supervision that are used to oversee and control employee behaviour.
7 *Identity.* The degree to which members identify with the organisation as a whole rather than with their particular work group or field of professional expertise.
8 *Reward system.* The degree to which reward allocations (i.e. salary increases and promotions) are based on employee performance criteria in contrast to seniority, favouritism and so on.
9 *Conflict tolerance.* The degree to which employees are encouraged to air conflicts and criticisms openly.

10 *Communication patterns.* The degree to which organisational communications are restricted to the formal hierarchy of authority.

These 10 characteristics include both structural and behavioural dimensions. For example, management support is a measure of leadership behaviour. Most of these dimensions, however, are closely intertwined with an organisation's design. To illustrate, the more routine an organisation's technology and the more centralised its decision-making process, the less individual initiative employees in that organisation will have. Similarly, machine bureaucracies create cultures with more formal communication patterns than do simple or matrix structures. Close analysis would also reveal that integration is essentially an indicator of horizontal interdependence. What this means is that organisational cultures are not just reflections of their members' attitudes and personalities. A large part of an organisation's culture can be traced directly to structurally related variables.

Do organisations have uniform cultures?

Organisational culture represents a common set of beliefs held by the organisation's members. This was made clear when we noted that culture was a system of *shared meaning*. We should expect, therefore, individuals with different backgrounds or at different levels in the organisation to tend to describe the organisation's culture in similar terms. Acknowledgement that organisational culture has common properties does not imply, however, that there cannot be subcultures within any given culture. Most large organisations have a dominant culture and numerous sets of subcultures.[12]

dominant culture the overiding core values shared by the majority of an organisation's members

core values the primary values expressed by an organisation's dominant culture

Subcultures separate cultures encompassed within organisational subunits

A **dominant culture** expresses the **core values** that are shared by a majority of the organisation's members. When we talk about an *organisation's* culture, we are referring to its dominant culture. It is this macro-view of culture that gives an organisation its distinct personality. Top management is often closely associated with either promoting or carrying the dominant culture.

Subcultures tend to develop in large organisations to reflect common problems, situations, technologies or experiences that members face. These subcultures can form vertically or horizontally.[13] When one product division of a conglomerate has a culture uniquely different from that of other divisions of the organisation, a vertical subculture exists. Transnational corporations also have vertical cultures, where different cultures exist in different countries. When a specific set of functional specialists—such as accountants or research and development personnel—have a set of common understandings, a horizontal subculture is formed. Of course, any group in an organisation can develop a subculture. For the most part, however, subcultures tend to be defined by departmental designations, tasks or geographical separation. The purchasing department, for example, can have a subculture that is uniquely shared by members of that department. It will include the core values of the dominant culture plus additional values unique to members of the purchasing department. Similarly, an office or unit of the organisation that is physically separated from the organisation's main operations may take on a different personality. Again, the core values are essentially retained but modified to reflect the separated unit's distinct situation.

If organisations had no dominant culture and were composed only of numerous subcultures, the influence of culture on organisational effectiveness would be far more difficult to determine and manage. Why? Because there would be no consistency of perceptions or behaviour. It is the 'shared meaning' aspect of organisational culture that makes it such a potent concept. However, we cannot ignore the reality that many organisations, and almost all large ones, also have distinct subcultures.

The fact that organisational members may share certain values need not mean that all organisations have a culture that is unique to them. Members of organisations are drawn from the local population, so it is not surprising that organisations reflect the culture and values of the population from which their members are drawn. For instance, if a country has been measured as being high in authoritarianism, then we will expect the organisations drawn from that country to have authoritarian values as well. There are also externally imposed restraints on the freedom of organisations to pursue certain forms of behaviour. Gender discrimination is illegal, for instance, as is a whole range of behaviours in the social sphere. Extensive consumer protection, employment and environmental laws restrict freedom of action by organisations and guide the behaviour of individual members. Additionally, many occupations have professional standards which guide and direct the behaviour of individuals within the organisation and over which organisations have little control.

When we examine the culture of organisations, we should not expect large variations between companies in the same industry. We would not expect there to be a large difference in culture between Coles supermarkets and Woolworths, for instance, as they undertake the same task using similar technologies serving a similar customer base. However, we would expect there to be large difference between the cultures of Woolworths and a university.

OT CLOSEUP

How cultures are seen by business people

We have listed the variables that academics have used to define culture. But business people and journalists have their own language to describe culture. The following descriptors, and their meanings, are among those commonly used in business journals.

Entrepreneurial culture. Constantly seeking new markets and products.

Conformist culture. Low tolerance of dissent.

Clubby and paternalistic culture. Exclusive, with the company looking after employees.

Cosy culture. Comfortable and stress-free.

Insular and consensus-driven. Isolated, inward-looking and agreement-seeking.

Slow-moving and arrogant. Slow to change and contemptuous of others.

Bureaucratic. Dominated by adherence to rules and procedures.

Complacent, sluggish and inward-looking. Uncaring of the organisation's environment and not prepared to change.

Performance-based. Goal- and target-driven behaviour.

Culture of hubris. Proud and dismissive of other organisations.

Shareholder culture. Seeking to maximise shareholder gains.

Hidebound, politics-ridden culture. Narrow-minded and conspiratorial.

Plodding, perfectionist culture. Stodgy but seeking constantly to improve products.

Aggressive culture. Pushy and assertive.

Culture and organisational effectiveness

What impact does culture have on organisational effectiveness? To answer this question, we need first to differentiate between strong cultures and weak ones.

A **strong culture** is characterised by the organisation's core values being intensely held, clearly ordered and widely shared. The more members that accept the core values, agree on their order of importance and are highly committed to them, the stronger the culture is. Organisations that have constant turnover among their members, almost by definition, will have a weak culture because members will not have shared enough experiences to create distinctive common meanings.[14] This should not be interpreted as implying that all mature organisations with a stable membership will have strong cultures, as the core values must also be intensely held.

Religious organisations, cults and Japanese companies are examples of organisations that have very strong cultures.[15] In extreme forms, these are very instructive about the role that culture can play in an organisation. For instance, when the Reverend Sun Myung Moon in South Korea can bring together and marry 30 000 couples where the bride and groom have never met, we see a degree of sharedness and an intensity of values that allow extremely high behavioural control. Other examples of extreme culture control are military organisations, which take recruits from a wide variety of backgrounds then isolate them for months while moulding them into an efficient fighting force. Of course, the strong cultural influences that can lead to mass marriages with strangers or the formation of elite military units can be directed positively, to create successful organisations such as the National Australia Bank and Virgin Blue—although of course the extreme mechanisms used by organisations such as military services must be modified in commercial organisations. Additionally, commercial organisations may not seek such a deep culture within their organisations.

If the culture is strong, how will it influence the organisation's effectiveness? In Schein's definition of culture given at the beginning of the chapter, we identified culture as playing an important role in internal integration and in the external adaptation of the organisation to its environment. We can see that effectiveness requires that an organisation's culture, strategy, environment and technology be aligned and appropriate to meet the organisation's goals.[16] The stronger an organisation's culture, the more important it is that the culture fit properly with the other variables.

The successful organisation will achieve a good *external fit*—its culture will conform to its strategy and environment. Market-driven strategies, for instance, are more appropriate in dynamic environments and will require a culture that emphasises individual initiative, risk-taking, high integration, tolerance of conflicts and high horizontal communication. In contrast, product-driven strategies focus on efficiency, work best in stable environments, and are more likely to be successful when the organisation's culture is high in control, minimises risk and conflict and emphasises conformance to standards. Successful organisations will also seek a good *internal fit*, with their culture properly matched to their technology. As noted earlier in this chapter, routine technologies provide stability and work well when linked to a culture that emphasises centralised decision making and limited individual initiative. None of us would be keen to fly with an airline that promoted and rewarded risk-taking. Non-routine technologies, on the other hand, require adaptability and are best when matched with cultures that encourage individual initiative and free-flowing communication and downplay control. Advertising agencies are good examples of this type of cultural fit.

Environments are rarely stable. Technology and the actions of competitors are constantly changing. Expectations of stakeholders, such as customers, shareholders, employees and government, change over time. And with the expansion of globalisation a whole new range of complexities have entered the organisation's external environment. From our definition we can see that the organisation's culture influences its ability to adapt to these changes. This indicates to us that the appropriateness of a culture is not set in stone. As environments and technologies change, then so too must the organisation's culture in order for the organisation to maintain its effectiveness. As we shall discuss later, the stronger the culture, the more difficult it is to change.

Many Australian and New Zealand companies that were in regulated industries or were government monopolies are faced with having to change strong cultures. In many cases, although the butt of many jokes about efficiency, these organisations (e.g. Telstra, the various water supply authorities, port authorities, and electricity-generation and supply organisations, to name a few), were strongly imbued with the ethic of service to the public. The stability that regulation had given them, combined in many cases with fairly static technology and a highly centralised and structured industrial relations system, led to very fixed and rigid ways of doing things. Any proposed change in the organisation's operations had to contend with the inertia of many layers of management and massive industrial relations problems. However, now that most of these organisations have been either deregulated or privatised, they must alter their way of operating in order to accommodate change more readily. Layers of management have been cut and labour awards negotiated on an enterprise basis. Whole organisations have had to come to terms with the fact that it is no longer sufficient just to get the job done, and that efficiency measures have to be met as well. The competitive marketplace is unforgiving of those organisations which do not use their resources effectively. In the new environment, the old culture was a liability, and a new culture of cooperation and wider job skills and responsibilities had to be learnt by those wanting to avoid redundancy.

Culture: a substitute for formalisation?

Another result of a strong culture is that it enhances behavioural consistency.[17] It conveys to employees what behaviours they should engage in, and tells them about things such as the acceptability of absenteeism.[18] Some cultures encourage employees to use their sick days, and do little to discourage absenteeism. Not surprisingly, organisations with such a culture have much higher absenteeism rates than those organisations where not showing up for work—regardless of reason—is seen as letting your co-workers down. As strong cultures enhance behavioural consistency, it is only logical to conclude that they can be a powerful means of implicit control and can act as a substitute for formalisation.

We know how formalisation's rules and regulations act to regulate employee behaviour. High formalisation in an organisation creates predicability, orderliness and consistency. A strong culture does the same but without any need for written documentation. Moreover, a strong culture may be more potent than any formal structural controls, because culture controls the mind and soul as well as an organisational member's actions. Many organisations that undertake work in which high levels of reliability are required have found that one of the most effective ways in which reliability is promoted is by the development of a strong culture.[19] Such organisations run nuclear power plants and oil rigs and operate air traffic control systems. As in most organisations, it is almost impossible to predict every eventuality and write a rule to cover it. This problem can be overcome by instilling a culture of reliability, which promotes making meaning of small changes or errors that may occur, and accommodates latitude for interpretation, improvisation and actions for which a precedent has not been set.

We have seen how some features of organisational culture can provide an intrinsic sense of belonging for the individual. Much of what is discussed as culture refers to the features of a modern form of tribe or clan, which acts as a source of identification for the individual employee.[20] Being a member of the organisation gives support through a sense of sharing goals, values and behaviour standards with other organisation members. This guides action through providing a set of sanctions and rewards to ensure that the organisation's behaviourial norms are being adhered to. Where such sharing of values is deeply embedded in the minds of organisational members, then the need for management virtually ceases to exist. We can see this in some religious organisations, such as the Jesuits. Those wanting to join the order spend years in isolation and contemplation, being ordained as priests only when they have been imbued with the values and beliefs of the organisation. Such values and beliefs are

OT CLOSEUP

McDonald's and the Kroc legend

McDonald's, the well-known hamburger chain, has been operating in Australia since 1971, when it opened its first hamburger restaurant at Yagoona in Sydney. Part of a worldwide chain, with 9800 restaurants in 46 countries, McDonald's was established in 1955 in the American state of Illinois by a hamburger salesman called Ray Kroc. So closely identified was Kroc to become with the setting of standards for the company that his influence lives on, long after his retirement from active involvement in the running of the company and many years after his death.

His office is preserved as a museum, with his reading glasses untouched in their leather case on his desk. New employees of McDonald's, by tapping rows of desktop computers, watch a 90-minute video made by Kroc. Photographs of Kroc's first hamburger restaurant, with Kroc cleaning the windows, are to be found in many of the administrative buildings. Kroc's obsession with cleanliness permeates McDonald's restaurants worldwide, and this, along with the concept of assembly-line production of food and a religious devotion to the hamburger, has kept the company in the leading position in the fast-food business for a number of years.

Kroc also encouraged innovation and was always coming up with new ideas, not all of them successful. He encouraged his franchisees to do likewise, and most of the McDonald's innovations have originated from this source.

McDonald's has shunned diversification and continues to adhere to the philosophies of its founder. The problem with this is that if these philosophies become dated or the hamburger goes out of fashion, changing the culture will be an extremely difficult task.

Adapted from: 'Paying Homage to the Hamburger God', *The Sydney Morning Herald*, 14 November 1989.

so strongly held that they are virtually impossible to eliminate, and Jesuit priests can almost always be relied on to always act in their Order's interests. This makes the traditional surveillance and supervision tasks of management redundant.

Many voluntary and not-for-profit organisations also have strong cultures which substitute for formalisation. Charities, environmental groups and local community associations have remarkably few rules and regulations and have low levels of coordination, hierarchy and formal management input. In this case those involved are guided by their identification with the goals of the organisation, and are prepared in many cases to self-manage their efforts.

It seems entirely appropriate to view formalisation and culture as two different roads to a common destination. The stronger an organisation's culture, the less management need be concerned with developing formal rules and regulations to guide employee behaviour. Those guidelines will have been internalised by employees when they learned the organisation's culture. But as we have seen, the downside of a strong culture is that, if it becomes inappropriate over time, it can be extremely difficult to change and in some circumstances will be so resistant to change as to threaten the organisation's existence.

Creating, sustaining and transmitting culture

An organisation's culture doesn't come out of thin air. Once established, it rarely fades away. What forces influence the creation of a culture? What reinforces and sustains these once they are in place? How do new employees learn their organisation's culture? The following summarises what we have learned about how cultures are created, sustained and transmitted.

How a culture begins

An organisation's current customs, traditions and general way of doing things are largely due to what it has done before and the degree of success it had with those endeavours. This leads us to the ultimate source of an organisation's culture—its founders.

The founding fathers or mothers of an organisation traditionally have a major impact on establishing the early culture. They have a vision or mission as to what the organisation should be. They are unconstrained by previous ways of doing things or by ideologies. The small size that typically characterises any new organisation further facilitates the founders' imposing their vision on all organisational members. Because the founders have the original idea, they also typically have biases about how to implement the idea. The organisation's culture results from the interaction between the founders' biases and assumptions, and what the original members that the founders initially employ learn subsequently from their own experiences.[21]

Sir Hudson Fysh of Qantas, Harry Seidler with his architectural firm and Franco Belgiorno-Nettis of Transfield are just some of the individuals who have had an immeasurable impact on the shaping of their organisation's culture. For instance, Sir Hudson Fysh's ideals in relation to taking the then risky venture of flying and applying modern technology and management methods to establish an airline is celebrated within Qantas' folklore. Harry Seidler has specialised in the design of large buildings and has managed to bring individuality to difficult architectural challenges. Franco Belgiorno-Nettis has recognised that the strength of his company is in construction, and it has never strayed from developing its skills in using people to manufacture and construct, even through the speculative boom of the 1980s.

Of course, not all firms that are founded by visionary individuals survive in the long run. And many that do need to undergo a cultural change along the way. As Bill Gates of Microsoft has found, the urge to be super-competitive and to dominate may have given his company an edge in the early stages of its formation and growth. But the culture developed to achieve this end proved to be a burden to Microsoft once this goal had been reached.

Keeping a culture alive

Once a culture is in place, there are forces within the organisation that act to maintain it by giving employees a set of similar experiences. In Table 13.1 we have identified the four forces that play the most important part in sustaining a culture are the organisation's selection practices, the actions of top management, the organisation's socialisation methods, and the use of appropriate rewards and punishments.[22]

Selection practices

The explicit goal of the selection process is to identify and hire individuals who have the knowledge, skills and abilities to successfully perform the jobs within the organisation. But typically, more than one candidate will be identified who meets any given job's requirements. When that happens, it would be naive to ignore the fact that the final decision as to who is hired will be significantly influenced by the decision maker's judgement of how well the candidates will fit into the organisation. This attempt, purposely or inadvertently, to ensure a proper match results in the hiring of people who have common values (ones essentially consistent with the organisations) or at least a good portion of them, and who are likely to acquire those which they do not have.[23] Moreover, the selection process provides applicants with information on the organisation. Candidates learn about the organisation and, if they perceive a conflict between their values and the organisations, they can self-select themselves out of the applicant pool. Selection, therefore, becomes a two-way street, allowing either employer or applicant to withdraw from the process if there appears to be a mismatch. In this way, the selection process sustains an organisation's culture by selecting out those individuals who might attack or undermine its core values.

For example, Macquarie Bank will hire only graduates with distinction averages. To get a distinction average, most students must be prepared to work hard, have ambition, be attuned to competition and have a fair measure of intelligence. These characteristics are those required by the bank of people who will work in the more complex areas of banking and finance, developing new products, interpreting financial trends and providing financial advice. In contrast, the police forces for many

TABLE 13.1 Ways in which a culture is sustained

Selection practices
Actions of top management
Socialisation
Use of appropriate rewards and punishments

OT CLOSEUP

Mayne and the surgeons: or the tricky business of hospital culture

One of the perennial underperformers on the Australian stock market is the former Mayne Nickless, now known as Mayne Group. As one of the conglomerates which dominated Australian business, Mayne has constantly struggled to determine what its core competencies are and in turn, extract reasonable returns from them. Its main businesses have been reduced to transport, logistic and its major division, health care which is based on 58 private hospitals and supporting diagnostic and pathology services.

After years of strategy changes and attempts at cost cutting, in 2001 the board of Mayne appointed Peter Smedley as managing director. Smedley established his reputation as a turnaround expert at Colonial Mutual, which he built from a sleepy insurance company to a major funds manager and which was subsequently sold to the Commonwealth Bank for $10 billion. Much of the growth at Colonial took place through acquisitions. Smedley, and the management team he brought with him, was expected to work a similar magic at Mayne.

However running a large health care group proved to be afar more difficult task than Smedley possibly imagined. The main reason for this was that the culture of the health industry proved to be radically different to that of banking. Hospitals are a service business and the main source of customers is not the patients but the surgeons who refer them to the hospital. The patients pay the surgeons and the health funds pay the patient. The patients go to the hospitals nominated by the surgeon. Keeping the surgeons happy therefore becomes the key to profitability. As they are not employees who can be managed in a traditional sense, they must be kept happy in other ways.

If anyone went out of their way to antagonise the surgeons, it is unlikely that they could have done a better job than Mayne. Their first structural move was to centralise all decision making in the Melbourne head office. The aim was to cut costs but it had the consequence of leaving little decision making at the local level. Surgeons were advised that if they wanted to speak to management they would have to write a memo, a complete contrast to just walking up to the hospital manager's office to discuss patient care. Many surgeons complained that their telephone calls were rarely answered and important meetings never held. Needless to say relations with medical staff deteriorated rapidly.

Another important downside from the centralisation strategy was that critical local issues were not identified and acted upon in time. Further, the remote management strategy gutted hospital management of its knowledge base.

Other health professionals have been put offside by constant cost cutting which many staff claim treats patients like cans off a conveyer belt and that the concentration on the bottom line has taken over and the important focus of patient care. Partly this attributed to Smedley and his team having little experience in managing a service industry like health. Ultimately a culture built on quality service to a patient is not going to take too kindly to bureaucratic type cost cutting. So antagonistic are health professionals to Mayne that potential take over targets, such as Brisbane based QML pathology group, are reluctant to become involved with a company such as Mayne. QML notes that most pathology services are managed by medical staff who are sensitive to medical issues and responsive to the needs of their clients.

The parallels which were drawn between banking ten years ago and health care in the past couple of years, and which underpinned Smedley's appointment, have proved to be elusive. A management model applicable to banking where margins can be shaved, customer inertia is high and money flows into funds management through government mandated superannuation, cannot be readily transferred to the health industry. As one doctor stated if your child has a brain tumour and you have a choice of the cheapest or the best, you don't think too long about your decision.

Adapted from: Beth Quinleven, *Medicine Man*, Business Review Weekly, April 4 2002, pp. 46–53; David Roe and Tom Noble, *How Dissatisfied Doctors Cost Mayne $1 Billion*, The Age 27th April 2002, p. 1.

years avoided hiring graduates. They preferred to educate the recruited rather than recruit the educated. Their idea was that those with just a basic education would be more easily socialised into the organisation and inculcated with police ways of thinking.

Actions of top management

Top management has a symbolic influence on an organisation's culture.[24] The actions and attitudes of the chief executive are closely observed for guides as to what behaviour is acceptable and how the problems of the organisation should be approached. Indeed, the chief executive is even looked to to define the problems of the organisation and what business it should be in. Although in a large organisation the chief executive is rarely seen, the pronouncements from the executive suite are often made available through annual reports, company profiles, e-mails and even videos for staff consumption. So important is this group in influencing the culture of the organisation that they have been termed 'culture carriers'.

The chief executive also has a major impact on culture through who is hired and fired.[25] Virtually all of the senior management of the organisation is chosen or approved by the chief executive. Those chosen almost always reflect the culture that the chief executive wants to promote.

Socialisation

No matter how good a job the organisation does in recruiting and selection, new employees are not hired fully indoctrinated into the organisation's culture. Perhaps most importantly, because they are least familiar with the organisation's culture, new employees are potentially most likely to disturb the beliefs and customs that are in place. The organisation will therefore want to help new employees adapt to its culture. As noted in Chapter 4, this adaptation process is called socialisation.

All new recruits in the army must go through recruit training. Recruit training camps are in country locations, such as Singleton or Puckapunyal, far from the family and society supports that have determined recruits' behaviour up to the time they enlisted. Once these supports are no longer there to fall back on, it is far easier for the army to mould the behaviour of the new recruit, so that the new, desired behaviours are more likely to dominate a soldier's actions. Similarly, the success of religious cults depends on effective socialisation, and this normally relies on isolation and a potential cult member always being in the company of an established cult member. Moonies have been consistently accused of kidnapping potential recruits and isolating them from family and friends while they are indoctrinated to place group loyalty above any other commitment. Most firms do similar things, in a very mild form, through such means as induction courses. These are designed to provide new employees with an understanding of what is expected of them, to tell them about the standards of dress and presentation required, how to treat customers, and to give them other information relevant to their job.

Socialisation continues throughout an employee's career in an organisation. However, socialisation is most explicit when a new employee enters an organisation. This is when the organisation seeks to mould the outsider into an employee 'in good standing'. Once on the job, a manager or senior colleague often becomes a coach to further guide and mould the new member. In some cases a formal training program will even be offered to ensure that the employee learns the organisation's culture.

Use of appropriate rewards and punishments

Rewards and punishments send a powerful message to organisational members. Employees are constantly observing events that are going on around them as well as experiencing praise and rebukes themselves. Such praise and rebukes may not be obvious: they can be as subtle as a glance or tone of voice. Events such as who is hired and fired, who is promoted and why, and actions that result in approval or admonition, both channel and direct behaviour. This time is also a very good predictor of likely future behaviour. If employees find that they cannot or will not change their behaviour to suit what they see around them, chances are they will have to leave.

Learning the deeper aspects of a culture

In addition to explicit orientation and training programs, culture is transmitted to employees in a number of other forms, the most potent being stories, rituals, material symbols and language.

Stories

If you worked at the Ford Motor Company during the 1970s, you would undoubtedly have heard the story about Henry Ford II reminding his executives, when they got too argumentative, that 'It's *my* name that's on the building'. The message was clear. Henry Ford II ran the company!

Stories such as this circulate through many organisations. They contain a narrative of events about the organisation's founders, key decisions that affect the organisation's future course and actions of top management. They anchor the present in the past and provide explanations and legitimacy for current practices.[26]

Stories serve a more important function than just being a narrative of occurrences or promoting coordination. Many events occur in organisations that defy logical analysis or simple behavioural explanation. Stories permit the explanation and interpretation of events and situations that are too complex for traditional linear analysis to explain.[27] Narratives and stories have been the main way in which humankind has passed on its experiences—and hence their culture and sense of meaning—since time immemorial. They allow the reconstruction of scenarios in a manner which enables them to be understood, interpreted and incorporated in the organisation's belief system. As a result they are powerful guides to action.

Rituals

We reviewed rituals in Chapter 4 in our discussion of formalisation. Just as rituals are used as a formalisation technique, so are they a means of transmitting culture. Activities such as recognition and award ceremonies, weekly Friday afternoon drinks and annual company picnics are rituals that express and reinforce the key values of the organisation, what goals are important, which people are important and which are expendable.[28]

Material symbols

In many cases, material symbols are used to transmit and reinforce the culture of an organisation. Anyone walking into a Kmart or Target store can see that it is obviously different from a David Jones or Country Road store. The workers in these chains know that working in each one is different as well. A David Jones employee acts differently towards customers and is expected to do different things from a Kmart employee.

An industry has arisen in recent times around generating image through office decoration and layout. Interior decorators design and fit offices to reflect the values and business philosophies of the client. Legal firms seek to create an image of high probity and low risk through muted tones and the isolation of staff. The decoration of an advertising agency tends to reflect originality, creative skills and the frenetic pace of the industry. It was traditional in older companies that the senior executive offices be wood-panelled, which led to lower-level staff referring to the accommodation as 'mahogany row'. Turn-of-the-century banking chambers were lofty, solid affairs, with substantial fittings to reflect an atmosphere of stability and permanence. Even the outsides of the buildings were made of heavy stone with solid Doric columns. In contrast, businesses such as Nike and Microsoft have built their offices in the style and form of universities, and have even gone as far as calling them campuses rather than offices.

Even such factors as the type of car driven by the senior management of the organisation reflect its standards and values. The advertising industry is famous for the number of executives who drive BMWs and Porsches. University vice-chancellors, however, drive far more sedate top-of-the-line Fords and Holdens.

Through the above means messages are conveyed to employees regarding such factors as who is important, the degree of egalitarianism desired by top management, and the kinds of behaviours (i.e. risk-taking, conservative, authoritarian, participative, individualistic, social) that are appropriate.

Observation and experience

Human beings are innately suited to functioning as members of social systems. Much of what they learn in organisations is a result of observation and experience. This is often a far more powerful teacher than written mission statements and policy and procedures manuals, which are often studied only at a superficial level and generally induce acute boredom. Where there is a conflict between what is observed and experienced and what is written, observation and experience will have the greater impact.

Language

Many organisations and units within organisations use jargon and terminology as a way to identify members of a culture or subculture. By learning language in this way, members attest to their acceptance of the culture and, in so doing, help to preserve it. In many cases the distinctive language of a culture or subculture derives from the tasks undertaken and technology used by the group.

The kitchen personnel in large hotels use terminology foreign to people who work in other areas of a hotel. Members of the army sprinkle their language liberally with jargon that readily identifies its members. Many organisations, over time, develop unique terms to describe equipment, offices, key personnel, suppliers, customers or products that relate to its business. New employees are often overwhelmed with acronyms and jargon that after six months on the job become a natural part of their language. But once assimilated, this terminology acts as a common denominator that unites members of a given culture or subculture.

When cultures collide: mergers and acquisitions

The contrast between two cultures is highlighted when organisations merge and an attempt is made to generate a common culture. In many cases the mergers do not go ahead because the culture clash is too great.[29] There have been a number of different proposals to combine the two professional accounting bodies in Australia— the Australian Society of Certified Practising Accountants and the Institute of Chartered Accountants in Australia. Although the merger makes considerable sense, all the proposals have so far been rejected by the membership because of differences in culture between the two organisations.

Similar differences in culture were exposed in the plan to merge the smaller former Colleges of Advanced Education (CAEs) in Australia into a larger university system. In many cases, the more traditional universities saw much of their strength in research and the CAEs saw their strength in teaching. Mergers were proposed by governments, in many cases with little thought as to whether the merged organisations would develop the necessary spirit of cooperation to operate effectively. High levels of conflict were often generated as a result of the mergers, with separate campuses of the same university being run virtually as autonomous bodies. Some mergers have actually had to be undone. The merger between the former Northern Rivers CAE, now Southern Cross University, and the University of New England was dissolved when it became apparent that the two institutions just could not work together.

Cultures may arise from geographical location and differing customer bases as much as from differing values. The merger between the former State Bank of Victoria (SBV) and the Sydney-based Commonwealth Bank of Australia shows that, even if on the surface organisations do much the same thing in the same way, problems can arise. The SBV was a long-established bank owned by the Victorian government and primarily serving the savings needs of ordinary Victorians. The Commonwealth Bank, owned by the federal government, undertook a similar function around Australia, although it was strongest in New South Wales. Through reckless lending policies, which most employees had nothing to do with, the SBV faced a financial crisis and was sold to the Commonwealth Bank. The fact that both banks served similar populations and undertook similar tasks in no way made the merger easy. Resentment was high at the SBV over the loss of identity and autonomy—the foundation of a culture—and the Commonwealth's managers were resentful of the amount of time they were spending in trying to make a merger, which they didn't want, work.

The preceding examples illustrate that there is more to a successful merger or acquisition than a favourable financial statement or product synergy. If the parties to a marriage both have strong cultures, the potential for 'culture clash' becomes very real. In fact, many senior executives are learning the hard way that a cultural mismatch is more likely to result in a disaster than is a financial, technical, geographical, product or market mismatch.[30] Recent research finds that 90% of these mergers fail to live up to the projections originally set by management.[31] Cultural clash is a major cause of this disappointment. The message this carries to management is to evaluate the culture of any organisation that is being considered as a merger or acquisition candidate.

Globalisation has added complexity, with many mergers now occurring across borders as companies seek to expand market share or achieve economies of scale. What looks on the surface to be a sound strategic move often proves difficult to implement. French-based Renault's acquisition of the Japanese-based Nissan, Daimler's acquisition of Chrysler and BP's merger with Amoco are just a few of the high-profile international mergers that have occurred recently. There are many smaller cross-border mergers that escape notice. Each of these mergers presents the additional problem of coping with the integration of those with different national cultures. In some cases firms don't try too hard to seek close integration; they run their overseas operations as separate divisions. CSR's and Boral's large-scale building material operations in the United States are run autonomously, with little day-to-day contact with the Australian operations. Most Australian overseas investment is aimed at operating as an insider in overseas markets, with very little integration with the Australian operations. This avoids many of the problems arising from differences in national culture. This approach has been called a multi-domestic strategy.

Probably the two most critical factors determining whether a merger or acquisition is successful are the strength of each organisation's culture and the degrees of difference that exist between the organisations' key cultural characteristics. Let's take a closer look at each of these factors.

In a merger or acquisition, if one or both of the organisations have weak cultures, the marriage is more likely to work. This is because weak cultures are more malleable and can therefore adapt better to new situations. Two strong cultures, on the other hand, can create real problems. The banking industry provides another example of this. Realising that reliance on low-margin traditional banking services would not deliver the growth desired, the large multi-product banks have, over the past 20 years, attempted to move into the higher-margin investment banking area. Investment banks provide such products as advising on mergers and acquisitions, managing funds, and providing general corporate advice. However, attempts by the large banks to merge with the investment banks have almost invariably resulted in failure. The reason for the failure was not a flawed strategy but the inability of the two cultures to merge. Mainstream banking promoted a culture of high control, application of rules and regulations, and risk avoidance. In contrast, investment banking relied on the skills of very talented, high-paid fast-moving individuals who would act on a perceived opening, which in many cases they themselves identified in the market. When the large banks tried to impose their culture of close control on the investment bankers, they felt restricted and unable to operate at their optimum level. High levels of defections and resignations among the investment bankers contributed to the failure of most of the mergers.

The merging of two strong cultures need not present problems if the cultures are very similar. BHP merged with the Utah minerals division of General Electric with a minimal amount of trauma. Both firms had strong cultures, but their compatibility was high and Utah enjoyed considerable autonomy in day-to-day operations. Thus, strong cultures are likely to hinder effectiveness in the newly merged organisation only when the cultures are at odds.

The incompatibility of two cultures need not be a problem when mergers are not within the same industry. For instance, when one company is taken over and added to another company as a division, the interaction with the rest of that company may be minimal. In this case, the new acquisition becomes a subculture of the larger

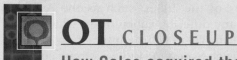

OT CLOSEUP

How Coles acquired the Myer culture

One of the more interesting mergers of the 1980s was the takeover of Myer by G.J. Coles in 1985. Although the merged group adopted the name of Coles Myer, Coles called all the shots in the merger.

Coles started out in the 1920s as a bottom-of-the-market retailer with the motto 'Nothing over 2/6'. It had a distinct discount image, with managers almost exclusively coming from the shop floor. The head office was situated over the company's main store in Melbourne, and all staff employed there, as well as visitors, had to pass rows of discount merchandise on vinyl flooring to get to the offices above.

By contrast, Myer was at the heart of the Melbourne establishment. It consisted of upmarket department stores whose name was a byword in the latest styles and merchandise. The Myer family was at the centre of Melbourne social life and while the offices of the staff could not be considered luxurious, they certainly reflected the ambience expected of a company with such a distinguished pedigree.

Observers of the merger expected a major cultural clash to occur, as it seemed that the cultures were not compatible. Although it was possible to run the various component shopping chains, such as Kmart, Target, Myer and Katies, as separate divisions, the nature and style of the head office were still to emerge.

What transpired was unexpected. What most analysts had failed to anticipate was that when Coles took over Myer it would throw off its cheap image. Brian Quinn, the managing director of Coles—and, after the merger, of Coles Myer—lost no time in moving away from the downmarket image he sprang from and developed a penchant for luxury. Typical of his actions was the move to build a new head office for the group in the Melbourne suburb of Tooronga. The Tooronga head office has a foyer the size of an aircraft hangar, complete with marble tables and leather armchairs, and is dotted with waterfalls. With its muzak and well-spoken and well-coiffed receptionists, it projects a glitzy Californian image.

The board of Coles Myer consisted of some of the more prominent entrepreneurs of the 1980s as well as a fair sprinkling of the Melbourne establishment. All of a sudden, the former Coles directors and their wives were surrounded by people who drove flash cars, collected expensive art and had their own planes. Somehow, Quinn and his colleagues from Coles had been seduced by the luxury. The directors' wives were treated to fashion and grooming advice and the men brushed up their image.

After the merger, there was a major disparity between the pay of the old Coles hands and the Myer executives. Rather than reduce the pay of the Myer executives, the group raised the pay of many former Coles staff by up to $80 000 per year to match that of their Myer counterparts, and Brian Quinn's pay rose astronomically. He was also famous for his collection of expensive cars, parked next to the lift in the Tooronga car park, and his Templestowe mansion became the talk of the town. He later faced criminal charges for using company money to renovate it.

Very little if anything of the old Coles culture remained. One Kmart buyer noted that trying to knock down suppliers half a cent a unit was useless after they had walked past the luxury cars and waited in the foyer. For a discount chain, the image was all wrong.

While Coles Myer was luxuriating in its surroundings, its market share, particularly in groceries and food, was being eroded by companies such as Woolworths and Franklins, with head offices perched above warehouses and with noisy window air-conditioners accompanying the price negotiations.

Adapted from: Colleen Ryan & Anne Lampe, 'Cache and Carry', *The Sydney Morning Herald*, 3 April 1993, p. 58.

organisation. Many of the conglomerates of the 1980s, such as the Adelaide Steamship Company, were made up of many differing subcultures, which made additions and disposals easier to accomplish. There is little interaction between Foster's beer and wine operations, allowing each to develop its own, strong culture.

Rarely is a merger a coming together of equals: there is generally a dominant party to the takeover. This can lead to feelings of superiority on the part of the company driving the takeover and a sense of loss and even defeat in those whose organisation is being taken over. This is often complicated by the difficulties that arise when the head offices are in different states or countries. Often senior managers are reluctant to move location for either family or economic reasons. This can spread hostility arising from the takeover to those who would not normally be affected by moving location. Moving to Sydney typically presents a greater problem than with other capital cities because of the cost of housing and the geographic spread of the city. The merger of the Sydney-based Advance Bank (later St George) and the BankSA was made more difficult because senior BankSA staff were reluctant to move to Sydney. BankSA staff were antagonistic also because they had lost the autonomy and status involved in being the largest locally owned bank in South Australia.

Although in many cases mergers are promoted as being the amalgamation of equals, this is rarely the case. One company generally emerges the strongest and manages to impose its will on the other. This is sometimes obvious from the financial strength of the companies concerned. But it can also be linked to the power plays surrounding who will become chief executive. Obviously there can be only one chief executive, and the one that emerges triumphant normally gets to stamp his or her personality on the merged company. Naturally, this means that the company from which the chief executive emerges is the stronger.[32]

How do we manage cultures?

We now turn to the essential issue in this chapter: are cultures manageable? Clearly, an organisation's culture has a marked influence on its employees. As we have seen, this influence is not only on the visible and measurable aspects of employee performance and behaviour. Culture also operates at a deeper level, which provides both meaning and a guide to action to employees. This contributes to making culture the organisational characteristic that is probably most difficult to change. It is far easier to change reporting relationships, introduce a new technology, draw up a budget or adopt a new strategy than to manage the supporting cultural changes. One of the reasons for this is that many features of culture are not easily understood and interpretable and hence not amenable to conventional management techniques. Further difficulties arise for managers in that culture is 'owned' by all members of the organisation and is not purely within management's capacity to change. In many cases management only played a part in creating the culture, with the organisational members themselves making a major contribution to many of its features. It almost tempts one to consider that culture should be treated as a given, in which case managers would be advised to try to understand their organisation's culture but to remember that there is very little they can do to change it.[33]

As our knowledge and experience of management has expanded, however, we realise that there are actions that managers can take to facilitate cultural change. Indeed, current thinking is that proactive steps should be taken by management to align the organisation's culture better with the organisation's strategy and environment. Many of those who are most admired in the business community are those who have introduced and sustained a program of cultural change in their organisations—although it must also be said that there are many cases of failure in this area.

When we discuss **managing culture**, we mean *changing* the culture. This has grown to become the prevailing definition, yet, as one writer has noted, managing culture need not be the same as changing culture.[34] In a time of transition, for instance, managing an organisation's culture may entail sustaining or reinforcing the present culture rather than making any change. So, in a very strict sense, managing a culture could entail stabilising the status quo as well as inducing a shift to another state. For our purposes, however, we will treat *managing* culture and *changing* culture as synonymous.

managing culture
changing the organisation's culture

What factors are likely to influence a cultural change program?

The foregoing discussion suggests that there may be circumstances which make culture easier for managers to change.[35] This leads us to a situational analysis of conditions that are necessary for, or will facilitate, cultural change. The ideas we offer are based on observation as well as substantive research. However, there seems to be increasing agreement among theorists about the importance of the following situational factors. Table 13.2 summarises the factors influencing cultural change.

A *dramatic crisis*

The condition that is most universally acknowledged as having to exist before culture can be changed is a dramatic crisis that is widely perceived by the organisation's members.[36] This is the shock that undermines the status quo. It calls into question current practices and opens the door to accepting a different set of values that can respond better to the crisis. Examples of such a crisis would include an unexpected financial setback, such as that suffered by BHP in the late 1990s, the emergence of a hostile takeover, the loss of a major customer (though such a customer would have to represent a significant proportion of the organisation's revenues—typically 25% or more). It could also include a dramatic technological breakthrough by a competitor. The crisis, of course, need not be real to be effective. The point is that it is *perceived* as real by the organisation's members.

TABLE 13.2 Factors influencing cultural change

A dramatic crisis
A long-term slow decline
Leadership turnover
Life-cycle stage
Age of the organisation
Size of the organisation
Strength of the current culture
Absence of subcultures

A long-term slow decline

Many successful cultural change programs have emerged from the realisation by management that its organisation has entered a period of slow or no growth. In many cases this does not arise from any particular management deficiency. For instance, demand for food or consumer products such as detergent and soap is linked to population growth. Should population growth slow, as it has in many countries in recent years, then firms producing these products face sluggish sales. Changing spending patterns are leading to a smaller proportion of income being spent in retail stores. What was high-technology, cutting-edge product in previous generations, examples being oil refineries or basic chemical manufacturing, has now turned into a commodity governed by commodity pricing. Pharmaceutical companies may find that over a period of 10 years their innovation rates have dropped and that they have not achieved a breakthrough in discoveries which would guarantee a future income stream. A charity such as Legacy, which was set up to cater for the needs of dependents of servicemen who had served overseas, is faced with the need to reinvent itself as this section of the population declines.

The origins of long-term loss of performance in many cases lies in the growth of a culture which reinforced the existing ways of doing things while losing sight of the importance of customers, shareholders and other stakeholders.[37] Success in the past has led to the growth of complacency at all levels in the organisation, leading to a slow deterioration in performance. Change in this case may be successfully undertaken only by changing the culture of the organisation to be more adaptive to changes in the environment.

None of the organisations in this situation have suddenly been faced with a dramatic crisis; rather, their environments have changed slowly over time and they have failed to adapt to these changes. Their senior management, through its review processes, has come to the realisation that major changes need to be made to the way its organisation operates, and this involves cultural change. It is part of management's cultural change program to create a sense of crisis in the organisation when none is necessarily felt by the majority of employees.

Leadership turnover

As top management has a major influence in transmitting culture, a change in the organisation's key leadership positions facilitates the imposition of new values.[38] But new leadership, per se, is no assurance that employees will accept new values. The new leaders must have a clear alternative vision of what the organisation can be; there must be respect for their leadership capabilities; and they must have the ability to translate their alternative vision into reality. New leadership without an alternative set of values is unlikely to result in any substantive change in the organisation.[39]

Leadership turnover must encompass the organisation's chief executive. But it is not limited to this position. The likelihood of successful cultural change typically increases with a purge of all major management positions. Rather than having previous executives accept the new leader's values, it is usually more effective to replace them with individuals who have no vested interest in the old culture. Of course, it is undesirable for all top managers to be replaced: some continuity is necessary for the ongoing health of the organisation. But selective replacement of key managers sends a powerful signal to the rest of the organisation.

Life-cycle stage

Cultural change is easier when the organisation is in transition from the formation stage to the growth stage and from maturity into decline.

As the organisation moves into growth, major changes will be necessary. These changes are more likely to be accepted because the culture is less entrenched. Additionally, a growing organisation is more likely to be hiring new employees, which gives management the opportunity to place those whose values are desired in key positions. However, other factors will facilitate acceptance of the change. One writer, for instance, has proposed that employees will be more receptive to cultural change if the organisation's previous success record is modest, employees are generally dissatisfied, and the founder's image and reputation are in question.[40] By contrast, organisations such as Microsoft and Nike can grow fast because their culture is attractive and easily transferable to those who seek employment with those companies.

The other opportunity for cultural change occurs when the organisation enters the decline stage. Decline typically requires cutbacks and other retrenchment strategies. Such actions are likely to highlight to employees that the organisation is experiencing a true crisis.

Age of the organisation

Regardless of its life-cycle stage, the younger an organisation is, the less entrenched its values will be. We should therefore expect cultural change to be more acceptable in an organisation that is only five years old than in one that is 50 years old. The reason for this includes the fact that young organisations have no long-serving employees and lower levels of formalisation.

Size of the organisation

We propose that cultural change is easier to implement in a small organisation. Why? In such organisations, it is easier for management to reach employees. Communication is clearer, and role models are more visible in a small organisation, thus enhancing the opportunity to disseminate new values.

Strength of the current culture

The more widely held a culture is and the higher the agreement of its values among members, the more difficult it will be to change. Conversely, weak cultures should be more amenable to change than strong ones.

Absence of subcultures

Heterogeneity increases members' concern with protecting their self-interest and resisting change. This observation is drawn from the power-control viewpoint. Therefore, we would expect that the more subcultures there are, the more resistance there will be to changes in the dominant culture. Trying to change three cultures is always going to be more difficult than changing one. This thesis can also be related to size. Larger organisations will be more resistant to cultural change because they typically have more subcultures.

What management techniques are available to change culture?

In describing culture, we have noted that many of its aspects are either difficult to observe or understand or otherwise are not interpretable. This presents a problem for managers, as it is difficult to change something that is intangible. Managers have little alternative but to work with the mechanisms available to them. As a consequence, those managers who successfully change cultures tend to concentrate on changing behaviour rather than values.[41] Changes in values will, it is hoped, emerge with changes in behaviour.

One study of cultural change in large organisations found that only a small number of the attempts at cultural change could be counted as a success.[42] Cultures were found to have a strong 'springback' quality: that is, they very quickly reverted to what they were originally. Those attempts at cultural change that were successful were multidimensional: that is, attempts to change the culture focused on a number of key variables which mutually supported the change process. These included changes in structure, rewards, leadership as well as in key personnel.

So how can cultural change be successfully undertaken? The following are those factors that have been found to be important when attempting a cultural change program and are summarised in Table 13.3.

Applying firm leadership

No successful attempts at cultural change have been made without strong leadership driving the change at the top of the organisation. As leadership is generally covered in organisational behaviour texts, we have paid little attention to it in this book. But it is of such fundamental importance to cultural change that it must be raised in this section. It is the role of a leader to raise fundamental questions in relation to the organisation. To do this a leader should have a good understanding of the present state of the organisation and a vision of the characteristics of the emerging culture. An extensive study of the leader's role in cultural change found that the leader often introduced cultural change by asking basic questions that challenged the status quo—for example, 'Are we meeting customer's needs better than the competition?', 'Can we produce product more efficiently?', 'Do our products incorporate the latest changes in technology?'. In many cases the leaders themselves have had to create a sense of crisis in what may have been a complacent organisation. The leader should be capable of communicating his or her vision to a wide variety of people and take every opportunity to do so.

Effective leadership cannot be imposed from the top of the organisation. Leadership lies in creating conditions in which people are inspired to follow. Consequently, leaders must work hard—communicating to a wide audience and constantly talking about and sharing their vision. The role of leadership is so important that rarely if

TABLE 13.3 Techniques of managing organisation culture

Applying firm leadership
Seeking political support
Changing key personnel
Implementing structural changes
Avoiding micro-managing the details
The need to be patient
Applying appropriate management skills

ever does cultural change emerge as a bottom-up initiative from those lower in the organisation. To be effective it must always be initiated and nurtured from the very top of the organisation.[43]

It is not surprising that leadership is so important in effecting cultural change, as it mirrors the intangible nature of culture itself. It draws on fundamental and poorly understood human values and perceptions and acts on us in ways that are difficult to define. The function of interpersonal influence is as old as humanity, and cannot be replaced by a computer program or a rule manual.

Seeking political support

Leaders cannot function without some political support in their organisation. We have seen that political activity is heightened during periods of organisational change. Not all of this activity need be aimed at resisting the proposed changes. Leaders introducing cultural change constantly seek out political support, either from individual managers or departments, as a base from which influence may spread. They often seek out early successes in which the benefits of the new culture may be observed by others and be adopted by the wavering.

Changing key personnel

It is inevitable in periods of cultural change that changes in management and other personnel take place. Those associated closely with the old culture are generally moved aside and newer, more sympathetic managers appointed. This even applies to the CEO, as very few cultural change programs are initiated without changes at the very top of the organisation.

Implementing structural changes

We have noted the tendency for cultures to resist change by reverting to their original characteristics. One of the ways in which managers can counteract this is by making supporting structural changes. Structure influences the ways in which people behave in organisations. The structure of an organisation allocates responsibilities, determines reporting relationships, defines tasks and determines the size of the management hierarchy. It also becomes the framework within which performance is assessed and rewards allocated in the organisation.

Cultural difficulties that can be addressed by structural change include problems arising from a large head office which is primarily involved in checking, an emphasis on the application rules and regulations rather than an outward focus on the customer, senior managers receiving out-of-date and filtered information, and managers being removed from markets and customers. It can also include lack of ownership of results on the part of managers.

So how can structural changes assist in addressing these problems? Reducing layers of managers can reduce the checking mentality prevalent in many organisations. It can also reduce the numbers involved in making decisions, leading to faster decision making. Reallocation of responsibilities can decrease the number of managers who can say 'no' but not 'yes'. By creating divisions and other profit centres managers become more responsible for results. Because of the close link between customer satisfaction and performance, managers should become more responsive to customer demands. If they are not, it becomes apparent from the poor results of their division.

Avoiding micro-managing the details

It is not possible for senior managers to micro-manage the details of cultural change. Micro-management is concerned with managing the small details of day-to-day processes and events. Senior management have little alternative but to create the conditions that establish and nurture the new cultural values and to constantly sell the advantages of a new way of doing things. As a result it is unreasonable to expect managers to manage myths, values or meanings. Organisational members, be they management or operatives, will create their own values, myths and meanings according to their own needs and experiences. Senior managers are limited to trusting that the deeper meanings of the new culture, as expressed in the values, myths and meanings, are aligned with what they are trying to promote in the organisation.

The need to be patient

All cultural changes take time; the bigger the change and the larger the organisation, the longer it takes. Large companies like General Electric have been working on cultural change for upwards of 15 years and still regard it as an ongoing process. Little in the way of sustainable cultural change can be accomplished in less than five years. This means that the change must often be steered by a number of successive senior managers. It also follows that one of the characteristics of successful leaders of cultural change is to have a good appreciation for what can be accomplished in any given period of time. Work too slowly, and momentum and interest in the change is lost. Work too fast, and the old culture is destroyed without replacing it with the new, more appropriate culture. Disillusionment and confusion is the result, followed by a loss of organisational effectiveness.

Applying appropriate management skills

The skills to introduce a major cultural change are not commonly possessed by managers. As a consequence, many companies faced with the need to quickly address the problem of a cultural change specifically appoint a chief executive whose task it is to quickly shake up the old culture and implant the new, then leave the task of consolidating the new culture to managers who skills are more appropriate to this task. Al Dunlap, who has earned the nickname 'Chainsaw' for his rapid and ruthless cost-cutting is such a manager. George Trumbull, the managing director of AMP from 1994 to 1999, is another example. Both operated with considerable speed in deconstructing much of the old culture, while leaving it to others to undertake the longer-term implementation and consolidation of the new culture.

Culture and the way ahead

This chapter has introduced and discussed the concept of organisations having cultures. Culture is, however, a tricky concept to define, as well as being difficult to measure and manage. Further, research is making only small advances in reducing what is a very complex issue into something that is more readily understandable. But research has highlighted that an organisation's culture makes a major contribution to its effectiveness and that culture needs to change over time, just as the organisation must change over time to adapt to changes in its environment.

It is difficult to successfully change an organisation's culture without changing other organisational features, such as its strategy, structure and management. Whichever way we approach it, changing a culture is a major task, involving significant upheaval over long periods of time. It requires leaders with outstanding communication and persuasion skills who have a good grasp of the problems facing the organisation and the way in which they may be solved.

Beneath the obvious surface of symbols, artefacts and structure lies a dense web of interactions drawing on, and satisfying, basic human needs. Managers have little alternative but to concentrate on those features of culture which can be manipulated while realising that the success of any cultural change lies very much in changing the deeper levels of culture.

Summary

Organisations have personalities, just like individuals. We call these personalities organisational cultures. An organisational culture is a system of shared meaning. Its key characteristics are individual initiative, risk tolerance, direction, integration, management contact, control, identity, rewards, conflict tolerance, and communication patterns.

Organisations have dominant cultures and subcultures. The former express the core values shared by a majority of the organisation's members, though most large organisations have additional values, expressed in subcultures. Strong cultures are those where values are intensely held, clearly ordered and widely shared. Strong cultures increase behavioural consistency and can therefore act as substitutes for formalisation.

The ultimate source of an organisation's culture is its founders. It is sustained by the organisation's selection and socialisation processes and by the actions of top management. It is transmitted through stories, rituals, material symbols and language.

The key debate surrounding organisational culture concerns whether or not it can be managed. Cultures can be changed, but there appear to be a number of conditions necessary for bringing about such change. Even where conditions for change are favourable, managers should not expect any rapid acceptance of new cultural values. Cultural change should be measured in years rather than months.

For review and discussion

1   Define *organisational culture*. Which of its key characteristics are structurally based? Which are behaviourally based?

2   Can an employee survive in an organisation if he or she rejects its core values? Explain.

3   What forces might contribute towards making a culture strong or weak?

4   Identify those parts of culture which are visible and interpretable and those which are hidden.

5   How is an organisation's culture maintained?

6   What benefits can socialisation provide for the organisation? For the new employee?

7   Can you identify a set of characteristics that describe your educational institution's culture? Compare them with those of your peers. How closely do they agree?

8   What is the relationship between culture and formalisation?

9   Why do management theorists and consultants have a vested interest in demonstrating that organisational cultures can be managed?

10 'Culture may change, but the change may not be planned or precipitated by management.' Discuss.

11 What factors work against changing an organisation's culture?

12 At what stage in an organisation's life cycle is cultural change most likely to be accepted? Why?

13 What condition is most necessary for cultural change to be accepted? Why?

14 Describe the conditions that would be most conducive to initiating cultural change.

15 A senior executive from a major corporation has hired you to give advice on how to change the organisation's culture. How would you approach this assignment?

CASE FOR CLASS DISCUSSION
The problems of building a common culture at BHP Billiton

The merger in 2000 of BHP of Australia and Billiton of South Africa, although headquartered in London, was not undertaken because the organisations were similar. It took place in order to build scale and financial size. Although they were both mining companies, the cultures of the two companies were very dissimilar. BHP reflected the Australian cultural traits of openness, mateship and questioning authority. Billiton, although formerly owned by Shell, reflected its South African heritage. It had a reputation for being strictly hierarchical with a culture that demanded respect for authority. There was little openness, a lack of exposure to outside criticism, and little experience of confrontational unions.

Merging the cultures was never going to be easy. It was complicated by the nature of the chief executive's role. Initially Paul Anderson, the American boss of BHP, was chief executive, but he was to be replaced in 2002 by Brian Gilbertson, the chief executive of Billiton. Seen as a talented opportunist, Gilbertson had risen to success mainly through takeovers and has yet to demonstrate that he can expand a company through organic growth. But it is his personality that will have the greatest impact on the emerging culture.

To assist in merging the cultures, BHP Billiton adopted a process known as 'feathering'. This involved alternating the placement of former BHP and Billiton staff throughout its organisational structure in an attempt to break down old company allegiances. Early emphasis was given to quickly combining key HRM processes, such as remuneration and performance management. Integration teams consisting of managers from each company were formed very soon after the merger. They were encouraged to abandon preconceived ways and to consider only what was good for BHP Billiton.

Integration was assisted to a certain extent by structural changes accompanying the merger. Both companies, being involved in mining, tended to concentrate on the mining operation. But after the merger the focus was changed to the customer and businesses built around customer groupings. The issue of administrative offices also had to be addressed. Some functions were located in London and some in Melbourne. And some functions had to be divided between the two, as well as with Billiton's operations in South Africa. The restructuring provided the opportunity to create new positions and spread the senior management task between members of both companies as well as some outsiders.

Adapted from: Stewart Oldfield, 'BHP Billiton Is No Feather Bed', *The Australian Financial Review*, 18 July 2001, p. 15; and Tim Treadgold, 'Falling out of Bed', *Business Review Weekly*, 6 July 2001, pp. 54–7.

QUESTIONS

1 What does the case tell you about how cultures originate and are sustained?

2 Evaluate the extent to which the cultural change program conforms to suggestions on managing culture discussed in this chapter.

3 Why is there likely to be a high turnover of managers during and immediately after the integration?

4 Discuss whether you consider the merger will be successful from a cultural consideration.

FURTHER READING

Paul Bate, *Strategies for Cultural Change*, Oxford: Butterworth Heinemann, 1995.
Terrence E. Deal & Allan A. Kennedy, *Corporate Cultures: The Rites and Rituals of Corporate Life*, Reading, MA: Addison-Wesley, 1982.
John P. Kotter & James Heskett, *Corporate Culture and Performance*, New York: Free Press, 1992.
Edgar H. Schein, *Organizational Culture and Leadership*, San Francisco: Jossey-Bass, 1985.
Edgar H. Schein, 'The Role of the Founder in Creating Organizational Culture', *Organizational Dynamics*, Summer 1983, pp. 13–28.

NOTES

1 Drawn from Murray Massey, 'Mt Isa Builds a New Harmony', *Business Review Weekly*, 14 October 1996, pp. 50–52.
2 Terrence E. Deal & Allan A. Kennedy, *Corporate Cultures: The Rites and Rituals of Corporate Life*, Reading, MA: Addison-Wesley, 1982.
3 R.T. Pascale & A. G. Athos, *The Art of Japanese Management*, New York: Simon & Schuster, 1981.
4 Marvin Bower, *The Will to Manage*, New York: McGraw-Hill, 1966.
5 Edgar H. Schein, *Organizational Culture and Leadership*, San Francisco: Jossey-Bass, 1985.
6 Linda Smircich, 'Concepts of Culture and Organizational Analysis', *Administrative Science Quarterly*, September 1983, p. 339.
7 Edgar H. Schein, 'Coming to a New Awareness of Organisational Culture', *Sloan Management Review*, Winter 1984, p. 7.
8 M. Rokeach, *The Nature of Human Values*, New York: Free Press, 1992.
9 Clifford Geertz, *Interpretation of Cultures*, New York: Basic Books, 1973.
10 William Ouchi, 'Markets, Bureaucracies and Clans', *Administrative Science Quarterly*, 25(1), 1980, pp. 129–41.
11 Based on George C. Gordon & W.M. Cummins, *Managing Management Climate*, Lexington, MA: Lexington Books, 1979; and Chris A. Betts & Susan M. Halfhill, 'Organization Culture: Theory, Definitions, and Dimensions', paper presented at the National American Institute of Decision Sciences Conference, Las Vegas, NE, November 1985.
12 See, for example, K.L. Gregory, 'Native-View Paradigms: Multiple Cultures and Culture Conflicts in Organizations', *Administrative Science Quarterly*, September 1983, pp. 359–76.
13 Meryl Reis Louis, 'Sourcing Workplace Culture: Why, When, and How', in R.H. Kilmann, M.J. Saxton & R. Serpa, eds, *Gaining Control of the Corporate Culture*, San Francisco: Jossey-Bass, 1985, p. 129.

14 Schein, 'Coming to a New Awareness of Organizational Culture'.

15 Charles A. O'Reilly III, 'Corporations, Cults and Organizational Culture: Lessons from Silicon Valley Firms', paper presented at the 42nd Annual Meeting of the Academy of Management, Dallas, 1983.

16 Bernard Arogyaswamy & Charles M. Byles, 'Organizational Culture: Internal and External Fits', *Journal of Management*, Winter 1987, pp. 647–59.

17 Karl E. Weick, 'Organizational Culture as a Source of High Reliability', *California Management Review*, Winter 1987, pp. 112–27.

18 Nigel Nicholson & Gary Johns, 'The Absence Culture and the Psychological Contract— Who's in Control of Absence?', *Academy of Management Review*, July 1985, pp. 397–407.

19 Weick, 'Organizational Culture as a Source of High Reliability'.

20 Ouchi, 'Markets, Bureaucracies and Clans'.

21 Edgar H. Schein, 'The Role of the Founder in Creating Organizational Culture', *Organizational Dynamics*, Summer 1983, pp. 13–28.

22 See, for example, Yoash Wiener, 'Forms of Value Systems: A Focus on Organizational Effectiveness and Cultural Change and Maintenance', *Academy of Management Review*, October 1988, pp. 541–3.

23 Benjamin Schneider, 'The People Make the Place', *Personal Psychology*, Autumn 1987, pp. 437–52.

24 Renato Tagiuri & G.H. Litwin, *Organizational Climate*, Boston: Harvard University Graduate School of Business Administration, 1968; Jerome L. Franklin, 'Down the Organization: Influence Processes across Levels of Hierarchy', *Administrative Science Quarterly*, June 1975, pp. 153–64; and 'Handing Down the Old Hands' Wisdom', *Fortune*, 13 June 1983, pp. 97–104.

25 Ralph H. Kilmann, 'Five Steps for Closing Culture Gaps', in Kilmann et al., *Gaining Control of the Corporate Culture*, p. 357.

26 Andrew M. Pettigrew, 'On Studying Organizational Culture', *Administrative Science Quarterly*, December 1979, p. 576.

27 Karl Weick & L.B. Browning, 'Arguments and Narration in Organizational Communication', *Journal of Management*, 12, 1986, pp. 243–59.

28 Pettigrew, 'On Studying Organisational Culture'.

29 See for instance Anonymous, 'The Daimler Chrysler Emulsion', *The Economist*, 29 July 2000, p. 65–6.

30 Anthony F. Buono & James L. Bowditch, *The Human Side of Mergers and Acquisitions: Managing Collisions Between People, Cultures, and Organizations*, San Francisco: Jossey-Bass, 1989.

31 Price Pritchett, *After the Merger: Managing the Shockwaves*, Dallas: Dow Jones-Irwin, 1985, p. 8.

32 See, in relation to the BHP Billiton merger, Tim Treadgold, 'Falling Out of Bed', *Business Review Weekly*, 6 July 2001, pp. 54–7.

33 Schein, *Organizational Culture and Leadership*, p. 45.

34 Caren Siehl, 'After the Founder: An Opportunity to Manage Culture', in Peter Frost et al., eds, *Organizational Culture*, Beverly Hills, CA: Sage Publications, 1985, p. 139.

35 Joanne Martin, 'Can Organizational Culture Be Managed?', in Frost et al., *Organizational Culture*, pp. 95–6.

36 Pettigrew, 'On Studying Organizational Culture', pp. 570–81.

37 John P. Kotter & James Heskett, *Corporate Culture and Performance*, New York: Free Press, 1992.

38 See, for example, W. Gibb Dyer, Jr, 'Organizational Culture', in W.G. Dyer, ed., *Strategies for Managing Change*, Reading, MA: Addison-Wesley, 1984.

39 Pettigrew, 'On Studying Organizational Culture', pp. 570–81.

40 Siehl, 'After the Founder: An Opportunity to Manage Culture', pp. 128–9.

41 This section is drawn from Kotter and Heskett, *Corporate Culture and Performance.*
42 ibid.
43 ibid.

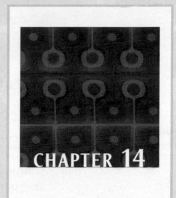

CHAPTER 14

Managing organisational growth and decline

After reading this chapter you should be able to:

1 identify four reasons why organisations seek growth;

2 describe the five-phase model of organisational growth;

3 discuss the applicability of the phases of growth;

4 define organisational decline;

5 describe environmental forces that might precipitate organisational decline;

6 explain how decline affects the administrative component;

7 outline the steps management is likely to follow in response to decline;

8 identify the potential problems managers face when organisations decline.

14

Introduction

Burns Philp: from island trader to yeast manufacturer

Burns Philp is one of Australia's best-known and longest-established companies.[1] It came into existence over 120 years ago to provide supplies to miners in North Queensland. The company subsequently branched out into island trading in the Pacific long before the Australian flag was seen there. It even had a major role in shaping Australia's foreign policy in the region. It was during this period that the company's strong traditions were established, built around plantations, stories of hurricanes, coral reefs, shipwrecks, copra and the eccentricities of expatriate staff. Burns Philp Trustee was established to look after the affairs of employees on overseas postings, and an insurance arm, QBE Insurance, was set up as a natural extension of what was, in many ways, a risky business.

Burns Philp had a reputation for being paternal but frugal. Once a certain age was reached, employees had a job for life. One managing director stayed in office until he was 92, making his deputy wait 24 years for promotion. It was common for employees and managers to be in their 80s. Bound by tradition, familiarity and past experience, there was a large measure of solidarity among the staff. Money wasn't wasted. Envelopes from letters written to the company were reused for memos and pay packets.

The quarter century from 1942 to 1966 was the most conservative in the company's history, with one year being virtually the same as another. By the time the 1970s came around, it was clear that the company needed to adapt to a changing environment. A decision was made to sell the shipping fleet because of continuing losses. The company, asset-rich but showing poor returns on capital, looked set for being taken over and broken up. It had a certain measure of protection from its ring of defensive shareholdings. These included a 10% shareholding by the descendants of the founders, and cross-shareholdings in the food group Mauri Bros and Thompson, as well as QBE Insurance. These defensive shareholdings were not all positive. They prevented Burns Philp from obtaining additional capital and, as earnings were declining, there was virtually nothing in the way of retained earnings to draw on.

Burns Philp had reached its nadir, but as least the board realised that the company must diversify from what had been its core business. Various acquisitions were made in the late 1970s, but these were opportunistic and few were successful or long-lasting. It bought various hardware stores, part of an iron ore mine, the Avis car rental group and had an interest in a cruise ship. Its greatest disasters were the purchase of Sun Electric and Hanimex. All these acquisitions cost money and management time and formed one of Australia's messiest conglomerates. In 1982 the company also purchased the balance of Mauri foods. Mauri had developed into a world-class food technology company, with significant interests in yeast and fermentation.

Throughout this period, the group had acquired assets worth $700 million, but in 1982 it generated only $5 million in profit. Debt had risen and the interest bill was running at $28 million per year.

The board, under the influence of Sir Peter Finley, realised that action needed to be taken to rationalise the holdings and put the company back on course. A new managing director, Andrew Turnbull, an engineer, was appointed. He went deeper into hardware by buying Nock and Kirby's and combining all the hardware stores into the BBC chain. He built on the food technology of Mauri and developed one of the world's largest suppliers of yeasts and fermentation products. He entered the spice trade by making a number of acquisitions around the world. He also sold underperforming assets, including many of the original South Pacific businesses. As a final break with the past, David Burns, grandson of the founder and only the third chairman of the company, stepped down in 1992.

But success was to be hard-won, even elusive. In attempting to concentrate on a few core businesses, Burns Philp sold its interests in QBE Insurance in 1991 and the BBC hardware chain in 1994. The trustee company, under pressure from the Estates Mortgage debacle, was put into liquidation in 1992. By trying to carve out for itself a position in the world spice industry, it came head to head with McCormick and Co in the United States. Burns Philp assumed that there was room for both companies in the US market, but McCormick's was not going to cede market share. A vicious price war ensued, leading to Burns Philp incurring significant losses. These losses were so significant that the company teetered on the verge of bankruptcy. In 1997 a New Zealand investor, Graeme Hart, bought 60% of the company at distressed prices, thinking he could release some of the value left in Burns Philp. The company proved difficult to turn around after the losses from the spice business. But there was a redeeming feature in Burns Philp, and that was its yeast business. It remained a world leader in yeasts, and this generated sufficient cash to keep the company in business. Burns Philp is now trying to exit its few remaining businesses, including spices. As a profitable and focused yeast company it now faces its next challenge in remaining in business: it is an attractive target for large food companies seeking to diversify. It may not yet see its 200th anniversary.

While managers seek growth and often use it as a criterion to assess organisational effectiveness, the Burns Philp case illustrates the often overlooked side of growth—the constant challenge to combat decline and stay in business. What makes the Burns Philp case unusual is that the company survived; most companies in the situation it found itself in would have been taken over or become insolvent. This other side—specifically, the managing of decline—is becoming a reality today. Terms such as *retrenchment*, *downsizing* and *merging* have become staples in many managers' vocabularies. The reality is that while growth may be widely sought, the contemporary manager is more likely than ever to be managing a shrinking organisation.

This chapter expands on the life-cycle concept, introduced in Chapter 1, to consider the impact of the life-cycle stage on an organisation. We demonstrate that the two most significant stages—growth and decline—create distinctly different organisational problems and opportunities for managers. We will begin by taking a closer look at society's growth bias and presenting two models of organisational growth.

Managing growth

Expectations favour growth

The association of growth with wellbeing and health is almost hard-wired into our brain. We rarely identify an organisation that is shrinking in size as having a great future. Managers and researchers alike have allowed the goal of growth to become a means of expressing this confidence in an organisational context. Growth has come to represent a way of making tomorrow's organisations better than today's.

But our concept of what constitutes growth has changed over time. No longer do we equate growth with an ever-expanding workforce. Growth is now more likely to be associated with measures that contribute to an organisation's survival than with numbers of employees. These include financial considerations such as turnover, profit, and low debt levels; or strategy measures such as market share.[2] It can also include production-oriented comparisons such as benchmarking, reaching world's best practice and quality of management. We now consider what factors have led to the emphasis on growth in organisations.

Bigger organisations derive economies of scale

In business, large size may also be justified in economic terms. Growth is desirable because with increases in size come economies of scale. Bigger, in fact, is often more efficient. We tend to view economies of scale as being associated with reductions in costs as production increases. But size may contribute to other economies. The costs of finance may be lower. Transport companies can offer more frequent services to more locations, thus becoming more attractive to passengers and freight forwarders. Banks and consultancies can offer a more comprehensive range of services, providing them with an advantage over their rivals. Retailers can lower the cost of goods sold by bulk buying. One interesting driver of growth is access to wider financial markets and an elevated share price. The main reason BHP and Billiton merged was to be of such a size that world financial markets would have to take notice of them.

Industries ranging from motor vehicles, wine, personal computers and mining have consolidated into a smaller number of large companies. There are, however, a few industries that are fragmenting into smaller-sized businesses. Some manufacturing has fragmented into clusters of smaller companies, which contribute to part of the supply chain. Of course, it does not automatically follow that large size provides economies. Few mergers and acquisitions provide the full benefits that were anticipated.[3] But they founder more for reasons of clashing cultures and management incompatibilities rather than on economies of scale not being achievable. But generally the opposite holds: larger organisations generally achieve some form of economies not available to smaller companies.

Growth increases the likelihood of survival

In our discussion of organisational effectiveness, we acknowledged the paramount status accorded to survival. If the organisation does not survive, issues of social responsibility and obligations towards stakeholders become meaningless. Growth becomes desirable, then, because it increases the likelihood of survival. Large organisations are rarely permitted to go out of existence in the way that small organisations are.[4] For example, the various state rail authorities and city transport services, even though they traditionally operate with large losses, still manage to survive. When Ansett went into administration in 2001, its large employment base meant that significant efforts were made by governments, unions and other interested parties to resurrect the company albeit unsuccessfully. A smaller company would have been allowed to disappear with no effort being made to save it. Also, the larger the organisation, the more likely it is to be taken over rather than fail. When Franklins, the grocery retail chain, decided to liquidate the group after continuing losses, it did not close shop. It sold off its businesses to various other parties, leading to little loss of employment. All that changed was the signage at the front of the shop.

In addition to providing a large constituency, growth facilitates survival by providing more resources with which the organisation can buffer itself against uncertainty. Large organisations can make mistakes and live to talk about them. They have sufficient financial and other resources to provide both a buffer against setbacks and time to respond to problems. Growing and healthy organisations also have slack resources that they can cut more easily than can small or stable organisations. The growing organisation that has to reduce its budget by 10% can often cut fat without threatening its survival. The stagnant organisation is often forced to cut to the bone. And larger organisations generally have better access to financial resources and to management skill and expertise. Finally, if size increases the likelihood of survival, it is not surprising that large organisations dominate, as they are the ones that survive.

Growth becomes synonymous with effectiveness

What is success? As we noted at the opening of this section, if an organisation is getting bigger, it is common to assume that it is being managed effectively.[5]

Business executives boast that 'sales are up significantly'. Hospital administrators produce charts showing that they are handling more patients than ever. Deans often like to boast about their university's growth in research output. Bankers are quick to tell anyone who will listen about their bank's growth in various lending categories. These examples all illustrate how organisations, rightly or wrongly, use growth as synonymous with effectiveness. If those in the specific environment on whom the organisation depends for continued support also equate growth with effectiveness, managers will obviously be predisposed to the values of growth.

The interaction of growth and effectiveness is seen explicitly in the systems concept, which we discussed in Chapter 1. In that chapter, organisations were described as open systems. In this context, organisations are analogous to living organisms, maintaining themselves by acquiring inputs from, and disposing of their output to, the environment. The systems approach favours growth. Growth is sought because it connotes youth and vitality.[6] Growth is evidence that the organisation is doing something right and is in good health. And expansion, again consistent with the systems perspective, increases the likelihood that the organisation will survive.

Growth is power

The arguments that growth can be consistent with economies of scale, can be used by the specific environment to assess the organisation's effectiveness and can increase the likelihood of survival are all economically rational explanations for the pro-growth bias. Now we want to present a political argument in favour of growth.

Growth is almost always consistent with the self-interest of the top management in the organisation. It increases prestige, power and income for this group. It should

OT CLOSEUP
How do organisations grow?

There are at least four distinct means by which organisations grow.[7] The first is expansion in the organisation's existing domain. Stripped of the jargon, it means growing bigger in the field in which the organisation operates. Coles followed this strategy when it merged with Myer, for instance. The operation of Kmart, Target, Coles Supermarkets and Myers Grace Bros, among others, provides greater concentration in the retail industry. As it is often difficult to grow organically, many organisations engage in mergers and acquisitions to grow.

The second means is growth through diversification into new domains, or areas of operation. This may take a variety of forms, including the development of new products and services, vertical integration and conglomerate diversification. Although popular in the past this means of growth has fallen from favour, and most companies seek to build on their core competencies.

Third is growth through technological development. This is most obvious for firms engaged in developing new products in the information technology and biotechnology industries. New products, provided they are successful, mean new markets and increased sales, often with substantial profit margins.

Fourth is growth through improved managerial techniques. This strategy seeks to improve the efficiency of the management process. Foster's Brewing and Fisher and Paykel are good illustrations of firms that have developed a large cadre of competent managers, which in turn has provided the impetus for the growth of the firms. As general rule, well-managed firms will find it easy to grow.

certainly be of more than passing interest to know that growth is undoubtedly linked to executive remuneration. Size, in fact, is a better predictor of executive salaries than is profit margin.[8] Even the heads of large organisations not showing a high return on capital are paid more than the heads of smaller companies that use their resources more effectively. Should we not expect, therefore, top business executives to be motivated towards expanding their firms?

The drive for expansion and growth is also driven by executive egos. Mergers and acquisitions are often motivated by the drive for power by questing CEOs. Needless to say, gratification of personal power needs is often the worst motive for undertaking a merger, but it plays a large part in expansion decisions.[9]

Growth also provides an organisation with more power relative to other organisations and groups in its environment.[10] Larger organisations have more influence with suppliers, unions, large customers, government and the like. And large corporations often prefer to deal with similarly large organisations. For instance, the wine industry has historically been fragmented into a large number of small producers. But most wine is now sold through large chains, which don't want to deal with small producers who can only supply in small amounts and who have good years and bad years. Large companies, such as Foster's and Southcorp, can produce in extremely large quantities and can blend seasonal differences out of the wine, thus providing product consistency. Needless to say, the large distribution chains prefer to deal with those companies which can supply a consistent quality of branded wines in large quantities.

The foregoing leads us to the obvious conclusion that growth is not a chance occurrence. It is the result of conscious managerial decisions. Growth typically provides economic benefits to the organisation and political benefits to the organisation's executive decision makers. Consequently, strong forces are continually encouraging organisations to grow and expand. However, we do need to qualify this observation. The maturity and lack of growth in many markets has led to a number of organisations realising that growth is difficult to come by. Examples of such markets are food processing, basic electronics and most building materials. Managers in these industries realise that their prospects for growth are limited, but their companies are still profitable and generating a considerable amount of cash. In many cases, firms such as these return capital to shareholders rather than use the capital for expanding into areas unfamiliar to them. In other words, they choose to remain the size they are instead of seeking expansion into unfamiliar areas.

But just as growth is the result of management choice, so too is the desire to stay much the same size. Research has indicated that, particularly in smaller companies, owners of businesses may be more comfortable with remaining small than seeking growth.[11] They may want to avoid losing control of their company and delegating management decisions, and they often want to operate a business that is more human in scale than a larger, more formal company. These businesses often have long life spans, far longer than many businesses that seek growth at any cost and then find that the management skills of the owner are not suited to running a larger decentralised business. For, as we shall see in the next section, each stage of growth presents its own particular problems and management challenges.

Models of organisational growth

Devising models that describe the various stages of growth is a prolific exercise in organisational theory. Most models proposed are theoretical in that while they possess face validity—that is, they appear logical—few are supported by extensive analysis. However, the models provide a useful taxonomy, or a classification scheme, that can act as a guide to research. We will discuss two models: one is basically a theoretical construct, and forms the basis for most subsequent theorising in relation to growth models; the second is supported by thorough research, and describes the experience of high-tech start-ups.

The first model we will discuss, that developed by Larry Greiner, is the best-known model of organisational growth.[12] Greiner studied a number of organisations and from his observations proposed that an organisation's evolution is characterised by phases of prolonged and calm growth, followed by periods of internal turmoil. The former he called **evolution**, the latter **revolution**. Each stage of evolution or growth creates its own crisis. The resolution of the crisis, however, initiates a new evolutionary phase. This evolution–crisis–evolution process creates the five-phase model shown in Figure 14.1.

evolution prolonged and calm growth

revolution periods of internal turmoil in an organisation's growth

Phase 1: creativity

The first stage of an organisation's evolution is characterised by the creativity of its founders. These founders typically devote their energies to the development of products and markets. Their organisation's design tends to look like the simple structure. Decision making is controlled by the owner-manager or top management. Communication between levels in the organisation is frequent and informal.

Figure 14.1 Five phases of growth

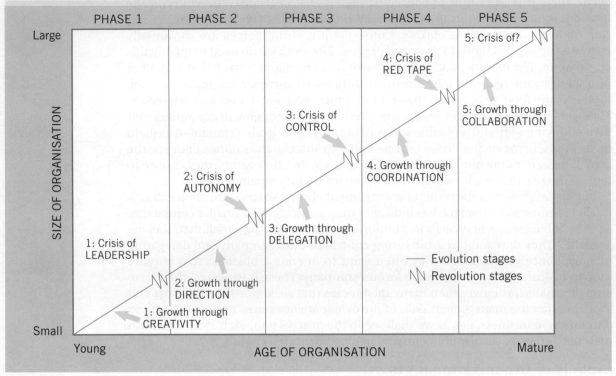

As the organisation grows, say to about 50–100 staff, it becomes difficult to manage by relying only on informal communication. The senior managers become overextended. There comes a *crisis of leadership*, as those who run the organisation no longer have the skills or interests to direct it successfully. Strong professional management is needed to introduce more sophisticated management and organisation techniques.

Phase 2: direction

If the leadership crisis is resolved, strong leadership will have been acquired. This new leadership will formalise communication and put accounting, budget, inventory and other systems in place. The organisation's design will become increasingly bureaucratic. Specialisation will be introduced, as will a functional structure, to separate horizontally differentiated units such as production and marketing activities.

This new direction, however, will create a crisis of its own making. As the organisation grows, lower-level managers will become frustrated and seek greater influence in decisions that affect them. The new management, however, is reluctant to give up authority and wants to maintain centralised decision making. The result is a *crisis of autonomy*. The solution tends to lie in decentralising decision making.

Phase 3: delegation

If decisions are decentralised, the crisis of phase 2 will have been resolved. A divisionalised structure will evolve and lower-level managers will now have relative autonomy to run their units. Top management will devote its energy to long-term strategic planning. Internal control systems will be developed to monitor the decisions of lower-level managers.

Delegation, however, eventually creates a *crisis of control.* Lower-level managers enjoy their autonomy, but top-level managers fear that the organisation is going in too many directions at the same time. Top management's response is to attempt to return to centralised decision making. Centralisation is viewed as the means to provide unity of direction. However, this is rarely realistic. Some other means of coordination needs to be found and implemented.

Phase 4: coordination

The control crisis is solved by establishing staff units to review, evaluate and control line-management activities and product groups to facilitate coordination. The head office starts to grow in size and influence.

These coordination devices create their own problems. Line–staff conflicts, for example, begin to consume a great deal of time and effort. Lower-level employees increasingly begin to complain that they are being overwhelmed by too many rules, regulations and controls. A *crisis of red tape* occurs, and unless it is resolved it can lead to goal displacement.

Phase 5: collaboration

The solution to the red-tape crisis is strong interpersonal collaboration among the organisation's members. A strong culture acts as a substitute for formal controls. Taskforces and other group devices are created to perform tasks and solve problems. The organisation's structure moves towards the organic form.

Greiner is unclear as to what crisis will evolve out of the collaborative and organic structure. It might well be a return to one of the earlier crises in the model.

The Greiner model demonstrates the paradox that success creates its own problems. As an organisation grows, it faces new crises. Each crisis, in turn, requires management to make adjustments in coordination devices, control systems and organisation design. But do organisations grow in standardised time spaces, as depicted in Figure 14.1? Moreover, do all organisations grow in the discrete stages that Greiner identifies? The answer to both questions is no. Greiner acknowledges that movement between the phases will vary both within and between organisations, but his diagram fails to reflect this. It is worthwhile remembering that organisations may face other types of crises arising from other causes. The types of crises Greiner identifies are internal ones linked to growth rather than from environmental or technological changes. An increasing number of organisations, as we see below, are unsuccessful in responding to a crisis. The result is often the beginning of organisational decline.

Hanks' growth model for high-tech organisations

Hanks and his colleagues developed a model of growth for firms involved in high-technology industries.[13] They defined high-technology industries as those having a higher than average number of technology-oriented workers than for manufacturing industries generally, and whose research and development spending was at least equal to the average of all industries. High-tech industries provide a useful sample, as they can move through the growth stages very quickly. Companies such as Microsoft, Apple, Yahoo and Dell went from start-ups to mature companies in the space of 10 years.

Hanks found that firms clustered into four main stages of growth, each with their own characteristics. Although the study was not a longitudinal one—that is, it did not follow firms over an extended period of time—there were strong indications from the research that the clusters represented stages that the various firms passed through.

- *Start-up stage.* This stage consisted of small young firms. They have a simple structure, are highly centralised around one or two people and have very low horizontal differentiation. They are oriented strongly towards research and development and their focus is on developing new products.
- *Expansion stage.* Spending at the earlier stage on research and development has produced a saleable product, and this stage is characterised by high rates of sales and employment growth. Firms at this stage have adopted a functional structure—that is, one where there are identifiable departments. Decision making is still highly centralised, but more formalisation has crept in compared to the start-up stage. More staff are involved in sales and accounting, indicating that firms are actively involved in the commercialisation of their product.
- *Late expansion/early maturity stage.* Firms in this stage are still growing rapidly. They average four levels of management and have a fully developed functional structure, with clearly identifiable departments. There is quite a high level of formalisation but the organisation is becoming more decentralised. At this stage there is an increase in those personnel concerned with large-scale production such as quality control, purchasing, customer/product service staff, finance, shipping, production planning, warehousing and payroll.
- *Maturity/diversification stage.* Firms at this stage have a mean of six organisational levels, and management is decentralised. Formalisation is high. At this stage there is greater horizontal specialisation, with the addition of personnel involved in such tasks as building maintenance, personnel, advertising, market research and inventory control. Early moves towards a divisionalised structure are becoming apparent. The average number of employees at this stage was 495.

Hanks found two other clusters that highlighted the difficulty of applying growth analysis to all organisation. One group had been established for a mean of 19 years but still only had an average of seven employees. They had a simple structure but their growth was slow, and employee numbers were tending to decline rather than expand. Centralisation was high. Hanks proposed that this group represented lifestyle firms, where the owners consciously kept their business small and capable of being managed by one person. A second group was about the same size as those in the expansion stage (a mean of 25 employees) but they were older, averaging 13 years since establishment. Some of these firms still adhered to a simple structure while others had adopted a functional structure. These firms appeared to rely on a more mature manufacturing process, and their research and development was aimed at contributing to incremental improvements to existing products rather than generating new ones. It was also possible that this group of firms was going through a success-disengagement substage, where the company had attained true economic health and had sufficient size and product market penetration to ensure average or above-average profits.

Hanks noted that there was not a continuous growth trajectory for firms. It was possible for organisations to go through cycles of stagnation or decline interspersed with stages of growth. Indeed, decline can occur at any stage. It was also possible to identify when organisational and structural considerations were important for the firm. In the early stages of growth, structure was not a major factor in the success or failure of the firm.[14] At the start-up and early elaboration stage, factors such as inadequate market knowledge, poor product performance, ineffective marketing and sales efforts, poor timing and financial difficulties were the major causes of failure. However, as firms moved to the later stages of growth, such as the delegation stage in Greiner's model or the late expansion/early maturity stage in Hanks' model, an appropriate organisational structure became more important. For instance, as they grew, if management did not delegate or put in place appropriate systems of control, decline could set in. So as a firm grew in size, so did the need to put in place appropriate organisational arrangements.

Organisational decline: accepting the new reality

Despite all the reasons that managers have for favouring growth conditions, organisational decline is becoming a fact of life in an increasing number of organisations, especially those in mature industries.[15] For example, most large organisations have engaged in some form of downsizing in recent years. In industries such as clothing and footwear, there have been large-scale plant closures, and almost every type of industry, including the service industries, has felt the need to rationalise by closing branches or factories, with consequent reduction in employment. Note that this does not mean that the output of the organisation is necessarily falling, rather that productivity in many cases has risen and there is need for fewer workers.

Twenty years ago, few managers or organisational theorists were concerned about decline. Growth was the *natural* state of things, and decline, when it occurred, was viewed as an aberration—a mistake created by poor management or merely a brief setback in a long-term growth trend. What, then, has changed? Have we merely ignored reality in the past, or have more organisations actually entered the decline stage of their life cycle?

Clarifying semantics

Before we look at the causes that may lead to organisational decline, let us clarify our terminology. When we refer to **organisational decline**, we refer to a long-lasting and ongoing decrease in the overall activity of the organisation. This can involve loss of customers or market share, a decline in competitiveness, or obsolescence in a firm's key technology, product or service. It is *not* meant to describe temporary slowdowns arising from changes in economic conditions or minor adjustments due to market forces.

organisational decline a long-lasting and ongoing decrease in the overall activity of the organisation

downsizing planned reduction in an organisation's staffing levels

Another term closely aligned with organisational decline, and sometimes used interchangeably with it, is *downsizing*. But, as we have seen in Chapter 6, we have given this term a more specific meaning. By **downsizing**, we mean a slimming down of the organisation by reducing the number of employees and organisational positions. Downsizing reduces the staff count, widens the organisation's average span of control and pushes authority downwards. When you hear about management reorganising to become 'lean and mean', the organisation is typically engaged in downsizing.

Decline and the changing environment

The empirical research into organisational theory which was conducted between the mid-1940s and the mid-1970s, was largely growth-oriented. Coincidentally, this same three-decade period was one of relatively uninterrupted growth in western economies. It should not be surprising, therefore, to find that the organisation theory literature is heavily growth-oriented, focusing almost exclusively on problems or benefits associated with expansion. However, since about the mid-1970s we have seen a distinct increase in the number of organisations shrinking their operations. The obvious question is, why?

One answer is *mature markets*. For instance, the appliance manufacturer Email now owned by Electrolux has found the Australian market for its products static. Everyone who wants a washing machine or refrigerator has one, and the market is limited to replacement sales. For many manufacturers, significantly lower production costs overseas have been an obvious factor precipitating a decline for their goods. Since 1980, approximately 300 000 manufacturing jobs have been lost in Australia to offshore competition. In some cases whole industries, such as consumer electronics, no longer exist in Australia. At one stage in the late 1960s Australia had more than 10 manufacturers of television sets. It now has none. Personal computer manufacturers are facing similar market maturity, leading to a round of mergers among some while others prefer to exit the market. Under such conditions, it is those organisations with better access to resources and which are better managed that survive.

The combination of mature markets and need to achieve economies of scale has led to *market ecology* supporting only a small number of players. This is particularly so in small markets, such as Australia and New Zealand. Returning to our whitegoods example, when we look at the number of refrigerators sold in Australia and then compare this with the size of factory necessary to achieve economies of scale, we can see that there is room for only one or at most two refrigerator manufacturers in Australia. The limitation on numbers of firms highlighted by market ecology applies to industries as diverse as airlines, building materials and telephone services.

Some organisations, especially those with a single product or those where a single product dominates sales, have been hit by *technological obsolescence*. Manufacturers of vinyl records, steam locomotives, aircraft propellers and wringer washing machines are just four examples of companies on the downside of the product cycle.

The end of the product life cycle does not apply only to product categories. The computer industry has seen the rise and decline of many innovative companies which dominated their field until new products were introduced by competitors. Examples of firms that have experienced decline caused by new product offerings are Wang, Digital, Apple and even IBM during the late 1980s.

Some organisations are forced to cut back as a result of *loss of market share*. The total market for their product or services may not be shrinking, but their failure to sustain their share of that market creates the need to retrench. Ford's loss of market share in the car market is such a case. Discount airlines have led to the near-elimination of interstate bus and rail services as mass movers of passengers. Deregulation has also had a major effect on Telstra as new players such as Optus have entered the industry.

Globalisation has introduced a whole new dynamic to business. It has had the effect of raising the levels of competition from both domestic and foreign businesses and of creating new opportunities overseas for Australian-based companies. The increase in competition has led to many firms realising that they have neither the scale nor scope to survive. They can seek merger partners or go out of business. But another effect has been for organisations to divest themselves of non-core businesses, allowing them to concentrate on those areas which they have a comparative advantage. The resulting organisation structure is more centralised and focused on a fewer number of products.

The recent rash of *mergers and acquisitions* has created redundancy in many companies. When banks merge or Mobil acquires Esso, efficiencies often dictate consolidating operations and staff personnel in functions such as legal, accounting, purchasing and human resources.

Local, state and federal government departments have additional problems to worry about. Changes in government priorities have led to a reduction in expenditure on public broadcasters such as the ABC and SBS. Forcing government business enterprises to compete has led to a major shift in the way they conduct their operations, in many cases involving large job losses. Privatisation (e.g. of the Commonwealth Bank or Qantas), has reoriented management to a more market focus. Even universities have been forced to seek more of their income from fees and services to industry. And previously protected industries such as electricity generation and gas distribution have been opened to competition.

Is managing decline the reverse of managing growth?

Until very recently, there was little research into the decline process. This was undoubtedly due to the growth bias and the reality that organisations undergoing contraction can rarely afford the luxury of sponsoring reflective research. Moreover, management does not see much to gain by permitting outsiders to chronicle its organisation's decline.[16] Our knowledge today about managing decline is essentially based on some preliminary research evidence and a good deal of insightful speculation.

We begin with the proposition that the management of decline is not merely a matter of reversing the process of managing growth. An organisation cannot be reduced piece by piece simply by reversing the sequence of activity and resource-building by which it grew.[17] Although the research is scant, there does appear to be enough evidence to conclude that activities within same-sized organisations during periods of growth and decline will not correspond directly. As a generalisation, there is a lag that typifies the rate of change in structure during prolonged decline that is not evident in growth.[18] As discussed in Chapter 6, changes in size have a significant impact on structure. But those conclusions were drawn from organisations that were all changing in the growth direction. During decline, size has an impact on structure, but it is not a reverse parallel of the growth pattern. This lag results in the level of

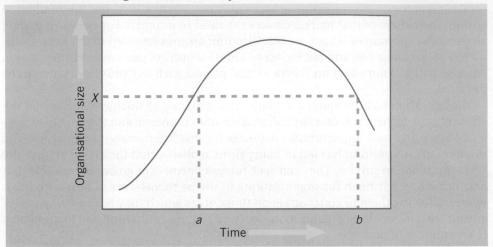

FIGURE 14.2 The organisation's life cycle

structure being greater in the same organisation for a given level of size during decline than for the same level of size during growth.[19] Referring to Figure 14.2, the lag thesis would state that at a given size, *X*, points *a* and *b* are not equal. More specifically, at point *b* in time, the organisation should have a greater degree of structure. For instance, we could expect a lag in the degree of formalisation. Typically, when an organisation goes from 100 employees to 1000, there is an increase in formal rules and regulations. But this is not easily reversible. We predict, therefore, that when an organisation is contracting, it will tend to have a higher degree of formalisation at each size level than it had at the same level in its growth stage. This lag factor is most evident, however, in recent studies of the administrative component in declining organisations.

The administrative component

The administrative component refers to the number of people in an organisation who engage in supportive activities. If there is a lag in decline, one would expect the administrative component to shrink at a slower rate than the whole organisation. Studies confirm this expectation.[20] In some cases, evidence has been found that the administrative component actually grew while organisations declined.[21] Although the exact nature of the relationship is not well established, it is clear that the relationship between size and the administrative component is different during decline from during growth. Interestingly, either a lag or an increase would be consistent with the conclusion that organisational politics distorts the effect of the decline process on the administrative component.[22] The administrative support group, because of its power, is more effective in resisting cutback pressures. As a result, the ratio of supportive staff to operatives will be higher at the same level of total organisational size in the decline stage.

An enhanced case for power-control

Organisational size is a major factor in determining an organisation's structure during growth, but not during decline. Thus, our conclusions in Chapter 6 on the size–structure relationship appear to be relevant only on the upside of an organisation's life cycle.

While the evidence is sketchy, we offer the following hypothesis: size is a key determinant of structure during growth, but it is replaced by power control in decline. The actions of vested interest groups to maintain or enhance their power are not nearly as visible during growth as they are in decline. A growing organisation allows most people to achieve at least part of their goals. In addition, there are more resources in

OT CLOSEUP
Why do companies fail?

The reasons for company failure are often difficult to determine. Researching the topic is fraught with methodological difficulties. Few managers of failing companies write memoirs explaining their role in their company's failure. They are often reluctant to give interviews, and those that do have a natural tendency to paint their statements in a positive light. Additionally, when a company fails, the staff of the company disperse and can be difficult to find. Contrast this with researching the histories of successful companies. The managers are more than willing to talk about the success of their organisation and their contribution to it. The organisation is still in existence, so managers and others are easy to trace. As well, archives and historical documents are readily to hand.

This does not mean that we do not have a good idea of why companies fail. One journal has identified the following six causes as contributors to organisational failure.[23]

1 *Identity crisis.* Senior management often does not have a clear idea of the business it is in and what makes it tick. Managers are often ill-informed as to the fundamentals of their business and what has made the business successful. They are therefore unaware of what actions need to be taken to ensure that the business grows.
2 *Failures of vision.* Few managers prepare their company for likely environmental or technological changes. Most do not anticipate threats to their core technology, such as diesels replacing steam locomotives and networked PCs replacing mainframes.
3 *High levels of debt.* Management and boards of directors often feel that unless they load their company with debt for expansion, the performance of the company will suffer and opportunities for expansion will be missed. Servicing the debt often becomes unsustainable during times of economic downturn and high interest rates, leading to corporate failure.
4 *Adhering to past practices.* Many companies continue to adhere to established customs and practices long after the circumstances that gave rise to them have passed. As a result, organisations find themselves out of alignment with actions of competitors and changes in market demand. This tendency increases with the size of the company.
5 *Failure to stay close to the customer.* This is an obvious failing and one which is the subject of dozens of management books and articles. But even companies that need to monitor customer demand, such as those in entertainment and fashion, still manage to get this fundamental wrong.
6 *Beware of the enemies within.* While the aphorism that employees are a company's greatest asset is true, many companies have been brought down by the actions of their own employees. Poor industrial relations, lack of incentives, misaligned rewards, uncontrolled risk taking, alienation and poor people management can lead to hostility and lack of cooperation from the workforce. Few organisations can thrive under these conditions.

the organisation, allowing the minimisation of conflicts. Confrontations can be resolved by all parties' winning. However, when the organisation is contracting, resources become scarce, leading to intense political activity over control around what few there are. Administrative rationality, which can explain the size–structure relationship in growth, is replaced by a power struggle. In decline, therefore, structure is more likely to reflect the interests of those in power, for they are best able to weather a political struggle.

Decline follows stages

Decline is not a continuous process, from some starting point through to the eventual dissolution of the organisation.[24] As environments and technologies are constantly challenging an organisation's legitimacy, all organisations will eventually face circumstances that can lead to decline. But there is nothing inevitable about decline. Management can and does have choices which, when exercised wisely and appropriately, can end or slow the decline process. The reason that organisational change is such a common part of management practice is that it is often associated with attempts to combat decline.

A useful model of organisational decline, proposed by Weitzel and Jonsson, sees decline passing through five stages. At each stage but the last, management can take corrective action to end the decline process. The model, shown in Figure 14.3,

FIGURE 14.3 Stages of decline and the widening performance gap

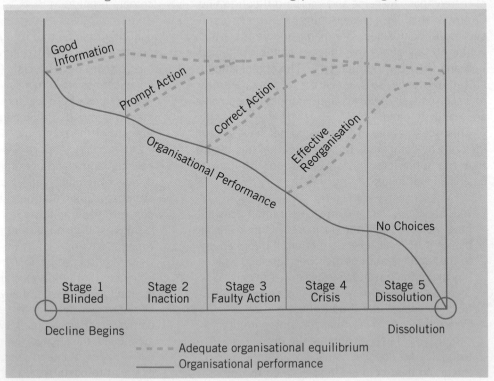

Source: William Weitzel & Ellen Jonsson, 'Decline in Organisations: A Literature Integration and Extension', *Administrative Science Quarterly*, 34(1), March 1989, p. 102.

identifies five stages of decline, with each stage having a corresponding action that the organisation can take to arrest the decline.

- *Stage 1. Blinded decline.* In this stage the organisation fails to anticipate or detect internal or external influences which can threaten the organisation's survival. Some of the signs that are often overlooked are the buildup of excessive numbers of personnel, a tolerance of incompetence, cumbersome administrative procedures, disproportionate staff power, poor productivity, unclear goals and decision benchmarks, fear of embarrassment and conflict, loss of effective communication, and an outdated organisational structure. One of the reasons for these signs being overlooked is that managers are trained to be attentive to quantitative changes in commonly gathered data, such as accounting measures of performance. But these data are historical, in that they reflect past performance. Decline may have set in long before it is reflected in performance statistics. Another feature of this stage of decline is that organisations often tend to focus their attention on meeting internal benchmarks rather than concentrating on adapting to the environment. However, management can overcome the problems of blinded decline by seeking good information; once this is obtained, overcoming the problems leading to decline is straightforward.

- *Stage 2. Inaction.* During this stage the signs of decline are apparent but the organisation chooses to do little or nothing about them. In profit-making organisations the signs can include declining profit, declining sales and surplus inventories. If the organisation is older and longer-established, the inaction stage is likely to be more pronounced and longer-lasting. Decline during this stage is by no means terminal, because prompt and appropriate management action can overcome the causes of the decline. One of the risks of this stage, however, is the likelihood of management increasing commitment to courses of action that contributed to the problem in the first place. This is why senior management is often changed during this stage.

- *Stage 3. Faulty action.* This stage sees the multiplication of the external signs of decline, even though action is being taken to arrest the decline. Differences of opinion regarding courses of action proliferate. This leads to an increase in political activity and power plays in the organisation as each faction lobbies to implement its preferred course of action. Employees experience uncertainty and morale deteriorates. Staff turnover increases. Organisation leaders are forced to consider substantive changes to ensure organisational survival. However, there is often difficulty in determining the most appropriate course to return the organisation to health. There is also pressure for quick action and decisions rather than well-thought-out ideas. Decisions may also be faulty because they concentrate on the indicators rather than the causes of the decline. Solutions may also concentrate on areas where slack resources are greatest or the power of resistance weakest. But effective action is still possible at this stage, provided that it correctly addresses the causes of decline.

- *Stage 4. Crisis.* At this stage opportunities to save the organisation are starting to run out. Arrival at this stage means that a major reorientation and revitalisation is necessary or the organisation will suffer certain failure. This inevitably involves a change in senior management. The staff suffer from divisiveness and the social fabric begins to break up. All those involved with the organisation, whether insiders or outsiders, begin to restrict their contact with it. As talented employees leave, turnaround becomes that much harder. Risk-taking increases as options run out. Customers and suppliers begin to desert the organisation. At this stage it may be subject to takeover if it has assets of value to other organisations, but this is not necessarily the case. Products may be old or out of date, technology or capital equipment obsolete, and brand names or market positioning of little worth.

● *Stage 5. Dissolution.* Decline at this stage is irreversible. The loss of capital, markets, reputation and talented personnel takes its toll and eventually the organisation collapses. Closing ceremonies, get-togethers and barbeques are often a feature of organisations that are closing up shop, and part of the skills of managing this stage of decline is in instituting constructive leave-taking processes.

Not all organisations follow precisely the stages identified in the model. In the case of a sudden shock, for instance, an organisation may find itself in stage 4 without going through the previous stages. An airline that experienced the crash of one of its aircraft for which it was found negligent would be a case in point. But the model does identify the difference between actual decline, the perception of that decline, and the actions necessary to restore the organisation to health. There are no formulas for doing this. It is very much a behavioural science, which relies on the important stakeholders of the organisation reading the situation correctly and taking appropriate remedial action. Reversing decline also requires that institutional support from the environment be available. Once an organisation loses the support of bankers, decline can be extremely fast. A bank itself can be put out of business in a week if depositors lose confidence in the bank's solvency. Organisations also rely on support from suppliers. Once this is lost and suppliers either won't supply or require cash in advance, the end of the organisation cannot be far off. Ratings agencies such as Standard & Poors' and Moody's do a brisk trade in assessing the risk of a business defaulting on its financial commitments.

Potential managerial problems when organisations decline

Some like the challenge of managing in adversity. Others merely find themselves in a leadership position when facts dictate that the organisation has entered its decline phase. While it is undoubtedly easier to manage an organisation during growth than during decline, the fact remains that decline is a reality, and when it occurs managers must be prepared to cope with its consequences. Table 14.1 lists some of these consequences. The remainder of this chapter looks in greater detail at some of these problems and considers what managers can do about them.

Increased conflict

A manager has the opportunity to really test his or her conflict-management skills during organisational decline. As we have noted before, growth creates slack, and that acts as a lubricant to smooth over conflict-creating forces. Management uses this slack as a currency for buying off potentially conflicting interest groups within the organisation. Conflicts can be resolved readily by expanding everyone's resources. However, in the decline phase, conflict over resources grows because there are fewer resources to divide up. For instance, conflict has been found to be higher in declining school districts than in growing districts.[25]

The increased conflict evident in decline is not necessarily dysfunctional. If managed properly, it can be directed towards slowing the decline. Out of the conflict

OT CLOSEUP

Do all companies follow the decline model?

Not all organisations appear to follow the stages of Weitzel and Jonsson's model. There have been some high-profile business failures that have not supported their contention of a long, slow decline process. Ansett Airlines' collapse in 2001 is a case in point. When it went into liquidation, it was not because of decaying morale, lack of appreciation of the problems, inappropriate technology or lack of customer support; it simply ran out of money and could not pay its bills. A similar situation applied to One-Tel and HIH Insurance. At a quick glance these businesses were in an established position in the market, finding new customers and operating normally. Their collapse was sudden and took many observers by surprise. So does this mean that decline does not follow stages?

Perhaps we are being a little unfair to Weitzel and Jonsson. Theoretical models are not intended to reflect immutable scientific principles but to act as a guide for most cases. Given this, we can identify the various stages of the decline model in Ansett's collapse. Ansett started to face problems when the airline industry was deregulated in the early 1990s. Qantas was reinvigorated by its merger with Australian Airlines and its privatisation created a new and important critical constituency, that of shareholders and financial analysts. This group monitored performance closely, and their evaluation was reflected in Qantas' share price. Additionally, Qantas operated an employee share ownership scheme, so few employees were kept in doubt as to how Qantas was faring in the market. This high level of public disclosure also kept Qantas' management attention firmly focused on profitability.

Ansett, which started the 1990s with a dominant position in the domestic market, was hampered by its ownership structure. Ownership passed during the 1990s from a joint ownership by TNT and News Ltd, Rupert Murdoch's company, to joint ownership with News Ltd and Air New Zealand, to full ownership by Air New Zealand. None of these owners gave Ansett the attention it deserved and all starved it of capital—either because they were not interested or, in the case of Air New Zealand, they did not have it.

All this time Ansett's performance was declining. It was slowly losing market share, its fleet was getting old and maintenance standards were slipping. Productivity rates were poor, a legacy of an outdated approach to industrial relations. But because of the lack of a need to disclose its performance, the full extent of losses was never fully appreciated by the public. On the surface, the airline was viable and indeed vibrant, with a strong brand name, a loyal workforce and, at worst, in need of stronger management and more capital. The reality was that, just prior to its collapse, it was losing over $1 million per day. The end saw the workforce and management and even Air New Zealand, its owner, stunned and stricken with disbelief.

Does Ansett fit Weitzel and Jonsson's decline model? In many respects it does, but we need to look at the 10-year time frame. What appeared to influence all those who worked for, managed or owned Ansett was that it would never fail: it was too big and too much of an institution in Australian business. Somehow it would pull through, and therefore the really hard decisions could be deferred. As a result the blinded and inaction stage was very long, extending at least five years. It seemed to skip the faulty action and crisis stage and moved very quickly to the dissolution stage. Weitzel and Jonsson's model highlights the fact that declining companies have choices, and it is one of the skills of management to take appropriate actions at the appropriate time.

TABLE 14.1 Dysfunctional consequences of organisational decline

Centralisation	Decision making is passed upwards, participation decreases and control is emphasised.
No long-term planning	Crises and short-term needs drive out strategic planning.
Innovation curtailed	No experimentation, risk-aversion and scepticism about non-core activities.
Scapegoating	Leaders are blamed for the pain and uncertainty.
Resistance to change	Conservatism and turf protection lead to rejection of new alternatives.
Turnover	The most competent leaders tend to leave first, causing leadership anaemia.
Low morale	Few needs are met, and infighting is predominant.
Loss of slack	Uncommitted resources are used to cover operating expenses.
Fragmented pluralism	Special-interest groups organise and become more vocal.
Loss of credibility	Leaders lose the confidence of their subordinates.
Non-prioritised cuts	Attempts to ameliorate conflict lead to attempts to equalise cutbacks.
Conflict	Competition and infighting for control predominate when resources are scarce.

Source: Adapted from Kim Cameron, David A. Whetten & Myung U. Kim, 'Organizational Dysfunctions of Decline', *Academy of Management Journal*, March 1987, p. 128; with permission.

can come changes that may revitalise the organisation: selection of a new domain, the creation of new products or services, and cost-cutting measures may make the shrunken organisation more efficient and viable.

Increased politicking

Less slack also translates into more politicking. There will emerge many organised and vocal groups actively pursuing their self-interest. As we noted earlier in this chapter, structural changes during decline are more likely to be determined by which coalitions win the power struggle for organisational control than by rational determinants such as size, technology or environment. Politically naive managers will find their jobs difficult, if not impossible, as they are unable to adjust to the changing decision-making criterion. Remember, in declining conditions the resources pie is shrinking. If one department can successfully resist a cut, the result will typically be that other departments have to cut deeper. Weak units will not only take a disproportionate part of the cut, but may be most vulnerable to elimination. In a 'fight-for-life' situation, the standard rules are disregarded. Critical data for decisions are twisted and interpreted by various coalitions so as to further their groups' interests. Such an environment encourages 'no-holds-barred' politicking.

Increased resistance to change

An organisation responds more slowly to environmental change in decline than in growth.[26] In its effort to protect itself, the dominant coalition fights hard to maintain the status quo and its control. Vested interests thwart change efforts.[27] Preparing the organisation for change becomes extremely difficult, as there is a genuine fear of the consequences of change. Generally, change in declining companies means redundancies and loss of status and position. Resistance to change seems to be related to the previously discussed 'stages of decline'.[28] Early in the decline, individuals follow a pattern of 'weathering the storm'. This is characterised by intensified efforts to follow the old, established procedures and may result in slowing the decline. But if it is truly of the prolonged variety, at best it can only delay the inevitable. Thus the early part of decline is a period of high resistance to change. Resistance should be reduced as it becomes clear that the decline is not temporary. It is part of management's task during decline to communicate the implications of decline widely.

One writer has noted that a major force for resisting change during the initial phase of decline will be those vested interests who have benefited most from growth.[29] As their power base is challenged, they are motivated to continue to push for growth-related policies, even though it no longer makes sense.

Loss of top management credibility

In its decline, members of the organisation will look to some individual or group on which to place the blame for the retrenchment. Whether or not top management is directly responsible for the decline, it tends to become the scapegoat. This leads to a loss of top management credibility. Members compare their organisation with organisations that are growing, or compare their plight with the situation of friends and relatives employed by healthy organisations, and then look for a place to vent their frustrations. If their organisation's senior management were competent, they seem to assume, retrenchment would not be necessary, or at least it would be of short duration.

The most obvious sign of this loss of credibility is a reduction in employee morale and organisational commitment. During retrenchment, job satisfaction tends to drop significantly, as does member loyalty to the organisation.

Change in workforce composition

Retrenchment requires workforce cuts. The most popular criterion for determining who gets laid off is seniority: that is, the most recent employees are the first to go. Laying off personnel on the basis of seniority, however, tends to reshape the composition of the workforce. As newer employees tend to be younger, seniority-based layoffs create an older workforce. If the industry is mature, large-scale layoffs of this nature can lead to a rise in the average age of the workforce of up to 10 years.

More recently, companies have been using voluntary redundancy, or variations of it, to reduce numbers. Although conventional wisdom has it that younger employees and those with more marketable skills are more likely to accept the packages offered, the results of research in the area are mixed. Many longer-serving employees, who often receive larger financial packages through the schemes, are attracted to them. Versions of early retirement schemes are also used to downsize the workforce, leaving a younger profile overall. Another method used to avoid the problem of changes in workforce composition is to make positions, and therefore their holders, redundant rather than specific individuals.

Increased voluntary turnover

Voluntary resignations are the other side of employee departures. This becomes a major potential problem in organisational decline, because the organisation will want to retain its most valuable employees. Yet some of the first people to voluntarily leave an organisation when it enters the stage of decline are the most mobile individuals, such as skilled technicians, professionals and talented managerial personnel. These, of course, are typically the individuals that the organisation can least afford to lose. Managers with a sharp eye on their career are particularly prone to 'jump ship' when it is clear that the growth days are over. The opportunities for advancement and increased responsibilities are obviously reduced greatly during decline. The upwardly mobile executive will look for an organisation where his or her talents are more likely to be used. This suggests that senior management will be challenged to provide incentives to ambitious junior managers if it is to prevent a long, slow decline from snowballing into a rapid descent.

Decaying employee motivation

Employee motivation is different when an organisation is contracting from when it is enjoying growth. During growth, motivation can be provided by promotional opportunities and the excitement of being associated with a dynamic organisation. During decline, there are retrenchments, reassignments of duties that often require absorbing the tasks that were previously done by others, and similar stress-inducing changes. It is usually hard for employees to stay motivated when they are uncertain whether they will still have a job next month or next year. When their organisation is experiencing prolonged decline, managers are challenged to function effectively in an organisational climate typified by stagnation, fear and stress.

What's the solution?

There are no magic techniques available to management that can overcome the many negative outcomes associated with organisational decline. However, some things seem to work better than others.[30] These include aligning the organisation's strategy with environmental realities, increasing communication, centralising decision making, redesigning jobs and work practices, and developing innovative approaches to cutbacks. Management also needs to improve the organisation's chances of survival by meeting the needs of critical constituencies in the environment.

Management needs to attack directly the ambiguity that organisational decline creates among employees. This is best done by clarifying the organisation's strategy and goals. Where is the organisation going? What is the organisation's future and potential? By addressing these questions appropriately, management demonstrates that it understands the problem and has a vision for what the new, smaller organisation will look like. Employees generally have a good idea of what the organisation's problems are, or at least can understand when told about them. They want to believe that management is not content to sit back and run a 'going-out-of-business' sale. If management loses credibility among the employees it will be so much harder to turn the organisation around.

Organisational decline demands that management do a lot of communicating with employees. The primary focus of this communication should be downward—specifically, explaining the rationale for changes that will have to be made. But there should also be upward communication to give employees an opportunity to express their fears and frustrations and have important questions answered. Remember, management's credibility is not likely to be too high. Moreover, rumours will be rampant. This puts a premium on management making every effort to explain clearly the reasons for, and implications of, all significant changes. That is not going to eliminate employee fears, but it will increase the likelihood that management is perceived as honest and trustworthy, which may be the best one can hope for.

During decline, organisations also need to sharpen their focus and clarify strategy. This may mean that unwanted or secondary businesses or undertakings are sold in order for management and workers to concentrate on what is worthwhile salvaging. This implies that it is common for managers to centralise decision making when a serious attack on decline begins. At such times, there is a significant need for the direction generated by strong leadership. This is reinforced by centralised decision making. Motivating and keeping staff focused requires extensive communication, but this does not imply an involvement in decision making.

You may also be thinking, wouldn't decentralisation and an increase in participation be a better solution? After all, participation is often proposed as a potent vehicle for facilitating change. We argue against participation during decline, especially in tough resource allocation and cutback decisions, because of the evidence that people cannot be rational contributors to their own demise.[31] The self-interest of participants is just too great to provide benefits that exceed the costs. Participation and decentralisation should be reintroduced only when it is clear to everyone that the decline has stabilised.

When cuts are made in personnel, there is an opportunity for management to consolidate and redesign jobs. If the decline appears to have been arrested and fears of further layoffs subside, the redesign of jobs to make them more challenging and motivating can turn a problem—eliminating functions and reassigning workloads—into an opportunity. For example, if the variety of work activities is expanded and people are allowed to do complete jobs, employees can find their new assignments offering a greater diversity of activities and develop a greater identification with their work.

Our final suggestion for managing organisational decline is for management to look for innovative ways to deal with the problems inherent in cutbacks. Some organisations, for example, have offered attractive incentives to encourage employees to take early retirement; have provided outplacement services to laid-off employees; and have set others up as contractors or suppliers to the organisation.

All of the above actions indicate that strong leadership is necessary if an organisation is to stop and reverse the decline process. The leader provides a focus for action and generates new ideas and courses of action. Leadership at this time may be even easier than in an organisation experiencing expansion. During decline, organisational members actively look to those in a leadership position for guidance and even hope. In times other than decline, the leaders may have difficulty getting those in the organisation to listen to them.

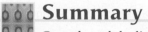

Summary

Growth and decline—the two most significant stages in the organisation's life cycle—create distinctly different problems and opportunities for managers.

The organisational theory literature has had a growth bias. 'Bigger is better' is consistent with that bias. So too are the beliefs that growth increases the likelihood of survival, is synonymous with effectiveness and represents power. This bias can be seen in Greiner's model of organisational growth. In this model, an organisation's evolution is characterised by phases of prolonged and calm growth, followed by periods of internal turmoil. Hanks' model of growth for high-technology firms does recognise that growth is not an inevitable outcome. It is only when firms start to expand beyond the start-up and early growth stage that organisational matters begin to be of importance for survival.

Managing organisational decline is not merely reversing what was done during growth. There is a lag that typifies the rate of change in structure during prolonged decline that is not evident in growth. This lag causes the level of structure to be greater in the same organisation for a given size during decline than during growth. In turn, this projects into a larger administrative component during decline; the increased importance of the power-control perspective in explaining structure; and the tendency for management to first ignore decline, then to treat it as an aberration and to respond appropriately only after some delay.

In decline, managers are likely to confront higher levels of conflict, increased politicking, stronger resistance to change, loss of credibility, changes in workforce composition, higher levels of voluntary turnover and decaying employee motivation. Suggestions for managing decline include clarifying the organisation's strategy, increasing communication, centralising decision making, redesigning jobs and developing innovative approaches to cutbacks.

For review and discussion

1   Why do Australian values favour growth?

2   How does growth increase survival?

3   How can growth be conceived as power?

4   In Greiner's model, what crisis does creativity create? Delegation? Coordination?

5   Discuss the applicability of Hanks' growth model to those organisations in other than high-tech industries.

6   Compare organisational decline and downsizing.

7   Describe how organisational decline can be interpreted as a reduction in organisational effectiveness.

8   Is decline more likely to occur in public-sector organisations than in business firms? Explain.

9   'Decline doesn't reduce slack; it increases it! In decline, organisations have more personnel and physical resources than they need.' Do you agree or disagree? Discuss.

10   How does the administrative component in decline differ from that in growth?

11   Describe how management typically responds to decline.

12   Why might a manager prefer to work in a growing organisation than in one that is in decline?

13   What positive outcomes, if any, can you see that retrenchment might provide for an organisation?

14   What solutions, other than those mentioned in this chapter, might management implement to manage decline better?

15   Contrast the role of the imperatives in determining an organisation's structure (discussed in Chapters 4–8) during growth and during decline.

CASE FOR CLASS DISCUSSION
Greenpeace faces its competition

Greenpeace seems to stand at the forefront of environmental groups. Its activism sets it apart from many other similar groups, such as the Australian Conservation Foundation and the World Wildlife Fund. Founded over 30 years ago, it has grown into the equivalent of a multinational corporation. Its headquarters are in Amsterdam and it has active branches in most parts of the world, although those in Western countries predominate. It is not afraid to undertake high levels of activism and its ships are seen at all the environmental hotspots around the world. Because of its activism, it attracts those who advocate a confrontational approach to environmentalism, rather than negotiation. Like markets, environmental problems are becoming increasingly international (note the issues of greenhouse gases, acid rain and ozone depletion). Greenpeace aims to bring a coordinated approach to environmental issues such as these.

Like any business corporation Greenpeace needs income, and this comes from donations and membership fees paid by supporters. As in any market, supporters can be fickle, and they must feel that they are getting value for their membership fees and donations or they will take their money elsewhere. Subscriptions to Greenpeace have been falling over recent years and there is evidence that environmentalists are supporting those who adopt a more cooperative approach to environmental problems. But Greenpeace has had some high-profile confrontations in which it is seen to come out in front. Examples are the protests against nuclear testing in the Pacific and the sinking of the *Rainbow Warrior*, and the win over Shell in 1995 over the disposal of the Brent Spar oil platform. Other protests are less clearcut. It associates trade with environmental degradation and has taken a prominent part in trying to stop world trade talks.

As it is dependent on donations, Greenpeace, like any business, thrives in time of economic growth. After rapid expansion in the 1980s, growth dropped back and some of the protest ships had to be disposed of. It has gone through traumas normally connected with profit-seeking organisations. It has downsized by

making 70 positions redundant and shut a number of shops selling Greenpeace products. It is also outsourcing certain functions such as data processing. And to boost income it is licensing its name to private firms to produce T-shirts, calendars and the like.

Greenpeace manages to balance centralisation and decentralisation better than many multinationals. Most decisions are taken locally, but when it needs to it acts in a highly centralised manner. It was one of the first organisations in the world to have an international computer network and, although regional bosses are given a fair amount of autonomy by the Amsterdam head office, they are never allowed to change Greenpeace's international policy to suit local conditions. The Greenpeace brand stays the same the world over.

The organisation also undertakes extensive long-term planning, realising that international conventions sometimes take up to 10 years to negotiate. But it can also react very rapidly when needs be. It has about $35 million dollars and 25% of staff time ready to allocate immediately to short-term issues as they arise. So Greenpeace has achieved a balance that many multinational businesses would envy; within the framework of long-term planning and goal achievement it has built an entrepreneurial and risk-taking culture.

Adapted from: 'Anonymous Environmentalism: Greenpeace Means Business', *The Economist*, 19 August 1995, pp. 65–6.

QUESTIONS

1 From the information in the case, evaluate the extent to which not-for-profit organisations face the same management problems as profit-seeking ones.

2 What problems of growth has Greenpeace faced, and how has it attempted to solve the problems?

3 How does Greenpeace fit Greiner's growth model and Weitzel and Jonsson's model of decline?

4 Is it likely that Greepeace will decline to the point of insignificance? If so, what factors may contribute to its decline?

FURTHER READING

Larry E. Greiner, 'Evolution and Revolution as Organizations Grow', *Harvard Business Review*, July/August 1972, pp. 37–46.

Michael T. Hannan & John H. Freeman, 'Internal Politics of Growth and Decline', in Marshall W. Meyer & Associates, eds, *Environments and Organizations*, San Francisco: Jossey-Bass, 1978, pp. 177–99.

Steven Hanks, Colin Warson, Eric Jansen & Gaylen Chandler, 'Tightening the Life-Cycle Construct: A Taxonomic Study of Growth Stage Configurations in High-Technology Organizations', *Entrepreneurship Theory and Practice*, 18(2), 1993, pp. 5–29.

William Weitzel & Ellen Jonsson, 'Decline in Organizations: A Literature Integration and Extension', *Administrative Science Quarterly*, March 1989, pp. 91–109.

NOTES

1 Based on Trevor Sykes, 'How Burns Philp Hit Terra Firma', *Australian Business Monthly*, September 1992, pp. 84–9; and Carolyn Cummins, 'Battered Burns to Quit the Spice Trade', *Sydney Morning Herald*, 20 May 1997.

2 James D. Thompson, *Organizations in Action*, New York: McGraw-Hill, 1967, p. 89.

3 Anonymous, How Mergers go Wrong, *The Economist*, July 22, 2002, p. 19.

4 Jeffrey Pfeffer, *Organizational Design*, Arlington Heights, IL: AHM Publishing, 1978, p. 114.

5 David A. Whetten, 'Organizational Decline: A Neglected Topic in Organizational Science', *Academy of Management Review*, October 1980, p. 578.

6 William G. Scott, 'The Management of Decline', *Conference Board Record*, June 1976, p. 57.

7 David A. Whetten, 'Organizational Growth and Decline Process', in Kim S. Cameron, Robert I. Sutton & David A. Whetton, eds, *Readings in Organizational Decline*, Cambridge, MA: Ballinger Publishing, 1988, p. 36.

8 Jeffrey Pfeffer & Gerald R. Salancik, *The External Control of Organizations*, New York: Harper & Row, 1978.

9 *The Economist*, op. cit.

10 Pfeffer, *Organizational Design*, p. 115.

11 Steven Hanks, Colin Warson, Eric Jansen & Gaylen Chandler, 'Tightening the Life-Cycle Construct: A Taxonomic Study of Growth Stage Configurations in High-Technology Organizations', *Entrepreneurship Theory and Practice*, 18(2), 1993, pp. 5–29.

12 Larry E. Greiner, 'Evolution and Revolution as Organizations Grow', *Harvard Business Review*, July/August 1972, pp. 37–46.

13 Hanks et al. 'Tightening the Life-Cycle Construct: A Taxonomic Study of Growth Stage Configurations in High-Technology Organizations'.

14 David Terpstra & Philip Olsen, 'Entrepreneurial Start-Up and Growth: A Classification of Problems', *Entrepreneurship Theory and Practice*, 17(3), 1993, pp. 5–20.

15 See, for instance, William Weitzel & Ellen Jonsson, 'Decline in Organizations: A Literature Integration and Extension', *Administrative Science Quarterly*, March 1989, pp. 91–109.

16 Whetten, 'Organizational Decline: A Neglected Topic in Organizational Science', p. 579.

17 Charles H. Levine, 'More on Cutback Management: Hard Questions for Hard Times', *Public Administration Review*, March/April 1979, pp. 179–83.

18 Jeffrey D. Ford, 'The Occurrence of Structural Hysteresis in Declining Organizations', *Academy of Management Review*, October 1980, pp. 589–98.

19 ibid., p. 592.

20 John H. Freeman & Michael T. Hannan, 'Growth and Decline Processes in Organizations', *American Sociological Review*, April 1975, p. 215–83; William McKinley, 'Complexity and Administrative Intensity: The Case of Declining Organizations', *Administrative Science Quarterly*, March 1987, pp. 87–105; and John R. Montanari & Philip J. Adelman, 'The

Administrative Component of Organizations and the Ratchet Effect: A Critique of Cross-Sectional Studies', *Journal of Management Studies*, March 1987, pp. 113–23.

21 Jeffrey D. Ford, 'The Administrative Component in Growing and Declining Organizations: A Longitudinal Analysis', *Academy of Management Journal*, December 1980, pp. 615–30.

22 Michael T. Hannan & John H. Freeman, 'Internal Politics of Growth and Decline', in Marshall W. Meyer & Associates, eds, *Environments and Organizations*, San Francisco: Jossey-Bass, 1978, pp. 177–99.

23 Kenneth Labich, 'Why companies fail', *Fortune*, 14 November 1994, pp. 152–68.

24 William Weitzel & Ellen Jonsson, 'Decline in Organisations: A Literature Integration and Extension', *Administrative Science Quarterly*, 34(1), March 1989, pp. 91–186.

25 Hannan & Freeman, 'Internal Politics of Growth and Decline'.

26 ibid.

27 John Gardner, 'Organizational Survival: Overcoming Mind-Forged Manacles', in John F. Veiga & John N. Yanouzas, eds, *The Dynamics of Organization Theory: Gaining a Macro Perspective*, St Paul, MN: West Publishing, 1979, pp. 28–31.

28 B.L.T. Hedberg, Paul C. Nystrom & William H. Starbuck, 'Camping on Seesaws: Prescriptions for a Self-designing Organization', *Administrative Science Quarterly*, March 1976, pp. 41–65.

29 Whetten, 'Organizational Decline: A Neglected Topic in Organizational Science', p. 582.

30 These suggestions are derived from Ronald Lippitt & Gordon Lippitt, 'Humane Downsizing: Organizational Renewal versus Organizational Depression', *S.A.M. Advanced Management Journal*, Summer 1984, pp. 15–21; Lee Tom Perry, 'Least-Cost Alternatives to Layoffs in Declining Industries', *Organizational Dynamics*, Spring 1986, pp. 48–61; Cynthia Hardy, 'Strategies for Retrenchment: Reconciling Individual and Organizational Needs', *Canadian Journal of Administrative Sciences*, December 1986, pp. 275–89; and George E.L. Barbee, 'Downsizing With Dignity: Easing the Pain of Employee Layoffs', *Business and Society Review*, Spring 1987, pp. 31–4.

31 Charles H. Levine, 'More on Cutback Management: Hard Questions for Hard Times'.

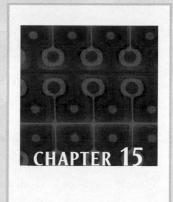

CHAPTER 15

Gender and organisations

After reading this chapter you should be able to:

1 explain why gender in organisations is a widely debated and important topic;

2 describe how workforces become gender-segmented;

3 identify the main barriers to women's promotion;

4 examine the main schools of feminist thought in relation to organisations;

5 describe feminist research methodologies;

6 identify the characteristics of masculine and feminine management;

7 identify the characteristics of equal opportunity programs;

8 evaluate whether organisations can become gender-free.

Introduction

Gender and the workforce

Organisations and their management are not renowned as topics of conversation which inspire rapt attention and heated debate. But one area that can be counted upon to draw contributions from a wide range of opinions is that of women in organisations. There are a number of reasons for this. One is that notwithstanding thirty years of activism and longstanding legislation outlawing gender discrimination, the employment outcomes for men and women are still far apart. A further reason is that the causes for this divergence in outcomes are not at all clear.

For instance, in management consulting firms, whilst an equal number of male and female graduates are hired, within five years the gender ratio has often shifted to 70:30 in favour of males. Further, although men and women start with the same salary, gaps soon start to open and men's pay starts to rise faster than women's. Whilst the most common explanation given for the disparity in outcomes is that of marriage and pregnancy, other factors are obviously present. Whilst many of these barriers are difficult to identify, a number have been proposed. Amongst them are that women lack role models, mentors and supporters at the top of organisations. Others have proposed that men network more efficiently than women and as a consequence are better informed on the internal workings of the organisation. Various work/life arrangements, such as lack of support for those who are pregnant and have young families have also been raised.

But others point to the fact that many male managers don't see gender balance as a problem. They have met the legislative requirements and put in place procedures and policies which are fair then they have just closed their mind to the issue. The sustained effort required to maintain the momentum of women in management progression is not forthcoming.

The subtle interplay of influences, motivations and agendas will ensure that gender in organsations will be a topic of debate well into the future.

Take a look at most organisations, and the chances are that the board of directors, the managing director, as well as most of the senior management, are male. The more senior the management, the fewer the number of women you are likely to see. Look at the studies quoted in this book, and most of them, with the notable exception of Woodward's studies quoted in Chapter 7, have been undertaken by men. Not surprisingly, you may be left with the impression that men have both defined and operationalised management and the way organisations are structured, and that they have done so in a way that has promoted male interests. In the process, this has excluded the participation of women.

The impact of gender on the way organisations are structured and managed forms the subject of this chapter. We have called it 'Gender and organisations', although it draws primarily on studies concerning women. In part this is because most of the literature on gender in organisations is drawn from feminist literature, and women have largely defined the nature and content of gender studies. The implications are that existing organisational knowledge, as it has been largely male-dominated and practised, reflects the male position. There have been many studies and theoretical writings about women in organisations. Few have men as their main source of inquiry.[1]

Most studies regarding women's participation in the workforce have concentrated on their absence from managerial and other positions of influence. In this area the statistics are quite clear: the higher the managerial position, the fewer women are to be found. In a recent Australian study it was found that 71% of supervisors were women. But they comprised only 13.7% of junior managers, 14% of middle managers and only 1.3% of senior managers.[2] Notwithstanding legislative provisions and equal employment programs this situation, according to some studies, is not changing. It is not as if women did not have the educational background for higher levels of responsibilities: in 1996, of those enrolled at universities, 53% were women.

But first we need a few definitions and explanations. Sex is a biological concept, which refers to whether we are male or female. **Gender** is a broader concept which, although including sex, addresses the various actions and roles of men and women in organisations and in society generally. It includes the different life experiences of men and women in terms of social conditioning, family roles and community expectations and the thought processes and orientations that can arise from these.

A branch of gender studies is feminism. There is no shortage of opinions as to what feminism is and what its impact has been over the past 20 years. It is more difficult, however, to come up with a definition that is acceptable to all parties. However, we shall define **feminism** as an active advocacy of the claims and aspirations of women. As with all social movements, feminism has adherents ranging from strong and politically vocal advocates through to those who espouse sympathy but little else. Feminism also has a negative image among some sections of the population, women included. But what is common to all interpretations of feminism is a promotion of the rights and interests of women. These rights and interests extend to all aspects of modern life, from political decision making to equal employment opportunity. A close reading of our definition identifies that you do not have to be a woman to be a feminist, although of course feminism is widely regarded as an exclusively female orientation. There are many men who adopt attitudes that are feminist in nature, just as there are many women who reject them.

In keeping with the theme of this book we will look at feminism as it applies to organisations. The literature on feminism has grown extensively over the past 20 years, with only part of it being relevant to organisation theory. In this chapter, we address two streams of feminist literature. The first is the feminist attack on rational scientific inquiry and methodology. And the second is the position that considers organisations having been developed and run as a patriarchy which marginalises female participation.

It is difficult to isolate the organisational theory aspect of organisations from that of organisational behaviour. After all, all organisational life is behavioural life. As with our chapter on culture, we will cross the boundaries between organisational behaviour and organisation theory in order to better understand the subject.

gender the various actions and roles of men and women in organisations and in society generally

feminism an active advocacy of the claims and aspirations of women

Why should we be concerned with gender and organisations?

The types of organisations discussed in this book have a central part to play both in the economy and in shaping society. Not only do they perform the essential functions of deciding what and how much to produce, but they are also the main mechanism for distributing income to the various sectors of the population. Most people's income and status are largely derived from the positions they hold in business and government organisations. If a section of society is excluded from holding positions of influence and power, then that section of society is disenfranchised from many of the benefits that society can provide. Also, significant decisions concerning the direction of society are not made by people representative of that society. It is, of course, no secret that women have been underrepresented in positions of formal power in the past. And through being the main carers and nurturers of children as well as the elderly, they have typically had a lower status in the community.

Further, to exclude, either by design or accident, one section of the population from the full range of opportunities available to members of society is an affront to the rights of the individual. Very few members of the workforce rise to senior management or decision-making positions, but it should be open to all members of society to aspire to such positions, or any other occupation, on the basis of their merits. Additionally, by widening the pool of available applicants we make the best use of the talent available, thus improving the chances of putting the best person in the job.

Another reason for taking gender in organisations seriously is that the issue has been highly politicised. Few readers are unaware of the extent to which women's issues have been publicly raised and discussed. None of the issues discussed in this book carries the same political, or emotional, connotations as that of gender. It is hard to imagine parliaments giving their attention to organisational size, technology or culture. But highly skilled lobbying on the part of feminist activists has led to a raft of legislation that forces organisations to take issues relating to women seriously. Managers are not able to ignore the legislative requirements, or community attitudes or expectations.

What has led to the gender segmentation of the workforce?

Australia has traditionally had one of the most gender-segmented workforces of the industrialised countries.[3] This has applied not only to occupations but also to the dominance of men in management. And, particularly as far as participation in management is concerned, women's inroads seem to be stalling.[4] It is useful to consider how this segmentation came about and why it appears to be perpetuated. In this book we have considered many different points of view about the influence of variables on organisation structure; equally there are debates about why organisations have come to be male-dominated. (From the factors we discuss, you can probably make your own evaluation as to their relative influence.)

We also draw a distinction between political and legal equality and the participation of women in business and employment. This distinction highlights the different stages in the progress of the women's movement. Feminists have been active for over 150 years in promoting legislation that treats men and women equally. Many protests in years gone past have been violent and disruptive. Suffragettes, those seeking the vote for women, often used to chain themselves to iron fences in London and throw away the key. One suffragette threw herself under the king's horse in a race at Ascot and was killed. In the early part of the 20th century, the women's suffrage movement dominated political discourse. So the legislation we have seen emerge over the past 20 years promoting equality in the workplace is the result of a long period of feminist activism. In Western countries up to the early part of the 20th century, the women's movement concentrated on the rights of women to own property and to vote. From 1883 in the various Australian colonies, legislation was passed to allow married women the same legal position in relation to property as unmarried women. Prior to this, the property of all married women could be claimed by their husbands. However, divorce and inheritance laws recognised women's dependence and provided income support for them. They were also provided with widow's pensions on the premature death of their husband.

Australia, along with New Zealand, was one of the first countries to give women equal voting rights with men. In 1894 South Australia was the first colony to allow women the right to vote (called suffrage). The other colonies, later states after federation in 1901, progressively followed, with Victoria being the last to grant female suffrage in 1908. Women were allowed the right to vote in the first federal elections in 1903. By contrast, female suffrage was not introduced in the United States until 1920, and in the United Kingdom not until 1928.

Despite legal and political progress, women saw little move to equality in the employment area. This was a combination of factors, both social and institutional. By institutional we mean that the barriers existed in legislation and in accepted organisational custom and practice. Societal expectations were such that women were primarily mothers and keepers of the household. Until 40 years ago, this demanded a fair amount of time. Family sizes were larger than today, leading to the care of children extending over a longer period.[5] Health standards were also poorer.[6] Few of the labour-saving devices we now take for granted existed. Washing machines, vacuum cleaners, refrigerators and motor cars did not reach full-scale commercialisation in Australia until the 1950s. Microwave ovens, take-away food and all-night shopping were well in the future. The better-off households could afford domestic help, but this was mostly provided by other women.

The notion of the 'housewife' and women and domesticity was entrenched in the social structures and expectations of the day. It was reinforced by advertising and the popular press, with many women's magazines promoting the role of the woman as housewife and mother. The etiquette and social standards of the day saw men and women treated differently. Men always raised their hats to women, stood for women in public transport and opened doors for women. As attitudes changed in the 1970s, these actions were interpreted by feminists as being condescending, and eventually died out.

To complement the caring role of women, men had their specialised tasks in relation to providing income and family support. In many cases, men were seen to be the 'disposable gender'. The most obvious example of this is 'women and children first' in relation to safety at times of danger. There was also extensive loss of male life during the two world wars of the 20th century. Typically males undertook the dirty, dangerous and physically demanding work, and few working-class men reached retirement age without at least one industrial disease having a major impact on their quality of life, if not their life itself.[7] Women, by legislation, were barred from employment in what were considered dangerous occupations such as mining and lead refining. Workers' compensation for women was not available in some industries, effectively banning their employment. But compared to those of women, male experiences have been poorly documented and theorised by gender researchers.

The idea that male and female labour in the paid workforce had a different economic value was entrenched in law by Justice Higgins in the Harvester Judgment in 1907 and subsequent additions to it. In determining the wage to be paid in the Harvester factory, Justice Higgins researched what it would cost for a man to keep a wife and three children in a reasonable standard of comfort. This became known as the basic wage. Because women were not seen to have the same economic responsibilities as men—in other words, either they had only themselves to look after or they supplemented the wage earned by their husband—their wage was subsequently determined to be 54% of the male rate. Equal pay for equal work was not introduced in federal awards until 1972.

Although men and women shared a common employer in factories and offices, rarely did they do the same job. Men dominated as clerks and managers, women as secretaries and typists. Women did virtually all the sewing in clothing factories, while men maintained the machines and drove the delivery trucks. As we have seen, in an age where occupational health and safety was neglected, men took on most of the higher-risk tasks and those requiring lifting or physical strength. Most organisations had rules determining that certain positions could be filled only by men, and in some cases women. Women could rise only to mid-level positions in the public service, for instance, not because of any subtle discrimination but because legislation was in force reserving the higher positions for men.

With the evolution of technology and society, we would expect many of these barriers to fall over time. However, in the 50 years up to 1950 there were enormous economic and political changes, which interrupted the normal evolutionary pattern of society. The two world wars saw large-scale dislocation of work responsibilities and the need to find employment for demobilised soldiers (almost all men) at the conclusion of hostilities. They were given preference in the workforce. The contribution of women to the war effort has been well documented. But after the wars, prompted by high marriage and birth rates, women were back in their traditional care-giver roles. And the shortage of jobs during the 1920s and the depression of the 1930s, in which unemployment rose to over 30%, saw scarce jobs being rationed on the basis of one job per family. In line with the expectations of the day, women were rarely seen as the ones to work, and on marriage most women had to leave the workforce. Married women were not allowed to join the Commonwealth public service until 1966.

The various legislative barriers we have discussed were kept in place long after the values of most in the community had changed. Once laws become enacted and institutionalised, they are not readily repealed; it requires a conscious effort on the part of law makers. The delays added to the politicisation of feminist activity.

Barriers through the nature of work

Participation of women in the workforce has generally been at the lower levels of responsibility. In some cases this has been set by award conditions which reflected prevailing, mainly male, attitudes and values. But in others it has emanated from the conditions of the work itself. For instance, Qantas cabin service was dominated by the use of stewards until the 1970s. This originated from the early Qantas experience of the use of flying boats.[8] These required men to handle anchors, stow mailbags and baggage and row the tending boats. The strength requirements precluded women from gaining entry to the occupation and therefore the higher levels of responsibility. Also in the aviation field, flying the early passenger aeroplanes required physical endurance and strength, which deterred many women. Further examples are the difficulties in steering and gear changing on a 1950s bus, operating points in signal boxes in the railways, and the lifting requirement of many store-keeping jobs. It was a short step for companies to institute a policy of hiring only men for certain occupations and women for others. In a further stereotype, women were seen to be superior in detailed manufacturing such as sewing and electrical assembly, leading to many being employed in such jobs in factories.

As the workforce was largely gender-segregated, the workplace facilities were similarly segregated. Engineering companies, for instance, did not have washrooms or change facilities for women, and thus could excuse themselves from hiring women. The odd requirement to lift a heavy load could act in a similar manner. For those occupations requiring accommodation away from home, such as train drivers, barracks were supplied only on a single-sex basis. Many occupations, such as that of police officer, had height, weight and strength requirements well in excess of that necessary to undertake the work. This acted as a barrier to hiring women.

As technology advanced, many of the physical barriers were eliminated. A person of a child's strength can now fly an aircraft, for instance. But attitudes and values proved more resistant to change than the technology, and it was in order to remove the remaining barriers to equal employment that affirmative action policies were introduced. The first sex discrimination act in Australia was passed by the South Australian parliament in 1975.

Biological differences

The biology of women, or more specifically their child-bearing role, has been identified as a major barrier to their promotion in organisations. Put simply, it is difficult to combine family and child-rearing responsibilities with forging a high-powered career. It was the expectation in previous generations that if women did not permanently leave employment upon marriage, they did so on pregnancy. Most women now expect to resume employment after taking time off to have children, but women are fortunate if they can re-enter the workforce at the level at which they left it. Generally, circumstances in organisations have changed in their absence, and career impetus may be lost. As a result, valuable experience, and promotion opportunities, are forgone. Motherhood is also not just a matter of maternity. The need to care for children during their long periods of dependency may drain energy, prevent travel and lead to the rejection of career-advancing assignments that require relocation to another geographic area. Men manage to escape the more onerous of these obligations because of their biology and domestic arrangements.

In many ways the child-rearing issue is the most intractable problem to overcome in promoting more women to senior management. Child rearing is not a simple task; it can be both demanding and draining and is often accompanied by health problems on the part of either mother or child. Accommodating both career opportunities and the many demands that motherhood places on women cannot easily be resolved by legislation, as it extends beyond the provision of maternity leave. Compensating for the time lost through child rearing requires new organisational practices and attitudes, which are proving slow to emerge. Current promotion

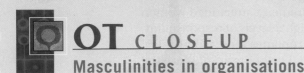

OT CLOSEUP

Masculinities in organisations

It might not be apparent from reading the literature on gender but there are actually two genders, one female and one male. Feminists have been highly successful politically in publicising their claims and having supporting legislation passed. But statistics still show continuing inequality of outcomes within organisations. Although they join organisations in equal numbers to men, their progression up the management ladder is slower. In particular they remain stubbornly underrepresented in the executive suite. But on a more mundane level, the gender segmentation of the workforce is obvious from everyday experiences. Men are giving up becoming educators in droves, with teaching becoming an increasingly feminised profession. Similar outcomes can be seen in the health industry, with men rarely seen in nursing and in allied health occupations. Welfare positions such as social work are almost exclusively female.

Why do we see such segmentation? This has been the subject of considerable theorising and research, but a valuable insight may be provided by studying masculinities—in other words, what defines and motivates men as a gender. This is not a new area of research, and increasing attention is being paid to it. One of Australia's leading researchers on masculinities is Professor Amanda Sinclair of the University of Melbourne. She notes that men are often not comfortable talking about themselves and other men but yet their experiences are crucial to understanding organisational life. She considers that this may be because the male management experience is considered the norm, and hence not worthy of separate consideration. Men consider that most management theory has been deducted from the research of men and deserves no special male focus. This is compounded by the fact that men in dominant positions have generally not thought of themselves as a category or identity group; gender is something women have and race and culture something non-whites and immigrants have. Men in prominent positions can also be defensive, bearing the brunt of criticism ranging from being a 'suit',

being white, being male, being senior and running exploitative corporations.

Not discussing masculinities leaves much of organisational life opaque, inaccessible and beyond negotiation and change. It also means that we can revert to familiar stereotypes such as 'the glass ceiling' and 'the pipeline' to understand what is going on. To contribute to greater understanding, Sinclair has identified three key areas that are revealing of masculinities in organisations. These are the role of heroic leadership, men's role in the new economy, and teamwork and the exclusion of diversity.

Male managers relate the management task to that of *heroic leadership*. They view management, and leadership, as demonstrating endurance, emotional toughness, self-reliance and a rejection of the feminine. The more endurance and stamina demonstrated as a leader, the more status is accrued to the person as a man. Sinclair sees this as deriving from the frontier mentality of history. She sees success in this culture as providing the attribute of invincibility and almost mythical status. Where professional heroic cultures have been defined by the absence of women, problems of invincibility can arise. Where leadership is defined by the myth of invincibility, alternate viewpoints are not considered and the organisation becomes inflexible. For women to succeed in this culture, they must exhibit traits similar to the dominant male culture. Of course there are other masculine subcultures within organisations, but that of the heroic leader dominates the executive levels.

The *new economy* presents a more complex picture for masculinities. On the one hand, new communication technologies are reducing status, racial and gender barriers to communicating. Alternatively, it is possible to work 24 hours a day, and work can overflow into personal and family life. Travel for work and answering e-mails is expected to be done in the evening and at weekends. Research indicates that under these conditions the emerging masculinities are as excluding of women as traditional work, but they may be more accommodating of racial and cultural diversity. Successful employees are those without a family and for those for whom work and play merge in a desire to be at the technological frontier.

Teamwork is also revealing of masculinities. Although Australian workplaces are diverse, the composition of teams within them is very homogeneous, particularly at the middle and senior levels. This homogeneity often extends to the way in which teams operate. Team behaviour is limited by the traditional and narrow template of expected behaviours and interactions, which include strong leadership, which rewards verbal assertiveness

and certainty as evidence of knowledge. This has emerged as part of the heroic and stoic culture of management in Australia. Many teams also function in hierarchical ways, where everyone knows their place and who is the boss. As well, teams often recruit members who are like themselves. Sinclair considers that, in this culture, the contributions of women are often marginalised and women's ways of doing things are rarely experienced.

Adapted from: Amanda Sinclair, 'Caution: Men at Work', Weekend Review, *The Australian Financial Review*, 5 January 2001, p. 1.

practices are developed around male notions of freedom from domestic constraints. At the present time, many women who aspire to senior management and leadership in the professions are deciding not to have children, thus eliminating motherhood as a barrier to promotion.

The problem-solving characteristics deriving from the biological differences of men and women has been identified as contributing to the gender segmentation of the workforce.[9] Unlike pregnancy, these are not clearcut and cannot be said to be the exclusive preserve of either gender. Specifically, the issue of right and left brain has been raised as a reason why men and women succeed in different occupations. Left-brain fields are those associated with rational, quantifiable, logical and analytical thought processes. Right-brain skills are those linked to intuition, emotional orientation and relationships. This may explain why men have an advantage in such areas as engineering and accounting and women are drawn to fields such as nursing, teaching and the health professions. Physiologists also claim that women are able to switch more easily between left and right brain skills than men. While the left-brain/right-brain dichotomy is a little speculative, it assists us in understanding why men and women may excel in different types of occupation.[10]

Barriers through societal attitudes

The attitude of society to women's roles also militated against their pursuing a career in the paid workforce. As we have discussed, women's main role in life was considered to be that of wife and mother. As a consequence, work was seen as a transition phase between leaving school and family responsibilities. This also led to fewer educational opportunities for women than for men, consigning them to jobs with reduced chances of promotion. In many cases, money spent on the education of women was considered to be wasted, as their participation in the workforce was expected to be short. These attitudes also led to the expectation of women being submissive and for it to be inappropriate for them aspiring to higher levels of responsibility. Nursing, teaching and secretarial work were the main career paths for women wanting more than domestic service and factory jobs.

Barriers through organisational practices

The paucity of women in top management has been a subject of considerable theorising. The statistics are clear, but the reasons behind them are often clouded. Most organisations, particularly large ones, have transparent management selection and promotion processes, and most senior managers genuinely believe that their organisations are free of discrimination. Although the visible impediments that women face in recruitment and promotion have been removed, they still have difficulty reaching the highest levels of management. The final hurdle has been called the *glass ceiling*, referring to the fact that the barriers are invisible but real nonetheless. A complicating factor in determining the reasons for the paucity of women in senior management is that traditional research techniques seem inadequate to the task. Subtleties in organisational practices and attitudes are difficult to identify and interpret. Actions may be motivated by unconsciously held beliefs, which are complex and puzzling. These subtleties of course are as much applicable to women as to men. It may be that, as one researcher has noted, many managers realise that environments may not be conducive to women, but suppress any moves to do anything about it because the whole issue is too messy.[11] Regardless of these difficulties, there has been sufficient research undertaken to provide a good guide to the particular problems faced by women in male-dominated organisations. Theorists have also

OT CLOSEUP

Where girls go

Recent research shows that the career choices of men and women tend to diverge at an early age, even before high school has been completed. The study, carried out by two Australian academic researchers, found that women's careers were far more complex than men's because of the greater number of variables they experience in education and through their career. What made the research unusual was that it was a longitudinal study: that is, it followed the careers of a sample of women, in this case 34, from when they left school in 1973 until 1990.

As a result of the study, three career predictors for women were nominated. The first was the study of maths, which gave girls multiple options and opportunities. Many jobs and courses depended on number literacy and computer skills. The second was the student's own motivation, sense of self and subjective values. The third predictor was the extent of sophisticated career advice via the computer, the family and the school. Many parents were found to influence the careers of children, with fathers particularly encouraging daughters to choose traditional female occupations.

The study found that women tended to fall into three categories as far as career and lifestyle were concerned. The first was the superwomen category—those who try to combine a fast-track career with child rearing. The second was women with no children who concentrate on their career. The third group was women who shift their focus from their career to spend more time with their family.

There was also evidence in the study that young women choose careers with family compatibility in mind. The study suggested that being in the superwomen category may be too difficult for many. They rather look for factors in a career such as flexitime and institutions with child care and maternity provisions.

Adapted from: Millicent Poole & Janice Langdon-Fox, *Australian Women and Careers*, Melbourne: Cambridge University Press, 1997.

been active in generating explanations. So while the research has been seen as confusing, episodic and contradictory, we can at least be confident that many barriers we identify do exist in many organisations.[12] To put this section into perspective, it should be stated that promotion positions in organisations are scarce. Many aspire to such positions, but in large organisations only a tiny proportion of the workforce of either gender reach top management.

Male management and behaviour standards

As men dominate management, it is not surprising that their preferred management style has come to dominate organisations.

Rosabeth Moss Kanter reported a classic study of organisational gender segmentation in 1977, which identified many of the arguments as to why male management is self-perpetuating.[13] The organisation she studied had a bureaucratic approach to management, with a tall hierarchy of many management layers. Female jobs were concentrated in secretarial and lower-grade clerical work. She found that the senior management of the company, which was almost exclusively male, tended to reproduce itself because people tended to understand, and trust, people who were most like themselves. As the management team required such trust, the cloning of management from one generation to the next became common, leading to men promoting other men. In other words, managers were reluctant to take a risk in promoting someone who was different from themselves.

Linguistics can also assist us in identifying why male management may become entrenched.[14] Shared language is an important guide to who is included, or excluded, from a group. (By language, we are referring to the subtle nuances and word usage that are part and parcel of shared experience and close working relationships.) One of the ways we can identify the sharing of a corporate culture is by the use of language. Kanter found that those in the management group in the organisation she studied spent most of their time in face-to-face communication. Time pressure was such that they had to derive as much as possible from the time spent communicating. This led not only to importance being placed on communication ability, but also to the sharing of a common symbolism, inflection and meaning which disadvantaged those outside the group.

Such symbolic language in organisations often draws on male interests.[15] For instance, football analogies and references to war are often used to make meanings of situations. 'Doing battle', 'no man's land', 'bringing the big guns to bear', 'going head-to-head', 'doing the hard yards' and 'taking your eye off the ball' are often used to describe management problems and responses. The use of words such as chairman and foreman also gives management a masculine flavour.

Needless to say, the linguistics associated with management has been mainly originated and defined by men, so it is not surprising that women might feel intimidated by the communication used in the executive suite. The failure to share the meaning of symbolic language and phraseology is a familiar way to make women feel excluded and marginalised. Feminists would argue that, even though procedures and policies may make an organisation 'facially neutral', in practice factors such as language perpetuate gender segregation in the workplace.

Choice of decoration may also act to make women feel intimidated in the executive suite. Dark tones and colourings, pictures reflecting male interests, furnishings to suit male tastes and a general bonhomie among the men can act to make even the most determined woman feel out of place. Many simply give up trying to achieve high levels of management and settle for a position with a greater comfort zone.

The male approach to management has also been identified as contributing to the paucity of women in management. Later in this chapter we consider in some detail the differences in management styles that have been attributed to men and women. We could summarise this research, however, by identifying that women have been linked to a management style that stresses teamwork, empathy and relationship building. Men, on the other hand, have been identified as emphasising results, placing great importance on control, and stressing the primacy of the task at hand. While these management styles are only generalisations (we do not have to look too hard to find exceptions) they do represent styles that are difficult to practise simultaneously. The male management style that tends to dominate in most organisations presents a challenge to women to adapt. Some women resolve the problem by leaving the organisation rather than fighting, many starting their own businesses where they can practise their preferred management style.

Women have found that the barriers to promotion are lower in those organisations which operate in fast-changing industries and those which are new start-ups.[16] In each of these types of organisations there are fewer entrenched practices and institutional barriers to change, hence promotion decisions are more likely to be made according to ability.

Management selection processes

It is probably fair to say that in most large organisations considerable effort has been expended on creating discrimination free selection and promotion criteria. But women are still underrepresented in promotion positions, particularly in senior management. What causes this situation is difficult to establish, as the subtleties stretch existing research methodologies. Theorists have of course been active in generating explanations, and there has been some research that has provided useful information. From these sources, the following indicate some of the barriers faced by women. Of course, men face many of the barriers as well, but they appear to be more pronounced in the case of female employees.

Uneven allocation of assignments. While selection and promotion criteria may be impartial, the allocation of challenging tasks that may lead to promotion is inequitable.[17] Track record and task accomplishments are important to promotion; candidates can point to these as evidence of capacity. It is also true that assignments that build a strong track record are hard to come by. It is at this level that women appear to be disadvantaged, as they are given fewer stretch assignments. As a result, when the time comes to apply for promotion, they are less able to demonstrate competence. Such tasks might be membership of key committees and taskforces, introduction of new machinery or techniques, coordination or liaison roles, and management responsibilities. The importance of these additional tasks is highlighted by the vague and ill-defined nature of management selection criteria. Such phrases as 'demonstrated competence', 'ability to communicate' and 'analytical skills' are tricky to nail down and assess. We usually rely on a candidate being able to demonstrate that he/she is able to do these things through previous assignments.

Along with uneven allocation of assignments, women are often left in particular jobs longer than men. This means that they lose significant experience and job knowledge, as well as contacts and opportunities for networking.[18]

Lack of line-management experience. All companies have core activities relating to their main area of competence. Managers in these areas are called line managers. They also have staff activities, with staff managers, which support the core. Typical staff tasks are human resource management, IT, payroll and most accounting functions, and the maintenance of facilities.[19] Female managers are more likely to be found in the staff areas, particularly the human resource management function. This puts them at a disadvantage in applying for senior management positions, as they lack experience in those areas critical to the organisation's effectiveness. Similarly, the fact that women tend to have a shorter employment history than men, often interrupted by family responsibilities, acts against them when applying for promotion.

Commitment and competence are overtested. The commitment of men to the organisation is often taken for granted. Career ladders are constructed around male career patterns, and by being the same gender as the dominant management team men are more likely to be judged as being similar in attitude to those in top management. Women find that they are constantly having to demonstrate commitment and competence.[20] Women's loyalty to the organisation is less likely to be taken for granted, and one or two career successes are insufficient to maintain a reputation. Although no-one can rest on their laurels, women find that the usual assumptions surrounding male employment do not apply to them.

Women are given less credit for achievements. The fact that less credit seems to be given to women for their achievements may be summarised as the problem of attribution.[21] Women must achieve more for their efforts in order to be given the same amount of credit as men. In effect, this means that the performance bar is higher for women than for men.

The nature of work

The nature of work also seem to be militating against the promotion of women. While it appears that work has become more team-oriented and less hierarchical in nature, both attributes which favour women, the time demands are also growing. Those with full-time jobs are expected to work longer and longer hours, while there are a growing number of part-time and contract positions that rarely lead to promotion. Women are overrepresented in these latter positions, partly because of their domestic arrangements. But it is from the full-time workforce that the management cadre is drawn. The IT industry, which should be open equally to either gender, often makes unscheduled demands on workers because of the 'crisis' nature of the industry. Employees have to be on call almost 24 hours a day for breakdown and support, making it difficult for women with family responsibilities to fully participate.

Barriers through patriarchal attitudes

Many feminists would question the above causes of gender segregation in the workforce as being the rationalisation of a deeper prejudice and animosity towards women. They would seek the explanation for the lesser roles of women, particularly in management, in the nature of gender relationships. They see men as forming a patriarchy, which seeks to marginalise and subordinate the roles of women and to keep them in subservient positions in both society and the workforce. They consider that the style of management which men adopt, emphasising control and competition, has become the dominant style. This acts to exclude the participation of women who prefer to manage in different ways. That such a small number of women reach senior management positions is the result of a conspiracy, either conscious or unconscious, on the part of men to keep women out of the executive suite. Breaking down the barriers to women's participation requires activism and the support of legislation, and will not be achieved by natural progression and the removal of obvious barriers. This position is clearly at variance with a number of those discussed in previous sections. It derives from a different ideology concerning the role of men and women. We discuss the different approaches to gender studies in the next section.

The above list seems to paint a fairly daunting picture for those women seeking senior management positions. However, these are mainly generalisations, and not all apply in any particular organisation. Rectifying the situation is not easy. Even though equal opportunity legislation has been in effect for almost 20 years, the statistics in relation to management and the gender distribution of those holding positions of influence show that men still attain management positions well in excess of their numbers in the workforce. Women are still overrepresented in part-time positions and work with lower levels of responsibility.[22] In response to the persistence of gender segregation, one researcher noted that men are given mixed and confusing signals as to how to behave. No doubt further research, perhaps involving examination of female-dominated organisations, will reveal ways to redress the disadvantages women may face.

Different approaches to gender studies

The above section may leave the impression that once the barriers we have discussed are removed, men and women will have an equal opportunity to compete for positions of responsibility within organisations. The literature concerning the gender and organisation studies area fits into a number of different streams. These will be identified and described in turn.[23]

Liberal feminist theory

The word *liberal* has had the traditional meaning of being associated with personal freedom and liberation, and it is on this sense that liberal feminist theory is founded. It is from this school of thought that most of the women-in-management literature is derived. Those studying and writing on organisations from the liberal feminist position take the structure of industry, and the organisations in it, as given. They do not seek to change the nature of industry or the economic system of private enterprise and market-based decisions by companies. Rather they seek to improve the access of women to appropriate conditions of employment and to remove barriers to promotion faced by women. They aim to further the interests of women as people and as valued employees of the organisation. Consequently there has been extensive data-gathering and statistical analysis on the participation of women in various occupational groups and levels in the organisation. It is on the liberal feminist tradition that most equal opportunity and affirmative action programs are based.

The liberal feminist view assumes that attainment of high positions in organisations is the aim of most women. It emphasises access to professional and management positions, and seeks to eliminate barriers to promotion that may act against women's interests. However, not all women, or men, are concerned with these issues.

Many women may look on their participation in the workforce as being secondary to other interests they have in life. At work they are more concerned with pay levels, safe and harassment-free working conditions, and flexibility issues than with striving to enter the executive suite or breaking the glass ceiling.[24]

Radical feminist theory

Radical feminism considers that society, and the organisations in it, have been defined by men. It considers that men in society have formed a patriarchy which seeks to consistently exclude, subordinate and marginalise the role of women, and that this has become the norm in society. Further, the organisations that men create reflect the designated male values of hierarchy, competition, an obsession with winning and highly defined mechanisms to control behaviour. The designated feminist values of equality, community, participation and integration of form and content are not seen to be practised in modern corporations, and consequently women will always be marginalised. Radical feminists say women will need to form their own organisations to be able to manage in ways that reflect their values.

A radical feminist would not research organisations in the manner described in most studies in this book. Rather she would start with an individual or group, in this case women, and theorise from their lives and experiences to create a feminist revision of organisational practices. Case studies are therefore the most commonly used research tool.

Psychoanalytic feminist theory

Although discounted in modern times, Sigmund Freud, the founder of psycho-analysis, introduced to the study of psychology the complex relationships between men and women based on their upbringing and their physical sexual differences. Children are born into the world either male or female and pass through a number of stages of psychosexual development, complicated by the fact of the observable sexual differences between them. Dealing with these differences forms much of Freudian analysis. Central to this analysis is the resolution of the Oedipal period, during which the mother is the object of love and desire. This occurs when a person is 3 or 4 years old, and differs between males and females. Freud considered that females had more difficulty in attaining maturity than males and had a less well developed sense of justice and ethics. He considered that women suffered from more neuroses and had limitations in their psychosexual development.

It is not surprising that feminists have rejected a theory that consigns them to a lesser state of psychological development than men. In response, psychoanalytic feminists look more to the social arrangements associated with the upbringing of children as the means by which men and women experience different psychological development. Psychoanalytic feminists would see women as being socialised to be passive and to view themselves as victims rather than as agents in charge of their own destiny. They also lack the drive for mastery that characterises men, and from this develops a female fear of success and the inconsistency between femininity and achievement.

However, some psychoanalytic theorists see these imputed gender traits as being positive in modern organisations. The increased emphasis on empathy and interpersonal sensitivity aligns with modern concepts of management. As well, participation and inclusion are seen to be superior to the male pyramid and chain style of management and structuring.

Anti-capitalist feminist theories

The liberal feminists accept our business system as being both the most productive and most conducive to personal liberties. They seek to remove inequalities rather than change the system. However, by its nature, such a system has many detractors. Therefore it is not surprising that socialist feminism has as its core a belief in the inherently exploitative nature of capitalism. Socialist feminists further link capitalism to patriarchy and male dominance, which conspire to exploit and marginalise women. A more extreme form of socialist thought is Marxism. Marxist analysis holds the view that a capitalist economy should not be described through such concepts as market forces, exchange patterns and supply and demand, but through the relationships between people. Using this form of analysis, emphasis is placed on inequality and the exercise of power. The capitalist business system is seen to reproduce an ongoing sex/gender inequality as measured by the outcomes of money and power. Adherents to this form of analysis favour case studies, which reveal informal and invisible processes, rather than survey analysis to gather data.

In addition to the studies in this book being largely undertaken by men, you will also have observed that they concentrate on profit-seeking organisations, in many cases multinationals. This reflects how the world is viewed from London, New York, Tokyo or Sydney. It is also no secret that the world viewed from these vantage points reflects the view of the economic elite of these cities. Combining race and gender in these centres, we find that this view of the world has been closely associated with white men, excepting of course the Asian centres in relation to race.

A feminist school of thought has developed that acts as a counterpoint to this economic view of the world. It could loosely be called the 'Third World postcolonial viewpoint'. It challenges both Western feminist views and the 'First World' view of the world. It also rejects the Western basis of knowledge and what feminists see as the economic system of exploitation. Holders of this view seek to deconstruct—that is, demolish or pull apart—Western tradition and the businesses it has created. This will allow a new world order to be built based on new perceptions of liberty and gender relations, particularly the role of women. This viewpoint is largely associated with non-white women, so called women of colour, who consider that their experiences give them a different point of view.

We summarise the various feminist schools of thought in Table 15.1. The liberal feminist ideas guide most government and private enterprise projects concerning women, and most people in Australia would probably identify with their aims and assumptions. The balance of the views provides an interesting contrast. With the collapse of communism and the move away from socialism, criticism of capitalism and its institutions has shifted from its economic to a social base. It is also not surprising to find that many in the Third World dislike capitalism, also the scientific and technological methodologies associated with its productive systems. It is the success and attractions of the technologies and outputs of the system that has led to the breakup of so many traditional, self-sufficient societies.

Most of the radical feminist viewpoints have been developed and nurtured in universities. The publications describing their theories are largely academic ones. To put many of the ideas into practice, deconstruction of the existing economic and social order would be necessary, which makes the probability of its occurring remote. However, an appreciation of the viewpoints can raise our awareness of matters we might otherwise not have considered.

TABLE 15.1 Comparison of the various ways in which feminists approach organisational studies

1. Intellectual roots	2. *Conception of sex and gender methodology*	3. Conceptions of good society	4. *Preferred research*

Liberal feminist theory
1. Evolved from 18th- and 19th-century political theory.
2. *Sex is part of biological endowment. Gender is socialised onto humans for appropriate behaviour.*
3. A just society which allows individuals to fulfil themselves through a system of individual rights.
4. *Positivist social science techniques with use of quantitative analysis.*

Radical feminist theory
1. Women's liberation movement of 1960s.
2. *'Sex class' is the condition of women as an oppressed class. Gender is a social construct that ensures women's subordination.*
3. A good society is a gender- or sex-free society (or maybe a matriarchy).
4. *Consciousness-raising groups and case studies.*

Psychoanalytic feminist theory
1. Evolved from Freudian and other psychoanalytic theories.
2. *Individuals become sexually identified as part of their psychosexual development. Gender structures a social system of male domination which influences psychosexual development.*
3. A good society will have no gender structuring because both parents are involved in upbringing.
4. *Clinical case studies concentrating on context-specific social relations and developmental processes.*

Anti-capitalist feminist theories
1. Emerged out of Marxism and postcolonial critiques of Western research theories and concepts of progress.
2. *Gender is part of class relationships, which perpetuate oppression under capitalism. This extends to the sex/gender aspects of globalisation.*
3. A good society is a classless society which allows for the full development of human nature. Western ideas of progress are not universal.
4. *Case studies, textual analyses, deconstruction and concentration of micro-social activities.*

Research methodologies and feminism

All of the studies we have described in this book are based on accepted scientific methodology. In this section we describe what this methodology is and what its assumptions are. We then consider feminist research methodologies as they apply to organisations and which act as a counter to existing scientific methodologies.

The sciences can be divided into two broad areas: the physical sciences and the behavioural sciences. The physical sciences are areas such as physics, biology and

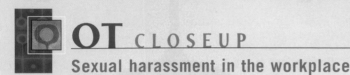

OT CLOSEUP

Sexual harassment in the workplace

An issue that often surfaces when integrating women into a predominantly male workforce is that of sexual harassment. Although it is not only women who are subject it, it is the women's movement that has largely defined what constitutes sexual harassment. It is this interpretation that has been incorporated in the Sex Discrimination Act. This considers such harassment as unwelcome sexual advances or requests for sexual favours, or engagement in unwelcome conduct of a sexual nature in which a reasonable person having regard to the circumstances would have anticipated that the person harassed would be offended, humiliated or intimidated.

The purposes of the provisions of the act were laudable, namely the protection of vulnerable women from intimidation in the workplace. Sexual harassment can include personally offensive verbal comments, sexual or smutty jokes, unsolicited letters, obscene phone calls, being followed from work to home, offensive hand or body gestures, provocative posters with sexual connotations, repeated comments or teasing about a person's private life or stares and leers. It can also include general discussion of sexual matters in the presence of those who may find it offensive.

Whereas there is broad community acceptance that certain behaviours are clearly unacceptable, there is a large grey area that makes it difficult for even a reasonable person to decide whether sexual harassment has taken place. This problem was broadly discussed by a Senate Standing Committee into alleged sexual harassment aboard HMAS *Swan* during its Asian deployment in 1992. The navy started to integrate female sailors into its crews in the early 1990s and there were a number of female sailors on HMAS *Swan* during this deployment. At the conclusion of the voyage a number of serious allegations of sexual assault and harassment were made, which were investigated by various boards of inquiry and finally the Senate Standing Committee. A number of charges were laid and censures made against naval officers, most of which were subsequently withdrawn. There were enormous emotional costs to all involved including the complainants, a number of whom suffered ill-health from the ordeal of repeatedly having to give evidence. Matters were not made easier for them by the wide publicity given to the case in the mass media.

One of the problems the Senate Standing Committee had was determining what actually constituted sexual harassment. It noted that there were a number of problems with the definition and its implementation. First, under the Act, whether sexual harassment had taken place was the subjective judgement of the person being harassed. This put sexual harassment into a different category from all other areas of the law, in that innocent intention was no defence. Given the wide variation among people in society, it is inevitable that different people would interpret the same act by a person in different ways. The Committee also found that either sex could experience difficulties in the behaviour of the opposite sex. For instance, if copies of *Penthouse* are offensive in the workplace, are copies of *Cleo* or *Cosmopolitan* also offensive? Persons from different cultures also have different interpretations of behaviour, including touching and comforting.

In reviewing the Committee's deliberations, Beatrice Faust, a feminist from the University of New South Wales, considers that one of the main problems with EEO and sexual harassment cases is that they accept a very low threshold for an offence to have occurred. By contrast, the prevailing community threshold appears to be much higher. For instance, popular shows and films such as *Sex/Life*, *Basic Instinct*, *Fatal Attraction*, *Sleepless in Seattle* and *Sex in the City* assume that women are more sexually autonomous than EEO legislation acknowledges. She considers that legislation is a top-down remedy which, if it is to succeed, must be met by a bottom-up change in values, attitudes and expectations. Often skilful lobbying by special-interest groups will lead to reform in an area which may result in a disjunction between the law, attitudes and practices.

Stung by the HMAS *Swan* case, the navy realised that it had had handled the integration of women into ship's crews poorly. It realised after the event that it required major organisational change rather than an approach to problems on a piecemeal, ad-hoc basis. The whole culture of the navy needed to be changed, from proper preparation for both men and women for seagoing appointments to changes in navy regulations. The expectations of men and women needed to be more clearly defined and genuine problems such as the different physiology of men and women openly addressed rather than assumed away. In a perverse way, the experience of the women on HMAS *Swan* led to improved working conditions for all concerned. Previously the navy was very much a macho environment, which expected too much of people and consistently breached reasonable occupational health, safety and ergonomic limits. Now emphasis is placed on better standards of supervision, ergonomic factors at work and improved avenues for addressing complaints.

engineering; the behavioural sciences include anthropology, psychology and management. Methodology can be classified into the two broad categories—quantitative and qualitative. In the behavioural sciences, quantitative techniques are based on measuring some phenomenon or form of behaviour and the use of statistics to analyse relationships within a sample. Qualitative techniques rely on an in-depth analysis and description of behaviour. The sample is either very small, or a single person or organisation. The results are mostly presented in a descriptive form and often require subjective assessments as to interpretation.

As a management text this book is part of behavioural science, and the majority of studies mentioned are qualitative in their approach to data-gathering. There are, however, some significant quantitative studies, prominent among them being Woodward's work and the Aston research. The studies have been drawn from the academic literature, which means that they have been through a reviewing process which accepts that their methodology and techniques of inquiry are appropriate to the aims of the study. Guiding scientific principles are the following assumptions:[25]

- objectivity and neutrality on the part of the researcher;
- a lack of emotional attachment to the topic so that independence is not compromised;
- replicable research methodology;
- inquiry from a position of rational hypotheses or propositions;
- lack of any political agenda;
- no preconception as to how research is used.

Most of the quoted research has proceeded on the basis of linear thinking. This sees a hypothesis or idea proposed which is often derived from previous research. A research methodology is then established. Data are gathered and statistically analysed. Conclusions are drawn from the data in relation to the hypothesis or proposition. The conclusions drawn should act as a guide for further research.

However, a feminist may look at the studies, both individually and as a group, and reject them as being unrepresentative of organisational life in general and women in particular. As a result, feminists have labelled research such as that found in this book 'malestream'.[26] Their criticisms may be grouped into the following categories.[27]

- The studies in this book are androcentric—that is, based on male experience and perceptions. They study organisations that are managed by men and use methodologies developed by men.

- The research is used to reinforce the white male view of the world through reproducing management exploitation, dominance and control. This is sometimes termed 'whitewash'.
- The researchers have defined the problem and created their research in their own image. They are part of the same culture of the organisations they study, and as researchers they are far from being disinterested observers.
- A large part of organisational structuring is excluded by the methodology. The definitions assume hierarchy and differences in power and position, and consequently give the 'view from above' of the organisation.

In contrast, a feminist may propose that methodologies used to study organisations should have the following research principles:

- No researcher should be objective. Researchers should have a 'conscious partiality' to their subjects which allows them to empathise with their subjects' experiences and thus obtain a greater insight into their problems and experiences.
- The values implicit in the research should be acknowledged and discussed along with the findings.
- It should be acknowledged that there is inequality between the researcher and the subject, leaving the researcher in a position of power.
- One should accept that organisational knowledge is socially constructed and that deconstructing this knowledge will permit new insight.
- The research should proceed on the basis of the view from below in the organisation, rather than the view from above.
- Research should emphasise more of the social implications of structuring, rather than trying to make hierarchies and structures more effective.

Many feminist researchers subscribe to the postmodernist belief that all knowledge is socially constructed. This means that there is no objective truth; causation, meanings and reality itself derive from the interpretation that a social group, or part of a social group, places on them. This permits multiple interpretations of the same event, depending on who we are, what our experiences have been and the point of view we adopt. Applying this approach to researching gender in organisation permits radically different interpretations of the same event. The social construction of reality underwrites research which finds that men and women can experience the same event in different ways. It rejects the idea that there is a fundamental underlying truth which may be identified through research.

Drawing on this construct, feminists would consider the contribution of women in organisations to be marginalised by the existing research methodology. Subtle power plays and indirect forms of discrimination are not identified using quantitative techniques. As well, it is not possible for male researchers to identify with women's perspectives sufficiently to undertake meaningful research on the issues involved. This is because they socially construct the world differently from women.

Application of feminist approaches to research

Many aspects of the feminist approach to research in organisations are not new and take us back to the techniques in use over 50 years ago. At that time, many of the studies on organisations were case studies, using techniques developed by anthropologists.[28] The researcher adopted the position of a participant observer and would report from the point of view of an insider in the organisation. The techniques were time-consuming and the specific nature of their findings meant that generalising from the results was difficult. However, they did reveal much of value in the way organisations operate and, after a lapse of up to 50 years, it may be time to revisit this methodology and reapply it in contemporary organisational settings. Indeed, many studies in recent times have used these techniques.[29]

Does the criticism levelled at the studies in this text render them of questionable value? In part, the assumptions and principles underlying the research of this book and those of its detractors are drawn from different viewpoints. Therefore, it is not surprising that they view the organisations discussed in this book differently. In evaluating this criticism we should bear in mind that many women, and some feminists, would not support the views of the more radical feminists. And no doubt many men would not be comfortable with the 'malestream'.

When we consider topics involving strategy and other management issues, we cannot help but take the perspective of a manager in the organisation. Further, most of the organisations referred to in this book are either business organisations seeking to make profits in competitive environments or government departments subject to budgetary restraints. We have made reference to organisations that have other aims, churches for example, but we have segmented our area of studies to concentrate on those of interest to the business student. Given business students' interests there is considerable benefit in considering such issues as strategy and the impact of technology on structure from a management perspective.

As well as acknowledging the ideological foundations of our research, we must admit that the research has not been undertaken by disinterested researchers. It has been conducted by those with sympathy for their topics and who have a large measure of identification with their subjects. Business as a topic for research has drawn some outstanding scientists with the aim of trying to improve business organisations by seeking to better understand how they work. To this extent business researchers are not impartial: they view business differently from the way a Third World feminist may view it. But this does not invalidate their point of view.

We, the authors of this text, have the goals of extending our knowledge of business organisations and improving the way they are structured and operated. We hope to make students more aware of the environments organisations operate in and to give some guidance as to how to manage organisations effectively. All books reflect a culture, and as this book is written for those who live and work in Western cultures, it is natural that we should draw on research in the Western tradition and write in terms that are familiar to our readers. Further, most of the studies have been undertaken by English-speaking researchers and reflect a laissez-faire view of the world. For instance, we do not have a chapter on how to form monopolies or the need of business to project government or nationalistic objectives. Rather, we concentrate on how to succeed in competitive and contested markets. However, as we have shown in Chapter 6, the problems faced by those companies engaged in international operations are similar no matter where they are domiciled, so much of what is written in this book is applicable to contemporary business everywhere.

Do men and women manage differently?

Over the past 20 years there has been a significant growth in the literature about women in management. This has seen research into how women manage, as well as the development of theories to explain women's management behaviour. The basic assumption has been that the existing literature reflects the male management style and attitudes. Much of the newer literature has sought to determine whether women have a different management style from men, and whether the organisation structures they would design and construct would be different from existing, male-dominated organisations.

All classifications of managerial styles are to an extent generalisations and stereotypes. And a female management style could only be defined as a counterpoint to what is an assumed male management style. Table 15.2 summarises the features commonly associated with male and female management styles.

Further differences have been proposed in the way men and women view organisation structures. Helgeson claims that women tend to view them as a spider's web, with concentric circles being held together by spokes.[30] By contrast, she claims, men view organisations as hierarchies held together by chains. Some feminists have even gone so far as to propose organisations without any form of hierarchy altogether. One of the often-used examples of 'female' organisations is that of women's centres and refuges.[31] At least on the surface, these centres are characterised by a lack of hierarchy, with democracy being the norm in decision making.

There is limited benefit to be gained in comparing the management of an autonomous work team in the community sector with that of a steel mill. However, a number of studies looking at similar organisations have shown that the management styles of men and women are largely the same,[32] although there is a consistent theme in gender studies that the preferred management styles of men and women are different. The proponents of such a position are largely feminist authors theorising on the topic. But based on empirical research it would appear the theoretical position that there are significant gender differences in management styles may be overstated.

Those who propose that gender-based differences in management are largely illusory would be challenged by those who argue that in order to succeed, women must conform to male values and behaviour standards. To further complicate

TABLE 15.2 Comparison of male and female management styles

	Female	Male
Operating Style	Cooperative	Competitive
Organisational structure	Team	Hierarchy
Basic objective	Quality output	Winning
Problem-solving style	Intuitive/ rational	Rational
Key characteristics	Lower control	High control
	Empathic	Strategic
	Collaborative	Unemotional
	High performance standards	Analytical

Source: Marilyn Loden, *How to Succeed in Business Without Being One of the Boys*, New York: Times Books Random House, 1985. Reprinted with permission.

comparisons, a new group of women has emerged who consciously put their career before relationships and family. Over 50% of senior women managers do not have children.[33] And the falling birth rate indicates that many women are putting career before family considerations, while the number of male managers who are married with children is overwhelming.

There has been much research into alternative organisational forms, and these studies have identified men as generating similar structures to the low hierarchy and control structures attributed to female management. Trist and Bamforth found that underground miners had developed a virtually hierarchy-free way of organising work and in mediating relationships between members.[34] This discovery led to the development of the sociotechnical system of organisation. Similarly, the Volvo experiment of creating semiautonomous work teams in a motor vehicle assembly plant in Sweden was instigated by men.[35] Its subsequent modification had more to do with cost than any failure of the behavioural dynamics. In the Australian experience, areas such as mining, sheep shearing, construction work and oil drilling have been characterised by high levels of teamwork and mutual dependence and low levels of hierarchy.

The features of the type of work identified above have much in common with the women's centres that figure in much of the feminist literature on organisations. It is undertaken by small groups, which share a common set of either values or task goals. It is often isolated in time and space from the rest of what may be a large organisation. In Volvo's case the factory at Kalmar was built on a greenfields site, with each part having the characteristics of a small workshop. Similarly, women's shelters have a clearly definable boundary with the outside environment. In addition, in all of the organisations identified, intensive socialisation and self-selection mean that people have a propensity to share organisational culture characteristics with each other, and this leads to a fall in communication barriers.

One of the problems in these types of organisation is that they cannot accept a wide variety of members and put them to work productively. Modern bureaucratic organisations have developed great expertise in breaking jobs down into identifiable tasks and then hiring a wide variety of people to undertake the tasks. Factories particularly have people of many different nationalities and of great diversity working productively within them. Forming such a wide diversity of people into self-contained teams would require a long time for socialisation.[36]

Another criticism of bureaucracies raised by feminists is that it is unreasonable to separate personal life from organisational life.[37] Ferguson, for instance, considers that Weber's proposition in relation to bureaucracy—that organisational life and personal life should be separated—unrealistic and reflecting male values of rationality and objectivity. Ferguson says it is not possible to separate the intimate aspects of human relationships and the various family and community demands placed on us from our role in organisations. Organisations should therefore be more responsive to the private needs of individuals.

If we accept the evidence that the management styles of men and women are largely similar, this makes the inequality of women in management positions even more difficult to understand. If men and women did not share similar management styles, it would be easier to explain the scarcity of women in high positions. But if they practise management similarly, the argument for significant barriers to women's promotion becomes stronger.

FIGURE 15.1 The two continuums of male and female management characteristics

Female management characteristics

- Collaboration
- Emphasis on teams
- Empathy
- Performance standards
- Emotional involvement

Male management characteristics

- Stress on hierarchy
- Emphasis on control
- Strategic thinking
- Emphasis on analysis
- Emphasis on winning

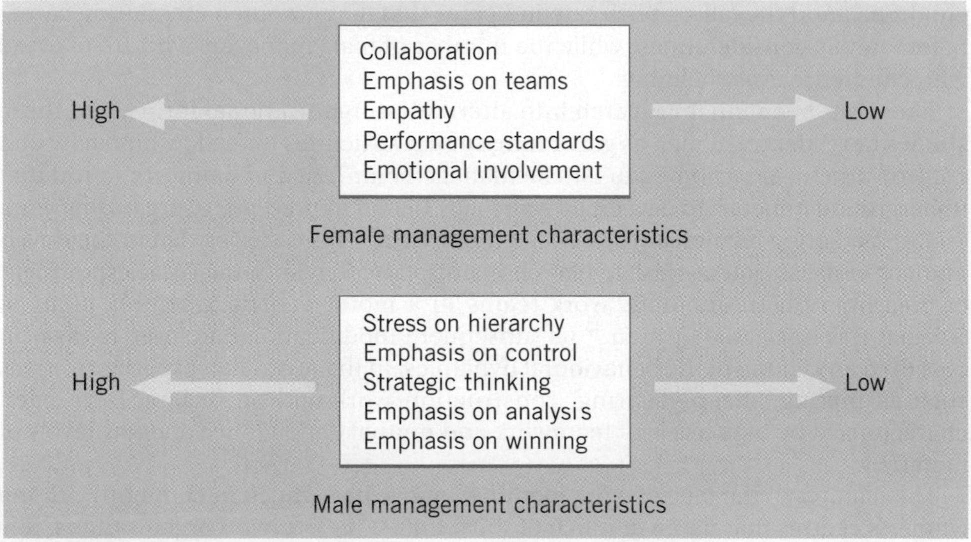

Gender management styles as different continuums

Advocates of different management styles for men and women have identified two different ways of managing, but research gives support to the proposition that the management styles of men and women are not radically different. How is it possible to reconcile these opposing views? It may be that male and female management styles are not the ends of a single continuum but are two separate continuums. We have shown this in Figure 15.1, which draws on the characteristics identified in Table 15.2. The continuums are independent of each other, allowing managers to be high or low on both. Female managers who practise the identified female management style would be high on female management characteristics but low on male ones. But this does not preclude a male manager from being similarly high on female characteristics but low on male ones. It would also allow a manager to be high on both male and female characteristics. Close examination of the features of male and female management styles shows that they are not mutually exclusive. For instance, it is still possible to have teamwork within an hierarchical framework: the matrix structure is evidence of this. Similarly, quality output and winning in many cases complement each other. This interpretation allows for the wide variation in management behaviour within genders to be accommodated without compromising the notion that male and female management styles are different.

What are the characteristics of equal opportunity programs?

Feminists have long felt that in order to compete equally for management and other positions in organisations, the prevailing culture of hiring and promotion must be changed. This reflects the position of the liberal feminists, who do not seek to deconstruct the organisation or the economic system but rather to make it more amenable to the aspirations and abilities of women. There is a difference between equal opportunity and affirmative action programs. Equal opportunity programs create environments that seek to make ability the main criteria for appointment to a job regardless of gender, ethnicity or physical disability. Affirmative action programs are aimed at taking positive measures to increase the participation of certain target groups in various occupational positions. Women have been the main target group of affirmative action programs in Australia. Quotas or targets are often set that specify how many women, and members of other nominated groups, should be hired or promoted.

The civil rights movement in the United States in the 1960s provided the major impetus in the Western world for opening organisations to a wider range of participants. However, the US programs differed from those introduced in Australia. Australian programs maintained the principle of the best person for the job being selected. The United States introduced affirmative action, which made the hiring and promotion of target groups such as women and Afro-Americans mandatory and subject to a quota. In Australia, the legislation of most relevance to business has been the federal government's *Affirmative Action (Equal Opportunity for Women) Act 1986*. This created the Affirmative Action Agency which, while it does not have any powers of enforcement, can name non-complying companies in parliament which can subsequently be denied government contracts. Public service departments follow the principle of hiring and promoting female over male candidates where both are equally qualified for a position.

The various acts and programs are aimed at making organisations gender-neutral. As well, they aim to cater for the specific needs of women in areas such as child care, and to create hiring and promotional conditions that concentrate on the ability of the person to do the job rather than on meeting irrelevant criteria.[38] The following summarises the main provisions that organisations must conform to in order to meet the various legislative criteria.

- Jobs must be defined and advertised in terms which concentrate on the requirements of the task. It is illegal to advertise for members of a particular gender, racial group or sexual preference except where this is necessary to undertake the task (i.e. women to work in lingerie, Aborigines to be youth workers to the Aboriginal community).
- Job descriptions should reflect the actual requirements of the task. Superfluous requirements, such as educational and strength criteria not necessary to carry out the job, should not be used.
- Advertisements should encourage women to apply.
- Interview panels should have members of both genders on them and should be stress-free.
- Washroom and change facilities must be provided for both genders.
- Employers are responsible for maintaining an environment that is harassment-free.
- Organisations are to have targets as to the numbers of women in various occupational positions, including management, and they are to report on the attainment of these targets regularly.

As women tend to have primary family care responsibilities, the provision of child care is a major factor when seeking employment. If such care is not available, women may lose valuable years of experience in involuntary absence from the workforce, thus harming later career opportunities. The provision of child care facilities is therefore an important part of affirmative action programs. Also because of family responsibilities, women are the major group seeking part-time work. It is, therefore, important for this group to be given equal access to in-house and external training courses in order to keep their skills and knowledge up to date. Maternity leave is provided by law, but employees taking maternity leave should be kept up to date with organisational changes.

The maternity and child care issues raise important implications for all employees: that is, that most organisations cater very poorly for those who would like non-standard work patterns. Difficulty in meeting the normal working week of 40 hours with unrestricted availability to travel may arise because of the need to care for parents (elder care), illness or recuperation, or the desire for less responsibility as retirement approaches. The need for coordination and control, supervision and negotiation and the requirement to work in teams place a premium on all employees being present at the same time. Work that can be isolated and undertaken without reference to other members of the organisation is typically poorly paid and undervalued. Examples of such work are unskilled clerical processing, answering inquiries and home workers in manufacturing. As the limitations on non-traditional work patterns affect women more than men, they are covered under affirmative action programs. Although most companies have provision for job sharing and part-time work, these generally do not extend into management ranks or other positions with higher levels of responsibility.

Overall, the processes described above have the aims of removing the barriers faced by women to employment and promotion because of their gender. Many feminists, however, feel that they do not address their main criticisms—that is, that the dominant gender in the organisation is male and that the requirements of affirmative action described above are forcing women to conform to male standards. As a result, feminine work practices are overlooked. They argue that women are still excluded from the 'malestream' of management by exclusionary practices and patriarchal attitudes and that women must conform to the male standard of management in order to gain promotion. They claim that women are excluded from informal networks of information by creating organisations that devalue the way in which women prefer to manage and by creating spatial physical characteristics, such as executive suites, which have obvious male characteristics in colour and decoration.[39]

Researching such propositions would be difficult, which indicates why feminists favour the case study approach to research rather than a survey method of data-gathering. As we have seen previously in relation to methodology, feminists would argue that objectivity would never be able to uncover such barriers and that a subjective approach by a sympathetic observer would be far more productive. The difficulty with the subjective approach, however, is in getting other researchers to accept the validity of the findings.

Much of the feminist literature discusses theoretical positions. However, there have been extensive data gathered on numbers of women in organisations, concentrating on those filling management positions. These data generally show extensive gender segregation of the workforce. Conclusions are often drawn that this is a prima facie case of discrimination. This line of reasoning assumes that the management of organisations should reflect the racial and gender characteristics of the society in which the organisation is based and that if this does not occur, discrimination must be present. However, such quantitative surveys give little guidance as to what gives rise to disparities in participation by different groups and how these can be eliminated. Statistics, particularly those from surveys, typically show association between the variables, not causation of events. For instance, a survey may show that 95% of those in the fishing industry are male, but it doesn't give us any guidance as to why, or how, the participation of women in the industry could be increased. We have already noted that many women in senior management positions do not have children. We need further qualitative research to determine what the reasons for this may be.

Are gender-free organisations possible?

Notwithstanding affirmative action and equal opportunity programs, there is still a wide gulf between the roles of men and women in organisational life. Drawing on the research that has been undertaken, and examining the literature, we can build a case both for and against the possibility of organisations becoming gender-free.

We should be clear in our mind about what we mean by the term 'gender-free'. There are two components that can be identified when considering this issue. The first refers to an organisation as being gender-blind. That is, in matters of gender, men and women are considered equally under its policies, procedures and culture, and no weight is placed on the gender of an employee. It would also include special provisions for women by taking into account their child care role. The second component is statistical equality between men and women at all levels in the organisation. This would see an end to the typical rise in the proportion of men holding senior positions in organisations.[40]

We could raise the following points to support the argument that organisations will become gender-free:

1   The active promotion of equal opportunity and affirmative action will inevitably see more women move into the full range of organisational life, including senior management. Their positions as decision makers will ensure that the interests of women are considered and that female approaches to management and organisational structuring are accommodated and given a far more sympathetic hearing in the organisation.

2   Modern human resource practices try to avoid the situation where women with children are absent from the workforce for long periods of time after having children. Even where women prefer to stay at home with children, attempts are being made by businesses, such as banks, to keep employees up to date, through providing part-time work for instance. This ensures continuity in their career. The long career breaks that previously put women at a disadvantage in promotion will no longer be a feature of corporate life. And, of course, families are becoming smaller and fewer women are choosing to have children.

3   New technologies allow women to compete equally with men in the labour force. For instance, using computers does not require strength or stamina, unlike shovelling coal. And automation and labour-saving devices have removed physical barriers to the employment of women in lower-level positions from which they can gain promotion. Also, with less gender segregation in the workforce men and

women use the new technology equally, unlike the days when women were often restricted to using typewriters.

4   The new management paradigms are closer to those associated with female management styles than with the male management style. Such management behaviours as the promotion of teamwork, empathy, cooperation and a lower emphasis on control will favour women as managers. We will therefore see more women promoted on their skill as managers.

5   Organisations reflect societal attitudes, and as societal attitudes change, then organisational practices will change. Women are participating more in education, and now form over half of university enrolments, as well as performing better at school. As more women move into the higher levels of organisational activity, so gender practices will become less of an issue.

6   Many feminists have overstated the case regarding discrimination against women in organisations. They have let their dislike of the business system generally, and in many cases dissatisfaction with male management styles, portray organisations as male-dominated patriarchies intent on perpetuating women's disadvantage. Such perceptions are not supported by the progress of women in organisations, and society, over the past 20 years.

7   Organisations are realising that there is much to be gained by having a staff profile similar to their customer base. For instance, women and men both buy cars and use banks, but the senior management of both car manufacturers and banks is heavily male-dominated. More women in senior positions would create products better suited to the substantial female clientele.

The case for organisations remaining gendered may be summarised as follows:

1   New technological developments are not favouring women. Since the Industrial Revolution in Europe, the nature of technological and scientific progress has been determined by men, and new technology is no different. The Internet is domi-nated by men;[41] men are shaping the nature of the new technologies, ranging from computers to biotechnology, and thus defining what is classified as progress. In addition, men dominate the older, established technologies based on the car, aircraft, railways and telecommunications. In turn, women are still concentrated in the 'caring' professions such as health, welfare and education. As the dominant determiner of new technology, men define the organisations they create to serve them in their own image.

2   Societal attitudes still devalue women's work. The greater the proportion of women in a profession, the lower its status.[42] Infant and primary school teaching indicate this trend. Also, the greater the number of women in a profession or occupation, the lower its pay. Social workers, occupational therapists and psychologists are examples. This devaluation of the attitudes and values of women has organisational implications. As society devalues women's work, so do organisations.

3   Organisational size is not really under the control of management. In order to achieve economies of scale, it is not possible to have a small bank, car plant or oil refinery. Where the size of the organisation is determined by the needs of the tech-nological core, rather than being a reasoned decision of management, there is a need for the traditional management skills of control through hierarchies, and unemotional, rational analytical decision-making styles to optimise the perform-ance of the organisation. These are characteristics attributed to male management.

4 Because of their nurturing and physical make-up, men and women are equal but different. It is natural that these differences in biology and nurturing would have an impact on the performance and interests of men and women in an organisation. Even where women are reaching the top rung of management, this is typically in human resources and other 'caring' areas of the organisation.

5 New organisational forms are acting as a deterrent to women's participation. Writing creative software, for instance, requires a discontinuous work pattern, with intense periods of work over weeks, often with workers not returning home for days on end. There may then be long breaks in the work. This pattern is common in many creative enterprises. Depending on the cooperation from her partner, this clearly doesn't suit a woman with family responsibilities. Women in similar situations are limited in their freedom to travel and take up overseas postings. Because women are the primary carers in the family, men are far less limited by time constraints. Promotion is therefore more difficult for women to come by.

6 There is little evidence that the female management style will find much applicability in the emerging organisational environment. The opening up of the world economy, and the emphasis of governments on competition and microeconomic reform, have created highly competitive organisations and workplaces. In this environment, choosing appropriate strategies and using all the resources in the organisation as productively as possible becomes important. There is little in the feminist literature that claims women are superior in all-round management to men: the feminist position relies on more sympathetic management of people than the management of resources. But the way the physical resources of the organisation are used is of major importance to the profitability of the organisation.

7 Despite over two decades of equal employment opportunity, labour markets remain stubbornly segmented.[43] Some, such as school teaching, are developing greater gender inequality rather than less. Women still show disdain for many of the lower-level jobs typically undertaken by men. Men are still not moving into the areas such as nursing, welfare services and part-time work which are dominated by women and which form the major area of workforce growth. As technological change has eliminated many typically 'male' jobs but created new positions in those typically filled by women, men as a gender have been the biggest losers.

Summary

Over the past 20 years, the role of gender in organisational structuring and operation has been the subject of considerable discussion and research. Part of the reason for this is that organisations form the core of power and reward in society, and women felt they were being disadvantaged by being denied equality of access to management and other senior positions. The removal of barriers to women's participation within organisations falls within the liberal feminist point of view. However, other feminist perspectives would view both the structure of business and the way organisations are run as being incapable of serving women's interests. Feminists have also criticised scientific methodology as failing to reveal the full extent of discrimination that occurs in organisations.

The gender segmentation of the workforce has a number of historical origins, but the evidence is that it is persisting beyond what could be expected given affirmative action legislation. Management is still dominated by men. And women still find themselves disadvantaged through their child caring responsibilities.

Research has failed to reveal a uniquely or dominant female style of management, although a feminine, as opposed to a masculine, approach to management is often referred to in the gender literature. Feminine styles are based on cooperation, empathy and intuition, while masculine styles emphasise control through hierarchies and stress winning.

Whether an androgynous, or gender-free, way of organising and managing is likely to emerge is not clear. Whereas there is progress in some areas, such as in minimising the absence of women from the workforce because of family responsibilities, there seems to be little progress in others. Management is still dominated by men, and the concept of 'male' and 'female' jobs still influences many members of the workforce.

For review and discussion

1   Define sex, gender and feminism.

2   Why should we be concerned with gender in organisations?

3   Identify and describe three factors that have led to gender segmentation of the workforce.

4   Debate with other members of your group the following proposition: 'The male patriarchy will never let women rise to top management'.

5   How has technological change assisted women's progress in the workforce?

6   Discuss the extent to which you feel that child-rearing and family responsibilities may disadvantage women who seek top management positions.

7   Identify barriers that may exist to the promotion of women in an organisation you are familiar with.

8   Are male and female language likely to be different, and if so how? Give illustrations. How is this likely to affect the roles of each in the workforce?

9   Contrast the approaches of the liberal feminist, radical feminist, psychoanalytic feminist and anti-capitalist feminist theories to women's expectations of access to management positions.

10 Identify the strengths and weaknesses of the feminist approach to research.

11 Build an argument either supporting or rejecting the proposition that men and women manage differently.

12 What are the differences between equal opportunity and affirmative action programs?

13 Argue a case either supporting or rejecting the proposition that affirmative action programs disadvantage men.

14 Why are men reluctant to enter traditionally female occupations?

15 Do you consider that gender-free organisations are possible? Be prepared to discuss your position.

CASE FOR CLASS DISCUSSION
Gender *inequality* goes underground

A conference on 'Women, management and employment relations' came to the conclusion that gender *inequality* in the workplace hasn't vanished— it's just gone underground. And without a concerted effort to change the fundamentals of organisations, including addressing the culture and behaviour of those in management, little will change that will benefit women. Further, one of the greatest problems was that many believed that the case for gender equality and diversity had already been addressed.

Ann Sherry, a senior Westpac manager, claimed that most male managers '. . . .do not see a problem. The frame of reference that our managers bring is the same as for many corporates. They're middle aged, they're male, many went to private schools and they spend their weekends hanging out with each other. If you attack this group with a hectoring, punishment approach it does not work. It actually sends the problem underground. They don't disagree openly, they close their minds and stop participating'. She went on to say that women's achievements are in danger of being mere talk if they are not underpinned by a framework that achieves sustainability, and this means making major cultural changes in organisations.

She claimed that achieving equality is easier when problems are more visible. The discrimination is now subtle, where what appears to be the status quo provides many barriers to women's progression. Work practices and cultural forms that may appear unbiased can create a subtle pattern of systemic disadvantage that blocks all but a few women from career advancement. Too often, sustaining diversity relies on the efforts of individuals, and once they leave there is no legacy in the company to sustain the transformation that is taking place.

Ann Sherry's comments were reported in: Catherine Fox, 'Gender Inequality Goes Underground', *The Australian Financial Review*, 24 July 2001, p. 50.

QUESTIONS

1 Why would changing an organisation's culture be necessary for improved equality for women? Identify what you think the barriers to such sustained cultural change would be.

2 What does Ann Sherry mean by the problems of gender inequality going underground?

3 What would be the likely characteristics of an organisation's culture with which women felt comfortable? Would men feel comfortable in this culture? If not, how can the two be reconciled?

4 Discuss whether it is possible to have a caring, supportive organisation in a demanding and unforgiving environment.

FURTHER READING

Marta Calas & Linda Smircich, 'The Women's Point of View: Feminist Approaches to Organisational Studies', in Stewart Clegg, Cynthia Hardy & Walter R. Nord, eds, *Handbook of Organisation Studies*, London: Sage, 1996.

D. Collinson & J. Hearn, *Men as Managers: Managers as Men*, Critical Perspectives on Men, Masculinities and Management, London: Sage 1996.

Susan Halford & Pauline Leonard, *Gender, Power and Organisations*, Houndmills, Basingstoke: Palgrave, 2001.

Sally Helgeson, *The Female Advantage: Women's Ways of Leadership*, New York: Doubleday, 1990.

Rosabeth Moss Kanter, *Men and Women of the Corporation*, New York: Basic Books, 1977.

Judy Wajcman, 'Desperately Seeking Difference: Is Management Style Gendered?', *British Journal of Industrial Relations*, September 1996, pp. 333–49.

NOTES

1 However, see David Collinson & J. Hearn, eds, *Men as Managers, Managers as Men: Critical Perspectives on Men, Masculinities and Managements*, London: Sage, 1996; and Cliff Cheng, ed., *Masculinities in Organisations*, Thousand Oaks, California: Sage, 1996.
2 Leonie Still, Cecily Guerin & William Chia, 'Women in Management Revisited: Progress, Regression or Status Quo?', in Alexander Kouzmin, Leonie Still & Paul Clarke, eds, *New Directions in Management*, Sydney: McGraw Hill, 1994.
3 See for instance Australian Bureau of Statistics Labour Force: Australia Catalogue 6291.0.40.001.
4 Leonie Still, Cecily Guerin & William Chia, 'Women in Management Revisited'.
5 In 1900 the average family consisted of four children.
6 In 1900 the average life expectancy was 55 years of age for women and 52 years of age for men. In 1992 the figures were 80 and 75 respectively.
7 Asbestosis, dust diseases of the lungs and industrial deafness were the three most common. To these were added muscular and skeletal problems arising from labouring and lifting. The average life expectancy of a working-class man up to 1945 was 65 years of age. Women who worked in factories also suffered from many industrial diseases, particularly in the 19th century. Smoking-related illnesses were common. Working-class people of both genders suffered from poor diet.
8 John Gunn, *Challenging Horizons: Qantas 1939–1954*, Brisbane: University of Queensland Press, 1987.
9 Sharon Moore, 'Closing the Gender Gap', *Australian Accountant*, 68(1), 1998, pp. 20–1.
10 Nigel Piercy, David Cravens & Nikala Lane, 'Sales Manager Behaviour Control Strategy and its Consequences: The Impact of Gender Differences', *Journal of Personal Selling and Sales Management*, 21(1), 2001, pp. 39–49.
11 Stephen Linstead, 'Comment: Gender Blindness or Gender Suppression? A Comment on Fiona Watson's Research Note', *Organization Studies*, 21(1), 2000, pp. 297–303.
12 Peter York, 'The Gender Agenda', *Management Today*, October 1999, pp. 56–63.
13 Rosabeth Moss Kanter, *Men and Women of the Corporation*, New York: Basic Books, 1977.
14 D. Tannen, 'The Power of Talk', *Harvard Business Review*, September/October 1995.
15 R. Evered, 'The Language of Organizations', in Louis R. Pondy, Peter J. Frost, Gareth Morgan & Thomas C. Dandridge, eds, *Organizational Symbolism*, Greenwich, CT: JAI Press, 1983, pp. 125–43.
16 Anna Smith, 'Gender Defender', *Management-Auckland*, 46(4), 1999, pp. 20–2.
17 Judith Oakley, 'Gender-Based Barriers to Senior Management Positions: Understanding the Scarcity of Female CEOs', *Journal of Business Ethics*, 27(4), 2000, pp. 321–34.
18 Catherine Fox, 'Gender Inequality Goes Underground', *Australian Financial Review*, 24 July 2001, p. 50.
19 ibid.
20 ibid.
21 ibid.
22 See Australian Bureau of Statistics, *Workforce Statistics* (such as Nos 4113, 6104 and 6259). In 1995 over three-quarters of jobs created were part-time or casual, and women filled most of these.
23 This section has been drawn from Marta Calas & Linda Smircich, 'The Women's Point of View: Feminist Approaches to Organisational Studies', in Stewart Clegg, Cynthia Hardy & Walter R. Nord, eds, *Handbook of Organisation Studies*, London: Sage, 1996.
24 See Claire Burton, *The Promise and the Price*, Sydney: Allen & Unwin, 1991.
25 Fred Kerlinger, *Foundations of Behavioural Research*, 3rd edn, New York: CBS College Publishing, 1986.
26 This term is commonly used in the feminist literature. But see Jeanne de Bruijn & Eva Cyba, *Gender and Organizations: Changing Perspectives*, Amsterdam: VU University Press, 1994.

27 The points in regard to methodology are drawn from the following sources: Gloris Bowles & Renate Klein, eds, *Theories of Women's Studies*, London: Routledge & Kegan Paul, 1983; Sandra Harding, *Feminism and Methodology*, Indiana: Indiana University Press, 1987; Sandra Harding, *The Science Question in Feminism*, Ithaca, NY: Cornell UP, 1986; Mary Fonow & Judith Cook, eds, *Beyond Methodology*, Indiana: Indiana University Press, 1991; Ruth Bleier, *Feminist Approaches to Science*, New York: Pergamon Press, 1986; Judy Wajcman, *Feminist Confronts Technology*, Cambridge: Polity Press, 1991; and S. Reinharz, *Feminist Methods in Social Research*, Oxford: Oxford University Press, 1992.

28 An early study using participant observation was L. Williams, *What's On the Worker's Mind?*, New York: Charles Scribner & Sons, 1920.

29 See, for example, Huw Beynon, *Working for Ford*, 2nd edn, Harmondsworth: Pelican, 1984; and Brian McVeigh, *Life in a Japanese Women's College*, London: Routledge, 1997.

30 Sally Helgeson, *The Female Advantage: Women's Ways of Leadership*, New York: Doubleday, 1990.

31 Helen Brown, *Women Organising*, London: Routledge, 1992; and Judith Pringle, 'Feminism and Management: Critique and Contribution', in Alexander Kouzmin, Leonie Still & Paul Clarke, eds, *New Directions in Management*, Sydney: McGraw Hill, 1994.

32 See, for instance, Judy Wajcman, 'Desperately Seeking Difference: is Management Style Gendered?', *British Journal of Industrial Relations*, September 1996, pp. 333–49.

33 de Bruijn, op. cit.

34 Eric Trist & K.W. Bamforth, 'Some Social and Psychological Consequences of the Longwall Method of Coal Getting', *Human Relations*, 4, 1951, pp. 3–38.

35 For the Volvo experiments in teams, see J. Matthews, *Tools of Change*, Sydney: Pluto Press, 1989; and J. Pontusson, 'The Politics of New Technology and Job Redesign: A Comparison of Volvo and British Leyland', *Economic and Social Democracy*, 11, 1990, p. 311.

36 A. Sinclair, 'The Tyranny of Teams', *Working Paper No. 4*, Melbourne: Graduate School of Management, University of Melbourne, 1989.

37 Kathy Ferguson, *The Feminist Case Against Bureaucracy*, Philadelphia: Temple University Press, 1984.

38 See the various publications of the Affirmative Action Agency, as well as the relevant legislation.

39 See, for instance, Ferguson, op. cit., de Bruijn and Cyba, op. cit., and Rosabeth Moss Kanter, *Men and Women of the Corporation*, New York: Basic Books, 1977.

40 For suggestions as to what constitutes gender-free management, see Alice Sargent, *The Androgenous Manager*, New York: Amacom, 1981.

41 Dale Spender, *Nattering on the Net: Women, Power and Cyberspace*, Sydney: Spinifex Press, 1995.

42 de Bruijn and Cyba, op. cit.

43 'Tomorrow's Second Sex', *The Economist*, 28 September 1996, pp. 25–30.

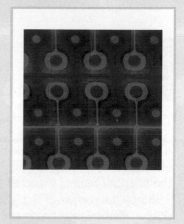

Case studies

CASE STUDY 1
Coles Myer Limited

Coles Myer is one of those unhappy companies that make the headlines for all the wrong reasons; it has proved to be incapable of introducing an effective change program and it has never achieved the financial returns expected of it. It was formed in 1985 by the merger of G.J. Coles, a Melbourne-based downmarket general goods and supermarket retailer, with Myer Limited, an upmarket department store chain which was part of the Melbourne establishment. It created a monster retailer, including Coles supermarkets, Liquorland, Myer and Grace Bros department stores as well as Kmart and Target discount chains. The anticipated benefits from the merger were significant. These derived from economies in shared services, purchasing, property and so forth. But almost from the start these benefits failed to materialise. Burdened with poor management, bad strategic decisions and internal conflict, the group had reached an all-time low by 2000. The share price was faltering, lagging behind a resurgent Woolworths. Profit had been stagnant for the previous three years. The board realised that it had one more chance to try to get the whole group performing at the same time or it would have to be broken up and sold, with each part going its separate way.

In September 2001 the board appointed John Fletcher as chief executive. Fletcher was well known to the Australian business community as the man who had done so much to turn Brambles into a successful international company. His first comment on being appointed chief executive was that he had not been inside a supermarket for 25 years, but that did not matter in his job: he was a change agent, and his job was to manage the company in order that it reach its potential.

So what were Fletcher's priorities? Doing something about Coles Myer's share price was the first one. But that would rise only when investors, particularly institutional investors, saw some improvement in the business. But his first steps were expected to include the sale of non-core businesses, such as Red Rooster fast foods and World 4 Kids.

Fletcher also made it clear that he wanted to break down the bureaucratic culture at Coles Myer. The inappropriate culture was personified by the headquarters of Myer in the Melbourne suburb of Tooronga. Nicknamed 'Battlestar Galactica', it was built in the early days of the combined group as a statement of purpose, place and status. It has a foyer reminiscent of a garish five-star hotel, vast executive office space, and a floor plan that stymies communication. Fletcher is unfortunately stuck with it, but he has made symbolic changes. He has turned the executive office floor into accommodation for 79 staff rather than the four it previously held.

On the merger of Coles and Myer, several 'silos' were allowed to develop, each with its own ethos, loyalties and culture. None of the silos cooperated with any other. Fletcher moved to dismantle these to make it a one culture/one company business. Previous management have tried to achieve this and have failed. This is not surprising, as successfully dismantling silos and moving towards a single culture is one of the most difficult tasks for management.

Trying to define where each business fits is also a challenge for Fletcher. After constant interference from previous management, they are being returned to the brand positioning they had five years ago. The role of the supermarkets is fairly obvious. But Kmart is to become a deep discounter, Target more oriented towards fashion and apparel with most of its sales being its own branded goods, and Myer Grace Bros moving into the middle and upper market.

Costs are also being tackled. In September 2001 Coles Myer introduced 'Operation Right Now' with the aim of saving up to $150 million in the non-food businesses. This involves optimising the supply chain by removing duplication in purchasing, processes and operational structures. Coordination among the various functions will also be improved. IT is to be standardised in order to simplify business processes. All computers will use a common platform and will be able to talk to each other. This will assist coordination of worldwide sourcing and will allow common supply-chain and logistics planning.

Clear structures, roles and responsibilities are to be defined so performance can be assessed. One of the obvious areas for savings is in purchasing. Myer Grace Bros, KMart and Target all sell common items, such as shoes and manchester. It seems logical to create a common buying team which can obtain greater discounts from suppliers. But early experimentation showed little promise: Kmart's needs were different from those of Myer Grace Bros. So it was decided that a better outcome could be achieved by improving coordination and communication between buyers for the chains than by having a common purchasing function.

Tackling the bureaucracy also means downsizing. Up to 1000 back-office staff will be made redundant in the first wave, with others to follow. The previous CEO had only three people reporting to him; Fletcher has increased his direct reports to eight. Some of his direct reports will be hired from outside the company. As it stands, Coles Myer is a mishmash of North American managers, who run the major businesses, and local managers further down the hierarchy.

Developing a consistent strategy is important. The way ahead for Coles supermarkets has always been reasonably clear. But the strategies for the other businesses have constantly changed, often from year to year, as managers have repositioned stores and changed stock levels and product ranges in an attempt at hitting on a successful formula. Consumers have ended up confused and staff disillusioned.

Fletcher sees himself as a change agent rather than a hands-on micro-manager. His previous role at Brambles emphasised his role as a careful manager of capital. This means seeking a return on funds greater than the cost of capital, being clear as to where you are making and losing money, and either fixing businesses or selling them. But it also means identifying areas for growth. Supermarkets have heavy traffic and can be used to sell other products, from financial services to bill paying. Tapping into these new sources of growth is fundamental to the future health of the company.

Cultural revolutions are fraught with difficulty. Morale can decline. Productivity can fall as people's thoughts turn inward, and new roles must be learned and old ones unlearned. Good people can resign or inadvertently be sacked. And the clash between the old and new staff, and those who benefit and those who lose, can be extremely disruptive. Fletcher must undertake this task while every analyst and reporter watches and assesses his moves. It is tough at the top.

QUESTIONS

1 What is an appropriate method of assessing the effectiveness of Coles Myer? Using the method you have nominated, how effective has Coles Myer been since it was formed?

2 Compare and contrast the changes proposed at Coles Myer with the model of change discussed in Chapter 12.

3 What would be easier to change, culture or business processes? Why?

4 Undertake sufficient research to determine to what extent Coles Myer has achieved its goals since the case was written.

CASE STUDY 2
The culture of being exclusive

LVMH (Louis Vuitton Moët Hennessy) makes an unusual living: it produces goods that no-one needs. LVMH is the manufacturer of such well-known luxury brand names as Moët champagne, Louis Vuitton, Dom Perignon, Givenchy, Dior and Tag Heuer. It also owns a raft of well-known perfume and fashion goods labels. All these products have two things in common: they are expensive, and they carry an air of exclusivity. No-one is going to pay large amounts of money for something that is fairly common. So designing and producing products that stand apart in the marketplace becomes a central part of managing the company.

Many of LVMH's management techniques tend to run counter to conventional business wisdom. New products begin with radical innovation. This is a highly emotional, unpredictable and unwieldy activity, which is not subject to management control. LVMH does not believe in setting limits on its creative types, believing that artists must be completely unfettered by managerial and financial concerns to do their best work. The managing director of LVMH, Bernard Arnault, believes that creators and innovators cannot be managed any more than Leonardo da Vinci or Michelangelo could be 'managed'. As an illustration of this, Arnault did not wince when the chief designer of Dior sent a model down the catwalk in a dress made from newspaper.

Arnault believes that if you act like a typical manager around creative types, with rules, policies, time cards, data on customer preferences and so on, you soon kill talent and innovation. As a result, designers are given freedom to innovate without limits. This leads to LVMH being highly decentralised. Each brand, headed by its own artistic director, is responsible for its own operations.

LVMH takes little notice of customer surveys or focus groups. It considers that you cannot charge premium prices for products that customers want. The premium comes from giving customers what is unexpected. Similarly, you will never have high-demand products that people queue around the block to buy if all you have done is listened to focus groups. The high-demand products are a result of the creative and innovative process uninhibited by marketing concerns. They are the output of the gut instincts of the creative team.

So what of the failures that emerge from the creative process? LVMH of course, like any other company, does not like failures, and most sales come from existing products that it calls its classics which have been around for years. It limits its new product introductions to no more than 15% of sales each year. That way the entire company is not put at risk in the event of a product not selling as expected. But failures are few and far between. More common is a demand for a new product, with a limited production run, well and truly exceeding supply. LVMH does run focus groups, but these are just one part of the decision-making process as to whether to introduce a new product. Ultimately the company has faith in its creators, who have the greatest input into whether to introduce a product or not.

The other key to LVMH's success is its manufacturing operations. No hiring casual labour and putting it on a production line in an LVMH factory (or *atelier*, as they are called in French). It goes without saying that the quality of LVMH products is high. But productivity is also high, because of the heavy reliance on modern engineering technology. And close study is made of every motion and process to remove unnecessary steps and ensure that quality is maintained. Hand production is still common, and it takes time to train the artisans who make the product. Quality emerges from hiring very dedicated people, training them and then keeping them for a long time. Such people, live, breathe and are the embodiment of the product, and cannot easily be replaced.

LVMH has grown fast through acquiring other firms. When absorbing them into LVMH, care is taken to maintain the traditions and practices that made the acquired company successful in the first place. LVMH considers that the brand is basically the people who design and manufacture it. As a result, LVMH eschews the practice of large-scale layoffs and management changes when making an acquisition. This way it maintains quality and the loyalty of those staff who have the brand in their bones. By making redundancies in acquired firms, LMVH considers it would be letting go those people who respect the brand the most and have contributed to its success.

Adapted from: 'The Perfect Paradox of Star Brands: An interview with Arnault of LVMH', *Harvard Business Review*, October 2001, pp. 116–23.

QUESTIONS

1 From the information in the case, create an organisational design for LVMH. Identify the major factors that have influenced your design choice.

2 Discuss how LVMH challenges conventional attitudes in relation to management and organisation design.

3 The products manufactured by LVMH are not price-sensitive. Discuss the extent to which this may influence its management practices.

CASE STUDY 3
The decline of Franklins

It is not too often that a dominant company within a stable industry loses its way and finally goes out of business. Franklins, an east-coast grocery retailer, managed to do that after being the leading grocery discounter for over 50 years. Franklins was founded in the early 1950s by Norman Tieck and Harold Cornock. Tieck was a successful buyer for Woolworths and Cornock an expert store manager for Coles. They made a formidable team, and their strategy was pure cost-cutting. They stocked the stores with a limited range of dry goods (i.e. packaged and tinned groceries) and sold them cheaper than their competitors. The success of Franklins' stores drew other retailers, such as greengrocers and butchers, to set up close by, thus forming self-contained shopping precincts.

Franklins operated a lean organisation. It was headquartered above a warehouse in the distinctly downmarket Sydney suburb of Chullora, and in the 1960s the head office had only one manual typewriter. Its stores were spartan and crowded with stock and it did not run advertising. Its success depended on its people and culture. These were closely aligned to the goals of the organisation. It was the archetypical machine bureaucracy, with costs squeezed to the bone. No-one was in any doubt as to the importance of frugality and sticking to the original vision of the company. Staff numbers were kept to a minimum and economies were achieved by carrying only a small number of essential items in each store.

By 1980 there were 60 stores across Sydney, and Franklins' success attracted the attention of those wanting an entry to the industry. In 1978 it was bought by the Hong Kong-based Dairy Farm group. Dairy Farm was a major owner of supermarkets in Hong Kong, where it had a controlling position in the industry. It also operated supermarkets in South-East Asia and the United Kingdom. Dairy Farm installed Paul Simons, an ex-Woolworths man, as managing director. Simons, during his 10-year stint at the top of Franklins, maintained the old Franklins culture. The business gradually added outlets and expanded into Victoria and Queensland. When he left, there were 120 stores and a 3% profit margin on turnover, which is fairly standard for the discount grocery industry.

As ultimate owner Dairy Farm had the final say on strategy, and in the late 1980s it introduced a worldwide strategy of moving its stores upmarket. Following the example of its British stores, Kwicksave, Franklins tried to reinvent itself by increasing the range and composition of goods sold. In particular, it tried to compete directly with Woolworths and Coles by moving into fresh foods such as fruit and vegetables. This greatly increased Franklins' costs. Greater warehousing space was required. Investment in IT had to be stepped up to track the larger number of items on sale. Capital expenditure had to be increased to accommodate the new items. Staff numbers expanded. As well, the greengrocery items required new storage facilities. Fruit and vegetables were labour-intensive to handle and had a short shelf life, unlike packaged groceries. They required refrigeration and other back-up infrastructure.

While this policy worked for Coles and Woolworths, Franklins stores were too small for the concept to be introduced throughout the chain. This required a selective roll-out of new stores which stocked the full range of products. Costs grew further as economies of scale were lost—the expensive new infrastructure serving only a few stores. A further blow to Franklins was the introduction of late-night trading. While Franklins could stay open until later at night, the specialist stores that supported Franklins, such as the butchers and bakers, could not. As a result, customers lost the benefit of being able to do all their shopping close by. Franklins' margins slowly eroded. Cost grew from 13% of turnover to 24%. Profits turned into substantial losses.

While this was occurring, there was continuous top management turnover. In the 1990s Franklins went through four managing directors. There was also substantial staff turnover, leading to a loss of experience and facilitating the drift away from the philosophies that had made Franklins successful in the past. The Hong Kong-based Dairy Farm also gave the chain less attention than it deserved. Dairy Farm made most of its money from supermarkets in Hong Kong, where it was one-half of a duopoly. Retailing requires extensive local knowledge and experience, and it is difficult being a mass retailer in a foreign market. Dairy Farm did hire local managers but appeared to have little faith in them. And there was the issue of what type of business Dairy Farm wanted to be in, and owning a downmarket deep discounter did not appeal. But the types of infrastructure and skills owned by Franklins did not easily lend themselves to moving up the value chain. There was also a suspicion that Dairy Farm was not prepared to finance its strategy of competing directly with Coles and Woolworths. As a consequence, Franklins never had the funds to buy and outfit the appropriate number of stores or invest in areas that needed investment. Local management also felt marginalised by Dairy Farm's lack of support and constant statements of dissatisfaction with the local operations.

By 2001 Dairy Farm was no longer prepared to sustain the losses being incurred by Franklins. No foreign company was prepared to buy the business outright, and local supermarkets were prevented by competition laws from buying the business as a whole. As a consequence Franklins was broken up, with various groups such as Coles and Woolworths buying stores to fit their portfolio. But as Franklins was disappearing, Aldi, a German-owned deep discounter which only stocked a limited range of house brand dry goods, started to increase its presence in the market.

QUESTIONS

1 Identify how Weitzel and Jonsson's theory, discussed in Chapter 14, may be used to explain the decline of Franklins.

2 Discuss the extent to which culture was a factor in Franklins' demise.

3 How did other business factors, such as strategy and finance, influence Franklins' ability to change? Discuss whether these were of greater or lesser importance than the general difficulties associated with organisational change.

4 What approach would you use to assess the effectiveness of Franklins? How could the balanced scorecard be used to advantage?

CASE STUDY 4
The DaimlerChrysler emulsion

When, two years ago, Daimler-Benz, Germany's most profitable car company, and owner of the world-beating Mercedes marque, revealed that it was merging with Chrysler, the smallest but most efficient of America's Big Three car producers, the two companies embarked on a cross-border deal based on what seemed to be impeccable industrial logic.

Cross-border mergers are notoriously tricky. For DaimlerChrysler to succeed requires cohesion not just between two headquarters, in Stuttgart and Auburn Hills, Michigan, but also between a host of offices and factories with different national and corporate cultures. To overcome such differences, the merged company took an unusual approach.

In its pre-merger planning Daimler put little weight on the fact that the deal would be a cross-border one. Apparently, it assumed that this would create no special problems. According to Eckhard Cordes, one of three Daimler managers to take part in the pre-merger discussions with Chrysler (the others were Jürgen Schrempp, the group's chairman, and Jürgen Hubbert, a board member responsible for Daimler's Mercedes-Benz car division), questions raised by the deal's cross-border nature were not specifically asked until after its broad terms had been agreed.

Mr Cordes says that three big issues preoccupied the Daimler team. First, against a background of consolidation in the car industry, they were trying to put together two companies with strong and distinctive heritages, so how best could they do this? Second, given that there was no precedent for such a merger, was the deal at all feasible? And third, were Daimler and Chrysler bold enough to manage the difficult task of post-merger integration successfully?

None of these issues, says Mr Cordes, had an explicit cross-border element: they would have applied equally had the deal been between two German companies. The solution to post-merger integration, for instance, was to be ruthless over efficiency and planning, no matter where the deal. At the same time, however, the questions were formulated in the knowledge that profound difficulties over differing locations and cultures would have to be tackled if the merger were to succeed.

These difficulties were aggravated by a justifiable feeling among those on the American side that this was no merger of equals, but rather a deal in which Daimler was calling the principal shots. Chrysler's middle managers and engineers saw it as a sell-out to foreigners, and feared an invasion of rigid Teutonic working practices into their own rather freewheeling company. The potential clash of cultures was thus corporate as well as national: could a bunch of process-led German engineers work effectively with Chrysler's hunch inspired, risk-taking bosses?

By some measures, the fact that DaimlerChrysler has got as far as it has since 1998 has been nothing short of miraculous. Despite plenty of bumpy moments, the combination has held together. 'We are absolutely happy with the development of the merger', says Mr Hubbert. 'We have a clear understanding: one company, one vision, one chairman, two cultures.'

DaimlerChrysler has surmounted barriers as simple but important as the time difference between Germany and America. Managers from both firms criss-cross the Atlantic in a stream of meetings and workshops, seeking ways to drive down expenses and share future development costs. To reduce the wear-and-tear of constant travel, a specially converted aircraft helps them to catch up on sleep. In an ironic twist, DaimlerChrysler has leased space in New York's Chrysler Building so that travel can be further reduced.

Moreover, the new firm has continued to expand. On 27 March, for example, it announced a deal with loss-making Mitsubishi Motors of Japan which should strengthen DaimlerChrysler's plans for small cars. And on 26 June it spent $428 million on a 10% stake in Hyundai of South Korea.

But by other measures, the merger has fallen far short of its designers' vision. Until last autumn the companies were talking about maintaining two head offices, and the word 'merger' was still in use. In fact, it is now acknowledged by people such as

Mr Hubbert that Daimler, seeking to solve strategic problems of its own, had engineered a friendly takeover of America's third car maker.

Two years on, problems abound. Some are financial. DaimlerChrysler has abandoned detailed discussion of the cost-saving targets it set for the new company, even though investors remain intensely interested. But the group has admitted that renewed and deep cost-cutting efforts have had to be undertaken to shore up the group's operating results.

On 26 July DaimlerChrysler duly announced second-quarter profits of $1.7 billion, slightly ahead of expectations. But it also said that it was struggling to meet earlier projections of operating performance for the full financial year. And, tellingly, Mr Schrempp said the group urgently needed to improve its efforts to communicate its story to investors. This remark came after an abysmal period for the group's share price, which has now fallen by more than 40% from a high of €95.5 ($106) in 1999. The stockmarket, at least, seems sceptical about the prospects for the merger.

Other problems are operational. Rumblings of discontent within the firm can still be heard. Competition in the car market is intensifying, especially in Chrysler's home market and in the high-margin minivan sector that it has long dominated. As competitors such as Honda of Japan have produced their own vans, Chrysler's efforts to hang onto market share have consisted largely of giving even bigger discounts to dealers. But sales have stalled, and Chrysler recently began a new $2 billion cost-cutting program to shore up its performance. A few vehicles, notably the retro-styled PT Cruiser, have been successes, but the firm's main roll-out of new models is still several months away.

Even the deal with Mitsubishi is an admission that the transatlantic marriage was not enough: it united two complementary sets of products in America and Europe, but failed to remedy the weakness of both companies in the faster-growing Asian and Latin American markets. Eighteen months ago, Mr Schrempp wanted to invest in Nissan as an answer to Daimler's Asian shortcomings. But he was overruled by his management board, which decided that Daimler could not digest two big acquisitions at once. To the surprise of Renault, the rival bidder, Daimler walked away from a deal that would have made its reach global in a way that its takeover of Chrysler has not.

Yet, despite these problems, it is too early to conclude that the merger has failed. Its true test will come in the next two or three years, when the first products developed entirely since the merger should start to roll off the production lines. If DaimlerChrysler can show that it has translated operational efficiency into successful new cars and higher levels of profit, it will have proved that the deal's underlying logic was sound. Even at this early stage, however, the merger offers some powerful lessons in the problems of combining firms in different countries.

The business background to the deal shows why both companies were willing to take on such problems. By the mid-1990s Chrysler had survived near bankruptcy and a failed hostile buyout launched by Kirk Kerkorian, a corporate raider who was its biggest single shareholder. Chrysler was lean and had trendy designs, but where was it going? Its advisers, Credit Suisse First Boston, prepared a paper outlining six strategic options. According to a recent book by two *Detroit News* journalists, they all consisted of some form of alliance with the Germans.

Desultory talks had taken place between the two companies in 1995. But Bob Eaton, Chrysler's chairman, believed that sooner or later he would have to throw in his lot with another car company. So when, in 1997, Mr Schrempp sought to reopen talks with Chrysler, he got a friendly reception. Not that everything was friendly thereafter. In particular, Mr Eaton took plenty of personal flak after he announced that he intended to stand down as co-chief executive within three years.

Yet, judging by DaimlerChrysler's performance since the merger, Mr Eaton may deserve more credit for strategic insight than he has had. In return for accepting junior status in the merger, he obtained a big premium for Chrysler shareholders. Had it remained independent, Chrysler would be in a horrid position today.

Even so, the merger could have been better handled. By focusing on general issues rather than cross border ones, the two companies underestimated a factor that would define, and could even scupper, the entire deal. Throughout the negotiations, even after integration began, cross-border problems surfaced, demanding attention. But top managers on both sides seemed to prefer sidling up to potential hurdles rather than meeting them head on.

Consider, for instance, the task of melding two distinct ways of doing business. Old Daimler was bureaucratic and formal. A standard meeting of senior managers would generate thick wads of papers and lengthy minutes. After months of influence by the Americans' more spontaneous behaviour, most presentations are now oral, and a one-page memo then summarises proceedings.

Some barriers have been harder to overcome. At the time of the merger, senior Chrysler managers became rich, as share options suddenly became hugely valuable. That triggered concern in Germany that Daimler bosses might become greedy. But it also served to highlight deep-rooted differentials in pay. Typically, the Americans were taking home two, three or even four times as much as their German equivalents. At the same time, the Americans were aghast at what they viewed as German profligacy over expenses. Some Daimler executives routinely travelled first class to get to meetings, or stayed at top-flight hotels over weekends. For these cultures to meet in the middle will take time and the acceptance by both sides of new approaches.

One thing that has made the merger easier is that neither company conformed entirely to the American or Teutonic stereotypes, particularly at the level of top management. By the time the two got talking, Chrysler was no longer the funky Detroit company that in the 1980s had come back from the dead through then chief executive Lee Iacocca's sheer flair. Its chairman, Mr Eaton, was a cautious, reserved former GM manager with all the buttoned-down instincts of a GM engineer. Daimler-Benz, for its part, was under the spell of Mr Schrempp, who had spent the formative periods of his adult life in South Africa and who still goes there to relax. He is a gutsy, earthy, wilful leader whose style is to listen before making up his mind and then dominating.

Viewed from outside Detroit, the merger seems to have caused relatively few arguments. DaimlerChrysler has had some high-profile departures, most of which occurred at the time of the merger when senior jobs were allocated. The exception was the controversial exit of Thomas Stallkamp, former president of Chrysler and a fervent believer in the importance of thoroughly integrating the two companies. He left last September, to be replaced by Jim Holden. Mr Stallkamp had been undermined by the Germans for weeks before Mr Schrempp gave Mr Eaton the order to fire him.

There has, however, also been a slew of departures further down the ranks. At one stage last year, talented Chrysler designers were defecting in droves. The flow has slowed to more of a trickle these days. Mr Hubbert says the Germans have learnt an important lesson: that they should not take workers' loyalty for granted. But it is also possible that the departures have distracted top managers' attention from the underlying problems in Chrysler's business.

The German dominance in the deal has also led to uncomfortable moments, such as when Mr Hubbert asserted last year that DaimlerChrysler would have a single headquarters in Stuttgart. But generally the Germans have been diplomatic, sensible even. From the outset, Daimler tried to apply lessons learned from other troubled deals. Hence, for instance, the insistence on clarifying in advance which managers would occupy which slots.

Hence, too, a determination to centralise and control decisions that might otherwise chip away at cohesion. To handle the hundreds of integration projects, DaimlerChrysler has formed a powerful automotive council of five senior managers to which all projects must report every four to six weeks. Mr Cordes, who sits on the council, says it has been critically important in helping the group to stay on course.

In the end, the lesson of DaimlerChrysler's merger may be that cross-border deals are, in essence, the same as all other mergers, only with extra layers of difficulty. Mr Schrempp and his team have concentrated on the deal's operational parts, downplaying cultural problems and management jockeying as inevitable but manageable.

The trickiest problems seem to have been largely about the details of doing things effectively. In May 1998, the merging companies forecast $1.4 billion of cost savings during 1999, a figure they duly delivered. Having set internal goals for further cost synergies by 2000 and 2005, DaimlerChrysler then decided not to make these public. One reason was that, to management's growing discomfort, investors and journalists alike were interested in little else.

A second, more acceptable, reason was that defining a true synergy becomes harder the more time has passed since a merger.

But another reason was more subtle. As DaimlerChrysler has tried to produce workable and cost-efficient ways of doing business as a single entity, it has run into a level of difficulty that was not anticipated when the deal was struck. Consider the apparently simple idea of component sharing. If Daimler and Chrysler have two similar vehicles, in theory they can save money by using the same component—an axle or fuel pump, say—in both. But what if one vehicle is scheduled for launch this year, the other not until next year? Should the product launches be coordinated to maximise efficiency? And how are development costs to be allocated?

It is on these nitty-gritty details that the deal's fate ultimately rests. If DaimlerChrysler gets it right, the merger might yet come to be seen as a masterstroke. If it fails, doubtless some blame will be laid on cross-border differences such as language and culture. And that, perhaps, is the true lesson of such mergers: the cross-border angle comes to the fore only when other things are already going wrong.

Source: 'The DaimlerChrysler emulsion', *The Economist*, 29 July 2000. pp.65–6.

QUESTIONS

1 From the information in the case, identify the factors that are important when considering a cross-border merger. Assess the importance of each one in the DaimlerChrysler merger.

2 Drawing on the case, discuss the importance of culture when merging two organisations.

3 Evaluate the extent to which the cultures of Daimler and Chrysler were influenced by national characteristics.

4 From the information in the case, prepare a brief model showing the major steps involved in merging organisations. Evaluate the viability of the model you have proposed.

CASE STUDY 5
Is IBM worth more than its parts?

IBM, often known metaphorically as Big Blue, is part of America's, and indeed the world's, industrial establishment. It grew to dominate the computer industry up to the 1980s through its supremacy in mainframe computing. Few others could match the breadth of services that IBM could offer in supplying the mainframe, the software and the support needed to make it work. But IBM always had problems. Its research laboratories were world class and produced some great inventions, but the bureaucracy at IBM was always slow in bringing the products to market. Its many management layers led to slow and cumbersome decision making and inhibited the company from adapting to change.

Poor performance caught up with IBM by the late 1980s, when the near collapse of the company made worldwide news. It 1993 it appointed an outsider, Lou Gerstner, to restructure and downsize the company in an attempt to restore profitability. One big decision Gerstner had to make was whether to break up IBM into its component parts. IBM, which is one of the largest companies in the world, has a divisionalised structure roughly based on product. The main divisions are mainframes, software, business services, servers, microchips, PCs and financing. Gerstner's opinion was that by remaining one company, IBM could leverage off its size and each part would benefit from being joined to the other. He argued that IBM's integrated portfolio was its greatest strength.

There are opinions that run counter to Gerstner's argument. Some analysts feel that freed-up divisions would work leaner and faster. Each division would react faster to its environment, and management would be able to respond to a smaller and better-defined range of problems; as it is, each division is struggling to match the performance of its more focused and nimble rivals. It also might end conflicts among competing businesses within the company. Overall, a breakup may lead to a far more competitive IBM.

Informing the argument is the poor financial performance of IBM in recent times. Each division is growing slower than the segment it is operating in, and profitability has stalled. Over the past 10 years, shareholders' equity has halved and only financial engineering, such as share buybacks and lower taxes, has boosted earnings per share. Splitting the company up may lead to the parts being worth more than the sum of the whole, which would be a financial windfall for shareholders. But the longer the decision is delayed, the more likely it is that the value of each component will fall. The poor performance of the company cannot continue indefinitely without something being done to rectify it.

Parts of this case were adapted from Daniel Lyons, 'Separating IBM's Parts Might Improve Its Sums', *Business Review Weekly*, 24 November 2000, p. 56.

QUESTIONS

1 Discuss how organisational theory can assist solving the breakup dilemma at IBM.

2 Drawing on the case, explore the relationship between financial structuring and organisational structuring.

3 Discuss whether the environmental pressures identified in the case prevent the company from incorporating social concerns in decision making.

CASE STUDY 6
Will the modern corporation survive?

Over its long history, the world has seen many different types of organisations evolve. Examples of different organisational forms include various church and religious groups, all manner and type of government organisations and military structures through to the modern industrial corporation which dominates the present day. All of these organisations reflect the environmental and technological capacities of the societies from which they emerged. And although all organisations do have some features in common—they require leadership, someone to manage day to day affairs and a means of coordinating people—in some ways they are all different in that they have features which are unique to the age in which they exist.

The dominant organisational form of the present day is the large business corporation. In attempting to address the question as to whether it will survive we need to be aware of the circumstances which have led to its dominance. We can identify a number of these. First the large amount of capital needed to establish plant and attain geographic spread is beyond the capacity of a small business or sole trader. Second, the large corporation, through its hierarchy of managers and agreed reward systems, could, in certain circumstances, mediate exchanges between various workers more efficiently than market forces. Third, because consumer's knowledge of products was limited, brands became important. If a consumer had confidence in a brand then they did not need to know the details of the product. As a result, large corporations grew to be the custodians of important brands. Fourth, corporations considered that as far as possible, all functions should be carried out by the company. This resulted in them carrying out their own accounting, transport and maintenance, as well as countless other functions.

The growth of the large corporation had certain sociological features as well. Industrialists sited their factories close to raw materials or sources of supply. This often resulted in them employing large workforces in isolated locations with the resulting loss of a labour market. Further, the requirements of the production process meant that employees had to arrive and leave at specified times leaving little flexibility in scheduling work. Employees often built their career around service to one company and spent a lifetime with one employer. This was reinforced by firms having what is termed an internal labour market. This is one where most employees enter at a low level in the organisation and promotion positions are filled by those already in the company.

So what is happening, and is likely to happen, which might radically change the nature of the corporation? First, all manner of new technologies have been introduced which improve communication. This removes friction both within and between companies. One of the main functions of the management hierarchy, that of a communication conduit, is now reduced in importance. As well, contractors to the company can receive instructions and information far easier than it was possible to transmit them within the company not so long ago.

Cheaper transport means that firms no longer need to locate close to raw materials. Firms have tended to agglomerate closer to customers, sources of labour and transport nodes. This has permitted the growth of a labour market with workers now shopping around for the best employment prospects. As a concept, as well as in practice, jobs for life is now a rarity.

Firms have also changed their attitudes towards what should be undertaken in-house. They realise that it is no longer possible to be efficient at everything; the new technologies have permitted many functions to be subcontracted to specialist providers who have greater knowledge and lower costs. Subcontracting can range from determination of strategy to IT services and debt collection.

On the other hand the forces leading to large size are still with us. Many businesses need to be big in order to attain economies of scale. Others seek large size in order to more successfully tap capital markets. Other industries, such as airlines, not only require enormous amounts of capital, but they experience extreme cycles of demand. During the periodic downturns in the cycle, the poorly capitalised and managed firms go out of business leaving the remaining participants stronger.

So what is likely to emerge from these conflicting pressures? We can expect to see the emergence of a number of different types of company. The first are specialist providers which concentrate on one task. These firms will range in size from small family companies to large consulting firms. They will be linked to the customer through dense communication channels and may have employees located on the customer's premises. Examples of specialist providers are contract manufacturers, maintenance firms, labour hire firms, recruitment specialists and payroll and accounting suppliers.

Brands still provide benefits for both consumer and producer and those firms with strong brand identification will probably become multinational companies. Managing the multinationals will pose many challenges but those that are succeeding are breaking into a federation of companies with a small head office and autonomous subsidiaries. No longer are we likely to see enormous head offices with a staff of thousands.

As many advances in products and technology are being made at the intersections of industries, we are likely to see the growth of strategic alliances. Rather than try to develop all advances in their products in house, firms are likely to seek suitable partners with which to pool knowledge and exploit new products and ideas.

And what of employment? Modern workforces have a high level of mobility. This applies not only within a country and region but also between countries. Workers and managers, particularly those with high levels of scarce knowledge, will need to be nurtured. Their loyalty cannot be taken for granted: they will need to be treated as volunteers in order to attract and keep them.

The role of top management and the demands placed on those who fill the key positions will need to be reassessed. The success of a few super managers who have achieved household name status disguises the more common experience which is the perceived failure of senior management. Most CEOs only hold office for a short number of years and then leave the organisation with the taint of failure. This is notwithstanding the fact that they were promoted to the position on the basis of their success in previous management roles. Too much appears to be expected from the chief executive and it is likely that both corporate and community expectations will need to change to accommodate a greater form of collegiate decision making at the top of the organisation accompanied by a downplaying of the role of an all powerful chief executive.

Some of the ideas for this case were drawn from Peter Drucker, 'Will the Corporation Survive?', *The Economist*, 3 November 2001.

QUESTIONS

1 Relate the material in the case to any three chapters in the text. Discuss whether the material in the chapters you have considered will no longer apply in twenty years' time.

2 Evaluate whether the points raised in the case will have a greater impact on relationships between organisations rather than the internal structure of any particular organisation.

3 How is the worker and employer likely to change? How will this affect areas such as societal expectations, industrial relations and family relationships?

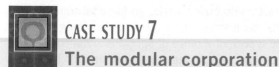

CASE STUDY 7
The modular corporation

In a leap of industrial evolution, many companies are shunning vertical integration for a lean, nimble structure centred on what they do best. The idea is to nurture a few core activities—designing and marketing computers, copiers or cars, for example—and let outside specialists make the parts, handle deliveries or do the accounting. The new breed avoid becoming monoliths laden with plants and bureaucracy. Instead, they are exciting hubs surrounded by networks of the world's best suppliers. Those manufacturing or service units are modular: they can be added or taken away with flexibility of switching parts in a child's Lego set.

Modular companies fit a fast-moving marketplace. Outsourcing non-core activities yields two advantages: first, it holds down the unit costs and investment needed to turn out new products rapidly; second, it frees companies to direct scarce capital where they hold a competitive advantage. Typically that means more money for market research, developing software used to design new products, hiring the best engineers, and training sales or service personnel. Using the modular model, companies can achieve rapid growth with small amounts of capital, and compact management companies such as Dell Computer and apparel and footwear company Nike have leveraged miniscule investments into big, fast-growing enterprises. One reason is that they don't have to invest in fixed assets; these costs are borne by the subcontractors.

Modular companies work best when they achieve a pair of tough objectives: collaborating smoothly with suppliers and choosing the right specialty. Depending on outsiders has its pitfalls. Companies need to find loyal, reliable vendors they can trust with trade secrets. If sales suddenly take off, they also need assurances that suppliers will stretch and rapidly retool plants to rush out new products. But like other companies, a modular one needs the vision to identify what customers will want, not what the companies are technically good at.

Modular companies are flourishing in two industries that sell fast-changing products: apparel and electronics. But a number of important industries are becoming more modular. Even in steel, chemicals, and photographic equipment—industries that have traditionally tried to do everything in-house—are avidly outsourcing services. Among the services most often outsourced are transport, catering, logistics, data processing and accounting. Oil companies no longer transport their own oil, and financial firms often subcontract their IT needs.

Apparel companies are modular pioneers. Nike and Reebok have prospered by concentrating on their strengths: designing and marketing high-tech, fashionable footwear for sports and fitness. Nike owns one small factory that makes some sneaker parts. Reebok owns no plants. The two rivals contract virtually all footwear production out to suppliers in Taiwan, South Korea and other Asian countries. Outsourcing helps Nike and Reebok keep up with changing tastes, as their suppliers are expert at rapidly retooling for new products. Sparse fixed assets translate into bountiful profitability. Nike and Reebok each earned a return on assets of up to 16% over the last decade.

The electronics industry is evolving into a web of modular companies. The trend is transforming the markets for IBM-compatible personal computers and high-powered workstations. Most of the growth in this segment is being met by modular companies rather than vertically integrated companies such as IBM.

Leading the revolution in PCs are such newcomers as Dell and Gateway, plus workstation innovators like Sun Microsystems. Those companies either buy their products ready-made or purchase all the parts from suppliers, then assemble the machines. Their big, established competitors—IBM, Hewlett-Packard and Compaq—produce many of their parts in-house, including disk drives that provide the computer's memory and microprocessors that furnish its speed and power. But the profitability of the modular companies is far greater than their opposition.

Dell Computers, which operates in Australia, demonstrates many advantages of being modular. Dell prospers by concentrating on two aspects of the computer business where the vertically integrated companies are vulnerable: marketing and service. Dell owns no plants and leases two small factories to assemble computers from outsourced parts. Investment in fixed assets is a tiny $55 million. Dell takes in $35 of sales for every dollar of fixed assets. For Compaq the figure is $3.

Freed from heavy spending on plants, Dell lavishes money on training salespeople and service technicians and furnishing them with the best computers, databases and software. Those relatively modest investments generate terrific returns. Dell sells IBM-compatible PCs in competition with Compaq, DEC and IBM, but while the others rely primarily on computer stores or dealers, Dell sells direct to consumers, who read about the products in newspaper ads or catalogues. Buyers call a toll-free number and place orders with salespeople. By eliminating the middleman and the typical retailer's 13% markup, Dell can charge lower prices than IBM or Compaq.

That's not all. Dell sells not a standard machine but custom PCs. Customers can choose a colour Mitsubishi monitor, an extra-powerful Intel microprocessor, or a host of other options. Dell also offers everything you can buy in a computer store— 650 software programs, a full range of modems and much else. But it doesn't make or even stock the products. It simply orders them from a big distribution company which often delivers direct to the buyer. The arrangement is luring customers, who find that dealing with a single supplier means fewer payments and better service.

For the modular model to work, contract manufacturers must maintain a delicate balance. To lower costs, they strive to run plants at near-full capacity. But they also need to plan for unforeseen shifts in business. Sales of a PC or workstation can jump unexpectedly. A client may need to launch a new PC on a crash schedule. If the supplier is caught short of capacity, customers can suffer setbacks from lost sales and late products.

It is not only in the PC industry that we can find modular corporations. The car manufacturers have long been moving towards outsourcing a large amount of their work. Motor car companies now specialise in design and assembly, with outside contractors providing most of the parts. Many of the outside contractors do their own design in collaboration with the car companies. The move to outsourcing has led to the growth of a range of specialised subcontractors, who concentrate on one area of car design. These range from styling and engine optimisation through to specialised companies which can calculate stresses and sources of vibration. This has allowed new entrants to find a niche in the industry that they otherwise might have found difficult. Daewoo is a recent maker of cars, but apart from providing assembly facilities most of the other work has been outsourced. The bodies of its cars are styled in either Los Angeles or Italy, the engineering is carried out in England or Germany and the supplies of components even stretch to Australia, with General Motors Holden providing the engine for many Daewoo models.

Other examples of modular companies can be found in the airline industry, with companies such as British Airways and Qantas buying in many of the services that they use, and the chemical industry, which is becoming more highly specialised. Even the pharmaceutical industry is moving towards a modular form. Large pharmaceutical companies are looking outside their companies for new ideas rather than generating them in-house. They can then use their expertise in product testing, regulatory approval and marketing, which requires the capital arising from large size.

Source: Shawn Tully, 'The Modular Corporation', *Fortune*, 8 February 1993, pp. 106–15. © 1993 Time Inc. Reproduced with permission.

QUESTIONS

1 What environmental and technological factors have led to the growth of the modular corporation?

2 Given that the modular corporation needs some coordination, what replaces the traditional coordinating mechanisms that exist in large corporations?

3 Can the virtual corporation be used to advantage in all industries? Why, or why not?

4 Research whether the use of the virtual corporation has been increasing over the past few years. Identify the reasons for your conclusions.

CASE STUDY 8
Organisational change in the navy

From the early 1990s, women were able to serve on all vessels of the Royal Australian Navy except submarines. Integrating women is a major change for any organisation, but this particularly posed the navy enormous problems. Virtually all naval vessels were built to be manned by men, or at least one gender. To embark women, ships up to 40 years old had to be modified to provide toilet, ablution and sleeping facilities for both sexes. This led to the women having either better or worse facilities than the rest of the ship's company. It even involved such details as whether to allow women more water for washing their hair.

If the integration of women into a ship's company was to be a long-term success it was imperative that women be seen to be doing a job that was equal to that of male crew members. This was not just a matter of training: there were obvious physiological differences between men and women. Men were stronger in areas such as the shoulders and arms and women were more likely to suffer leg injuries in carrying heavy loads or shifting material.

The navy was the archetypal masculine environment. For hundreds of years, warships had been the preserve of men. Cramped into confined spaces for months on end, jocularity often centred on sexual references and exploits. Bad and lewd language accompanied virtually every conversation. Even tattoos often had a sexual connotation. It was also the natural home of the macho management style. Top-down, directive, tough, uncompromising and often abusive with little show of emotion or compromise, it was justified on the basis that war situations demanded such management behaviour.

Any aggravation festered in the environment of a warship at sea. The same people in a cramped, sometimes non-air-conditioned space, operating 24 hours a day often at the limits of physical endurance, tested the levels of tolerance. Crew members were isolated from home comforts and there was emotional trauma in separation from loved ones. Seasickness was often a problem. Any difference was grasped at as a source for releasing frustration. Introducing women into such an environment was always going to be hard.

Perhaps the greatest potential area of difficulty was that of sexual harassment. The language commonly used on a warship would not be acceptable in a mixed workplace in civilian life. Given the nature of seagoing life, the possibility of unwelcome sexual advances would be high. But within the confined spaces of a warship people often have to brush past one another or otherwise inadvertently come into physical contact. Handling complaints arising from this would be difficult. Another problem was fraternisation (a services codeword for sexual relationships). Harassment was harassment only if it was unwelcome. Fraternisation involved consenting adults. The possibility of fraternisation splitting the crew and creating havoc with morale could not be discounted.

Given all of the above considerations, it was considered that no woman should be allowed at sea without other female members of the ship's company as support. The navy relied on the divisional system to identify and correct any problems. The divisional system basically relies on the hierarchy of command identifying and acting on problems.

It was not as if women were new in the navy. The WRANS (Women's Royal Australian Naval Service) had long been a feature of service life. Women joined the WRANS as a branch of the service but had female officers and were close to their own support network. What was being attempted by the navy was their seamless integration into all branches of the service.

In the early days of women at sea, the navy basically relied on people knowing what was right and doing it. In many cases common sense prevailed and this worked well. In other cases it failed. A woman being transferred between ships at sea almost fell in the water because crew members were reluctant to grab hold of her to steady her. They had been told that any touching of women was tantamount to sexual harassment. Female sailors watched as men did the heavy work, leading to resentment among the men.

Sometimes men did not know which way to look as a female sailor let forth with a string of bad language.

During the time it was trying to integrate women into the service the navy had other major problems on its hands. It was introducing a complex quality control system and was grappling with program budgeting. It was faced with a high attrition of skilled staff and had had its funding allocation cut. At the same time, more was expected of it.

In 1992 the events on HMAS *Swan* (briefly described in the OT Closeup in Chapter 15) revealed that the navy's approach to integrating women was flawed. In subsequent inquiries it became clear that events on HMAS *Swan* were the product of a whole range of factors coming together on the one ship. Allegations of sexual harassment intermixed with discontent over the working conditions of female crew members. Standards of supervision and handling of complaints were found wanting. Some women were poorly trained for their job and others inadequately prepared for seagoing life. Men were often confused and unsure of what was acceptable conduct and what was not. In some areas of the ship standards of management were poor, and these happened to be those where women were present. Some of the male officers' language and conversation in the wardroom drew complaints even from male colleagues.

The captain of the ship was censured by the Chief of Naval Staff for the events that occurred on HMAS *Swan*. However, this was later seen to be an exercise of looking for someone to blame in order to send a powerful message to the rest of the service that sexual harassment was not to be tolerated. The Senate Standing Committee inquiring into the affair found that making a scapegoat of someone who had tried to do his best and did not deserve censure was hardly an appropriate message to send to the fleet. Most officers felt that any reasonable person would have acted the same way as the captain, and were relieved that they were not in his shoes. The real problem was the culture of the navy and the management system it supported.

Adapted from: 'Sexual Harassment in the Australian Defence Force', *Report of the Senate Standing Committee on Foreign Affairs, Defence and Trade*, AGPS, August 1994.

QUESTION

1 Assume that it is 1990 and you have been appointed by the navy to advise them on how to successfully integrate women into their ships. The first women are to be posted to ships in 1992. It is to be a navy-wide project. Draw up a plan of action identifying the main points you feel need addressing and how you will tackle them. The navy has approximately 12 000 members, of whom 12% are women.

Glossary

Adaptive activities Change activities that allow the system to adapt over time.

Adhocracy An organisational form characterised by high horizontal differentiation, low vertical differentiation, low formalisation, decentralisation and great flexibility and responsiveness.

Administrative innovation The implementation of changes in an organisation's structure or its administrative processes.

Alienation A feeling held by employees that their work is meaningless and that they are powerless to correct the situation.

Analysers Organisations whose strategy is to move into new products or new markets only after their viability has been proven.

Appeals system The right of redress on grievances through formal channels.

Aston Group Researchers at the University of Aston in Great Britain who supported the theory that size was a major determinant of structure.

Authority The formal rights inherent in a managerial position to give orders and expect the orders to be obeyed.

Autonomy The degree to which a job provides substantial freedom, independence and discretion to the individual in scheduling the work and in determining the procedures to be used in carrying it out.

Balance scorecard The balanced scorecard seeks to balance the various demands on the organisation with its capabilities.

Biological school A work-design approach that emphasises the comfort and physical wellbeing of the worker.

Boundary spanners People who operate at the periphery of the organisation, performing organisationally relevant tasks, and relating the organisation to elements outside it.

Bridging The process by which managers endeavour to regulate their environments through negotiation, cooperation, exchange of information and other forms of mutual benefit.

Buffering Protecting the operating core from environmental variations in supply and demand.

Bureaucracy An organisational form characterised by division of labour, a well-defined authority hierarchy, high formalisation, impersonality, employment decisions based on merit, career tracks for employees and distinct separation of members' organisational and personal lives.

Bureaupathic behaviour Adherence to rules and regulations by individuals to protect themselves from making errors.

Business-level strategy Refers to those strategies adapted by business units of the organisation.

Capacity The degree to which an environment can support growth.

Centralisation The degree to which decision making is concentrated in a single point in the organisation usually top management.

Change agents Those in power, and those who wish either to replace or constrain those in power, who initiate structural change.

Change process The unfreezing of the status quo, moving to a new state and refreezing the new change.

Closed system A self-contained system that ignores its environment.

Coalescing The combining of an organisation with one or more other organisations for the purpose of joint action.

Complexity The degree of horizontal, vertical and spatial differentiation in an organisation.

Computer-integrated manufacturing A manufacturing process controlled by computers and which brings together all aspects of the production process.

Configuration A complex clustering of elements that are internally cohesive and where the presence of some elements suggests the reliable occurrence of others.

Conglomerate A divisional structure where the autonomous units engage in diverse businesses and are completely independent.

Contracting Protects the organisation from changes in quantity or price on either input or output side.

Co-opting The absorption of those individuals or organisations in the environment that threaten a given organisation's stability.

Coordination The process of integrating the objectives and activities of the separate units of an organisation in order to achieve organisational goals efficiently.

Core values The primary values expressed by an organisation's dominant culture.

Corporate-level strategy Attempts to define the nature of the businesses in which the firm seeks to operate.

Cost-leadership strategy Aims to achieve the lowest cost within an industry.

Craft technology Containing relatively difficult problems but with a limited set of exceptions.

Critical theory An approach to studying organisations which concentrates on their perceived shortcomings and deficiencies

Decentralisation Low centralisation.

Defenders Organisations whose strategy is to produce a limited set of products directed at a narrow segment of the total potential market.

Differentiation Task segmentation and attitudinal differences held by individuals in various departments.

Differentiation strategy Aims to achieve a unique position in an industry in ways that are widely valued by buyers.

Disturbed-reactive environment An environment characterised by many competitors, one or more of which may be large enough to influence that environment.

Division of labour Functional specialisation; jobs broken down into simple and repetitive tasks.

Divisional structure A structure characterised by a set of self-contained, autonomous units, coordinated by a central headquarters.

Domain An organisation's niche that it has staked out for itself with respect to products or services offered and markets served.

Dominant coalition That group within an organisation with the power to influence the outcomes of decisions.

Dominant culture The overriding core values shared by the majority of an organisation's members.

Downsizing Planned reduction in an organisation's staffing levels.

Employee alienation The distance an employee feels between themselves and their work.

Engineering technology Containing a large number of exceptions, but can be handled in a rational and systematic manner.

Entropy The propensity of a system to run down or disintegrate.

Environment Those institutions or forces that affect the performance of the organisation but over which the organisation has little or no direct control.

Environmental change Ranges from static (little change) to dynamic.

Environmental complexity The degree to which the environment is concentrated on just a few elements.

Environmental scanning Scrutinising the environment to identify actions by factors that might impinge on the organisation's operations.

Environmental uncertainty The degree to which an environment is characterised by a large number of heterogeneous and rapidly changing factors.

Equifinality A system can reach the same final state from differing initial conditions and by a variety of paths.

Evolution Prolonged and calm growth.

Evolutionary mode A strategy that evolves over time as a pattern in a stream of significant decisions.

External strategies Management alters the environment to fit better with the organisation's capabilities.

Feedback Receipt of information pertaining to individual or system effectiveness.

Feminism An active advocacy of the claims and aspirations of women.

Focus strategy Aims at cost advantage or differentiation advantage in a narrow segment.

Formalisation The degree to which jobs within the organisation are standardised.

Functional specialisation The breaking up of work activities into simple and repetitive tasks.

Gender The various actions and roles of men and women in organisations and in society generally.

General environment Conditions that potentially have an impact on the organisation.

Global strategy Lowering costs by selling a common product on a global basis.

Goal-attainment approach An organisation's effectiveness is appraised in terms of the accomplishment of its goals.

Goal displacement The displacement of organisational goals by subunit or personal goals.

Hawthorne studies A series of studies which identified the behavoural basis of organisational outcomes.

Hierarchy The graded layers of management within an organisation.

Hierarchical control Control by management prerogative.

Horizontal differentiation The degree of differentiation among units based on the orientation of members, the nature of the tasks they perform and their education and training.

Human-relations model Organisational effectiveness is defined in terms of a cohesive and skilled workforce.

Imperative A variable that dictates structure.

Incremental change Small step-by-step changes to an organisation's practices.

Information processing The manipulation of information from one form to another. In its modern use, this normally involves the use of computers.

Information technology (IT) A generic term covering the application of computerised information-processing techniques to organisational operations.

Innovation The adoption of ideas that are new to the adopting organisation.

Institutional theory An approach which integrates an organisation's past actions and the social and environmental pressures on it to explain organisational practices.

Instrumental values Desired modes of behaviour.

Insurance A contract where, by paying a premium, an organisation may spread the risks of the insured activity with other organisations.

Integration The quality of collaboration that exists among interdependent units.

Intensive technology The utilisation of a wide range of customised responses, depending on the nature and variety of the problems; reciprocal interdependence.

Interlocking directorate Two or more organisations having one or more directors in common.

International strategy Attempts to achieve maximum local responsiveness while achieving worldwide economies of scale.

Internal strategies Managers adapt and change organisational practices to better fit the environment.

Intervention strategies The choice of means by which the change process takes place.

Interpreneurship Creating the spirit and rewards of entrepreneurship within or alongside a large bureaucracy.

Large organisation An organisation having approximately 2000 or more employees.

Lobbying Using influence on an external party to achieve favourable outcomes for an organisation.

Long-linked technology A fixed sequence of connected steps: sequentially interdependent tasks.

Machine bureaucracy An organisation that has highly routine operating tasks, very formalised rules and regulations, tasks that are grouped into functional departments, centralised authority, decision making that follows the chain of command, and an elaborate administrative structure with a sharp distinction between line and staff activities.

Maintenance activities Activities that provide stability to a system and preserve the status quo.

Management audit A systems application that appraises organisational performance in 10 key areas.

Management by objectives (MBO) A philosophy of management that assesses an organisation and its members by how well they achieve the specific goals that have been jointly established.

Managing culture Changing the organisation's culture.

Market control Control by the operation of the price mechanism and market forces.

Mass production Large-batch or mass-produced technology.

Matrix A structural design that assigns specialists from functional departments to work on one or more interdisciplinary teams that are led by project leaders.

Mechanistic structure A structure characterised by high complexity, high formalisation and centralisation.

Mediating technology The process of linking together different clients in need of each other's services; pooled interdependence.

Metaphor Is a figure of speech in which a descriptive term is used to refer to another object to which it seems to bear no relationship.

Middle line The part of an organisation that encompasses managers that connect the operating core to the strategic apex.

Multidomestic strategy Aims to achieve maximum local responsiveness with products customised to meet local conditions.

Mutual problem solving Conflicting parties come face to face with the underlying causes of their conflict and share responsibility for seeing that the solution works.

Mutual task dependence The extent to which two units in an organisation depend on each other for assistance, information, compliance or other coordinative activities to complete their respective tasks.

Network centrality The degree to which a position in an organisation allows an individual to integrate other functions or reduce organisation dependencies.

Networks Groups of companies that pool their resourfces in various ways.

Non-rationality A process of decision making that does not follow the principles of logical deduction.

Non-routine technology Containing many exceptions and difficult-to-analyse problems.

One-way task dependence The condition in which one unit in an organisation is unilaterally dependent on another unit in the organisation.

Open system A dynamic system that interacts with and responds to its environment.

Open-systems model Organisational effectiveness is defined in terms of system flexibility and ability to acquire resources.

Operating core The part of an organisation encompassing employees who perform the basic work related to the production of products and services.

Organic structure Flexible and adaptive structures, with emphasis on lateral communication, non-authority-based influence and loosely defined responsibilities.

Organisation A consciously coordinated social entity, with a relatively identifiable boundary, that functions on a relatively continuous basis to achieve a common goal or set of goals.

Organisation design The construction and change of an organisation's structure.

Organisation size The total number of employees in the organisation.

Organisation structure The degree of complexity, formalisation and centralisation in an organisation.

Organisation theory The discipline that studies the structure and design of organisations.

Organisational behaviour A field of study that investigates the impact of individuals and small-group factors on employee performance and attitudes.

Organisational culture A system of shared meaning within an organisation.

Organisational decline A long-lasting and ongoing decrease in the overall activity of the organisation.

Organisational economics The application of economic theory to explain the structuring and operation of organisations.

Organisational effectiveness The degree to which an organisation attains its short- and long-term goals, the selection of which reflects strategic constituencies, the self-interests of the evaluator and the life stage of the organisation.

Organisational life cycle The pattern of predictable change through which the organisation moves from start-up to dissolution

Organisational slack A cushion of excess resources that enables an organisation to adjust to environmental change.

Planned change Change efforts that are proactive and purposeful.

Planning mode Strategy as an explicit and systematic set of guidelines developed in advance.

Policies Statements that guide employees, providing discretion within limited boundaries.

Politics Efforts of organisational members to mobilise for or against decisions in which the outcome will have some effect on them.

Pooled interdependence Two or more units that contribute separately to a larger unit.

Population-ecology view The environment selects certain types of organisations to survive and others to perish based on the fit between their structural characteristics and the characteristics of their environment.

Postmodernism An approach to studying organisations which emerged from European philosophical origins and which rejects traditional approaches to studying organisations

Power An individual's capacity to influence decisions.

Power-control An organisation's structure, at any given time, is to a large extent the result of those in power selecting a structure that will, to the maximum degree possible, maintain and enhance their control.

Principles of organisations Developed by Fayol to identify the functions which a manager should perform.

Problem analysability The type of search procedures followed to find successful methods for adequately responding to task exceptions; from well-defined and analysable to ill-defined and unanalysable.

Procedures Specific standardised sequences of steps that result in a uniform output.

Process production Highly controlled, standardised and continuous processing technology.

Product innovation Designing, development, production and marketing of new products and services.

Professional bureaucracy A structural form that has highly skilled professionals, high complexity, decentralisation and the use of internalised professional standards in place of external formalisation.

Prospectors Organisations whose strategy is to find and exploit new product and market opportunities.

Psychological school Work-design approach that emphasises employee satisfaction.

Radical change Significant changes to an organisation's practices and ways of doing things.

Rational-goal model Organisational effectiveness is defined in terms of the existence of specific plans, high productivity and efficiency.

Rationality The belief that decisions are goal-directed and consistent.

Rational-planning perspective A model of organisation based upon the development of clear goals and plans to achieve those goals.

Rationing The allocation of organisational products or services according to a priority system.

Reactors A residual strategy that describes organisations that follow inconsistent and unstable patterns.

Reciprocal interdependence The output of one unit becomes the input for another unit.

Refreezing Stabilising and sustaining a change action.

Revolution Periods of internal turmoil in an organisation's growth.

Rituals A process in which members prove their trustworthiness and loyalty to the organisation by participating in various behaviours in which predetermined responses are expected.

Routine technology Containing few exceptions and easy-to-analyse problems.

Rules Explicit statements that tell an employee what he or she ought or ought not to do.

Scientific management A movement, initiated by Frederick Taylor, to achieve production efficiencies by systematising and standardising jobs to achieve the 'one best way' they should be done.

Sequential interdependence Procedures are highly standardised and must be performed in a specified serial order.

Simple structure A structure that is low in complexity, low in formalisation, and in which authority is centralised in a single person.

Smoothing Levelling out the impact of fluctuations in the environment by offering incentives to environmental units to regularise their interactions with the organisation.

Socialisation An adaptation process by which individuals learn the values, norms and expected behaviour patterns for the job and organisation of which they will be a part.

Span of control The number of subordinates that an individual manager can supervise effectively.

Spatial differentiation The degree to which the location of an organisation's facilities and personnel are dispersed geographically.

Specialisation Grouping of activities performed by an individual.

Specific environment The part of the environment that is directly relevant to the organisation in achieving its goals.

Stability The extent to which there is little change in the environment.

Strategic apex The part of an organisation encompassing top-level managers, who are charged with the overall responsibility for the organisation.

Strategic choice Managers have considerable discretion in which to choose their organisation's structural design.

Strategic-constituencies approach An organisation's effectiveness is determined by how successfully it satisfies the demands of those constituencies in its environment from which it requires support for its continued existence.

Strategy The adoption of courses of action and the allocation of resources necessary to achieve the organisation's goals.

Strong culture A cultures characterised by intensely held, clearly ordered and widely shared core values.

Stuck in the middle Organisations unable to gain a competitive advantage through one of various strategies.

Subcultures Separate cultures encompassed within organisational subunits.

Superordinate goal A common goal held by two or more parties that is compelling and highly appealing and cannot be attained by the resources of any single party.

Support staff The part of an organisation that encompasses people who fill the staff units that provide indirect support services for the organisation.

System A set of interrelated and interdependent parts arranged in a manner that produces a unified whole.

Systems approach Evaluating an organisation's effectiveness by its ability to acquire inputs, process the inputs, channel the outputs and maintain stability and balance.

Task uncertainty The difference between the amount of information required to perform a task and the amount of information already possessed by the organisation.

Task variability The number of exceptions encountered in performing a task.

Technology The information, equipment, techniques and processes required to transform inputs into outputs.

Technological innovation The use of new tools, techniques, devices or systems to produce changes in products or services or in the way those products are produced or services rendered.

Technostructure The part of an organisation that encompasses analysts who have the responsibility for effecting forms of standardisation in the organisation.

Terminal values The desired end-state or outcome that people try to attain.

Transnational strategy Attempts to achieve maximum local responsiveness while achieving worldwide economies of scale.

Turbulent-field environment An environment in which change is ever-present and elements in the environment are increasingly interrelated.

Unfreezing Overcoming resistance to change.

Unit production Technology wherein units are custom-made and work is non-routine.

Vertical differentiation The number of hierarchical levels between top management and operatives. Sometimes referred to as layers of management.

Index